AMERICA'S
Wonderful
LITTLE
HOTELS
& INNS
1991

The Middle Atlantic

States Covered in this Edition

Delaware	New York
District of Columbia	Pennsylvania
Maryland	Virginia
New Jersey	West Virginia

Also in this Series

America's Wonderful Little Hotels & Inns, U.S.A. and Canada
America's Wonderful Little Hotels & Inns, The Midwest, The Rocky Mountains, and The Southwest
America's Wonderful Little Hotels & Inns, New England
America's Wonderful Little Hotels & Inns, The South
America's Wonderful Little Hotels & Inns, The West Coast
Europe's Wonderful Little Hotels & Inns, Great Britain & Ireland
Europe's Wonderful Little Hotels & Inns, The Continent

AMERICA'S
Wonderful
LITTLE
HOTELS
& INNS
1991

The Middle Atlantic

Edited by Sandra W. Soule

Associate Editors:
Nancy P. Barker
June C. Horn
Matthew Joyce

Contributing Editors:
Suzanne Carmichael
Susan Waller Schwemm

Editorial Assistants:
Kirstin O'Rielly
Amy Phillipps
David Phillipps
Hilary Soule

St. Martin's Press
New York

ISBN 0-312-05048-8

First Edition: December 1990

10 9 8 7 6 5 4 3 2 1

Maps by David Lindroth, © 1991, 1990, 1989, 1988, 1987 by St. Martin's Press.

This book is dedicated to the people who take the time and trouble to write about the hotels and inns they've visited, and to my children—Hilary and Jeffrey—my husband, and my parents.

It's also dedicated in memory of Betty Rundback, a special person who introduced me to the world of B&B.

Contents

Acknowledgments

I would like again to thank all the people who wrote in such helpful detail about the inns and hotels they visited. To them belong both the dedication and the acknowledgments, for without their support, this guide would not exist. If I have inadvertently misspelled or omitted anyone's name, please accept my sincerest apologies.

I would also like to thank Hilary Rubinstein, who originated the concept for this series. Also thanks to my helpful and supportive editor Anne Savarese; to my colleagues Nancy Barker, June Horn, and Matt Joyce; to Kirstin O'Rielly, Amy Phillipps, David Phillipps, and Hilary Soule, my invaluable assistants; to Suzanne Carmichael and Susan Schwemm, my colleagues in the field; to Judith Brannen, April Burwell, Marjorie Cohen, Dianne Crawford, Arlyne Craighead, Pat Fink, Willis Frick, Kathryn and Bob Gearhead, Pam Harpootlian, Nancy Harrison, Nelson Ormsby, Debbie Joost, Keith Jurgens, Zita Knific, Pat and Glen Lush, Betty Norman, Carolyn Mathiasen, Carolyn and Bill Myles, Ed Okie, Janet Payne, Mary Louise Rogers, Joe Schmidt, Laura Scott, Jeanne Smith, Lee Todd, James and Janice Utt, Wendi Van Exan, Hope Welliver, Diane Wolf, Rose Wolf, and Eileen Yudelson, and the many others who went far beyond the call of duty in their assistance and support; and to Melania Lanni, for without her help, I'd never get anything done.

Introduction

Reading the Entries

Each entry generally has three parts: a description of the inn or hotel, quotes from guests who have stayed there, and relevant details about rooms, rates, location, and facilities. Occasionally you may find that no general description is given or that the factual data are incomplete. There are two reasons for this: Either the descriptions supplied by guests made this unnecessary, or the facility failed to supply us with adequate information because of time limitations or other problems.

Please remember that the length of an entry is in no way a reflection of that inn or hotel's quality. Rather, it is an indication of the type of feedback we've received both from guests and from the innkeepers themselves. Some hotel owners are totally unaware of this guide; others take an active role in encouraging their guests to write.

Wherever a location is of particular tourist interest, we've tried to include some information about its attractions. If we have only one listing for a town, this description usually falls within the body of the entry. If there is more than one inn or hotel listed for a town, the description of the town and information about its location precede the individual entries.

In some areas the magnet is not a particular town but rather a compact, distinct region. Travelers choose one place to stay and use it as a base from which to explore the area. But because this guide is organized by town, not by region, the entries are scattered throughout the chapter. When this applies, you will see the name of the region noted under the "Location" heading; check back to the introduction for a description of the region involved. For example, inns and hotels in Bucks County, Pennsylvania, start with Erwinna near the beginning of the chapter and extend to Upper Black Eddy at the end, but the description of the area itself is found at the beginning of the chapter.

The names at the end of the quotations are those who have recommended the hotel or inn. Some entries are entirely or largely quoted from one report; if several names follow the quotation, we have distinguished the writers of the quoted material by putting their names first. Some writers have requested that we not use their names; you will see initials noted instead. *We never print the names of those who have sent us adverse reports, although their contributions are invaluable indeed.*

1

Although we have tried to make the listings as accurate and complete as possible, mistakes and inaccuracies invariably creep in. The most significant area of inaccuracy applies to the rates charged by each establishment. In preparing this guide, we asked all the hotels and inns to give us their 1991 rates, ranging from the least expensive room in the off-season to the most expensive peak-season price. Some did so, while others just noted the 1990 rate.

Since the process of writing and publishing a book takes nearly a year, please don't rely solely on the figures printed. *You should always double-check the rates when you make your reservations; please don't blame the hotel or this guide if the prices are wrong.* On the other hand, given the current level of inflation, you should not encounter anything more than a 5% increase, unless there has been a substantial improvement in the amenities offered or a change of ownership. Please let us know immediately if you find anything more than that!

If you find any errors of omission or commission in any part of the entries, we urgently request your help in correcting them. We recognize that it takes extra time and effort for readers to write us letters or fill in report forms, but this feedback is essential in keeping this publication totally responsive to consumer needs.

Inngoers' Bill of Rights

We've read through a lot more brochures for inns and hotels than the average bear, and can attest to the fact that not one makes mention of its possible drawbacks, however slight. And rightly so. A brochure is paid advertising, no more obligated to provide the full picture—both pros and cons—than a TV ad for diet soda. Furthermore, unlike this guidebook, *which accepts no fee of any kind for an entry,* most inn guidebooks charge a listing or membership fee of some kind, making them basically paid advertisements. Despite brochure promises and glowing listings in other books, we all know that perfection isn't possible in this world, but we feel that (despite the irate reactions of some innkeepers) complete and honest reporting will give readers *reasonable* expectations, ones that are often surpassed in the best of hostelries.

On the other hand, although perfection may not be on the menu, as guests (and customers), travelers have the right to expect certain minimum standards. These rights are especially important in hotels and inns at the top end of the rate scale; we don't expect as much from more modestly priced places, although it certainly is often received.

So, please use this Bill of Rights as a kind of checklist in deciding how you think a place stacks up on your own personal rating scale. And, whether an establishment fails, reaches, or exceeds these levels, be sure to let us know. These rights are especially important because of the financial penalties levied by most establishments; with the exception of the larger hotels, nearly every establishment listed in this book requires a substantial advance deposit, yet travelers have little or no recourse if facilities prove to be substandard. We would also hope that innkeepers will use this list to help evaluate both the strong points and shortcomings of their own establishments, and are grateful to those who have already done so.

The right to suitable cleanliness. An establishment that looks, feels, and smells clean, with no musty or smoky odors. Not just middle-of-the-room clean, but immaculate in all the nooks and crannies—under the radiators, in the dresser drawers, out on the balconies. Rooms should be immaculate prior to check-in, and kept as close as possible to that standard during your stay. You also have the right to prompt maid service, and should not have to wait until mid-afternoon for your room to be made up.

The right to suitable room furnishings. A comfortable bed with a firm mattress and soft pillows (preferably two per person), fresh clean linens, and blankets is a minimum. On *each* side of a double or larger-size bed should be a reading lamp (minimum 60 watts; ideal are three-way bulbs), along with a night table (or its equivalent) giving you a place to leave the bedtime necessities—a glass of water, a box of tissues, your eyeglasses and watch. Two comfortable chairs with good reading lights are a welcome addition, as is a well-lit mirror and readily accessible electric outlet in a room without a private bath. A well-equipped room also has adequate storage space for clothes, both in drawers and closets, along with extra pillows and blankets and a rack for your luggage.

The right to comfortable, attractive rooms. Guest rooms and common rooms that are not only attractive, but livable as well. Not just a visually handsome museum set piece, but a place where you'd like to spend some time reading, chatting, relaxing. You should be as comfortable as you are at home, without having to do any of the work to make yourself so.

The right to a decent bathroom. Of course, cleanliness heads the list here, followed by reliable plumbing, adequate and even supplies of hot water, decent lighting, an accessible electric outlet with wiring that can take a hair dryer, a fixed or hand-held shower added to old-fashioned tubs, a shelf or table for toiletries, and an ample supply of soft, absorbent towels. In more expensive accommodations, an "amenities kit" is a reasonable expectation.

The right to privacy and discretion. Even in the most familial of inns, you are entitled to conduct private conversations in common rooms, and even more private ones in your own room—and you have the right *not* to hear the equally private conversations of your neighbors. The right to discretion precludes prying hosts' questions about one's marital status or sexual preference. A truly offensive intrusion on a guest's privacy is the practice of displaying proselytizing religious brochures, tracts, and signs.

The right to good, healthful food. Fresh nutritious food, ample in quantity, high in quality, attractively presented, and graciously served in enjoyable smoke-free surroundings—whether the offering is a cup of coffee and a roll, a seven-course gourmet dinner, or anything in between. An end to dessert masquerading as breakfast and ample supplies of brewed decaffeinated coffee and herbal teas is applauded. Freedom from pretentious menus written in fractured French menuspeak would be a welcome companion.

The right to comfortable temperatures and noise levels. Rooms should be reasonably cool on the hottest of summer nights and warm on the coldest winter evenings. Windows that open, screens without holes, fans, air conditioners, and heating systems that run quietly are all key; although not always possible, individually controlled thermostats are ideal. In locations where traffic noise is a problem, double- or even triple-glazed windows, drapes, and landscaping should all be in place.

The right to fair value. People don't stay in inns or small hotels because they are cheap, which is good, because very few of them are. What is expected, though, is a good value, with prices that are in reasonable relation to the facilities offered and to the cost of equivalent accommodation in the area. This right extends to the times when things go wrong. Even when the problem is beyond the innkeepers' control, guests have the right to an apology at the minimum, and restitution at a maximum, depending on the situation. Guests do not have the right to perfection, but they have the right to innkeepers who are concerned and solicitous when a problem arises.

The right to genuine hospitality. Owners and staff who are sincerely glad you've come, and who make it their business to make your stay pleasant and memorable without being intrusive. Innkeepers who help guests to get to know each other when appropriate and who leave the less sociable to their own thoughts. Resident owners are best, resident staff is often acceptable; someone should be readily available for emergencies around the clock.

The right to a caring environment and little luxuries. Seeing that the little extras have been attended to—asking about pet allergies and dietary restrictions, making dinner reservations, providing inside and accurate information on area activities and events. Offering afternoon or evening refreshments, and welcoming new arrivals with refreshments appropriate to the season. Leaving a personal note, fresh flowers, or candies to greet guests is another way of saying welcome. Being there to provide toothpaste or a toothbrush to guests who have forgotten theirs at home. A good hostelry is more than accommodation. It's an end in itself, not just a means to an end. Amenities are more than imported soaps; innkeepers who are attuned to guests' needs and wants, anticipating them before they're even expressed, are the most important amenity of all.

The right to personal safety. Facilities in large cities need to be located in reasonably safe neighborhoods, with adequate care given to building security. Where caution, especially at night, is advisable, innkeepers have an obligation to share this information with guests.

The right to professionalism. Running an inn or hotel is not a business for amateurs, and guests have the right to receive requested brochures promptly, after one request, and to have their room reservations handled efficiently and responsibly. Check-in and check-out should be smooth, with rooms available as confirmed.

The right to adequate common areas. One of the key distinctions between a motel and an inn is the existence of at least one common room where guests can gather to read, chat, or relax, free of any pressure (implied or otherwise) to buy anything.

The right of people traveling alone to have all the above rights. Those traveling alone usually pay just a few dollars less than a couple, yet the welcome, services, and rooms they receive are often less than equal.

The right to a reasonable cancellation policy. Before booking, get the details. Penalties levied for a cancellation made less than 7–14 days before arrival is relatively standard at most inns; the 2–7 day policy found at many Western inns is preferable. Most inns will refund deposits (minus a processing fee) even after the deadline if the room is rebooked. We feel that all should offer the chance to rebook within a few months as an alternative to cancellation penalties. To be avoided are inns with policies such as this: "On cancellations received less than 45 days in advance, the deposit [approximately 50%] is not refundable, regardless if the room is re-rented or not."

Of course, there is no "perfect" inn or hotel, even when every provision of the bill of rights is met, since people's tastes and needs vary so greatly. But one key phrase does pop up in the hotel/inn reports over and over again, whether the writer is describing a small hotel in the city or a country inn: "I felt right at home." This is not written in the literal sense—a commercial lodging, no matter how cozy or charming, is never the same as one's home. What is really meant is that guests felt as welcome, as relaxed, as comfortable, as they would in their own home. One writer put it this way: "Where does one start in describing this inn? With mixed feelings. (It's a wonderful place, and I don't want the world to discover and spoil it.) But I'll tell you about this grand hideaway. It's clean, quiet, isolated, warm, and comfortable. The fireplaces work and the owners seem intent on making your stay happy. They describe dinner specials with smiles, remember you from trip to trip, and are willing to help in any way they can. The unique qualities of each room make you want to try them all. It's a wonderful place. Please don't take my room."

What makes for a wonderful stay?

We've tried our best to make sure that all the hotels and inns listed in this guide are as wonderful as our title promises. Inevitably, there will be some disappointments. Sometimes these will be caused by a change in ownership or management that has resulted in lowered standards. Other times unusual circumstances, which can arise in the best of establishments, will lead to problems. Quite often, though, problems will occur because there's not a good "fit" between the inn or hotel and the guest. Decide what you're looking for, then find the inn that suits your needs, whether you're looking for a casual environment or a dressy one, a romantic setting or a family-oriented one, a vacation spot or a businessperson's environment, an isolated country retreat or a convenient in-town location.

We've tried to give you as much information as possible on each hotel or inn listed, and have taken care to indicate the atmosphere each innkeeper is trying to create. After you've read the listing, write, if there is time, for a copy of the establishment's brochure, which will give you more information. Finally, feel free to call any inn or hotel where you're planning to stay, and ask as many questions as necessary.

A good guest is a good traveler

We travel because we want to see new places, meet new people, experience new sensations. When we travel we encounter many things that are different from the way they are at home. If we respond to these experiences in a positive way, our travels are enriching, entertaining, memorable. If we respond with endless adverse comparisons to "the way it is at home," our travels are doomed to disappointment before the key is out of the front door lock.

Some people prefer to stay in an endless succession of almost identical motels and hotels to insulate themselves from the possible good and bad surprises of travel. They are rarely disappointed because their expectations are so modest. Readers of this guide have chosen a different path. Each hotel or inn listed here is very different from the next in a dozen different ways. Pick the ones that you'll enjoy visiting and then let them surprise you!

Hotels, inns . . . resorts and motels

As the title indicates, this is a guide to exceptional inns and hotels. Generally, the inns have 5 to 25 rooms, although a few have only 2 rooms and some have over 100. The hotels are more often found in the cities and range in size from about 50 to 200 rooms.

The line between an inn or hotel and a resort is often a fine one. There are times when we all want the extra facilities a resort provides, so we've added a number of reader-recommended facilities to this edition; they tend to be on the small side for resorts and are highlighted in "Appendix 2: Resorts" at the back of the book.

You'll also find that we've listed a handful of motels. Although they don't strictly fall within the context of this book, we've included them because we received letters strongly endorsing their positive qualities, particularly their concerned and involved owners and friendly atmosphere, two qualities usually lacking in even the best of motels. A number of these recommendations have come for properties in the Best Western chain. Please don't be put off by this; Best Western is a franchise operation, with no architectural unity from one property to the next. Those listed in this guide have substantial architectural or historical appeal, and concerned, professional management.

Although we do not provide full coverage of hotel chains, we do want to point out that the Four Seasons and Ritz-Carlton hotels are almost impossible to beat at the luxury end of the spectrum. Readers consistently rave about their unbeatable combination of unparalleled service, and plush accommodation.

Rooms

All hotel and inn rooms are not created equal. Although the rooms at a typical chain motel or hotel may be identical, the owners of most of the establishments described in this book pride themselves on the individuality of each guest room. Some, although not all, of these differences are reflected in the rates charged.

More important, it means that travelers need to express their needs clearly to the innkeepers when making reservations and again when checking in. Some rooms may be quite spacious but may have extremely small private baths or limited closet space. Some antique double beds have rather high footboards—beautiful to look at but torture for people over six feet tall! Many inns are trading their double beds in for queens and kings; if you prefer an oversize bed, say so. If you want twin beds, be sure to specify this when making reservations and again when you check in; many smaller inns have only one or two twin-bedded rooms.

Some rooms may have gorgeous old bathrooms, with tubs the size of small swimming pools, but if you are a hard-core shower person, that room won't be right for you. Many others have showers but no baths, which may be disappointing if you love a long, luxurious soak in the tub. If you are traveling on business and simply must have a working-size desk with good light, speak up. Some rooms look terrific inside but don't look out at anything much; others may have the view but not quite as special a decor. Sometimes the best rooms may look out onto a main road and can be quite noisy. Decide what's important to you. Although the owners and staff of the hotels and inns listed here are incredibly hard-working and dedicated people, they can't read your mind. Let your needs be known, and, within the limits of availability, they will try to accommodate you.

Our most frequent complaints center around beds that are too soft and inadequate reading lights. If these are priorities for you (as they are for us), don't be shy about requesting bedboards or additional lamps to remedy the situation. Similarly, if there are other amenities your room is lacking—extra pillows, blankets, or even an easy chair—speak up. Most innkeepers would rather put in an extra five minutes of work than have an unhappy guest.

If your reservation is contingent upon obtaining a particular room, make this very clear to the innkeeper. Some inns will not accept such reservations, feeling that they are too difficult to guarantee. Those that do accept them have an obligation to meet their guarantee; if circumstances prevent them from following through on the promised room, make it clear that you expect some sort of remuneration—either the return of your deposit or a reduction in the price of another room.

If you really don't like your room, ask for another as soon as possible, preferably before you've unpacked your bags. The sooner you voice your dissatisfaction, the sooner something can be done to improve the situation. If you don't like the food, ask for something else—in other words, you're the guest, make sure you get treated like one. If things go terribly wrong, don't be shy about asking for your money back, and be *sure* to write us about any problems.

What is a single? A double? A suite? A cottage or cabin?

Unlike the proverbial rose, a single is not a single is not a single. Sometimes it is a room with one twin bed, which really can accommodate only one person. Quite often it is described as a room with a standard-size double bed, in contrast to a double, which has two twin beds. Other hotels call both of the preceding doubles, although doubles often have queen- or even king-size beds instead. Many times the only distinction is made by the number of guests occupying the room; a single will pay slightly less, but there's no difference in the room.

There's almost as much variation when it comes to suites. We would like to define a suite as a bedroom with a separate living room area and often a small kitchen as well. Unfortunately, since suites are now a very popular concept in the hotel business, the word has been stretched to cover other setups, too. Some so-called suites are only one large room, accommodating a table and separate seating area in addition to the bed. If you require a suite that has two separate rooms with a door between them, specify this when you make reservations.

Quite a few of our entries have cabins or cottages in addition to rooms in the main building. In general, a cabin is understood to be a somewhat more rustic residence than a cottage, although there's no hard-and-fast rule. Be sure to inquire for details when making reservations.

What is a B&B anyway?

There are basically two kinds of B&Bs—the B&B homestay, and the B&B inn. The homestay is typically the home of an empty nester, who has a few empty bedrooms to fill, gaining some extra income and pleasant company. B&B inns are run on a more professional basis, independently marketed and subject to state and local licensing. Guests typically have dedicated common areas for their use, and do not share the hosts' living quarters, as in a homestay. We list very few homestays in this guide. Full-service or country inns and lodges are similar to the B&B inn, except that they serve breakfast and dinner on a regular basis, and may be somewhat larger in size; dinner is often offered to the public as well as to house guests. The best of all of these are made special by resident owners bringing the warmth of their personalities to the total experience. A B&B is *not* a motel that serves breakfast.

Making reservations

Unless you are inquiring many months in advance of your visit, it's best to telephone when making reservations. This offers a number of advantages: You will know immediately if space is available on your requested dates; you can find out if that space is suitable to your specific needs. You will have a chance to discuss the pros and cons of the available rooms and will be able to find out about any changes made in recent months—new facilities, recently redecorated rooms, non-smoking policies, possibly even a change of ownership. It's also a good time to ask the innkeeper about other concerns—Is the neighborhood safe at night? Is any renovation or construction in progress that might be disturbing? Will a wedding reception or other social function be in progress during your visit that might affect your use of the common areas or parking lot? If you're reserving a room at a plantation home that is available for public tours, get specifics about the check-in/out times; in many, rooms are not available before 5 P.M. and must be vacated by 9 A.M. sharp. The savvy traveler will always get the best value for his accommodation dollar.

If you expect to be checking in late at night, *be sure to say so;* many inns give doorkeys to their guests, then lock up by 10 P.M.

We're often asked about the need for making advance reservations. If you'll be traveling in peak periods, in prime tourist areas, and want to be sure of getting a first-rate room at the best-known inns, reserve at least three to six months ahead. This is especially true if you're traveling with friends or family and will need more than one room. On the other hand, if you like a bit of adventure, and don't want to be stuck with cancellation fees when you change your mind, by all means stick our book in the glove compartment and hit the road. If you're travelling in the off-season, or even mid-week in season, you'll have a grand time. But look for a room in the early afternoon; never wait until after dinner and hope that you'll find something decent.

Payment

Many innkeepers don't like plastic any better for payment than they do for decorating. Some accept credit cards for the initial deposit but prefer cash, traveler's checks, or personal checks for the balance; others offer the reverse policy. Still others have accepted credit cards as a part of modern living. When no credit cards are accepted at all, you can settle your bill with a personal check, traveler's check, or even (!) cash.

When using your credit card to guarantee a reservation, be aware that some inns and hotels will charge your card for the amount of the deposit only, while others will put a "hold" on your card for the full amount of your entire stay, plus the cost of meals and incidentals that you may (or may not) spend. If you're using your card to reserve a fairly extended trip, you may find that you're well over your credit limit without actually having spent a nickel. We'd suggest inquiring; if the latter is the procedure, either send a check for the deposit or go elsewhere.

Rates

All rates quoted are per room, unless otherwise noted as being per person. Rates quoted per person are usually based on double occupancy, unless otherwise stated.

"Room only" rates do not include any meals. In most cases two or three meals a day are served by the hotel restaurant, but are charged separately. Average meal prices are noted when available. In a very few cases no meals are served on the premises at all; rooms in these facilities are usually equipped with kitchenettes.

B&B rates include bed and breakfast. Breakfast, though, can vary from a simple continental breakfast to an expanded continental breakfast to a full breakfast. Afternoon tea and evening refreshments are sometimes included as well.

MAP (Modified American Plan) rates are often listed per person and include breakfast and dinner. Only a few of the inns listed serve lunch, although many will prepare a picnic on request for an additional charge.

State and local sales taxes are not included in the rates; the percentage varies from state to state and is noted in the introduction to each state chapter or in the individual listing. When budgeting for your trip, remember that taxes can easily add 10% to the cost of your travels, and even more in many big cities. *When inquiring about rates, always ask if any off-season or special package rates are available.* Sometimes discounted rates are available *only* on request; seniors and AAA members often qualify for substantial discounts. During the week, when making reservations at city hotels or country inns, it's important to ask if any corporate rates are available. Depending on the establishment, you may or may not be asked for some proof of corporate affiliation (a business card is usually all that's needed), but it's well worth inquiring, since the effort can result in a saving of 15 to 20%, plus an upgrade to a substantially better room. Another money-saving trick can be to look for inns in towns a bit off the beaten path. If you stay in a town that neighbors a famous resort or historic community, you will often find that rates are anywhere from $20 to $50 less per night for equivalent accommodation.

If an establishment has a specific tipping policy, whether it is "no tipping" or the addition of a set service charge, it is noted under "Rates." When no notation is made, it's generally expected that guests will leave about 5 to 10% for the housekeeping staff and 15% for meal service. A number of inns have taken to leaving little cards or envelopes to remind guests to leave a tip for the housekeepers; some readers have found this objectionable, others don't seem to mind at all. Reported one reader: "An envelope was left out for tips for the chambermaids, a practice I dislike very much. I would much rather they paid their employees a living wage and add a service charge if they must. I don't wish to be told that the maids rely on my generosity to pay their rent." And from an innkeeper: "We don't tip chambermaids when we stay overnight, and we don't expect our guests to tip our chambermaids. If and when our guests leave a tip, we feel a sense of pride that our staff has done an exceptional job. In lieu of shaming guests into leaving a tip, we pay our chambermaids a gratuity for every room they make up or change (a different rate because there's different work involved) out of what we collect for the room rate, and do not add a percentage to the room rate for 'service.' This has been an item we debate every time we meet with other innkeepers, and as yet we have not gone the way others are going." Comments?

A few readers have indicated that they feel some innkeepers have taken advantage of the current popularity of B&Bs with a disproportionate increase in their rates: "I've encountered a few American B&Bs without a private bath and serving only a barely adequate continental breakfast that charge two people as much or more than a good chain motel would. Granted, there's a more personal touch, but given the lack of motel amenities, I think the price should be somewhat lower. Even some B&Bs with private baths and considerable charm are, I fear, suffering delusions of grandeur when pricing themselves in the range of a grand hotel." *(AD)* We agree. Comments, please?

Deposits and cancellations

Nearly all innkeepers print their deposit and cancellation policies clearly on their brochures. Deposits generally range from payment of the first night's stay to 50% of the cost of the entire stay. Some inns repeat the cancellation policy when confirming reservations. In general, guests canceling well in advance of the planned arrival (two to four weeks is typical) receive a full refund minus a cancellation fee. After that date, no refunds are offered unless the room is resold to someone else. A few will not refund *even if the room is resold,* so take careful note. If you're making a credit card booking over the phone, be sure to find out what the cancellation policy is.

We would like to applaud many of the inns of the Northwest, where only two to seven days' notice of cancellation is required, and would love to see other areas follow suit. We also feel that even if you cancel on short notice, you should be given the opportunity to rebook within a reasonable time period rather than losing your entire deposit.

Sometimes the shoe may be on the other foot. Even if you were told earlier that the inn at which you really wanted to stay was full, it may be worthwhile to make a call to see if cancellations have opened up any last-minute vacancies.

Minimum stays

Two- and three-night minimum weekend and holiday stays are the rule at many inns during peak periods. We have noted these when possible, although we suspect that the policy may be more common than is always indicated in print. On the other hand, you may just be hitting a slow period, so it never hurts to ask if a one-night reservation would be accepted. Again, cancellations are always a possibility; you can try calling on a Friday or Saturday morning to see if something is available for that night.

Pets

Very few of the inns and hotels listed accept pets. When they do we've noted it under "Extras." On the other hand, over one-half of the country inns listed in this book have at least one dog or cat, sometimes more.

11

If you are highly allergic to animals, *we strongly urge that you inquire for details before making reservations.*

Children

Some inns are family-style places and welcome children of all ages. Others do not feel that they have facilities for the very young and only allow children over a certain age. Still others cultivate an "adults only" atmosphere and don't even welcome children at dinner. When inns and hotels do not encourage all children, we've noted the age requirement under the heading "Restrictions." If special facilities are available to children, these are noted under "Facilities" and "Extras"; we've also listed these establishments in "Appendix 1: Places That Welcome Families" at the back of this book. If an inn does not exclude children yet does not offer any special amenities or rate reductions for them, we would suggest it only for the best-behaved youngsters.

Whatever the policy, you may want to remind your children to follow the same rules of courtesy toward others that we expect of adults. Wall-to-wall carpeting was not a Victorian specialty, and the pitter-patter of little feet on an uncarpeted hardwood floor can sound like a herd of stampeding buffalo to those trying to sleep in a bedroom on the floor below.

Children used to the indestructible plastics of contemporary homes will need to be reminded (more than once) to be gentle with furniture that dates back 100 years or more.

For some reason, Southerners seem to be more tolerant of children than are New Englanders. Of the dozens of exquisitely decorated, antique-filled inns in the South, there are very few that exclude kids. In the North, nearly all do! And California innkeepers apparently would prefer it if children never crossed the state borders at all! Most inns there won't take any children under 12, and some are strictly for adults only.

State laws governing discrimination by age are affecting policies at some inns. To our knowledge, both California and Michigan now have such laws on the books, although this was rarely reflected in the brochures sent to us by inns in those states. Some inns get around this by limiting room occupancy to two adults. This discourages families by forcing them to pay for two rooms instead of one. Our own children are very clear on their preferences: although they've been to many inns that don't encourage guests under the age of 12, they find them "really boring"; on the other hand, they've loved every family-oriented place we've ever visited.

Porterage and packing

Only the largest of our listings will have personnel whose sole job is to assist guests with baggage. In the casual atmosphere associated with many inns, it is simply assumed that guests will carry their own bags. If you do need assistance with your luggage—because you have a bad back, because your bags are exceptionally heavy, or for any other reason at all—don't hesitate to say so; it should be gladly given. Ideally, innkeepers and their staff should ask you if you need help, but if they forget, don't suffer silently; just say "Could you give us a hand?"

If you're planning an extended trip to a number of small inns, we'd suggest packing as lightly as possible, using two small bags rather than one large suitcase. You'll know why if you've ever tried hauling a 50-pound oversized suitcase up a steep and narrow 18th-century staircase. On the other hand, don't forget about the local climate when assembling your wardrobe. In mountainous and desert regions, day- and nighttime temperatures can vary by as much as 40 degrees. Also, bear in mind that Easterners tend to dress more formally than Westerners; if you'll be traveling in New England or the South, men should pack a tie and jacket, women a skirt or dress.

Meals

If you have particular dietary restrictions—low-salt, vegetarian, or religious— or allergies—to caffeine, nuts, whatever—be sure to mention these when making reservations and again at check-in. If you're allergic to a common breakfast food or beverage, an evening reminder will ensure that you'll be able to enjoy the breakfast that's been prepared for you. Most innkeepers will do their best to accommodate your special needs, although, as one innkeeper said to us, "We're not operating a hospital."

In preparing each listing, we asked the owners to give us the cost of prix fixe and à la carte meals when available. An "alc dinner" price at the end of the "Rates" section is the figure we were given when we requested the average cost, in 1990, of a three-course dinner with a half bottle of house wine, including tax and tip. Prices listed for prix fixe meals do not include wine and service. Lunch prices, where noted, do not include the cost of any alcoholic beverage.

Dinner and lunch reservations are always a courtesy and are often essential. Most B&B owners will offer to make reservations for you; this can be especially helpful in getting you a table at a popular restaurant in peak season and/or on weekends. Some of the establishments we list operate restaurants fully open to the public. Others serve dinner primarily to their overnight guests, but they also will serve meals to outsiders; reservations are essential at such inns, usually eight or more hours in advance.

Quite a number of restaurants require jackets and ties for men at dinner, even in rather isolated areas. Of course, this is more often the case in traditional New England and the Old South than in the West. Unless you're going only to a very casual country lodge, we recommend that men bring them along and that women have corresponding attire.

Breakfast: Breakfast is served at nearly every inn or hotel listed in this guide. Those that do not, should. No inn is truly "wonderful" if you have to get in your car and drive somewhere for a cup of coffee and a roll, and early-morning strolls should be the choice of the guest, not the host! Nor do we consider the availability of coffee and tea alone an appropriate substitute. The expense and effort involved in providing a minimal continental breakfast are more than compensated for by the civilizing influence it provides.

The vast majority of lodgings listed include breakfast in their rates. We haven't noted in the "Rates" section whether the breakfast is full or continental. The reason for this is that the definitions have become hopelessly blurred in current American usage.

Continental breakfast ranges from an inadequate offering of coffee and store-bought pastry to a lavish offering of fresh fruit and juices, yogurt and granola, cereals, even cheese and cold meats, homemade muffins and breads, and a choice of decaffeinated or regular coffee, herbal and regular tea. There's almost as much variety in the full break-fasts, which range from an uninspired offering of eggs, bacon, and toast, plus juice and coffee, to three-course gourmet extravaganzas. If the innkeeper or the guests feel that a breakfast is something special, you'll see it described in the write-up. If there's no particular mention of it, then either it's nothing special or we've missed it—so please let us know.

We've received occasional complaints about the lack of variety in the breakfasts served. No one likes to have pancakes three days in a row, and doctors advise against having eggs every day. Sweet breads and muffins are the only breakfast offering at some establishments, yet many would prefer a roll or slice of toast. As one reader put it: "Bed and breakfast hosts seem to think that in order for a breakfast to be special, it has to be sweet. They should make plain toast or unsweet-ened rolls available to guests without the guest having to ask for them. People feel funny about making special requests—they don't want to cause trouble. What about diabetics? What about people like my hus-band who simply don't care much for sweets? There are plenty of good things for breakfast that don't have to be made with sugar." We agree. Do make your preferences known!

Lunch: Very few of the inns and hotels listed here serve lunch. Those that do generally operate a full-service restaurant, and you'll see some mention of it in the listing. Quite a number of B&B inns are happy to make up picnic lunches for an additional fee. We've noted this where we know about it; if we haven't, just ask if they can do one for you.

Dinner: Meals served at the inns listed here vary widely from simple home-style family cooking to gourmet cuisine. We are looking for food that is a good, honest example of the type of cooking involved. Ingredi-ents should be fresh and homemade as far as is possible; service and presentation should be pleasant and straightforward. We are not inter-ested in elaborate and pretentious restaurants where the descriptions found on the menu far exceed the chef's ability to prepare the dishes.

Here's how one of our readers put it, reporting on an inn in Virginia: "The inn had changed owners from our first to our second visit, a few years later. Although the rooms were much improved, the food was not.

Dinner was of the type I describe as 'American pretentious,' the sort of ambitious would-be haute (and haughty) cuisine that a regional inn without a fine professional chef and kitchen staff is ill-advised to attempt. The innkeepers would have been much better off keeping the old cooks who were still in the kitchen the first time we visited, preparing the same delicious Southern home cooking they'd been doing for at least 30 years." *(Ann Delugach)*

Drinks

With a very few exceptions (noted under "Restrictions" in each listing), alcoholic beverages may be enjoyed in moderation at all of the inns and hotels listed. Most establishments with a full-service restaurant serving the public as well as overnight guests are licensed to serve beer, wine, and liquor to their customers, although "brown-bagging" or BYOB (bring your own bottle) is occasionally encouraged, especially in dry counties. Bed & breakfasts, and inns serving meals primarily to overnight guests, do not typically have liquor licenses, although most will provide guests with setups, i.e. glasses, ice, and mixers, at what is often called a BYO (bring your own) bar.

Overseas visitors will be amazed at the hodgepodge of regulations around the country. Liquor laws are determined in general by each state, but individual counties, or even towns, can prohibit or restrict the sale of alcoholic beverages, even beer.

Smoking

Most of the larger inns and hotels do not have any smoking restrictions, except to prohibit cigars and pipes in dining rooms; restrictions at smaller establishments are becoming quite common. Where prohibitions apply we have noted this under "Restrictions." When smoking is prohibited in the guest rooms, this is usually for safety reasons; when it's not allowed in the common rooms, it's because your hosts don't care for the smell. A growing number of inns prohibit indoor smoking entirely. This has become quite common in California, Oregon, and Washington. We suggest that confirmed smokers be courteous or make reservations elsewhere. One reader noted with dismay that although smoking was not prohibited at one inn, no ashtrays were in evidence, making her feel very uncomfortable about lighting up.

When making reservations at larger hotels, nonsmokers should be sure to ask if nonsmoking rooms are available. Such rooms, which have been set aside and specially cleaned, are becoming very common.

Physical limitations and wheelchair accessibility

We asked every innkeeper if the hotel or inn was suitable for the disabled, and if yes, what facilities were provided. Unfortunately, the answer was often no. A great many inns dating back 80 years or more have far too many steps and narrow doorways to permit wheelchair access. If you do not need a wheelchair but have difficulty with stairs, we urge you to mention this when making reservations; many inns have one or two rooms on the ground floor. Similarly, if you are visually handicapped, do share this information so that you may be given a room with good lighting and no unexpected steps.

Where the answer was positive, we have noted under "Extras" the facilities offered. In some cases the response was not nearly as complete as we would have liked. Wheelchair access (via ramp) to inn and hotel restaurants tends to be better than guest room accessibility. City hotels often have street-level entrances and, of course, elevators. Some innkeepers noted that ground-floor guest rooms were wheelchair accessible but did not note whether that applied to the bathrooms, as well. Please do inquire for details when making reservations, and please share your findings with us.

Air conditioning

Heat is a relative condition, and the perceived need for air conditioning varies tremendously from one individual to the next. If an inn or hotel has air conditioning, you'll see this listed under "Rooms." If it's important to you, be sure to ask when making reservations. If air conditioning is not available, check to see if fans are provided. Remember that top-floor rooms in most inns (usually a converted attic) can be uncomfortably warm even in relatively cool climates.

Transportation

A car is more or less essential for visiting most of the inns and hotels listed here, as well as the surrounding sights of interest. Exceptions are those located in the major cities. In some historic towns, a car is the easiest way to get there, but once you've arrived, you'll want to find a place to park the car and forget about it.

If you are traveling by public transportation, check the "Extras" section at the end of each write-up. If the innkeepers are willing to pick you up from the nearest airport, bus, or train station, you'll see it noted here. This service is usually free or available at modest cost. If it's not listed, the innkeeper will direct you to a commercial facility that can help.

Parking

Although not a concern in most cases, parking is a problem in many beach resorts and historic towns. If you'll be traveling by car, ask the innkeeper for advice when making reservations. If parking is not on-site, stop at the hotel first to drop off your bags, then go park the car. The compact size of these cities will allow you to forget about it until it's time to leave. In big cities, if "free parking" is included in the rates, this usually covers only one arrival and departure. Additional "ins and outs" incur substantial extra charges. Be sure to ask.

If on-site parking is available in areas where parking can be a problem, we've noted it under "Facilities." Since it's so rarely a problem in country inns, we haven't included that information in those listings.

Christmas travel

Many people love to travel to a country inn or hotel at Christmas. Quite a number of places do stay open through the holidays, but the extent to which the occasion is celebrated varies widely indeed. We know of many inns that decorate beautifully, serve a fabulous meal, and organize all kinds of traditional Christmas activities. But we also know of others, especially in ski areas, that do nothing more than throw a few token ornaments on a tree. Be sure to inquire.

Is innkeeping for me?

Many of our readers fantasize about running their own inn; for some the fantasy may soon become a reality. Before taking the big plunge, it's vital to find out as much as you can about this very demanding business. Experienced innkeepers all over the country are offering seminars for those who'd like to get in the business. While these can be very helpful, they tend to be limited by the innkeepers' own experience with only one or two inns. (Some examples are the Chanticleer in Ashland, Oregon; the Wildwood Inn in Ware, Massachusetts; the Wedgwood Inn in New Hope, Pennsylvania; the Lord's Proprietors Inn in Edenton, North Carolina; and the Big Spring Inn in Greeneville, Tennessee; see entries for addresses.) For a broader perspective, we'd suggest you contact Bill Oates (P.O. Box 1162, Brattleboro, VT 05301; 802–254–5931) and find out when and where he'll be offering his next seminar entitled "How to Purchase and Operate a Country Inn." Bill is a highly respected pro in this field and has worked with innkeepers facing a wide range of needs and problems; his newsletter, *Innquest,* is written for prospective innkeepers looking to buy property. Another good source is Pat Hardy and Jo Ann Bell, publishers of *Innkeeping Newsletter,* as well as a number of books for would-be innkeepers. They also offer a biannual workshop in Santa Barbara, California, entitled "So, you think you want to be an innkeeper?" For details contact them at 1333 Bath Street, Santa Barbara, CA 93101; 805–965–0707.

For more information

The best sources of travel information in this country and in Canada are absolutely free; in many cases, you don't even have to supply the cost of a stamp or telephone call. They are the state and provincial tourist offices.

For each state you'll be visiting, request a copy of the official state map, which will show you every little highway and byway and will make exploring much more fun; it will also have information on state parks and major attractions in concise form.

17

Ask also for a calendar of events and for information on topics of particular interest, such as fishing or antiquing, vineyards or crafts; many states have published B&B directories, and some are quite informative. If you're going to an area of particular tourist interest, you might also want to ask the state office to give you the name of the regional tourist board for more detailed information. You'll find the addresses and telephone numbers for all the states and provinces covered in this book in Appendix 4, at the back of this book.

You may also want to contact the local chamber of commerce for information on local sights and events of interest or even an area map. You can get the necessary addresses and telephone numbers from the inn or hotel where you'll be staying or from the state tourist office.

If you are one of those people who never travel with less than three guidebooks (which includes us), you will find the AAA and Mobil regional guides to be helpful references. The Mobil guides can be found in any bookstore, while the AAA guides are distributed free on request to members. Both series cover hotels, restaurants, and sightseeing information, although we find the AAA guides offer wider coverage and more details. If you're not already a AAA member, *we'd strongly urge you join before your next trip;* in addition to their road service, they offer quality guidebooks and maps, and an excellent discount program at many hotels (including a number listed here).

We'd also like to tell you about a guidebook that makes a delightful companion to our own. *The Traveler's Guide To American Crafts*, by contributing editor Suzanne Carmichael, is divided into eastern and western editions. Suzanne leads readers to the workshops and galleries of outstanding craftspeople in every state.

Guidebooks are published only once a year (or less frequently); if you'd like to have a more frequent update, we'd suggest one of the following:

The Discerning Traveler (504 West Mermaid Lane, Philadelphia PA 19118; 215–247–5578), $50, 8 issues annually, $6 single copy. Picks a single destination in the New England and Mid-Atlantic states and covers it in real depth—sights, restaurants, lodging, and more.

Uncommon Lodgings (P.O. Box 181329, Dallas TX 75218; 214–343–9766), $15.95, 11 issues annually, $1.50 single copy. Lots of information on inns all over the country, from a delightfully opinionated editor; an excellent value.

Innsider (821 Wanda, Ferndale MI 48220; 313–541–6623), $18, 6 issues annually. Country inns, B&Bs, historic lodgings; inn-depth articles & lots of pictures; also recipes, book reviews, misc.

Country Inns/Bed & Breakfasts (P.O. Box 182, South Orange NJ 07079; 800–435–0715), $15, 6 issues annually. As above. Exceptional photography and paper quality.

Regional itineraries

We are excited by a brand-new addition to our guides this year—suggested vacation itineraries, prepared by contributing editor Suzanne

Carmichael. We hope to lead you from the best-known towns and cities through beautiful countryside, over less-traveled scenic highways to delightful towns and villages, to places where sights both natural and historic outnumber the modern "attractions" which so often litter the contemporary landscape. Try them and let us know what you think; the hardest part was picking the three itineraries in the following pages—here are lots more we want to add next year if you find them helpful.

To get a rough idea of where each itinerary will lead you, take a look at the appropriate map at the back of this book. But to really see where you'll be heading, pull out a detailed full-size map or road atlas, and use a highlighter to chart your path. (If you're hopeless when it comes to reading maps, ask the AAA to help you plan the trip with one of their Triptiks). Some of our routes are circular, others meant to be followed from one end to another; some are fairly short, others cover hundreds of miles. They can be traveled in either direction, or for just a section of the suggested route. You can sample an itinerary for a weekend, a week, or even two, depending on your travel style and the time available. For information on what to see and do along the way, refer to our state and local introductions, and to a good regional guidebook. For a list of places to stay en route, see the list of towns at the end of each itinerary, then refer to the entries in the state chapters for full details.

Finger Lakes Loop: A contemporary haven for travelers who like quiet towns and top-notch wineries, the Finger Lakes region was shaped both by ancient glaciers which carved out eleven skinny lakes, and local 19th century events which left their mark historically. Begin the tour in Syracuse, where you can see the country's most comprehensive collection of American ceramics at the Everson Museum. Head west on Route 175, then follow Route 20 to Skaneateles (pronounced Skinny-atlas) to the tip of its namesake lake. Continue west on Route 20 through Auburn, where the Republican Party was founded and escaped slave Harriet Tubman helped other slaves flee to Canada. Skirting the top of Cayuga Lake, Route 20 next passes through Seneca Falls, where the women's rights movement was born during an 1848 suffragist convention. Recommended are the Women's Rights National Historical Park and the National Women's Hall of Fame.

Route 20 next goes through Waterloo, where the Mormon Church was organized, to Geneva, situated on the northern shore of Seneca Lake. Known for its South Main Street Historic District, Geneva is surrounded by vineyards and farmland. From here head south on Route 14 along the lake, then jog west at Dresden on Route 54 to follow the shore of Keuka Lake into the heart of upstate wine country. Tour the Wine and Grape Museum in Hammondsport, then detour north on Route 54A for more lake views and winery tours.

From Hammondsport take Route 54 south to Bath, then Route 415 (or speed along Route 17) southeast to Corning, the U.S. glass capital. Families will enjoy the Corning Museum of Glass and tours of the Steuben Glass Factory. Head towards Seneca Lake on Route 414 north to Watkins Glen, known for its auto racing and multi-waterfalled state park. Cross over to Cayuga Lake on Route 227, then follow Route 89

19

south, stopping at Taughannock Falls, and continue to Ithaca, home of Cornell University.

Time to stop lake hopping and see some of the area's rolling farmland. Head east from Ithaca on Route 13, north at Dryden along Route 38 to Groton, then east on Route 222 to Cortland. Continue northeast on Route 13 through small sleepy towns such as Sheds, and on to Cazenovia, situated at the south end of yet another picturesque lake. From here return to Syracuse via Route 92, turning west at Fayetteville on Route 5.

Suggested overnights included in this region (in order of their appearance above): Skaneateles, Geneva, Hammondsport, Corning, Trumansburg, Ithaca or Groton, and Cazenovia. See entries for full details.

Marvelous Delmarva: Get away from metropolitan stress for a week or a weekend by visiting what locals call the Delmarva peninsula. Taking its moniker from the letters of *DEL* aware, *MAR* yland and *Vir-giniA*, this three-state peninsula is surrounded by the Chesapeake Bay and the Atlantic Ocean. Our route takes you through historic towns and small Chesapeake villages, across lush farmland and to popular ocean beaches. Try the region's famous crabcakes or, in season, softshell crabs. And bring along your bicycle—the flat but scenic back roads are a perfect way to explore the peninsula. For an introduction to the area from pre-European settlement to modern times, read *Chesapeake* by James Michener.

Begin your sojourn from Washington DC, or Baltimore by driving to Annapolis to watch Naval Academy pomp and see 18th-century colonial architecture. Follow Route 50 east across the Chesapeake Bay Bridge, through Stevensville on Kent Island and on to the peninsula. Turn north on Route 213 to Chestertown, a genteel town with historic riverfront brick homes, then wend your way north on Route 213 with a possible detour to bayside Betterton (Route 292, just after Kennedyville).

Continue to explore the upper peninsula by driving north on Route 213, stopping at Chesapeake City to see an 1832 canal still used by boats traveling between Chesapeake Bay and Delaware Bay. In Elkton, turn east on Routes 40, then 13 and 273 to New Castle, Delaware where William Penn first arrived to explore his colonial lands. Preserved rather than restored, New Castle is a charming 17th century town, centered around The Green laid out in 1655 by Peter Stuyvesant. If time permits, a recommended detour is to drive north on Route 9 to Wilmington to see DuPont family homes, gardens, and other treasures at Winterthur, Hagley, and the Nemours Museums.

If you crave ocean beaches and the hoopla of busy vacation villages, head south along Routes 13, 113 and 1 to bustling Rehoboth Beach or quieter Lewes; then continue south on 528 to Ocean City. From here take Route 50 west to Route 113 and Snow Hill, a sleepy river town not far from Chincoteague Bay. If you prefer quieter environs for the whole trip, go directly from New Castle to Snow Hill on Routes 13 and 113. During the fall, scan the sky and fields for huge flocks of migrating Canadian geese.

Continuing on Route 113 south to Pocomoke City, you can extend your explorations by driving south on Route 13 to Virginia's Cape Charles near the peninsula's tip, or turn north on Route 13. If you choose Route 13, jog south on Route 413 to Crisfield. Sample local oysters here, or board a boat to visit Smith Island, a virtually unsullied Bay retreat. Back on Route 13 stop by Princess Anne's historic district, then turn northwest onto Route 50 at Salisbury.

As you drive through evergreen forests, farms and marshlands, turn towards the Bay on Route 333 to visit 17th-century Oxford, then cross the Tred Avon River on the country's oldest continuously operating, privately-owned ferry. A few miles farther (turn left on Route 33) is isolated St. Michaels, a haven for sailing enthusiasts and home to the Chesapeake Bay Maritime Museum. Another option is to leave Route 50 at Easton, and head up Route 328 to Denton, a quiet town near the Choptank River. Complete your trip by following Route 50 north and back across the Chesapeake Bay Bridge.

A slew of great accommodations can be found in this area including those in (in order of their appearance above): Annapolis, Stevensville, Chestertown, Betterton, and Chesapeake City (Maryland); New Castle, Wilmington, Lewes, and Rehoboth Beach (Delaware); Snow Hill (Maryland); Cape Charles (Virginia); Princess Anne, Oxford, St. Michaels and Denton (Maryland).

Shenandoah Sojourn: Nature outdoes herself in the 200-mile long Shenandoah Valley: majestic Blue Ridge Mountains, glittering limestone caverns, and lush green valleys. Scattered through the area are important historical sites, small inns and posh resorts. Only a short drive from Washington, DC, the area can be explored in a series of weekend jaunts or on a leisurely loop as we suggest here.

Leave DC on Route 50 going south, then go west through Aldie, where you can visit one of James Monroe's homes, or continue on to Middleburg, near three of the state's finest wineries. Follow Route 50 west, then Routes 340 and 277 west to Route 11 which will be your path south into Shenandoah country. Consider stopping first in Middletown where there is another winery as well as Belle Grove, an unusual 1794 limestone-fronted mansion.

Route 11 now heads south through numerous small towns including Woodstock (great summer music festival), Edinburg (another winery here), Mt. Jackson, and historic New Market with its nearby caverns (Endless and Shenandoah). Route 11 next passes through Harrisonburg, known for its great river fishing; Mt. Crawford; and on to Staunton, birthplace of Woodrow Wilson. Stop by Staunton's Chamber of Commerce for a map outlining a self-guided walking tour of the town's 19th-century architecture.

Turn west on Route 250 into the state's Highland Country, the heart of the Allegheny/Shenandoah Mountains. Pass through forests and small river valleys to Monterey, a center for maple syrup production. Go south on Route 220, along the Jackson River, to Warm Springs and Hot Springs, towns known for their medicinal springs and pampering resorts.

INTRODUCTION

From Warm Springs, take Route 39 east to Lexington, home of Washington and Lee University. Go north on Route 11, past Vesuvius to Steeles Tavern, then east on Route 606 to the Blue Ridge Parkway. A 470-mile scenic road that starts in Asheville, North Carolina, the Parkway joins Virginia's Skyline Drive north of Afton, winding through pristine forests and along mountain crests.

We suggest you follow the Parkway/Skyline Drive north to its terminus in Front Royal, stopping at overlooks which double as perfect picnic sites. Optional diversions include a detour on Route 664 east, passing through Nellysford and on to Charlottesville to visit both Ash Lawn-Highland, James Monroe's home, and Thomas Jefferson's Monticello. Return to the Parkway on Route 250 and continue north. Another detour, which children will especially enjoy, is Route 211 west to Luray to explore the east coast's largest caverns. From here you can return to Washington on Routes 211 east, 522 and 29, or complete the Skyline Drive to Front Royal, taking I-66 back to town.

Overnight options along this route include (in order of their appearance above): Aldie, Middleburg, Middletown, Woodstock, Edinburg, Mt. Jackson, Mt. Crawford, Staunton, Swoope (just west of Staunton), Monterey, Warm Springs, Hot Springs, Lexington, Vesuvius, Nellysford, Charlottesville, Luray, and Stanley (just south of Luray).

Where is my favorite inn?

In reading through this book, you may find that your favorite inn is not listed, or that a well-known inn has been dropped from this edition. Why? Two reasons, basically:

—In several cases very well-known hotels and inns have been dropped from this edition because our readers had unsatisfactory experiences. We do not list places that do not measure up to our standards. Feel free to write us for details.

—Others have been dropped without prejudice, because we've had no reader feedback at all. This may mean that readers visiting these hotels and inns had satisfactory experiences but were not sufficiently impressed to write about them, or that readers were pleased but just assumed that someone else would take the trouble. If the latter applies, please, please, do write and let us know of your experiences. We try to visit as many inns as possible ourselves, but it is impossible to visit every place, every year. Nor is the way we are received a fair indication of the way another guest is treated. This system only works because of you. So please, keep those cards, letters, and telephone calls coming! As an added incentive, we will be sending free copies of the next edition of this book to our most helpful respondents.

Little inns of horror

We try awfully hard to list only the most worthy establishments, but sometimes the best-laid plans of mice and travel writers do go astray.

22

Please understand that whenever we receive a complaint about an entry in our guide we feel terrible, and do our best to investigate the situation. Readers occasionally send us complaints about establishments listed in *other* guidebooks; these are quite helpful as warning signals.

The most common complaints we receive—and the least forgivable—are on the issue of dirt. Scummy sinks and bathtubs, cobwebbed windows, littered porches, mildewed carpeting, water-stained ceilings, and grimy linens are all stars of this horror show.

Next in line are problems dealing with maintenance, or rather the lack of it: peeling paint and wallpaper; sagging, soft, lumpy mattresses; radiators that don't get hot and those that could be used for cooking dinner; windows that won't open, windows that won't close, windows with no screens, decayed or inoperable window shades; moldy shower curtains, rusty shower stalls, wornout towels, fluctuating water temperatures, dripping faucets, and showers that only dribble top the list on our sh-t parade.

Food complaints come next on this disaster lineup: poorly prepared canned or frozen food when fresh is readily available; meals served on paper, plastic or worst of all styrofoam; and insensitivity to dietary needs. Some complaints are received about unhelpful, abrasive or abusive innkeepers, with a few more about uncaring, inept, or invisible staff. Innkeeping complaints are most common in full service inns when the restaurant business can dominate the owners' time, leaving guest rooms and overnight guest to suffer. More tricky are questions of taste—high Victorian might look elegant to you, funereal to me; my collectibles could be your Salvation Army thriftshop donation. In short, there are more than a few inns and hotels that give new meaning to the phrase, "having reservations"; fortunately they're many times outnumbered by the many wonderful places listed in this guide.

Criteria for entries

Unlike some other very well-known guidebooks, *we do not collect a membership or listing fee of any kind from the inns and hotels we include.* What matters to us is the feedback we get from you, our readers. This means we are free to write up the negative as well as the positive attributes of each inn listed, and if any given establishment does not measure up, there is no difficulty in dropping it.

Key to Abbreviations

For complete information and explanations, please see the Introduction.

Rates: Range from least expensive room in low season to most expensive room in peak season.

Room only: No meals included; sometimes referred to as European Plan (EP).

B&B: Bed and breakfast; includes breakfast, sometimes afternoon/evening refreshment.

MAP: Modified American Plan; includes breakfast and dinner.

Full board: Three meals daily.

Alc lunch: A la carte lunch; average price of entrée plus nonalcoholic drink, tax, tip.

Alc dinner: Average price of three-course dinner, including half bottle of house wine, tax, tip.

Prix fixe dinner: Three- to five-course set dinner, excluding wine, tax, tip unless otherwise noted.

Extras: Noted if available. Always confirm in advance. Pets are not permitted unless specified; if you are allergic, ask if pets are in residence.

We Want to Hear from You!

As you know, this book is only effective with your help. We really need to know about your experiences and discoveries.

If you stayed at an inn or hotel listed here, we want to know how it was. Did it live up to our description? Exceed it? Was it what you expected? Did you like it? Were you disappointed? Delighted?

Have you discovered new establishments that we should add to the next edition?

Tear out one of the report forms at the back of this book (or use your own stationery if you prefer) and write today. Even if you write only "Fully endorse existing entry" you will have been most helpful.

Thank You!

Delaware

The Lord and Hamilton Seaside Inn, Rehoboth Beach

Delaware is a small but historic state. The Brandywine Valley, overlapping both Delaware and Pennsylvania, is particularly rich in sites of cultural interest such as Winterthur, the Hagley Museum, and the Nemours Mansion. Wilmington, Delaware's major city, has restored many of its historic areas in recent years and is small and very manageable in size. History buffs will also enjoy the 18th- and 19th-century houses of Odessa (including a Muskrat Skinning Shack), and the Victorian architecture in Dover's Historic District. If you're traveling through on I-95, be sure to stop in historic New Castle for at least an hour or preferably overnight.

The beaches of Rehoboth and Lewes are favorite escapes from the heat and humidity of summertime Washington. They are 120 miles (approximately 3 hours) from Washington, Baltimore, and Philadelphia. If you're coming from New York or New Jersey, take the New Jersey Turnpike over the Delaware Memorial Bridge, then take Route 13 to Route 1 to Lewes and Rehoboth. An alternate route (recommended for the trip home) is to take the 70-minute ferry ride from Lewes to Cape May to the Garden State Parkway (call 302–645–6313 or 609–886–2718 for details); it's about a 5-hour drive to New York City. A recommended short detour is the Bombay Hook National Refuge (northeast of Dover) where migrating ducks and geese stop by in spring and fall, and herons, egrets and other wading birds spend the summer.

Peak rates generally run from June 15 to September 15; off-season rates are considerably less. Rehoboth is a favorite family resort, combining all the boardwalk stuff kids love with chic shops and gourmet restaurants; Lewes is a bit more sedate.

Rates do not include 6% room rental tax.

Information please: The Towers (101 Northwest Front Street, Milford 19963; 302–422–3814) is a magnificent mauve mansion (how's that for alliteration) dating back to 1783, but elaborately remodeled a century ago in the Steamboat Gothic style, with more gingerbread, towers, and gables than you can imagine. Rooms are furnished with French Victorian decor, and the original walnut and cherry woodwork has been fully restored. There are five guest rooms, and guests are welcome to cool off in the swimming pool or relax in the gazebo.

Another possibility in the southwest corner of this little state is the **Spring Garden Inn** (Delaware Avenue Extension, Rte. 1, Box 283A, Laurel 19956; 302–875–7015) an 18th century "country manor" listed on the National Register of Historic Places. The five guest rooms are furnished in either Victorian or colonial decor, and rates include a full breakfast and afternoon wine and cheese.

LEWES

New Devon Inn   *Tel:* 302–645–6466
2nd and Market Streets, P.O. Box 516, 19958

Located in the historic Dutch seaport of Lewes, the New Devon is in the old market section of town, not far from the canal which carries fishing and pleasure boats to sea. The New Devon was built in 1926 as the Lewes Hotel, and was in use as a boarding house when Dale Jenkins and Bernard Nash bought and restored the inn in 1988 in the style of a small European hotel. The common areas are eclectically decorated with tiled floors, Oriental carpets, glass brick dividing walls, crystal chandeliers, and period decor, while the guest rooms have antique beds, fine linens and other collectibles. Rates include a continental breakfast of fresh fruit and juice, coffee and tea, and breads and pastries.

"We felt as though we were guests in a fine private home, a feeling enhanced by the friendliness and personal attention of the staff." *(Ann & Arthur Mackey)* More comments please.

Open All year.
Rooms 2 suites, 23 doubles—all with private bath and/or shower, telephone, air-conditioning. Some with desk.
Facilities Dining room, lobby with TV, games. Off-street parking on weekends.
Location Historic district, center of town.
Restrictions Light sleepers should request rooms away from street. No children under 17.
Credit cards Amex, MC, Visa.

Rates B&B, $80–125 suite, $65–90 double. Extra person in room, $25.
Extras Wheelchair accessible; some rooms equipped for the disabled. Station pickups by prior arrangement. Cribs available.

Savannah Inn   *Tel:* 302–645–5592
330 Savannah Road, 19958

This is the eighth season Dick and Susan Stafursky will be operating the Savannah Inn. They describe it as being "friendly and casual, furnished with a mixture of antiques and old furniture. It is fairly modest, but intentionally so. There are no private baths, TVs, phones, or air-conditioning. Most of our guests enjoy the atmosphere here. Some also enjoy socializing with us or with other guests, although it is certainly not required."

"The Savannah is located in the quiet, quaint town of Lewes, away from the hubbub of the busy boardwalk, yet within walking distance of the beach, interesting shops, and fine restaurants. The inn is a large, rambling structure with a homey, informal atmosphere. It has light, warm sitting rooms with large windowed areas and wood floors. The rooms are simply furnished and immaculate, as are the shared baths. The informal atmosphere encourages socializing through games, cards, and conversation. There are scrumptious vegetarian breakfasts with homemade bran muffins, granola, jams and jellies, and fresh fruit. The innkeepers are available, well informed, friendly yet unobtrusive. We joined one of their weekly 'jellyfish hunts,' a chance to see the wildlife along Cape Henlopen by boat." *(Zvi & Jacqueline Geismann)* Reports most welcome.

Open Memorial Day through Sept. 30; fall weekends (no breakfast served).
Rooms 7 doubles, with a maximum of 5 people sharing bath. All with fans.
Facilities Living room, glassed-in porch, patio, flower garden. Games, piano.
Location DE shore. 110 m E of Washington, DC. Enter Lewes on Rte. 9, which becomes Savannah Rd. Inn on left at Orr St. intersection.
Restrictions No smoking in common rooms. Traffic noise might disturb light sleepers in rooms at front of house.
Credit cards None accepted.
Rates B&B, $38–54 double, $38–48 single, tax included. 15% discount for stays of 7 nights or more. 2–3 night weekend minimum. Off-season rates. Tipping not expected.
Extras Bus station pickups. Food allergies accommodated if possible.

NEW CASTLE

New Castle is a delightful town, an ideal spot to stop for lunch or for the night if you're traveling along I-95 between Washington and New York. In the few minutes it takes to drive from the highway to the historic section, you can travel back 250 years to a living colonial village.

The town was founded in 1651 by Peter Stuyvesant. It was claimed alternately by both the Dutch and the Swedish governments, until the Duke of York took it for the British in 1664 and renamed it New Castle. The town served as Delaware's first capital until the early eighteenth century, when the capital shifted to Wilmington. Development stopped, and a lovely piece of history was preserved. The town is built right along the Delaware River, nearly under the Delaware Memorial Bridge. In the colonial-era Battery Park, along the river, the modern bridge looms almost overhead—a strange but beautiful juxtaposition.

"Within easy walking distance in the historic area are a magnificent 1732 Court House, Delaware's colonial capitol, with informative and amusing free guided tours; the home of George Read II, built between 1797 and 1804; a lovely and inspiring Presbyterian Church built in 1707. Be sure to see how the Dutch settlers lived by visiting the Amstel House and the Old Dutch House museums." *(Nancy Harrison & Nelson Ormsby)*

While in New Castle, be sure to stop for a leisurely meal at the **Newcastle Inn**, built as an arsenal in 1809—crab cakes and walnut rum pie are specialties (1 Market Street; 302–328–1798).

Also recommended: Received too late for a full entry was a report on the **Ross House** (129 East Second Street, 19720; 302–322–7787), a 270-year-old home which also overlooks the Delaware. Restoration has uncovered both the Victorian tin ceiling, and colonial fireplaces and brick work. "This warm and interestingly restored home is furnished eclectically with colonial, contemporary, and traditional decor, along with ethnic artifacts from the owners' international travels. There's a sitting room with a guest refrigerator and TV, and rates include a continental breakfast. Innkeepers Julia Cripps and Lu Jones are delightful, as are Shnookie and Shady, their two small dogs. Enjoyable whether you're traveling for business or pleasure." *(Susan Weil)*

Although we were unable to obtain enough information to complete a full writeup, the **Terry House** (130 Delaware Street, 19720; 302–328–2505), an 1860s townhouse, is also highly recommended. "Furnished with well-chosen antiques in a clean, comfortable setting. Our room was large with a fireplace, and faced the common. Towels were plentiful and the service friendly. The full breakfast included fresh raspberries, served in the gracious dining room, while the living room made us feel right at home."

Information please: We're disappointed to report that recent feedback on the **The David Finney Inn** (216 Delaware Street at Third, 19720; 302–322–6367), listed in this guide for many editions, has not been good. One reader felt that the food in the tavern was overpriced and underwhelming, another complained that his room in the annex was unappealing because of deficiencies in the furnishings, housekeeping, and general maintenance. Reports please.

The Janvier-Black House   *Tel:* 302–328–1339
17 The Strand, 19720

Following an old tradition, the Janvier-Black House was a wedding gift from John Janvier to his daughter Ann and her new husband Dr. Henry

Black. The inn is on the quiet street that parallels the river. Several rooms have water views. The inn has been owned by Annabelle and Henry Kressman since 1987, and rates include a continental breakfast and evening sherry and port.

"The Kressman's warm and inviting Janvier-Black House, a high-style Federal townhouse built in 1825 and listed on the National Register of Historic Places, is set on one of the prettiest streets on the East Coast. While you will want to eat at the deservedly popular David Finney Inn, The Janvier-Black House is the place to stay. Wonderful Federal architecture, spacious, well-appointed rooms with a warm period feel, and perfect hosts. Definitely merits a return trip."*(Nancy Harrison & Nelson Ormsby)*

Open All year.
Rooms 2 suites—both with private bath and/or shower, telephone, radio/stereo, TV, VCR with movies, air-conditioning. 1 with desk.
Facilities Breakfast room, enclosed porch, deck, riverfront garden.
Location Historic district, on river.
Restrictions No smoking. No children under 12.
Credit cards None accepted.
Rates B&B, $75–105 double. Extra person in room, $25. Discount for 5-night stay. 2-night weekend minimum.

William Penn Guest House
206 Delaware Street, 19720

Tel: 302–328–7736

When you consider that the William Penn House is one of the oldest buildings listed in this guide, it seems especially appropriate that its owners, Irma and Richard Burwell, have been in the B&B business longer than almost any other innkeepers.

"This historic townhouse is where William Penn stayed the very first night after landing in America (and we stayed in the very same room he did). The house was built a year or so before he arrived. The center section of the house is the oldest, consisting of just two rooms—one up, one down; you can see the original fireplace in the bedroom. In the 1700s, a front section was added, including the large guest sitting room nicely furnished in antiques. Our bedroom (William Penn's) had beige wallpaper and extremely tiny closets on either side of the fireplace, and a mantel typical of the period—a simple board about 18' above the fireplace. The comfortable furnishings included a dried flower arrangement, some antiques and twin beds, each with its own electric blanket. The bathroom was clean but old fashioned. We saw another bedroom facing the street, with a double bed and cozy rag rug. Our breakfast included melon, orange juice, tea and coffee, and a croissant. All in all a pleasant place to stay at a very reasonable price." *(SC)*

Open All year.
Rooms 4 doubles—1 with private bath, 3 with a maximum of 6 people sharing bath. All with TV, air-conditioning, fan.
Facilities Living room with fireplace.
Location Historic district. 1 m from I-95.
Restrictions No smoking in guest rooms.
Credit cards MC, Visa.

Rates B&B, $40 double.
Extras Italian spoken.

ODESSA

Cantwell House   *Tel:* 302–378–4179
107 High Street, 19730

Odessa was one of the principal trading ports on the Delaware River
until the 1890s, when a viral disease destroyed its principal export,
peaches; hastening the decline of the port was the earlier construction
of a railway line in nearby Middletown. The early commercial success
of the town created not only wealthy traders but also access to the latest
architectural styles and trends; there are many examples of Colonial,
Federal and Victorian design as well as vernacular adaptations. As industrial progress bypassed Odessa, these fine 18th- and 19th-century
homes were left behind, and have now been restored as part of the
Winterthur Museum.

The Cantwell House, named after the man with the first toll bridge
in town, is a small B&B owned since 1983 by Carole Coleman, who has
been described by some as a "Renaissance woman"; she is an auction-
eer, interior designer, architectural drafter, and former antiques dealer.
Guest rooms are furnished with country antiques and are supplied with
firm mattresses. Rates include a breakfast of homemade breads and
muffins and fruit dishes; favorites include poached fresh peaches,
sugar-top oatmeal muffins, and almond granola. *(MW)* Reports most
welcome.

Open All year.
Rooms 3 doubles—1 with private bath and/or shower, 2 with a maximum of 4
people sharing bath. 1 with whirlpool tub, TV, air-conditioning, refrigerator. 1
with fireplace.
Facilities Dining room with fireplace, living room with games; screened porch.
1 block to tennis.
Location N DE, New Castle County. 25 m S of Wilmington, 25 m N of Dover.
1 block from historic district.
Restrictions No smoking in guest rooms. No children under 6.
Credit cards None accepted.
Rates B&B, $50–75 double. Extra person in room, $10.

REHOBOTH BEACH

Rehoboth is located on the Delaware's Atlantic shore, 125 miles east of
Washington D.C., and has been a mecca for Washingtonians escaping
the oppressive summer heat and humidity ever since the Chesapeake
Bay Bridge was completed in 1952. Rehoboth's beautiful white sands
are bordered in most areas by shady pine forests, offering a welcome
respite from the summer sun. Children love the mile-long boardwalk,
complete with snack bars of all persuasions alternating with miniature

golf courses and video games and capped with the rides at Funland. Those in search of more sedate entertainment will prefer the weekend evening concerts at the bandstand nearby on Rehoboth Avenue. Area activities center on the water, and include swimming, surf-casting, sailing, windsurfing, clamming, and fishing.

As is the case in most beach towns, parking is a pain in season, when Rehoboth's population zooms from 3,000 to 90,000. Once you've found an unmetered parking space, just leave your car where it is, and walk or bicycle to in-town destinations. To avoid congestion, visit mid-week.

Information please: At the **Tembo Guest House** (100 Laurel Street, 19971; 302–227–3360) owner Gerry Cooper's elephant collection highlights the decor of this cozy beach cottage; the atmosphere is peaceful, with no TVs and plentiful reading lights. Five air-conditioned guest rooms share 2 baths; beach chairs, guest refrigerator, off-street parking, and kitchen privileges are some of the amenities available. Rates range from $50 to $90, based on room and season, and include a buffet continental breakfast. A block from the ocean is the **Royal Rose** (41 Baltimore Avenue, 19971; 302–226–2535), a recently opened B&B in a 65-year-old beach cottage; eight air-conditioned guest rooms have private and shared baths. Off-street parking and a continental breakfast are included in the rates, which range from $65 to $110 double occupancy. Your opinions?

The Corner Cupboard Inn
50 Park Avenue, 19971

Tel: 302–227–8553

The Corner Cupboard Inn was built as a private home for Alice and Jess Gundry, aunt and uncle of the present innkeeper, Elizabeth Gundry Hooper. An inn for over 50 years, Mrs. Hooper describes the Corner Cupboard as the "inn that was in before inns were in. "Today, the inn's guest rooms are spread among several buildings and cottages. Mrs. Hooper describes her inn as a place where people are encouraged to gather for conversation and refreshments in front of the fire in the winter and on the patios in summer. Only breakfast is included in the off-season rates; summer rates include both full breakfast and dinner. Dinners feature good home-style cooking, with lots of seafood dishes (crab is a favorite), plus a beef and chicken entrée, and home-baked desserts.

"Located in a beautiful, quiet residential section of Rehoboth, the inn is about [a] fifteen minutes' walk away from the hubbub on Rehoboth Avenue. Rooms vary considerably in decor; the Blue Room, with a four-poster bed, is quite nice, while others are more basically furnished." *(Mike Spring)*

"A truly small inn, graciously kept, homelike and comfortable. Mrs. Hooper carries on the traditional hospitality of her late uncle and aunt. It offers fine food, a convenient location near the uncrowded beach, and reasonable rates. Guests are treated as friends." *(Paul Podgus)* More comments please.

Open All year, except Christmas, New Year's. Restaurant open Memorial Day weekend to mid-Sept.
Rooms 18 doubles, all with private bath and/or shower, air-conditioning; several with desk, TV. 9 rooms in inn, 4 in annex, 5 in cottages.
Facilities Restaurant, living room with fireplace, breakfast room, Ping-Pong, patios. 1½ blocks to beach for swimming, fishing. Tennis, golf nearby.
Location 8 blocks from town center. Between 1st and 2nd Sts.
Credit cards Amex, MC, Visa.
Rates B&B, $75–115 double, $70–100 single; extra person in room, $25 (Sept. 15–late May). MAP, $130–210 double, $100–180 single; extra person in room, $60 (Memorial Day–Sept. 15). Alc dinner, $35.
Extras Pets permitted in some rooms, $7.50 daily. Cribs, babysitting available. Airport/station pickups.

The Lord and Hamilton Seaside Inn
20 Brooklyn Avenue, 19971

Tel: 302–227–6960

The Lord and Hamilton was opened in 1982 by Marge and Dick Hamilton after considerable restoration work. Marge says, "We named the inn the Lord and Hamilton because we need all the help we can get."

"We were greeted warmly by the Hamiltons, and their friendly shepherd Bianca, proudly outfitted in her purple neck bandana. Marge and Dick are extremely witty and fun; their gregarious personalities invite guests to lounge around the cozy sitting room or sunny, sprawling veranda for convivial breakfasts or lazy afternoon conversations. There's plenty of sturdy, comfortable wicker furniture on the wrap-around veranda, and the hammock for two is always in demand. All the rooms are beautifully decorated with family antiques, comfortable beds—most of them canopies—showcased by charming quilts and spreads, with overstuffed chairs and lounges. Plenty of sunlight streams through the windows, and Laura Ashley curtains lend delicacy to the decor. Marge's special touches include antique lamps, candles, baskets of potpourri, antique dolls and collectibles, and plenty of reading material.

"Our room had a huge canopy bed high off the floor, with an antique wardrobe with its own latchkey. Right around the corner was the community fridge, convenient for the late-night munchies. Another fun thing about the inn is the spacious outside shower and dressing room, which really puts you in touch with nature. Nobody thinks twice about meeting a fellow guest wrapped only in a towel on their way up the back stairs. Less adventuresome B&Bers will prefer the rooms with indoor plumbing, one with a shower, the other housing an old-fashioned tub, perfect for a relaxing bubble bath. The location is very quiet, yet is just a half-block from the beach, and two from the town center, so you can forget about your car. Marge gladly made recommendations for local outings and dinner reservations!" *(Victoria Berman)*

"Immaculately clean, lighting and plumbing above average and perfect location. I stayed in a large room on the top floor, with ocean views. It had an antique white iron bed and two twins with wicker headboards, Victorian lamps and furnishings; linens and towels were all a Laura-Ashley type lavender print. I had a chance to see all the rooms and my favorite was #1, with a canopy bed, porch entrance, beautiful wood, and special decor. The breakfast buffet is served in the front parlor and includes lots of fresh fruit, juice, coffee, pastry, bagels, cheese, toast and muffins. The front parlor is filled with antiques, yet is still homey and cozy." *(Mrs. John Wooley, also Mary Winterstein)*

"Our favorite room is the Elizabeth Barrett Browning Room, with a beautiful four-poster canopy bed and overstuffed chairs. Sharing a large hall bathroom was no problem; there was plenty of hot water and electric outlets." *(Harriett Joy)*

Open May 1 to Oct. 31.
Rooms 2 suites, 5 doubles—1 with private bath and/or shower, 2 with private half-bath room, 4 with a maximum of 4 people sharing bath. All rooms with desk; 2 with air-conditioning, 5 with fan.
Facilities Dining/living room, wraparound porch, grill, picnic tables, guest refrigerator. Beach, fishing ½ block away. Tennis, golf nearby. Unmetered parking 1 block away.
Location 3 blocks to center of town. 3 blocks S of Rehoboth Ave.
Restrictions No smoking. No children.
Credit Cards None accepted.
Rates B&B, $40–70 suite, $30–60 double. Extra person in room, $15. 2–3 night weekend, holiday minimum. 7th night free.
Extras Bus station pickup.

WILMINGTON

Christina House   *Tel:* 302–656–9300
707 King Street, 19807   800–543–9106

Wilmington, long a sleepy small city dominated by the DuPonts, has started to grow. Christina House is its first all-suite luxury small hotel, created from three commercial buildings, gutted to form a variety of suites and a three-story glass and brick atrium. Furnishings are contemporary, and the spacious rooms are supplied with all modern amenities, including a television in both the living room and bedroom, three telephones (one in the bath, of course), plus built-in hair dryers and makeup mirrors. Rates include a continental breakfast brought to your room or served in the restaurant; a full breakfast is available for an additional charge.

"The atrium gives the hotel a spacious feeling, although the restaurant sounds at lunchtime can make it a bit noisy. Once your door is closed though, you don't hear them. Our top-floor suite had an unusual window angled into the roof, giving us a night-time view of the stars. The location, right across from the Radisson, is very convenient, and the bistro-style restaurant has a health-conscious, but tasty menu. At lunch, I enjoyed a grilled chicken breast in raspberry sauce, while my companion had a stir-fry dish, cooked with a light hand. For a taste of old Wilmington, do go back to the Hotel DuPont for an Old World dinner in the Green Room." *(Diane Wolf)*

And a suggestion: "Be sure to ask for a room with an outside window; a few face the atrium with 'windows' done in glass brick."

Open All year.

Rooms 39 suites—all with private bath and/or shower, telephone, radio, TV, desk, air-conditioning, wet bar, refrigerator, hair dryer.

Facilities Restaurant, bar, atrium lobby/lounge with fireplace, banquet, meeting rooms, health and fitness club with sauna, business services. Valet parking, $5.

Location Central business district. Take Exit 7A off I-95. Go downtown on Delaware Ave. bearing left for 11th St. Turn right on King St.; hotel is between 7th and 8th on King.

Restrictions No smoking in some guest rooms.

Credit cards Amex, DC, Discover, MC, Visa.

Rates B&B, $95 suite. $75 weekend rate. Extra person in room, $10. Corporate, long-term rates available. Alc lunch, $10; alc dinner, $25. Getaway, spa weekend packages.

Extras 1 suite equipped for the disabled. Free airport/station pickups and downtown limo service. Crib available.

Key to Abbreviations

For complete information and explanations, please see the Introduction.

Rates: Range from least expensive room in low season to most expensive room in peak season.

Room only: No meals included; sometimes referred to as European Plan (EP).

B&B: Bed and breakfast; includes breakfast, sometimes afternoon/evening refreshment.

MAP: Modified American Plan; includes breakfast and dinner.

Full board: Three meals daily.

Alc lunch: A la carte lunch; average price of entrée plus nonalcoholic drink, tax, tip.

Alc dinner: Average price of three-course dinner, including half bottle of house wine, tax, tip.

Prix fixe dinner: Three- to five-course set dinner, excluding wine, tax, tip unless otherwise noted.

Extras: Noted if available. Always confirm in advance. Pets are not permitted unless specified; if you are allergic, ask if pets are in residence.

District of Columbia

Kalorama Guest House,
District of Columbia

Everyone needs to visit "DC" at least once in their lives. Early spring is the prettiest time, with cherry blossoms adding color and softness to a city that can seem rather cold and impersonal. In addition to the obligatory monuments, museums and other famous tourist spots, add some less-visited stops to your itinerary: see hundreds of water plants at the Kenilworth Aquatic Gardens, wander through sprawling Rock Creek Park, stroll along the B&O Canal just west of Georgetown, or drive up MacArthur Parkway to Great Falls—a spectacular setting for picnics. If Congress is in session when you're in town, be sure to watch your lawmakers in action (night sessions are particularly intriguing). From late June to early July, join the throngs at the Festival of American Folklife. For a more sedate cultural experience, attend a performance at the Folger Shakespeare Theater (September to June).

Washington is one of the many cities where weekend rates drop dramatically at most hotels. Spring and fall are peak periods; weekday rates also drop considerably from December through February and during the summer, when Congress adjourns and many Washingtonians escape the city's infamous heat and humidity. When making reservations always ask if any special rates are in effect. If cost is a concern, and you will be in Washington during the week, then one of the smaller guest houses will offer you a better value than a hotel.

Reader tip: *Dianne Crawford* recommends booking a 90-minute weekend Scandal Tour offered by a political comedy group called the Gross National Product, highlighting Washington's lowlife (202–783–7212).

Information please: Over the past few years, new hotels have been sprouting in Washington faster than mushrooms after a rain. Most are modern, but one, the **Willard** (1401 Pennsylvania Avenue, N.W.; 800–327–0200), is one of Washington's oldest and most famous hostelries, which reopened late in 1986 after a $113 million restoration. Managed by Inter-Continental Hotels, this 365-room hotel is really on the large size for this guide, but given its background, we would like to request comments from readers who have stayed there. A smaller hotel we'd like to hear more about is the **Georgetown Marbury House,** in the heart of Georgetown with a swimming pool (3000 M Street, N.W.; 800–368–5922). We've heard good things but have had no feedback.

We'd also like to hear more about the **Inn at Foggy Bottom** (824 New Hampshire Avenue, N.W. 20037; 202–337–6620 or 800–426–4455), a small, luxurious all-suite hotel close to the State Department and the Kennedy Center. Rooms are furnished in soft colors and traditional decor; lunch is served in the courtyard and in the hotel restaurant. Amenities include a welcome bottle of champagne, chocolates and cognac at turndown, and the morning paper. Comments?

Bristol Hotel	*Tel:* 202–955–6400
2430 Pennsylvania Avenue, N.W., 20037	800–822–4200

Originally built as an apartment house, the Bristol was converted into a hotel in 1985. Rooms are furnished with reproductions of classic English furniture and art and have kitchenettes, including a coffee maker and mini-bar. Terry robes are available with the bath, and rates include the *Washington Post* and overnight shoe shine service. Although the Bristol advertises itself as an "all-suite" hotel, many of the rooms are actually doubles with the extras noted above. "Executive" suites have dining alcoves, and only the one-bedroom suites have a living room separate from the bedroom. The Bristol Grill serves breakfast, lunch, and dinner, and has gained a reputation for good food, especially their mesquite grilling; the Grill was recently chosen by the *Washington Post* as one of the city's top new restaurants.

"The Bristol is a beautiful place, warm and friendly with an elegant ambience. The suites are very spacious and comfortable, and they're all organized for the guests' convenience, from multiple telephones and remote-controlled television to large, comfortable, and well-lit working areas for business travelers. The rooms are very quiet, an unusual pleasure in a city with many parties and emergency vehicles with loud sirens. The location is excellent, just a short walk from the Kennedy Center, Georgetown, and the Metro. Room service and maintenance are excellent; should a problem arise, it's fixed immediately. Best of all is the staff, who are well trained and exhibit a real commitment to serve their guests." *(Charles Head)* More reports requested.

Open All year.
Rooms 37 suites, 203 doubles and singles—all with full private bath, telephone, radio, TV, desk, air-conditioning, mini-bar, hair dryer, coffeemaker, kitchenette.
Facilities Restaurant, bar/lounge, lobby, gift shop, meeting room. Guest laundry room. Concierge, facsimile services. Room service. Valet parking; self-park garage. Health club privileges.
Location West end of DC. 1 m to downtown.
Credit cards Amex, CB, DC, MC, Visa.
Rates Room only, $230–875 suite, $155–185 double. No charge for children under 17 in parents' room. Extra person in room, $20. Corporate rates. Weekend packages. Alc breakfast, $6–10; alc lunch, $15; alc dinner, $45.
Extras Spanish, Italian, French, Chinese, Vietnamese, Farsi spoken. Crib, baby-sitting available. Member, Wyndham Hotels.

The Canterbury Hotel
1733 N Street, N.W., 20036

Tel: 202–393–3000
800–424–2950

A modern apartment house, the Canterbury was converted into a hotel in 1983. It was built on the site of the former residence of presidents Teddy and Franklin D. Roosevelt, known as "the Little White House." All rooms are described as suites, which means that all are large enough to accommodate a stocked wet bar, separate sitting and work areas, and queen- or king-size beds; only the very largest are actually two separate rooms. Rates include continental breakfast, evening (5 P.M) cocktail, champagne at 10 P.M., the *Washington Post* in the morning, bathrobes, and chocolates. Rooms are furnished with eighteenth-century reproduction English furniture.

"The Canterbury is a charming, European-style hotel right in the middle of downtown Washington." *(Rosemary Mazon)* "Excellent location, close to Dupont Circle, yet on a quiet, tree-lined residential street. The lobby area is compact, yet offers ample seating space if you are meeting friends." *(SWS)*

"A lovely inn in the heart of Washington, with a very attentive, helpful staff, all in a gem of a neighborhood: one block from shopping on Connecticut Ave., a 10-minute walk to Georgetown, and a $4 cab ride from Kennedy Center. Strawberries and champagne were provided in a charming, large room with a complete kitchen, which can be closed off by shuttered doors if needed. Plenty of peace and quiet; a nice, safe location for a woman travelling alone." *(M.D. Stuart, also Millie Bryant)*

Open All year.
Rooms 99 suites—all with full private bath, telephone, radio, TV, desk, air-conditioning, wet bar, hair dryer.
Facilities Restaurant, lobby, bar, meeting rooms. Health club privileges. Valet parking, $9 daily.
Location 2 blocks from Dupont Circle. Between 17th & 18th Sts.
Credit cards Amex, CB, DC, MC, Visa.
Rates B&B, $280–350 suite, $160–220 double, $140–200 single. Maximum of 2 children under 12 free in parents' room. Extra adult in room, $20. Corporate, monthly rates. Alc lunch, $12; alc dinner, $28–35. Weekend packages.
Extras 1 suite equipped for the disabled. Spanish, French spoken.

The Hampshire Hotel
1310 New Hampshire Avenue, N.W., 20036

Tel: 202–296–7600
800–368–5691

The Hampshire is a small, modern hotel that has developed a good reputation since its opening in 1983. Most rooms have king-size beds or two doubles, sitting and dressing areas, and kitchenettes; guest rooms are decorated with traditional furniture and coordinating flowered drapes, valances, and bedspreads. Ample storage space is provided, and although the baths are small, they're well equipped with amenities and big, thirsty towels. Lafitte, the hotel's French-Creole restaurant, has been well reviewed by the Washington food critics. The Hampshire is owned by Taj International Hotels, the same company that owns the Canterbury.

"This quiet hotel is located in the downtown area, within walking distance of the White House, Kennedy Center, Georgetown, numerous restaurants, and many offices. Park your car at the hotel and enjoy the immaculate, well-lighted rooms, the comfortable bed, the ample hot water, the toilets that flush, and the TV that works. Also enjoy Lafitte, the hotel restaurant serving superb creole cooking, for breakfast, lunch, and dinner. The staff is courteous, friendly, and helpful." *(Glenn Matter)*

"The Hampshire is a delightful small hotel. The rooms are large and have small kitchenettes with complimentary coffee and tea, and the newspaper at the door each morning is a great help. Valet parking is convenient, quick, and appropriately priced. But nothing is as important as the staff, which is genuinely concerned with your comfort and well-being. Bellmen, front-desk people, and housekeeping staff all make clear that they are there to help you and do so efficiently and cheerfully." *(Walter Lambert, also Sidney & Mary Flynn)*

"While its modern architecture was not especially appealing or inviting from the outside, it is well-situated for walking around; the weekend rate makes it attractive for a Washington weekend. Our room was very light, and being at the back of the building, was very quiet. Service at their parking garage was fast and efficient." *(Ellie Freidus)* "At the Hampshire, you can sleep with the windows open, and awaken to the sounds of birds chirping. Its small size ensures that noisy convention-goers are not among the guests." *(Peter Detmold)*

And some minor niggles: "Only minor problems are small lobby and bar area for meeting friends, occasional fluctuations in water temperature, and the typical big-city noises of fire engines and police sirens." And: "We were frustrated by the fact that room service does not begin until 8 A.M. and that we could not place our breakfast order the night before."

Open All year. Restaurant closed Christmas and New Year's Day.
Rooms 82 suites—all with full private bath, telephone, radio, TV, desk, air-conditioning, kitchen, wet bar. Some with balcony.
Facilities Lounge, restaurant with live music nightly, meeting rooms. Room service, valet laundry, concierge service. Valet parking, $6. Health club, swimming pool privileges.
Location 1 block SW of Dupont Circle.
Restrictions No smoking in some guest rooms.
Credit cards Amex, CB, DC, Discover, MC, Visa.
Rates Room only, $138–184 suite (for 2 people), $121–169 single. No charge for

children under 12 in parents' room. Extra person in room, $15. Weekend, monthly, long-term rates. Alc breakfast, $5–12; alc lunch, $20; alc dinner, $40–50.
Extras Crib available. French, German, Spanish, Italian spoken.

Hay-Adams Hotel
1 Lafayette Square, 20006

Tel: 202–638–6600
800–424–5054

"An island of civility in a sea of power" is the opening line of the Hay-Adams' brochure, a beginning unique among such publications, and a key one in understanding the role filled by this elegant establishment. Built on the sites of the homes of John Hay and Henry Adams, this hotel dates back to 1927, when it was built in the Italian Renaissance style. In 1983, it was restored to its original grandeur and has developed a reputation for its luxurious atmosphere and excellent service. The lobby is decorated in shades of ivory and rose, punctuated by massive carved walnut pillars, polished brass, English antiques, and a seventeenth-century tapestry. The more expensive guest rooms offer a view of the White House and the Washington Monument beyond, but all are furnished with antique reproductions and plush fabrics. The hotel has several different restaurants: the Adams Room for 'power breakfasts'; the piano lounge for afternoon tea with scones, strawberries, and cream; the John Hay Room for elegant dining; and the English Grill, for British fare in club-like surroundings." *(Anne Borchardt)* More comments please.

Open All year.
Rooms 21 suites, 138 doubles—all with full private bath, telephones, radio, TV, desk, air-conditioning. Some with balcony, fireplace.
Facilities Restaurant, grill, lounge with piano, lobby, library. Valet parking.
Location Directly opposite White House facing Lafayette Square Park.
Credit cards All major cards accepted.
Rates Room only, $425–1,500 suite, $205–340 double, $155–315 single. Extra person in room, $25. Alc breakfast, $10–20; alc lunch, $25; alc dinner, $65. Weekend, holiday packages.
Extras Wheelchair accessible; many bathrooms equipped for disabled. Airport/station pickups, for a fee. Pets permitted with prior approval. Spanish, French, German, Italian, Japanese, Arabic, Chinese, Hebrew, Greek, Hungarian, Rumanian spoken. Cribs, babysitting available. Member, Preferred Hotels.

The Henley Park Hotel
926 Massachusetts Avenue, N.W., 20001

Tel: 202–638–5200
800–222–8474

A Tudor style building constructed in 1918, the Henley Park was restored in 1982. Its exterior is ornamented with 119 gargoyles and plaques. The common areas include a spacious parlor where afternoon tea and scones are served. Rooms are traditionally furnished in shades of beige, taupe, and mauve—colors that are present throughout the hotel. "Comfortable accommodations, friendly professional service at the front desk." *(PH)* "Fantastic food and service at the hotel's Coeur de Lion restaurant." *(RR)* Reports would be most helpful.

Open All year.
Rooms 7 suites, 89 doubles—all with full private bath, telephone, radio, TV, desk, air-conditioning. Some with four-poster beds.
Facilities Lobby, parlor with fireplace, restaurant with atrium, lounge with entertainment. Valet parking. Concierge service.

Location Downtown. At intersection of 10th Street and Massachusetts Ave. 1½ blocks from Convention Center; 6 blocks from Union Station; 4 blocks from Metro Center subway station.
Restrictions No smoking in some guest rooms.
Credit cards Amex, Choice, MC, Visa.
Rates Room only, $295–425 suite, $155–215 double, $135–195 single. Extra person in room, $20. Senior discount available. Alc breakfast, $6–12; alc lunch, $22–33; alc dinner, $45. Holiday, anniversary packages; seasonal brunch, dinner events.
Extras Cribs, babysitting available by prior arrangement. French, Spanish spoken. Member, The Classic Collection.

The Jefferson Hotel
1200 16th Street, 20036

Tel: 202–347–2200
800–368–5966

The Jefferson was built in 1923 as an apartment building for the wealthy. Totally renovated during the past decade, it features elegant, individually decorated rooms, many with Scalamandre fabrics, canopy beds, original paintings, and antique desks. The hotel has been popular for years with the rich and famous of the political, social, literary, and theatrical worlds, with H. L. Mencken, Helen Hayes, and Leonard Bernstein among its better-known fans. The Hunt Club, the hotel's restaurant, is a place for Washingtonians to see and be seen; it recently developed a reputation for fine regional cooking as well, under supervision of chef Will Greenwood.

There have been lots of changes at the Jefferson in the past year or two: new owners; a new manager (Rose Narva, the hotel's long-time manager, left the Jefferson for New York City not long ago); refurbishing of the lobby; and the installation of a state-of-the-art phone system. Some of the guest rooms have been recently redone, others may still be a bit tired. *(MW)* Comments, please, on how things are holding up under the new regime.

Open All year.
Rooms 32 suites, 68 doubles—all with full private bath, telephone, radio, TV/VCR, desk, air-conditioning, mini-bar, hair dryer, computer and facsimile machine hookups. Suites with stereo, CD player. 12 rooms in annex.
Facilities Restaurant, breakfast room, bar/lounge, video library. Health club with indoor swimming pool. Valet parking. Laundry service, 24-hour concierge, room service.
Location Downtown. At corner of 16th and M Sts. 4 blocks N of White House.
Credit cards Amex, DC, MC, Visa.
Rates Room only, $375–1,000 suite, $225–285 double, $175–260 single. Weekend, $180 suite; $145 double; $125 single. Weekend packages. Extra person in room, $20. Alc breakfast, $8–12; alc lunch, $30–35; alc dinner, $55–65.
Extras Small, well-behaved pets permitted, by prior arrangement. Crib, babysitting available. French, Spanish spoken. Member, Leading Hotels of the World, Small Luxury Hotels.

Kalorama Guest House
1854 Mintwood Place, N.W., 20009

Tel: 202–667–6369

The Kalorama is made up of two connecting townhouses, renovated in 1982 by Roberta Piecznik; also under the same ownership is the Kalorama at Woodley Park (202–328–0860), near the Washington Zoo.

"Guests are accommodated in one of the two beautiful Victorian houses, lavishly furnished with antiques and old-world memorabilia. On the wall of both the hallways and individual bedrooms you can peruse old cartoons, magazine covers and family photographs from the last century. The bedrooms are elegantly furnished with Liberty-style prints; you can relax in the sitting room and watch a little television. Breakfast is taken downstairs in the main house, at pretty French-style tables; there's always an interesting conversation to join over continental breakfast of juice, fruit, coffee, muffins, and the morning papers." *(Tessa Lamb)*

"I stayed in the Kalorama–Woodley Park. The innkeeper was very helpful, giving guests instructions to the subway, sightseeing information, and directions to the many nearby ethnic restaurants. I felt she really cared about the place and wanted guests to like it too. The decor is largely Victorian antiques; my room was quiet, medium in size, with a king-size bed and a small bathroom. Overall, an excellent value." *(Robert G. Schwemm)*

"I like staying in a real neighborhood instead of an anonymous high-rise area, and this guest house met this requirement nicely. After a wearying journey, I was met with a friendly welcome and a glass of sherry, taken in the lovely parlor." *(Judith Trent)* "I enjoy the diversity of rooms available; each tends to have its own special features, charm and idiosyncrasies, which is the reason I prefer B&Bs over standardized hotels. The ethnic character of the neighborhood, with its many restaurants, add to the fun." *(Michael A. Gomez)*

One caveat: "An auto is a liability in this area—parking spaces are scarce and parking regulations are tough. Still, public transportation is just fine so give the place a silver star for location."

Open All year.
Rooms 3 suites with private bath, 28 doubles—9 with private bath and/or shower, 19 with a maximum of 6 people sharing bath. All with clock/radio, desk, air-conditioning.
Facilities Parlors with library, games; breakfast room, courtyard. Limited pay parking.
Location Residential area, 10 min. by Metro from Smithsonian and White House. Between Columbia Rd. and 19th St. N.W.
Restrictions No children under 5. Light sleepers should request rooms at the front of the inn at Woodley Park.
Credit cards Amex, DC, MC, Visa.
Rates B&B, $65–95 suite, $50–85 double, $45–80 single. Extra person in room, $10. 10% AARP discount. 2–night weekend minimum Mar.–Nov.

The Morrison-Clark Inn
Massachusetts Avenue and Eleventh Street, N.W., 20001

Tel: 202–898–1200
800–332–7898

The Morrison Clark Inn, based in two grand townhouses dating to 1864, was carefully restored in 1987; a new structure complementing the graceful lines of the historic buildings houses 42 of the guest rooms.

A variety of dining rooms offers the elegance of a private club or the pleasures of outdoor dining. The Conservatory and the Solarium are fully enclosed, while the Courtyard enables diners to enjoy the perennial garden and cast iron balcony reminiscent of New Orleans. American cuisine is served, with accents from the South and Southwest.

Guest rooms feature authentic period furnishings, original artwork, honor bars—even computer-access data ports. Rates include a continental breakfast, morning paper, bath amenities, and turndown service.

"The guest rooms and public areas of the hotel are furnished with antiques and period furniture. Service is uniformly good to excellent. The spacious lobby is an excellent place to meet friends, and the hotel parlor, where complimentary continental breakfast is served, is well suited for an afternoon business meeting. The restaurant is elegant without being too formal and the food is excellent. My single room in the modern addition was quite small, but I understand that those in the original building are quite a bit larger. The location is central, and cabs are easy to find." *(Sam Mandel)*

"Outstanding restaurant. We ate there three nights in a row. We never repeated a dish, and everything was excellent. Although expensive, we felt it was worth every penny. Our suite was extraordinary, with stunning decor, and comfortable bedding. The bathroom had an unending supply of hot water, and the towels were fluffy." *(MAA)*

And some areas for improvement: In response to earlier comments regarding inadequate bedside lighting, we understand that additional lamps were on order, and should be installed by now.

Open All year.
Rooms 54 suites and doubles—all with full private bath, telephone, radio, TV/VCR, desk, air-conditioning, wet bar. Hair dryers available. Rooms in 2 adjacent townhouses.
Facilities Restaurant with fireplace, parlor, conservatory, solarium, courtyard, veranda, balcony. Concierge and room service, laundry, dry cleaning service. Business services. Valet parking. Morning limousine service to business district, Capitol Hill. Personal car with driver for hire.
Location Adjacent to downtown office district, close to Convention Center.
Restrictions Street noise in front rooms.
Credit cards Amex, DC, MC, Visa.
Rates B&B, $195 suite, $115–195 double. Extra person in room, $20. Weekend rates, $99–135.
Extras Limousine service to business district, Capitol Hill.

Normandy Inn
2118 Wyoming Avenue, N.W., 20008

Tel: 202–483–1350
800–424–3729

Like many of Washington's small hotels, the Normandy was built as an apartment building, then converted to a hotel in 1981. Complimentary tea and coffee are available in the tea room from 11 A.M. to midnight; cookies are added at 3 P.M.

"The Normandy has very clean, comfortable rooms, on the small side but well appointed with the amenities one expects. It is the atmosphere here that really makes it stand out—in some ways it resembles a European pensione. The location is ideal, right off Connecticut Avenue, in the Embassy District. It's within easy walking distance of the Metro and bus routes, yet its side street location ensures quiet. It is truly an international hotel; this is apparent any morning in the breakfast room, when one normally hears five or six languages being spoken. But the truly remarkable thing about this hotel is the management and staff, who treat guests with great courtesy, going out of their way to make each guest's stay pleasant. I received many telephone messages with no problems; if I was in the lobby or breakfast room, the call was forwarded to me; if I was out, an accurate message was relayed upon my return." *(Robert A. O'Connell, also Bob Schwemm)*

"Tuesday wine and cheese gatherings offer guests the opportunity to meet one another. There is a wonderful variety of restaurants nearby, both north and south on Connecticut Avenue, and in Adams Morgan— all within easy walking distance, reasonably priced, and inviting dinners with a whole world of ethnic variety." *(Gerald E. Hillier)*

Open All year.
Rooms 4 suites, 35 doubles, 35 singles—all with full private bath, telephone, radio, TV, desk, air-conditioning. Some rooms with refrigerator.
Facilities Lobby, breakfast room, patio with plants. Underground parking (extra fee), car and limousine rentals, sightseeing tours.
Location Adjacent to French Embassy, Dupont Circle (Metro); 20-min. walk to center. 8 m S of I-495. Just off Connecticut Ave.
Credit cards Amex, MC, Visa.
Rates B&B, $180 suite, $90 double, $80 single. Extra person in room, $10. No charge for children under 12 sharing room with parents. Weekend rate, $65.
Extras 2 rooms equipped for disabled. Crib, babysitting available. Arabic, French, German, Spanish spoken.

The River Inn   *Tel:* 202–337–7600
924 Twenty-Fifth Street, N.W., 20037   800–424–2741

A small, all-suite hotel of recent construction, The River Inn combines modern convenience and old-fashioned service. Rooms are spacious, decorated with comfortable contemporary decor, and most have views of the Potomac and Washington. Amenities include complimentary shoe shines, terry robes, and the morning paper. A membership in the "Club," designed for frequent travelers, provides complimentary continental breakfast and afternoon cocktails in the Club Salon. *(MW)* More comments please.

Open All year.
Rooms 128 suites—all with full private bath, telephone, radio, TV, desk, air-conditioning, fully equipped kitchens with microwave ovens. Some kitchens with coffee grinder, fresh coffee beans.
Facilities Restaurant, bar, sun deck. Private business lounge, business services. Concierge, room service, grocery shopping service, shoe shines, laundry services. Valet parking, $10. Boat rentals nearby.
Location Historic "Foggy Bottom" district, on Potomac. 2 blocks to Washington Circle, 6 blocks to Georgetown. Around the corner from Foggy Bottom Metro Station.
Restrictions No smoking in some guest rooms.
Credit cards Amex, CB, DC, MC, Visa.
Rates Room only, $122–175 suite. Extra person in room, $15. Weekend rate, $85–125. Theater, sightseeing, conference packages. Long-term rates available. Alc lunch, $10–15; alc dinner, $30.
Extras Crib, babysitting available. Italian, French, Spanish, Arabic, German, Pakistani spoken.

Swiss Inn
Tel: 202–371–1816
1204 Massachusetts Avenue, N.W., 20005

The Swiss Inn, a small, reconstructed townhouse with high ceilings and
bay windows, is located just a block or two from Franklin Park and
within walking distance of the White House and the Convention Center.

"A find for those on a budget; a good location in the downtown area,
with clean rooms, fluffy towels, and lots of lights. While the hostess
may be difficult to understand over the phone, she is very nice. With
the money you save on accommodation, walk over to the Morrison-
Clark [see entry], and splurge on their delicious restaurant." *(Dianne
Crawford)* More comments please.

Open All year.
Rooms 6 doubles—all with private bath and/or shower, telephone, TV, air-
conditioning, kitchenette.
Facilities Lobby. On-site parking.
Location At intersection of Massachusetts Ave., 12th & L Sts. 2 blocks to Con-
vention Center.
Credit cards Amex, MC, Visa.
Rates Room only, $58 double, $48 single. Weekly, monthly rates.

Tabard Inn
Tel: 202–785–1277
1739 N Street, N.W., 20036

During World War I, three Victorian townhouses were linked to form
the Tabard Inn. Efforts to demolish the inn were successfully defeated
in the early 1970s, and the Tabard is now Washington's oldest hotel in
continuous operation. Rooms at the Tabard vary widely in size and
decor—some are very spacious and are beautifully furnished with period furniture, while others (originally the servants' rooms) are nothing
special. These differences are reflected in the range of rates, which
include continental breakfast. The Tabard Inn Restaurant is also home
to one of Washington's top restaurants; during the summer its produce
comes from its own farm in Virginia.

"To find such a place in downtown Washington is rare. It has all the
charm of Victorian Washington. Excellent bar and restaurant." *(A.W.
Burton)*

"Those who find Washington an overly marbled and somewhat ster-
ile environment will find the Tabard to be an ideal oasis. In fact, the
mood here is much like a small hotel in London or Paris. But it is most
definitely not a hotel for everyone. The decor is emphatically not the
American concept of 'European elegance'; rather, it's the more truly
European setting of faded gentility, perhaps a tad on the tacky side. The
downstairs lounge is dark and cozy, with lots of comfortable seating;
you're welcome to browse through the papers, or order wine and a plate
of hors d'oeuvres. Upstairs, most rooms are large and are furnished with
turn-of-the century antiques. Ours had a huge armoire, about the size
of a New York City kitchen, fronted with gently silvered mirrors, an
old-fashioned double bed, and comfortable seating area in front of the
fireplace." *(SWS)*

"You get what you pay for—some of the less expensive rooms are tiny."

Open All year. Restaurant closed Jan. 1, Memorial Day, July 4, Labor Day, Thanksgiving, Christmas.
Rooms 33 doubles, 9 singles—22 with private bath, 20 with maximum of 4 people sharing 1 bath. All with telephone, desk, air-conditioning.
Facilities Lounges, bar, restaurant, outdoor patio.
Location 1 block from Dupont Circle. From Dupont Circle, follow CT Ave. S. to N St. Inn is between 17th and 18th Sts.
Restrictions Street noise might disturb light sleepers in some rooms. No cigar or pipe smoking in restaurant.
Credit cards MC, Visa.
Rates B&B, $69–119 double. Additional person in room, $15. Weekend rates. Alc lunch, $12–16; alc dinner, $35–40.
Extras Cribs available. Spanish, Portuguese, German spoken.

The Windsor Inn
1842 16th Street, N.W., 20009

Tel: 202–667–0300
800–423–9111

Renovated in accordance with the historic preservation standards of the National Park Service, the Windsor's rooms are decorated in the art deco style of the 1920s, while the **The Embassy Hotel** (1627 16th Street, N.W.; 202–234–7800) is a similar hotel, done in the Federalist style, located four blocks south and owned by the same company.

"Conveniently located in a very quiet neighborhood, with easy access to taxis and neighborhood shops, within walking distance of major streets and areas. Coffee was always available in the lobby, along with the morning papers, and afternoon sherry, all very nicely served and presented. Rooms are fairly large, very clean, well equipped, and attractive." *(D.A. Haight)*

"The lobby, where continental breakfast is served, is more akin to someone's living room. The staff takes a genuine interest in accommodating the needs and questions of guests." *(Norton Stone)* "The hotel has no parking facilities, but we had little problem finding a spot in front of the hotel." *(Willen Uilenbroek)* More comments please.

Open All year.
Rooms 9 suites, 27 doubles, 10 singles—all with private bath and/or shower, telephone, radio, TV, air-conditioning. One suite with kitchen.
Facilities Lobby/lounge/breakfast room, meeting room. Laundry, concierge services. On-street parking.
Location 16th Street Historic District. 1/2 m from center. Approx. 7 blocks NE of Dupont Circle; 1 block E of New Hampshire Ave.
Credit cards Amex, CB, Choice, DC, MC, Visa.
Rates B&B, $105–150 suite, $79–99 double, $69–79 single. Extra person in room, $10. No charge for children under 12 in parents' room. $55 weekend rate.
Extras Crib available.

Maryland

The Inn at Buckeystown, Buckeystown

In addition to Baltimore, historic Annapolis, and the gracious countryside of western Maryland, the Eastern Shore is the state's main area for attractive inns and hotels. This area is actually part of a large peninsula, extending south from Pennsylvania and Delaware like a fist with one long pointing finger. Delaware is on the western side of this peninsula; Maryland is on the east; the "finger" itself is part of Virginia. The entire area is very flat, ideal for bicycling, and, of course, fishing and other water sports are always options. It's also rich in history, with many well-preserved eighteenth- and early nineteenth-century houses to be found in Chestertown, Easton, St. Michaels, Oxford, and Cambridge. For a change of pace, stop in Crisfield, self-proclaimed "Crab Capital of the World," and a departure point for ferries to Smith and Tangier Islands, both pleasant afternoon excursions. If you visit the Delmarva Peninsula in late Fall you may see hundreds of snow geese during their annual migration.

Information please: In northern Maryland, about 25 miles northwest of Baltimore, and about the same distance northeast of Frederick, is the **Winchester Country Inn,** a 200-year-old home beautifully decorated to the period (430 South Bishop Street, Westminster 21157; 301–867–7373). It's been accurately restored (perhaps too accurately in the area of bedside lighting) to its 1760 origins, with handsome colonial antiques complementing the original moldings and hand-blown window glass. The reasonable rates include a full breakfast and afternoon refreshments. Area activities include the Carroll County Farm Museum, re-creating rural life a century ago, the Greenway Arboretum, local wineries, and Cascade Lake for water sports.

If you'd prefer a touch of the country just 12 miles north of Washington D.C., the **Thoroughbred B&B** (16410 Batchellors Forest Road, Olney 20832; 301–774–7649) is an interesting possibility. This 175-acre horse-breeding farm offers five guest rooms, a game room with full-size pool table, a hot tub, and a swimming pool. Rates include a full breakfast, and the Metrorail into DC is just 6 miles away if you don't want to fight rush-hour traffic.

Rates do not include 5% sales tax; some areas have additional lodging taxes.

ANNAPOLIS

Annapolis is an historic city with restored buildings spanning three centuries—a large section has been named a National Historic District. It's full of interesting shops and galleries; there's the Maryland State House and several eighteenth-century mansions, along with the harbor to tour, and, of course, the U.S. Naval Academy. Once known as Hell's Point, the only thing hellish about the area these days is the parking—streets in the historic district are narrow, and on-street parking is limited to two hours during the week. Unload your luggage at your inn, then park at the Navy Stadium and ride a trolley shuttle back. Forget your car—it's a compact area and everything's in easy walking distance.

Information please: A small but historic B&B is the **Jonah William's House,** dating back to 1830, owned and run by Dorothy Robbins (101 Severn Avenue, 21403; 301–269–6020). We'd also like comments on the **Historic Inns of Annapolis,** a group of restored inns and private homes, ranging in size from 9 to 44 rooms, including the **Maryland Inn,** dating to 1776, with an equally venerable restaurant, the Treaty of Paris (Church Circle and Main Street, 21403; 301–263–2641 or 800–847–8882). One reader stayed at the Robert Johnson House in this complex, but complained that the room was small, with no table, so they had to sit on the rug to eat the continental breakfast delivered to the door. Comments?

Gibson's Landing   *Tel:* 301–268–5555
110 Prince George Street, 21401

Three adjacent 18th and 19th century homes, furnished with antiques and highlighted by stained glass windows make up Gibson's Landing. Rates include a breakfast of juice, fruit, cheese, cereal, English muffins, croissants, and a selection of homemade goodies including muffins, banana walnut bread, and hot bread pudding.

"Adjacent to the U.S. Naval Academy, Gibson's is within walking distance of the Capitol and historic sites. Rooms are filled with interesting antiques and artifacts, and the newer sections of the inn were restored to match the older parts. Breakfast is great and the atmosphere is warm and homey. The personnel are delightfully friendly and seem like family." *(Les Long)* "Great restaurants are within walking distance, and Gibson's is unique in having ample free parking. The water taxi to Eastport is great fun and just 75 yards away." *(Geri Homa)*

"A charming place with friendly staff and delicious breakfasts. Our pretty room was furnished in period decor, and our shared bath was spotless. The location is ideal, central to everything." *(Elisabeth McLaughlin)*

Open All year.
Rooms 2 suites, 18 doubles - 7 rooms with private shower and/or bath, 13 rooms with a maximum of 4 people sharing a bath. All with air-conditioning. Some with telephone, radio, TV, desk, fan. Rooms in 3 houses centered around courtyard.
Facilities 2 living rooms/parlors in each house. 2 dining rooms, 1 conference room. 2 acres with courtyard, garden. Off-street parking. Boating, fishing, swimming nearby.
Location Downtown historic district. On Severn River and Chesapeake Bay.
Credit cards Amex, MC, Visa.
Rates B&B, $120 suite, $68–85 double, $58–75 single. Extra person in room $10. 2-night minimum USNA graduation and homecoming.
Extras Wheelchair accessible. Some Spanish, French spoken.

Prince George Inn
232 Prince George Street, 21401

Tel: 301–263–6418

Built in 1884, the Prince George is located in the heart of the historic area and has been carefully restored and handsomely decorated with Victorian antiques and art. Long-time owners Bill and Norma Grover-mann are very knowledgeable about the city and can suggest sights and activities to enhance your stay. Rates include a generous continental buffet breakfast.

"A jewel of a B&B. The guest rooms are nicely furnished, the shared baths are quite comfortable. The parlor is filled with an interesting selection of current and vintage reading material. All the sights of historic Annapolis are within walking distance." *(James & Janice Utt)* More comments please.

Open Feb. 15–Dec. 31
Rooms 4 doubles sharing 2 full baths. All rooms with radio, air-conditioning, fan.
Facilities Parlor with TV, fireplace; breakfast porches, bricked courtyard area. 4 blocks from city dock for cruising and dining.
Location 45 min. S of Baltimore, E of Washington, D.C. In historic district, 1½ blocks from State Circle. From Rtes. 2/50/301 (John Hanson Hwy.) take Rte. 70/Rowe Blvd. exit. Follow Rowe Blvd. (name changes to Bladen St.) to College St. Go left on College, right on King George, right on Maryland Ave., right on Prince George to inn on right.
Restrictions Smoking on 1st floor only. Children over 12 preferred. Parking limited.
Credit cards MC.
Rates B&B, $75 double, $60 single (midweek only). Extra person in room, $10.

William Page Inn
8 Martin Street, 21401

Tel: 301–626–1506

Robert Zuchelli and Greg Page renovated the William Page Inn and opened it as a B&B late in 1988. They've decorated this turn-of-the century home with period antiques and reproductions. Rates include a buffet continental breakfast and afternoon tea or lemonade, to be enjoyed either in the common room or on the wraparound porch.

"Comfortable rooms with beautiful furnishings and decor. The food is delicious, and the innkeepers take great care and pride in their establishment. They are also very knowledgeable about the area and provided expert advice on food and historic sights." *(Nancy Stickel)* "Spacious clean rooms. When leaving and returning at night a porch light automatically goes on, making you feel very safe. The tasty breakfast included fresh fruit, cereal, and muffins. Rob and Greg were friendly, informative, and very gracious." *(Lura & Bill Reddington)*

Open All year.
Rooms 1 suite, 4 doubles—3 with private shower and/or bath, 2 rooms with a maximum of 4 people sharing a bath. All with clock/radio, desk, air-conditioning.
Facilities Common room, porch. Off-street parking.
Location Historic district.
Restrictions No smoking.
Credit cards MC, Visa.
Rates B&B, $95–120, $55–80.
Extras Airport/station pickups, $30–40.

BALTIMORE

Baltimore has changed considerably in the past decade. Once a city tourists deliberately bypassed on their way to Washington, it is now a tourist attraction, thanks in part to the stunning National Aquarium (with its new marine mammal pavilion) and the shop-filled Harborplace, along with the renovation of many of its historic areas. Other attractions include the Revolutionary War frigate U.S.S. *Constellation,* the Maryland Science Center, the Power Plant indoor amusement park, the Baltimore Museum of Art, the Walters Art Gallery, and the Edgar Allan Poe House. Of no less importance is Baltimore's remarkably varied cuisine, with seafood houses and the restaurants of Little Italy among the leading contenders. Although cabs are reasonable priced, another good way to get around is the old-fashioned and inexpensive trolleys.

Baltimore is located 37 miles northeast of Washington, D.C., 67 miles southwest of Wilmington, Delaware, and 96 miles southwest of Philadelphia, Pennsylvania. Rates do not include 11% sales tax.

Reader tip: Baltimore enjoys an active night life, and from time to time, readers visiting on a weekend have reported being awakened by the noise of rowdies at 2 A.M. when the bars close. If you're a light sleeper, be sure to request a room away from the street.

Information please: If your idea of the ideal B&B combines brand-new plumbing with historic ambiance, then visit **Celie's B&B** (1714 Thames Street, 21231; 301–522–2323) and tell us what you think. Located on the waterfront in Fell's Point, rooms are furnished with antiques and collectibles, highlighted by such amenities as fresh flowers, down comforters, flannel sheets, and terry robes. The breakfast of fruit and fresh-squeezed juice, fresh-baked breads and pastries can be enjoyed in the dining room, courtyard, or on the rooftop deck with skyline and harbor views. Rooms have balconies, fireplaces, and/or whirlpool tubs; one is wheelchair accessible with a private garden.

We're also curious about the **Hotel Belvedere** (Charles Street At Chse, 21202; 301–332–1000 or 800–692–2700), a turn-of-the century hotel listed on the National Register of Historic Places. Its Owl Bar is a long-time favorite, and rooms are reasonably priced, with traditional (if a tad dreary) furnishings. Your comments?

Admiral Fell Inn
888 South Broadway 21231

Tel: 301–522–7377
800–BXB–INNS

The Admiral Fell Inn ("don't ask how, the staff has heard it before") is a good example of the kinds of changes Baltimore has undergone in recent years. The inn is located on the waterfront in Fell's Point, among Market Square's historic town houses. The town of Fell's Point was Baltimore's original seaport on the Chesapeake Bay, and dates back to the 1730s. Some of the earliest wharves, taverns, and shops are still in operation, and the area remains a working seaport today.

The inn consists of seven contiguous buildings, the oldest of which dates back to 1770. The interiors have been renovated to combine historical accuracy with modern comfort. Rooms are individually decorated with antiques and reproductions. The inn also houses a pub serving drinks and casual food, and a restaurant providing more elaborate meals. Rates include a continental breakfast and the morning paper.

"The inn is in a wonderful old section of town that shouldn't be missed. Though it's still rough in certain parts, they have done a terrific job of snapping up these old buildings for renovation. The staff was very helpful, although it is more of a hotel than a family-run inn. And we left the car parked the whole time. The staff will take you anywhere in their van and an antique trolley car runs all over town. Returning to the hotel in the evening was a treat; we found five or six old seamen's pubs still in operation, each with its own brand of live music. All very small, but extremely friendly. A terrific evening." *(Wendi Van Exan)* More comments please.

Open All year.
Rooms 1 suite, 39 doubles—all with full private bath, telephone, TV, desk, air-conditioning. 2 nonsmoking rooms. 4 rooms with Jacuzzi baths.
Facilities Restaurant, drawing room, library with games, atrium, pub, reception areas on each floor, courtyard garden. On the water.
Location Downtown, in Fell's Point. 1 m from Harborplace. From I-95 S, go N (downtown) on Russell St. to Pratt St. Turn right and go E 1 m around Inner Harbor on President St. (I-83) and Fleet St. to Broadway. Go right on Broadway to end at Thames St.
Restrictions Occasional late Saturday night street noise in some rooms.
Credit cards Amex, MC, Visa.
Rates B&B, $145 suite, $94–120 double. Extra person in room, $10. Alc lunch, $9; alc dinner, $25–35. Weekend packages available.
Extras Entrance accessible to handicapped. 4 guest rooms equipped for disabled. Free station pickups; free van transportation within city. Cribs, babysitting available.

51

Ann Street B&B
804 South Ann Street, 21231

Tel: 301–342–5883

Her home since 1978, Joanne Mazurek has welcomed bed & breakfast guests since 1988. Consisting of two adjacent 18th century houses, Joanne notes that the inn "offers travelers the opportunity to stay in an authentic colonial home atmosphere. Our inn has 12 working fireplaces, including two in the suite, and one in a bathroom. Hardwood floors and antiques highlight the decor."

"A jewel of a B&B just around the corner from the waterfront in Fell's Point. A trolley runs every 15 minutes to the Inner Harbor and downtown. Joanne is a thoughtful, friendly innkeeper who has thought of all possible needs and wants of her guests. The house was immaculate, well lighted and the spacious rooms were freshly decorated and furnished. She serves a full breakfast of juice, fruit, hot entrée (different each day), and muffins in the common room in cool weather, and in the walled courtyard in the summer months." *(Monna Hormel)*

Open All year.
Rooms 1 suite, 3 doubles—all with private shower and/or bath, radio, air-conditioning. 1 with desk.
Facilities Commom room, garden. Boat dockage nearby.
Location Historic waterfront area.
Restrictions Smoking in designated areas only. Children 10 and up preferred.
Credit cards None accepted.
Rates B&B, $95 suite, $75–90 double, $65–80 single. Extra person in suite $15.

Peabody Court
612 Cathedral Street at Mt. Vernon Place, 21201

Tel: 301–727–7101
800–732–5301

Created from a 1920s apartment house, the Peabody is a small luxury hotel that opened in 1985 and is owned by Morton Sarubin. Rooms are furnished with high-quality reproductions of the French directoire style. The headboards and armoires are built of cherry, topped with brass finials. The lobby is highlighted by a 6-foot Baccarat chandelier, and the hotel has two restaurants. The Brasserie serves from early-breakfast to late-night snacks, and the Conservatory, an elegant and expensive rooftop French restaurant, is open for lunch, tea, and dinner.

"The rooms are quiet, well appointed, clean, and tastefully furnished; the location is excellent." *(GB also W.F. Searle)* "Small, first-class hotel with impeccable furnishings, rooms, and service." *(Sheryl Gill)*

Open All year. Restaurant closed Sundays.
Rooms 25 suites, 79 doubles—all with full private bath, telephone, radio, TV, desk, air-conditioning, fan. 68 rooms with Jacuzzi tubs.
Facilities Lobby, sitting room, bar/lounge with pianist, 2 restaurants, guest passes at health club. Valet parking.
Location Downtown, theater area. 2–3 blocks from Symphony Hall, Lyric Theatre, Peabody Conservatory, Walters Art Gallery. 2 blocks to Civic Center. At corner of Monument and Cathedral Sts.
Credit cards Amex, CB, DC, MC, Visa.
Rates B&B, $125–1000 suite, $90–180 double. Weekend B&B packages. Corporate rates. Alc lunch, $15–22; alc dinner, $30–60. Extra person in room, $20.

Extras Member, Leading Hotels of the World. Complimentary limousine service to station, financial district, Inner Harbor; $25 to airport. Cribs, babysitting available. Wheelchair accessible; baths specially equipped for disabled. French, German, Italian, Spanish, Arabic, Dutch spoken.

The Shirley Madison Inn
205 West Madison Street, 21201

Tel: 301–728–6550

This beautifully restored hotel offers a warm and friendly atmosphere; it has been owned by Roberta Pieczenik since 1986, and is managed by Ellen Roberts. Trees, shrubs, and lots of flowers brighten the front of the building; interior highlights include stained glass windows, mirrored fireplaces, and a polished oak staircase. If you'd rather skip the stairs, you can ride the 100-year-old lift, original to the building. The rooms are furnished with Victorian and Edwardian antiques and collectibles; most have kitchenettes. Continental breakfast is served in the sitting room, and complimentary cocktails are offered in the parlor.

The Shirley House is part of the historic Mt. Vernon neighborhood, within walking distance of nearly all of downtown Baltimore, including the Inner Harbor, as well as numerous art galleries, antique shops, concert halls, and some of the city's best restaurants.

"The atmosphere lends itself to relaxation and a warm friendly feeling. The staff goes out of their way to assure you of a pleasant stay. Friendly conversation over a good continental breakfast or an evening glass of sherry or lemonade was always enjoyed and appreciated." *(Nina James)*

"A charming dining room for breakfast. Our suite had a bed, night stands, desk and chairs, reading chair, armoire with TV, and decorative fireplace, all facing a colonial-era church. Adjoining was a large room with a dining room table, four chairs, kitchenette, and modern bath. Rooms are decorated in beautiful colors—mint green, rose, mauve, soft teal. The inn is two blocks from Antique Row, the Maryland Historical Society, and Mount Vernon park." *(MM, also Alvin Safran)* "The inn lived up to the writeup you gave it in last year's edition." *(Sally Sieracki)*

Open All year.
Rooms 8 suites, 17 doubles—all with full private bath, radio, desk, air-conditioning. Most with kitchenettes. Many with telephone and TV. 9 rooms in courtyard house.
Facilities Breakfast room, 2 parlors with TV, living room with library, fireplace. Landscaped courtyard. Garage, $3.
Location Mt. Vernon district. 10 min. walk to center, Inner Harbor. From I-95 S, take I-695 W, Exit 23 (I-83 S/Baltimore). Take St. Paul St. exit, go S on St. Paul, right onto Madison.
Restrictions Occasional late Saturday night street noise in rooms facing Park St.
Credit cards Amex, DC, MC, Visa.
Rates B&B, $105–125 suite, $75–95 double, $55–75 single. Extra person in room, $10. Children under 12 stay free. Weekend, weekly, discounts. 10% senior discount.
Extras French, German, Polish spoken. Cribs available.

Society Hill Hotels   *Tel:* 301–837–3632
58 West Biddle Street, 21201
Hopkins–3404 St. Paul Street 21218   301–235-8600
Government House–1125 Calvert Street 21202   301–752-7722

The two Society Hill Hotels are owned by Thomas Kleinman, Howard Jacobs, and Kate Hopkins, who also own the Society Hill in Philadelphia (see Pennsylvania chapter). Rooms at all three properties are individually decorated with traditional wood furniture and Victorian antiques, brass beds, brass fixtures in the bathroom, and fresh flowers. Rates include a continental breakfast (of juice, coffee cake or croissant, fresh fruit, and coffee or tea, delivered to your room) and free parking.

The Society Hill at 58 Biddle was built as a private home at the turn of the century; its restaurant, Grille 58, serves casual American and Cajun cuisine. Innkeeper Kate Hopkins asks guests to let her know of stairs are a problem, since the inn is a walk-up and rooms are located on the first through the fourth floors. Nearby attractions include the Maryland Institute College of Art, the Theater Project, the School of Performing Arts, and the Meyerhoff Symphony Hall. Boutique Row and Antique Row are a short walk away.

Hopkins is located in the Johns Hopkins University area, in a Spanish revival-style 1920s apartment house; and Government House comprises three townhouses, dating back to 1827, and is set in the Mt. Vernon Historic District.

"Society Hill (58 Biddle) is a lovely small hotel, redone in the old way and in very good taste. Restaurant has good food and is extremely attractive." *(BP, also Wendy Robbins)*

"Service at 58 Biddle is excellent and friendly, and the continental breakfast (served when you want it) makes for a comfortable morning. The bar and restaurant provide both good food and a friendly atmosphere—in fact, the bar reminds me of the TV show, 'Cheers.' " *(Mark Pennels)*

"Government House is immaculately clean, with an extremely kind, accommodating, and gracious innkeeper. My delicious continental breakfast was brought to my room just on time." *(Dr. George Ludlam)*

"The Society Hill Hopkins is a very private, out-of-the way hotel with invisible management, unless you care to chat in the parlor. The furniture is real; the baths modern yet done in period, with an ample supply of soaps, shampoos, and toothbrushes." *(Nicholas Miller)*

Open All year. Restaurant closed Christmas Day.
Rooms 59 suites & doubles (total of all 3 hotels)—all with private bath and/or shower, telephone, radio, TV, air-conditioning. Some with desk.
Facilities Restaurant, piano bar (58 Biddle). Each with parlor. Free parking lot adjacent.
Location 58 Biddle: Across street from Symphony Hall; Government House: Mt. Vernon district; Hopkins: Johns Hopkins University area. Call for directions.
Credit cards All major cards.
Rates B&B, $135 suite, $100–120 double, $80 single. 10% senior discount. Alc lunch, $8–18; alc dinner, $15–25. Weekend packages.
Extras Free station pickups. Cribs available. French and Italian spoken.

For an additional Baltimore area listing, see entry for **Twin Gates B&B** in Lutherville, 15 minutes north of downtown Baltimore.

BETTERTON

Lantern Inn   *Tel:* 301–348–5809
115 Ericsson Avenue, 21610

Ann and Ken Washburn restored the Lantern Inn, built as a guest house in 1904, and opened it as a B&B in January 1987. While the guest rooms are decorated with country fabrics and period antiques, the common rooms have been modestly furnished with comfortable contemporary furniture.

"The inn is impeccably clean, and freshly ironed linens and fluffy towels are replaced daily." *(Jo Anne Parke)*

"Terrific breakfasts—possibly the best waffles we've ever eaten. The Washburns steered us towards good restaurants and local spots of interest. Betterton is a small village on the Chesapeake Bay that is devoid of any traffic or tourists in the off-season, although we'd imagine it's fairly busy in the summer, because it has the only public beach on the Eastern Shore. Still, the Lantern is the only visible business in town, so things can't get too hectic." *(Tom Wiener)*

Open All year.
Rooms 13 doubles—2 with private shower, 11 with maximum of 4 people sharing bath. All rooms with air-conditioning; 1 with desk.
Facilities Dining room with piano; 2 living rooms with TV, books, games. 1/2 acre with picnic table. 2 blocks to tennis. 1 1/2 blocks to sandy beach and pier on Chesapeake Bay for swimming, boating, fishing. Goose hunting (in season), hiking, bicycling nearby.
Location Upper Eastern Shore. 1 1/2 hrs. to Philadelphia, Baltimore, and Washington.
Restrictions Smoking on 1st floor only. No children under 12.
Credit cards MC, Visa.
Rates B&B, $60–75 double, $45–60 single. 2-night minimum stay, holiday weekends.

BUCKEYSTOWN

The Inn at Buckeystown   *Tel:* 301–874–5755
3521 Buckeystown Pike (Route 85), 21717

The village of Buckeystown is listed on the National Register of Historic Places. Buckeystown was founded before the Revolution; because of the many battles fought nearby, it was greatly affected by the Civil War.

The Inn at Buckeystown is a restored Victorian mansion opened in 1982 by Dan Pelz, now assisted by innkeepers Rebecca Shipman-Smith and Chase Barnett. Dan reports that "60–70 percent of our guests are

55

repeats. They have preferred seasons or rooms, and some even have special dishes they especially enjoy. We celebrate all seasons with gusto, but my personal favorites are spring (dogwood) time, October foliage, and our glorious full-month Christmas celebration with elaborate Victorian decorations. Antiquers, Civil War buffs, old house lovers and Victorian romantics are our favorite guests."

All rooms are furnished with period pieces, choice art, and collectibles, along with such modern conveniences such as air-conditioning and electric blankets. An additional suite is found in St. John's Cottage, a short stroll from the inn, in a converted nineteenth-century church, complete with a hot tub, fireplace, and VCR. Rates include complimentary port in the guest rooms, and wine served with dinner. Guests enjoy dressing for dinner, so it's advisable to bring a jacket and tie. The inn is noted for its good food and hospitality; holidays are celebrated with special gusto.

"The inn is our favorite retreat when we want to be pampered in elegant simplicity. Dress can be either elegant or casual and the atmosphere is of the relaxed, 'put your feet up in front of the fire and chat' type. All of the rooms are unique, but the 'Love' room is our favorite." (Mr. & Mrs. George Robinson)

"The inn is located in a small village that has three streets and lovely Victorian homes. It is only eight minutes from Frederick, for those who want to shop or explore historical sites. The service is excellent, and the food is presented on a lovely collection of old china and antique silver." (Sylvia & Martin Tulkoff) "Never have we had two finer consecutive meals than were served us (family-style) here. Dinner was a pork roast with excellent red cabbage; breakfast was superb French toast with genuine maple syrup. Rooms old, well furnished, with true antiques." (Mark Slen)

"Thanksgiving here is a tradition for us—it's like coming home. The food is fabulous—there's always something new to try. Dan is a marvelous host, who has the knack of making all this guests feel at home. The rooms are very comfortable and relaxing." (Leonora Welsher)

Open All year.
Rooms 8 doubles, 1 cottage—5 with private bath and/or shower, 4 sharing 3 baths. All rooms with air-conditioning; cottage with radio, TV, desk, fireplace, hot tub.
Facilities Library, 2 parlors with fireplaces, stereo, games; wraparound porch. Gardens, wooded grounds. Cross-country, downhill skiing, swimming, tennis, skating nearby.
Location W MD. 1 hr. W of Baltimore and NW of Washington, DC. 5 m S of Frederick, MD. Take Buckeystown exit off I-270 or I-70 to MD Rte. 85.
Restrictions No smoking in dining rooms. No children.
Credit cards MC, Visa.
Rates MAP, $125–185 double, $90–135 single. Cottage, $225 for 1 couple, $375 for 2 couples (MAP). Extra person in room, $40. Service charge $10 per person per night. 2-night minimum on some weekends and holidays. Set dinner available to outside guests with 24-hour notice, $30.
Extras Limo service to D.C. airports, $50 per party.

CHESAPEAKE CITY

Started in 1803, the Chesapeake and Delaware Canal was dug to connect these two major bays, saving ships the nearly 300-mile trip around the Delmarva peninsula. Chesapeake City, long known as Canal Town, first housed the workers who dug the canal, and was later home to the men who operated the canal's locks and engines. Widened and deepened many times over the years, the canal is now used by over 150 ocean-going ships monthly. When the locks and engines needed to operate the canal were eliminated in the 1920s, the town became a sleepy backwater, only recently rediscovered by tourists and boaters.

Reader tip: "Chesapeake City has a real Maryland crab house, The Tap Room, of the sort that's increasingly hard to find. The Village Cafe serves a good breakfast and offers the Philadelphia, Baltimore, and Washington Sunday papers for those who don't entirely want to get away from it all." *(Carolyn Mathiasen)*

Inn at the Canal
104 Bohemia Avenue, 21915

Tel: 301–885–5995

"Overlooking the Canal, the Inn at the Canal is owned by Al and Mary Toppolo—friendly, quiet innkeepers. Their 19th century home was built by a local tugboat captain as a present to his wife upon the birth of their first son. The Toppolos have restored its beautiful pine floors, and have furnished the inn with period decor. The common room has round oak tables with spindle back chairs, and the original ceiling has a classic design dramatically painted in shades of blue, gold, and green. The guest rooms have antique quilts hung on the wall, coordinating with quilts Mary has made for the queen-size beds. The bathrooms are new, with the sinks installed in antique oak bureaus, and everything is spotlessly clean. The two rooms in the rear wing overlook the water, and share a private staircase. One has its original tub in the bathroom, over six feet long and enclosed in a beaded board frame with oak railing. The inviting front porch has white wicker furniture—the perfect spot to sip an iced tea." *(NB)*

Rates include a full breakfast, morning papers, and afternoon refreshments.

Open All year.
Rooms 6 doubles—all with private bath, radio, air-conditioning. 5 with TV. 2 with desk.
Facilities Living/breakfast room, front porch. Antique, miniatures shop. Off-street parking.
Location NE MD. 30 min. S of Wilmington DE. On Bohemia Ave., between 1st & 2nd St. On Chesapeake and Delaware Canal. 1 block from harbor.
Restrictions Smoking permitted only on ground floor. No children under 10.
Credit cards Amex, MC, Visa.
Rates B&B, $65–100 double, $60–95 single. Extra person in room, $15. Corporate rates.

CHESTERTOWN

A quiet colonial town on the Eastern Shore, Chestertown's area attractions include walking tours of its historic homes, the Eastern Neck Island Wildlife Refuge and the Chesapeake Bay Maritime Museum, while boating, fishing, crabbing, bicycling, hiking, hunting, golf, tennis, and swimming are among the favorite activities.

Reader tip: The Chestertown area is quiet and peaceful, but not isolated. Lots of historic buildings in town, and a wildlife refuge full of migrating waterfowl (in season), deer, and other creatures. Stay to watch the magnificent sunset from the little one-lane wooden bridge leading into the refuge." *(Brad Freden)*

Chestertown is 90 miles east of Washington, DC; take the Chesapeake Bay Bridge to Route 301 north to Route 213 North.

Information please: For elegant American cuisine and guest rooms lavishly decorated in high Victorian style, try the **Imperial Hotel** (208 High Street, 21620; 301–778–5000). Dating to 1904, the inn was elaborately restored in 1984, and is listed on the National Register of Historic Places. 20th-century creature comforts were not forgotten during reconstruction; rooms are supplied with towel warmers, terry robes, in-room telephone and TV, even heated kennels for Fido. Comments?

Another nearby possibility is the **Widow's Walk Inn** (402 High Street, 21620; 301–778–6455), a Victorian guest house, furnished with "antiques and family treasures." Rates include breakfast and afternoon refreshments.

Finally, we haven't had any recent feedback on **The Country Inn at Rolph's Wharf** (P.O. Box 609, 21620; 301–778–1988), one of three inns marketed under the name of **Chesapeake Inns**, and listed in earlier editions. Rolph's Wharf dates back to 1830; a family restaurant on the property has a patio and serves Eastern Shore as well as American and continental cuisine. Rates include a continental breakfast, and all rooms have private baths. Comments?

Brampton   *Tel:* 301–778–1860
Route 20, RR 2, Box 107, 21620

Listed on the National Register of Historic Places, Brampton is a handsome red brick Victorian home, owned by Michael and Danielle Hanscom since 1987, and decorated with antiques, period reproductions, and well-chosen contemporary pieces.

"Danielle and Michael make Brampton a special place. It's elegant in design and decor, without a trace of fussiness. Once you enter Brampton's curving driveway, you encounter a peaceful mini-forest of very old trees, including many taller (and probably older) than the three-story house. The breakfasts include full carafes of coffee, fresh fruit (homegrown cantaloupe in August), and eggs, pancakes, or waffles, bacon or sausage from an Amish market, and always fresh baked muffins and toast, beautifully presented on blue and white floral porcelain china. Danielle does all the cooking, and makes her own jams and jellies from fruits grown on the property." *(Winifred DaVia)*

"Great owners—friendly and attentive, but not overwhelming; the inn itself is one of the nicest I've ever seen. They have two gregarious dogs, ready to chase sticks and play as long as your throwing arm holds out. Breakfast was delicious—bread pudding, fresh strawberry sauce, thick bacon, fresh-squeezed orange juice, and blueberry muffins that were 50 percent berries. We were welcomed with soda and peanuts in the parlor. Later in the evening we sipped sherry before the fireplace. The owners were helpful with directions, suggestions of activities, and making dinner reservations." *(Kristen Pendleton & Brad Freden)*

"Our comfortable airy room was beautifully decorated with a lace-covered canopy bed, and we were pleased and surprised that from our room we could not hear another sound in the house despite the fact that the inn was fully booked."*(WS)*

Open All year.
Rooms 1 suite, 4 doubles— suite with full bath, doubles with private shower. All with desk, air-conditioning. Most with fireplace or woodstove. Telephone, TV available.
Facilities Dining room with fireplace, living room with fireplace. 35 acres. Close to river and public beach.
Location 1½ m S of Chestertown.
Restrictions Smoking in public rooms only.
Credit cards MC, Visa.
Rates $125 suite, $100 double. Extra person in room, $25. 2 night weekend minimum.
Extras Crib available. French, German spoken.

The Inn at Mitchell House   *Tel:* 301–778–6500
Tolchester Estates, RD 2 Box 329, 21620

This imposing manor house was built in 1743, with an addition in 1825, and was bought by Tracy and Jim Stone in 1986. It's set on a sweeping lawn, next to a pond, and Tracy notes that "the inn is right for people who wish to get away from the fast pace of the city. We are away from everything, so guests should be looking for a bit of seclusion. Plenty of restaurants are within a short drive for dinner, though." The inviting rooms are furnished in a colonial motif with antiques and period reproductions. Rates include a full breakfast. Waffles, French toast, and eggs Bearnaise are all specialties.

"Set well back from the road, down a long, long driveway is this delightful retreat. The Stones are gracious hosts, the food is excellent, and the decor—a mixture of antique and traditional furnishings—is lovely. Each guest room has a special touch; I especially liked the flapper dresses from the twenties hung on the walls. Our room had a four-poster bed with an extremely comfortable mattress, good reading lights and was immaculately clean." *(Madeleine Hart)* More comments please.

Open All year.
Rooms 6 doubles—4 with private bath and/or shower, 2 with maximum of 4 people sharing bath. All with air-conditioning. 4 with fireplace.
Facilities Dining room, 2 parlors with TV/VCR, games, 1956 jukebox. 10 acres

with pond, stream, woods. 1/2 m to Chesapeake Bay for swimming, fishing, boating, crabbing. Tennis, golf nearby.
Location 10 m from Chestertown. From the Delaware Memorial Bridge, take Rte. 13 S to Rte. 301; connect with Rte. 291 W to Chestertown. Turn right on Rte. 20 S, right again on Rte. 21 (3 m on right).
Restrictions Children of all ages welcome by special arrangement.
Credit cards MC, Visa.
Rates B&B, $75–90 double, $70–85 single. Extra person in room, $15. 2-night minimum stay, holiday weekends.
Extras Free marina pickups.

The White Swan Tavern
231 High Street, 21620

Tel: 301–778–2300

The White Swan is one of those historic restorations you usually get to see only from the wrong side of a velvet rope. At this one, you get to take afternoon tea, stay overnight, and enjoy continental breakfast in the morning!

The restoration of the White Swan began with an archeological dig in 1978, which indicated that the site was used prior to 1733 as a tannery (the original room is now one of the inn's guest rooms); in 1793, the building was expanded to its present size for use as a tavern. After several years of professional renovation and reconstruction work, the White Swan reopened in 1981 as a B&B inn. Rooms are handsomely decorated in period antiques and reproduction pieces.

"We stayed in the John Landgrove Kitchen, the oldest part of the tavern. It has a walk-in fireplace, enormous hand-hewn beams, a hand-made brick floor, and charming decorative touches. We had a delicious dinner across the street at the Imperial Hotel." *(Diane Gayles)* More comments please.

Open Open all year. Closed late Jan. to mid-Feb.
Rooms 2 suites, 4 doubles—all with full private bath, desk, air-conditioning; 1 room in annex.
Facilities Breakfast and tea room, living room, game room, family room with TV and working fireplace, museum room. Courtyard with small garden, terrace. Fishing, swimming, sailing nearby. On-site parking.
Location Eastern Shore, 1 1/2 hrs. W of Baltimore, Washington, DC, and Philadelphia. Downtown historic district.
Credit cards None accepted.
Rates B&B, $125 suite, $75–110 double. Extra person in room, $25. Children under 3 stay free. Afternoon tea, $3.50.
Extras 2 rooms suitable for handicapped. Airport/station pickups. French spoken. Cribs, babysitting available.

DENTON

The Sophie Kerr House
Route 3, Box 7-B, 21629
Fifth Avenue and Kerr Avenue

Tel: 301–479–3421

The Sophie Kerr House is a large center-hall colonial, dating back to 1861, owned by John and Thelma Lyons since 1984. They have converted the old smokehouse, which is connected to the main house, into a honeymoon suite, and offer wine and candy to all newlyweds (with advance notice). Their B&B is also popular with bicyclists, who enjoy the country roads and easy riding of the Eastern Shore's flat but scenic countryside. Mr. Lyons notes that three of the guest rooms and two of the baths are on the ground floor, making life easier for senior guests. Rates include a full breakfast and afternoon wine and cheese.

"A beautifully restored old home, offering a relaxed atmosphere with an elegant country flavor. Our room was sparkling clean, and the lighting and plumbing are adequate and in good working order. The inn is situated on two acres, with mature trees and beautiful plantings." *(C. David Glaeser)* "Breakfasting in the formal dining room with fine china and silverware is a pleasure matched only by the quality and quantity of the food. But the inn's greatest treasure is the Lyons themselves. It is their welcoming nature which provides the atmosphere which makes a visit such a joy." *(A.P. Burkinshaw)* "From the crackling fire that greeted our return from dinner at a nearby colonial pub, to breakfast accompanied by Mr. Lyons' wonderful stories, our stay was a delight." *(Robert & Pauline Lucas)*

Open All year.
Rooms 5 doubles share 3 full baths. All rooms with radio, air-conditioning.
Facilities Dining room, living room, TV room. Gardens, badminton, croquet. Fishing nearby.
Location Eastern Shore. 60 m SE of Baltimore, 50 m E of Washington, DC. 1 m from Denton. Take Rte. 404 (downtown) to Fifth Ave.
Restrictions No smoking in common areas.
Credit cards None accepted.
Rates B&B, $40 double. Extra person in room, $5. Family discounts available. No tipping.
Extras Pets allowed with prior approval. Cribs available. Airport pickups available, $20.

FREDERICK

Frederick is a historic town, located just 46 miles west of Baltimore. A prosperous agricultural center, it boasts a number of restored eighteenth-century buildings, many now open as museums. It was also a center of fighting during the Civil War and changed hands between the Union and Confederate forces several times. According to local legend, it was here that Barbara Fritchie dared the forces of Stonewall Jackson to shoot her "old gray head" before she would take down her Union flag. Plan ahead if you want to visit the third weekend in May, when the craft fair is in full swing, or in late September, during the county fair. Stop at the Visitor Center (19 East Church Street, 21701; 301–663–8703) for information on walking tours and other activities. Traveling families will enjoy the Rose Hill Manor Children's Museum, where the 19th century is brought to life by costumed docents and hands-on displays. The town of New Market, billed as the antiques capital of Maryland, is nearby.

Information please: The **Tyler-Spite House** (112 West Church Street, 21701; 301–831–4455) is named for Dr. Tyler, as well as for the reason he built this three-story mansion in 1814—to spite the town fathers, who wanted to build a road across his land. Now restored as a B&B, it features marble fireplace mantels, carved woodwork, and period decor, with both canopied and Victorian beds. Weekend rates include a full breakfast, afternoon tea, and an evening carriage ride; midweek rates have fewer extras, but are more reasonably priced. Reports?

For a more rural setting, try **The Marameade** (2439 Old National Pike, Middletown 21769; 301–371–4214), a 200-year-old mansion built of brick and slate with French mansard styling, set on 26 acres with gardens, patios, a swimming and fishing pond, and an ancient oak tree. Rates are reasonable, and the inn restaurant is open for three meals daily. Comments?

Spring Bank   *Tel:* 301–694–0440
Harmony Grove, 7945 Worman's Mill Road, 21701

Spring Bank Farm is home to an 1880 mansion listed on the National Register of Historic Places. Owned by Beverly and Ray Compton since 1980, the rates include a continental breakfast, served in your room, and afternoon sherry.

Beverly describes the quiet, relaxing atmosphere of Spring Bank as being particularly appealing to guests. "Paths to walk, expansive lawns, a grand house of spacious proportions and architecturally significant features—such as plaster ceiling medallions and moldings, marbled fireplaces, and grained woodwork. We've tried to achieve an 1880s touch in the 1990s, which our guests seem to appreciate."

Beverly describes the house as a restoration: "What that means is that the antique beds are double size, and that our hexagonal white tile bathroom had a charming old upright sink but little shelf space for hair dryers or toilet articles. More importantly, it means enormous bedrooms, homey antique furniture, stenciled ceilings, interior room shutters that disappear into casements, hardwood floors, Oriental carpets, floor moldings, and bay windows."

"Breakfast included home baked muffins, fresh fruit, and coffee served on china and cut glass with linen napkins, and delivered on an antique tray. A particularly pleasant moment of our stay came around 5 P.M. when we plopped down on the back porch and opened a cold beer. Beverly and Ray came out to chat and we were soon joined by other guests returning from their jaunts. One guest entertained us with his description of Antietam Battlefield; a National Geographic photographer pulled up to ask about the house, and a neighboring farmer stopped by on his tractor to say hello." *(Diane Camp)* "The inn is set on a country road that parallels a major highway. Our rooms were on the main floor and had 12-foot ceilings." *(SHW)*

"The outstanding thing about Spring Bank (besides the architecture) is the owners, Beverly and Ray Compton. Both are very knowledgeable about the region and have shelves full of books on the area. Our room was huge, with a large bed, comfortable chairs, fresh linens, and tall windows with lace curtains. Ray Compton has done much of the restoration of the home himself, and took us on a tour of the house, telling us about its history, its architectural engineering features, and its resident ghost." *(Dale & Virginia Wright)* More comments please.

Open All year.
Rooms 6 doubles—1 with private bath, 5 share 2½ hall baths. All with air-conditioning.
Facilities Double parlors, 10 acres with gardens, walking paths. Swimming, fishing, hiking nearby.
Location Take I-70 or I-270 to Rte. 15 to Frederick (near Mile Marker #16), then Rte. 355 S for ¼ m; inn on left. 2½ m to center.
Restrictions No smoking. No children under 12.
Credit cards Amex, MC, Visa.
Rates B&B, $75–90 double. 2-night weekend minimum in spring and fall.

Turning Point Inn   *Tel:* 301–874–2421
3406 Urbana Pike, 21701   301–831–8232

Ellie and Bernie Droneburg, owners of the Turning Point since 1984, report that they "enjoy the majority of our guests, but seem to have a special rapport with those who seem to love life, appreciate beauty, and have genuine curiosity and interest in our multifaceted area, with its rolling farmland, historic towns and battlefields, antique meccas, and nearby cultural offerings." The Droneburgs have now turned the role of active innkeepers over to their son Charlie and his wife Suzanne Seymour.

A Victorian mansion with Georgian colonial features, the Turning Point was built in 1910. Food is just as important as decor here, and guests enjoy full breakfasts with specialties ranging from eggs Benedict to sautéed apples. Lunches include everything from original salad creations to Maryland crab, and the four-course dinners offer a choice of such entrées as veal with mushrooms and sherry, and swordfish with herb butter and sun-dried tomatoes.

"Our bedroom was furnished with two four-poster beds (firm and comfortable) and period furniture that reminded me of my grandmother's. The private bath was modern and spacious. Six large windows gave us views in three directions of rolling hills, barns, and country fences. We had a chance to inspect the whole house, which is filled with antiques. Each of the upstairs bedrooms is coordinated around a different soft pastel color, enhanced by wallpapers and draperies of matching patterns. Lighting throughout the house is controlled by rheostat, so one can have brightness or coziness, as desired. Books are everywhere, and the background music downstairs is subtle and gentle." *(Jody Adams)*

"Our room, at the top of the house with lots of light and two lovely quarter-circle windows, giving lovely views of peaceful farmland, was very pleasantly decorated and sparkling clean. Although the overnight trade was slow during our off-season visit, the restaurant business was booming. The inn's three dining rooms were full, and all waitresses were scurrying around non-stop. Despite the pressure, they were un-

failingly courteous and pleasant, and the food was very good indeed—
interesting, delicious, and plentiful. We also enjoyed the breakfast of
oatmeal, pancakes, and spicy potatoes." *(Ellie & Bob Friedus)*

Open All year. Restaurant closed Christmas, New Year's, July 4.
Rooms 5 doubles—all with private shower and/or bath, air-conditioning. Radio,
TV on request.
Facilities Restaurant, living room with TV, games, books; garden room with
piano. 4 acres with gardens, lawn games. Golf, fishing nearby.
Location From I-270, take Exit 26 to inn in Urbana, at junction of rtes. 355 &
80.
Credit cards MC, Visa.
Rates B&B, $75–85 double. Extra person in room, $15. Alc lunch $9. Prix fixe
dinner, $22. 1/2 price meals for children.
Extras One dining room wheelchair accessible. German, French spoken.

GEORGETOWN

Kitty Knight House   *Tel:* 301–648–5777
Route 213, P.O. Box 97, 21930

Kitty Knight was an unusual woman for her time. Born to a prominent
family, instead of marrying, she left home at 16 to live on her own, first
as a society belle, later as hero of the War of 1812. The inn itself has
had a more checkered history, and was last listed in our 1987 edition.
Re-opened in 1988 after a change in ownership and decor, it encompasses both the original building and an addition of more recent construction.

"This mid-18th century inn on Maryland's Eastern Shore has been
through many incarnations. Recently refurnished once again, it's not
particularly elegant, but the price is reasonable and we liked it. Our
good-sized room had a fireplace, pretty flowered wallpaper, a comfortable bed, and a lovely view of the Sassafras River marina, forming the
heart of Georgetown.

"There is a lot of pretty country in the Georgetown-Chesapeake City
area, and an intriguing colonial plantation, Mount Harmon. The house
has graceful proportions and fine Chippendale furniture, as well as a
dazzling lavender St. Charles kitchen and sunken baths installed in the
1960s by its then-owner, a Du Pont family member. For meals, we'd
suggest driving north 15 minutes to Chesapeake City [see entry]."
(Carolyn Mathiasen)

Some areas for improvement: "The plumbing in the room next door
was noisy, and the ceiling fixture was the only light fixture. Breakfast
is not served and we thought the restaurant meals uninspired."

Open All year. Restaurant closed Mondays Nov. to March.
Rooms 2 suites, 9 doubles—all with private shower and/or bath, TV, air-condi-
tioning.
Facilities Restaurant, tavern—both with weekend entertainment.
Location NE MD. 1 hour S of Wilmington, DE. From I-95 in Elkton, go S on
Hwy 213.
Restrictions Smoking in designated areas only.
Credit cards Amex, MC, Visa.

Rates Room only, $85 suite, $65–75 double, $65 single.
Extras Yacht charters available.

GRANTSVILLE

Information please: An interesting possibility in the Allegheny Mountains of the Maryland panhandle (about 20 miles east of Grantsville is the **Castle B&B** (P.O. Box 578, Mount Savage, 21545; 301–759–5946), a century-old copy of a Scottish castle, recently restored as a B&B. Rooms are furnished with antiques and rates include a full breakfast and afternoon tea. Use it as a base for riding the Allegany Central steam train through the Frostburg gap, or for hiking the C & O canal tow path, and let us know what you think.

The Casselman   *Tel:* 301–895–5055
Main Street (U.S. Route 40), 21536   301–895–5266

Grantsville is located along the route of the old National Road, in Maryland's hilly western panhandle. Settled in the 1850s by German-speaking Amish and Mennonites from Pennsylvania, their influence remains strong in the area today.

   To serve the many travelers on the busy route west, a tavern was built in 1790 which has survived as The Casselman. Rooms in the original building are decorated with Victorian antiques, while those in the motel are equipped with locally hand-crafted furnishings. The inn's restaurant serves three meals daily, at extremely reasonable prices, while its bakery will sate your sweet tooth without denting your pocketbook.

   "It's a rare treat to find country inn atmosphere at budget motel prices. We had a delicious lunch of homemade broccoli cheese soup and roast beef with mashed potatoes and gravy. We stopped in the bakery and brought home a walnut pie and a dozen sugar cookies. Only the mushroom soup, which tasted canned, was a disappointment." *(SHW)* More comments please.

Open All year. Restaurant closed Sunday.
Rooms 5 doubles in original building—3 with private bath, 2 sharing 1 bath. 40 rooms in adjacent motel with private bath, TV, telephone.
Facilities Parlor, restaurant, bakery, antique shop.
Location W MD (panhandle). On Rte. 40 at E end of town.
Restrictions No alcohol.
Credit cards Discover, MC, Visa.
Rates Room only, $20–45 double.
Extras Wheelchair accessible.

HAVRE DE GRACE

Vandiver Inn   *Tel:* 301–939–5200
301 South Union Avenue, 21078

Although founded in the 18th century, Havre de Grace grew prosperous in the 19th because of its strategic location, where the Susquehanna

River meets Chesapeake Bay. Many of the buildings from this period have been restored as homes or offices, while sailing and seafood continue as the town's favorite indulgences. In addition to a historic lighthouse, several waterfront parks and marinas, worth visiting is the museum devoted to carved wooden waterfowl decoys, including a workshop where you can see works in progress.

"The Vandiver Inn is a large Victorian home, and has been an inn since 1886. The parlor is filled with period furniture, and looks like the home where your grandmother might have lived. Our room, named after John O'Neill, the first keeper of the Havre de Grace light house, was spacious and comfortable. It contained a fireplace and full bath, with an unusual and amusing bath/shower apparatus, and a firm and attractive double bed.

"The innkeeper, Charles Rothwell, handles the cooking superbly. Every meal was a delight. Our dinners included osso bucco (braised veal shanks), roast beef tenderloin, with baked Alaska and Irish cream cheesecake for dessert. The breakfasts include fresh fruit, cheese omelets, bacon, sausage, and light-as-a feather biscuits and apple muffins. Our meals were served at large tables, and meeting and conversing with the other guests was pleasant, particularly after a day of sightseeing.

"The best part of the Vandiver Inn experience was the treatment we received from assistant innkeeper Lilyann Laye, a wealth of information on area activities. She is charming, caring, and gives the impression that her day would have been incomplete without your visit." *(Paul Starr)*

Open All year.
Rooms 8 doubles—all with private bath and/or shower, telephone, air-conditioning. Radio, TV on request.
Facilities Restaurant,
Location NE MD. 35 min. N of Baltimore. From I-95, take Exit 89 (Rte 155 E). Cross Rte 40 onto Ostego St. Follow to end at Union Ave. Go right then 7 blocks to inn on left.
Restrictions No children under 12.
Credit cards Amex, MC, Visa.
Rates B&B, $65–85 double. Extra person in room, $20. Prix fixe dinner, $20.

LUTHERVILLE

Twin Gates   *Tel:* 301–252–3131
308 Morris Avenue, 21093   800–635–0370

Built in 1857, the Twin Gates is a Second Empire mansard-roofed Victorian, owned and operated by Gwen and Bob Vaughan since 1985. Each room is decorated in the theme of one of the Vaughans' favorite locales: the California room, the Cape May room, and the Maryland Hunt room. Be sure to ask Gwen to show you the "secret room." Rates include a full breakfast and afternoon wine and cheese. Lutherville is a Victorian village, a northern suburb of Baltimore.

"The town and this house are steeped in history—the inn was part of the Underground Railroad; our hosts were delighted to share their

knowledge with us. The inn is tucked away on a quiet street, and we were not bothered by noisy cars or barking dogs." *(John & Susan Eberle)*
"A magnolia tree was in bloom right outside our window. A short brisk walk brought us to a very good seafood restaurant; we returned home to find sherry and chocolates by the bed." *(Mae Horns)*

"The dining room is one of the loveliest rooms in the house, and the table was beautifully set. The Vaughans enjoy chatting with guests after breakfast, and were very warm, friendly, and entertaining. They offered any help needed with directions, places to see, restaurants, and reservations." *(Harriet Ten Hoeve)*

"Twin Gates was superlative—all your readers' praises and more. When we came into the house from the August heat and humidity we were welcomed by Gwen into the cool, bright, clean and magnificently decorated surrounding. Our suite—the California Room—had been pre-cooled by the in-room air-conditioner and was wonderfully fresh, clean, and inviting. Lush carpeting, a comfortable bed with an excellent mattress, fine fabric and lace curtains and drapes, and a spacious bathroom supplied with soap, shampoo, powder, and even Q-tips, comprised the decor. Each detail beautifully, artfully, and thoughtfully orchestrated. Bob and Gwen reside at Twin Gates, which contributes to the home-like ambience. We truly felt more like guests in their beautiful home than visitors at an inn. The grand finale was breakfast served in the dining room with lit tapered candles, hazelnut coffee, fresh fruit berries compote, refreshing juice, warm homemade peach/blueberry muffins and zucchini bread, and a perfect egg and cheese soufflé. All this with Baltimore's Inner Harbor just 16 minutes away on the expressway." *(Humane Zia)*

Open All year.
Rooms 5 doubles with private bath and/or shower, radio, air-conditioning, ceiling fans.
Facilities Living room with fireplace, dining room, greeting room with TV, fireplace. 1½ acres with gardens, magnolia trees. Off-street parking.
Location Suburb 15 min. N of downtown Baltimore. From I-695 (Baltimore Beltway) take Exit 25N (Charles St.) Take immediate right onto Bellona Avenue. In 3 blocks turn left onto Morris Ave. 3 blocks to inn.
Restrictions No smoking. No children under 12.
Credit cards Amex, MC, Visa.
Rates B&B, $85 double. 2-night weekend minimum.

NEW MARKET

Strawberry Inn   *Tel:* 301–865–3318
17 Main Street, P.O. Box 237, 21774

Innkeepers Jane and Ed Rossig describe their B&B as the oldest in Maryland, established well before the "trend," in 1972. Rooms are decorated with some Victorian antiques and reproduction wallcoverings; the baths are modern. Rates include a light breakfast of fruit, coffee or tea, and homemade muffins served on the porch or delivered to your bedroom door at the hour requested.

The town of New Market dates back nearly two hundred years and is listed as a Historic District on the National Register of Historic Places—all the houses are over one hundred years old. It's also known as the antiques capital of Maryland, and makes a convenient base from which to explore the Civil War battle sites of Antietam, South Mountain, and Monocacy.

"We had a spacious room upstairs in the rear, with large bath and sitting room. The Rossigs directed us to the town tea room for a tasty lunch, and to Mealey's Inn for an outstanding meal." *(WW)* "Be sure to visit Ed's framing and print shop in the log cabin he has restored behind the inn." *(Pat & Cramer Riblett)*

"The very friendly innkeeper showed us his collection of decoys and antiques, and filled us in on local activities. Our room was clean and spacious, though not decorated with lots of antiques. Several delightful shops in town." *(PD)*

Open All year.
Rooms 5 doubles with private bath and/or shower, air-conditioning. Telephone on request.
Facilities Common room with fireplace, books, magazines. Back porch. Fully equipped restored 1840 log cabin available for meetings. 3/4 acre of shade and quiet. Tennis 2 blocks away, golf 1/4 m.
Location Halfway between Baltimore and Frederick. 35 m W of Baltimore on I-70, Exit 62. Center of town.
Restrictions Smoking in first-floor rooms only. No children under 7.
Credit cards None accepted.
Rates B&B, $60–90 double. Extra person in room, $15.
Extras First-floor guest room wheelchair accessible.

OXFORD

Information please: We'd like to hear more about the **1876 House,** a restored Queen Anne Victorian B&B, furnished in period and owned by Eleanor and Jerry Clark (110 North Morris Street, P.O. Box 658, 21654; 301–226–5496). Another possibility further south is the **Glasgow Inn** (1500 Hambrooks Boulevard, Cambridge 21613; 301–228–0575 or 800–225–0575), a six-guest room B&B built in 1760.

Another possibility overlooking the Town Creek and marina is the **Oxford Inn** (P.O. Box 627, 21654; 301–226–5220), a century-old home with a restaurant and rooms decorated in period reproductions and antiques. There's a second-floor sitting room for guest comfort, and rates include continental breakfast, sherry, chocolates, and fresh fruit.

Robert Morris Inn   *Tel:* 301–226–5111
Morris Street, P.O. Box 70, 21654

The Robert Morris Inn is one of the oldest buildings in one of Maryland's oldest towns. The earliest part of the inn was built prior to 1710 by ships' carpenters using wooden pegged paneling, ships' nails, and hand-hewn beams. Several fireplaces were made from English bricks used as ballast in the early sailing ships. Robert Morris, Sr., moved into the house in 1738 and became prominent in the shipping business. His son, Robert Morris, Jr., achieved fame as the financier of the Continental Army during the Revolutionary War and was a close friend of George Washington. Oxford is also the home of one of the oldest ferries in the U.S. The line, which connects Oxford with Bellevue, was started in 1760 by Elizabeth Skinner, who collected her fares in tobacco, the currency of the time.

Long-time owners Wendy and Ken Gibson describe Oxford as "one of the most relaxed places on the Eastern Shore. We offer quiet walks along the beach, peaceful spots to read, and breathtaking sunsets. The inn is couple-oriented, providing good food in a charming colonial atmosphere." In the past twenty years, the Gibsons have expanded so that rooms are available in a number of buildings. The Sandaway, built in 1875, located one block away from the inn, offers larger and more luxurious rooms at correspondingly higher rates. Newest are the River Rooms, overlooking the Tred Avon River, but other rooms are found in several additional buildings.

"The inn offers clean, comfortable rooms with wonderful views of the bay and village. The drawing rooms are old and attractive, filled with antiques. The menu in the dining room is typical of this area—crab soup, crab cakes and fresh fish." *(Mrs. John M. Schmunk)*

"We had a lovely, large, ground-floor room in the River Cottage, with a screened porch and view of the river. Breakfast was good but quite expensive." *(SHW)* "Guest rooms in the main house are small, but very authentic; Sandaway is more spacious, remote and romantic, with private balconies overlooking the water. The food is excellent—the best soft shell crab we've ever had, and the staff is very friendly. There are lots of little shops and places to go antiquing nearby, and good bicycling available." *(Pat Drake)*

"Though the inn's least expensive, our room smelled musty, with window shades apparently nailed shut. The food was good but over-priced."

Open All year. Restaurant closed week after Thanksgiving, Christmas Day, mid January–mid February.
Rooms 34 rooms—21 doubles with full private bath, 12 with private shower, 1 with private tub. All rooms with air-conditioning, 4 with desk. 15 rooms in inn, 8 rooms at Sandaway, 10 rooms in 5 cottages.
Facilities Sitting room. 3/4 acre by Tred Avon River, tennis, golf nearby.
Location Eastern Shore. 80 m SE of Baltimore, E of Washington, DC.
Restrictions No-smoking rooms available. No children under 10.
Credit cards MC, Visa.
Rates Room only, $70–170 double, plus 8% tax. Extra person in room, $20. Alc breakfast, $5–10; alc lunch, $15; alc dinner, $30. Children's menu available.
Extras Dining room, some guest rooms wheelchair accessible.

PRINCESS ANNE

Information please: Budget travelers may want to check into the Washington Hotel (Somerset Avenue, 21853; 301–651–2525), dating back to 1744. Some of its 12 rooms have antique decor, while others are standard motel issue. The $40 rate includes a room with air-conditioning, TV, and private bath, and the hotel has a dining room and coffee shop serving reasonably priced meals.

Elmwood
Locust Point County Road, P.O. Box 220, 21853

Tel: 301–651–1066

Arnold Elzey began construction on Elmwood in the early 1800s, and took over ten years to complete it. The house stayed in the Elzey family until the 1950s, and was restored as an inn in 1985 by Helen and Stephen Monick. Rooms are furnished with art and antiques, highlighted by Mrs. Monick's needlework.

"A stunning piece of early Federal architecture, Elmwood overlooks the wide and picturesque Manokin River. Lovingly restored by the Monicks, the exterior brick and interior architectural details will delight the most sophisticated connoisseur of period construction. The rooms are large, bright and handsome; little touches such as ring stands for jewelry are welcome additions. Be sure to make the short drive to Crisfield and the Captain's Galley for some of the freshest seafood the Chesapeake Bay has to offer—broiled or fried, the imperial-style crab cakes are not to be missed. Although it's tempting just to stay and relax at Elmwood, it's worth making an appointment to visit Teackle Mansion in Princess Anne, built in 1801 and modeled after a Scottish manor house." *(Nancy Harrison & Nelson Ormsby)*

"Located along the Chesapeake Bay, just up from the mouth of the Manokin River, Elmwood is a near-perfect country inn. The architecturally significant house was added onto three times. Throughout the house the impeccable taste of the owners can be seen in every detail of its restoration and decorating. The double living room has high ceilings, fine antiques, and exquisite hand-made moldings. Some of the window panes are original, done by the same glazier who Thomas Jefferson used. In fact, in the dining room you can see TJ's initials scratched into one pane (a practice once common among fine craftsmen who worked primarily for one person/patron).

"We had two large bedrooms upstairs. One had a handsome carved poster bed that was high enough off the ground that even our six-foot son said he used the two-step assist to get into bed. The enormous and sunny room had attractive rugs and quilts (hung on a special quilt rack), a large fireplace, a small antique highboy, comfortable chairs, beautiful embroideries, large closets, and a huge bath with a marble counter. You can see out to the river/bay while lounging in bed. Our equally spacious room had a private entrance to the large second floor of a two-story screened-in porch. There was a walnut bedstead, ample closets, fireplace, a rocking chair and an old-fashioned pedestal rocker, marble-topped dresser, attractive Austrian-style curtains, lots of little antique objects (covered dishes, old pictures), handmade quilt (again on its own rack), and large and comfortable bathroom.

"The ample grounds are pleasant to explore. We visited in the fall, and could hear and see Canada geese flying over in huge V-formations.

Lawns filled with old stately trees sweep down from the house to the water. The river is edged with tall grasses, and roses climb a fence. We put our canoe in the river and paddled upstream to see other old estates (in various stages of repair).

"Breakfast the first morning included a choice of freshly squeezed orange juice, cantaloupe, or puff pancakes with imported Italian cherries on top, little Smithfield ham sausage patties, nicely presented in the formal yet warm dining room, with a fire roaring in the fireplace. The second day we feasted on orange juice, an apple torte with flaky pastry and thin-sliced apple, eggs cooked with shallots and two kinds of cheeses and topped with caviar, plus bacon, and homemade croissants."

A small niggle: "A larger hot water tank would be helpful; we ran short one morning."

Open All year. Closed Christmas and New Year's Day.
Rooms 2 1-2 bedroom guest houses with kitchen, living room with fireplace. 4 doubles—all with private shower and/or bath, air-conditioning. 1 with fireplace, screened porch.
Facilities Dining room with fireplace, living room, library with fireplace, TV, games; screened porches. 10 acres with gardens, picnic table. On river for boating, fishing, crabbing.
Location Lower Eastern Shore. Take Rte. 13 S from Salisbury to Princess Anne. Go W 5 m on Rte. 363, then S 1 m on Rte. 627 to Locust Pt. Cty. Rd. Go 1 m to inn.
Restrictions No smoking. No children under 12 in main house.
Credit cards MC, Visa.
Rates B&B, $95 guest house (double), $75–85 double. 2-night minimum in guest houses. Weekly rates. Picnic lunches, $15–25.

ST. MICHAELS

Founded in 1632, St. Michaels was a noted shipping center throughout the 1700s. Under British attack during the War of 1812, the townspeople saved their homes by blacking out the town and hanging lanterns in treetops, causing the enemy to overshoot the town. Today, excitement in St. Michaels is more likely to ensue when a neophyte sailor overshoots a buoy, but visitors are attracted to its historic heritage, and the Chesapeake Bay Maritime Museum, devoted the history of the Bay and its ships.

Information please: The **Two Swan Inn House** (Foot Carpenter Street, P.O. Box 727, 21663; 301–745–2929) is a 200-year-old home overlooking the harbor, with antique furnishings and original flooring. The **Hambleton Inn** (202 Cherry Street, 21663; 301–745–3350) is a turn-of-the-century inn with antique decor, and a fireplace in one of its guest rooms. The **Parsonage** (210 North Talbot Street, 21663; 301–745–5519) was built in 1883 of red brick with white gingerbread trim, and was converted into a B&B nearly a century later. Rooms are furnished with Victorian antiques and reproductions, and guests have ample common areas—indoors and out—for relaxation. The **St. Michaels Harbour Inn & Marina** (101 N. Harbor Rd. 21663; 301–745–9001) offers motel-style rooms with balconies overlooking a fleet of pleasure boats. The **Victoriana Inn** (205 Cherry Street, P.O. Box 449, 21663; 301–745–3368) dates from 1865; guests enjoy relaxing on the porch and gardens, overlooking the harbor. Rooms are furnished in period and rates include a full breakfast.

In an even smaller hamlet than St. Michaels is the **Wades Point Inn**, an easy bike ride to the west. Built in 1819, the inn's setting is very quiet, overlooking the water and surrounded by 120 acres of field and woodland (Wades Point Road, McDaniel; mailing address: P.O. Box 7, St. Michaels 21663). Owners Betsy and John Feiler offer 12 guest rooms in the main house, with an additional 14 in a recently constructed annex. The reasonable rates include a buffet breakfast of fruit, juice, cheeses, fresh-baked rolls and muffins; children under 12 stay free, and senior discounts are available.

Finally, if you like the feeling of staying at the end of the road, follow Route 33 to its terminus on tiny Tilghman Island. **Sinclair House** (Main Street, P.O. Box 145 Tilghman Island 21671; 301–886–2147) is a welcoming homestay B&B; its modest rates include a full breakfast. **The Black Walnut Point Inn** (P.O. Box 308, Tilghman Island 21671; 301–886–2452) overlooks the bay. Both cottages and rooms are available, and guests are welcome to enjoy the swimming pool, tennis court, and bayside hammocks. We await your opinions!

The Inn at Perry Cabin
308 Watkins Lane, 21663

Tel: 301–745–2200
800–722–2949

Laura Ashley aficionados may have a new Mecca when they discover that Sir Bernard Ashley, co-founder of the Ashley decorating and clothing business, has purchased The Inn at Perry Cabin, making it the first Ashley inn to debut on this side of the Atlantic. Originally an eighteenth century farmhouse, the inn sits right on the banks of the Miles River and is surrounded by country gardens. Familiar Ashley patterns can be found throughout the inn, decorating everything from the antique furnishings to the bathroom towels. Rates include a full breakfast, daily newspaper, and afternoon high tea.

"St. Michaels has many things to offer, not the least of which is Perry Cabin Inn. Sail and motor boats anchor offshore, or dock at the inn's pier." *(JF)* More comments please.

Reader tip: At press time, we learned that the new management planned to expand the existing guest rooms to a total of 41, completing the project by June 1991.

Open All year.
Rooms 19 doubles—all with full private bath, telephone, TV, air-conditioning.
Facilities Restaurant, veranda. 27 acres with gardens, docking facilities, bicycles. Golf, tennis, hunting, sailing nearby.
Location Eastern Shore, 50 m E of Baltimore, Washington, DC. 1/4 m from town. On Miles River.
Restrictions No children.
Credit cards Amex, DC, MC, Visa.
Rates B&B, $160–385 double. Alc dinner, $50.

Kemp House Inn   *Tel:* 301–745–2243
412 Talbot Street, Box 638, 21663

Built in 1805, the Kemp House Inn was recently restored as an inn. Rooms are decorated with period antiques, many with four-poster rope beds with trundle beds underneath, patchwork quilts and down pillows. Old-fashioned night shirts are also provided. "A handsome old stone house on the main street of St. Michaels. We had a most attractive room on the first floor (near the front door), with a canopied bed, working fireplace with the original mantel, two comfortable chairs and a sink in an old wooden cabinet. A lavatory with toilet and shower had been added in one corner of the room. The floor was brick and the curtains, bedspreads, and decorations had been chosen with taste and care. A good continental breakfast is brought to the room in a wicker basket at whatever hour you request between eight and ten A.M., or you may eat on one of the porches. All of the rooms have been turned into accommodations, so there are no communal rooms indoors, possibly a drawback in poor weather. Next time we'll request a room on the second floor; they're quieter and equally attractive.

"We thought the Kemp House and St. Michaels were splendid places to spend a pretty fall weekend, not least because they were an easy walk from the area's famous seafood restaurant, the Crab Claw, where the food is well worth the wait." *(Carolyn Mathiasen)*

Open All year.
Rooms 7 doubles, 1 cabin—3 with private shower, 5 with a maximum of 6 people sharing a bath. All with air-conditioning.
Facilities No common facilities.
Location Eastern Shore, 50 m E of Baltimore, Washington, DC. 2 blocks from town center.
Credit cards MC, Visa.
Rates B&B, $55–95. Extra person in room, $10. 2-night weekend minimum March to Dec.

SHARPSBURG

Information please: We'd like to know what you think of **Lewrene Farm B&B** (R.D. 3, Box 150, Hagerstown 21740; 301–582–1735) about ten miles to the north. Irene and Lewis Lehman invite guests to their 125-acre crop farm and their southern colonial-style home. Rates for their five guest rooms—some decorated with canopy beds and homemade quilts—range from $50–75, and include afternoon refreshments and a full breakfast. Reports?

Inn at Antietam   *Tel:* 301–432–6601
220 East Main Street, P.O. Box 119, 21782

This turn-of-the-century Victorian has been owned and run by the Fairbourns since 1984, and has been recommended with exceptional enthusiasm by our readers:

"The inn is set at the edge of the picturesque town of Sharpsburg in the Potomac Valley, overlooking the Antietam battlefield. This rambling Victorian farmhouse is spotless and beautifully decorated. Particularly handsome is the suite created from the old summer kitchen/smokehouse with a huge fireplace and bedroom loft.

"The Fairbourns serve a good hearty breakfast of Belgian waffles or blueberry pancakes, with fresh squeezed orange juice; in the afternoon they offer tea, coffee, cider, or lemonade with homemade cookies. A high point of our weekend was our tour of the battlefield, arranged by the Fairbourns; a local Civil War historian, John Powell, arrived in a Union army uniform and gave us a fascinating tour for a very reasonable price." *(David Fogle, also Dr. & Mrs. Marvin Sears)*

"The hospitality of the owners can hardly be surpassed. Rooms are furnished with carefully selected antiques, and the home-cooked breakfast is served in elegance on beautiful china. Nearby is the battlefield tour route, including Burnside's Bridge and Bloody Lane. The Visitor Center displays and films explain the events as they took place nearly 125 years ago. Outdoor enthusiasts will also find the inn an ideal location for hiking and bicycling excursions along the C & O Canal, just a few miles away, where they will pass deserted locks and quiet natural areas along the Potomac." *(Esther Bittinger, also Betty Norman)*

Open All year. Closed Dec. 20 through New Year's Day.
Rooms 3 suites, 2 doubles—4 with full private bath, 1 with tub only. All with air-conditioning, 1 with TV, 2 with desk.
Facilities Sitting room, sun-room, dining room, porches. 8½ acres with patio, gardens. Fishing, swimming, hiking, bicycling, cross-country skiing nearby.
Location W MD. 4 m E of Shepherdstown, WV. 13 m from intersection of I-70 and I-81. From Washington or Baltimore, take I-70 to Braddock Heights, Exit 49 and turn left to Alt Rte. 40 W. Go W through Middletown and Boonsboro to Rte. 34. Turn left onto Rte. 34, 6 m to Sharpsburg. Approaching Sharpsburg is the Antietam Battlefield Cemetery on left; inn is just past it.
Restrictions Smoking in common rooms only.
Credit cards Amex. 5% service charge.
Rates B&B, $85–95 suite, $65–75 double. Extra person in room, $10–20. No tipping.
Extras Airport/station pickups, $25.

SNOW HILL

Information please: About 15 miles north of Snow Hill, the **Atlantic Inn** (2 North Main Street, Berlin 21811; 301–641–3589) is a historic hotel and restaurant, providing an elegant alternative to Ocean City's motels. Located in the center of the historic district, its 16 guest rooms combine the charm of antique decor with private baths, air-conditioning, and in-room telephones. A restaurant and lounge occupies the first floor, on the second guests can relax by the fireplace in the parlor.

Chanceford Hall   *Tel:* 301–632–2231
209 West Federal Street, 21863

Michael and Thelma Driscoll opened Chanceford Hall as a B&B in 1986, after completing a major restoration of their Georgian-style home, built in 1759. "The house was a wreck when we bought it from a judge who had lived here for thirty years—no heat, ivy growing through the doors, crumbling plaster, and more. The good part was that no one had ever 'K Marted' it. All is original—the floors, woodwork, plaster, glass, all ten fireplace mantles, and so on." The inn is decorated with period antiques and reproductions, lots of comfortable wing chairs, canopied beds, and handmade quilts.

"Everyone whom we met in Snow Hill was awed by the large restoration project, which they accomplished almost single-handedly. Founded in 1642, Snow Hill is an quiet harbor town on the Pocomoke River, with over 100 historic homes; its sidewalks are made with bricks used as ballast in the early English sailing ships." (Dr. Gunter Born) "Tongue and groove paneling, moldings, mantels, and plank flooring have been renovated in the most delicate manner of the cabinet maker, a skill readily demonstrated by Mr. Driscoll in numerous fine furniture pieces through this home. If you take the opportunity to extract the details of the restoration process from this couple, you will find the labor of love and the satisfaction of accomplishment. Oil lamps, comfortable queen-sized beds, spotless linens and draperies are found in all rooms." (John Callander)

"The grounds are private and beautifully landscaped, the parking plentiful. The house is impeccably clean, and both the air-conditioning and the heating are most effective. The plumbing and wiring is all new, the lighting excellent. The full breakfast of fruit, juice, eggs, and bacon or sausage is served in the high-ceilinged dining room." (M.A. Filippino) "Our delicious dinner included a tasty salad and a seafood platter, followed by a rich dessert. Our bedroom was furnished with a Hepplewhite four poster bed, in the English style of about 1750." (L. Ingerslev Madsen)

"Mr. and Mrs. Driscoll were extremely pleasant and were happy to show us around the whole house. Our room had a four-poster bed which had been made by Mr. Driscoll, a highly accomplished cabinetmaker. We had a working fireplace with a carefully laid fire all ready to be lit. We settled into our room and were brought tea and cookies. The Driscolls recommended an excellent local seafood place for dinner that suited us very well. We were most impressed with the flexibility of breakfast times, and their sensitivity to our dietary requests. Mrs. Driscoll is justly famous for her ring cake, a dried fruit and cinnamon-perfumed confection which she served warm for breakfast, wrapping the leftovers for our journey. The plumbing was in fine working order, the street absolutely silent, the bed firm with lighting on *both* sides. Parking is under cover, and we were given a map and ferry timetables for our trip north." (Ellie & Bob Friedus, also Joan Barnes and others)

Open All year.
Rooms 1 suite, 4 doubles—all with private shower and/or bath, air-conditioning, desk. Some with fireplace.
Facilities Dining room, kitchen, living room, solarium/family room. 1½ acres with heated lap pool, bicycles. Pocomoke River for canoeing. 6 m to Chincoteague Bay, 30 min. to Chincoteague, Assateague National Wildlife Refuge. Golf, tennis, swimming nearby.

Location S Eastern Shore. 90 m S of Wilmington DE, 130 m SE of Baltimore. Historic district.
Restrictions No children under 12.
Credit cards None accepted.
Rates B&B, $105–115 suite, $95–105 double. No tipping. Prix fixe dinner, $44 (prior notice required). 20% discount for 3-night stay; 10% discount midweek; 20% Jan., Feb.
Extras 1 bedroom & bath wheelchair accessible. Airport/station/dockside pickups. Free use of bicycles.

Snow Hill Inn
104 East Market Street, 21863

Tel: 301–632–2102

Built in 1790, with a second larger section built later, the Snow Hill Inn is owned by George Mojzisek and managed by Elizabeth Quillen. Its popular restaurant is open for lunch and dinner, serving the requisite Maryland crab cakes and traditional American food.

"We had a chance to see a number of guest rooms. All have wide board floors, many authentically uneven. The Delotte Room has nice blue wallpaper, a working fireplace (with logs but no kindling), oak furniture, and five windows. Another, the Pocomoke Room was rather small, with a brass bedstead, an oak dresser, and school teacher's desk. One of our favorites was under the eaves, in the oldest section, prettily done in whites and blues, with a big oak double bed, comfortable chairs and a rocker. Those avoiding stairs might enjoy the first floor room off the dining room, with a huge carved walnut headboard, full floor-length drapes, huge marble-topped antique dresser, fancy armoire, hooked rugs, and a charming bath with striped wallpaper." *(SC)* "Courteous, kind, caring staff. Warm atmosphere and good food." *(Tracy Zylinski)*

A few caveats: "Be sure to ask if you need a firm mattress—ours was not. Also no one from the staff stayed overnight at the inn when we were there on a Monday, off-season."

Open All year. Restaurant closed Sun. - Mon.
Rooms 7 doubles—2 with full private bath, 5 rooms sharing 2 baths. All with desk, air-conditioning, fan. Some with fireplace.
Facilities Dining room, living room, lounge. Off-street parking. Swimming, camping, boating nearby.
Location S Eastern Shore. 90 m S of Wilmington DE, 130 m SE of Baltimore. Historic district. 1 block from town center.
Restrictions Light sleepers should request room away from street. No children under 13.
Credit cards MC, Visa.
Rates B&B, $70–81 double. Alc lunch $6, dinner $16.
Extras Wheelchair accessible.

STEVENSVILLE

Kent Manor Inn
Route 8, Box 815, 21666

Tel: 301–643–5757

Thanks to the Chesapeake Bay Bridge, access to the Kent Manor Inn is a little easier now than it was when the original building was constructed in 1820. A large wing was built in 1870, and a matching wing was completed in 1987, after the property was purchased by Fred Williams. Williams has long experience in the hotel business, and when he saw the falling-down structure in 1986, he felt it presented too good an opportunity to pass up. During the extensive restoration process, all of the original bull-pine flooring was saved, along with the walnut staircase and marble fireplaces. Rooms have been individually decorated with four-poster beds, reproduction armoires and bureaus, Oriental rugs, and coordinating drapes and wallcoverings, combining period elegance with modern comfort.

"Friendly, courteous staff. Excellent food and service. Our room had a beautiful four-poster, king-size bed with a quilt and matching drapes. Parking is conveniently situated and the lot is well lighted. The location is convenient for a visit to Annapolis, yet away from its hustle and bustle." *(Susan Moss)* More comments please.

Open All year.
Rooms 1 suite, 24 doubles—all with full private bath, telephone, radio, TV, air-conditioning. Many with balcony, fireplace.
Facilities Dining room, parlor, lounge/bar. 226 acres with gazebo, tennis court, swimming pool, gardens. On Thomas Creek for fishing, boating (docking facilities).
Location Eastern Shore. Kent Island, near Bay Bridge. 10 m E of Annapolis, 35 m S of Baltimore, 40 m E of Washington. From E side of bridge, take Rte. 50 to Rte. 8 S to inn on left (turn just before Jones Realty).
Credit cards MC, Visa.
Rates B&B, $125–149 suite, $99–119 double, $79 single. Ask about senior discounts, special occasion packages.
Extras Wheelchair accessible; 2 guest rooms equipped for disabled. Cribs available.

We Want to Hear from You!

As you know, this book is only effective with your help. We really need to know about your experiences and discoveries.

If you stayed at an inn or hotel listed here, we want to know how it was. Did it live up to our description? Exceed it? Was it what you expected? Did you like it? Were you disappointed? Delighted?

Have you discovered new establishments that we should add to the next edition?

Tear out one of the report forms at the back of this book (or use your own stationery if you prefer) and write today. Even if you write only "Fully endorse existing entry" you will have been most helpful.
Thank You!

New Jersey

The Queen Victoria, Cape May

Those who have seen New Jersey only from the turnpike have given the state a bad reputation. Others, familiar with Atlantic City and the more raucous beach towns, assume that it simply is not their sort of place. In truth, the state has quite a lot more to offer. Gracious beach resorts are found from Bay Head to Spring Lake to Cape May; many pleasant country towns along the Delaware River invite you to relax and explore; and shoppers may find Nirvana in the bargain shops of Flemington. To the south, the Pine Barrens include lush marsh and woodlands; in the northwest, New Jersey shares the impressive Delaware Water Gap National Recreation area with Pennsylvania. Since this is the 'Garden State,' be sure to stop by one of the region's most impressive horticultural centers: Leaming's Run Gardens in Swainton (16 miles north of Cape May) which has 25 different gardens spread over 50 acres.

The rates listed here do not include the 6% state sales tax. Most inns at beach resorts provide beach badges or passes to guests, which eliminates the need for guests to buy expensive nonresident passes. Two- and three-night minimums are the rule in most beach towns and resorts.

Information please: If you'd like to visit the 17 miles of white sand beaches to be found on Long Beach Island, we'd suggest you head for the historic district of Beach Haven, at the southern end of the island, where several Victorian homes and boarding houses have been restored as B&Bs. Two possibilities are the **Bayberry Barque** (117 Centre Street 08008; 609–492–5216), a homey relaxing place; and the **Magnolia House** (215 Centre Street 08008; 609–492–0398) a Greek Revival Cottage built in 1867 with gingerbread trim and a wraparound veranda. Its

12 guest rooms have ceiling fans to catch the ocean breezes, and rates include continental breakfast.

In Stewartsville, a tiny village just a ½ mile from Interstate 78, near the Pennsylvania border, is the **Stewart Inn**, a casual family-style inn in a stone manor house dating to 1770. Children will enjoy the farm animals and swimming pool; all will appreciate the farm-fresh eggs and blueberry pancakes (South Main Street, R.D. 1, Box 571, Stewartsville 08886; 201–479–6060).

BAY HEAD

Only an hour away from New York City, Bay Head offers a quick trip back to the turn of the century. The town was developed in 1879 by a group of wealthy Princeton men as a summer retreat for their families; many homes are still owned by these families. Bay Head has no neon signs, no supermarkets, no movie theaters, no parking meters, and no fast-food restaurants. It does have beautiful, uncrowded beaches and Victorian summer "cottages" and gardens. Area activities include swimming, fishing, sailing, windsurfing, tennis, and golf.

Bay Head is located 60 miles south of New York City via the Garden State Parkway, and 65 miles east of Philadelphia.

Bay Head Gables   *Tel:* 201–892–9844
200 Main Avenue, 08742

An elaborate Newport-style cedar-shake "cottage" with art deco furnishings and ocean views, the Gables has been owned by Don Haurie and Ed Laubusch since 1984. Built in 1914 and attributed to Stanford White, the three-story inn has a 150-foot wraparound porch overlooking the flower gardens and a white sand beach, just 75 yards away. Don describes it as "an elegant B&B. Each guest room is a personal statement with fine art and furnishings. The front rooms have ocean views and the rear ones overlook the lake. The ambiance is informal with the emphasis on hospitality." Guests can start the day with an expanded continental breakfast on the enclosed porch in summer, and a full one in the cooler months. All are welcome to relax on the overstuffed chairs and couches of the art-filled living room.

"Cheery, comfortable, easy-going atmosphere. Prompt and cordial service. Immaculately clean. The beautifully served breakfast tastes as good as it looks."*(AR Horesta, also E. & R. Hall)*

Open All year.
Rooms 11 doubles—all with private shower and/or bath, air-conditioning. Some with private decks.
Facilities Breakfast room, living room with fireplace, wraparound porch. Lawns and gardens. On-site parking. Beach, tennis passes. Close to central area for shopping and watersports.
Location On Rte 35S. 75 yards from beach.
Restrictions No smoking in guest rooms. No children under 14.
Credit cards Amex, MC, Visa.

Rates B&B, $85–130 double, $75–120 single. 2-3 night minimum stay weekends/holidays.
Extras Train station pickups.

Conover's Bay Head Inn
646 Main Avenue, 08742

Tel: 201–892–4664

Carl and Beverly Conover, who have operated the Bay Head Inn for many years, describe it as "a small place where we can pay attention to detail. We try to equip rooms as you would the guest room in your own home. Everything is home-baked for breakfast every day. Our continental summer breakfast includes local fruits in season; winter breakfast is full and hearty, and afternoon tea is also served."

"Everything is tidy and beautifully kept up. Rooms are decorated with a mixture of reproduction wicker, English chintz, and Victorian furniture. Beverly Conover hand-quilted the bedspreads and color-coordinated the sheets and towels. Carpeted hallways keep noise at a minimum. Breakfasts are luscious. Altogether a charming place to stay." *(Michael Spring)*

"The beach is one of the nicest in New Jersey, and the well-kept yard offers shade on hot sunny days; shopping is nearby for rainy ones. Beverly and Carl made us feel very welcome." *(Susan Klimley)*

Open All year, weekends only in winter.
Rooms 1 suite, 11 doubles—6 with private bath and/or shower, 6 with maximum of 6 people sharing bath. All air-conditioned.
Facilities Living, sitting rooms with fireplace, books, porches. Shaded yard with flower gardens, lounge chairs, picnic tables, grill, croquet. 1 block to swimming, fishing, water skiing. Beach passes. Horseback riding nearby.
Location 3 blocks from town. 1½ blocks past the 3rd traffic light on Rte. 35 S out of town.
Restrictions No children under 13. No smoking.
Credit cards Amex, MC, Visa.
Rates B&B, $95–135 suite, $70–125 double; $5–10 less for single occupancy. Extra person in room, $30. 2-3 night minimum weekends and holidays. Sunday to Friday stay, 1 night free.
Extras Train station pickups.

BELMAR

The Seaflower
110 Ninth Avenue, 07719

Tel: 201–681–6006

Pat O'Keefe and Knute Iwaszko have owned this B&B since 1986. A Dutch colonial built in 1907, the Seaflower features rooms furnished with a casual seaside mixture of antiques, wicker, and other pieces collected over the years. Some have ocean views; others are decorated with flowered or paisley wallpapers, and one has a canopy bed. Rates include a full breakfast, with fresh fruit and juice, cereal, home-baked breads or muffins, plus a daily special—perhaps blueberry pancakes or seafood quiche. Those who enjoy the shore off season will want to visit in early December, when five nearby inns sponsor holiday workshops covering the Victorian arts of Christmas.

"Behind the Seaflower's unassuming yellow facade, innkeepers Pat and Knute provide an ambiance that is both friendly and intelligent. The common rooms are attractive and inviting. The living room has two cozy love seats and a window seat filled with board games. The dining room is decorated with the sun, moon and stars (ask Pat why) and it has a small blackboard with a saying of the day, provided by Knute, and a listing of local events. Pat's fabulous three-course breakfasts include fresh fruit, then an omelet, French toast or perhaps potato fritatta, and a 'dessert,' such as raspberry chocolate chip muffins. My room was appealingly decorated in the Victorian manner, and the other rooms had similar motifs—in one room the bed has a wicker headboard, in another an unusual string canopy. All amenities were of the highest order, and the off-street parking is a special plus." *(Mark Rinis)*

"We received pleasant, friendly, and thoughtful care. While not elaborate, the house is in good condition, clean, and knowledgeably arranged." *(Edward Townsend)* "One of the most homey and friendly places I've ever stayed in. They offered us a glass of wine before dinner, and were able to advise us about all the local restaurants and night spots." *(James Bovaso)* "A calm and uncrowded beach, a comfortable living room, and a relaxing front porch overlooking the flowers and ivy—what more could you want?" *(A. She)* "Pat is very friendly and accommodating, and is a fabulous cook." *(Mr. & Mrs. James Hanley)*

Open All year.
Rooms 2 suites, 6 doubles, 1 single—7 with private bath and/or shower, 2 with maximum of 4 people sharing bath. All rooms with fan.
Facilities Breakfast room, parlor with TV/VCR, movies, games; porch, deck, off-street parking. Beach passes, bicycles. 1/2 block to beach for swimming, fishing.
Location Central NJ shore. From NYC, take Garden State S to Exit 98, then Rte. 138 E to Belmar. From Philadelphia take NJ Turnpike to Exit 7A, then go E on I-195 to Rte. 138 E into Belmar. From Belmar, go left on Rte. 35 N to 4th light. Go right on 10th Ave., left on Ocean Ave., left on 9th Ave. to inn on right.
Restrictions No children under 10. Smoking in guest rooms only.
Credit cards None accepted.
Rates B&B, $110–150 suite, $55–90 double, $35–50 single. 5% senior discounts. 2-3 night minimum summer weekends.
Extras Station pickups.

CAPE MAY

Cape May has so many Victorian gingerbread houses that the town has been designated as a National Historic Landmark. Cape May's heyday as a beach resort stretched from 1850 to 1900, when thousands of visitors arrived by train or steamer each summer from Philadelphia and points farther south. Many of today's guest houses date from a disastrous fire in 1878. From the ashes rose this extraordinary collection of elaborate beach "cottages" designed by Philadelphia's best architects, built by the town's master carpenters, and paid for by the millionaires of the day. These "cottages" actually come in three sizes: cottage, villa, and mansion, or big, bigger, biggest.

Cape May has an unusually large number of high-quality owner-operated inns. When calling for reservations you may find that your first choice is full; inn owners are very good about referring you to a nearby establishment of equal appeal, and you'll do well to follow their suggestions. Almost none of Cape May's inns serves dinner; there are so many good restaurants within an easy walk that there's no need. People usually name the Chalfonte, Maureen's, and the Mad Batter among their favorites. One respondent did note that "many of Cape May's best restaurants do not have liquor licenses, a fact which we were dismayed to learn after we'd been seated for dinner." We suggest you ask when making reservations, and, if necessary, stop by a liquor store on your way to dinner.

Activities in Cape May include swimming, fishing, birding, and bike riding on the town's flat roads, and, of course, touring the Victorian mansions. The Mid-Atlantic Center for the Arts sponsors walking tours, summer theater, and special Victorian programs. The walking tours are a special treat; many are guided by the innkeepers of the establishments listed below. A number of the most famous inns serve afternoon tea along with an afternoon tour; we recommend that you give it a try. Many special events are sponsored at Christmas time; call the Chamber of Commerce (609–884–5404), or ask your favorite inn for details.

Most guest houses require a two- to three-night minimum stay on weekends and holidays during the spring, summer, and fall. Quite a few inns restrict smoking; this number has risen in recent years because of strict state fire regulations. Be prepared for parking problems during the summer; once you find a spot, leave the car and forget it until it's time to go home. Peak season crowds also create noise, as people walk around at night from place to place; if you want a more peaceful visit, we urge you to visit before Memorial Day or after Labor Day. Keep in mind that few of these inns are air-conditioned. Although ceiling fans and the ocean breezes are normally cool enough for comfort, if you hit a real August heat wave, you will be hot. Most inns in Cape May provide an outside shower, and refrigerators for guest use.

Cape May is at the southernmost tip of New Jersey, 3½ hours from New York and Washington, 2 hours (90 miles) from Philadelphia, and 38 miles south of Atlantic City. To get there, follow the Garden State Parkway to the very end, when it becomes Lafayette Street. From the south, take the ferry from Lewes, Delaware; call (302) 645–6313 for information.

Information please: Although we need more Cape May entries about as much as a dog needs fleas, we were intrigued by a newly reopened Cape May establishment, the **Virginia Hotel** (25 Jackson Street, 08204; 609–884–5700). Built in 1879, a recent restoration has produced a small elegant and expensive hotel, with 24 luxurious bedrooms, combining period decor with all 20th century amenities, along with a restaurant offering seafood and regional American cuisine. Comments?

Even more interesting is the **Carroll Villa Hotel** (19 Jackson Street, 08204; 609–884–9619) adjacent to the well-known Mad Batter restaurant. Its 24 rooms are reasonably priced ($55–95) and furnished with

83

Victorian antiques. There's a wicker-filled living room and garden terrace for relaxing, and rates include a creative full breakfast at the Mad Batter.

The Abbey   *Tel: 609–884–4506*
Columbia Avenue and Gurney Street, 08204

Built in 1869 by a Philadelphia coal baron, the Abbey is easy to find because of its 60-foot high tower. Authentically restored by Jay and Marianne Schatz, who've owned the inn since 1979, they've complemented the original stenciled and ruby glass windows with high Victorian antiques, ornate glass fixtures, 12-foot mirrors, tall walnut beds, and marble-topped dressers. Most guest rooms are spacious and attractive, with a comfortable seating area. Although the furnishings are formal, the Schatzes try hard to create a warm atmosphere; guests meet at breakfast, for croquet, and at afternoon tea, and are introduced by first names. Jay feels he's done his work well if guests start going out to dinner together after a few days' stay. Rates include a continental buffet in summer, and a full breakfast in winter.

"Jay and Marianne Schatz totally involve you in their splendid Victorian home. Concern for their guests is always first in their minds. Plumbing, parking, lighting, and safety have all been taken care of in a most pleasing manner." *(Mr. & Mrs. Frank M. Mancini)*

"Once the doors close behind you, the present is erased from your mind as you face a house full of Victorian treasures. The rooms, with their striking colors, are decorated with period antiques. The authentic decor does not stop on the first floor, but continues throughout the house. Our room, the New Orleans room, had a four-poster canopy bed, a green velvet seat, spacious wardrobe and dressing table, plus a private bath and refrigerator. To their credit, the innkeepers had no problem entertaining fourteen guests at breakfast. The food was excellent and the service couldn't have been better." *(Tim & Kay Miller)*

"Rooms are light, airy, and meticulously maintained. Breakfasts are pure joy, complete with juice, fresh fruit, warm muffins, and the most imaginative entrees. Our favorites were the caramel French toast and the cream cheese strata with strawberries. Marianne gladly shares her recipes. Don't miss afternoon tea." *(Mr. & Mrs. Craig Campbell, also Gina & Ken Wright)*

Open April through Nov.
Rooms 2 suites, 12 doubles—all with private shower and/or bath, fan. Some with desks, air-conditioning. 7 doubles in McGreary Cottage annex.
Facilities Parlors, library, dining room. Croquet court, flower garden. On-site parking. Beach passes, beach chairs.
Location Historic district; 1 block from beach.
Restrictions No smoking. No children under 12.
Credit cards Amex, MC, Visa.
Rates B&B, $140–150 suite, $75–85 double, 3-4 night minimum stay in summer. 10% weekly discount.
Extras Station pickups.

Abigail Adams B&B   *Tel:* 609–884–1371
12 Jackson Street, 08204

Recent changes at the Abigail Adams, owned by Donna and Ed Misner since 1982, include the addition of another private bath, and the redecoration of several guest rooms.

"The Abigail Adams sits at the end of Jackson Street, only 100 yards from the water. The front of the house faces away from the street, toward the ocean. It has a very relaxing atmosphere that is enhanced by the sound of the waves on the shore. There is a great front porch, which tends to be a gathering place. The decor is more Victorian country than straight Victorian, with clean, restful colors—peaches, pale greens, clear blues. There is a fantastic circular staircase that goes all the way to the third floor. Our favorite room, on the second floor, has a private bath, with a large bay window and a breathtaking view of the ocean." *(Linda Lee Moran)*

"Donna and Ed Misner are excellent innkeepers who do everything to make our stay comfortable. We always linger over breakfast for at least two hours—chatting, laughing, and drinking an endless amount of their good coffee. Donna bakes her own muffins, scones, and coffee cake. The inn's decor is casual country and Victorian, the beds comfortable and clean, the location close to the beach and restaurants. It's quiet and one feels very safe in Cape May, a very family-oriented place." *(Mary Jane Reep)*

Respondents have noted one small drawback: "After you unload your car in front of the inn, you must drive it several blocks and park it in a private lot." Most everyone gets around in Cape May by walking, so it's usually not a problem. If it is, the innkeepers are happy to drive guests back and forth between the inn and parking lot.

Open April to mid-Oct.
Rooms 2 suites, 3 doubles—3 with full private bath, 2 with maximum of 4 people sharing bath. 3 rooms with ocean view.
Facilities Living room, dining room, sitting room, porch with ocean views. Herb garden. Parking in nearby lot, beach tags.
Location Historic district, 100 feet from beach. At corner of Atlantic Terrace.
Restrictions No smoking. No children under 16.
Credit cards MC, Visa.
Rates B&B, $95–105 suite, $85–95 double, $75–90 single. Extra person in room, $25. 2-night minimum stay, weekends and holidays.
Extras Station pickups.

The Brass Bed   *Tel:* 609–884–8075
719 Columbia Avenue, 08204   609–884–1852

The Brass Bed is a sixteen-room Carpenter Gothic cottage built in 1872 as two separate buildings and joined together some time in the early 1900s. The innkeepers, John and Donna Dunwoody, want their guests to feel relaxed and at home (in fact, innkeeper Donna Dunwoody used to describe a visit to the inn as being like a visit to Grandmother's house—until she became a grandmother herself!). Some of the rooms are furnished with pieces the Dunwoodys found when they restored the inn in 1980; shipping tags confirmed that they belonged to Lewis Dannenbaum, the house's original owner. These have been supplemented by other pieces of similar style and character. Of course, all the rooms have nineteenth-century brass beds, along with reproduction Victorian wallpapers, reading lights and bedside tables.

"John and Donna run an immaculate inn, serve huge and delicious breakfasts, encourage friendly contact among guests at tea, and regale us with hilarious Cape May stories. John is a mini-historian of New Jersey Victoriana, and isn't bad at ghost stories either. The inn has been lovingly restored with beautiful period pieces, without losing its homey feeling." *(Veronica and Victor Strozak)* "I enjoy the wide porch furnished in wicker for summer visits, but no matter when I visit, John and Donna always provide warm hospitality, clean comfortable accommodations, and excellent service." *(Thomas King)*

Open All year.
Rooms 8 doubles—4 with private bath or shower, 4 rooms sharing 2 baths.
Facilities Parlors with piano, games; dining room, sun-room, library, veranda. Outside shower.
Location Historic district. 2 blocks to shops, beach.
Restrictions Smoking in sun parlor, veranda only. "Caters to adult couples."
Credit cards MC, Visa. 3% service charge.
Rates B&B, $55–115 double, $5 less for single. Extra person in room, $20. 10% weekly discount; 3rd night 30% off in winter. Christmas packages. Minimum stay requirements.
Extras Airport/station pickups.

Chalfonte   *Tel:* 609–884–8409
301 Howard Street, 08204

The Chalfonte is the oldest hotel in Cape May; it has accommodated guests since 1876. There has been a certain amount of restoration work, but not a great deal has changed since then. In fact, the Chalfonte's landmark status is such that students from the University of Maryland still come every spring to work on the hotel as part of one of their architecture courses! You can come too—for a $15 fee (including room and board, you can spend a spring or fall weekend painting and plastering, sewing or gardening, to help get the hotel in shape). Projects (for professionals) last year included restoring the front porch floors, adding ceiling fans, and upgrading the hotel's electrical and plumbing systems.

The hotel was owned for over 80 years by the Satterfield family, and was taken over in 1983 by Judy Bartella and Anne LeDuc. No major changes were instituted by them; Judy and Anne, who had managed the Chalfonte for years, first started visiting the hotel as children!

The Chalfonte is known for its traditional southern cooking, served in the enormous dining room, originally built as a ballroom. Both breakfast and dinner are included in the very reasonable rates. Breakfast often consists of eggs, biscuits, fried fish, bacon or sausage, and a big bowl of spoon bread. Family-style dinners offer a choice of either of three entrees: the fish of the day in a lemon sherry sauce; a scallop or crab dish; and a meat dish, typically roast beef, turkey or lamb, fried chicken, or country ham. Even if you're staying elsewhere, come here at least once for dinner. Cooks Helen Dickerson and her daughter Dorothy Burton have been working at the Chalfonte for 45 and 40 years, respectively; a (relatively) new arrival to the team is Lucille Thompson. Gentlemen wear jackets at dinner, and children under 7 eat in the supervised children's dining room.

Many of the common rooms are decorated with furniture original to the building, while the reading room mixes equally venerable titles with those of more recent vintage. Guest rooms are very simply furnished in period decor, much original to the hotel.

Often, aficionados of the Chalfonte started visiting as children and are now continuing the tradition with their own kids. "I have returned to the Chalfonte every summer since my family's first visit when I was 13 years old. There may be newer hotels in Cape May but none are equal to the Chalfonte for wonderful southern cooking, congenial atmosphere, and warm hospitality." *(Rosemary Mazon)* "For character, there is no place like the Chalfonte. The people, the food, the place, the tradition, all add up to the state of mind that *is* the Chalfonte. If you are looking for beautiful beaches, gorgeous rooms, and incredible service, go to the Cloisters at Sea Island. But if you want to fall in love, go to the Chalfonte. My grandparents, my parents, my kids, and soon my grandchildren all are, will be, or were Chalfonters." *(W. Richard Sattler)*

"I worked at the Chalfonte while in college, and now return as a guest. I have witnessed guests come through the front door into the simple yet inviting lobby with expressions that range from pure shock to divine delight. Upon arrival at the hotel you are briefed as to what your Chalfonte experience will include, from mealtime to quiet hours. Meals are served family-style, and often times guests are seated together as strangers. As a waitress, I have seen the apprehension in the eyes of some; to my delight, by the end of the meal, addresses are being swapped so that new friends can keep in touch until their return the coming year." *(Kate Fralin)*

"Though my room had only the essentials, and the hallways were a bit creaky, this only added to an overall ambience, shared by actors from New York City, proper Bostonians, Main Line Philadelphians, and Southern ladies and gentlemen. When joined together for dinner, cocktails, or conversations on the porch, the atmosphere is always interesting, and people watching a favorite Chalfonte sport." *(Gerry Wolf)*

"Where else can you find a quaint, affordable stay in an historic landmark where children are welcomed? The concept of a children's dining room (all children under seven must eat there) is perfect for us—a vacation both from and with the children!" *(Katherine Bliss)*

And another opinion: "Our room was not clean, and the shared bath had a broken shower."

Open April through Nov.
Rooms 67 doubles, 5 singles—11 with private bath and/or shower, 61 with maximum of 6 people sharing bath; all with fan. 21 rooms in 3 separate cottages.
Facilities Dining room, main lobby, solarium, library, reading room, bar, TV room with VCR, playroom, children's program, porches, garden with swings. Concerts and comedy weekends; Victorian Marionette Opera; wine tastings mid-

week in summer; painting, craft, personal growth workshops. 2 blocks to ocean. Outside bathhouse. Beach tags available on a first-come, first-serve basis.

Location 2 blocks from ocean and town center. From Lafayette, turn left on Madison, right on Columbia (at water tower), left on Howard.

Restrictions Smoking in public rooms only.

Credit cards MC, Visa.

Rates MAP, $77–135 double, $59–65 single, plus $5 per person per night service. Extra person in room, $27. Reduced rates for children. Set price full breakfast $6.50, dinner $16.95. 25% discount midweek June 10–July 12, Sept. 3–13, excluding holidays. Weekly, monthly, group discounts. 2–night weekend minimum.

Extras Limited wheelchair access. Bus/airport pickups. Cribs, babysitting, play equipment available. French, German spoken.

Colvmns by the Sea

Tel: 609–884–2228

1513 Beach Drive, 08204

Built in 1910, the Colvmns was one of the last "cottages" to go up in Cape May before the town's slide into twentieth-century obscurity. No architect was used in the construction, and the result is a brick mansion with fluted columns, colonial revival accents, and a touch of Italian palazzo. Barry and Catherine Rein, owners since 1983, have decorated the rooms with Victorian antiques, reproduction beds and baths, and Oriental highlights. Guests are invited to use the kitchen to store snacks and drinks, and to get ice. One breakfast might include grapefruit juice, baked apple, asparagus strata, and date-nut bread, while the next morning might bring orange mimosas, honeyed bananas, blintz soufflé, and sour cream coffee cake. Afternoon tea might be accompanied by finger sandwiches and homemade pizza, and evening sherry and port is offered with cookies or cheesecake.

"Our hosts were warm, informative, and helpful. Service was excellent and went beyond the usual hospitality we have found at other B&Bs. Breakfast was sumptuous and gourmet in quality. Tea included wonderful snacks, and, when we returned from dinner, our hosts had sherry and port ready, which we enjoyed along with their lively conversation." *(Marshall & Doris Rosenberg)* "The lighting was soft in keeping with the Victorian era, yet ample for reading. Plumbing was great—it appeared to be period but worked like new. The large porch and rocking chairs were an added plus. Best of all was the beauty and charm of this authentically reconstructed Victorian home." *(Betty P. Benson)*

Open April 26 to Dec. 31.

Rooms 2 suites, 9 doubles—all with private shower and/or bath, ceiling fan. 6 with desk.

Facilities Dining room, formal parlor, TV/VCR room with nickelodeon, upstairs parlors, reading foyer, wraparound veranda. Directly across from ocean; beach passes, bicycles, beach towels. On-site parking.

Location 1 m from center.

Restrictions No smoking. No children under 13.

Credit cards MC, Visa.

Rates B&B, $115–145 suite, $88–125 double, $70–115 single. Extra person in room, $30. 3-night weekend, holiday minimum. 10% discount for weekly stay; also for Penn State grads.

Extras Bus station pickups. German spoken.

The Duke of Windsor Inn   *Tel:* 609–884–1355
817 Washington Street, 08204

If you've always wanted to stay in the tower room of a Queen Anne Victorian mansion, Bruce and Fran Prichard and Barbara Hughes, owners of the Duke of Windsor Inn, will be delighted to show you to the guest rooms in their 45-foot-high tower. Other highlights of their nearly century-old inn include hand-crafted woodwork, tiled fireplaces, Tiffany stained glass, and elaborate plaster ceiling medallions. Rates include a breakfast of fresh fruit and juice, cereal, home-baked goodies, and in cool weather, a hot entrée.

"The parlor and dining rooms are decorated in authentic Victorian fashion, with dozens of interesting collectibles. Soothing music plays from an antique victrola; iced tea and cookies await in the dining room or on the wide porch, with rocking chairs and books galore. Our lovely bedroom was done in pink and rose, with ocean breezes wafting through the lace curtains of five sunny windows." *(Lisa Chipolone)*

Open Feb. 15 to Jan. 2.
Rooms 9 doubles—7 with private bath and/or shower, 2 with maximum of 4 people sharing bath. All with desk, fan.
Facilities Parlor with fireplace, library, dining room, game room, foyer with fireplace, porch. 4 blocks to beach. Off-street parking.
Location Historic district. Take Garden State Parkway to end; take first left; first right is Washington St.
Restrictions Smoking permitted in parlor only.
Credit cards None accepted.
Rates B&B, $55–98 double. Extra person in room, $15. 3 night weekend/holiday minimum. 10% weekly discount.

The Mainstay   *Tel:* 609–884–8690
635 Columbia Avenue, 08204

There are wonderful inns in Cape May, and then there is The Mainstay, which really is in a class by itself. It's one of those "velvet rope" inns—the kind with furnishings you'd normally only see, and not touch, in a museum. Although the environment is a bit intimidating at first, the owners' goal is to offer a relaxing, fun vacation experience. Innkeepers Tom and Sue Carroll were pioneers in Cape May's redevelopment, having opened The Mainstay in 1971.

The Mainstay was built in 1872 as a private club for wealthy gentlemen gamblers. They spared no expense; the villa was complete with 14-foot ceilings, ornate plaster moldings, and lavish furnishings, many of which are still in place today. Some, such as the 14-foot-high hall mirror, would be virtually impossible to move.

Advance reservations are imperative at The Mainstay, at least several months ahead for summer weekends. Rates include a full breakfast in spring and fall (continental in summer), and afternoon refreshments. If you're staying elsewhere in Cape May, stop at The Mainstay at 4 P.M. on Tuesdays, Thursdays, Saturdays, or Sundays for a tour of the downstairs rooms, and afternoon tea.

"Sue and Tom Carroll are superb innkeepers. Their knowledge of and commitment to Victoriana is infectious and they welcome guests as friends, but balance that with a perfectly run hostelry. On each visit we have chosen a different room and enjoyed its individual decor; it would be hard to name our favorite. The elegance of The Mainstay is matched by the charm of The Cottage, next door. They are connected by a lovely garden, and guests may use the common areas of both houses. The large rooms are authentically decorated, beautifully furnished with choice Victorian pieces yet totally comfortable for relaxing." *(Dr. & Mrs. Robert Dunn)*

"The Mainstay exudes relaxation, yet has been painstakingly restored to its original elegance; the lawns and gardens are immaculately kept. The service, cleanliness, lighting, etc., are the nicest we have encountered in all our travels. Breakfast on the veranda is the key event of the day. During the hour or so of serious munching, Tom and Sue make sure that no inquiries relative to what's going on around town, or who is serving the best softshell crabs, go unanswered. Everyone compares notes on last night's dining or carousing and plans their day accordingly—browning at the beach, napping on the oversize veranda swings, or sauntering downtown for a book." *(John & Linda Kelleher)*

"Staying at the Mainstay is like living in a museum. The historic restoration is elaborate, and includes fine antique pieces not only in the common rooms but in many of the guest rooms. It's worth staying here just to explore the collection. Probably for insurance purposes, some of the smaller pieces are kept behind locked glass doors, and the common rooms are closed at 11 P.M.. But the inn runs on its own schedule, and I was a little disappointed that they could not accommodate my need for breakfast (or even a cup of coffee) before 8 A.M.." *(AF)*

Open Mid-March to mid-Dec.
Rooms 3 suites, 9 doubles, all with private shower and/or bath. 10 with desk, all with fans. 6 rooms in Cottage.
Facilities Dining room, library, music room, parlor, veranda. Flower garden with fountain, croquet, swings. Beach passes; 2 blocks to ocean.
Location Historic district, 3 blocks to center, 2 blocks to beach. Turn left at first light after Canal Bridge, then right 3 blocks later onto Columbia.
Restrictions No smoking. No children under 12. On-street parking tight in summer. Occasional street noise in summer.
Credit cards None accepted.
Rates B&B, $95–140 suite, $80–125 double, $70–115 single. Extra person in room, $20. 3-night minimum stay, June–Sept.

Manor House   *Tel:* 609–884–4710
612 Hughes Street, 08204

The Manor House was built in 1906 in a classic colonial revival/American shingle style, a less ornate structure than early Victorian buildings. Owned by Mary and Tom Snyder since 1984, it features rooms furnished with late Victorian pieces and decorated with period reproduction wallpapers and burnished oak trim. Mary's breakfasts here are a highlight, with freshly baked breakfast buns and entrées such as apple-cheese pancakes or asparageggs—poached eggs and sauce Mornay over asparagus and homemade English muffin bread. Tom accompanies the meal with a mirthful morning monologue, "an attempt to make up for his inability to contribute much else to the enterprise," according to Mary.

"The instant you arrive Tom is there to help with your luggage and provide you with a tour of this handsomely decorated home. Rooms are decorated with brass and canopy beds, wonderful antiques, and lace curtains. The bed linens are beautiful, while thick, luxurious towels and lovely soaps and shampoos awaited in the bath. A warm robe and piping hot coffee and tea, to be sipped either in the privacy of your room or down by the fireside, awaited early risers." *(Claire Sparano)*

"Tom and Mary strike the perfect balance between attentive service and blissful privacy. The house itself is charming and unpretentious, with enough fun touches (like the old-fashioned barber chair) to invite exploration. The fireplace room always has several East Coast newspapers that are a perfect complement to the cozy fire that blazes during the colder months." *(Amy & Rich Alpers)*

"Tom and Mary are friendly, charming, and very gracious hosts. The rooms are beautifully furnished, and the quilts are wonderful. An almost invisible staff keeps it spotlessly clean. Nightly cookies on our pillow are an anticipated treat. Breakfast is worth the trip: mashed potato sticky buns, savory omelets, and exquisite French toast. Tom and Mary serve tea in the parlor from 4 to 5 P.M.; conversation is lively and Mary's baked Brie and special teas are a treat. They provide beach tags, towels, and chairs, and good dining information. The house is centrally located; you can park your car and forget it the entire stay." *(Susan Bevilacqua)*

Open All year except January.
Rooms 2 suites, 7 doubles—6 with private bath and/or shower, 3 with maximum of 6 people sharing bath. 2 rooms with air-conditioning, all with fans.
Facilities Foyer, parlor/living room, fireplace room, dining room, porch, herb patio. Small garden with lawn furniture. Outside showers, beach tags, bicycles. Off-street parking several blocks away.
Location Historic district, 1½ blocks from beach, 1 block to shops. Go 8 blocks down Lafayette St. to Franklin St. Turn left and go 2 blocks to Hughes St.
Restrictions No smoking. No children under 12.
Credit cards MC, Visa.
Rates B&B, $105–145 suite, $65–130 double, $50–130 single. Weekly rates. 2–3 night minimum stay on weekends and holidays. 10% weekly discount.
Extras Station pickups.

The Queen Victoria
102 Ocean Street, 08204

Tel: 609–884–8702

The Queen Victoria is a complex of three neighboring Victorian homes from the 1880s, restored a century later as a B&B inn by Dane and Joan Wells. They have decorated the rooms with authentic Victorian furnishings, attractive wallpapers and quilts, and antique iron, brass, and four-poster beds. The Wellses take their innkeeping seriously; they are very involved in the operation of their inn and most knowledgeable about the town's activities. Dane and Joan always have a new project underway to upgrade the inn. Recently, they redid all the plumbing, bringing it up to modern standards, and many baths now have whirl-pool tubs. To provide guests with their choice of relaxation, the inn has two parlors, one for quiet sitting in front of the fireplace, the other with TV, games, and puzzles. Guests comment consistently on their excep-tionally high housekeeping standards, the attentive service, the deli-cious food, the handsome decor, and the friendly atmosphere.

"Dane and Joan Wells really understand what hospitality is about, and have created an inn that is truly a home away from home. The small things stand out—always a bowl of fruit and a supply of club soda, well stocked bookshelves (including an extensive collection of Victoriana), and a book where guests can record their experiences at local restau-rants. When I was up early, coffee just seemed to appear. Guests are welcome to use the inn's facilities (including a shower) throughout the day they check out. Everything is spotlessly clean and well main-tained." (Arthur Fink)

"We were very graciously received by Joan Wells, and were given all kinds of necessary information right away. After settling in, we enjoyed a cup of hot tea accompanied by a variety of homemade cookies and crackers with deviled ham spread. Our room was decorated with nu-merous antiques and a handmade quilt for the bed." (Nancy W. Gulino)
"Joan and Dane are pleasant and informative conversationalists and excellent sources of knowledge and lore about both the area in particu-lar and Victoriana in general. Breakfast is an exceptionally pleasant time, with the guests and innkeepers gathered around the dining room table exchanging views and eating . . . and eating. Breakfast includes one egg dish, one fruit dish, several breads, homemade granola, juices, and plenty of coffee and tea. Tea, with little sandwiches, is served in the afternoon. The inn is within walking distance of most of Cape May's attractions; you can park your car and not use it for your entire stay." (Sharon & Michael Henry)

"We had the carriage house, which was perfect for us with a young daughter in tow. The downstairs had a large living room with TV, refrigerator, and full Jacuzzi bath. Upstairs was a large bedroom with an alcove area for a cot." (Marie Marhan Dropkin) "The rooms are won-derfully decorated, with scented bayberry soaps and chocolates on your pillow in the evening." (Barbara & Mark Titus)

"Among the little but influential niceties that we have particularly enjoyed is the fact that we always returned to a freshened room, regard-less of what time of day or evening we left it." (Laura & Thomas McMillan)
"Especially appealing were the free bicycles, beach tags, and equip-ment." (Sandra S. Grant)

"Your write-up on the Queen Vic in last year's edition was most accurate. We stayed in the Cottage, just right for two couples, with ample privacy and a nice layout." (Nina & Ernest Spinelli)

Open All year.
Rooms 7 suites, 17 doubles—20 with private bath and/or shower. 4 rooms have sink in room with maximum of 4 sharing bath; some rooms have desk, refrigera-tor, air-conditioning, fan. Suites in adjacent carriage house & cottage with tele-phone, TV, air-conditioning, kitchenette.
Facilities Dining rooms, "quiet" parlor with fireplace, parlor with TV, library,

games. Victorian flower garden, beach passes, chairs, towels; beach shower with changing room, bicycles. On-site parking for handicapped only; free parking 5 blocks away.
Location Historic district, 1 block to beach, 2 blocks to shops. Turn left at second stoplight off of Lafayette St. onto Ocean St. The inn is 3 blocks down on the right.
Restrictions No smoking. Children in suites only. "Toddlers usually aren't happy here."
Credit cards MC, Visa.
Rates B&B, $110–190 suite, $65–130 double, $55–85 single. Extra person in room, $10. Winter packages. 2- to 4-night weekend minimum.
Extras 1 suite fully equipped for disabled. 1 block to bus. Cribs, babysitting, beach toys available. French, some Spanish spoken.

The Seventh Sister
10 Jackson Street, 08204

Tel: 609–884–2280

The Seventh Sister, built in 1888, features a three-story central circular staircase. Rooms are furnished with a mixture of antiques—many of them wicker and original to the house—and contemporary pieces; nearly all have an ocean view. Longtime owners Bob and Jo-Anne Myers describe themselves as "artists with a sense of humor and a very informal way about us."

"The Seventh Sister has been our favorite inn for a long time. Through the years we have seen many B&Bs open up, but we are just as happy with one B only, enjoying our breakfast elsewhere in one of Cape May's great eating places. This inn is literally a pebble's throw from the beach; you can see your sand castle wash away with high tide from your bedroom window. The decor is Victorian summer house—white wicker, pastel colors, and Jo-Anne's ever-changing artwork and wonderful art projects. I find this more refreshing than some of the 'authentic' dark Victorian style we see elsewhere in Cape May. Everything is spic-and-span. The sheets are pretty flowered ones, and the towels are like the ones you have at home. Nothing is nicer than sitting on the front porch swing, soothing your sunburn, with a wine cooler from the guest refrigerator. Parking is tight all over Cape May; a lot at a nominal fee is not far away, but we usually manage to find a free spot on the street somewhere." *(Michelle Braverman)*

"Our room, #2, had floral bedding and window treatments, and overlooked the beach. Sometimes in the early morning you can spot schools of dolphins swimming by. Jo-Anne's artistic touches range from her colorful paintings to the Victorian music softly coming from the kitchen. You can always find fresh fruit on the coffee table, delicate flowers in unusual vases, and Jo-Anne and Bob somewhere nearby to chat with. The house plumbing is not modern, but the claw foot tub adds a bit of adventure; I prefer the downstairs shower, something each guest should experience. Guests enjoy sitting on the porch in the evening, planning the next day's activities and meals." *(Olga Forte)*

Open All year.
Rooms 6 doubles—all with desk, fan, and shared bath, with maximum of 4 people sharing bath.
Facilities Living room, porch, large yard with flower garden, croquet. Remote parking provided.

NEW JERSEY

Location Historic district, 100 feet from ocean.
Restrictions Well-behaved children over age 7.
Credit cards None accepted.
Rates Room only, $40–75 double, $40–65 single. Extra person in room, $10. 3-night minimum stay on weekends, June–Sept., holidays.
Extras Spanish, French, German spoken.

White Dove Cottage
619 Hughes Street, 08204

Tel: 609–884–0613

The White Dove was built in 1866 in the Second Empire style, with a mansard roof faced with original hand cut octagonal slate tiles, and has been a guest house for over forty years. Joyce and Spurgeon Smith re-opened the White Dove in 1988, after a year-long restoration job. Spurgeon notes that "breakfast at the White Dove is a sumptuous affair. Guests dine together over an antique banquet table set with lace, fine china, and heirloom crystal. Breakfast is different every day, and consists of fruit, juice, perhaps quiche or baked French toast, meats, vegetables, eggs, herbs from our English garden, home-baked breads, assorted desserts, coffee, and tea. To set the mood breakfast is accompanied by soft piano music in the background. Breakfast varies with the season—lighter in summer, long and leisurely in the quiet months."

"The ocean breeze gently moving the white lace curtains at our windows, the player piano in the parlor announcing a delicious breakfast in half an hour, relaxing on the porch on the white wicker chairs and rockers, chatting with new friends while watching the horse-drawn carriages go by, are all part of the White Dove's charms." *(Charlie and Kay Vandlik)* "This inn is cheerful, light, and airy, rather than heavy and dark, as are so many Victorian homes. Our suite was quiet, comfortable, and cozy, decorated with appropriate and useful antiques and beautiful linens. The former butler's pantry made a very attractive bathroom. Hughes Street is quiet and is one of the oldest and most charming streets in Cape May." *(Ronald B. Miller)*

"Each room has a private bath, with towels and washcloths changed daily. The water pressure was fine, even on the third floor, and there was plenty of hot water. Our room was well lighted, as were the hallways. Cleanliness is obviously a byword with the Smiths—and that applies to every part of the house and property, including the well-kept gardens at the front and side of the house. To ensure privacy, we were given a key both to our room and to the inner front door for use at night, and the combination to the screen door lock as well. It was a pleasure to park our car on arrival, and then not to use it, since everything that we needed was close by—restaurants, the boardwalk and ocean, and the mall.

"Spurgeon Smith is an excellent woodcarving craftsman, and many of his works are exhibited throughout the house. Joyce displays her collection of antique dolls, dressed in period attire, along with the many quilts she has collected." *(Rosemary & John Robinson)* "We were cordially greeted by Mr. Smith and shown to our room. He told us about afternoon tea at 5 P.M., sherry at 7 P.M., and breakfast at 9 A.M.. After settling in, it was delightful to sit on the veranda—furnished with wicker and shaded by old sycamore trees—listening to the horse-drawn carriage going by." *(Joyce DeVivo)*

Open All year.
Rooms 2 suites, 3 doubles—1 with full private bath, 4 with private shower. All with desk; some with TV, air-conditioning.
Facilities Dining room, parlor with piano, books; veranda. Beach passes, outside shower. English garden. Free off-street parking. Bike rental nearby.
Location Center of historic district, 2 blocks from beach. From Lafayette St. turn left on Franklin, right on Hughes.
Restrictions No smoking. No children under 8.
Credit cards None accepted.
Rates B&B, $110–180 suite (sleeps up to 4), $75–125 double. 3-night weekend minimum June–Sept. Tipping encouraged. 10% weekly discount.
Extras Airport/station pickups.

The Wooden Rabbit
609 Hughes Street, 08204

Tel: 609–884–7293

Although a few other Cape May inns tolerate children, The Wooden Rabbit is the only B&B in Cape May (to our knowledge) that actually welcomes children of all ages. Owners Greg and Debby Burow explain: "We have a comfortable (unbreakable) country decor that is practical for children but is still very special for adults. We have two young sons of our own who enjoy being playmates, but we try to keep them out of the way of adult guests." In a high Victorian town, The Wooden Rabbit is also unusual in that it was built by a sea captain in 1838; Robert E. Lee spent summers here, and the house was also used by the Underground Railroad.

"The Wooden Rabbit is a cozy inn, decorated in countrylike cheeriness with Peter Rabbit collectibles throughout. Just 1½ blocks from the beach and close to the shopping mall and antique stores, this inn is very convenient to all attractions—park your car on arrival, and your feet can do the rest. Our room was spacious and spotless, decorated in small country prints with coordinating borders. Lovely handmade accents—quilts, pillows, and wall hangings—highlight the decor; the furnishings are mainly wicker, except for the beds and bureaus. Our suite had a sitting room, which accommodated our children nicely.

"A buffet-style breakfast is served from 8:00 to 9:30 A.M. and consisted of homemade blueberry muffins, quiche (a different variety daily), fresh fruit salad or apple crisp, orange juice, and a delicious granola cereal blend. Coffee and an assortment of herbal teas topped off the meal. While the children recall the piece of fudge left on their pillows in the evening, I remember fondly the clip-clop of the horses going past the inn and the aroma of fresh-baked breakfast goodies emerging from the kitchen." *(Beverly Lang)*

"The room decor, bathrooms, and common areas are superb, with Greg and Debby filling you in on local history and best restaurants during the 4 P.M. tea-and-treats gathering on the sun porch. Greg is the house baker, and I couldn't decide if his sticky buns, cookies, or nut breads were the best." *(Stephanie Lesiga and others)* "The living room has a variety of reading materials, including children's books and a child-size rocker." *(Arlette & Gary Braman)* "Although the inn is quite large, it only has three guest rooms, making it very quiet and friendly." *(William Straus)*

Open All year.
Rooms 1 suite, 2 doubles, all with private bath and/or shower, TV, air-conditioning, fan.
Facilities Dining room with fireplace, living room with fireplace, enclosed sun porch. Flower garden with sandbox, outside shower. Beach passes, off-street parking.
Location In historic district, 2 blocks from beach. From Lafayette St., turn left on Franklin St., then right onto Hughes St.
Restrictions No smoking.
Credit cards MC, Visa (for deposits only).
Rates B&B, $80–135 suite, $65–115 double. Extra person in room, $15. Thanksgiving, Christmas packages available. Minimum stay requirements.

FLEMINGTON

Peaceful rural relaxation is well and good in its place, but there are days when nothing gets the adrenalin going like a serious round of bargain hunting. Flemington, with over 150 outlet shops in two colonial-style shopping centers, fits the bill perfectly. When you're all shopped out, you'll awake to notice that you're in a National Historic District town with a self-guided tour of its varied Victorian and Greek Revival architecture. You can view the peaceful farms on a historic steam train ride, or visit in mid-September for the New Jersey State Agricultural Fair. Flemington was famous in the early 1900s for its cut glass, and you can stop by the Flemington Glass Company, one of the companies still in operation, for a free demonstration.

Flemington is located in west central New Jersey, about 60 miles southwest of New York City, and the same distance northeast of Philadelphia. About 15 minutes to the west is the Delaware River, Bucks County, and the town of New Hope.

The Cabbage Rose Inn   *Tel:* 201–788–0247
162 Main Street, 08822

Named for its prevailing decorative motif, the Cabbage Rose Inn was bought by Pam Venosa and Al Scott in 1988. Gallons of paint, uncounted rolls of wallpaper and fabric, and unending quantities of elbow grease were needed restore a shine to this restaurant's oak floors and carved staircase, and to bring the charming Victorian spirit of its rooms back to life. From the stained glass window that illuminates the foyer, to the antique-filled parlor, to the sun room furnished with white wicker, Pam and Al take pride in the old-fashioned charm of their inn. The inn's exterior combines a dozen angles, and includes porches and gables with gingerbread trim. Most unusual is the third-floor turret: although these usually were enclosed, this one is open and heavily ornamented with trim, much in the style of a roof-top gazebo.

Rates include a breakfast of fruit salad with granola and yogurt, cold cereal or hot oatmeal, and home baked breads and muffins; afternoon tea or lemonade; and bedtime sherry and chocolates. *(MW)*

"The inn is filled with delightful Victorian touches. The spacious yellow and blue room contrasts with the cozy charm of the pink room with its private claw-foot bathtub. We looked forward to breakfast each morning as Al and Pam's genial manner encouraged animated and diverse conversation over delicious sweet breads and coffee." *(Jean Elemendorf)* More comments please.

Open All year.
Rooms 5 doubles—3 with private tub and/or shower, 2 with maximum of 4 people sharing bath. All with desk, air-conditioning, fan.
Facilities Dining room with piano, parlor, sun-room, porch. Near river for canoeing, rafting, and tubing.
Location In center of town.
Restrictions No smoking. No children under 10.
Credit cards Amex, MC, Visa. "Checks preferred."
Rates B&B, $65–85 double, $60–80 single. Extra person in room, $15. 2-night weekend minimum from May to Nov.

Jerica Hill   *Tel:* 201–782–8234
96 Broad Street, 08822

After a hard day of shopping, you may feel the need to get a new perspective on things, and how better to do so than from the basket of a hot-air balloon? Innkeeper Judith Studer, owner of Jerica Hill since 1985, will happily make all the arrangements for your flight; all you have to do is hope for good weather. Of course, you don't have to leave terra firma to enjoy the relaxing atmosphere of this B&B. A turn-of-the-century Victorian home painted gray with dark red trim, the interior features a beautiful center hall staircase; surprisingly, the antique decor is colonial in its simplicity, not Victorian. Rates include a breakfast of fresh fruit, yogurt, cereal, homemade pastry and breads, with fresh fruit and flowers provided in the guest rooms.

"Judith grew up in Flemington, and really knows her way around the area's shops, restaurants, historic sites, and attractions, from the local vineyards to canoeing on the Delaware. Our spacious room at the front of the house had lovely bay windows with adjustable shutters, a four-poster bed with lace canopy, handwoven coverlet, and blanket; an old-fashioned wooden rocker, and an antique upholstered chair. In the morning, we had breakfast on the plant-filled screened porch, cool and inviting with white wicker furniture and a flagstone floor." *(MW)* More comments please.

Open All year.
Rooms 5 doubles—2 with private shower and/or bath, 3 rooms with a maximum of 6 people sharing a bath. All rooms with radio, air-conditioning, fan.
Facilities Living room with fireplace, library, TV; screened porch. Off-street parking. Close to tennis, golf. River nearby for tubing, rafting, bicycling.
Location 2 blocks E of Main St.
Restrictions No smoking. No children under 12.
Credit cards Amex, MC, Visa.
Rates B&B, $55–85 double, $50–80 single. Extra person in room, $15. Corporate rates. 2-night weekend minimum.
Extras Station pickups.

FRENCHTOWN

For more information on area attractions, please see the Bucks County section of the Pennsylvania chapter introduction.

The Old Hunterdon House
Tel: 201–996–3632
12 Bridge Street, 08825

The Old Hunterdon House is a three-story Italianate brick Victorian, built in 1865 and restored as a bed & breakfast inn 120 years later. Since it opened in 1986, we've received enthusiastic reports about the inn and particularly previous innkeeper/owner, Rick Carson. In 1990, the inn was sold to Tony and Gloria Cappiello, who recently undertook a major change in lifestyle by becoming innkeepers. Tony's background is in advertising, design, and photography (Gloria says he's a great cook too), while Gloria worked as a talent agent in Hollywood, and as a banquet manager at New York's famous Russian Tea Room.

"I found the Hunterdon to be charming, clean, and faithfully deco-rated in period. Tony and Gloria make a visit here feel special. They are enthusiastic in their hospitality, combining the feel of both home and hotel to make their guests feel most welcome. A delightful breakfast was accompanied by great conversation. I had to tear myself away at the last minute to make my business contact on schedule." *(Thomas Dewey, also Laura Farrington)*

"Frenchtown is a quaint small town with a few excellent restaurants of its own, and many more in the area. The surrounding countryside and towns of Lambertville and New Hope are wonderful for weekend strolling and browsing." *(Louise & John Clark)*

Open All year.
Rooms 1 suite, 6 doubles—1 with full private bath, 6 with shower only. All with air-conditioning.
Facilities Dining room, study/library with fireplaces, porch, garden with patio. Near Delaware River for tubing, canoeing, fishing, swimming. Cross-country skiing nearby; 25 min to downhill skiing.
Location W central NJ, Hunterdon Cty. 70 min. W of NYC, N of Philadelphia. Approx. 15 m N of New Hope, PA. Near intersection of rtes. 12 & 29.
Restrictions No children under 15.
Credit cards MC, Visa.
Rates B&B, $80–100 double. Mid-week singles rates. 2- to 3-night weekend/holiday minimum.
Extras NYC bus stops next door.

HADDONFIELD

The Queen Anne Inn
Tel: 609–428–2195
44 West End Avenue, 08033

Bordering Camden, the historic town of Haddonfield was founded in 1713 by Elizabeth Haddon—an unusual woman in an era when women

had few if any rights to own property in their own names. The Queen
Anne was built as a private home in 1870, and served many uses over
the years: a maternity hospital in the 1930s, a guest house in the 1940s,
and a rundown boarding house by the 1980s. In 1984, Haddonfield
native Mark Lenny bought the house for conversion into a B&B; it's
been a long haul, but the inn seems on the right path now, under the
day-to-day management of innkeeper Jenny DeVos. Authentic clap-
board and fishscale shingles for the third-floor turret have replaced
asphalt shingles; the house is painted in shades of buff, soft yellow, and
red; and the wraparound veranda is once again filled with white wicker
furnishings and lots of plants.

Inside, the decor is light, airy, and eclectic. The living room and the
foyer is colonial in mood, with stenciled walls and decor that evokes
the early 18th century; others, particularly the bedrooms, have flowered
wallpapers and elaborately carved Victorian beds and bureaus. Many
have two upholstered chairs so that guests can relax in their rooms.
Rates include a breakfast of fruit, juice, bagels, breads, pastries, and
muffins; terry robes are supplied for the trip to the bath.

"This lovely inn is clean, warm, and cozy. Lots of variety is offered
for breakfast, and everything was good and fresh. Jenny helped me to
find places, and really went out of her way to make my stay as comfortable as possible." *(Patricia Perez)*

Open All year.
Rooms 11 doubles—all with shared bath, radio, fan, in-room sink. 3 first floor
rooms share 2 baths; 7 second floor rooms share 2 baths. 3 with desk.
Facilities Breakfast room, living room with TV, books.
Location 20 min E of Philadelphia. 2 blocks from center off Kings Hwy-Rt. 41.
2 blocks from PATCO train to Philadelphia.
Restrictions No smoking. No children under 5.
Credit cards Amex, MC, Visa.
Rates B&B, $55–80 double. Extra person in room $10. 10% AARP discount.

HOPE

Inn at Millrace Pond   *Tel:* 201–459–4884
Route 519, P.O. Box 359, 07844

For the mood of Bucks County without the crowds, head out Interstate
80 to the historic hamlet of Hope, founded in 1769 by Moravian settlers, and listed on the National Register of Historic Places. During the
Revolutionary War, grain from the mill in Hope was hauled over Jenny
Jump Mountain to Washington's troops in Morristown. In 1985, local
developers Dick Gooding and Gloria Carrigan decided that the long-
vacant complex of cut limestone buildings would be perfect for a country inn. The arduous two-year restoration combined authentic period
detail with such modern comforts as queen-size beds and Jacuzzi tubs.
Williamsburg colors of blue, soft reds, grayish green, and cream were
used to accent the antiques, Oriental rugs, and colonial reproduction
furnishings—wing chairs, Queen Anne tables and bureaus, and four-

99

poster beds. Some rooms are done in a mix of formal and "country" colonial styles.

Most of the guest rooms are found in the restored miller's and wheelwright's houses, while the original mill building is home to the restaurant, tavern, and additional guest rooms. A recent dinner included such treats as corn and mussel chowder, with diced tomato and dill; roast duck with glazed apples and peppercorn sauce, with fresh vegetables, salad, and sorbet; and such desserts as Linzer torte with raspberry jam, or strawberry cheesecake.

"We were welcomed by Dick Gooding, and given a packet that included a walking tour of the area, and information on local wineries and places of interest. Our room (#8) in the Millwright House had wide pine floors (a bit splintery), a canopy bed with open work crochet top, light-colored walls and woodwork in a lovely colonial teal blue, and a comfortable chair. The bathroom was large with a whirlpool tub. There's also a living room on the first floor; rather formal but with a fireplace, TV, and books. We had a light dinner of a variety of appetizers, including perfectly seasoned wild mushroom bisque, pâté with stone ground mustard, marinated shrimp, homemade bread, and a green salad with freshly-crushed raspberry vinaigrette. Both service and food were excellent. The breakfast of juice, fruit, croissant and sticky bun was adequate, although they were extremely nice about supplying extra cheese by special request.

"Most interesting of all is the way these buildings have been restored. You can walk along the original millrace, and see where the water was diverted to run the millwheel. You can also see the millwheel from inside the restaurant. It's rare to see a group of industrially related buildings on their original site, and in this Moravian style, and the owners are to be complimented on their efforts. The town itself is two blocks away, and is very pleasant, truly historic, yet totally non-commercial and non-touristy." (SC)

"The staff was down-to-earth, personable and friendly; the owners were formal, yet smiling and helpful. The inn is exceptionally clean; even the cracks and corners of the beautiful wooden floors were clean. Despite its location near the road, the inn is quiet and peaceful; lighting is good in the bedrooms and throughout the inn." (Cindy & Frances McEachern)

Open All year. Restaurant closed Christmas Day.
Rooms 1 suite, 16 doubles, all with full private bath, desk, air-conditioning. 5 with whirlpool tubs; 9 with telephone, radio. Rooms in 3 separate buildings.
Facilities Dining room with weekend music, tavern, parlor with fireplaces. 23 acres with picnic areas, paths, brook. 10 m to Delaware River for canoeing, rafting, swimming, fishing. Tennis, golf, downhill and cross-country skiing nearby.
Location NW NJ, Skylands Region, Warren Cty. 50 m W of NYC, 70 m N of Philadelphia. In center of town. From Rte. 80, take Exit 12 to Rte. 521 S. Go 1 m to blinker light in town, then left on Rte. 519 1 block to inn.
Credit cards Amex, MC, Visa.
Rates B&B, $90–100 suite, $75–95 double, $65–90 single. Extra person in room, $10. 2-night holiday weekend minimum. Alc dinner, $37.
Extras Restaurant wheelchair accessible.

LAMBERTVILLE

Just across the river from New Hope, Lambertville was settled in 1705, and grew into an industrial center with the development of the Delaware & Raritan Canal. After years of neglect, its many fine homes are being restored, and its factories reused as artists' studios, shops, and restaurants.

Information please: Those who prefer larger establishments may wish to try the **Inn at Lambertville Station**, a country hotel and restaurant (11 Bridge Street 08530; 609–397–4400). The well-known **Colligan's Stockton Inn**, on the Delaware River, has undergone a variety of management changes in recent years, and we'd like to hear more from recent guests on both the food and lodging experience before reinstating them for a full entry (Route 29, Stockton 08559; 609–397–1250).

Another possibility is **The Bridgestreet House** (67 Bridge Street, 08530; 609–397–2503), a 19th century Federal-style house with rooms eclectically decorated with antiques. Guests have the use of a sitting room with fireplace, and a hot tub in the back yard garden. The menu offers an intriguing choice of creative entrées.

Chimney Hill Farm   *Tel:* 609–397–1516
Goat Hill Road, RD 3, Box 150, 08530

A quiet river town just across the Delaware from New Hope, Lambertville has much of the same bucolic scenery, with a fraction of Bucks County's summer hustle and bustle. Chimney Hill Farm began as a small farmhouse in 1820, but was greatly expanded in 1927, giving it the imposing presence of a stone manor house. In 1988 it was bought by Frederick Root and Kenneth Turi, and owes much of its distinctive furnishings—highlighted by chintz florals and antiques—to the fact that it was decorated as a designer showcase prior to opening as a B&B. The decor combines 18th century American Queen Anne and Chippendale reproductions with antique furnishings, rich flowered fabrics, and plenty of comfortable seating. Guest rooms are lavish, many with canopied beds and love seats. Rates include a breakfast of freshly squeezed orange juice, homemade muffins, and jam made from the farm's own raspberries, as well as extras like fresh flowers, all-cotton sheets, robes, and a continual supply of coffee, tea, soda, snacks, and ice. "Beautiful place; the innkeepers are delightful and attentive yet not overbearing." *(Rochelle Mason)*

Open All year.
Rooms 7 doubles, all with private bath and/or shower, air-conditioning, fan. 2 with fireplaces, 1 with porch.
Facilities Dining room with fireplace, sun room with fireplace, guest pantry. 10 acres with gardens, terraces, greenhouse.
Location 1½ hours W of NYC, 45 min. N of Philadelphia. ½ m to town. From town, go S on River Rd. to Swan St. Turn left on Swan St. to Studdiford–Goat Hill Rd., inn on left.
Restrictions No smoking. No children under 12.

Credit cards MC, Visa.
Rates B&B, $105–150 double. 2-3 night weekend/holiday minimum. Corporate, long-term rates.

York Street House
Tel: 609–397–3007

42 York Street, 08530

Built in 1909 by a local coal baron as an anniversary present for his wife, the York Street House was featured in *House and Garden Magazine* in 1911. Today, the red-brick serves as a B&B, offering quiet lodging to travelers who prefer the more relaxed atmosphere of Lambertville over the bustle of nearby New Hope, Pennsylvania.

"Gardens and trees surround the outside of York Street House, while the inside is filled with eclectic antique furnishings. Found throughout the house are English chintzes, chandeliers, original oil paintings, cherry wood panelling, china, linen, and flowers. The bedrooms are neat and clean with four-poster beds, ceiling fans, and comfortable chairs for reading. The manager, Peg Pierce, is a wonderful hostess, who serves a full English breakfast each morning. She gladly offers restaurant recommendations and makes reservations once you have decided where to eat. The location is ideal for walking to antique shops, restaurants, and across the river into New Hope." *(Valerie Cauley, also Pegi Costantino)*

Open All year.
Rooms 6 doubles—2 with private shower and/or bath, 4 rooms sharing 2 baths. 3 with air-conditioning, 3 with ceiling fan. Some with desk.
Facilities Dining room with fireplace; library with fireplace; parlor with fireplace, TV; screened porch, gardens.
Location In town center. 2 blocks from river.
Restrictions "Smoking discouraged in bedrooms." No children under 12.
Credit cards None accepted.
Rates B&B, $65–85 double. Senior discounts. 2-night holiday minimum.
Extras On bus line from New York City. Some French, Spanish spoken.

LYNDHURST

The Jeremiah Yereance House
Tel: 201–438–9457

410 Riverside Avenue, 07071

This tiny house, listed on the National Register of Historic Landmarks, consists of a north wing, which was probably moved to this location around 1840, and a south wing, built in 1841. Rates also include a breakfast buffet of homemade breads and muffins, fresh fruit and juice, plus coffee or tea. Evelyn and Frank Pezzolla bought the house in 1984, and had to replace the roof, structural supports, plumbing, wiring, and heating before any restoration work could begin. Rooms are simply furnished with Victorian antiques. Guests enjoy the inn's location, just five minutes from the Meadowlands, ideal for sports fanatics with a sense of history!

"Mrs. Pezzolla pays attention to guests' needs and is responsive to suggestions for improvement. I've enjoyed staying in a fully restored historic landmark which is also clean, well-maintained, and reasonably priced." *(Mark L. Darrow)*

"The Pezzollas are among the most gracious hosts I've encountered in years of bed & breakfasting. They even called local restaurants for us to find one were we would feel comfortable with our small child. The inn's atmosphere is never intimidating; it's charming and livable." *(Lester Gabis-Levin)* More comments please.

Open All year.
Rooms 1 suite, 2 doubles, 1 single. 3 standard rooms share 1 bath. Suite with private bath, telephone, radio, TV, desk, air-conditioning, fireplace, separate entrance.
Facilities Breakfast room, sitting room with TV. Wisteria arbor with benches. Next to park with tennis courts, jogging, bike paths.
Location Central NJ, 5 min. from Meadowlands Sports Complex, 12 m W of NYC. 5 blocks from center. From NJ Turnpike, take Exit 16W to Rte. 3 W, follow to Riverside Ave. Exit, and go left off ramp. From Garden State, take Exit 153A to Rte. 3 E; exit at Riverside Ave. and go left.
Restrictions No smoking. No children under 13.
Credit cards Amex.
Rates B&B, $75 suite, $55 double, $50 single. Extra person in room, $15. Weekly, monthly rates.
Extras Airport/station pickups for fee.

MILFORD

Chestnut Hill on the Delaware
63 Church Street, P.O. Box N, 08848

Tel: 201–995–9761

Long-time owners Linda and Rob Castagna invite guests to share their romantically decorated Victorian home, built in 1860 and furnished with beautiful Victorian decor. One of its key attractions is the wrap-around veranda overlooking the Delaware River, where guests can relax on the antique rockers for hours, sipping a glass of iced tea. Next door, Rob has restored a Victorian cottage, painting its porch in eleven delicate colors and decorating it in period. The full breakfast varies daily, and might include fresh fruit salad, juice, German apple pancakes, and home baked muffins. It is served on the front veranda during fine weather, and inside on the candlelit table in the Victorian dining room during the cooler months. Each guest room has individual charm, with a name that reveals its color scheme: several have spindle spool beds, braided or Chinese rugs, or river views.

"Linda is one of the finest, most caring innkeepers we've ever met. Her concern for her guests' well being makes Chestnut Hill the kind of place that guests keeping coming back to—over and over again. All the rooms are lovely, but our favorite is the very private Teddy's Place, with over 75 bears in residence, many sent by past guests. Crisply ironed, white cotton, lacy, designer sheets and monogrammed toothbrushes are typical special touches." *(Linda & David Glickstein)*

Open All year.
Rooms 1 cottage, 2 suites, 3 doubles—3 with private bath, 2 with maximum of 4 sharing bath. Some with desk, fan, TV. Telephone on request.

Facilities Dining room, parlor with fireplace, drawing room with gift gallery, library, fireplace, piano, pump organ; wraparound veranda. Dock on river for swimming, tubing, canoeing. Hiking, cross-country skiing nearby.
Location W central NJ, Hunterdon Cty. 70 min. W of NYC, N of Philadelphia. Approx. 20 min. NW of Flemington, 30 min. N of New Hope, PA. From I-78, take Exit 11 to Rte. 614 S (toward Pattenburg). Go 7.9 m to Rte. 519. Go left, 2.3 m to Bridge St. & turn right. Follow Bridge Street to end, turn right to inn on right facing river.
Restrictions No smoking. No children under 12.
Credit cards None accepted.
Rates B&B, $120 cottage, $70–95 double. Extra person in room, $10.
Extras Station pickups.

MONTCLAIR

Marlboro Inn   *Tel:* 201–783–5300
334 Grove Street, 07042

Set in a residential neighborhood of suburban Montclair, the Marlboro Inn is an English Tudor-style structure, restored to a 1920s ambience with exposed beams and some antiques. Rates include continental breakfast.

"This inn has a real 1920s feeling—comfy, cozy, muted, and genteel. The public rooms are lovely, particularly the warm and relaxing living room. The bedrooms are large and comfortable, but some are decorated better than others. The two rooms I've seen certainly don't look like the suites in the brochure. Still, the fourth floor rooms have views of the city. The staff are all very accommodating and willing to do a bit extra to make your stay memorable. The food is satisfactory, sometimes even good." *(RD)* More comments please.

Open All year.
Rooms 8 suites, 30 doubles—all with private bath. Some with fan, desk.
Facilities Living room with fireplace, restaurant, sun porch, patio. 3 acres with lawns, shade trees.
Location 30 min. W of NYC. From Garden State Parkway take Exit 151 to 1st light. Turn right on Watchung Ave. Go 3 lights to Grove St. Inn on corner.
Restrictions Smoking in designated areas only.
Credit cards Amex, DC, MC, Visa.
Rates B&B, $130–150 suite, $105–120 double, $90–100 single. Extra person in room, $15–25.
Extras Cribs, babysitting available.

NORTH WILDWOOD

Candlelight Inn   *Tel:* 609–522–6200
2310 Central Avenue, 08260

An imposing four-story Queen Anne Victorian home awaits visitors to this quiet, residential part of the Wildwoods. Central Avenue is a broad boulevard, with wide borders and a landscaped center island. Built by

Leaming Rice at the turn of the century, it remained the family home until it was restored as a B&B in 1985 by Paul DiFilippo and Diane Buscham. They've decorated the inn in period, including an 1855 sofa and Eastlake piano in the parlor, and the original built-in oak break-front and chestnut pocket doors in the dining room. Guest rooms are individually furnished with brass or antique wood beds, period pieces in oak, mahogany, walnut, and pine, accompanied by Oriental rugs, old prints, and lace. Rates include a breakfast of fresh fruit and juice, cereal, eggs, waffles, pancakes, French toast, homemade breads, jams, and freshly brewed coffee and tea; afternoon refreshments; and in-room evening sherry, chocolates, and fresh flowers.

"Tastefully restored and decorated. Enjoyed great breakfasts, late afternoon lemonade and cookies. Diane was friendly without being intrusive and was very helpful with restaurant recommendations." (Janet Payne)

One small area for improvement: "Our bathroom needed a shelf or small table on which to place toiletries."

Open Feb.–Dec.
Rooms 1 suite, 9 doubles—8 with private bath and/or shower, 2 with maximum of 4 sharing bath. All with ceiling fans. Suite with living/dining area, TV, kitchen, jacuzzi.
Facilities Dining room, parlor with piano, deck with gas grill, hot tub, outside shower. On-site parking. Short walk to beach, tennis. Bicycling, fishing, boating, golf nearby.
Location Jersey Shore. 40 m S of Atlantic City, 6 m N of Cape May. Take Garden State Pkwy. S to Exit 6 (Rte. 147.) Go E on 147 to end, then turn S on Central Ave. to inn on right. From Garden State Parkway N take Exit 4. Turn left on New Jersey Ave to 24th Ave. Turn right. Inn on left.
Restrictions No smoking. Children in suite only.
Credit cards Amex, MC, Visa.
Rates B&B, $80–150 suite, $70–105 double. 2-3 night minimum July, Aug., holiday weekends. 10% senior discount midweek.
Extras Station pickups. French spoken.

PITTSTOWN

Seven Springs Farm B&B
Perryville Road, R.D. 3, Box 223, 08867

Tel: 201–735–7675

If the idea of holding a drinking bucket for a newborn calf, riding a tractor, and catching tadpoles from the pond appeals to you and your family, read on. Just an hour and a half from either New York City or Philadelphia is the Seven Springs Farm, owned by James and Dina Bowers for thirty years. Open as a B&B since 1984, the farm has been in the Bowers family for several generations. Any antiques that furnish its rooms are the kind that came with the house. Guests are served a hearty breakfast of the farm's own eggs, bacon or sausage, and fresh fruits, along with pancakes and home-baked breads. As the Bowers describe it: "Ours is a working farm. Many families no longer have relatives living on the land and a stay with us opens doors for youngsters and their parents. We spend time explaining the farm. Kids love to collect eggs, climb hay bales, maybe get a ride on a hay wagon. Folks also enjoy boating and swimming at local reservoirs, visiting the local museum and art center, and discount shopping in Flemington."

"A warm caring environment in the disappearing farm country of New Jersey. Healthy breakfasts, comfortable accommodations with privacy, and a real sense of 'home.' " *(Steven Putrich)* "This is a place where you can leave your belongings in the morning and be sure to find them in the evening, where someone says 'Good Morning' and really means it, and where you can relax with a cup of coffee in the evening. Dina is a wonderful hostess; she keeps the rooms nice and tidy and will do anything she can to make your stay comfortable." *(J.Paul)* "The countryside reminded me of the wooded hills of South and Southwest England. Good showers!" *(John Dobson, and others)*

One delighted guest did note that the guest rooms are on the small side, and can be warm on humid summer nights.

Open All year.
Rooms 3 doubles share 1½ baths. All with radio, fan; 2 with desk.
Facilities Living room with library, TV, VCR, game table, toys; dining room with fireplace, piano; sun porch. 110 acres with farm buildings, gardens, play equipment, pond for fishing. Cross-country skiing on property.
Location W NJ. 45 m W of Newark, 30 m N of Trenton. 5 min from Clinton, NJ. From Rte. 78, take Exit 15 (Clinton) left to Rte. 513 S. Turn right at third road; continue to farm ¾ m on right.
Restrictions No smoking.
Credit cards None accepted.
Rates B&B, $25 per adult; $25 per child first night, then $10 each subsequent night.
Extras Bus station pickup for fee. Crib, babysitting available.

PRINCETON

Information please: The **Nassau Inn** (Palmer Square, 08542; 800–922–3432 or 609–921–7500) is unquestionably the best-known hotel in Princeton. Members of the Continental Congress came here to eat in 1783, when taking a break from meetings across the street at Nassau Hall. Over the years, though, it grew to a 217-room hotel, and lost much of its sense of history under the ownership of an assortment of hotel chains. Now locally run again, many of the rooms have been beautifully refurbished with handmade quilts and period furnishings. Reports, please.

Peacock Inn   *Tel:* 609–924–1707
20 Bayard Lane, 08540

Built in 1775 as a private home, the gambrel-roofed Peacock Inn was moved to its present location a century later, and opened its doors to the public in 1912. Illustrious guests over the years included Bertrand Russell, Albert Einstein, and F. Scott Fitzgerald. In 1985, the inn was purchased by Michael Walker and his wife Candy Lindsay. They redecorated with French, early American, and English antiques, crafts, and carefully chosen fabrics and wallcoverings. Le Plumet Royal restaurant occupies the main floor, serving fine French cuisine in an elegant atmosphere, with well spaced Queen Anne tables and chairs, ornate silverware, and fresh flowers; the peacock theme runs throughout its decor.

"Friendly, knowledgeable staff. The rooms are furnished with interesting antiques; some of the bathrooms are new, others old, but all were spotless. Our room had good lighting for reading in bed, and tables on each side, along with two comfortable wing chairs for relaxing. Rooms have been decorated with much care. The wallpaper in bedrooms coordinates with bathroom; in our room, the pink ribbon theme was repeated on the towels. Our bath was newly redone with a stall shower, pedestal sink, and medicine cabinet. Our self-service breakfast included granola, fresh fruit, juice, English and sweet muffins, quiche, coffee, and tea. The inn is in a great location for antiques lovers, with many shops in easy walking distance. Also nearby is the Princeton University Art Museum, the Firestone Library, and interesting sculpture and architecture on and about campus. We found a musty, antiquarian bookstore, housed in a former bank vault, and browsed happily.

"Our dinner was expensive but superb. My duck—marinated in citrus, honey, and white wine and served with currant mustard sauce—was the best I've ever had. We split an appetizer of wild mushrooms and goat cheese in phyllo with tomato coulis that was also outstanding. Portions were small, but beautifully presented and delicious." *(Diane Wolf)*

Open All year.
Rooms 17 doubles—9 with private bath and/or shower, 8 rooms with maximum of 4 people sharing bath. All with air-conditioning, alarm clocks, desk, telephone, ceiling fan.
Facilities Restaurant, bar/lounge, sitting room with TV, porch. Off-street parking.
Location Central NJ. 1 block from Princeton campus. On Rte 206.
Credit cards Amex, MC, Visa.
Rates B&B, $125 double, $90 single. MAP, $165 double, $115 single. Extra person in room, $105. Weekly, off-season (summer) rates. Prix fixe dinner $20. Alc lunch, $10–20; alc dinner, $40–50.
Extras Airport/station pickups. Pets accepted. Cribs available. Czechoslovakian, French, Spanish spoken.

SOUTH BELMAR

Hollycroft
506 North Boulevard, 07719

Tel: 201–681–2254

Along a shoreline where motels and bungalows predominate, a country lodge like Hollycroft comes a surprise. Built by a prosperous lumber baron in 1908 as a private summer retreat, and sheltered by trees and holly bushes, this inn seems transplanted from the Adirondacks, with its log beams and columns, knotty pine walls, and massive stone fireplace. Linda and Mark Fessler have owned the inn since 1985 and have furnished the guest rooms with country Victorian wallpapers and antique and reproduction beds. Although all rooms have private baths, guests are welcome to use the inn's original bathroom, complete with two antique claw-foot tubs (robes and bubble bath provided). In addition to the beach, nearby attractions include the restored 1853 village at Allair State Park, and fishing in adjacent Lake Como.

"In the living room, we stood by the huge stone fireplace and gazed through the window, past the majestic trees and onto the shimmering lake and ocean beyond. Wooden beams, brick and mahogany floors, a double-sided staircase, and many restored architectural details form the background for the lovely antique furnishings and modern accoutrements that make Hollycroft a showplace. We stayed in the Windsor Rose room with a brass queen-sized bed, white wicker furniture, private screened-in porch, and large bathroom. The rose and green color scheme is completed by hand stenciling, lace curtains, flowers, pictures, lamps, and all sorts of whimsical accessories. The attention to detail was evidenced by the white eyelet pillow shams, new mattress and pillows, sparkling clean glasses, and immaculate bathroom.

"Breakfast includes a variety of fruits, freshly squeezed orange juice, cold cereals, freshly baked breads, muffins, cakes and assorted edible surprises. The carafes of freshly brewed coffees and tea, both regular and decaf, are always steaming hot and limitless. The food is so plentiful, the conversations so congenial, and the company so enjoyable that breakfast just goes on and on. Linda and Mark Fessler are gracious, generous, helpful, yet unobtrusive hosts. They are always available to offer tips on dining, sightseeing, shopping, recreation and local lore. Guests are immediately made to feel at ease, and often explore the public rooms admiring the collection of handmade dolls, miniature English cottages, ceramic tea pots, antique beaded bags, and the old-time player piano. " *(Stephen & Marsha Meyers)*

"Hollycroft is located in a beautifully private wooded lot, two blocks from the ocean, overlooking a small lake. Plumbing is both modern and old-fashioned, with claw foot tubs, but all bathrooms have an abundance of beautiful color coordinated towels. The interior lighting is very pleasant and low key." *(Dr. & Mrs. Bruce Morgan)*

Open All year. Closed Christmas.
Rooms 7 doubles—2 with full private bath and/or shower, 5 with shared bath. 2 rooms with desk; some with radio.
Facilities Dining room, sun-room, living room with fireplace, sitting room, breakfast patio. 1 acre with hammock. Beach badges, ocean swimming, lake and ocean fishing, golf, tennis nearby.
Location NE NJ, on Jersey Shore. 50 m S of NYC, 50 m N of Atlantic City, 70 m N of Philadelphia. From Garden State, take Exit 98. Follow Rte. 34 to traffic circle. Go around circle to Rte. 524 E (Allaire Rd.). Go 3.3 m to 2nd traffic light (Rte. 71) and turn left, then right onto Church St. Follow Church St. to 3nd Ave., then left. Go 2 blocks, then turn right onto North Blvd. Follow North Blvd to inn.
Restrictions Smoking in common rooms only. No children under 12.
Credit cards Amex.
Rates $65–95 double. 2-3 night weekend/holiday minimum in season.
Extras Station pickups.

SPRING LAKE

Spring Lake is one of New Jersey's most pleasant shore towns. It offers a 2-mile-long boardwalk (with no commercial facilities) for strolling along the ocean; wide, tree-lined streets, with many turn-of-the-century houses; and, in the center of town, a lovely lake, surrounded by a park. Outdoor activities include golf, tennis, horseback riding, and canoeing. Joggers will enjoy the path around the lake or the boardwalk. Peak season in Spring Lake extends from Memorial Day through mid- to late September. The town is located in Monmouth County, 1½ hours south of New York City, 1½ hours north of Philadelphia and Atlantic City. Take Exit 98 off Garden State Parkway to Route 34. Go 1½ miles to traffic circle and go left on Route 524 (Allaire Rd.). Go east on Route 524 for 3 miles into town.

Information please: Sea Crest by the Sea (19 Tuttle Avenue, 07762; 201–449–9031) is a 12-bedroom Victorian mansion decorated with French and English furnishings from the 1880s. Outside is a croquet court and a rack filled with bicycles; the beach is just a block away. Rates include a continental breakfast. Reports?

Ashling Cottage   *Tel:* 201–449–3553
106 Sussex Avenue, 07762

George Huelett, who was responsible for much of Spring Lake's architecture, built Ashling Cottage in 1877. Goodi and Jack Stewart have owned this B&B since 1984 and have furnished it with period antiques.

"Visiting Spring Lake is like traveling to another world. All the hustle and bustle of the modern world are left behind, and sun, sand, and surf exist for your quiet enjoyment rather than as choice sites for hot dog stands and video arcades. Ashling Cottage offers the charm and appointments of another era, with creature comforts of today. Sunken bathrooms, private porches, scrumptious breakfasts, and friendly, helpful hosts make this our most special hideaway." *(Tom & Dana Bogany)*

"The house is a mansard-style Victorian, and rates include a hearty continental breakfast of two or three kinds of bread, cereal, fruit, juices, coffee, tea, and eggs. Newspapers and porches encourage a relaxed breakfast time. We've never seen anything other than spotless rooms, and have always enjoyed the pretty antiques, lovely lace curtains, and cool ocean breezes." *(Mr. & Mrs. Joseph Mulay)*

"Jack and Goodi Stewart greet all comers as old friends, be it their first visit or their twentieth. A welcoming glass of wine on the veranda with Jack or a detailed note of dining suggestions from Goodi are just some of the touches that made the Ashling unusual. You can choose to join in with the convivial spirit of the cottage, or you can quietly enjoy the lovely views of the ocean from the comfort of your own brass bed." *(M. Stannard Doyle)* More comments please.

Open March through Dec.
Rooms 10 doubles—8 with private bath and/or shower, 2 sharing 1 bath.
Facilities Living room with TV, VCR, library, games; parlor; solarium. Patio with barbecue. 1 block to ocean, 1 block to lake.

Location 3 blocks from town. Follow Rte. 524 to 1st Ave. Turn right on 1st, again right on Sussex.
Restrictions No smoking in guest rooms. No children under 12.
Credit cards None accepted.
Rates B&B, $60–105 doubles, $58–98 singles. Extra person in room, $25. 3-night minimum stay weekends in July and Aug.
Extras Train station pickups; free pickup from Newark Airport for guests staying at least a week.

The Chateau   *Tel:* 201–974–2000
500 Warren Avenue at Fifth, 07762

Longtime owner Scott Smith has combined turn-of-the-century atmosphere with modern amenities at The Chateau, a Victorian hotel built in 1888. Nestled between two parks and overlooking the lake, The Chateau has received a three-star rating from Mobil and three diamonds from AAA. Rooms are done in colorful contemporary florals and wicker.

"To us, Spring Lake is the most attractive resort town on the Jersey Shore—immaculate, a bit sedate, and with innumerable Victorian homes and hotels, yet still close to New York City, Atlantic City, and Philadelphia. The Chateau's accommodations are attractive and comfortable, and the housekeeping is excellent. The owners are most friendly and accommodating." *(Henry W. Satchwell)*

"The Chateau is one of the most charming, cozy, and attractive places I've visited, and is especially unique for a shore town. I've seen a number of the guest rooms, and all are delightful, perhaps because of the constant renovation and redecoration efforts." *(LM)*

One suggested improvement: "In-room coffee pots would be delightful for fixing an early morning drink."

Open April through Oct.
Rooms 16 suites, 24 doubles, all with private shower and/or bath, telephone, radio, TV, air-conditioning, fan, refrigerator. Many with porch or balcony. Suites have wet bars, VCR's, hair dryers; 2 have kitchens, most have fireplaces. 6 rooms in annex.
Facilities Lobby with library. Tennis courts, fishing nearby. 4 blocks to beach; beach passes provided. Bicycle rentals. Room service.
Location 3 blocks from center.
Restrictions Smoking in guest rooms only.
Credit cards Amex, MC, Visa.
Rates Room only, $70–165 suite, $55–109 double, $50–104 single. Extra person in room, $10. First child under 12 free. Continental breakfast $5.00. Pre-season senior discount. 3-night weekend/holiday minimum during July, Aug. 1–week minimum for kitchen units, June–Oct.
Extras Free station pickups. Some rooms wheelchair accessible. Cribs, babysitting available.

The Normandy Inn   *Tel:* 201–449–7172
21 Tuttle Avenue, 07762

The Normandy Inn was built as a private home in 1888, and was moved to its present site—just four houses from the ocean—in the early 1900s. Michael and Susan Ingino have owned the inn since 1982, and have decorated it with period wallpaper and furniture. White wicker tables and chairs furnish the wraparound porch; antique clocks, stained glass lamps, and gilded mirrors grace the parlor; and brass, walnut, and mahogany beds can be found in most of the bedrooms. The Inginos also restored the outside of the house, painting it with accurate Victorian colors—shades of green, burgundy, and terra-cotta. Breakfast items are featured on a menu, with guests choosing their favorite style of eggs, omelets, or pancakes—blueberry, chocolate chip, or pecan.

"Anytime you go 60 miles out of your way to stay at an inn for one or two nights, that says something about the inn—its innkeepers, location, food, and calm and beautiful surroundings—only a block from the Spring Lake boardwalk. Where else can you get porridge to go along with an outstanding full breakfast—served in a fine dining room with classical music—extremely courteous waitresses, and a fine presentation by the chef-owner? Others enjoy the two large TV's in the living room and family room, the VCR and library. The inn is extremely clean, from its antiques to its six-foot towels." *(Bill Wagner)*

"Susan and Mike are friendly and most gracious in meeting your every need. The inn is clean and comfortable, pleasant and homey. Mike's breakfast will hold you till dinner if you let it. The pancakes are the size of the plate and the freshly baked muffins are a perfect way to start the day." *(Bob & Bonnie Larson)*

Open All year.
Rooms 15 doubles, 2 singles, all with private bath and/or shower, radio, air-conditioning. 2-bedroom apartment in separate building.
Facilities 2 parlor areas, with TV. Dining room, open and enclosed porches, flower gardens, bicycles. Beach is 4 houses away. Golf, tennis, horseback riding, fishing nearby. Parking for 1/2 of guests on property, remainder at beach.
Location 1½ hrs. from NYC, Atlantic City, and Philadelphia. 4 blocks from town. Take Rte. 524 E to Ocean Ave. Go right 1 block and right again on Tuttle.
Restrictions No smoking in dining room. Limited parking.
Credit cards Amex, MC, Visa. 5% discount for checks, cash.
Rates B&B, $71–125 double, $47–115 single. Extra person in room $20. Child under 12 in room, $1 per year of age additional; family of four needs 2 rooms. 2–4 night weekend minimum. 15% discount for 7-day stays. Full breakfast for outside guests, $7.00
Extras Station pickups available. Cribs available.

STANHOPE

Whistling Swan Inn   *Tel:* 201–347–6369
110 Main Street, P.O. Box 791, 07874

Paula Williams and Joe Mulay restored this Queen Anne Victorian, built in 1905, and opened it as a B&B in 1986. Guest rooms are decorated in different themes—Oriental, Art Deco, brass, and white iron— and are named after historic locations nearby. The inn itself was named for an old-fashioned sign Paula had long admired in an antique shop, but hadn't purchased because of its high price. When it disappeared from the shop, she assumed someone had bought it; her assumption was correct, but fortunately that someone was Joe, who had bought it for her as a birthday present. Rates include a buffet breakfast with a hot egg, fruit, or cheese dish; homemade breads; juice and fruit; coffees and tea. Paula is happy to provide an early weekday breakfast for business travelers.

"A delightful inn and innkeeper. Paula went above and beyond the call of duty, treating us like family. Airline problems delayed our arrival substantially, yet she greeted us warmly, despite the late hour." *(Marylin & Don Root)*

"Very clean, charming decor, comfortable beds. The owners always had time to visit, offering tea or whatever throughout the day. They provided lots of local information, and helped us arrange transportation to NYC." *(Susan & Richard Spencer)* "Breakfast on the porch is a special treat in good weather. Also a delight are the two claw-footed tubs in the original large bathroom." *(Barry & Rosemary Baker)*

Open All year.
Rooms 1 suite, 9 doubles, all with private bath and/or shower, air-conditioning, fan. Most with radio, desk. Telephone on request.
Facilities Breakfast room; parlor with TV/VCR, piano; porch. 1 acre with picnic table. 3 blocks from lake swimming, boating, fishing. 3 m to cross-country skiing.
Location NW NJ, Skylands Region. 1 hr. W of NYC; 27 m E of Poconos. In center of town. From I-80, take exit 27 or 27B to Rte. 183/206. Follow Rte. 183/206 past traffic circle and continue N one block past stop light. Turn left after brownstone church onto Main St.
Restrictions No smoking. No children under 12.
Credit cards Amex, MC, Visa.
Rates B&B, $95 suite, $70–90 double. Extra person in room, $20. $5 senior discount. 2-night holiday weekend minimum. Weekly, corporate rates.
Extras Airport/station pickups.

SUMMIT

The Grand Summit Hotel
Tel: 201–273–3000
570 Springfield Avenue, 07901-4599

Just 45 minutes from Manhattan, Summit is very much a part of the New York City metropolitan area; a plethora of chain hotels and motels have sprung up to fill the needs of travelers doing business with area companies. A special pleasure, then, to find a hotel of history and distinction. The Grand Summit dates back to 1868, when New Yorkers traveled by train to what was then a resort area. Many wealthy guests settled in the area, attracting even more visitors. In 1929, the present hotel was built in Tudor style, with detailed brick work, a vaulted beamed ceiling and leaded glass in the lobby, and elaborate detailing. In 1986, the hotel's ownership changed, and the hotel was modernized and upgraded at considerable cost, bringing back its original elegance; Franz Eichenauer is the general manager. Guest rooms are furnished in period decor, some with four poster beds and cherry wood armoires. Rates include a complimentary morning newspaper and freshly brewed coffee delivered to your room after your wakeup call; afternoon tea and pastries served in the lobby; and nightly turndown service with home-made chocolate chip cookies.

The hotel is known for its eclectic regional American cuisine, prepared by chef Steven Jilleba. Possible entrées include lamb with wild mushrooms, herbs, mustard, and Cabernet Sauvignon sauce; chicken breast stuffed with spinach and shrimp and chive sauce; or veal with glazed apples and hazelnut sauce.

"The hotel is located in a modest, but safe neighborhood. Much restoration work has already been done on the hotel, although a few projects still await. The rooms are pleasant, but the food, which is outstanding, makes the hotel worth a detour." *(PG)*

Open All year.
Rooms 15 suites, 129 doubles all with private bath, telephone, radio, TV, desk, air-conditioning, fan. Some with Jacuzzi.
Facilities Dining room, bar/lounge with entertainment nightly, lobby with fireplace, pool, fitness center.
Location Center of town. 45 min. W of Manhattan. From NYC, take NJ Trnpke. (I-95) S to Exit 14, then I-78 W into Rte. 24/124 W. Exit at Summit Ave. (2nd exit). Go left at light; go straight on Summit Ave 1 m to Springfield Ave. & turn right. Go straight past 4 lights (about 1/2 m) to hotel on left immediately after 4th light.
Credit cards Amex, DC, MC, Visa.
Rates Room only, $180–300 suite, $135 double, single. Extra person in room, $15. Weekend rates, packages. Alc lunch $13, alc dinner $26.
Extras Free airport pickup by advance reservation. Cribs, babysitting available.

VENTNOR CITY

Mayfair by the Sea   *Tel:* 609–822–0611
105 South Little Rock Avenue, 08406

"This charming 10-room house is decorated with Laura Ashley fabrics and wallcoverings. On the second floor is a balcony that overlooks the ocean; out back is a courtyard patio with chairs. The beach has soft white sand and is very clean. Within walking distance are several moderate to high-priced ethnic restaurants. Last and most important are the warm and vivacious hosts of this establishment, Sam and Jill Staufenberg and Donovan Rankin. Breakfast is served in a sun-room with lacy tablecloths and fresh-cut flowers; tea is served at five in the family room. A light snack of fresh-cut vegetables with dip, assorted crackers and cheeses, and various juices is offered." *(Pam Ungeleider)*

"Exceptionally clean rooms and crisp linens. The rooms are good-sized, and at night they turn down your bed and place a flower on your pillow. The atmosphere is the best part; everybody is friendly and socializes in the main sitting room. Breakfast consists of fresh fruit, breads, cereals, yogurt, waffles, and omelets made to order. Coffee and tea are available all day long. During breakfast and throughout the day Sam plays piano music." *(Yvette Rocca)* "The Staufenbergs really made us feel at home, offering us everything from a back massage to directions for restaurants and places to go." *(Cathleen Moser)*

"Fully endorse your existing entry. The outside doesn't foretell the lovely inside." *(Janet Payne and others)*

Open All year.
Rooms 10 doubles—6 with private bath, 4 with maximum of 4 sharing bath.
Facilities Living room, sun-porch, tea room, den, courtyard. ½ block from beach, boardwalk. Bicycling, tennis nearby.
Location NJ Shore, 1½ m S of Atlantic City. 1 m S of closest casino. From Atlantic City Expressway, go S on Atlantic Ave. to Little Rock Rd. & turn left.
Restrictions Limited & metered on-street parking.
Credit cards MC, Visa.
Rates B&B, $75–125 double.

WOODBINE

Henry Ludlam Inn   *Tel:* 609–861–5847
Rural Delivery 3, Box 298, 08270

The homestead of prominent local family—active in the area since the 1700s—the Henry Ludlam Inn is an early 19th century farmhouse owned by Ann and Marty Thurlow since 1984. Hand-stenciled walls, plank doors, antiques and collectibles convey a sense of the past, while Anne's hearty breakfast, served by the fire in the common room or on the porch, will energize you to face the present. Birdwatchers will want to visit in spring or fall; this area is on the north/south flyway, and several nature sanctuaries are just a short drive away. Rates include a full breakfast (stuffed French toast a speciality), afternoon wine and sherry, and evening beverages and fruit.

"Ann and Marty welcomed us warmly to their historic inn. Our room was supplied with fluffy towels, night-time mints, and fluffy featherbeds. Ann's delicious breakfast included cream-topped peaches filled with fresh berries, homemade muffins, crispy bacon, and a choice of omelets. The inn makes a terrific base from which to explore Atlantic City, Cape May, and Delaware Bay. Returning to the inn after a day of exploring, you feel like the innkeepers are sincere in their inquiries as to how your day has been." *(LS)* More comments please.

Open All year.
Rooms 5 doubles—3 with private shower and/or bath, 2 rooms sharing 1 bath. All with air-conditioning, fan. 3 with desk, fireplace.
Facilities Living room with fireplace, common room with wood-burning stove, TV, games; screened porch. Lakeside swing. On lake for canoeing, fishing. All water sports, golf, tennis, hiking, horseback riding nearby.
Location S NJ, Cape May Cty. 18 N of Cape May, 40 min S of Atlantic City.
Restrictions Smoking in common room only. No children under 12. Traffic noise might disturb light sleepers in front rooms.
Credit cards Amex, MC, Visa.
Rates B&B, $65–95 double. Extra person in room, $15. MAP, $145 double. 2-night holiday minimum. Prix fixe dinner, $30.
Extras Airport pickups.

New York

The Sedgewick Inn, Berlin

Although to some people New York is synonymous with New York City, the state is an exceptionally diverse one. In fact, the New York State Tourism Council divides the state up into the following distinct regions (not counting the Big Apple, which most consider a region unto itself): Long Island, the Hudson Valley, the Catskills, the Capital (Albany)/Saratoga, the Adirondacks, Thousand Islands Seaway, Central/Leatherstocking, the Finger Lakes, the Niagara Frontier, and Chautauqua/Allegheny. The New York State Tourism Division publishes first-rate materials on all these regions; see the appendix for the address and telephone.

If you don't belong to the 'see-everything-in-one-visit' club, you might want to design a trip, even within a single region, around a specific theme. Possibilities abound but might include: New York gardens (branch out from the Brooklyn Botanic Garden to the sculpture gardens in Harrison or the formal Sonnenberg Gardens in Canandaigua); craft museums (begin with New York City's American Craft museum for contemporary work, Old Chatham's superb Shaker Museum, or East Aurora's historic Roycroft crafts community); historic architecture (from Manhattan's many landmarks to the Adirondack "Great Camps" and FDR's Hyde Park mansion); ethnic New York (in addition to the Big Apple's myriad ethnic neighborhoods, seek out Albany's Dutch heritage, and sample some of the ethnic food in Buffalo's Polish and German communities); New York's Native Americans (visit the Iroquois Museum in Schoharie, and Niagara Falls's outstanding Native American Center for the Living Arts, housed in a turtle-shaped building).

Information please: We're distressed to note that we have no entries for Lake Placid, a major summer and winter resort in the Adirondacks, and would like reports on the **Stagecoach Inn** (Old Military Road, Lake Placid, 12946; 518–523–9474), a historic inn dating from 1833 and decorated with Victorian antiques; and the **South Meadow Farm** (Cascade Road, Lake Placid, 12946; 518–523–9369) with 5 double rooms and rustic cabins. It's a working farm with home-grown food; the cross-country ski trails used in the 1980 Olympics cross over the farm, and the hiking is terrific.

Two inns on **Long Island** we'd like to hear more about are the **Three Village Inn** (P.O. Box 801, Stony Brook, 11790; 516–689–3441) on Long Island's North Shore near Port Jefferson. Its 32 rooms are decorated with antique reproductions, and New England-style seafood is the specialty at its restaurant. In the same area is the **Captain Hawkins House** (321 Terryville Road, Port Jefferson Station, 11776; 516–473–8211). Built by a successful sea captain in 1867, the mansion stayed in the Hawkins family until the 1950s, when it was bought by Cornelius family; Ralph Cornelius opened it as a B&B in 1989. Guest rooms are furnished with brass or four poster beds, with antiques and ceiling fans; rates include a breakfast of fresh fruit and juice, yogurt, croissants, and homemade muffins, served in the dining room or out by the swimming pool.

New York State sales tax is 7%, plus additional local taxes applicable in most counties.

ADAMS BASIN

Canalside Inn B&B   *Tel:* 716–352–6784
425 Washington Street, 14410

The Canalside Inn, listed on the National Register of Historic Places as the Adams-Ryan-Nichols House, is a post-and-beam-construction building that dates back to the early 1800s. The Greek Revival–style north portion of the house was added in 1858, when the house was converted to an inn and tavern. In those days, the bar and card room were for men only; women and children had to wait in the "Loafing Room" while the men refreshed themselves. The inn was closed to the public in 1916, when the canal had fallen into disuse because of the railroads.

In 1972, Bud and Elsie Nichols purchased the house and began an extensive restoration effort; they did not open the inn until July 1985. Each guest room is furnished with a different type of wood—walnut, chestnut, tiger maple, and pine—and is named accordingly. Guests are welcome to visit Bud's carpentry and antique restoration shop at the back of the inn. "The inn, steeped in local history, made a lovely place to stay for my first visit to this part of the U.S. The hospitality, service, and accommodation were of the highest order." *(Brenda Knott)* "I felt very much at home here, had a marvelous stay, and enjoyed the excellent food." *(Russell Franks)*

Open All year.
Rooms 4 doubles—all with private shower. 3 with fan, 1 with TV, 1 with air-conditioning.
Facilities Parlor with TV, bar, dining room, porches, lighted dock with boats, canoes. ½ acre with fish ponds. Hiking, bicycling on canal towpath. Golf, tennis, swimming, cross-country skiing nearby.
Location W NY, on Erie Canal. 20 m W of Rochester. Take Rte. 31 W from Rochester. Turn N on Rte. 36 to town on canal.
Restrictions No smoking. No children under 12.
Credit cards None accepted.
Rates B&B, $55 double, $45 single, plus 10% tax. Extra person in room, $15. Packages available.

ALBANY

Mansion Hill Inn   *Tel:* 518–465–2038
115 Philip Street, 12202

Built in 1861 for brush-maker Daniel Brown, the Mansion Hill Inn was used as a tavern for many years. In 1984, Maryellen and Steve Stofelano restored it as a restaurant and inn, and plan to expand the number of guest rooms to 15 by February 1991. They note that "our inn is especially convenient for the business traveler, due to our downtown location; our suite accommodations are ideal for families." The inn restaurant offers Italian cuisine and New York state wines; veal, shrimp, and pasta dishes are specialties.

"The inn is small with a homey atmosphere; very friendly owners and staff. The food is excellent—fresh, well prepared and attractively presented; rooms are completely renovated, sparkling clean, and large." *(Jim Goacher)* "Ample parking, welcoming atmosphere." *(Diane Fleming)*

"The inn comprises two buildings in a hilly area with lots of brownstone houses, many in the process of being renovated. It's a good area for walking, and the Governor's Mansion is right up the street. The corner building has a nice informal dining room with an appealing menu; it's very popular with neighborhood residents. My room was decorated with reproduction antiques, wall-to-wall rose carpeting, ruffled rose curtains, and a quilted floral bedspread—pleasant and immaculate. It had a state-of-the-art air conditioner, remote-control cable TV, and a good clock-radio next to the bed. Breakfast was the standard bacon-and-eggs type menu, but was very tasty." *(Kathie Desmond)*

Some suggestions for improvement (from an otherwise delighted guest): "The decor lacks the personal touches that would give the rooms more individual flavor. Hopefully, some twin-bedded rooms will be available in the new wing; none were so equipped when we visited. Finally, we were surprised that our in-room phone was a wall phone, across the room from the bed."

Open All year. Restaurant closed Sun. evening, Mon.
Rooms 2 suites, 5 doubles—all with full private bath, telephone, radio, TV. Most with desk, air-conditioning. Suites with kitchen, deck.
Facilities Dining/breakfast rooms with fireplace. Room service. Off-street parking. Hiking, boating, fishing nearby.
Location South End; "Mansion Neighborhood," around the corner from the Governor's Mansion. From NYS Thruway or I-787, exit at Madison Avenue; follow Rte. 20 (Madison Ave.) through 4 traffic lights; turn left onto Philip St.; continue to 2nd blinking light and inn on right at corner of Park Ave.
Credit cards Amex, DC.
Rates Room only, $135 suite, $115 double, $95 single. Extra person in room, $10. 15% service charge. 10% senior discount. Alc lunch, $7; alc dinner, $25. 2-night midweek minimum.
Extras Wheelchair accessible. Station pickups. Crib, babysitting available. Spanish, German, Italian, French spoken.

AMENIA

Troutbeck
Leedsville Road, P.O. Box 26, 12501

Tel: 914–373–9681

Once a gathering place for the literati and liberals of the 1920s, Troutbeck has a dual personality: It's a gracious country estate on weekends and an executive retreat for conferences and seminars during the week. The main house is a slate-roofed, leaded-windowed Tudoresque manor built from 1918 to 1920; there are also rooms in a farmhouse dating back to the eighteenth century, with a modern addition. Both the common and the guest rooms are furnished traditionally, with pleasing colors and consciously comfortable chairs and sofas. The dining room is open to outsiders too, with sumptuous five-course dinners, devilish desserts, and a half-dozen appealing entrées. A recent dinner included wild mushroom tart, scallop bisque, endive salad, baked pheasant with lingonberries and cranberries, and baked pears with three sauces.

Troutbeck had been vacant for 35 years when James Flaherty and Robert Skibsted bought and restored it in 1979. Although they often fill all the rooms for midweek executive seminars, they claim they never book more than 20 to 25 couples on weekends in high season.

"Every room is different, but most have their own bright sun porches. The inn is filled with books—it was a private residence for years and still feels much like one. In the winter all the cozy common rooms have blazing fires in beautiful stone fireplaces." *(Julie Clark)* "The food was perfect—quality, presentation, service, the works. Absolutely nothing to criticize. The main house is beautiful, both inside and out; guest rooms vary in size but all are most inviting and livable." *(Lars Nilsson)*

Another reader enjoyed the inn but was disappointed by the room he and his wife had in the modern addition. "Although comfortable in every way, it lacked the old-fashioned charm of guest rooms in the main house." More comments please.

Open All year. Closed Christmas weekend.
Rooms 6 suites, 28 doubles, most with full private bath, radio, desk, air-conditioning. 18 rooms in annex, 3 in guest house. Some with canopy bed, fireplace.

Facilities Dining room; living room with fireplace, piano; bar/lounge with fireplace; library with fireplace, TV, VCR. 442 acres with gardens, indoor and outdoor swimming pools, tennis courts, sauna, exercise room, greenhouse, hiking, jogging, cross-country skiing, lake for fishing.
Location SE NY; Dutchess County, on NY/CT border, near Sharon, CT. 2 hrs. N of NYC, 1½ hrs. N of White Plains & W of Hartford, 1½ hrs. E of Albany, 3½ hrs. SW of Boston. Take I-684 W to Rte. 22. In Amenia, go right (E) on Rte. 343 2.4 m to inn driveway on right.
Restrictions No children between the ages of 1 and 13. No cigars or pipes in dining room.
Credit Cards Amex.
Rates Full board and open bar, $325–475 per couple, plus tax and 12% service. 2-night stay, $575–790. Lower rates for 2 couples sharing one bath. Prix fixe lunch, $26; dinner, $39.50. Weekend packages.
Extras Spanish, Portuguese, French, Italian spoken. Station pickups. Cribs available.

AVERILL PARK

The Gregory House   *Tel:* 518–674–3774
Route 43, P.O. Box 401, 12018

The Gregory House was built by Elias Gregory around 1830 and remained in the family for three generations. Bob and Bette Jewell bought the house in 1964, and in 1976, after their children were grown and had left home, they converted it into a small restaurant. In 1984 they expanded the building to include the guest rooms and a common room. The restaurant at the Gregory House is as popular with locals as with the inn's overnight guests—always a good sign. The menu is continental, with such entrées as veal with basil cream sauce, steak au poivre, and chicken tarragon.

"Innkeepers Bob and Bette Jewell are very friendly people who care about comfort, cleanliness, and atmosphere. With a decanter of sherry always available in the common room, and a fire in the fireplace, guests are sure to become friends." *(Mr. & Mrs. David Pierce)* "The food is excellent, varied, and reasonably priced. Mrs. Jewell is always in the dining room, seeing that the needs of guests are being met. Mr. Jewell oversees the operation of the kitchen, and you are always welcome to go back and meet him. The rooms are bright and airy, the furnishings simple yet appealing. In the summer, you can enjoy your favorite beverage by the small pool just outside the main door. In the winter, you can relax by the fire in the common room, and talk all night if you desire." *(James J. MacArevey)*

"I want to mention the cleanliness—the sparkling modern bathrooms, where everything works, the well-maintained grounds, with gorgeous flowers and swimming pool area (with a handy basket of giant, fluffy towels)." *(Elaine & Jack Schwartz)* "A continental breakfast of juices, coffee and tea, and delicious breakfast rolls is served in the common room; hot entrées are available for an extra charge." *(Bradley & Dorinda Whisher)* More comments please.

Open All year. Restaurant closed 3 days at Christmas; 2 weeks in winter.
Rooms 12 doubles with full private bath, radio, air-conditioning; some with desk.
Facilities Restaurant, common room with fireplace, TV, games. ½ acre with swimming pool. Nearby lake for swimming, windsurfing. Golf, cross-country skiing nearby; ½ hr. to downhill.
Location E central NY; Hudson Valley. 13 m E of Albany, 10 SE of Troy. In center of village on Rte. 43.
Restrictions No children under 6.
Credit cards Amex, CB, DC, MC, Visa.
Rates B&B, $60–75 double, $55–70 single. Extra person in room, $10. 7% service charge. 7th night free. Alc dinner, $27.

BERLIN

The Sedgwick Inn

Tel: 518–658–2334
Route 22, P.O. Box 250, 12022

Bob and Edie Evans left careers in psychiatry and hospital management in 1981 for the "retirement" career of running a country inn. The Sedgwick Inn was built as a stagecoach stop in 1791, and was originally part of the Van Rensselaer estate. For many years it was operated as a restaurant called the Ranch Tavern. Full breakfast is included in the rates, and lunch and dinner are available as well. Meals are served on the airy sun porch, and in the coach tavern dining room. There is a choice of five entrées at dinner; Viennese-style desserts are a specialty.

"Lovely setting. Edie, who is Viennese, produces meals of note. Her artistic touches are evident at every turn, from the fresh rosebud on each table to the beautiful Christmas tree we shared one holiday. The inn is a handsome old building, with several bedrooms on the second floor. We stayed in the motel section at the back; it has comfortable clean rooms, and is far enough from Route 22 to ensure a quiet night. The gift and antique shops are fun for browsing, and are products of Bob's interest in assembling the unusual. The Evanses are most considerate hosts, with an interest in the community to which they have brought a special contribution." *(Mr. & Mrs. Richard Weinland)*

"Edie greeted us at the door and give us a nice tour of the common rooms. The inn was warm, friendly, and very welcoming. After settling in, we visited the library to browse through their large assortment of books and magazines. Our visit was made complete by the queen-size bed with a firm mattress. Our dinner was beautifully presented and delicious. When I had a problem with the duck I had ordered, Edie quickly replaced it with a delicious New York strip steak. Very impressive innkeepers! Bob was more visible in the morning and served a delicious and relaxing breakfast." *(Mrs. Joan Bond)* More comments please.

Open All year. Restaurant closed Mon., Tues.
Rooms 1 suite, 10 doubles, all with private bath and/or shower, telephone, radio, fan. Many with desk, TV. 6 rooms in annex.
Facilities Dining rooms, 2 sitting rooms, with fireplace, TV, videodiscs. Dinner

pianist weekends. 12 acres. Hiking, skiing, swimming, fishing, cross-country skiing nearby. 12–14 m to downhill skiing.

Location E central NY. Approx. 30 m E of Albany, 15 m W of Williamstown, MA, 25 m NW of Tanglewood. On Rte. 22, 5 m S of intersection with Rte. 2.
Restrictions No smoking in inn guest rooms. Children welcome in motel only.
Credit cards Amex, DC, MC, Visa.
Rates B&B, $100 suite, $60–80 double, $50–70 single. Extra person in room, $10–12. Alc lunch, $6–10; alc dinner, $20–25. 2-night minimum summer, fall weekends.
Extras Limited wheelchair access. German, French spoken. Pets OK in motel.

BLUE MOUNTAIN LAKE

Information please: Similar to Hemlock Hall, described below, is **The Hedges,** once a private estate turned a summer lodge with cottages in a beautiful lakeside setting (Blue Mountain Lake, 12812; 518–352–7325). Reports?

Hemlock Hall *Tel:* 518–352–7706
Route 28N, 12812 Winter: 518–359–9065

"The Hall is owned and operated by Paul and Susan Provost. Paul had been a regular visitor since the 1950s, before he bought it for himself just a couple of years ago. The cottages are equipped with range and refrigerator, should you decide to cook for yourself . . . but who would want to? Breakfast and dinner are served in a sunny room at the lodge. Every morning we were called to breakfast by the large bell on the porch of the lodge (usually rung by one of the visiting kids). We had bacon, eggs made to order, pancakes, and hot cereal both days. Home-made bread is served with dinner each evening. They seated us at a different table at each meal so that we could meet other guests. We also considered it a real bonus that children are welcome here. Their meal-time conversations were often humorous and added much to the charm. Each evening Paul would place a snack of fresh fruit or homemade cookies out for us to serve ourselves. There was no shortage of activities to keep us occupied—they provide free use of their canoes, sailboats, paddleboats, and rowboats. Children and adults enjoyed relaxing on the private beach complete with lounge chairs. There are numerous hiking trails in the area, including Blue Mountain. If the weather isn't favor-able to outdoor activities, you can curl up in a chair by the fireplace in the lodge and read one of the books from their library, or go shopping in any of the many art and craft stores in the region. The Adirondack Museum is also just five minutes away.

"Hemlock Hall is definitely a jewel in the rough, tucked away in the Adirondack wilderness and combining companionable comfort far from the tourist crowds." *(Tim & Susan McDaniel)* More comments please.

Open May 15 to Oct. 15.
Rooms 23 rooms in motel units, lodge rooms, and 1- and 2-bedroom cabins, with private or shared bath. Some with kitchen, porch, fireplace.
Facilities Restaurant, living room, game room, library. Lakefront with beach, canoeing, boating, sailing, fishing, hiking.

Location N NY, Adirondacks. From S & W: take I-90 to Exit 31 at Utica; take Rte. 12 N 20 m to Alder Creek; go N on Rte. 28 to Blue Mt. Lake. From E, take I-90 to Exit 24 at Albany. Go N on I-87 to Exit 23 at Warrensburg. Follow sign to Rte. 28 & go N. At intersection of Rtes. 28, 30, & 28N, go N on 28N ¾ m and look for sign. Lodge is 1 m off road on N shore of lake.
Credit cards None accepted.
Rates MAP, $101–113 cottages, $70–97 doubles. For single rate deduct $15. Extra person in room, $27; child 2–8, $18. 3-night minimum for advance reservations. Alc breakfast $5, alc lunch $5, alc dinner $10.

CAZENOVIA

Founded in 1793, lakeside Cazenovia became a summer retreat for wealthy big-city families after the Civil War, and many of its finest mansions date from this period. The lake remains a focus of activity to this day, with fishing, swimming, and sailing leading in popularity, along with golf, hiking, tennis, and horseback riding. Winter favorites include ice-skating, hockey, ice-fishing, sleigh rides, downhill and cross-country skiing.

Information please: We've received mixed reports on the **Brewster Inn** (6 Ledyard Avenue, 13035; 315–655–9232), an elaborate mansion-turned-inn with antique-filled rooms, a lakeside restaurant, and a beautiful setting. More comments please.

Cazenovia is in central New York state, 20 miles southeast of Syracuse.

Brae Loch Inn
5 Albany Street, Rte. 20, 13035

Tel: 315–655–3431

With so many innkeepers falling victim to burnout, and uncounted inns changing hands every few years, we have a special fondness for long-time family-owned inns. The Brae Loch was opened in 1946 by Scottish-born Adam Barr; 44 years later, the inn is still run with a Scottish theme by Adam's son Grey and his grandson Jim. Dinner specialities change nightly but might include Cornish game hen with apricot sauce or salmon grilled with fresh vegetables and sauced with bearnaise.

"We arrived on a hot, humid day and were shown to our air-conditioned suite, with a king canopy bed in a huge room, decorated in antiques. I had a chance to see the other rooms and even the least expensive, with two antique sleigh beds, is delightful." *(Wendi Van Exan)*

"The old country Scottish theme, the delicious meals, the warmth of owner Grey Barr and his staff take you back to a quieter time. Everything, from parking to plumbing to the peaceful lakeside location, makes for a delightful stay." *(Richard Streeter)*

And a suggested improvement: "Our spacious room was very clean and well-equipped, but breakfast consisted only of coffee and cold pastries."

Open All year. Restaurant closed Dec. 24, 25.
Rooms 1 suite, 13 doubles. 12 with private bath and/or shower, telephone, radio, TV, air-conditioning. 6 with desk.

Facilities Parlor with fireplace, restaurant, lounge, bar, banquet room, gift shop. Golf nearby, 1 block to Lake Cazenovia for water sports.
Location 3 blocks from town center.
Restrictions Smoking restricted. Traffic noise in some rooms.
Credit cards Amex, DC, MC, Visa.
Rates Room only, $80–125 suite, $69–80 double. Extra person in room, $10. Cot, $5. 15% service charge. Alc dinner $25–35.
Extras Crib available.

Lincklaen House
79 Albany Street, P.O. Box 36, 13035

Tel: 315–655–3461

Built in 1835 as a luxurious stopover for travelers, Lincklaen House has provided lodging for many prominent figures over the years, including President and Mrs. Grover Cleveland and John D. Rockefeller. The main floor has high ceilings with handsome classical carved moldings, painted wood panels, and impressive Williamsburg chandeliers. Afternoon tea is available in the East Room, decorated with carved woodwork, beautiful antiques, comfortable sofas, and often a fire in the fireplace. Traditional American cuisine is served in the main dining room, and a continental breakfast is offered to guests in the more casual Delft Room. A quiet backyard courtyard is pleasant for a pre-dinner drink in good weather. The colonial-style guest rooms have stenciled walls, swagged window treatments, and white chenille spreads; most of the bathrooms and a few of the guest rooms are quite small.

The hotel has been owned by the Tobin family since 1956, and is now managed by Howard Kaler.

"From the time we entered the newly-restored front lobby to the time we reluctantly left the next morning, we felt at home and welcomed by the friendly, helpful staff—the very hospitable and patient manager, Howard, sets the tone here. Our room was decorated with period furnishings, stenciling, plenty of reading lamps, thick towels, new blankets; extra pillows were cheerfully brought up to our room after a last minute request at 10 P.M. There was a selection of muffins, fruit, and juice for breakfast, appealingly displayed on the dining room table; the private patio was a peaceful spot to start the day, enjoying good conversation with the other guests. From the inn it was easy to walk around the village, browsing in the antique shops and just savoring the beauty of the area." *(Tom & Mary Jane Tesoriero, also John Voorhes)*

Open All year. Closed Christmas, Jan. 1.
Rooms 3 suites, 18 doubles—all with private bath and/or shower, telephone, TV, desk, air-conditioning.
Facilities Dining room, living room, TV room, tavern with live music in winter, patio. Golf, water sports nearby. 5 min. to cross-country, 25 min. to downhill skiing.
Location Center of town.
Restrictions Traffic noise might disturb light sleepers in front rooms.
Credit cards MC, Visa.
Rates B&B, $100–130 suite, $70–95 double, $65–90 single. Extra person in room $8. Alc lunch, $6–9; alc dinner, $21. Mid-week discount; corporate rates. 2-night weekend minimum May, October.
Extras Pets permitted by prior arrangement. Crib, babysitting available.

CHESTERTOWN

Information please: Built in 1860, **Friends Lake Inn** (Friends Lake Road, 12817; 518–494–4751), owned by Sharon and Greg Taylor, offers intricate tin ceilings and original chestnut woodwork in a country Victorian setting, along with access to the areas innumerable outdoor pleasures—hiking, bicycling, white-water rafting, golf, and skiing. In Chestertown's historic district is the **Chester Inn** (Main Street, P.O. Box 163, 12817; 518–494–4148), a handsome Greek Revival home built in 1837 and listed on the National Register of Historic Places. The interior features solid Honduran mahogany woodwork, period antiques, and Shaker reproduction furnishings; rates include a full breakfast. Reports?

The Balsam House	*Tel:* 518–494–2828
Friends Lake Road, 12817	494–4431

The Balsam House was built as the Valentine Hotel in 1891, a typical Adirondack hotel of the period, with 39 rooms and four baths. Frank Ellis bought the building in 1981 and gutted it, leaving mainly doors, woodwork, and hardwood floors from which eleven layers of paint were scraped. The interior is furnished eclectically, with Victorian pieces, comfortable couches, and Oriental rugs. During the winter, Saturday night sleigh rides are offered to guests (at an extra charge). Summer attractions include the inn's private beach, with lunches served at the beach house. The cuisine is "country French," including such entrées as shrimp in cream sauce with Pernod, garlic, and white wine; braised sweetbreads with bordelaise sauce; and veal cordon rouge. The inn is managed by Shaun Green.

"We had a comfortable room up under the eaves, with windows on the fall foliage we had come to see, and skylights to let in the morning sun. The inn provides bicycles, rowboats, picnic baskets, and all sorts of other amenities, along with menus of local restaurants. We chose to eat at the inn, and we chose well. Every part of our dinner, from the cold smoked fish plate and hot shrimp appetizers, through fine continental main dishes, to peach melba and *poire Hélène,* was well prepared. The wine list contains a good selection of California wines, fairly priced. The service was terrific, careful but not smothering." *(Hillary Huebsch Cohen)*

"The inn and its setting are beautiful, and the food is excellent. Our room was small but adequate. It's run like a small hotel; service is not as personalized as some places we've been." *(DM)*

Open All year.
Rooms 1 suite, 19 doubles, all with private bath and/or shower.
Facilities Restaurant; living room; breakfast room; TV room with movies, games; lounge with guitar music weekends in winter, nightly in summer. 22 acres on Friends Lake, with croquet, shuffleboard, beach, swimming, boating, fishing, cross-country skiing, and skating. 15 m to downhill skiing at Gore Mt. Horseback, carriage riding nearby.

Location Adirondack region, NE NY. 70 m N of Albany, 18 m NW of Lake George. 5 m S of town. Off I-87, take Rte. 9 to Rte. 28. Turn right off of Rte. 28 onto Potter Brook Rd. 4 m down on left is The Balsam House.
Credit cards Amex, DC, MC, Visa.
Rates All rates based on double occupancy. B&B, $95–145 suite, $75–95 double, $60–80 single. MAP, $145–185 suite, $125–145 double, $75–95 single, plus 7% tax and 18% service. Extra person in room, $10. 2-night minimum on weekends. Ski free midweek packages. Alc lunch, $8; alc dinner, $33.
Extras Cribs, babysitting, games available.

CLARENCE

Asa Ransom House
10529 Main Street (Route 5), 14031

Tel: 716–759–2315

A country inn that combines good food and comfortable lodging in a pleasant and welcoming atmosphere is the kind of inn we are most pleased to list in this guide, and the Asa Ransom House fits the bill to a "T." Longtime owners Robert and Judith Lenz have decorated the inviting rooms with antiques and period reproductions, country wallpapers and colonial motifs. The inn is popular with visitors and locals alike for its good country cooking. Prices are extremely reasonable, and among the many house specialties are a variety of tempting deep-dish pot pies—chicken and leek, steak and kidney, and salmon and vegetable topped with cheese pastry. As might be expected from an inn located in a wine-growing region, the cellar features an excellent selection of New York's finest labels at very fair prices.

"From your time of arrival, when Judy brings a basket of fruit and cheese to your room, to the regretful time of departure, guests are treated with concern and attention." *(Dave & Lou Hardman)*

"Bob and Judy Lenz are a charming couple who obviously care deeply about high-quality inn service. Beds are excellent, lighting is good for reading in bed, the bathrooms are modern—spotlessly clean without a hint of wear. The food is consistently well prepared and delicious, with interesting menu innovations. Particularly outstanding are the dessert selections, including homemade ice creams; the special breads; and the beautiful presentation." *(Mr. & Mrs. David McConnell)*

"Our room had just been refurbished, and the bathroom had new plumbing. Parking is ample and the inn's location well back from the highway was quiet. The sitting room invites guests with its blazing fire, jigsaw puzzles, and comfortable chairs for reading." *(Ronald & Shirley Martin)*.

Open Feb. through Dec.
Rooms 4 doubles, all with private bath and/or shower, radio, air-conditioning. 1 with desk. 2 with telephone.
Facilities Restaurant, tap room, library with games, gift shop. 2 acres with herb & flower gardens, pond. Swimming pool, tennis nearby; 2 m to golf.
Location W NY. 16 m NE of Buffalo, 28 m SE of Niagara Falls. Take Exit 49 from I-90. Go N on Rte. 78 (Transit Rd.) to Rte. 5. Go E 5 m to inn at corner of Main and Ransom Rd.
Restrictions No smoking. No children under 6.

Credit cards Discover, MC, Visa.
Rates B&B, $85–95 double, $65–75 single. MAP, $125 double. Extra person in room $15. 11% service charge. Alc lunch, $6–9; alc dinner, $14–22. Children's menu.
Extras Station pickups. Crib available. Spanish spoken.

COLD SPRING

Just 90 minutes north of New York City is the charming Hudson River village of Cold Spring. Its main street runs steeply downhill from Route 9D to the river, and is lined with charmingly restored (for the most part) 19th century buildings and intriguing shops. The bandstand overlooking the river offers beautiful views of the Hudson Highlands. Do come here for a delightful escape from Manhattan. Good restaurants abound—and there's a long list of sights worth seeing: Boscobel Restoration, FDR's home and library and the Vanderbilt Mansion in Hyde Park; the quiet little village of Garrison's Landing; and across the river, West Point and Storm King Art Center. For a breath of fresh air, hike the stream-side trails at Manitoga, on Route 9D just south of the Garrison turn-off. But don't come to this area looking for bargains. Room rates are very high (and still climbing) for what you get, and parking in Cold Spring is inconvenient at best.

Information please: The **Olde Post Inn** (43 Main Street, 10516; 914–265–2510) is an 1820s tavern known for its terrific weekend jazz and comfortable restaurant; four basic rooms are available for B&B. The **Hudson House** (2 Main Street, 10516; 914–265–9355) is just across from the river, and about 6 of its 15 guest rooms have magnificent river views. The inn was extensively restored several years ago, and the guest rooms are sparely decorated with delicately flowered wallpapers, natural pine furniture, and oversize cookie cutter ornaments; bathrooms are new but basic. The downstairs restaurant area bustles on weekends (there's no parlor) when rates start at $100. We thought it overpriced but welcome additional reports.

We'd also like reports on **Plumbush** (Route 9D, 10516; 914–265–3904) a gracious mansion built in 1869 and best known known for its superb French and Swiss cuisine. Its three guest rooms are decorated in period, and the rates ($95–125) include a breakfast of fresh fruit and juice, granola, baked goods and pastries. Reports please.

Pig Hill B&B   *Tel:* 914–265–9247
73 Main Street, 10516

"Although Pig Hill is right in the middle of town on Main Street, we drove by it twice before finding either its name or street number. Watch instead for the gift shop devoted to little oinkers and other collectibles at the front of the inn. Wendy O'Brien has owned this B&B since 1986, and has done a stunning job of decorating it with antiques, nearly all of which are for sale. When we were there, a massive English pine table took up a good section of the spacious dining room, where guests gather for the full breakfast—which might include souffle rolls, egg pot pies, fresh fruit and juice, and homebaked breads. The parlor is small and formally decorated, so guests tend to relax in the lovely backyard garden, or in their rooms. Each room is very different, but all are stunning. One is rustic, with unpeeled birch log furnishings and a oil painting of a friendly Holstein; another is elegant, with flowered chintz headboard, matching tables and pillow shams, and an antique crazy quilt; a third is more masculine, done in bold shades of green and red (looks much better than it sounds). All rooms have two comfortable chairs and a small table (many guests take breakfast here), and we'd guess that quite a few guests come to spend a special weekend alone with their significant other. Each bathroom has an adorable bar of soap shaped like a little pink pig; we saved ours, and used the other soaps provided for washing." (SWS)

"We arrived late in the afternoon with winter light slanting from the river and glowing on the bricks of the inn. Our room was like a small cabin in the wilderness, complete with antlers over the fireplace and logs ready to burn. The little seating area had Adirondack style furniture, a coffee table, an original painting on the wall, and shelves with books and magazines. An old map and history book on Cold Spring were especially enjoyable. Each item in the room was carefully and thoughtfully chosen. Many were for sale, an extension of the antique shop downstairs. Since we like a cool room at night, we were delighted that the windows opened, and that our room had its own thermostat. Our sleep was also enhanced by the brand-new mattress. The manager suggested we have dinner at the Riverview, within walking distance of the inn—like a meal in NYC's Soho, but at half the cost. The innkeeper was polite and helpful with a good sense of humor, but she respected our privacy. Breakfast, brought to our room on a tray, was memorable—hot homemade muffins and toast, a ramekin of coddled eggs with sliced tomato and cheddar cheese, fresh-squeezed orange juice, and at our request, fresh brewed decaf." (Katherine Desmond)

Open All year.
Rooms 8 doubles—4 with private bath, 4 with maximum of 4 sharing bath. Most with fireplace or woodstove. All with air-conditioning, fan.
Facilities Dining room, parlor, gift shop, garden patio.
Location In town. S side of Main Street. Walking distance to train.
Restrictions Limited off-street parking.
Credit cards Amex, DC, MC, Visa.
Rates B&B, $140 suite, $115 double, $90 single. Extra person in room, $25. Picnics for two, $50; dinner, $60 per person.

Three Rock B&B
3 Rock Street, 10516

Tel: 914–265–2330

"A fabulous place, with magnificent views of the Hudson. The house is very unusual architecturally, with hundreds of small-paned windows to take in the vistas. It was originally intended as a private home, but the building/owner is away too much, and he now offers magnificent suites for B&B. Very relaxed, low-key service. It's right in the village and a short walk to shops and restaurants. Although the price was above our normal budget, we were not disappointed and would recommend it highly." (Sally Sieracki)

Open All year.
Rooms 3 suites—all with private whirlpool tubs.
Facilities Dining room, living room with fireplace, deck.
Location In town. 2-minute walk to train. From traffic light on Rte. 9D, turn down Main St. and take 3rd left onto Rock St. #3 is 1st drive on right.
Restrictions No smoking.
Credit cards None accepted.
Rates B&B, $100–135 suite. No charge for children under 6 in parents' room.

COOPERSTOWN

Cooperstown was founded in 1786 by William Cooper. His son, James Fenimore Cooper, became world famous as the author of a series of books known as the Leatherstocking Tales. Cooperstown is also the place where Abner Doubleday invented the game of baseball in 1839, and the home of the National Baseball Hall of Fame. The Glimmerglass Opera Theater, noted for its original productions of operas, has a beautiful opera house, right on the lake. Other attractions include the Farmer's Museum, a working museum depicting eighteenth- and nineteenth-century life; Fenimore House, with a collection of American folk art and Cooper memorabilia; and Otsego Lake, with three areas for public swimming, boating, and good fishing. There's plenty of hiking, bicycling, golf, and tennis in summer, and cross-country skiing, skating, and snow-tubing in the winter.

Cooperstown is in New York's Central/Leatherstocking region, 30 miles south of the NY State Thruway (I-90), 20 miles north of Oneonta, and 70 miles west of Albany. From the west, use Thruway Exit 30 at Herkimer (Route 28); from the east, Thruway Exit 25A at Route I-88.

We'd like to get some recent reader reports on **The J.P. Sill House** (63 Chestnut Street, 13326; 607–547–2633), listed for several years in this book, now under the new ownership of Laura and Angelo Zucotti. A restored, late-19th-century Italianate Victorian built of brick and cut stone, the J.P. Sill House has original handcrafted woodwork, marble fireplaces, and etched glass. Previous owners Joyce Bohlman and Robert Lake wallpapered the house with magnificent Bradbury & Bradbury period reproduction papers, with striking results. The inn is within walking distance of the town and the large yard provides ample off-street parking. "One might think that the most memorable moments of a trip to Cooperstown would be spent in the Baseball Hall of Fame. To our pleasant surprise, it was the J.P. Sill House that gave us the most memories. We marveled at the long staircase with a massive balustrade, which is the first thing one sees upon entering the house." *(Jim & Cindy Blank)*

Briar Hill Farm   *Tel:* 607–264–8100
Briar Hill Road, RD 2, Box 634, 13326

"Briar Hill Farm is a lovingly restored historic farmhouse in the Mohawk Valley between the Adirondacks and the Catskill Mountains. The warm, individual attention given guests by the owners, Nancy and Web

Tilton, makes visiting this inn an unusual experience. The views of the lake to the south and the mountains of Vermont and upper New York State are marvelous. The guest room is furnished with antiques, including a comfortable four poster Sheraton arched canopy bed, a Chippendale mahogany bachelor's chest, good reading lights, and comfortable chairs. Adjoining it is a very large private bath equipped with luxurious, fluffy bath towels and a selection of toiletries.

"The Tiltons came to their Cooperstown location from Washington, D.C. Both are very involved locally and can point out the spots worth seeing, including the many historical points of interest. The house is spotless, breakfasts delicious." *(Betty & Pete Moran)*

Unusual extras included in the B&B rate are a complimentary car wash and vacuuming—courtesy of Web—and a ride in Nancy's jeep to hilltops offering limitless views. Breakfast includes fresh-squeezed orange juice, melon, cereal, pancakes or waffles, eggs, bacon, sausage, or kippers, muffins and toast.

Open All year.
Rooms 1 double with full private bath, telephone, clock/radio, TV, desk, fan.
Facilities Country kitchen. 130 acres with pond, woods, old smokehouse. Golf nearby. 6 m to cross-country skiing.
Location 10 m N of town, 5 min. from Glimmerglass State Park. From Cooperstown, go 9½ m N on East Lake Rd. (Rt. 31) to Briar Hill Rd. Turn right and go 1 m to inn.
Restrictions No smoking in guest rooms. No children under 9.
Credit cards None accepted.
Rates B&B, $75 double. Extra person in room, $25. Free car wash with night's stay (no kidding). No tipping.

Creekside B&B
Fork Shop Road, RD 1, Box 206, 13326
Tel: 607–547–8203

Although all are welcome, musically-oriented travelers will especially enjoy the Creekside B&B, owned by Fred and Gwen Ermlich, founders of and performers with Glimmerglass Opera. Residents of Cooperstown since 1970, the Ermlichs opened their colonial-style home to B&B guests in 1983. In addition to three guest rooms in the house, there's a three-room cottage which, Gwen reports, is "for those looking for something extra special. It has a canopy bed, living room with wet bar, and a private deck overlooking acres of lawn and creek." Rates include a full breakfast prepared by Fred (perhaps scrambled eggs with herbs or cinnamon French toast) and afternoon refreshments. A low cholesterol breakfast is also available upon request.

"Gwen is a gracious innkeeper who did everything she could to make our stay a happy one. Our room was clean and comfortable." *(Nancy Thomas)*

Open All year.
Rooms 1 cottage, 1 suite, 2 doubles—all with private bath and/or shower. Some with ceiling fan, deck, or TV. Cottage with wet bar, private deck.
Facilities Dining room, living room, guest refrigerator, deck. Creek for swimming, fishing.
Location 3 m from town. From Cooperstown, turn right onto Rte. 26. Go 2.5 m and turn left on Fork Shop Rd. Inn is 1st house on left.

Restrictions No smoking.
Credit cards Amex, MC, Visa.
Rates B&B, $100–110 cottage, $85–95 suite, $65–85 double. Extra person in room, $10. 2-3 night weekend/holiday minimum. Discount for extended stay.
Extras Crib, babysitting available. French, German spoken.

The Inn at Brook Willow
Tel: 607–547–9700
RD 2, Box 514, 13326

Brook Willow is a Victorian "cottage" house, owned by Jack and Joan Grimes since 1976. Guest rooms are airy and spacious, furnished with antiques and lots of homey touches. It's located in a part of Cooperstown known as Lentsville, whose population peaked in 1878 at 36 inhabitants. Joan notes that "after a stay at our inn, guests should return to their worlds refreshed, unstressed, and peaceful. Ours is a place where reflections on the past and plans for the future unfold."

"If you don't slow down, you'll likely miss the hidden driveway and small white sign to Brook Willow, but once you make the turn, go over the bridge and up to the house, you'll slow down for sure. The lovely main house and cozy barn are completely surrounded by willows, oaks, and maples, and the grounds with pond, meadow, and babbling brook are perfect." *(Emily Zacharda)* "Antiques and carefully chosen combinations of wallpapers, fabrics, and colors abound, right down to the changes in china to match the breakfast tablecloth. Plan to enjoy relaxed conversation with the other guests, and with Joan and Jack." *(Jo-Ann & Lloyd Jaeger)*

"This Victorian-style B&B has such personal touches as family pictures in antique frames, doilies on the table, and plants and flowers in each room. We loved the pond with the ducks and frogs." *(Cynthia Ziegler)* "Our spacious room has a queen-size bed, closet, dresser, desk and chairs. Small touches such as pictures, an old washbasin, chamber pot, and coat tree gave it a homey old-fashioned touch. Extra touches included a tray of fruit and herbal shampoos." *(Lisa Fadelici)* "After an early morning walk around the property, we were greeted by the aroma of blueberry muffins baking as we entered the house. We breakfasted on those melt-in-your-mouth muffins, with fine china and silver service complementing the candles and flowers on the table." *(Marcia & Albert Lichtsinn)*

"Our room in the restored barn had a queen-sized bed with an antique headboard, coordinating wallpaper, floral sheets and comforter, and a very firm mattress. The ceiling fan and generous-sized window kept us cool on a hot day. Our bathroom had excellent plumbing and lighting; we were impressed by the antique fixtures on the marble sink. Impeccable cleanliness everywhere." *(Patricia A. Moran)*

"Joan and Jack Grimes are the quintessential hosts, making you feel warm and welcome and introducing you to your fellow baseball fans. Breakfast-time is filled with funny anecdotes about the town and tips on how to get a great buy at an antiques auction." *(Mary & Roger Bow, and others)*

Open All year.
Rooms 1 suite, 1 double in main house with private bath. 3 doubles in restored barn with private bath and/or shower, desk, ceiling fans.

Facilities Dining area, living room, family room with TV, games; fireplaces; wicker garden room, porch, barbecue. 14 acres with pond, brook, gardens, meadows, cross-country skiing.
Location 6 m to town. Turn E on Rte. 33 and follow to inn.
Restrictions No smoking.
Credit cards None accepted.
Rates B&B, $55–80 suite or double, $40–55 single. Extra person in room, $15. No charge for children under 2. No tipping. 2-night minimum stay on weekends.
Extras Station pickups. Cribs, babysitting, games available.

The Inn at Cooperstown
16 Chestnut Street, 13326

Tel: 607–547–5756

Innkeeper Michael Jerome restored and reopened this inn in 1985. Although used for a time as an apartment house, it was built in 1874 as the annex to the Fenimore Hotel, which was then across the street. The building was designed with a mansard roof and detailing typical of the Second Empire style. The architect, Henry J. Hardenbergh, was also responsible for New York City's Plaza Hotel, Dakota apartments, and Waldorf-Astoria Hotel.

"The towels were good-sized, the beds firm, the plumbing new. The public rooms are pleasant and comfortable. The inn is within walking distance of most of the area's attractions and restaurants. The credit for everything goes to the innkeeper, Michael Jerome. He was pleasant, friendly, knowledgeable, and concerned." *(R.M. Hannan)* "Pleasant large rooms; ample off-street parking. The continental breakfast was prompt, with endless cups of coffee and juice and freshly baked muffins."*(Mary Saunders)*

"The inn was clean, quiet, and the window in our room could be opened for fresh air—a big plus for us. The beds were excellent, the continental breakfast undistinguished. This inn has great possibilities, but could use a little more decorating before it's really "finished.' " *(ELC)*

"We found the inn to be exactly as you've described it—spotlessly clean, pleasant, and conveniently located, with an accommodating innkeeper. The only part that we'd like to take issue with is the comment about the inn's decor. While this may be true, one gets the impression that it's not simply an oversight. Instead, you get the feeling that Michael is taking his time to decorate the inn slowly, carefully, and thoughtfully." *(Jane Fyffe)*

Open All year.
Rooms 17 doubles with private shower, fan.
Facilities Dining area; 2 sitting rooms with TV, books, fireplace; conference room; veranda. Nearby lake for swimming, fishing, boating. Cross-country skiing nearby, 1 hr to downhill.
Location Center of Cooperstown Historic District, on W side of Rte. 80. 3 buildings N of the traffic light.
Credit cards Amex, DC, Discover, MC, Visa.
Rates B&B, $75–90 double, $65–80 single, plus 6% tax. Extra person in room, $10. Weekend and midweek ski packages in winter and spring.
Extras Ramp, specially equipped bathroom for disabled. Station pickups. Crib, babysitting available.

Lake View Motel
RD 2, P.O. Box 932, 13326

Tel: 607–547–9740

Patty and Doug Muehl have owned the Lake View since 1976. They note that this "is a small country motel owned and operated by our family. The difference between our motel and others of similar size is the feeling of deep personal satisfaction in knowing our guests have had more than a place to sleep—someone's guest bedroom, not an impersonal motel room. Our attention to detail extends to extra amenities and care in decorating. Our grounds and flowers are lovely, and rooms have breathtaking views of Otsego Lake."

Mrs. James McAllister persuaded us to add the Lake View to the very short list of motels listed in this guide, because of its "cleanliness, comfort, and home-away-from-home feeling, along with the moderate prices essential to retirees on a fixed, modest income." She also recommends "visiting the nearby village of Laurens. Travel winding country roads to an abandoned cemetery where three Revolutionary War heroes are buried. One is Jonas Hodgskin who fought as a lad of 16 at the Battle of Stoney Point with General Anthony Wayne." More comments please.

Open April 1 to Nov. 15.
Rooms 2 cottages, 12 doubles, 2 singles, all with private bath and/or shower. All with telephone, radio, TV, desk, air-conditioning.
Facilities Porch with deck chairs. 1.3 acres with beach on Lake Otsego, fishing dock. Boat livery for water sports.
Location 6 m N of Cooperstown on Rte. 80E.
Restrictions No smoking in some rooms.
Credit cards MC, Visa.
Rates Room only, $50–85 double, $48–82 single. Extra person in room, $5. Cottage, $350–450 weekly. 2-night weekend minimum.Continental breakfast available off-season.
Extras Crib available, $5.

The Phoenix on River Road
RR 33, RD 3, P.O. Box 150, 13326

Tel: 607–547–8250

Phoenix Mills was a bustling village a century ago, with a hotel, store, school, several mills, and a factory. Today, only the hotel remains, its name virtually the same, although its focus has shifted. Under the ownership of Mary Dunkle and Meg and Jim Myers, the tavern, which once served mill workers, has been restored as a cheery Williamsburg blue and white breakfast room; a casual common room with comfortable couches and wing chairs is adjacent. The guest rooms have all been furnished simply, but with considerable care and attention to detail, including colonial-style muslin tie-back curtains and gentle floral bedspreads. Furniture is mostly white wicker, with some freshly painted older bureaus.

"Professionally and beautifully done. The inn is completely restored in soft country colors. The curtains and bedspreads were designed and sewn by the mother-daughter owners. Breakfast included fresh fruit, corn muffins, and coffee, served in the tavern room." *(Rosemary Schlegel)* More comments please.

Open All year.
Rooms 8 doubles—3 with private shower, 5 with maximum of 5 people sharing bath. All with ceiling fan.
Facilities Breakfast/tavern room; common room with TV, wood-burning stove, games, books; balconies. 9 acres. Swimming, boating, fishing, cross-country skiing nearby.
Location 2½ m from center. From Susquehanna Ave., take Rte. 33 S 2 m to inn.
Restrictions No smoking.
Credit cards None accepted.
Rates B&B, $90 suite (sleeps 4), $45–60 double. Extra person in room, $10. 2-night holiday weekend minimum.
Extras Crib, babysitting available. Some French spoken.

CORNING

Rosewood Inn   *Tel:* 607–962–3253
134 East First Street, 14830

Built in 1855 as a Greek Revival home, and then redone as an English Tudor style in 1917, the Rosewood is furnished in Victorian antiques and handmade quilts. Each guest room has a special theme, from railroading to whaling to antique glass. Owners Winnie and Dick Peer are knowledgeable about Corning and will gladly assist with dining, shopping, or sightseeing plans.

"Best part was the intellectual milieu at the elaborate breakfast table, from our affable host to the other guests who included a tinsmith, a violinist turned engineer, and a stock broker. A stimulating two-hour conversation carried us through baked apples with cinnamon, maple syrup, walnuts, and raisins; scrambled eggs with pesto cheese, fresh baking powder biscuits, pumpkin bread, brandied sweet butter, and orange scented coffee. Breakfast was accompanied by Dick's own morning paper with weather forecast, headlines of the day and local sights." *(Zita Knific)*

"Mrs. Peer welcomed us and invited us to help ourselves to hot tea and cookies. Each elegantly furnished guest room has individual character, named after a well-known person of the Victorian era. We stayed in the Herman Melville room, decorated with whaling memorabilia, walnut beds, and a spacious private bath. Located at the back of the inn, it was very quiet and comfortable with plenty of storage space, and good reading lights. The inn is within walking distance of the restored downtown area, the glass museum, the Rockwell Museum, outlet shopping, and many good restaurants. At breakfast we were treated to a concert of glass music, a perfect complement to the granola, fresh fruit, and delicious bread pudding. Mr. Peer hosted breakfast while Mrs. P. served and then visited with each guest. There were at least ten of us at breakfast, so this personal touch was remarkable. We also enjoyed the guest sitting room on the second floor, a great place to visit with fellow guests, and to browse through the menu basket provided. A lovely inn with very personable, caring owners." *(April Burwell)*

"The inn's location is perfect—just two blocks from Main Street, yet on a quiet, tree-lined street; two suites have private entrances adjacent to the driveway. The Victorian decor in the living room is striking, from the rust-colored velvet swag curtains to a proper (for Victorians, that is) velvet and lace mantel drape. The rooms are furnished with period antiques; the Frederick Carder suite has beaded board panelling and a marble sink built into a rosewood bureau. The Peers have thoughtfully provided lighting on both sides of the bed, using wall sconces where there isn't enough room for a bedside table." *(NB)*

Note: The Peers recently decided to take things a little easier, and placed the inn on the market. Inquire further when making reservations.

Open All year.
Rooms 2 suites with private bath; 5 doubles—3 with private bath and/or shower, 2 with a maximum of 4 people sharing bath. All with air-conditioning. Some with telephone, TV, fireplace. 1 suite with kitchen and private entrance.
Facilities Dining room, sitting room with TV. Off-street parking.
Location C NY, Finger Lakes Region. Town center. Follow Rt. 17 to downtown Corning. Turn S on Chemung St., go 1 block, turn right on First St. to inn.
Restrictions No smoking in guest rooms.
Credit cards Amex, DC, MC, Visa.
Rates B&B, $90–95 suite, $68–85 double, $60–75 single, plus 7% tax. Extra person in room, $15. 2–night weekend minimum June–Oct.
Extras Station pickups. Crib available.

DOVER PLAINS

Old Drovers Inn   *Tel:* 914–832–9311
Old Drovers Inn Road (Old Post Road), 12522

Named for the professional middlemen or "drovers" who purchased herds of cattle and swine from New England farmers and "drove" them down the post roads to New York City's markets, this inn has been welcoming travelers for 250 years. Well known for its restaurant, the Tap Room, the second floor has guest rooms furnished with antiques. The breakfast room is decorated with hand painted murals by artist Edward Paine, depicting Hudson Valley landmarks. Innkeeper Alice Pitcher notes that guests are pleasantly surprised to find such a romantic getaway so close to the New York metropolitan area.

"While many people seem to prefer the 'Old Meeting Room' for an evening's stay, my favorite is the 'Cherry Room' with its generous proportions, richly colored decor, slightly sloping wide-planked floor and fireplace. The real atmosphere of Old Drover rests in proprietors Alice Pitcher, Kemper Peacock, and long-time host Charlie Wilbur. They are professional, elegant, witty, and fun. They're knowledgeable about Dutchess County and can direct visitors to the many charms of the countryside as well as the best spots for antiques." *(Nora Kennington)*

"The food is better than ever, and the new owners have done an authentic job of redecorating. Nothing was painted that shouldn't have been, and no architectural 'improvements' altered the structure. In short, an absolutely impeccable old inn." *(Janet Gaillard)*

134

"It's worth a detour just to stop at the tavern for a dish of their signature turkey hash with mustard sauce, and the truly colonial atmosphere. The inn is furnished with antiques throughout, and lovely murals in the breakfast room, where omelets with wild mushrooms and Belgian waffles are served. Though not at all fancy, the guest rooms have true country inn charm." *(SWS)*

Some areas for improvement: "We loved our stay here, but expected better bedside lighting and a shower, considering the rates."

Open All year. Restaurant closed Tues., Wed.
Rooms 4 doubles, all with private bath, desk, air-conditioning. 1 with shower/ tub combination, 3 with tub only.
Facilities Restaurant, breakfast room, sitting room with fireplace, library. 12 acres. Tennis, golf nearby.
Location E NY, Dutchess County. 15 m E of Poughkeepsie. From New York City, take Hutchinson River Pkwy to I-684. Take I-684 N to Brewster. Turn N on Route 22 and continue 21 m N to inn. Watch for sign.
Credit cards MC, Visa.
Rates B&B, $110–170 double, $90–150 single. Extra person in room $25. 15% service. 2-night minimum May-June, Sept.-Oct., holiday weekends. Alc lunch $30, alc dinner, $50.
Extras Station pickups. Small dogs allowed by prior arrangement. French spoken.

DRYDEN

Sarah's Dream   *Tel:* 607–844–4321
49 West Main Street, 13053

Owned by Judi Williams and Ken Morusty since 1987, Sarah's Dream was built in 1828 and is listed on the National Register of Historic Places. Opening a B&B was Judi's mother's idea, and the source of its name. Rooms are furnished primarily with Victorian antiques, including marble-topped tables, wicker chairs, and elaborately carved canopy beds. Judi notes that "our many antiques lend an atmosphere of grace and elegance, though we are relaxed, casual hosts." Breakfasts vary daily, but might include melon with raspberries and kiwi, oatmeal cookies, granola, biscuits, apple tarts, and sweet pepper quiche. Refreshments available throughout the day include hot and cold beverages, fruit, cheese and crackers, cookies, and fruit breads.

Judi doesn't confine her very considerable baking talents to the breakfast table. Tea is served mid-week (by reservation only, at 1 and 2:30 P.M.) with antique china, heirloom silver, and fine linens, a choice of a dozen traditional and herbal teas, and an array of goodies that might include scones, shortbread, walnut pie, cucumber and watercress sandwiches, quiche, cheese and crackers, chocolate torte, banbury tarts, cream puffs, and madeleines.

"This lovely home reflects the caring and personable characters of its owners. Each room has an interesting collection of furnishings, pictures, books, and more, combining cleanliness and comfort with Victorian charm." *(Ethel & Marshall Weiss)* "Breakfast was delicious, a tin of chocolate chip cookies was always available to munch on, and evening mints were placed on our nightstand. Ken and Judy went beyond the call of duty to make our stay pleasant. This area is lovely year-round, but fall foliage, combined with the pleasures of hiking, bicycling, and wine-touring, make autumn my favorite." *(Leslie Kaufman)*

Open All year.
Rooms 2 suites, 4 doubles—all with private bath and/or shower, air-conditioning, fan. 4 with radio, 3 with desk, 2 with TV, telephone.
Facilities Dining room, living room, library with fireplace, TV/VCR. Tennis, golf nearby. 9 m to Cayuga Lake for water sports. 3 m to cross-country, 8 m to downhill skiing.
Location Finger Lakes region. 9 m NE of Ithaca on Rte. 13. 9 m SW of Cortland. From I-81, exit at Whitney Point and take Rte. 79 W to Richford. Then take Rte. 38 N to Dryden & Rte. 13. 2 blocks to center.
Restrictions Traffic noise in front rooms might disturb light sleepers. No smoking. No children under 10.
Credit cards MC, Visa.
Rates B&B, $85–120 suite, $65–85 double, $55–80 single. 2-night minimum some weekends. Tipping not encouraged. Afternoon tea, $9.
Extras Airport/station pickups.

EAST HAMPTON

Although known best for its beaches and fashionable restaurants and shops, East Hampton actually has many historic homes dating back to the eighteenth century. If you're visiting on a rainy day, stop by to see the Mulford House, dating back to 1680, now a museum of architectural history. East Hampton is on the South Fork of eastern Long Island, reached via the Long Island Expressway or the Southern State Parkway to Route 27.

"The Hamptons are best enjoyed off season, either in the late spring or early autumn. My favorite time is September, when the weather is usually good and the ocean temperature is still relatively high. July and August can be a nightmare on weekends, with unbelievable traffic jams and mobs of trendy people everywhere, although things are much quieter during the week." *(SWS)*

Typical for a resort town, two- and three-night weekend minimums are the rule in season, with four or five nights required for July 4th and Labor Day weekend. Be very sure of your plans before booking; most East Hampton inns give *no refunds* on canceled space (which we find to be a really distasteful policy).

Bassett House Inn   *Tel:* 516–324–6127
128 Montauk Highway, 11937

Unlike traffic today, a passing vehicle was probably a big event when the Bassett House was built back in 1830. Several additions were completed over the years, the last in 1926. Owner Michael Bassett has furnished the rooms with antiques and curios of varying periods, with everything from an old barber's chair to an antique wood-burning stove. A long-time veteran of the innkeeping business, Michael says: "I think my ability to have guests feel at home and comfortable as soon as they arrive is my best asset. I try to encourage a pleasant atmosphere of camaraderie, especially around the long breakfast table. I enjoy what I do and plan to keep on doing it for some time." "Outstanding hospitality, relaxing atmosphere." *(GR)*

"The inn's antiques give it a delicate feeling, yet the mood is relaxed, touched by Michael Bassett's personal style. My room was sparkling clean, service was splendid, and the breakfast not to be missed." *(Jennifer Moriarty)* More comments please.

Open All year.
Rooms 2 suites, 6 doubles, 2 singles—8 with full private bath, 2 with shared bath. All have desk, air-conditioning; 2 have telephone. Radio on request. Suites have Jacuzzi or fireplace.
Facilities Dining room; living room with woodburning stove, TV, game room. 1½ m from ocean.
Location 1½ m from center.
Restrictions Light sleepers should request back rooms.
Credit cards Amex, MC, Visa.
Rates B&B, $125–135 suite, $79–115 double, $42–95 single. Extra person in room, $15. 3-night weekend minimum in season. Off-season rates.
Extras Airport/station pickups. Pets allowed at extra cost. Cribs, play equipment available.

Centennial House
13 Woods Lane, 11937

Tel: 516–324–9414

David Oxford and Harry Chancey have worked hard to restore this 1876 summer cottage to its original elegance and grace. As Harry describes it, "marble bathrooms adjoin bedrooms with English and French furnishings, while the formal parlor boasts two crystal chandeliers and an Italian marble hearth. The spacious Georgian dining room is wainscotted and draped with Williamsburg fabrics."

If you're in the Hamptons, don't try to visit here without an appointment or a reservation. Notes Harry Chancey: "Above all else, we respect our guests' needs for privacy. In order to preserve such privacy in the ambience of a private home, unannounced visits are out of the question. Otherwise, the peace and quiet that draws our guests would be destroyed."

"Exquisite rehabbed Victorian, with magnificent antique furnishings in the guest rooms and baths. Fresh flowers, chocolate truffles, three bottles of liqueurs, and plush robes in our room. Our bath was tremendous, with thick towels, fresh plants, and authentic fixtures. David and Harry were warm, gracious hosts, and provided many helpful hints to enrich our stay . . . charming people. Breakfast, served buffet-style in an elegant setting, was delicious." *(Edith & David De Mar, also Susan Shotzbarger)* More comments please.

Open All year.
Rooms 1 2-bedroom, 2-bath cottage, 3 doubles—all with full private bath, telephone, desk, air-conditioning.
Facilities Dining room, parlor, porch. 4 blocks to ocean.

NEW YORK

Location Entering East Hampton historic district, inn is at 1st traffic light. 4 blocks to beach or shopping.
Restrictions No smoking. Children discouraged.
Credit cards MC, Visa.
Rates Room only, $375 cottage. B&B, $185–250 double. 2–5 night minimum depending on season.
Extras Airport/station pickups. French spoken.

Hedges Inn
74 James Lane, 11937

Tel: 516–324–7100

A flower lined walk leads to the yellow clapboard Hedges Inn, named for William Hedges who held the original land grant in 1652. The property remained in the Hedges family for over 270 years, until 1923. The inn is now home to the Palm Restaurant and fourteen guest rooms.

"Fabulous staff—friendly, delightful people who couldn't do enough for us. The beautifully presented continental breakfast included the best fruit muffins I've ever eaten. Our room was clean but very basic, with an exceptionally comfortable bed and a passable bathroom." *(Laura Bard)* More comments please.

Open March through Dec. Restaurant open Memorial Day through Sept.
Rooms 14 doubles, all with private bath, air-conditioning, clock/radio. Some with desk.
Facilities Restaurant, TV/sitting room, breakfast room, patios. 2½ acres with pond.
Location Between main beach and village business district. ¾ m to center.
Restrictions Light sleepers should request rooms in back.
Credit cards All major credit cards.
Rates B&B, $85–150 double. Extra person in room $15. 3-night summer weekend minimum; 5 nights summer holidays. Alc dinner $35.
Extras Spanish spoken.

Maidstone Arms
207 Main Street, 11937

Tel: 516–324–5006

The Maidstone is set across from the town pond and village green in East Hampton's National Historic District. It was originally built as a private home, then converted to a hotel in the 1870s. Rates include a continental breakfast, served on the plant-filled wicker sun porch. The inn's deservedly popular restaurant, run by Morris Weintraub, serves French cuisine, emphasizing fresh fish and local produce. Innkeepers Rita and Gary Reiswig have owned the Maidstone since 1979; Donna Cullum is the manager.

One of our English readers reports: "Thoroughly in the style of what this book is after—homey and comfortable, with sound, unobtrusive hospitality by the management. This New England–style inn has a clapboard exterior, kept warm with double glazed windows and no drafts. Interior doors never quite fit, but that's all part of the charm. Our room had pleasantly crisp if slightly frilly furnishings (the late Laura Ashley would undoubtedly have approved), old-style but thoroughly serviceable bathroom fittings, a large comfortable bed, and no shortage of hot water.

"The public rooms are very pleasant, and include a considerable library. There is a front sitting/breakfast room, mainly glass on one side, with a large woodstove. The dining room is well frequented, and dinner conducted with style, close attention, and gently self-confident humor." *(Jeremy Larken)*

"Excellent dinners, beautiful glassware. Mrs. Reiswig was warm and gracious. A minor annoyance—the bed sheets were too small for the mattress, and came off without much encouragement; a thoughtless neighbor played his radio or TV too loudly for comfort late one night. Overall a fine choice; we wish we could have stayed longer." *(DF)* More comments please.

Open April to mid-Jan.
Rooms 5 suites, 11 doubles—all with full private bath, telephone, air-conditioning. Some with radio, TV, desk. 3 cottages available for weekly rental.
Facilities Restaurant, bar, sun porch, library. 2 acres with lawn furniture.
Location 15-min. walk to beaches, shops, entertainment. Take Rte. 495 E from NYC to Exit 70. Continue E on Rte. 27 to East Hampton. ½ m from town.
Restrictions Some traffic noise in front rooms.
Credit cards Amex, MC, Visa.
Rates B&B, $150–230 suite, $95–140 double, $90–130 single, plus 7½% tax and 3% service. Extra person in room, $15. Senior discount midweek, off season. Alc dinner, $35.
Extras Airport/station pickups.

1770 House
Tel: 516–324–1770
143 Main Street, 11937

Dating back to the 18th century, the 1770 House served such diverse functions as a general store, private home, and even a boarding school dining hall. It became popular as an inn in the 1940s and '50s with show business and society types, then declined until Sid and Miriam Perle restored it in 1977. Guests enjoy relaxing in the Tap Room, with its open Dutch hearth and old hickory beams, or by the cozy fireplace in the wood-panelled library. Additional accommodations are available in the Philip Taylor House, dating to 1650, just a few doors down on Main Street. Guest rooms are furnished with antiques—four with canopy beds—and rates include a continental breakfast. "Good food in a lovely atmosphere, with pleasant comfortable rooms." *(Janet & Bob Bernstein)* More comments please.

Open All year. Restaurant open Thurs.-Sun. in July, Aug,; Fri.-Sat. from Sept. through June; also holiday Sundays.
Rooms 7 doubles—all with private bath, air-conditioning. 2 with fireplace, 3 with private entrance.
Facilities Restaurant, tavern with fireplace, library with fireplace, gift/antique shop.
Location 1 block from center town. 1 m from ocean.
Restrictions Smoking discouraged. No children under 12.
Credit cards MC, Visa.
Rates B&B, $95–165 double. 2–4 night holiday, summer weekend minimum; 2-night minimum all other weekends. Deposits are non-refundable.

EAST WINDHAM

Point Lookout Mountain Inn   *Tel:* 518–734–3381
Route 23, Box 33, 12439

Although the original Point Lookout Inn was a landmark dating back to the 1920s, a fire destroyed it totally in 1965. Although quickly rebuilt with spacious guest rooms and picture windows to maximize the view, a series of financial setbacks left it on the verge of collapse when Rosemary Jensen, Mariana and Lucio DiToro bought it in 1980. Little by little, they rebuilt and refurnished the motel-style rooms with country decor, swagged window treatments and ladder back chairs and rockers. Rates include a self-service breakfast of yogurt, granola, and pastries. An extensive menu is offered at lunch and dinner, with both Mexican and Italian specialities available; the owners are exceptionally sensitive to dietary needs, and will gladly cater to special requirements.

Rosemary notes that "our most important features are our spectacular setting on a cliffside, overlooking a 270° view encompassing five states, and our caring attitude towards food preparation. We cater to those seeking real food, prepared from scratch, with good nutrition in mind. Our atmosphere is casual and comfortable, to reflect the lifestyle of the mountains. Bicyclists, hikers, skiers, and family vacationers especially enjoy staying with us."

"The dining room with its huge fireplace has a comfortable atmosphere, excellent service, a menu to suit most tastes, and a magnificent view. Our room was large, airy, well appointed and clean, and the same view as the dining room. The bathroom was modern and clean with a memorable shower." *(Kevin Halloran, also Robert Wilk)*

Open May through March.
Rooms 14 doubles—all with private bath and/or shower, radio, TV, desk, fan.
Facilities Dining room, bar/lounge with occasional live music, deck. 5 acres, birdwatching. Swimming nearby. 2 m to cross-country, 5 m to downhill skiing.
Location 2½ hrs. north of New York. From I-87 take Exit 21 to Rt. 23. Go west 16 m to inn.
Credit cards All major credit cards accepted.
Rates B&B, $55–115 double, $45–105 single. Extra child in room $10, adult $20. Senior discount. 3-night minimum holiday weekends. Alc lunch $9, alc dinner $25. Mid-week non-holiday ski packages, $45 per person including meals and lift tickets; kids ski free mid-week non-holiday.
Extras Station pickups. Pets by prior arrangement ($25 security). French, Italian spoken.

ELKA PARK

Redcoat's Return   *Tel:* 518–589–6379
Dale Lane, 12427

Built as a summer boarding house in 1910, the Redcoat's Return is well known for its hospitable English atmosphere and delicious food. Rooms are small but comfortably furnished with brass or iron beds, period oak dressers, and cheerful prints and fabrics, and rates include a full English breakfast. The inn borders the Catskill Game Preserve, and many trails lead up from the grounds into the mountains. Long-time owners Tom and Peggy Wright note that "our inn reflects our British origins and interests. It's full of books and antiques. Winston, our Bernese Mountain dog is well loved by our guests. We are basically a quiet place offering good conversation, food, and beautiful scenery."

Once a chef on the *Queen Mary*, Tom's cooking is well known; the menu includes such traditional favorites as prime rib and Yorkshire pudding (Saturday night) and steak and kidney pie, as well as nightly specials—perhaps shrimp in Dijon mustard or quail with grapes and wild rice. *(Mary Fitzgerald)* More comments please.

Open Closed April 1 to Memorial Day. Restaurant closed Tues., Wed.
Rooms 14 doubles—all with full bath and/or shower, fan.
Facilities Restaurant with fireplace, bar with fireplace. 17 acres with trout fishing, children's play equipment. Golf nearby. 4 m to downhill skiing, 3 m to cross-country skiing.
Location Greene Country, Catskills Mt. region. 100 m N of NYC. 4 m S of Tannersville. In Tannersville, turn S on Rte. 16, continuing along river to Dale Ln. on the right. Turn right to inn on the left.
Restrictions No smoking in dining room. No children under 6.
Credit cards Amex, MC, Visa.
Rates B&B, $80–95 double, $65–75 single. 2-night weekend minimum. Alc dinner, $30–39 plus 7% tax, 15% service.
Extras Station pickups.

FREDONIA

The White Inn
52 East Main Street, 14063

Tel: 716–672–2103

Despite its classic white exterior accented with black shutters, the White Inn was not named for its appearance, but for its founder, Dr. Squire White, who built the original dwelling on this site in 1809. The current building dates to 1919, and was refurbished by current owners David Palmer and David Bryant. Rooms are furnished with antiques and quality reproductions; three newly refinished rooms have such features as a double Jacuzzi, all wicker decor, or a rice carved poster bed.

The inn's restaurant is a long-time favorite of local inhabitants. One of the charter members of Duncan Hines "Family of Fine Restaurants" back in the 1930's, the inn grows its own herbs and uses the freshest of local ingredients. Some of the more creative entrees include pork medallions with ginger and apples; lamb stuffed with spinach, almonds, shallots, and garlic; and shrimp with smoked salmon and shallot cream sauce.

"Our room, a very large double with two brass beds and antique bureau, had a fresh new bathroom; a vanity with sink was unobtrusively tucked away in the corner of our bedroom. An efficient, quiet air conditioner kept our room delightfully cool, and a tiny but quaint elevator eased our journeys to and from the third floor. Dinner was excellent and creatively prepared, and our waiter helpfully suggested children's portions. The complimentary continental breakfast was nothing special, but the waitress was very friendly, and my children loved the blueberry pancakes she recommended." *(Nancy Barker)*

"Exceptionally helpful staff, outstanding food." *(Deanna Smith, also Mrs. Gilbert Olson)* "The Bridal Suite is wonderfully romantic with a canopied four-poster bed all in white ruffles." *(Sharon McConomy)*

An area for improvement: One reader noted that rooms are sometimes made up quite late in the day; if you're staying more than one night, request that your room be done early.

Open All year.
Rooms 9 suites, 14 doubles—all with full private bath, telephone, TV, desk, air-conditioning.
Facilities Restaurant, lobby, bar/lounge, craft shop. Herb and flower gardens. Off-street parking. Tennis, golf, playground, vineyards, Lake Erie beaches nearby. Summer sailing on inn's sloop. 20 min. to cross-country, downhill skiing.
Location W NY, Chautauqua County. In town. 40 m SW of Buffalo. From I-90, take Exit 59 and go S on Rt. 60. At Rt. 20, turn right and continue 1.3 m to inn on right.
Restrictions Traffic noise in front rooms might disturb light sleepers.
Credit cards Amex, MC, Visa.
Rates B&B, $75–145 suite, $50–85 double or single. Extra person in room, $5. Children under 12 free in parents' room. Minimum stay required on college weekends. Alc lunch, $7; alc dinner, $40. Children's portions.
Extras Limited wheelchair accessibility. Cribs available.

FULTON

Battle Island Inn
Route 48, RD 1, Box 176, 13069
Tel: 315–593–3699

Many business travelers love the ambiance of B&Bs, but are reluctant to give up such conveniences as an in-room phone, desk, and television. Richard and Joyce Rice, owners of the Battle Island Inn have taken care to provide such amenities, accompanied by the charm of a 1840s Italianate mansion decorated with period antiques. Rates include a full breakfast: a typical menu might include hot homemade applesauce, blueberry pancakes with maple syrup and sausages; or fresh fruit cup, ham and cheese souffle, toasted homemade bread, and herb potatoes, and homemade jam. "Warm hospitality, beautiful home, delicious breakfast." *(GR)* More comments please.

Open All year.
Rooms 6 doubles—all with private bath and/or shower, telephone, radio, TV, desk, fan.
Facilities Parlor with music, 2 sitting rooms, dining room, porch. 3 acres with patio, herb gardens, fountain. Golf across the street. Charter boats nearby.
Location N NY, Oswego County. 7 m S of Lake Ontario, 3 m N of Fulton. On Rte. 48 N of town.
Restrictions No smoking.

Credit cards Amex, MC, Visa.
Rates B&B, $65–85 double, $55–60 single. Extra person in room, $15.

GENEVA

Set at the head of Seneca Lake, one of the larger Finger Lakes, Geneva makes a good base for visits to the many excellent area vineyards. It's also home to Hobart and Smith College, and to Rose Hill, a restored Greek Revival mansion. Geneva is located in the Finger Lakes region of western New York, 50 miles west of Syracuse, and 35 m southeast of Rochester.

Information please: About 17 miles west of Geneva is Canandaigua, at the north end of the lake of the same name. The **Wilder Tavern** (5648 North Bloomfield Road (County Road 30), Canandaigua 14425; 716–394–8132) is a stage coach inn built in 1829. Its four guest rooms are furnished with handmade quilts, samplers, and family memorabilia. Rates are reasonable, and include a full breakfast, served by the fireplace, with homemade breads and preserves and local produce. Comments?

Geneva-on-the-Lake *Tel:* 315–789–7190
1001 Lochland Road, P.O. Box 929, 14456   800–3–GENEVA

Cozy and quaint are just what inngoers enjoy most of the time, but every now and again its fun to stay in a place that's truly grand. Geneva-on-the-Lake is a slightly scaled-down replica of the Lancellotti Villa of Frascati, Italy, built from 1910 to 1914, when Geneva was the source of great fortunes. Although a lovely town today, Geneva never became the great city its boosters prophesied, and by 1974, the mansion was in a sorry state indeed. Now impeccably restored by Norbert Schickel, assisted by his son Bill, the inn combines comfort and elegance in balanced measures. The furnishings are primarily Queen Anne and Stickley reproductions, with soft coral, ivory, and celadon among the favored colors. Although available only on weekends, the restaurant has an equally good reputation for creative continental cuisine, under the supervision of chef Richard Lerman.

"A true replica of an Italian Renaissance palazzo. The rooms are very fashionably decorated, and the staff is very friendly. A great place." *(Dr. Levent Cakmur)*

Open All year. Restaurant open Fri. through Sun.
Rooms 29 suites—all with private bath and/or shower, telephone, radio, TV, desk, fan, kitchen. Some with air-conditioning, fireplace, patio, or balcony. Some rooms in 4 townhouses.
Facilities Restaurant with piano, violin, vocal entertainment; living room. 10 acres with formal gardens, swimming pool, lawn games, lake swimming, dock on Lake Seneca. Bicycles, $10/day. Boat rentals and instruction, fishing charters. Tennis privileges at nearby Hobart & William Smith Colleges. Ice skating rink, golf nearby. 29 m to skiing.

Location NW NY, Finger Lakes region. 42 m SE of Rochester, 45 m W of Syracuse. 1 m to center of town. On Rte. 14 S of Geneva.
Restrictions No smoking in living or dining rooms.
Credit cards Amex, Discover, MC, Visa.
Rates B&B, $149–322 double, $139–312 single. Extra person age 16 and older in room, $52; age 10–15, $29; age 4–9, $17; under age 4 free in parents' room. Crib, $6. Discount for 3-night stay. Getaway packages. 2-night weekend minimum, May 15–Oct. 31. Sunday brunch, $17. Alc breakfast, $6–10; alc dinner, $45–60.
Extras Airport pickups, $40. Crib, babysitting available. Member, Great Inns of America.

The Inn at Belhurst Castle
Lochland Road, P.O. Box 609, 14456

Tel: 315–781–0201

Over a century ago, fifty craftsmen labored for four years to construct a mansion of red Medina stone at a cost of $475,000—in 1885 dollars. The result, a castle built in the Richardson Romanesque style, was the private home of Mrs. Carrie Collins until 1926. Red Dwyer, her nephew, was the next owner, and turned the place into a restaurant, speakeasy, and gambling casino. In 1975, Robert and Nancy Golden bought Belhurst and set about transforming it into a gracious inn. Fortunately, all the original leaded glass, marble fireplaces, and hand-carved woodwork were well preserved, and needed only a thorough cleaning—to remove layers of tobacco smoke—to restore them to their original beauty. Once again in working order is the spigot on the second floor landing that delivers—not water—but white wine. Rooms are decorated with period antiques, including canopied four-poster beds and leather wingback chairs.

The popular restaurant serves hearty portions of prime rib, a variety of Italian-style veal dishes, and a nice choice of fresh seafood entrées; we'd suggest a bottle of wine from one of the nearby Finger Lakes wineries as an appropriate accompaniment.

"We splurged on the sumptuous Tower Suite. Sparkling clean, Oriental rugs, and not one damn goose, grapevine, or crocheted toilet paper holder in sight. The decor defies description. Good service too. The only thing lacking was a make-up mirror. The restaurant was over-extended when we were there, but the maitre d' was accommodating about providing us with a romantic dinner in our room. The food was just average, but by candlelight, who cared?" *(KZ)*

Less favorably: "Furnishings and grounds show signs of neglect; food uneven."

Open All year.
Rooms 3 suites, 9 doubles—all with private bath and/or shower, telephone, radio, TV, desk, air-conditioning. Most rooms with fireplace. 1 room in annex.
Facilities Dining room, bar/lounge. 23 acres on lake for fishing, swimming, boating. Golf nearby.
Location On Rte. 14, 2 m S of center of town.
Credit cards Amex, DC, MC, Visa.
Rates Room only, $185–235 suite, $90–135 double. Prix fixe lunch, $7–10; alc dinner, $30–40.

Extras Airport/station pickups. Crib, babysitting available. French, Spanish spoken.

GROTON

Benn Conger Inn
206 West Cortland Street, 13073

Tel: 607–898–5817

New owners Alison and Peter van der Meulen plan to maintain the reputation for fine lodging and outstanding French and Italian food developed by the previous owners. The limited-choice menus change with the seasons, but are mouth watering year-round.

"The exterior of the inn is impressive: a well-maintained Greek Revival structure with several large and unusual arched windows. The grounds are attractively planted. We particularly enjoyed conversing with the other guests by the fireplace in the comfortable library. The dining rooms are spacious and attractively furnished. A handsome center hall staircase leads to the guest rooms. Each of the oversized rooms is well appointed and offers its own distinctive charm—an old-fashioned fireplace, a reading porch, or Empire antique furnishings. Care is taken to anticipate any guest's needs, seen in the surfeit of fluffy towels and the fine bed linens." *(Jane & Tom Jacobs)*

"Built in 1921, the inn is beautifully furnished with country antiques, large, comfortable beds, handsome prints, and floral arrangements." *(Mark & Amy Frankel)* "All of the rooms are excellent, but our favorite is the suite with the fireplace and living room." *(Larry & Rox Kagel)* Additional reports most welcome.

Open All year. Restaurant closed to public on Sun., Mon.
Rooms 3 suites, 1 double—all with private bath and/or shower, desk, fan. 1 suite with fireplace.
Facilities Restaurant, bar/library with fireplace, upstairs common room with TV. 18 acres with hiking, cross-country skiing. Tennis, golf, water sports nearby.
Location Central NY, Finger Lakes. Approx. halfway between Ithaca and Cortland, 45 min. S of Syracuse. From Cortland, take Rte. 222 to Groton. Cross Rte. 38, making no turns; inn is up hill on right. From Ithaca, take Rte. 13 N to Rte. 366E to Rte. 38. Turn left on Rte. 38; go N about 4 m to Groton. Stay on Rte. 38 to Rte. 222. Turn left to inn up hill on right.
Restrictions No smoking in guest rooms. No young children.
Credit cards Amex, DC, MC, Visa.
Rates B&B, $90–150 suite, $75 double. Extra person in room, $25. 2-night weekend minimum; 3-night holiday, special university weekend minimum. Alc dinner, $35–40.

HADLEY

Saratoga Rose B&B Inn
4870 Rockwell Street, 12835

Tel: 518–696–2861

Built in the late 1800's, the Saratoga Rose was restored as an inn by Tony and Nancy Merlino in 1988, and has been decorated in Victorian country decor. Grand Marnier French toast and eggs Anthony are breakfast favorites, while dinner entrées have an Italian accent, with homemade pastas a speciality.

"The Saratoga Rose is built on top of a hill overlooking the little town of Hadley, just a short drive from Saratoga Springs. The interior furnishings of the inn look like they had just been photographed for *Country Living* magazine. Our bedroom had a big, cozy four-poster bed covered with an old-fashioned quilt and strewn with fluffy, ruffled throw pillows. The fireplace was well-supplied with logs for chilly nights. We awoke to the smell of freshly brewed coffee and Tony's full breakfast. He and Nancy were invaluable assistants in planning our daily activities and excursions." *(Ligaya & Ronald Duncan)*

"Charming building, in a quiet setting just across the bridge from Lake Luzerne, with equally charming owners. We were in the Blue Room, which was lovingly appointed and spotlessly clean, as was the bathroom. The pleasant library is well supplied with reading materials." *(Vreni Ness)*

"Our room had Victorian wallpapers and furnishings, highlighted by lovely Christmas decorations. The restaurant alone is worth a visit. The chef tries all kinds of specialty dishes, and the food was exceptional. Last but not least was the Merlino's exceptional warmth and hospitality." *(Carol Shepard)*

Open All year.
Rooms 5 doubles—all with private bath, radio, fan. Some with desk.
Facilities Library with TV, restaurant with fireplace, foyer, veranda. 1 acre with woods. Tennis, golf, cross-country skiing nearby. 5 min. to Lake Sacandaga for water sports. 5 m to downhill skiing.
Location NE NY, in Adirondack Park. 45 m N of Albany, 15 m N of Saratoga, 10 m S of Lake George. From Saratoga, take Rte. 9N N through Corinth to Lake Luzerne. Left on Bay Rd. to Main St. Turn left on Rockwell St. Inn is 500 yards on left, past Rockwell Falls Bridge.
Restrictions No smoking in guest rooms. No children under age 12.
Credit cards Amex, MC, Visa.
Rates B&B, $65–95, double. Extra person in room, $7–10. 2-night summer weekend minimum. Picnic lunch by prior arrangement, $10. Alc dinner, $25. Off-season packages.

HAGUE

Trout House Village Resort   *Tel:* 518–543–6088
Lake Shore Drive (Route 9 N), 12836

Those underwhelmed by the overdeveloped town of Lake George should head directly north to Hague, where the natural beauty of the lake is not obscured by dozens of tacky t-shirt shops. Trout House is an old-fashioned family resort, owned by Lynn and Bob Patchett since 1971, and managed by son Scott and daughter Alice Patchett. Rooms are furnished with comfortable "colonial-style" upholstered furniture, although some guest rooms in the main lodge have four-poster and brass beds. Although no organized children's programs are offered, kids will keep busy for days with all the lake has to offer; be sure to save a day for visiting nearby Fort Ticonderoga.

"Spread out along the lake front, the resort consists of the comfortable old lodge, basic motel rooms and handsome new log cabins. We stayed in the Library Room with a spectacular view of the lake, shelves of great books, and good lighting. We spent a pleasant summer evening in rocking chairs on the big veranda." *(Gladys & Jim Gilliland)*

Open All year. Restaurant closed July, August.
Rooms 13 suites, 11 doubles, 13 cabins—most with private bath. 3 rooms share 1 bath. All with TV, fan. Some with kitchens, telephone, radio, desk, porch. 2 with whirlpool bath, fireplace.
Facilities Dining room, living room, TV/game room, lounge. 5 acres with putting green, lawn games, bicycles. 400-foot beach/lake front for swimming, canoeing, kayaking, sailing, fishing. Cross-country skiing, snowmobiling, hiking. Golf, tennis nearby.
Location NE NY. N end of Lake George. 8 m S of Ticonderoga. From I-87 take exit 25 and follow Rte 8 to Hague. Turn left onto Rte. 9. Resort on right.
Credit cards Amex, Discover, MC, Visa.
Rates Room only, $79–204 suites and cabins, $41–83 double, $35–75 single. Full breakfast, $5. Extra person in room $5. 5% senior discount. Weekly rates. 2-night minimum summer holiday weekends.
Extras Airport pickups. Cribs, babysitting available.

HAINES FALLS

Huckleberry Hill Inn
Route 23A, P.O. Box 398, 12436

Tel: 518–589–5799

Owners Mary Crisanto and Hank Nooe have restored their turn-of-the-century summer boarding house with country-comfortable decor. Owners since 1987, they choose the inn's name after the train, known as the Huckleberry Express, that once ran alongside the property. The train had to climb the steep incline so slowly that passengers could reach out and pick the huckleberries that grew by the tracks.

"Mary Crisanto couldn't do enough for us. I casually mentioned that I like a hot cup of tea before retiring, and she made sure that I had the makings for tea by my bed each night. The outstanding breakfast includes sausage, bacon, pancakes or French toast, fruit, cereal, juices, and home-baked breads." *(Jean Harkins)* More comments please.

Open All year.
Rooms 2 suites, 16 doubles—most with private bath. Some with kitchen facilities, TV, private entrance. 4 in cottage.
Facilities Breakfast room, living room, library with TV, VCR. 5 m to Hunter Mt. ski area.
Location SE NY, Northern Catskills, Greene County. 2¾ hours N of NYC, 50 m S of Albany. 2 m E of Tannersville. Near Mountain House Road and North Lake State Park. From NY Thruway, take Exit 20, Rte. 32 to Rte. 32A to Rte. 23A to inn.
Restrictions Light sleepers should request a room at the back.
Credit cards Amex, MC, Visa.
Rates B&B, $50–70 suite, double, $35–50 single. Extra person in room $20. Reduced rates for children.

Extras Station pickups. Pets, babysitting by prior arrangement. Crib available.

HAMMONDSPORT

Blushing Rosé   *Tel:* 607–569–3402
11 William Street, 14840   607–569–3483

The Blushing Rosé is an Italianate Victorian home built in 1843, painted just the shade of pink you'd expect given this B&Bs name. Ellen and Bucky Laufersweiler opened it in 1986, and did a lovely job of decorating it with Victorian antiques and country decor, including handmade quilts, ruffled curtains, grapevine wreaths, braided rugs and period oak furnishings. Rates include a full breakfast of fresh fruit and juice, homemade granola, jams and jellies, and a hot entrée, perhaps baked French toast or cheese strata.

"We were delighted to find this friendly B&B in the heart of the Finger Lakes Wine Country. Bucky, retired from Corning Glass, and Ellen made us feel right at home, and were very knowledgeable about area activities and local restaurants. Our spotless room had a comfortable bed with a handmade quilt and good lighting, a small sitting area, and private bath with thirsty towels and quality soaps. We took one of the many magazines out to the large porch and relaxed on the wicker chairs. Ellen served us a delicious breakfast of quiche and delicious oatmeal pie." *(Nancy Ellen & Jeff Seiden)*

Open All year.
Rooms 4 doubles—all with private bath and/or shower, clock/radio, air-conditioning. 2 with desk, 2 with fan.
Facilities Dining room, living room with TV/VCR, stereo, books, guest refrigerator; porch. 1 block to beach, boat launch.
Location Steuben County, Finger Lakes region. 45 min. NW of Corning. Approx. 2 hrs. S of Rochester. 1 block from Keuka Lake, 1/2 block to Village Sq.
Restrictions No smoking. "Children only if specific room available."
Credit cards None accepted.
Rates B&B, $55–75 double, $45–65 single. Extra person in room, $20. 2-night weekend, special event minimum.
Extras Airport/station pickups; fee charged. Babysitting available.

HIGH FALLS

Captain Schoonmaker's B&B   *Tel:* 914–687–7946
County Route #213 West, Box 37, 12440

Sam and Julia Krieg are both educators—he an animal behaviorist at SUNY New Paltz, and she a third grade teacher—who got into the B&B business about seven years ago. Their B&B occupies three historic landmark buildings—a 1760 Revolutionary War hero's home, a converted barn/carriage house, and the old lock tender's house on the 1840 Delaware Hudson Canal."

Breakfast is an event at the Captain's: The seven-course meal might include a cheese-broccoli soufflé, honey sausages, baked apples in maple syrup with whipped cream, juice, home-baked bread, strudels, and fresh-fruit Danish.

"This B&B inn is full of early American furniture, plants, books, pictures, and interesting artifacts. Sam and Julia Krieg are warmhearted and welcoming hosts who draw guests into a relaxed family atmosphere. All guests are invited to wine and cheese on Saturday evening before going off for dinner; everyone gathers in the main house sitting or dining room in front of roaring log fires in the winter or the solarium full of flowers in summer.

"Breakfast is served in the main dining room. Everything is home-made and there's enough to carry most people through to dinner. Guests have a tendency to linger after breakfast just to chat with each other and with Sam and Julia. The rooms are clean and comfortably lit, as well as being full of charm. Bathrooms are modern, with plenty of hot water. Although Route 213 runs directly behind the main house, traffic noise is not obtrusive. Several good restaurants and antique shops are within easy driving distance." *(Patrick & Sarah Swan)*

"This is an average B&B made better by the genuine friendliness and helpfulness of the innkeepers, Sam and Julia Krieg. We stayed in one of the rooms in the main house; it was small but attractively decorated with a wide assortment of antiques and collectibles. Afternoon snacks are served in a pleasant patio area, and there is a good selection of restaurants within a ten-mile radius—the Kriegs willingly help with recommendations and reservations." *(JJU)*

One reader noted that their room in the main house was rather cramped; Julia responded that these rooms, dating back to 1760, are "only rented in peak season, and are the last rooms filled."

Open All year.
Rooms 2 suites, 11 doubles, 1 single—2 with full private bath, 12 with maximum of 4 people sharing bath. All with fan. Some rooms with desks, fireplaces, private verandas. 3 guest buildings with 4 rooms and 2 baths in each.
Facilities Dining room; family room with TV, solarium, canopied patio, decks. 11 acres with flower gardens, croquet, woodlands. Remains of 1760 grist mill. Stocked trout stream for fishing and "country dipping." Hiking, cross-country skiing nearby. 5 m to Mohonk Preserve.
Location SE NY; Hudson River Valley. 80 m N of NYC, approx. 10 m N of New Paltz. ½ m to village.
Restrictions Smoking discouraged. No children on weekends; infants and children over 5 permitted Sun.–Thurs.
Credit cards None accepted.
Rates B&B, $85 suite, $75 double, $45 single. Extra adult in room, $20; no charge for children staying in parents' room. Extra charge for fireplace rooms in season.
Extras Bus station pickups.

HILLSDALE

Hillsdale is an attractive resort area, located on the New York/Massachusetts border, 100 miles north of New York City, and 45 miles southeast of Albany. The area is pleasant in winter for skiing at Catamount, and popular in summer for golf, swimming, fishing, and hiking. It is also within driving distance of Tanglewood and the other Lenox area attractions.

L'Hostellerie Bressane
(Dutch Hearth Inn)
Corner routes 22 and 23, P.O. Box 387, 12529

Tel: 518–325–3412

In the nearly twenty years that Chef Jean Morel and his wife Madeleine have been the chef/owners at L'Hostellerie Bressane, they have built a reputation for serving outstanding French cuisine in a charming atmosphere. Rates include a continental breakfast of a croissant and small French roll, freshly squeezed juice, fresh fruit, jams and butter, plus coffee, tea, or hot chocolate.

"This is the closest we have found in the U.S. to a fine French inn. Our room was large, with a good sitting area near the fireplace. The meals are extraordinary—well-prepared, imaginative dishes, and very attentive service. We were served an excellent continental breakfast in a welcoming atmosphere, and were remembered and specially welcomed on our second visit." *(Elizabeth Ring, also Liz Rollins)*

"This beautiful red brick colonial house, built in 1783, sits at the crossroads of Routes 22 and 23. All the original common rooms are now a series of intimate dining rooms, several with non-working but handsome fireplaces. One has an exposed brick wall and wood paneling, another is more formal with French green wallpaper and matching swagged drapes. Service is very correct and formal, yet the atmosphere is warm and casual; Chef Morel emerges from his kitchen frequently to greet diners personally. The food is classic French, and the six-course prix fixe dinner (available every night but Saturday) an incredible value. Come hungry. The guest rooms are basic but clean and comfortable—much as you'd find a French country hotel." *(SWS)*

Open May through Feb.
Rooms 6 doubles—2 with full private bath, 4 with maximum of 4 people sharing bath. All with air-conditioning.
Facilities Restaurant, bar, flower gardens with lounge chairs. Hiking, swimming, fishing, skiing nearby.
Location E central NY; Hudson Valley region. 2¼ hrs. N of NYC, 2½ hrs. W of Boston, 1 hr E of Albany. 3 m from MA border.
Restrictions No children under 12. Weekday traffic noise in 4 rooms.
Credit cards None accepted.
Rates B&B, $75–95 double. Alc dinner, $40. Sunday–Friday night 6-course dinner, $22.
Extras French spoken.

Swiss Hutte
Route 23, 12529

Tel: 518–325–3333

The Swiss Hutte was purchased in 1986 by Gert and Cynthia Alper. Mr. Alper, a former Swiss ski racer, is just as proficient in the kitchen as he was on the slopes, and the menu features many Swiss and French specialties, including Wiener schnitzel and chicken with wild mushrooms, along with home-baked desserts. Cynthia notes that "we are a young couple with a lot of energy and desire to show our guests a delightful stay. When we are not in the restaurant you can usually find us on the grounds, working in the gardens, or fixing up things."

The inn overlooks the slopes of the Catamount ski area, and is literally set on the New York/Massachusetts border. It is made up of the main inn building, which houses the restaurant and several guest rooms, plus an adjacent two-story motel wing, just renovated last year. Additional rooms are available in a separate house overlooking a pond and tennis courts. The grounds are especially lovely, with two small ponds and perennial gardens with over 150 varieties of flowering plants and shrubs.

"We enjoyed a refreshing early morning swim in the skillfully landscaped pool, then returned for a delightful breakfast on the covered patio. It included fresh fruit and juice, our choice of eggs or pancakes and breakfast meat. After too many overly sweet breakfasts, we savored the toasted home-baked white bread, served with sweet butter in a little crock and marmalade. Service was both friendly and professional. Our room was comfortable but unattractive, but we were told they've been redecorated since we visited." (SWS) Comments?

Open Mid-April–mid-March. Restaurant closed Tues.
Rooms 1 suite, 15 doubles—all with full private bath, telephone, TV, desk, air-conditioning.
Facilities Restaurant, living room with TV, bar/lounge; all with fireplaces. 11 acres with rose/perennial gardens, heated swimming pool, 2 tennis courts, putting green, hiking trails, 2 spring-fed ponds with beach area.
Location 2 m from town, on Rte. 23. From the Taconic Pkwy or Rte. 22, go E on Rte. 23 to inn on right; from Rte. 7, go W on Rte. 23 to inn on left.
Credit cards MC, Visa.
Rates Room only,$85–110 suite, $65–100 double, $65–85 single. MAP, $150–170 suite, $150–160 double, $95–120 single, plus 15% service. No charge for 3rd person in room. Children's rates. 2- to 3-night weekend minimum. Alc breakfast, $2.50–6.50; alc lunch, $7–12; alc dinner, $38.
Extras Bus station pickups. French, German, Swiss-German spoken. Babysitting available.

ITHACA

Known best as the home of Cornell University and Ithaca College, Ithaca is also a lovely place to visit in the summer months, when the students are gone and the pace slows down. Follow Route 89 north along the west side of Cayuga Lake, past the 400-foot falls at Taughannock Falls State Park, and on to visit the several wineries of the Cayuga Wine Trail. The same glaciers that created the Finger Lakes left the Ithaca area with a combination of steep hills and deep gorges, making for beautiful waterfalls and occasionally treacherous driving in the hilly sections.

Ithaca is located at the southern tip of Cayuga Lake, in the Finger Lakes region of central New York, 55 miles south of Syracuse.

Also recommended: For an additional area entry, see listing under **Dryden**, 9 miles east of Ithaca.

Another charming possibility in Ithaca is the **Hanshaw House** (15 Sapsucker Woods Road, 14850; 607–273–8034), an antique-filled 1830s farmhouse overlooking a gardens and a quiet pond, just a short walk from Cornell's Ornithology Lab and hiking trails in beautiful Cayuga Heights. Each of the four bedrooms have private baths, down comforters and pillows; owner Helen Scoones prepares a breakfast of fresh-squeezed orange juice, fresh fruit, homemade muffins and jams, and a hot entrée. "Beautifully painted and most attractive, inside and out." *(Hope Welliver)*

Buttermilk Falls B&B
110 East Buttermilk Falls Road, 14850

Tel: 607–273–3947
      607–272–6767

A sturdy brick house built in 1825, Buttermilk Falls B&B has been owned by the Rumsey family for five generations. Owner Margie Rumsey notes that she came to her grandfather's home as a newlywed in 1948. "I raised three sons here, and now have five grandchildren who come to visit and help out." Located just across the street from Buttermilk Falls (with its 500-foot drop), summertime visitors enjoy a refreshing swim, or hiking up the gorge to Pinnacle Rock. Rooms are decorated with family heirlooms—some antique, and some heirlooms-to-be. Some of the latter are the hand-crafted authentic reproduction Windsor chairs, created by Margie's son Ed, which grace the dining room, surrounding a long plank Shaker table. The living room, with its more eclectic furnishings and Oriental rugs, boasts a first rate collection of games, puzzles, and magazines. Rates include a breakfast of hot whole grain cereals with nut and fruit toppings, egg dishes or cheese souffles, and popovers. "While just around the corner from a busy road, this B&B provides a totally private hideaway, tucked behind high hedges and set back from the street. Margie is a charming, witty lady who has her very own hideaway—a small treehouse in the yard—where she goes to read; my two children were very envious and wanted to sleep there, but alas, it is off-limits to guests.

"The large yard, with garden swing, provided plenty of playing space; right across the street is Buttermilk Falls for swimming, climbing, and exploring. The falls are very dramatic as they cascade down various rock formations into a swimming hole, where a lifeguard is on duty until the park closes at 5 P.M.

"Our room was simply furnished with antiques; Margie has ingeniously tucked a small bathroom with stall shower and excellent lighting into the corner of the room. The other guest rooms which we saw had a variety of antiques and more contemporary furnishings. Breakfasts here are a treat to behold and to consume; everything is orchestrated to be at exactly the right temperature, at the right time. We had a choice of three juices, two kinds of melon, blueberries, fresh apple fritters (which are delivered at dawn from the farmer's market), whole-oat oatmeal with raisins (with a choice of toppings), cheese soufflée with salsa, sausage, bacon, and homemade bread. Margie tries to use only locally grown produce, meat and dairy products; the quality is superb. Margie's hospitality and personality warmed the atmosphere;

her congeniality was contagious among the houseful of guests." *(Nancy P. Barker)*

"This lovely old home has lots of charm, atmosphere, and antiques. The old-fashioned kitchen really buzzes with the preparation of the lavish breakfast goodies. The charming cottage at the year of the yard is very secluded and quiet; one first floor guest room in the house has a double Jacuzzi in the room, in addition to a fireplace, making it a very romantic retreat." *(Hope Welliver)*

One tiny niggle: "The cottage seemed a touch damp; a dehumidifier might help."

Open All year.
Rooms 4 suites, 3 doubles—all with private bath and/or shower. 4 with desk, 3 with air-conditioning. 2 rooms in cottage.
Facilities Living room with CD, games; library, kitchen with TV, dining room, screened porch. 2 acres with croquet, picnic table, swing. Swimming, hiking, cross-country skiing nearby.
Location N NY, central Finger Lakes region. 3.5 m from Cornell/Ithaca College. At foot of Buttermilk Falls, just off of Rte. 13.
Restrictions Light sleepers should request rooms away from street. No smoking.
Credit cards MC, Visa accepted for reservations only; not for payment.
Rates B&B, $65–150 suite or double. Extra person in room, $20–25.
Extras Airport/station pickups by prior arrangement; small fee charged.

The Peregrine House
140 College Avenue, 14850

Tel: 607–272–0919

A red brick three-story townhouse, built in 1874 in the French mansard style and furnished in period, the Peregrine House has been owned by Nancy Falconer since 1986. Nancy notes that "because of our proximity to Cornell, our guests include professors, scientists, writers, and actors from all over the U.S. and the world, making for fascinating breakfast-time conversation."

"Just three blocks from the Cornell campus, the Peregrine is ideal during the school year if you're visiting Cornell; in the summer, the pace slows down and the setting is more peaceful. Our room in this three-story house was compact but comfortable. Breakfast was a highlight, and we feasted on our choice of juice, melon with strawberries, cereal, our choice of an omelet with asparagus, mushrooms, and cheddar cheese or cornmeal waffles with berry sauce, crisp bacon, delicious sweet rolls, blueberry muffins with strawberry butter, and excellent brewed decaf." *(Nancy Ellen & Jeff Seiden)*

"Our room was clean, comfortable and beautifully decorated; there are terry robes for the shower and candies by the bed. Area parking is difficult but the small guest parking lot saved the day. Breakfast was a highlight, with unique choices such as red bananas with toasted almonds, tangerine juice, and blueberry cornmeal pancakes." *(Jennifer Carnevale)*

Open All year.
Rooms 8 doubles—4 with private bath and/or shower, 4 with half-bath sharing 2 shower rooms. All with radio, TV, desk, air-conditioning.
Facilities Dining room with fireplace, living room with fireplace. Off-street parking.

Location 3 blocks from Cornell campus, 5 blocks to center of town.
Restrictions Traffic noise might disturb light sleepers in some rooms. No smoking in dining room or guest rooms. No children under 10.
Credit cards MC, Visa.
Rates B&B, $55–99 double, $49–95 single. Extra person in room, $15. Cots, $15. Family rate for 2 rooms (1 full price, 1 half-price). 2-night special event weekend minimum. Thanksgiving, Christmas, reunion packages.
Extras Airport/station pickups, $8. French spoken.

Rose Inn
Tel: 607–533–7905
Route 34 North, P.O. Box 6576, 14851-6576

Since opening the Rose Inn in 1983, Charles and Sherry Rosemann have worked hard to create an exceptionally luxurious and somewhat formal inn, with four diamond/star ratings from both AAA and Mobil. Charles, who was born in Berlin, is delighted to help guests plan tours of the Finger Lakes wineries; Sherry is an interior designer specializing in pre-Victorian nineteenth-century furniture.

"The inn is situated in beautiful farm country north of Ithaca, overlooking Lake Cayuga. The house was built by a wealthy farmer during the 1800s; a remarkable spiral mahogany staircase (completed in 1924) runs through the core of the building. Throughout, Rose Inn is furnished in antiques. More important is the feeling of gracious comfort found in each of the inn's rooms. Both Charles and Sherry Rosemann contribute to the absolutely superb food served at the inn. Charles's breakfast features French toast, eggs Benedict, and German apple pancakes, accentuated by Sherry's homemade preserves, and accompanied by cider from the inn's orchard. Their personal blend of coffee has a subtle hint of almonds. Sherry's dinners are a joy. Creatively designed menus and superb food beautifully presented are the norm—from sweetbreads with black butter to chateaubriand." *(William Bennett)*

"Mr. and Mrs. Rosemann greeted us on arrival and showed us to our charming room with a spectacular bath. The grounds are as magnificent as the decor of the house. The food was delicious with unusual variety at breakfast." *(Barbara Neish)* "The food is definitely a four-star rating—breakfasts are excellent, dinners superb. This is an elegant and gracious inn, with spacious rooms, decorated in excellent taste." *(Jack Weber)*

Open All year. Restaurant closed Sun., Mon.
Rooms 3 suites, 12 doubles—all with full private bath, radio, fan. Suites have double Jacuzzi; 1 has fireplace. Some rooms with desk.
Facilities Dining room, 3 public rooms with TV, stereo, library, games, guest refrigerator. 20 acres with lawns, fishing pond. 4 m to sailing, fishing, swimming on Lake Cayuga. 15–20 m to cross-country, downhill skiing.
Location 9 m to town, Cornell University. 12 m to Ithaca College. From Ithaca, take Rte. 34 N for 5.7 m to a "T," turn right, go ½ m to fork, stay left. Go 3.5 m to inn.
Restrictions No smoking. No children under 11.
Credit cards Not accepted for deposit. Amex, MC, Visa.
Rates B&B, $165 suite, $90–150 double. Extra person in room, $25. Family discount Monday–Thursday. 10% senior discount Sunday–Thursday. 2–3 night minimum weekends, holidays. Prix fixe dinner, $50; by advance reservation.
Extras Airport pickup. Babysitting available. German, Spanish spoken.

KEENE

The Bark Eater   *Tel:* 518–576–2221
Alstead Mill Road, 12942

Originally built in the 1800s as a stagecoach stopover between Lake
Champlain and Lake Placid, The Bark Eater gets its name from the
English translation of the Indian word "Adirondack." For 55 years, the
Wilson family has been providing a simple, relaxing atmosphere for
enjoying the rugged, wooded Adirondacks countryside, along with a
full complement of outdoor activities for adults and families to enjoy.
Breakfast choices include homemade granola and muffins, sausage or
bacon, hot yogurt cereal, and blueberry pancakes. A typical dinner
might be broccoli-apple soup, Cornish game hen with currant sauce,
wild rice and hot cheese bread. *(MA)* Comments appreciated.

Open All year.
Rooms 8 doubles, 3 singles, 1 cottage—5 with private bath, 7 with a maximum
of 6 people sharing a bath. 10 with desk, 4 with fan. 4 rooms in carriage house.
Facilities Dining room with fireplace, living room with fireplace, game/TV
room, library, porches. 200 acres with gardens, bicycling, horseback riding, cross-
country ski shop and trails, canoeing, white water rafting, fishing. 10 min. to
downhill skiing.
Location NE NY, Adirondack region. 5½ hrs. N of NYC, 2 hrs. N of Albany,
2 hrs. S of Montreal. From Albany via I-87, take Exit 30 (Rte. 9N) to Keene. Turn
W (left) on Rte. 73, then left on Alstead Mill Rd. and follow signs to inn on right.
Restrictions No alcohol is available; BYOB. No smoking in guest rooms or
dining room.
Credit cards None accepted.
Rates B&B, $45–55 per person, double occupancy. MAP, Sun.–Fri., $285–329 per
person (for 5 nights). 13% service additional. Midweek B&B rates for 5-night
stay. Skiing, white water rafting, climbing, horseback riding packages. 2-night
weekend/holiday minimum. Trail lunch, $6; prix fixe dinner, $24.
Extras Some rooms equipped for the disabled. Small pets permitted by prior
arrangement. Airport/station pickups by prior arrangement. Cribs, babysitting
available.

LAKE LUZERNE

The Lamplight Inn   *Tel:* 518–696–5294
2129 Lake Avenue (Route 9N), P.O. Box 70, 12846

In 1984, Gene and Linda Merlino left jobs in the textile printing business to renovate The Lamplight, a Victorian summer cottage built in
1890 by Howard Conkling, a wealthy lumberman and summer resident.
Conkling was a very eligible bachelor, and his home was designed for
entertaining. Five doors off the parlor lead out to the wraparound porch.
The first floor has 12-foot beamed ceilings, with chestnut wainscotting,
moldings, and a keyhole staircase all crafted in England. Linda reports
that "we have tried to make our inn as comfortable as we can, with good

mattresses, reading lights on both sides of the beds, individual thermostats, and modern baths. Flannel sheets and fluffy comforters are provided for winter warmth."

"The atmosphere is very friendly, comfortable, and warm—a perfect place for couples to get away and relax. Parking is less than 100 feet from the house. Gene and Linda have all the activities of the town and region posted; they're familiar with area restaurants and are happy to set up dinner reservations." *(MB)* "Location is optimum. Off the beaten path yet accessible to all the things the Adirondack region has to offer." *(Joseph DiRocco)*

"A fire was usually roaring in the fireplace in the parlor; the TV is discreetly tucked away in an antique cabinet. The hardwood floors are beautiful, covered with Oriental rugs, and the antique furnishings are comfortable. Gene cooks breakfast, served on the sun porch or in the dining room. The weekend specials were waffles and strawberries, peach crepes, and raisin French toast, but you could also order any style of eggs—including superb omelets and home fries." *(Nancy Sosinski)* "Loved reading the room diaries and adding our own comments!" *(Clare Beck)*

"We were helped in with our luggage and ushered upstairs to our room, named for its rose-patterned wallpaper, fluffy rose comforter and rose-flowered sheets and towels. In the morning, we feasted on hot fruit compote, nut bread, eggs Benedict with the creamiest hollandaise I've ever tasted; Belgian waffles with fresh raspberries the next day were just as good. The dining room table was beautiful with white eyelet linens, fresh flowers, and lovely china. We especially enjoyed looking through the Merlino's restoration albums. The addition (built in 1988) has enhanced the original building so completely that one cannot imagine the house without it." *(Lorraine & Justin Tavino)* "We loved the convenience and charm of our room's gas fireplace. Usually we are the 'jump out of bed' type, but here we turned on the fireplace and lounged in bed, enjoying the peaceful atmosphere." *(Joanne Van Zandt)* "We stayed in the sunny Coral Room, a large coral and white room with double and single iron beds, oak dressing table, and a private bath across the hall (bathrobes provided). There was always hot water, and the housekeeping was very efficient." *(Carrie Kries)*

Open All year. Closed Christmas.
Rooms 10 doubles—all with private shower, ceiling fan. 5 with fireplaces. 1 with full bath, 2 with double showers.
Facilities Breakfast room; living room with fireplace, TV; library with fireplace, chess table; sunporch; wraparound veranda. 4 acres with perennial garden. 1 block to Lake Luzerne for swimming, fishing. White-water rafting, cross-country, downhill skiing nearby.
Location E central NY. S Adirondack Region. 45 min. N of Albany, 17 m NW of Saratoga Springs, 9 m SW of Lake George village. Take the Northway I-87 to Exit 21; go left & follow Rte. 9N W 10 m to inn on right. 1 block from town.
Restrictions Traffic noise in front rooms might disturb light sleepers. Smoking in living room only (no cigars or pipes). No children under 12.
Credit cards Amex.
Rates B&B, $60–125 double. Extra person in room, $25. 2-night weekend minimum. Except Aug., 10% discount for 5-night stay; 1 night free with 7-day stay.
Extras Station pickups.

LEONARDSVILLE

The Horned Dorset Inn   *Tel:* 315–855–7898
New York State Route 8, 13364

The Horned Dorset is a restaurant and inn, the former housed in a restored nineteenth-century commercial building, the latter in a neighboring restored 1875 Italianate home, furnished with antiques from the same period. Rates include a continental breakfast of fresh-squeezed orange juice, croissants, and coffee. The cuisine at dinner is French, and veal is a particular specialty.

"The Horned Dorset is located in the tiny village of Leonardsville—population about fifty. The cuisine is both ambitious and expensive, the service excellent, and the building itself interesting and attractive. The guest rooms are luxurious. The surrounding countryside is attractive, and people come to this inn to eat from all over upstate New York." *(Elizabeth Ring)*

"By buying here and there from old hotels and historic buildings, the owners have added everything from antique fireplace mantels to staircases, to make a very attractive restaurant. The food is outstanding." *(Michael Willis)*

And another opinion: "Although we've enjoyed this restaurant for years, two recent visits were disappointing. Our waiter described each dish in excruciating detail, which was either irritating or amusing, depending on your point of view. Unfortunately, we felt that the food was disappointing. The expensive ingredients did not work together to bring out the best in the whole." *More reports please.*

Open All year. Restaurant closed Mon.
Rooms 2 suites, 2 doubles—all with private shower and/or bath. 2 rooms with working fireplace, desk, TV.
Facilities Restaurant, bar/library, sitting room with reading material, piano. 1 acre with gardens, lawn, surrounded by 300 acres of woods with trails, horseback riding, cross-country skiing. 25 minutes to lake fishing, boating, swimming.
Location Central NY, Leatherstocking region. 4½ hrs. NW of NYC, 45 min. S of Utica, 90 min. SE of Syracuse, 30 min. NW of Cooperstown, 25 min. S of NYS Thruway.
Restrictions No children under 12.
Credit cards MC, Visa.
Rates B&B, $95 suite, $75 double. Alc dinner, $35–45.
Extras Pets permitted with prior approval. Spanish, French, Russian spoken. Airport/station pickups.

LOWVILLE

Hill Top Bed & Breakfast   *Tel:* 315–376–6364
Route 12, North, Postal Route 1, Box 14, 13367

After 32 years as Connecticut residents, Robert and Rita McLaughlin moved to upstate New York and opened a cozy B&B. Rates include a full breakfast and afternoon tea.

"This B&B is set atop a hill, and the view of the surrounding area was magnificent. Its location is very convenient for those en route to the big army base at Fort Drum.

"Rita and Robert McLaughlin are charming and hospitable people. A warm, homey atmosphere permeates their inn. Our bedroom was neat, clean, and cheerful and even had a few plants. Breakfast was served as early in the morning as desired, and included bacon and eggs, with homemade cinnamon buns and breads. The owners are so very easy to talk to that it was hard to tear ourselves away when it was time to leave." *(Mr. & Mrs. Joseph Day)* More comments please.

Open Dec.–Oct.
Rooms 3 doubles—1 with full private bath, 2 with maximum of 4 people sharing bath. All with desk.
Facilities Dining room, living room with TV. 1 acre. Boating, fishing, golf, hunting, snowmobiling, skiing nearby.
Location N NY. 1 hr. SE of Thousand Islands. 45 m N of Utica. On Rte. 12, 1¼ m N of town.
Restrictions No smoking. No children.
Credit cards None accepted.
Rates B&B, $30–35 double.
Extras Airport pickups.

MALONE

The Carriage House
PO Box 433, 12953

Tel: 518–483–4891

Arthur and Barbara Mead welcome guests to their magnificent Greek Revival home, in the remote town of Malone, in northernmost New York. Once owned by a U.S. Congressman, guests are welcome to relax in the Mead's 32-foot living room with fireplace and handmade needlepoint rug. A simple continental breakfast of juice, coffee or tea, and a choice of cinnamon buns, English muffins, toast, or cereal, is served in the dinette or in the formal dining room under the brass chandelier.

"The Meads are gracious hosts who did everything possible to make our stay a happy one. Clean, comfortable rooms." *(Nancy Thomas)*

Open All year.
Rooms 2 suites with private bath, radio, TV.
Facilities Dining room, living room with fireplace. 3 acres on Salmon River, swimming pool, golf nearby. 5 m to cross-country, 8 m to downhill skiing.
Location Northern Adirondacks, 50 m N of Lake Placid, 11 m S of Quebec border.
Restrictions Smoking in dining room only. No children.
Credit cards None accepted.
Rates B&B, $40 suite. No tipping. 10% senior discount.

MILLERTON

Simmons' Way Village Inn   *Tel:* 518–789–6235
Main Street (Route 44 East), P.O. Box 965, 12546   800–533–INNS

Originally built in 1852 as a simple farmhouse, this inn was transformed in 1892 into a Victorian showplace, complete with elaborate
porches and gingerbread trim, by E.H. Thompson, a bank clerk-turned-
president. It was first restored as an inn in 1983. Current owners Nancy
and Richard Carter, who bought the inn in 1987, have done an exceptional job of redecorating the inn in a country Victorian style, with lots
of white wicker, soft floral chintzes and wallcoverings, and white iron
beds, complementing the inn's original marble fireplaces, oak trim,
stained glass, and hardwood floors.

Menus at the inn restaurant change with the seasons; recent entrées
included sautéed medallions of venison in brandy butter sauce; poached
shrimp and scallops served on fresh curry pasta with a sauce of crème
fraîche, capers, garlic, and wine; or roast duck with blackberry brandy
sauce.

Millerton's location, close to the Connecticut/Massachusetts border,
makes it convenient to a wide variety of activities, both along the
Hudson to the west, in the Litchfield Hills to the east, and up into the
Berkshires to the north—all within a 15- to 30-mile drive. In addition
to the usual outdoor favorites, area activities include movies at Millerton's art cinema, visits to the Roosevelt and Vanderbilt estates, summer
stock theater in Sharon, music at Tanglewood, and dance at Jacob's
Pillow in the Lenox area, along with the ever popular pastime of antiquing.

"On the main street of town, set high up on a hill away from traffic
noise and commercial distractions sits this lovely inn. Beautifully restored, the house combines Victorian charm with the comfort of central
air-conditioning, making it delightfully cool and quiet on a sweltering
July day. Common rooms include a cozy tea room with an impressive
cappucino maker, a gracious living room with overstuffed couches, and
an inviting breakfast room. The restaurant is in an extension at the very
back of the house, and is very light and airy in mood. The guest rooms
continue the country Victorian mood, with good reading lights and
lamps on both sides of the bed, down pillows and quality linens, flowered chintz window treatments, and English antiques and reproduction
furnishings. Bathrooms are given extra flair by the sinks set in period
dressers instead of modern vanities. Attention to detail in the decor
include the lace curtains, the brass fixtures, and the television discreetly
tucked in a cabinet. The town of Millerton is a typical working town,
and is not a tourist destination in itself: some will enjoy the lack of
chi-chi boutiques, others will lament it."*(SWS, also Dave & Cheri Kendall)*

Open All year. Restaurant closed Tues.
Rooms 9 doubles, all with private bath and/or shower, radio, desk, air-condi-
tioning. 2 with private porch, some with Japanese soaking tub.
Facilities Dining room; breakfast room; living/TV room with games, fireplace;

lounge with fireplace. 1 acre. Taconic State Park nearby for swimming, boating, sailing, fishing, hiking. Tennis, golf, skiing nearby.
Location 60 m S of Albany, 100 m N of NYC, 55 m W of Hartford, CT. In center. From S, take Rte. 22 N to Rte. 44 E.
Restrictions No smoking in guest rooms.
Credit cards Amex, MC, Visa.
Rates B&B, $115–160 double. MAP, $220 double. 15% service. Extra person in room, $25. 2–3 night weekend/holiday minimum. Alc dinner, $30; Sunday brunch, $10. Midweek rates.
Extras Pets allowed with prior approval. Crib, babysitting available. 2-block walk from bus station. Member, Great Inns of America.

MT. TREMPER

Mt. Tremper Inn   *Tel:* 914–688–5329
Corner Route 212 and Wittenberg Road, P.O. Box 51, 12457

The Mt. Tremper Inn was built in 1850 as a 23-room summer guest house. After extensive renovation and redecorating, innkeepers Lou Caselli and Peter La Scala reopened the Mt. Tremper in May of 1985. Rooms are furnished with period decor throughout, including authentic Victorian furnishings, red velvet wallcoverings, and French lace curtains. The area offers dozens of antique shops, as well as a number of excellent French restaurants.

"Lou and Pete are warm and wonderful hosts. Rooms are filled with antiques, and soft classical music plays in the background. You can play shuffleboard, sit on the wraparound porch, or take a walk in the beautiful countryside." *(Sharon & Anthony Tsengoles)* "This inn's outstanding feature is the personal attention and hospitality of the two gracious and friendly hosts, who greet you and take care of all your needs. Our downstairs corner bedroom and private bath were impeccably clean. Having breakfast on the porch, enjoying the mountain air, evoked pleasant memories of childhoods in the Catskills. Breakfast was completely homemade and consisted of granola, juices, fruit breads, baked cheddar cheese omelet, coffee, and tea. Sipping complimentary sherry in the evening, and chatting with our hosts and the other guests, was a highlight of our stay.

"Lou and Pete helped us choose places to dine, and guided us to sights that would particularly suit our interests. The inn was quiet; we slept deeply, and appreciated the cool mountain night air from our open windows." *(Barbara & Elliott Wolfe)* "Comfortable firm beds, good bathroom facilities with hot water and cold well water available in seconds. Books, magazines, and local brochures and newspapers are readily available." *(Max & Helen Benaroyo)*

And an area for improvement: "It may have been taken care of by now, but our bathroom needed updating. The metal stall shower appeared rusty, and we found sink faucets that were hard to use." More comments please.

Open All year.
Rooms 1 suite, 11 doubles—2 with private bath or shower, 10 with maximum of 6 people sharing bath. Sinks in rooms.

Facilities Breakfast room, parlor with fireplace, game room, library, veranda. 3 acres with lawn games. Swimming, fishing, tubing in creek across street. 16 m to Bellayre, Hunter Mts., for cross-country, downhill skiing.
Location S NY, Catskill Mts. 120 m N of NYC, 60 m S of Albany. 20 m NW of Kingston, 8 m W of Woodstock.
Restrictions No smoking in guest rooms or dining area. No children under 16.
Credit cards MC, Visa.
Rates B&B, $90 suite, $60–75 double, plus 7% tax. 2-3 night minimum stay on weekends/holidays.

MUMFORD

Genesee Country Inn
948 George Street, P.O. Box 340, 14511

Tel: 716–538–2500

The Genesee Valley was settled by Scots in the early 1800s; one of them, Philip Garbutt, built a plaster mill in 1833. It was later used for the manufacture of hub and wheel spokes, then for making paper. One hundred and fifty years later, the sturdy stone building was converted into a bed and breakfast inn. Rooms combine country antique decor with twentieth-century favorites—queen- and king-size beds, telephone and TV, and baths supplied with oversize towels, shampoos, and soaps. Rates include full breakfast and afternoon tea.

"Innkeeper Glenda Barcklow is very accommodating and sociable, but respects your privacy. Rooms are beautifully furnished—one is stenciled in blue and overlooks the old mill stream; another is decorated with Laura Ashley fabrics. Each room has a guest diary, filled with notations ranging from places to eat and visit, to impressions of the inn. Our breakfast of cheese omelets, croissants, fruit, and good coffee was served on the breakfast porch, overlooking the mill stream and grounds. In the afternoon, cheese and crackers were served in the cozy parlor. All the common rooms have been stenciled by a local artist." *(Mrs. William Dix)*

"The upstairs guest rooms are quite small, but have charm. Our room was one of the new downstairs rooms, complete with fireplace and canopy bed. The Genesee Country Village and Museum (not connected to the inn) just down the road was an unexpected delight. It's made up of over 50 19th century farm and villages buildings moved to the museum's 150 acres. Costumed docents demonstrate the period's essential skills." *(KG)* More comments please.

Open All year.
Rooms 10 doubles—all with private shower and/or bath, telephone, radio, TV, air-conditioning. 1 with fireplace.
Facilities Living room, breakfast room, conference/card room. 6 acres with gardens, waterfall ponds, trout streams. Bicycling, tennis nearby. 20 min. to Letchworth State Park for swimming, cross-country skiing, hiking.
Location W NY. 17 m SW of Rochester. In center of town. From Rochester Airport, take Brooks Ave. E to Rte. 390 S. Take Exit 17 to Scottsville Rd. (Rte. 383). Continue S through Scottsville into Mumford.
Restrictions No children on weekends; older children welcome midweek.
Credit cards Amex, MC, Visa.

Rates B&B, $85–115 double, $80–110 single. Extra person in room, $10. 2-night weekend minimum in May. Senior discount off-season. Weekend, celebration packages.

NEW PALTZ

Mohonk Mountain House *Tel:* 914–255–1000
Mohonk Lake, 12561 212–233–2244

"How can I recommend a hotel with 300 rooms for a book about 'little' hotels and inns? The idea may seem ridiculous, but once you've spent time at Mohonk you'll understand why this very special place belongs here. This venerable hotel on the mountain, sitting since 1869 on its perch alongside a beautiful glacial lake is the perfect retreat from the crush of city life. Well over a century after its founding, the hotel still belongs to the Smiley family, descendants of the two brothers, Albert and Alfred, who started it all. The interior, a reminder of a more gracious time, is full of comfortable places to sit, perfect places to catch a view of the lake or the valley. Outside are trails for hiking, cross-country skiing, and horseback riding. You can join in a full range of summer sports, or just sit at one of the gazebos that dot the property and admire the surroundings. When I was there the evening entertainment was a local actor reading a Sherlock Holmes short story in front of the fireplace in the beautiful Lake Lounge. Earlier, we had enjoyed tea and cookies, along with the Sunday *New York Times,* in the lounge after a day of cross-country skiing. Our room had a fireplace and a generous supply of wood, plus a balcony with rocking chairs." *(Marjorie A. Cohen, also Laurie Grad)*

"The view of the lake from our room was beautiful, and I liked the old-fashioned character of our room. Although provided with free shampoo and pretty soap, the bathroom was just adequate. But you don't come here to stay in your room—just to hike a portion of the available trails makes it worthwhile. Afternoon tea in the lounge was relaxing and appreciated. The food in general was good, not great, but with enough options available so that we happily stuffed ourselves with things we enjoyed. In sum, Mohonk is huge, interesting, and fun. The grounds are seemingly endless, gorgeous, and delightful to explore." *(Emily Clement)*

"There's simply no place like it for the incredible atmosphere combined with the extensive range of activities and facilities. It's ideal both for families and for couples looking for a romantic getaway. Your description of the common rooms is very accurate, but your readers should know that the decor of most of the guest rooms is very basic, and the baths are quite dated." *(KF)* "A real experience just being there, but a little pricey considering the food is mediocre at best. So many places to sit, wander, and get lost. The rooms are fine, the staff enthusiastic, the carriage house museum a real treat." *(WB)*

Some areas for improvement: "At $200 a day, we found the extra rental charges for a one-hour paddle boat ride annoying!" And: "Although the grounds are exceptional, the rugs and furnishings were worn, the walls needed repair, and the couches needed replacing. We resented paying a 15% service charge when no one was even around to carry our bags."

Open All year.
Rooms 300 rooms—250 with private bath, 50 with sink in room & sharing hall baths. 150 with working fireplaces, 200 with balcony.
Facilities 3 dining rooms, verandas, parlor, library with TV. 22,000-acre preserve with private lake for fishing, swimming, boating; gardens, greenhouses, picnic area, hiking trails, museum, stables, fitness center, game room, tennis, golf, ice-skating, cross-country skiing. Children's programs. Special interest programs (foreign languages, fitness, nature, music, tennis, cooking, photography).
Location SE NY, Hudson River Valley. 6 m W of New Paltz. Approx. 90 min. N of NYC. From NY Thruway, take Exit 18 and turn left on Rte. 299 and go through New Paltz. Take 1st right after bridge, go ¼ m and bear left at the fork in road. Continue up road to hotel.
Restrictions No smoking in common rooms. Casual attire not appropriate for evening meal.
Credit cards MC, Visa.
Rates Full board, $180–345 double, $95–240 single, plus 15% service charge. Child in room, age 2–12, $45; over age 12, $55. 2-3 night weekend, holiday minimum. Weekly rates, midweek packages. Extra fees for some activities.
Extras Airports/station pickups, fee charged. Cribs available.

NEW YORK CITY

There are many very wonderful things to be found in New York City, but little hotels are unfortunately not at the top of the list. An unusually high number of hotels can't even be bothered to return questionnaires, and change—both good and bad—seems to happen more quickly in the context of corporate ownership than in the case of long-term family-owned establishments. So *please*, keep those cards and letters coming; your reports are the heart of every entry in this guide.

In making our selections, we considered anything under 300 rooms small by Big Apple standards; more important was the attentiveness of the staff and the quality of the rooms and public areas. You may want to think of a visit to New York City as a lesson in assertiveness training. Particularly in the older hotels, the quality of the rooms is uneven, and you may be shown to a room that appears dirty or stained, or has sagging beds, or is in otherwise poor repair. Reject it immediately on one of these grounds, and ask to be shown one that has been more recently redecorated. Before the bellhop leaves, check to make sure that the bed is firm, and that TV, air-conditioning, and shower are working well; if there's a problem, it's better to change rooms early than to attempt to have it repaired—especially at midnight!

Another decision in selecting a room is the choice of light or quiet. Ideally, a room on a top floor will provide both; if one is not available, front rooms will usually be noisier, back rooms darker. Don't be shy about making your preferences known.

When booking a room, expect to pay a $100–150 for a single on weekdays; weekend, summer, and Christmas week rates offer considerable savings, so always ask about any promotional rates when booking. To further reduce the pain, *always* ask if any discounts rates are available: senior citizen, family, AAA, corporate, whatever. You'll always get a better deal by calling the hotel directly, rather than a central reservation service. Budget-conscious travelers will want to plan their NYC visits to spend the weekend in the city, when rates are lowest, and weekdays exploring the countryside, when country rates are lower. Nevertheless, if the hotel rates quoted here are beyond your means (not at all difficult), we'd advise booking a room in a B&B through one of the half-dozen agencies available. One frequent contributor stayed in a pleasant, unhosted apartment that she found through **City Lights, Bed & Breakfast Ltd.** (P.O. Box 20355 Cherokee Station, 10028; 212–737–7049). If booking through an agency, try to get a building with a doorman or security guard, and ask for a room that is set up as a bedroom, with adequate storage space, rather than a den or at-home office. Drop us a line if you'd like more names and addresses.

Rates do not include city, state, and local hotel taxes, which total 13.25%, plus a $2 room fee, and a 5% special hotel occupancy tax on rooms costing over $100, which just went into effect last June; in other words, the daily cost of a $150 hotel room (including tax but exclusive of tips) is $178. Considering the income tourists and business travelers bring to the city, we're reminded of the old adage about biting the hand that feeds you!

Information please: In the luxury price range is one of Manhattan's hottest hotels, the **Royalton** (44 West 44th Street, 10036; 800–635–9013 or 212–869–4400), a totally renovated version of a hotel originally built in 1898. Some critics feel that style here has won out over comfort, others find it a refreshing change. Just across the street from the Algonquin, rooms have been done with art deco flair, and weekday rates start at $220.

Re-opened in 1990 after a lengthy, $5 million dollar restoration, the **Hotel Wales** (1295 Madison Avenue, 10128; 212–876–6000 or 800–223–0888) was renovated by stripping layers of paint from woodwork and marble, restoring mosaics and tiling, in order to return to its turn-of-the-century Edwardian elegance. Guest rooms have original golden oak or gleaming mahogany moldings, fireplaces, and ornate mantels over (non-working) fireplaces. The Wales is one of the few hotels to offer guests a well appointed living room on the second floor (where the light continental breakfast of coffee, juice, and pastry is served). Despite great press coverage, an early visitor was not impressed: "The 'doorman' was attired in sweatpants, and the halls smelled musty; I saw one small room which was OK."

An intriguing possibility for budget travelers is the **Herald Square Hotel** (19 West 31st Street, 10001; 212–279–4017). Built in 1893 in the Beaux Arts style, and the long-time home of Life Magazine, it lingered for decades as a rundown hotel. It now has a new name and ownership, and has been totally redone. Although they vary in size, its newly renovated 130 rooms have been decorated in pastel tones; most have private baths, and all have air-conditioning, and color TV. Although there are no frills, management is very security conscious, and double rates range from $65–80. The location is not bad, with Macy's and the Empire State Building nearby. *Reports, please.*

Also recommended: Although there wasn't time to complete a full write-up, we received an enthusiastic recommendation for the **May-flower** (15 Central Park West at 61st Street, 10023; 212–265–0060). It enjoys a prime West Side location, with beautiful views of Central Park, just two blocks from Lincoln Center. Rates are reasonable and rooms are quiet, good-sized, attractively decorated with traditional furnishings; many have refrigerators. The lobby is handsome and the staff quite friendly; the hotel restaurant offers a reasonable pre-theater dinner. *(Rose Wolf)*

Recommended with equal enthusiasm is the **Salisbury** (123 West 57th Street, 10019; 800–223–0680 or 212–246–1300) offering spacious, well maintained rooms—many recently refurbished—at very reasonable prices for its top location. "Rooms are extremely pleasant but unremarkable, done in traditional American furnishings. Rates are very reasonable, and the staff is extremely attentive. Lots of great restaurants—in every price range, in the neighborhood." *(Dianne Crawford)*

B&B on the Park
Tel: 718–499–6115

113 Prospect Park West, Brooklyn, 11217

If you're visiting friends or family in Brooklyn, or simply want to experience New York the way New Yorkers do, a stay here will give you a totally new perspective. A classic New York brownstone, built in 1895, B&B on the Park has beautiful stained glass windows and richly detailed oak woodwork and floors. Owner Liana Paolella has furnished it with 19th century Victorian antiques, Oriental rugs, original oil paintings, formally swagged drapes with lace curtains, brass or lace canopied beds, and down comforters. Rates include a full breakfast of home-baked bread and rolls, homemade jams and jellies, bacon or ham, and German pancakes, quiche Lorraine, crepes, or omelets, served on Irish linens with period silverware and china.

"Wonderful atmosphere and ambiance, with immaculate rooms and beautifully appointed. The dining room is one of the most beautiful rooms I have seen with glorious stained glass window and magnificent fretwork and furnishings; breakfasts are delicious." *(Gerri Luther)*

Open All year.
Rooms 2 suites, 4 doubles—5 with private bath and/or shower, 1 with shared bath. All with telephone, TV, desk, air-conditioning, ceiling fan. 1 suite with kitchen.
Facilities Dining room, living room, roof garden. Tennis, bicycle, canoe rental across street in Prospect Park. Parking garage 4 blocks away.
Location Park Slope. From Manhattan: FDR Drive to Brooklyn Bridge. Turn left on Atlantic Avenue. Turn right on 4th Avenue. Go 1 m, turn right on 5th Street, continue to end. Turn left on Prospect Park West, 2 blocks to inn. 10-min. walk from Brooklyn Museum.
Restrictions Smoking in common room only. No children between ages 2–6.
Credit cards MC, Visa for deposit only.
Rates B&B, $135 suite, $100–125 double, $90–125 single. Extra person in room $35. $10 surcharge for 1-night stay midweek; 2-night weekend minimum.
Extras French, Finnish spoken.

The Box Tree *Tel:* 212–758–8320
250 East 49th Street, 10017

We can promise one thing to all guests at the Box Tree for sure—you
won't have to look at a matchbook to remember where you're staying.
From the formal Louis XVI sitting room to the Gaudí-style art nouveau
sculptured staircase, to the opossum fur throws for each bed, owner
Augustin Paege has slowly created a miniature masterpiece which some
have compared to a Fabergé egg. Paege has operated the Box Tree
restaurant at this location since 1982; the hotel was opened in 1988.
Each guest room has a different decorating theme—Chinese, Egyptian,
Japanese, and so on, but all offer such extravagances as a choice of Irish
linen, Egyptian cotton, silk or flannel sheets, Guerlain toiletries, Dead
Sea bath salts, and in the evening, a marron glacé on your pillow. Some
readers may think it precious or pretentious, but all will find it memorable. Rates include continental breakfast, and a $100 credit towards
dinner in the Box Tree restaurant.

"We spent two nights in the Egyptian Suite and I was astounded with
the beauty, no less the details, surrounding us, and every moment I
discovered more perfection. Let's start with the Tiffany key ring, the
engraved stationary and Montblanc pen, the leather-bound TV guide
and leather 'do not disturb' sign, the No. 4711 soap and tissues, the
porcelain water glasses, the enormous European shower head, and the
wonderful monogrammed towels. Service was exceptional and the food
incredibly good at dinner. I could go on and on about the superb
detailed molding, the mirrors, the soft pillows and more." *(Paula Murad)*

A few minor niggles: "At these rates, I would have liked the option
of a newspaper, a radio, robes, sherry, or a cocktail upon arrival. And
perhaps a housekeeping oversight—the refrigerator needed a good
scrub." Also: "After a long day of sightseeing, the two flights of stairs
up to our room seemed very long and steep."

Open All year.
Rooms 12 suites—all with full private bath, air-conditioning, fireplace. All with
choice of bed linens (Egyptian cotton, silk, flannel or Irish linen).
Facilities Restaurant, sitting room with piano, meeting rooms. 24-hour room
service. Butler, valet, florist service. Chauffeured Rolls-Royce or Bently for hire.
Fitness instructor.
Location Midtown Manhattan. On 49th St. between Lexington & 3rd Ave.
Restrictions No elevator. Jacket & tie required in dining room at all times.
Credit cards Amex.
Rates B&B, $230–300 suite. 20% service additional. Alc dinner, $125–145. Rates
include $100 credit in dining room.
Extras Chauffeur service. Pets welcome.

Chelsea Inn *Tel:* 212–645–8989
46 West 17th Street, 10011

Advertised as "a small inn in a big city," the Chelsea Inn was opened
in 1988 by Linda Mandel and Mindy and Harry Chernoff, whose past
experience involved commercial real estate, not the hotel business.
They felt that Manhattan offered a market for clean, comfortable accommodations in an informal, inexpensive setting. Two side-by-side

brownstones were restored, and the rooms—some spacious, some small—were refurbished with brightly painted walls, and abstract wall-papers, and a decor that ranges from natural-wood furnishings with patchwork-style quilts to finds from antique stores, yard sales, and flea markets. The neighborhood is an interesting one; within an easy walk is the wholesale flower market, the Flatiron district, and Greenwich Village. Manager David Zirlin or another staff member is at the front desk until 9 P.M. nightly to assist with theater tickets, dinner reservations, and sightseeing information.

"If you had business or family in this area, the Chelsea would be a comfortable place to stay. Although the street is a busy one, the area is quiet at night, but not deserted. Although I wouldn't recommend the first-floor suite, I saw two upstairs bedrooms which shared one bath. They were cheerful, and very clean but not 'decorated'—more like a friend's guest room than a hotel. The weekday rates are reasonable compared to most midtown hotels; for a weekend stay, I think you'd do better uptown." *(AS)*

Open All year.
Rooms 6 suites, 7 doubles—2 with private bath, 11 with maximum of 4 sharing bath. All with kitchenette, telephone, radio, TV, air-conditioning.
Facilities Lobby. 1/2 block to public parking lot.
Location Chelsea district.
Credit cards Amex, MC, Visa.
Rates Room only, $135–140 suite, $78–105 double. Extra person in room, $10.

Doral Tuscany
120 East 39th Street, 10016

Tel: 212–686–1600
800–847–4078

Very much a small hotel by New York City standards, the Doral's location on a relatively quiet residential street is convenient to most city activities. Rooms are decorated with traditional furnishings, and vary considerably in size—but not in price. A nearby hotel under the same management and similarly recommended is the **Doral Court,** (130 East 39th Street, 10016; 212–685–1100 or 800–624–0607) with oversize rooms and a pleasant courtyard cafe.

"The doorman, desk folks, and elevator man were so friendly and helpful that we felt very much at home. They are older professionals who take their work seriously. We had a pleasant room, fairly large by New York City standards, with a decorative fireplace. The housekeeping staff were very responsive. There's a lovely little lobby with brass and wood paneling and fresh flowers, and the midtown location is great." *(Kathleen Novak, also Ethel Aaron Hauser)* "Based on your recommendation, we tried the **Doral Court**, and were very pleased. Our room— spacious by Manhattan standards—had been newly redone in soft pastel tones, and had such extras as a VCR, refrigerator, bathrobes, and refrigerator. It not only looked fresh, but smelled fresh, with individual touches that avoided the institutional look of many hotels." *(MW)*

Open All year.
Rooms 7 1–2 bedroom suites, 112 doubles—all with full private bath, telephone, radio, TV, desk, air-conditioning, refrigerator. Exercise bikes on request.

167

Facilities Restaurant, bar/lounge, meeting rooms. Valet parking, health club privileges. Concierge service.
Location Midtown Manhattan, Murray Hill, just E of Park Ave.
Credit cards Amex, DC, MC, Visa.
Rates Room only, $375–750 suite, $225–240 double, $205–220 single. Lower weekend rates; free parking on weekend. Corporate rates. Alc breakfast, $6–12; alc lunch, $45; alc dinner, $75.
Extras Wheelchair accessible. French, Spanish spoken. Crib, babysitting available.

Dumont Plaza
150 East 34th Street, 10016–4601

Tel: 212–481–7600
800–ME–SUITE

Nine family-owned hotels throughout midtown make up the chain of Manhattan East Suite Hotels. The Dumont is the newest, having been completed in 1987. The 2-bedroom suites are particularly recommended for families or for two couples traveling together; the extra space and the weekend rates make this a very good option. If the location of the Dumont isn't convenient, call their reservations number for the addresses of their other properties.

"Our room was surprisingly large for New York, and refreshingly decorated in muted green, gray, and peach. The mattress was firm, the pillows comfortable. There was a desk that could convert to a dining table and a comfortable armchair, in addition to the color television and full-size dresser. For the best view, I'd recommend a room above the 15th floor. The kitchenette was compact, but had a full-size stove and refrigerator, and was outfitted with a toaster and coffee maker (including coffee, filter, creamer, and sugar). The bathroom was also quite large and very clean. In addition to the usual toiletries, there was a disappearing clothesline in the tub/shower area. Security is well-considered and includes a peephole on the door, as well as a security officer who pleasantly greets (and verifies) all guests after midnight. The neighborhood is well lighted and feels residential because of its proximity to Park Avenue. The restaurant is pricey but quite good, although the portions were small. The rolls were crusty and the entrées nicely garnished." *(Amy Peritsky)*

Open All year.
Rooms 252 suites—all with full private bath, telephone, radio, TV, desk/table. Some with kitchenettes.
Facilities Restaurant, lounge, health club, garden terrace. Concierge service.
Location Midtown, East Side. 5–10 min. walk from Grand Central, Penn Station.
Restrictions Light sleepers should request back rooms.
Credit cards All major cards.
Rates Room only, $195–415 suite. Extra person in room, $20. Weekend rates, $100–225. Monthly rates.
Extras Limited wheelchair access. French, Spanish spoken. Crib, babysitting available.

Hotel Algonquin
59 West 44th Street, 10036

Tel: 212–840–6800
800–548–0345

Though it dates back to 1902 and served as the gathering place for a famous group of American writers in the 1920s and 1930s, the Algonquin long remained a relatively friendly and unpretentious establishment. Much of the staff has been there for over thirty years; longtime owner Ben Bodne, who bought the hotel in 1946, sold it late in 1987 to Caesar Park Hotels, a subsidiary of a large Tokyo corporation. During 1990, the restaurant and all the guest rooms were renovated, and plans to refurbish the common areas are also anticipated. "When we stopped by to visit, in June of 1990, many of the guest rooms were closed for renovation, as was the Oak Room. We saw a few rooms, and they were small; their decor a bit tired and dated. The lobby has long been a famous place to meet for drinks, but it seemed in need of refurbishing as well. The reports below predate the renovations, so reports are urgently requested.

"The handsome wood-paneled lobby has the aura of a well-loved club. Comfortable chairs and sofas are grouped informally for tea or cocktails or after-theater drinks; having guest status helps one to snare one of those groupings. Many of the guest rooms have matching flowered bedspreads and draperies with pale salmon or pale yellow backgrounds, both very attractive. Rooms are equipped with a number of reading lamps, a small desk, brass bedsteads, at least one chair with arms, a television set in a cabinet, and, invariably, the latest *New Yorker*. Our most recent bathroom was a bit shabby, but perfectly clean and satisfactory. The double room rate seemed well worth the cost of the comfort, tradition, and splendid location that it buys. Light sleepers might be bothered by plumbing noises; the radiators do clank a bit, and our bathroom pipes muttered noisily when the water was turned on next door." *(Carolyn Mathiasen)*

"The public rooms give you everything you could want, and the food in the Rose Room was excellent. My room overlooked the street and was very noisy; it was extremely small—the bathroom door wouldn't even open the whole way; it could have been cleaner and no amenities (shampoo, hand lotion) are provided. I'd recommend coming for drinks and dinner and staying elsewhere." *(DC)* More comments please.

Open All year.
Rooms 24 suites, 141 doubles—all with full private bath, telephone, TV, air-conditioning. Most with desk.
Facilities Lobby, restaurants, entertainment. Room service 7 A.M.–11:30 P.M. Parking garage across the street with special rates for guests; free weekend parking with 2-night stay (5 P.M. Fri.–10 A.M. Mon.)
Location Midtown. Between Fifth and Sixth Aves.
Restrictions Light sleepers should request rooms at back.
Credit cards All major cards.
Rates Room only, $320–350 suites, $175–185 double, $165–175 single. Extra person in room, $25. Alc dinner, $40–50.
Extras Wheelchair accessible. Crib available. French, Spanish, Italian spoken.

Hotel Beverly   *Tel:* 212–753–2700
125 East 50th Street (at Lexington Avenue), 10022   800–223–0945

Although so-called European-style hotels are springing up faster than mushrooms after the rain, the Beverly has been one for many years. Family owned for over twenty years, it has an inviting wood-paneled lobby with traditional furniture and crystal chandeliers, and tradition-ally styled guest rooms with large, comfortable couches for relaxing. The one-bedroom suites are just that; the junior suites have a separate sitting alcove. Although certain frills are cut to save costs (e.g., extra charge for cable TV), this is compensated for by the warm, friendly staff, the value offered (especially on weekends), and the safe, central location. *(CD)* "The lobby is inviting, the staff friendly, and the hotel offers such conveniences as a coffee shop and drug store. My room was clean and comfortable, although it smelled a bit musty until aired out." *(MW)*

Open All year.
Rooms 100 1-bedroom suites, 75 junior suites, 22 doubles—all with full private bath, telephone, TV, refrigerator, in-room safe. All suites with kitchenettes, desk/table.
Facilities Restaurant, lounge, drugstore/coffee shop, hair stylists, concierge. Room service, 7 A.M.–11 P.M.
Location Midtown, East Side.
Credit cards All major cards accepted.
Rates Room only, $180–225 1-bedroom suite, $149–179 double, $139–169 single. Extra person in room, $10. AARP discount. Weekend rates, $129 suite, $119 double. Alc lunch, $8–12; alc dinner, $30–40.
Extras French, Italian, Spanish, Greek, Hebrew spoken.

Hotel Empire
44 West 63rd Street (at Broadway), 10023

Tel: 212–265–7400
800–545–7400

The key reason for the Empire's inclusion here is its location, a superb one, just across the street from Lincoln Center. Within easy walking distance are Carnegie Hall and the dozens of restaurants and boutiques of Columbus Avenue. Just a bit farther are the theater district and Fifth Avenue. The hotel was fully renovated in recent years, and once drab and dingy rooms have been redone in soft shades of rose, green, and blue—the effect is clean and cheerful. The Empire's drawback is the fact that it attracts a certain number of tour groups, rendering service some-what inefficient, and the front desk area chaotic during group check-ins.

"While the check-in and check-out was disorganized, the staff was very helpful in providing other arrangements for me until my room was ready."*(Dianne Crawford)* "We had a chance to see a number of guest rooms, and, although small, all were beautifully decorated with fresh new furnishings and fabrics. Definitely an excellent value in the New York hotel market, and I'd recommend it highly." *(RW)*

And from the nothing's perfect department: "My bed was very tippy—if I moved at all, I went sliding into the headboard! The TV was broken, and after four calls, someone arrived but could neither fix or replace it. The bathroom was so cramped I bruised my shins from hitting the toilet paper holder." Comments?

Open All year.
Rooms 25 suites, 350 doubles, all with private bath and/or shower, telephone, radio, TV/VCR, desk, air-conditioning, CD/cassette player, hair dryer, mini-bar. Suites with whirlpool or soaking tub.

Facilities Restaurants, lobby, guest lounge. Meeting rooms, business services. Valet, laundry, 24-hr. room service. Health club privileges, private exercise studio. Valet parking.
Location Upper West Side, at Lincoln Center.
Restrictions No smoking in public areas. Inside rooms are quieter, darker, less expensive.
Credit cards Amex, CB, DC, MC, Visa.
Rates Room only, $210-350 suite, $165–215 double, $145–195 single. Extra person in room, $15. Holiday packages. Corporate, weekend rates. Alc lunch, $20; alc dinner, $40–50.
Extras Airport transfers. Crib available. Spanish, French, German spoken.

Hotel Iroquois
49 West 44th Street, 10036

Tel: 212–840–3080
800–332–7220

A quiet hotel overshadowed by its famous neighbors, the Iroquois offers an excellent value in a first-rate location. Refurbished rooms are decorated in Queen Anne reproduction decor, primarily in shades of buff, soft rose, and dusty blue.

"A real discovery for the money. Fabulous location just off Fifth Avenue, next to the famous Algonquin and across the street from the stylish Royalton. The hotel is slowly being refurbished, so make sure you get a room that's been renovated. My suite was large with new drapes, bedspreads and furniture; it was fresh, clean, and relatively quiet. The staff was very pleasant and helpful; the lobby was bright and attractive." *(Dianne Crawford)*

Minor niggles: "Typical of older hotels in New York, my room could have used more electrical outlets. There was no bathtub stopper and the hot water flow was uneven."

Open All year.
Rooms 90 suites & doubles—all with full private bath, telephone, television, air-conditioning. Some with kitchenette.
Facilities Lobby, restaurant, bar, barber shop. Parking garage nearby.
Location Midtown, just off 5th Ave.
Credit cards Amex, MC, Visa.
Rates Room only, $120–$175 suite, $85–$95 double, $75–$85 single. Extra person in room, $10. Weekend rate, $75.
Extras Babysitting available.

Hotel Plaza Athénée
37 East 64th Street, 10021

Tel: 212–734–9100
800–CALL–THF

Once the site of a rundown old hotel, the Plaza Athénée opened in 1984 with hardly an inch of floor space unrestored. A definite five-star luxury hotel, it's very European in style, clientele, and ownership. Guest rooms are elegantly and tastefully decorated, with many French touches, and are intended to look more like the rooms in a private home than a hotel. Bathrooms are spotless, faced with gleaming marble. The hotel restaurant, Le Regence, serves fine French cuisine, and there's a lounge to repair to for afternoon tea and evening cocktails. Finally, it's worth noting that the weekend rate for the suites, $325, is a very good value, all things considered. *(MW)* More comments please.

Open All year.
Rooms 37 suites, 120 doubles, all with full private bath, telephone, TV, radio, desk, air-conditioning.
Facilities Restaurant, lobby, lounge with pianist. Concierge service; 24-hour room service. Valet parking.
Location Upper East Side.
Credit cards Amex, CB, DC, MC, Visa.
Rates Room only, $590–1,950 suite, $285–355 double, $245–315 single. Extra person in room, $40. Weekend B&B rate, $325 suite, $230 double. Call for children's rates. Alc breakfast $13–17; alc lunch, $37; alc dinner, $90.
Extras Pets permitted. Airport/station pickups. Crib, babysitting available. Nearly all foreign languages spoken. Member, Trusthouse Forte Hotels, Leading Hotels of the World.

The Lowell
East 63rd Street 10021

Tel: 212–838–1400

Exceptionally small for New York, with 60 suites and doubles, the Lowell is able to offer truly personalized service to guests. Built in 1928, the building was overhauled in 1984 in a no-expense-spared renovation. Rooms are individually and distinctively furnished, with an eclectic mixture of French and Oriental pieces, eighteenth- and nineteenth-century prints, and Art Deco light fixtures. The Pembroke Room, tastefully dripping with chintz and lace, is open for breakfast, lunch, and English-style afternoon tea, complete with de rigueur crustless watercress and cucumber sandwiches along with more inventive offerings.

"From the moment I arrived, and was personally escorted to my room by the manager, to the time we left, I have never been treated so royally in New York. Our suite was beautiful and room service exceptional." *(DH)* "We've eaten several times in the Pembroke Room and have always found the surroundings elegant, the service impeccable, and the food very good." *(Gerald, Ilene, & Emily Bahr)*

Open All year.
Room 47 suites, 13 doubles, all with full private bath, telephones (2 lines), radio, TV, desk, air-conditioning. Most with kitchenette, wood-burning fireplace; some with terraces.
Facilities Tea room, restaurant, room service, 7 A.M.–2 A.M. Health club nearby. Valet parking, $29 daily.
Location Upper East Side. Between Park and Madison.
Credit cards Amex, DC, MC, Visa.
Rates Room only, $360–1200 suite, $280 double, $220–260 single. Extra person in room, $20; crib, $20. Alc lunch, $35; alc tea, $10–15; alc dinner, $50.
Extras Small pets permitted. Cribs, babysitting available. French, Italian, Spanish, German, Dutch spoken.

Parc Fifty-One
152 West 51st Street, 10019

Tel: 212–765–1900
800–237–0990

Imagine leaving the hubbub of midtown Manhattan, lined with faceless glass towers, for a totally calm and elegant marble-floored lobby, done in soft salmon and taupe, lined with plush Oriental carpets. To the side is a quiet lounge, with conversational groupings of period furniture and soft couches, eighteenth- and nineteenth-century art, and a discreet service bar, should you care for a drink or afternoon tea. The attentive staff awaits you at the thankfully small registration area—the intimate (by Big Apple standards) size of the hotel eliminates check-in lines. The hotel is built inside the gutted shell of the old Taft Hotel; virtually the only thing left of the old hotel are the carved bronze panels in the lobby. Although re-opened originally as the Grand Bay, the hotel was sold in 1990 to Park Lane Hotels, headquartered in Hong Kong, and the name changed to the Parc Fifty-One.

Guest rooms are spacious by New York City standards, and supplied with every conceivable luxury—two-line telephones, one TV discreetly concealed in the armoire, another on a swivel base in the bathroom; the bathrooms also have a make-up mirror, hair dryer, Crabtree and Evelyn toiletries, and robes. Mineral water and a bucket of ice are left when the beds are turned down at night. Room decor varies from country French to Art Deco to modern; all are very handsome and supplied with oversize beds and comfortable reading chairs.

Another advantage here is the location, an easy walk from the theater district, yet far enough removed from the 42nd Street sleaze. Fifth Avenue and Rockefeller Center are also close by, and it's a reasonable walk to Carnegie Hall, Central Park, Lincoln Center, and many of the city's museums. *(SWS)* More comments please.

Open All year.
Rooms 52 suites, 126 doubles—all with full private bath, telephone, TV/VCR, radio, desk, air-conditioning, hair dryer.
Facilities Restaurant, lobby/lounge with piano music, beauty salon, gift shop, meeting room. Concierge services. Valet parking. Health club nearby with heated swimming pool, hot tub, exercise equipment.
Location Midtown Manhattan. At corner of 7th Ave.
Restrictions No smoking on some guest floors.
Credit cards Amex, DC, Encore, MC, Visa.
Rates Room only, $385–925 suite, $275–305 double, $255–285 single. Extra person in room, $30. Weekend packages. Corporate rates. Alc breakfast, $15.
Extras Wheelchair accessible. Crib, babysitting available. Spanish, French, Portuguese, Italian, German, Arabic, Chinese spoken. Small pets allowed. Member, Preferred Hotels.

Park Avenue Sheraton   *Tel:* 212–685–7676
(formerly the Sheraton Russell)   800–325–3535
45 Park Avenue (at 37th Street), 10016

"Quiet, elegant accommodation is the hallmark of this small hotel. The lobby is dark and clubby, with handsome wood-paneled walls; although it's small, with limited seating, two leather wing chairs hidden in a back corner would be ideal for quiet conversation. The bar and restaurant are similarly intimate, and coordinate well with the overall atmosphere of the hotel. The entire hotel was completely redone in 1987—and it shows. Our room, a standard double, was small (i.e., average size by New York City standards) but beautifully decorated in gentle coordinating patterns of ivory and dark red, with traditional mahogany furnishings and ample lighting. The all-white bath was very compact, but sparkling clean. The staff is highly trained and extremely responsive." *(SWS)*

"Very good area, with all the amenities, a good restaurant, and excellent service. Enjoyed an English-style tea as well." *(Ethel Aaron Hauser)*

Open All year.
Rooms 18 suites, 113 doubles, all with full private bath, telephone, radio, TV, desk, air-conditioning, fan. Some with fireplace; VCR on request.
Facilities Restaurant, bar/lounge with live jazz 4 nights weekly. Tennis available. Valet parking, $24 daily. 24-hour room service.
Location Midtown, Murray Hill.
Credit cards Amex, CB, DC, Enroute, JCB, MC, Visa.
Rates Room only, $325–600 suite, $215–270 double, $195–240 single. Extra adult in room, $30; no charge for 1 child under 17 staying in parents' room. AARP 25% discount (excluding weekends). Weekend rate, $149 double. Alc lunch, $25; alc dinner, $50.
Extras Wheelchair accessible; 2 rooms specially equipped for disabled. Small pets permitted by prior arrangement. Crib, babysitting available. French, German, Spanish, Italian spoken.

The Pierre
5th Avenue and 61st Street, 10021

Tel: 212–838–8000
800–332–3442

Many New York City hotels have become newly elegant after multi-million-dollar renovations—the Pierre has *always* been that way. From the neoclassic decor of the Café Pierre for dining to the frescoed charm of the Rotunda for drinks or tea to the handsome guest rooms traditionally decorated with muted fabrics, formal draperies, Chippendale and Chinoiserie furnishings, the Pierre offers all the luxuries and extra amenities you'd expect from a hotel of this caliber: twice-daily maid service, shoe shine service, terry robes, and more. *(Zacharias Rossner)*

Open All year.
Rooms 196 1- and 2-bedroom suites, doubles, singles—all with full private bath, telephone, TV, radio, desk, air-conditioning, refrigerator, in-room safe.
Facilities Restaurants, reception/meeting rooms. Business services. 24-hour room service. Multilingual concierge service. Valet parking. Hair styling salon, boutiques.
Location Midtown Manhattan, opposite Central Park.
Credit cards Amex, CB, DC, MC, Visa.
Rates Room only, $550–1,000 suite, $295–395 double, $265–360 single. 2-night weekend package, including continental breakfast, wine and cheese 1st night, $480–650; service additional. Alc breakfast, $7–14; alc lunch, $18–30; alc dinner, $27–48.
Extras French, German spoken. Member, Four Seasons Hotels

The Stanhope
995 Fifth Avenue, 10028

Tel: 212–288–5800
800–828–1123

Opulent luxury describes the Stanhope, built in 1926 and located across the street from the Metropolitan Museum of Art and Central Park. In November 1986, the Stanhope opened under new ownership, sporting a $26 million restoration. In 1990, the ownership changed again, to that of Grand Bay Hotels. Managing Director Guenter Richter plans to take the hotel's four diamond/star rating from AAA and Mobil up to the five diamond/star level, by offering even more in the way of amenities, service, and luxurious decor. The lobby is furnished with authentic eighteenth-century French antiques, with 24-carat gold leaf gilded moldings. Guest rooms are supplied with custom-designed French furniture, thick bath towels, terry robes, flowers and plants from the in-house florist, and lots of sunlight, a precious New York commodity. Le Salon is open for breakfast, and also serves what may well be New York's best afternoon tea, the perfect ending to an day at the Met. Plans for the hotel restaurant were under review at press time; a grill room atmosphere with light fare was under consideration.

"Exceptionally luxurious English atmosphere; staff very attentive." (RW)

Open All year.
Rooms 94 suites, 23 doubles—all with full private bath, telephone, radio, TV, desk.
Facilities Restaurant, tea room, bar/lounge. 24-hour room service. Health club access. Limousine service.
Location Upper East Side, across from Central Park.
Credit cards All major credit cards accepted.
Rates Room only, $400–2,000 suite, $250–325 double. Extra person in room, $40. Weekend rates, $195–295, including continental breakfast, museum tickets.
Extras Small pets permitted by prior arrangement. Crib available. Numerous foreign languages spoken.

Wyndham   *Tel:* 212–753–3500
42 West 58th Street, 10019

In a city of hype, the Wyndham's profile is so low as to be almost invisible. The management is not interested in publicity of any kind, and does not even publish a brochure or rate card. But the homey lobby, individually decorated rooms and reasonable rates make the hotel very popular with those in the know, including more than a few celebrities from California and England. Its location is ideal—a relatively short walk (5–20 minutes) to Carnegie Hall, City Center, Lincoln Center, and the Broadway theaters. Advance reservations are essential.

"The Wyndham is small and European in character and traditional in decor. The service is good and personal." *(Elizabeth Ring)* "A wonderful hotel. Women traveling alone like the security. My suite had a living room, bedroom, bathroom, and little eating area with a refrigerator. I found it quiet, compared to other New York City hotels; the staff was very friendly, more like staying in an apartment." *(Dianne Crawford)* "While not as luxurious as some of the city's top hotels, our room was spacious, comfortable, and an excellent value for the money." *(AS)* "The lobby is beautifully furnished, and looks more like a beautiful living room than a hotel lobby.

"Great location. Rooms are clean, quiet, large, comfortable and decorated in flowered chintz. We had a two-bedroom suite which provided a private bedroom and bath for each couple in our group and a shared living room with TV, kitchen area with refrigerator. Make reservations far ahead." *(Jack & Sue Lane)*

A minor niggle: The hotel restaurant is closed on weekends, which is a bit of an annoyance at breakfast.

Open All year. Restaurant closed Sat., Sun.
Rooms 148 suites, doubles, and singles—all with full private bath, telephone, TV.

NEW YORK

Location Midtown Manhattan.
Restrictions Traffic noise in some rooms.
Credit cards Amex, CB, DC, MC, Visa.
Rates Room only, $165–195 suite, $120–130 double, $105–115 single.

NORTH HUDSON

Elk Lake Lodge   *Tel:* 518–532–7616
North Hudson, 12855

Margot Paul, one of the owners of the Elk Lake Lodge, describes it as
"a great place for grandparents and toddlers alike, with cabins for two
to twelve people, and good wholesome food. The main lodge is furnished with Adirondack furniture, a large roaring fire, and a friendly
atmosphere. There are over 12,000 acres available for a maximum of 50
guests. This offers a great deal of freedom, but people who like planned
activities are better off in a large resort. Elk Lake is for the nature lover,
photographer, and people who enjoy solitude, hiking, boating, and
exploring the seasonal changes of the high peaks of the Adirondacks."

A frequent guest writes: "For over fifteen years we have enjoyed the
peace and quiet of Elk Lake. No motorboats are allowed on the lake;
you hear only the cry of the loon. People who come to stay at Elk Lake
Lodge come back year after year, bringing children and grandchildren.
Often the young couples who come have been at the lodge as children
in the past. The rooms in the lodge are small, but a friendly living room
has space for everyone, with a large fireplace and library to make the
evenings and rainy days comfortable. The cabins all have double bedrooms and living rooms, several with fireplaces. The wood supply is
brought in as needed. The cabins and rooms are tended to daily; fresh
towels every day and clean sheets several times a week. Plenty of hot
water and warm heating systems.

"We find the owners and the help most friendly and efficient, with
warm greetings for us when we arrive and interest in our day-to-day
requirements and activities. The extensive trail system offers superior
hiking in some of the most beautiful surroundings anywhere. High
Adirondack peaks frame the lake and the canoeing is a constant delight.
Rowboats for fishing are also supplied. The table d'hôte menus in the
dining room are not fancy, but the food is ample and well prepared.
Trail lunches are supplied if needed." *(Mr. & Mrs. Richard Weinland)*
Additional reports needed.

Open May to Nov.
Rooms 26 rooms. 6 in main lodge with private shower, 7 cottages with a total
of 20 bedrooms. Each cottage with 1 or 2 full baths.
Facilities Lodge dining room, living room, library, with games, fireplace. On
12,000 acres with two lakes, for walking, mountain climbing, fishing, boating,
canoeing, hunting, swimming. Ornithology workshop.
Location NE NY, Adirondack Mts. Exit 29 of the Northway, 2 hrs. N of Albany.
10 m to North Hudson.
Credit cards None accepted.
Rates Full board, $180–200 cottage (for 2 people), $90–100 single. No charge for

176

children under 2; age 2–6, 50% discount; age 7–12, 25% discount. 15% service additional. 2-night minimum in cottage. 2-night weekend minimum.
Extras Limited wheelchair access. Airport/station pickups. Crib available.

NORTH RIVER

Information please: Built as a private home in 1933, **Highwinds Inn** (Barton Mines Road, 12856; 518–251–3760) sits high in the hills overlooking the Adirondacks in a secluded country setting. In the Barton family for over a hundred years, over 1600 acres are available for cross-country skiing, hiking, fishing, canoeing and tennis. The reasonable rates for the inn's four guest rooms include a full breakfast and dinner. Comments?

Garnet Hill Lodge
13th Lake Road, 12856

Tel: 518–251–2821

Garnet Hill Lodge was built in 1936 to house workers from the nearby garnet mine; both the Log House and Big Shanty (the original mine owner's house) have huge fireplaces built of garnet rock. Although visitors can still hike to an abandoned mine to search for garnets, most guests are seeking treasure of a different kind: the spectacular view of 13th Lake and the surrounding mountains, the relaxing setting of a classic Adirondack lodge, and the outdoor pleasures of hiking, boating, fishing for landlocked salmon or trout, rafting on the Hudson, or skiing, depending on the season. Rates include a hearty breakfast and dinner; the menu changes seasonally, but home-baked breads, pastries, and desserts are year-round favorites. Guest rooms are simply done in pine paneling, wallpaper, or split-log walls with cheerful curtains and spreads; some have brass beds. *(ML)* More comments please.

Open All year.
Rooms 27 doubles—all with desk. 20 with private bath and/or shower, 7 with shared bath. 6 with balconies, some with fan. 14 rooms in main lodge, 13 in 3 other buidlings. 2 with whirlpool tubs.
Facilities Dining room, game room with ping pong, pool; TV room. 580 acres with gazebo, tennis court, nature trails, 50 km. cross-country ski trails with rentals; private beach on lake, swimming, canoeing, sailing, fishing. 10 m to downhill skiing. Whitewater rafting, tubing nearby.
Location Central Adirondacks, 90 m N of Albany, 35 m NW of Lake George. Take Exit 23 off I-87. Go N on Rte. 9 to Rte. 28. Go 21 m to 13th Lake Road, turn left. 5 m to inn.
Restrictions Smoking permitted in lounge and smoking section of dining room only.
Credit cards None accepted.
Rates MAP, $108–174 double, $67–130 single. Extra person in room $40. 12% service additional. Reduced rates for children in room with parents. 2-night minimum weekends mid-Nov. to April. Packages available. Alc lunch $8, alc dinner $20.
Extras Station pick-ups for fee. Cribs available.

ONEIDA

The Pollyanna Bed & Breakfast   *Tel:* 315–363–0524
302 Main Street, 13421

If you're looking for a pleasant overnight to break up the long haul up the New York State Thruway, consider the Pollyanna. It's a good example of what B&Bs are all about—well-traveled, multi-faceted hosts with a large and architecturally distinctive house to share with guests. Ken Chapin is a business consultant who also collects canes and makes English baskets, while Doloria is a textile artist and craftswoman who plays the dulcimer and tends their beautiful gardens of roses, lilies, and 100 kinds of iris. Their home is a turn-of-the-century brick Italian mansion with the original woodwork, crystal chandeliers, and eclectic detailing. Rates include a full breakfast.

"A delightful place, quiet and well-maintained, with large, comfortable rooms, high ceilings, and lots of light. Doloria & Ken are warm, friendly, and bring you right into their family (and kitchen). Doloria makes the lightest and most delicious waffles I've ever had. The inn is surrounded by lovely gardens; don't miss the Japanese garden—complete with lantern, Zen pond, and the Window of Heaven." *(Jeanette Lurier)* "Very gracious hosts—Ken is always open to a game of chess and Doloria will gladly show you her loom or play her dulcimer for you." *(Trudy Staples)*

Open All year.
Rooms 1 suite, 4 doubles—all with private bath and/or shower, fan. 4 with air-conditioning, 1 with telephone.
Facilities Parlor, dining room, common room with library, games, organ. Perennial, rose, Japanese gardens. Laundry facilities available. Off-street parking.
Location N NY, Leatherstocking region. 25 m E of Syracuse, 23 m W of Utica. Historic district. From Utica, take I-90 to Exit 33. Turn right on Rte. 365A. At 3rd light turn left and go 2 blocks to inn at corner of Stone & Main Sts. From Syracuse, take Exit 34 and turn left on Peterboro. Go to Rte. 5 and turn left. Go 5 m to Rte. 46 and turn left. Go through 1st light to end of block to inn on left.
Restrictions No smoking. Some traffic noise on summer weekend evenings. "Well mannered children welcome."
Credit cards Amex, MC, Visa; preferred for deposit only.
Rates B&B, $60–75 suite, $50–100 double, $45–60 single. Extra person in room, $10. 10% discount for 4 day visit. 2-night college, holiday weekend minimum.
Extras Some pets permitted, off-season, by prior arrangement. Airport/station pickups, $10–25. Playpen available.

PHILMONT

Harmony House Inn   *Tel:* 518–672–4577
Schnackenberg Road, P.O. Box 707, 12565

After many years teaching school, Lee and Richard Dixon decided a life in the country was what they really wanted. They remodeled a contemporary lodge-style home, added bedrooms and baths, and became full-time innkeepers in 1987. The Dixons note that breakfast, served from 7:30-9:30, is a "special time." Buttermilk pancakes, eggs Benedict, quiche, or another favorite is accompanied by home fries, assorted breakfast meats, fresh fruit and juice, homemade baked goods, and preserves.

"Very charming bucolic setting, warm and wonderful hosts, huge and terrific breakfasts." *(Rick Balkin)* "A comfortable place to visit again." *(PDA)*

Open All year.
Rooms 1 2-bedroom suite, 2 doubles—all with private bath and/or shower, radio, air-conditioning. 1 with desk. Suite has fireplace, private entrance.
Facilities Breakfast room; 2 living rooms with fireplace, TV; sun room; decks, patio. 8 acres with gardens, woods. Swimming in state park nearby. 10–30 m to downhill, cross country skiing. 30 m to Tanglewood.
Location SE NY. Hudson River Valley W of Berkshires. 38 m S of Albany, 109 m N of NYC, 10 m E of Hudson. From Taconic State Parkway, exit at Rte. 217. Turn left and continue to Schnackenberg Rd. and turn R. ½ m to inn.
Restrictions No smoking in guest rooms.
Credit cards None accepted.
Rates B&B, $115–150 suite, $50–70 double, $40–60 single. No tipping. Family discount midweek.
Extras Suite is wheelchair accessible. Crib available.

PITTSFORD

Oliver Loud's Inn
1474 Marsh Road, 14534

Tel: 716–248–5200

In its first life, Oliver Loud's Inn was located in the village of Egypt, which was on a busy stagecoach route in days past. When the Erie Canal was completed, the stagecoach business died out, and the once busy tavern lost much of its trade. In 1985, the inn was scheduled for demolition, but the owners of Richardson's Canal House decided to move it next to their four-star restaurant, to provide luxury lodgings in a historic setting.

"A restored nineteenth-century building, the inn has been decorated with reproduction furniture and colors documented from the period. The owners have done much research into the history of the building. The Erie Canal, a beautiful backdrop in any season, is close to Rochester and many activities." *(Bonnie Gibson)* "Freshly painted in an appealing yellow color, the inn has an extremely inviting appearance. The hostess warmly welcomed us into a beautifully furnished sitting room, decorated with historic mementos relating to the history of the inn. Our second-floor room was furnished with a four-poster canopy king-size bed, with appropriate lamps, tables, and desk completing the decor. It was evident that much skilled planning had gone into the furnishing of the inn. Our dinner at Richardson's Canal House was superb. The wonderful breakfast served in our room included fresh fruit and juice, coffee, homemade rolls and muffins, cheese, and jam." *(George & Myra Trautman)*

"Our smallish room had a private porch facing the canal; it had good reading lamps (with three-way bulbs that worked) on either side of the king-size bed, a good TV with remote control, a well-conceived closet with built-in dresser, and a clean and efficient bath with an extra vanity counter, and good soaps. In-room amenities included complimentary fruit, a split of champagne, and afternoon cheese and crackers. Turn-down service with fresh towels." *(Judith Turner, and others)*

"Personal extras like homemade cookies, sherry and a well-equipped closet and immaculate bath were welcome surprises. The superb breakfast hamper contained just enough food, and the dishes and linens were of the best quality. I was especially impressed by the discreet service and warm hospitality of the people at the inn. Dinner at the restaurant was delicious. The wine list was not extensive, but good; the atmosphere is rustic, and tavern-like. Since I visited during the off-season, I took advantage of a special package which significantly reduced the price of the room and dinner, yet I never felt that I was receiving bargain treatment in any way." *(Lisa Tilton)*

And from the 'Nobody's Perfect Department': "Service at dinner was slow, and our waitress had to be asked to bring such essentials as butter and the wine list."

Open All year. Restaurant closed Sun., also Jan. 1, Dec. 25. Year's Day; closed for lunch on Sat.
Rooms 8 doubles—all with full private bath, telephone, desk, air-conditioning.
Facilities Common room with fireplace, books, games; porch, restaurant adjacent with weekend musical entertainment. 5 acres on Erie Canal, with towpath for walking, bicycling, cross-country skiing, fishing.
Location NW NY. Finger Lakes region. 12 m SE of Rochester, 3½ m from Pittsford. From I-90, take I-490 W to Bushnell's Basin exit. Turn right and go 400 yds to Richardson's Canal House Village, where inn is located. From downtown Rochester, take I-490 E to Bushnell's Basin; proceed as above.
Restrictions No smoking in some guest rooms. No children under 12.
Credit cards Amex, CB, DC, MC, Visa.
Rates B&B, $125 double. Alc lunch, $8–10; alc dinner, $25–30. Off-season packages.
Extras 1 room wheelchair accessible. French, Spanish spoken.

POUGHKEEPSIE

Inn at the Falls
50 Red Oaks Mill Road, 12603

Tel: 914–462–5770
800–344–1466

Poughkeepsie is not a town that comes readily to mind when one summons up visions of romantic weekend escapes; it's not even a place you'd suggest as an ideal spot for a midweek executive seminar. Yet that is just what the Inn at the Falls is all about. In 1985, owner/manager Arnold Sheer opened this newly built brick and shingle inn set on the banks overlooking an old mill pond and waterfall on Wappingers Creek. The hotel's main living room is a two-story affair, with lots of windows, comfortable conversation groupings, soft rose-toned walls and draperies, lots of plants, and a handsome brass chandelier. Guest rooms are done in either country-style, English, contemporary, or Oriental motifs, but all are spacious, luxurious, and comfortable with nightly turndown service and chocolates, terry robes, personal toiletries, and whirlpool tubs. A continental breakfast is served in the living room or brought to your room at the time you've requested. The inn is just five minutes' drive from Vassar College, and many other Hudson area attractions, such as the Roosevelt home at Hyde Park, are just an easy drive away.

"The inn is a stone's throw from one of the messiest traffic snarls in the county, but you wouldn't know it when you're inside. Our room had a great view of Wappingers Creek and the falls beyond (really a dam spillway). The inn is beautiful, very quiet, and service is excellent." *(Geoff & Sue Meissner)* "We thoroughly enjoyed the living room type lobby where we breakfasted on fresh breads, coffee, juice, fruit, and cereals. The staff was friendly and professional, but not stiff." *(Jeffrey & Ruth Ann Smith)*

"The living room with two-story atrium is stunning, and the rooms exceptionally handsome and spacious. We saw one dramatically modern one with a black lacquer headboard and a slate gray bath with a black Jacuzzi, another done in country Victorian style with a king-size bed with brass headboard, and a third with a four-poster, lace-canopied bed." *(SWS)*

And a few minor niggles: "We would have liked this inn even better with a little more attention to detail. The supply of towels and robes could have been more generous; beds were not turned down at night, though fresh towels and chocolates were provided; and breakfast pastries were served unheated right out of the box."

Open All year, except Christmas through New Year's.
Rooms 14 suites, 22 doubles—all with full private bath, telephone, radio, TV, desk, air-conditioning, fan. Whirlpool tubs in suites.
Facilities Living room with fireplace, bar, meeting room. 3 acres with swimming pool, waterfalls, creek for fishing.
Location Dutchess County. 85 m S of Albany. 5 m from center. Take Taconic State Pkwy. N to Rte. 55, Poughkeepsie Exit. Go W on Rte. 55 3 m, then turn left on Titusville Rd. Go 2 m and turn left on Red Oaks Mill Rd. Inn is ¼ m down on right.
Credit cards Amex, DC, MC, Visa.
Rates B&B, $135 suite, $105 double, single. Children stay free in parents' room. 10% senior discount.
Extras Wheelchair accessible; two rooms equipped for disabled. Station pickups. Cribs available.

RHINEBECK

Rhinebeck combines the charms of a beautifully preserved historic village with the modern-day appeal of first-class craft shops and galleries and innovative restaurants. The village recently celebrated its 300th birthday, and dozens of its buildings, ranging in style from Dutch colonial to Federal to Gothic and Greek Revival, are listed on the National Register of Historic Places. A key annual event in Rhinebeck is the Dutchess County Fair, held since 1919 during the third week of August; it's a real old-fashioned country fair, with ox-pulling contests and flower and vegetable displays (expect rate surcharges). From May through October, there's some kind of festival on the calendar nearly every month—crafts, antiques, and others. Be sure to catch an air show at the Old Rhinebeck Aerodrome, highlighting aircraft from World War I and earlier. Other area activities include bicycling, golf, and boating on the Hudson.

Rhinebeck is about 100 miles north of New York City, and is easily accessible by train from Grand Central Station. By car, take the NY State Thruway (I-87) to Exit 19 (Kingston-Rhinecliff Bridge). Continue to light. Right onto Rte. 9G to light. Right onto Route 9 to Rhinebeck. Another route is the Saw Mill Parkway to the Taconic to Route 199 west to Route 308 west into Rhinebeck.

Note that you pay a premium for the town's proximity to New York, and rates are high and still climbing faster than the rate of inflation. Let us know if you think it's worth it!

Information please: About 12 miles north of Rhinebeck is the **Inn at Blue Stores** (Route 9, Box 99 Star Route, Hudson, 12534) built in 1908 with distinctive Spanish style architecture and highlighted by stained glass, black oak woodwork, and handsome Arts & Crafts decor. Rates include a continental breakfast, and guests will enjoy relaxing on the front porch or swimming in the backyard pool.

Beekman Arms   *Tel:* 914–876–7077
4 Mill Street, 12572

Founded in 1766, the Beekman Arms is one of the oldest inns in America; Revolutionary War soldiers held drills on the front lawn, William Jennings Bryan orated here, and Franklin Roosevelt spoke from the porch steps.

"The inn is impeccably landscaped and maintained with a profusion of flowers. Downstairs is the colonial-style restaurant, the historic tap room, and an enormous parlor, filled with elegant yet comfortable couches and easy chairs, both beautiful antiques and quality reproductions. The guest rooms upstairs have an authentic 'old inn' feeling to them. Additional accommodations are found in the motel wing and another building in the back parking lot, and at the Delamater House and Courtyard one block away. The motel rooms are adequate but uninspired, while the rooms at the Delamater Courtyard have the quietest setting. Recently built, these neo-Victorian townhouses are set around a grassy common, and have Shaker-style pencil post beds, a comfortable sitting area, and country decor. Best of all is the recently redecorated Delamater House, built in 1844 and an excellent example of early American Gothic architecture. The decor is stunning; not a literal reproduction of Victorian country style, but rather an exuberant re-interpretation, with bright, airy color, textures, and patterns; tones of soft rose, green, and cream are used frequently.

"Rates in the Rhinebeck area are very high, and we felt that rooms at the Beekman were by far the best value in the area, even though they don't include breakfast; the staff is very helpful and accommodating, although there is no contact with the owners." (SWS)

"We chose to stay in the original building, preferring character over amenities. Our room was in excellent condition, pleasantly wallpapered and curtained. The bed, a canopied four poster with two pillows for each of us, was well-lit for reading. Other furnishings were a large desk, suit valet, a full-length standing mirror, and real plants. No bathtub, but the shower pressure was fine and we made use of the ample supply of toiletries and complimentary brandy. The inn is warm and inviting, a well-maintained colonial building, but it was hard to imagine George Washington tying his horse in front of the atrium greenhouse. We enjoyed a dinner of swordfish and apricot ginger chicken." (Emily & Jeff Clements)

"We stayed in an enormous suite on the second floor of the firehouse gift shop. Although somewhat oddly furnished with a canopied four poster bed and a very modern oil painting, it had a separate room with a brass bed, and a fold-out couch as well. There was plenty of room for the kids to spread out, and we didn't have to worry about them disturbing anyone." (NB)

Some areas for improvement: "We enjoyed our lovely condo-style suite in the Delamater Courtyard, but felt that more insulation between rooms would have made for a quieter stay." And: "A stay in the Delamater House is recommended, but our dinner was uninspiring; what was called white chocolate mousse was actually vanilla pudding."

Open All year.
Rooms 47 suites and doubles—all with private shower and/or bath, telephone, desk. Most with TV, air-conditioning; some with fireplace. 12 rooms in main inn; remainder in 5 buildings nearby.
Facilities Parlor, tap room, restaurant, meeting rooms.
Location In town, at intersection of Rtes. 9 & 308.
Restrictions Traffic, restaurant noise in some rooms.
Credit cards Amex, Discover, MC, Visa.
Rates Room only, $55–110 double. Midweek corporate rates. 2-night weekend minimum, May 15–Oct. 31 and holidays.
Extras Limited wheelchair access.

Village Victorian Inn
31 Center Street, 12572

Tel: 914–876–8345

Built in 1860, Judy and Rich Kohler bought the Village Victorian in 1987, decorating it lavishing with period decor. Guests report great satisfaction with the inn, and the food, service, and hospitality provided by innkeeper Julie Kirsh.

An additional venture of the Kohlers that we'd like to receive feedback about is the Lakehouse Inn on Golden Pond, in Stanfordville, about 10 miles east of Rhinebeck. A luxury lakeside accommodation with 4 suites, the Lakehouse offers privacy and seclusion, including private island for sunbathing, picnicking, and blueberry picking, on 22 wooded acres. Rates range from $275 to $350 per night, with full breakfast. Comments?

"The inn is set on a quiet street in the middle of town, within walking distance of the Fairground, the revival movie theater, and two charming restaurants. We had the downstairs bedroom, a Victorian suite with a king-size reproduction canopy bed, a huge, fascinating armoire, and a small bath—pretty wallpapers, nice colors, all spotlessly clean. There's a nice dining room and a small but pleasant parlor with a sofa, several upholstered chairs, and a card table, all antiques of various vintages and value. The owners live in Stanfordville, about twenty minutes away." *(JR)* "Julie, the innkeeper, never intruded on our privacy, but was always there to take care of our needs. Our room had an Oriental mauve rug, a gorgeous and comfortable brass bed with Victorian-style sheets trimmed with ruffles and lace. The pillows, with satin shams, were artfully arranged on the bed, and the quilt, a slightly different print than the sheets, was beautiful, as was the matching dust ruffle and coordinating wallpaper. The potpourri gave the room a lovely clean aroma. The bath was handsomely done with dusty rose towels and white wicker, and the closet was even supplied with peach-colored satin hangers." *(Debra Segal)* "The decanter of sherry and glasses in the sitting room to sip as you please is a delightful touch." *(Don & Rachel Shive)*

"This yellow house with wraparound veranda is surrounded by a white picket fence. Inside are the original hardwood floors, moldings, and paneling, all polished and shining. Every corner of the inn shone and sparkled, starting with the crystal drops that hung from the lamp next to the guest book. We awoke in the morning to the aroma of fresh coffee and all kinds of wonderful baking smells wafting through the house. We entered the dining room to find a sideboard overflowing with a variety of fruits, fresh croissants, and fresh-baked muffins. We were then served French bread toast, accompanied by fresh strawberries and whipped cream, followed by any style of eggs, potatoes, and bacon (for those who could find room). Along with all of this came homemade jellies, preserves, and jams, tasty coffee, and a choice of fine teas." *(Olivia & Carl Johnsen)*

"The rooms provide time travel to a Victorian past yet utilities are modern and in good working order; all the details have been attended to and everything is spotlessly clean. The breakfasts rival the meals served at the Culinary Institute nearby." *(Robert Buckley)*

"As lovely as described in last year's book. Julie, the manager, is helpful, competent, and made our stay delightful." *(Mrs. Leonard Paul, also Brian & Charlotte Hommel)* "We would love to return, but don't see how we could afford to. Rates here have increased from $85 to $120 in the last year!"

Open All year.
Rooms 7 doubles—all with private bath and/or shower, air-conditioning, fan. 2 rooms in cottage.
Facilities Dining room with fireplace; parlor with games, TV; porch. 2 m from Hudson River for swimming, fishing, sailing. 3 m to cross-country skiing; 25 min. to downhill.
Location 18 m N of Poughkeepsie, 4 m E of Kingston, 15 m SW of Berkshires. 1 block from center of town. From Rte. 308 in Rhinebeck, turn right on Center St. Inn is on corner on right. From Rte. 9, turn left on Livingston St. to inn on right at corner.
Restrictions No smoking. No children under 16.

Credit cards Amex, MC, Visa.
Rates B&B, $120–170 double. Extra person in room, $40. 10% senior discount.
2-night weekend, holiday minimum.
Extras Airport/station pickups.

Whistle Wood
Tel: 914–876–6838
Pells Road, 12572

"Maggie Myer has had horses as guests on her little ranch since she bought Whistle Wood in 1975; in 1982, she decided people could come too, and since then, has rarely stopped feeding one or the other. Guests follow the long drive up to the house, past pastures of grazing horses, to the contemporary ranch-style home that Maggie has furnished and upgraded with love and care. Entering through the sun porch, past oversized rockers, we tried hard not to track any barn mud into the house. From there you enter the sunken living room, with ample comfortable seating, quilts hung on the walls, and a cozy fire burning in the woodstove. The whole house is filled with a delightful collection of antique quilts, farm primitives, and collectibles. Our spacious room was the nicest (and most expensive), with a rough-hewn queen-size canopy bed made by Maggie herself, a beautiful blue and white quilt serving as a partial canopy at the head of the bed, and luxurious blue and white linens and pillow shams. An armoire, desk and chair, day bed, table and chairs completed the decor, along with an old poster for an 1884 farm journal, a rustic barrel bedside table, and other charming touches. We had a chance to peek into the other rooms, which were also very inviting. After a delicious dinner at Il Parmegiano in Rhinebeck, an idiosyncratic and original pizza/pasta restaurant in a converted church, we gathered with the other guests to sing around the player piano in the dining area, and nibble on Maggie's delicious homemade almond cake and deep-dish apple pie. In the morning we went for an early walk on the country road, past a pond where wild ducks paddled, returning in time for a hearty breakfast of fresh fruit salad, cereal, blueberry corn muffins, and egg/cheese strata. The food was set out on an antique cookstove, and we took our dishes out back to the sunny deck to savor." (SWS)

Open All year.
Rooms 4 doubles—all with private bath and/or shower, ceiling fan. 1 with bath across hall. 2 with clock/radio, 1 with air-conditioning.
Facilities Living room with woodstove, dining area with TV/VCR, player piano, sun porch, deck, gardens. 13½ acres with barns, paddocks, horses.
Location 3 m E of town. From Taconic Pkwy, exit at Rte. 199 (Rhinebeck/Red Hook) and go W for 3 m to Rock City (traffic light). Bear left on Rte. 308 and continue for 3 m. Look for caboose on right, then turn right on Pells Rd. to inn (5th driveway on right). From Rhinebeck, take Rte. 308 3 miles to Pells Rd. & turn left.
Restrictions Smoking in common rooms only.
Credit cards Amex, MC, Visa.
Rates B&B, $75–125 double. Extra person in room, $15. 10% discount 3-day stays, seniors. Midweek discounts. 2-night weekend minimum late May through Dec.
Extras Wheelchair accessible. Pets permitted with prior approval; boarding kennel available. Station pickups. Some German, Spanish spoken.

ROSCOE

The Open Door B&B   *Tel:* 607–498–5772
Old Route 17 at Blinker Light, 12776

Anglers heading for "Trout Town U.S.A." no longer need feel guilty about leaving their spouses at home or in non-nondescript motels. *Eugene Gardner* reports that "Ellen Pusey runs a beautiful country Victorian B&B in the heart of town. Although the inn is located just minutes from some of the most popular trout fishing streams in New York, she does not cater only to fishermen. The living room is filled with books and magazines on virtually every subject; the guest rooms are very clean and beautifully decorated. A tiny gift shop offers potpourri, dried flowers, jams, honey, and mementos. Breakfast consists of a wide variety of cereals, fresh fruit and juices, coffee, teas and an incredible helping of freshly baked biscuits and muffins and the most varied array of jellies, jams, and honey I've ever seen under one roof. Breakfast can be eaten in the small dining room or taken to your bedroom on a tray. A nice little afternoon extra is the selection of light beverages and snacks put out around 4 P.M. The owner's friendliness is very sincere and she is quick to offer advice on local fishing hot-spots and places to eat." More comments please.

Note: We learned at press-time that the inn had been sold and would suggest inquiring further when making reservations, initial reports were disappointing.

Open All year.
Rooms 5 doubles—4 with private half-bath, 1 with shared bath.
Facilities Dining room, living room with TV, veranda, guest refrigerator. 1 acre with gazebo. 1 block to swimming pool, tennis court, Beaverkill River for trout fishing. Golf nearby. 20 min. to downhill, cross-country skiing.
Location 100 m N of NYC, Sullivan County. 5 blocks from town at blinker light.
Restrictions No smoking.
Credit cards None accepted.
Rates B&B, $45–60 double, $40–55 single. Extra person in room, $10. Children under 3 free; $3–7 for ages 3–16.
Extras Port-a-crib, babysitting available.

SARANAC LAKE

The Point   *Tel:* 518–891–5674
Star Route 30, 12983   518–891–5678
                                                       800–255–3530

If you've always wanted to live like a Rockefeller, The Point is the place to do it. This Adirondack camp was built in the 1930s by William Avery Rockefeller, as a place to "modestly" entertain the elite during the summers (although one reader informed us that few, if any, guests were ever received). Today, in keeping with the tradition of this remarkable home, The Point continues to accept paying guests in an elegant, yet relaxed, house party atmosphere. Early morning coffee, and breakfast are brought to your door. Lunch, cocktails, and dinner are served at set times; there is no choice of menu. Guests dress for dinner; coat and tie are de rigueur for men, and many wear black tie Wednesday and Saturday night. The food is excellent, the service first-rate, and the atmosphere extraordinary.

The Point was bought by David and Christie Garrett at the end of 1986, and is hosted by Bill and Claudia McNamee. The Garretts have improved the facilities by upgrading and adding fireplaces to all rooms, and adding more antiques to the furnishings.

"Very exclusive retreat situated in a wooded area overlooking Lake Saranac. The day begins with a light knock on the door announcing the arrival of morning coffee. About an hour later comes a louder knock and outside your door awaits a rolling cart loaded with breakfast goodies—freshly squeezed orange juice, homemade muffins and rolls, and other assorted fruits. Breakfast can be eaten in front of your fireplace or on the screened porch in warmer weather. Truly romantic. The guests usually make it out of their rooms in time for a leisurely walk and then a grand luncheon, sometimes preceded by a round of Bloody Marys from the always open bar. There are only two tables and all the guests are seated together for lunch and dinner. The host and hostess each head one table and interject interesting trivia on the area and keep the conversation stimulating. The guests come from all over the country and have very diverse backgrounds. You might take a boat ride along the scenic lake, possibly with a picnic prepared by the chef, take a walk in the woods, or just lay in the hammock with a good book. Or drive to Lake Placid, 20 minutes away, stopping at the Adirondack stores along the way. In the evening, you dress for dinner, then meet for cocktails before an exquisite meal. Cordials and conversation around the twin floor-to-ceiling stone fireplace cap off a wonderful and romantic day. Perfect for a honeymoon—first, second, or otherwise!" *(Susie & Robert Preston)*

"The main lodge has all the marvelous twiggy, woodsy and warm Adirondack atmosphere you could want. The service is complete, unobtrusive and professional (with a homey touch). The rooms range from cozy and comfortable with a little stone fireplace to huge, with a walk-in fireplace and picture window overlooking the lake. Bathrooms are well equipped and clean. The McNamees are most accommodating and attractive; the staff is young and eager to please." *(Julia & Coleman Walker)*

"The food is spectacular. The soups are incredible, especially the scallop bisque and the creamed asparagus; both are served piping hot and cloud-light. A smoked salmon mousse was just outstanding, and the desserts are 'to die from.' Most guest rooms are done in 1930s Adirondack camp style, and while very attractive, are not as luxurious as some people might expect. Bathrooms are well supplied with hot water, stacks of giant towels, and thick terry robes, although the facilities themselves are fairly basic. Our room was called The Trapper and was designed to look like the inside of a slab-sided, peak-roofed 1800s cabin, with stuffed critters here and there. It was cozy and fun; the weather was rainy and cold, and we just kept the fire going all weekend." *(Dave & Cheri Kendall)*

One area for improvement: "Given the price tag, I thought the bathroom amenities, though of good quality, were a bit skimpy—a tiny bar of soap, and one-ounce shampoo and conditioner."

Open All year.
Rooms 11 doubles all with full private bath, desk, fan; all with fireplaces and/or decks. 4 rooms in main lodge, 7 in 3 adjacent buildings.
Facilities Living/dining room with two fireplaces, piano, bar; pub with billiards, games, TV/VCR. Sailing, fishing, canoeing, boating, waterskiing, badminton, croquet, and sauna, ice-skating, cross-country skiing, snowshoeing, including equipment. Downhill skiing, tennis, and golf nearby.
Location NE NY, Adirondack region. 6 hrs. N of NYC, 3 hrs. N of Albany, 2½ hrs. S of Montreal. Directions only on confirmation.
Restrictions No smoking at dinner. No children (call for information on exceptions).
Credit cards Amex.
Rates $525–675 including all meals, wine, liquor, liqueurs, and facilities. 15% service. $100 reduction for singles. Extra person in room, $150. 2–3-night weekend/holiday minimum.
Extras Airport pickups. Pets allowed by prior arrangement. Some French spoken. Member, Relais et Chateaux.

SARATOGA SPRINGS

"Queen of the Spas," and one of the most popular and fashionable resorts of late Victorian America, the heritage of Saratoga Springs was nearly destroyed by the wrecker's ball in the 1960s. Fortunately, the voice of the preservationists was heard before all was lost, and the town has not only restored much of its past glory, but has added some important new attractions as well. In August, horse lovers head early in the morning for the 127-year-old track to watch the horses work out, return in the afternoon for the races, then move on to the polo fields at 6 P.M. for world-class matches. (If you can't make it in August, the Saratoga Harness Track has races nearly year-round). Culture buffs are equally delighted with the summer program at the Saratoga Performing Arts Center, with the Philadelphia Orchestra and the New York City Ballet in residence during much of July and August. Open most of the year are the town's museums, including the country's first dance museum, the National Museum of Racing, and the Casino in Congress Park, with exhibits depicting the town's heyday. Last but certainly not least are the famous waters—sample them in town at Hathorn Spring No. 1, or head to Saratoga Spa State Park for a soak or a swim in the baths or swimming pools. Contact the Chamber of Commerce, (494 Broadway; 518–584–3255) for more details. Another good source of information is the Preservation Foundation (6 Lake Avenue, P.O. Box 442, 12866; 518–587–5030) which sponsors walking tours, house tours, and workshops.

For an especially good meal in Saratoga, a reader suggests **Eartha's Kitchen,** a tiny place serving exceptional food.

August is the season in Saratoga Springs, when room rates *triple*. Unless you expect to make up the difference at the track, consider staying in a neighboring town, where prices are more reasonable (see suggestions below). Another alternative, if you are something of a gambler, is to not make reservations and just see which hotels still have rooms available after six o'clock; we have heard that the Adelphi drops rates on unbooked rooms in the evening.

Information please: The good news on the spa front is that TW/ Recreation Services, competent operators of the parks and lodges in many national parks, has invested millions in renovating the historic 132-room **Gideon Putnam Hotel** and adjacent spa buildings (P.O. Box 476, Saratoga Spa Park, 12866; 518–584–3000). Another possibility is the century-old **Inn at Saratoga** (231 Broadway, 12866; 518–583–1890) with a handsome restaurant and 38 luxuriously equipped rooms.

Seven miles west of Saratoga is the **Mansion Inn**, an elegantly restored and decorated Victorian home, built in 1866 in the style of a Venetian villa by a man who had made a fortune from his invention—the folded paper bag (Route 29, P.O. Box 77, Rock City Falls 12863; 518–885–1607).

Saratoga is in eastern New York, about 35 miles north of Albany and about 30 south of Lake George via I-87. Take Exit 13 to South Broadway.

For additional Saratoga area listings, see the entries for the **Inn on Bacon Hill**, a 15-minutes drive away in **Schuylerville**, and the **Saratoga Rose Inn**, a similar distance away in **Hadley**.

Adelphi Hotel   *Tel:* 518–587–4688
365 Broadway, 12866

When Gregg Siefker and Sheila Parkert bought the Adelphi in 1979, this century-old hotel was badly run down and neglected. Since then, little by little, these two energetic innkeepers have restored the hotel, starting with the piazza overlooking Broadway, to the three-story columns supporting a maze of Victorian fretwork and airy verandas, to the grand lobby and spacious guest rooms. The Adelphi's two restaurants, the Saratoga Club and the Cafe Adelphi, specialize in imaginative entrées and home-baked French desserts.

"Since the 1960s, the town of Saratoga has undergone a rebirth, resurfacing with much of the glamour, elegance, and pure fun that characterized it in the 1870s. Perhaps the most marvelous reincarnation is the Adelphi—the only remaining grand hotel. You approach its Italianate villa–style veranda and enter a small-scale Victorian world. After checking in at the antique desk, amid palms and fascinating decor, we quickly mounted the high Victorian staircase and were shown to our luxurious rooms, with 15-foot ceilings, very tall doors, and French doors opening onto the second-story veranda overlooking Broadway. Gregg and Sheila have carried out a detailed restoration effort—their goal is to return the hotel to its original grace and elegance. They have been undeniably successful. Elegant fabric bed hangings and draperies (along with a very firm and comfortable bed) set the mood in our airy bedroom and sitting room. The furnishings are an eclectic collection of attic and auction finds rather than expensive antiques, and it all works very well. The updated 1920s bathroom had a good shower and Caswell Massey soaps and treats (not renewed the second day), while our modernized sink was in our room.

"A continental breakfast of fresh muffins and breads is served in the

NEW YORK

fabulous second-floor parlor, but we took ours outside to the veranda in front of our room. We also enjoyed the veranda for late afternoon drinks brought up from the bar. I'd suggest asking for a front or court-yard room. We didn't try their restaurant, but other Saratoga favorites include Hattie's Chicken Shack, Mrs. Long's Bake Shop, the Ash Grove Inn, Charles, and, for a splurge, Chez Sophie, a 45-minute drive away."
(Deborah Reese)

Another reader, visiting during the height of the season, in August, felt her room was overpriced and noisy, with an uncomfortable bed. More comments please.

Open May to Oct. Restaurant open July, Aug.
Rooms 17 suites, 17 doubles, all with private bath and/or shower. All with telephone, TV, air-conditioning. Most with desk.
Facilities Restaurants, bar, lobby, breakfast room, veranda, courtyard. Parking in public lot ½ block away.
Location 35 m N of Albany. Downtown Saratoga Springs.
Restrictions Light sleepers should request back rooms. "Older children preferred."
Credit cards Amex, MC, Visa.
Rates B&B, $85–230 suite, $70–190 double, $60–150 single. Extra person in room, $15. 2–3 night weekend minimum. Alc dinner, $30.
Extras Cribs, babysitting available.

Six Sisters B&B   *Tel:* 518–583–1173
149 Union Avenue, 12866

Kate Benton named the B&B she and husband Steve Ramirez opened in 1989 in honor of her siblings. Built in 1890, the house has "Saratoga porches" with basket weave railings on the first and second floors, and an unusual Dutch-influenced, scalloped-edge roof. Rooms are fur-nished in period; the dining room, where a full breakfast is served, has an inlaid wood table, Oriental carpet, black marbleized fireplace and mantel. The menu might include French toast with honey-nut bread, topped with fresh fruit, and accompanied by maple sausage; or quiche with fresh vegetables and bacon, accompanied by home-baked apple crisp, juice, and a variety of fresh fruit.

"The Maureen Anita is our favorite room, with a fireplace, sitting area, refrigerator, and private porch. The bathroom is large, and storage space ample. The owners have added many thoughtful touches—a night light, clock radio, extra blankets and pillows, even a neck pillow for the bathtub and a jar of bubble bath. In each room they leave a detailed list of restaurants and local attractions. The other rooms are just as nice, especially the Elizabeth Marie room with white wicker furniture and foam green walls—reminiscent of the owners' many years in Hawaii. The location is ideal. While on a busy street, there is ample parking on a small street behind the inn, and we had no noise problems. It's right across the street from the racetrack, four houses away from the National Museum of Racing, and within walking distance of Congress Park and downtown shops and restaurants.

"The best part of the Six Sisters are the owners, Kate and Steve. They are warm and funny and full of suggestions for things to do and see.

190

Having grown up in Saratoga, Kate knows much about the area. Thanks to her, early morning walks took us to the training track, where, binoculars in hand, we watched the horses at their morning workouts. Breakfast is also a highlight. The food and company are equally satisfying, and Kate serves the best coffee in town." *(Martha & William Poole, and others)*

Open All year.
Rooms 2 suites, 2 doubles—all with private bath and/or shower, radio, desk, air-conditioning, fan. 1 with TV, balcony, refrigerator, fireplace.
Facilities Dining room, parlor, verandas, gardens. Off street parking. Swimming pool, lakes, golf, tennis, cross-country skiing nearby.
Location In town, walking distance to downtown, racetrack. Take I-87 to Exit 14. At 3rd light turn right onto Nelson Ave. and an immediate right onto Morton Place. First white house on right.
Restrictions Traffic noise may disturb light sleepers in downstairs room in summer. No smoking. No children under 10.
Credit cards None accepted.
Rates B&B, $65–170 suite, $60–150 double. Extra person in room $15. 10% senior discount Mon–Thur. 4-night minimum in Aug. Off-season rejuvenation package.
Extras Limited wheelchair access. Station pick-ups, airport pick-ups $15. Babysitting available.

SCHROON LAKE

The Schroon Lake Inn
RD 1, Box 274, 12870

Tel: 518–532–7042

The Schroon Lake Inn opened in 1989, and is owned by Louise Cronin and managed by Pat Savarie. Visitors enter the inn via the veranda, hung with flowering plants and supplied with antique wicker furniture. Guests enjoy relaxing on the comfortable couches in front of the living room fireplace or viewing a movie on the VCR in the den. Guest rooms are furnished with quilted coverlets, custom window treatments, Tiffany-style lamps, and Victorian dressers; Oriental rugs contrast with the polished wood floors. Bathrooms are supplied with toiletries, velour robes, and thick towels, and truffles are provided as a bedside treat.

Rates include a full breakfast, with an extensive menu to choose from—everything from Irish porridge with brown sugar and cinnamon to strawberry cheese blintzes to Louisiana French toast with bananas and bacon. Dinner entrées are varied and creative, including shrimp sautéed with peppered vodka and roasted peppers, salmon in green peppercorn sauce, and pork medallions with apple mustard.

"The inn was warmly decorated with a personal touch. The rooms were spotless, comfortable, and well equipped. Breakfasts were superb and plentiful. The owner, innkeeper, and cook were very friendly and made us feel right at home. At night we sat in front of the fire and talked with the staff and fellow guests." *(Pat Lucisano)* More comments please.

Open All year. Closed Dec. 25.
Rooms 6 doubles—5 with private bath and/or shower, 1 with shared bath. All with air-conditioning, fan.

Facilities Dining room, living room with fireplace, den with TV/VCR, porch. 2 acres with lawn. Public beach, boat launch, tennis, golf nearby.

Location N NY, Adirondacks region. 90 m N of Albany. 2 m from town. From I-87 (Northway) take Exit 28 and make a quick right turn on Rte. 9 to inn on right.

Restrictions No children under 12.

Credit cards Amex, MC, Visa.

Rates B&B, $65–75 double or single. 10% senior discount. 2-night weekend minimum. Prix fixe dinner, $16. Alc dinner, $35.

Extras 1 room wheelchair accessible; equipped for the disabled. Station pickups.

SCHUYLERVILLE

The Inn on Bacon Hill   *Tel: 518–695–3693*
200 Wall Street, 12871

If you're looking to combine the excitement of the Saratoga season of horse racing and performing arts with a quiet country getaway, The Inn on Bacon Hill, opened in 1987 by Andrea Collins-Breslin, may fit the bill perfectly. Andrea says that her "primary goal is making each guest feel special. I meet guests as they pull into the driveway, and provide a tour of the house. Then we chat over a glass of wine to help them feel at home." Andrea's efforts are paying off: we heard from a number of her guests, all of them enthusiastic about the warm hospitality, comfortable and immaculate accommodations, and good food they found here.

A mid-Victorian home built in 1865 by a prominent New York state legislator, the inn was fully restored by Andrea and her mother. A number of the original features have survived, including the high ceilings, mahogany woodwork, ceiling moldings and border wallpaper, marble fireplaces, and kerosene chandelier. One parlor is furnished primarily with Victorian antiques, the other with Queen Anne reproductions, while the guest rooms have both antiques and pieces of more recent vintage, plus fresh flowers and an amenities basket.

"Andrea and her mother are charming, witty, down-to-earth good cooks. After a day of sightseeing, it was so good to return to the house for wine and cheese in relaxed surroundings. The exceptional breakfasts included a hot entrée, plus homemade muffins, toast, and croissants. The location is excellent, set on a quiet country road amidst cornfields and cows." *(Frances Gallagher, also Roseann Butera, Dave Powell & Kate Fitzgerald)*

"Warm, welcoming, beautifully and comfortably decorated. Every need is attended to, even the ones you didn't know you had. Andrea has thought of everything, down to a book of local restaurants into which guests add their comments. She even takes a picture of you which she sends home after your visit. Books and games galore are available in the living room. There's even a barn to put the car in when snow threatens." *(Eloise Kay, also Nadine & Manny Schultz)*

"We stayed in the Tulip Room which had beautiful early morning light, a wonderfully comfortable four-poster bed, and a reading light that you could really read by." *(Judith Pratt)* "The guests mingled easily with each other and the owners, who went out of their way to provide information and directions." *(Dr. & Mrs. Stanley Goldman)*

Open All year.
Rooms 4 doubles—1 with full private bath, 1 with private shower, 2 sharing 1 bath.
Facilities Dining room, 2 parlors with fireplace, piano, library, stereo, games; porch. 5 acres. 15–30 min. to cross-country/downhill skiing.
Location E Central NY. Saratoga County. 10 min. E of Saratoga Springs, 45 min. N of Albany. Take NY State Thruway to I-87 (Northway) Exit 24. Take I-87 N to Exit 14 (Rtes. 9P and 29). Follow signs for Schuylerville/Rte. 29 and go E on Rte. 29. At sign for Grangerville, turn left and go 1.3 m N to inn, opposite a red barn.
Restrictions No smoking. No children under 16.
Credit cards MC, Visa for final payment.
Rates B&B, $55–100 double. No tipping. 2-night weekend minimum in August.

SHELTER ISLAND

With over ⅓ of Shelter Island set aside as a nature preserve, the area has maintained a more peaceful mood than the more frantic Hamptons, yet is still convenient for such activities as bicycling, walking, tennis, horseback riding, and all water sports.

Information please: Although the **Chequit Inn's** restaurant has long been a Shelter Island favorite, two buildings adjacent to this 120-year-old inn—The Cedar House and the Cottage—have been recently newly restored and redecorated with antiques and light country decor. Rates range from $75–150, with midweek discounts available. Reports?

Ram's Head Inn   *Tel:* 516–749–0811
Ram Island, 11965

The short ferry ride to Shelter Island will take you back to a quieter era; even more peaceful is the causeway leading to Ram Island. The Ram's Head Inn is set on a hill overlooking the water. Most guest rooms have flowered wallpapers and old-fashioned beds; the furnishings are clean and adequate, and the grounds are lovely, with plenty of big trees, lounge chairs, and hammocks.

Unless you have the stamina to deal with Long Island summer weekend traffic (or can get away during the week), we recommend a visit during the inn's off-season, from May to mid-June, or after Labor Day through October (excepting Columbus Day and Memorial Day weekends), when you and the locals may have the island to yourselves. "Shelter Island is accessible only by ferry and it is necessary to drive from the ferry slip to reach the inn (unless you have your own boat and can use their moorings or dock)." *(DM)*

"This is a charming inn, in a pleasant, quiet, romantic location. It is attractive, and the staff is very nice; it is well run, and the food is excellent. We ate outdoors on the terrace, overlooking the hotel lawn. I was a bit dubious when I saw the rather elaborate menu, but dinner turned out to be delicious with an appealing freshness and delicacy.

NEW YORK

"Beautiful, peaceful location. The common areas charmingly done with lots of wicker. Guest rooms are spartan—clean and adequate, but nothing special." *(AF)*

Open May through Oct.
Rooms 17 suites and doubles with shared and private baths.
Facilities Bar, restaurant with occasional entertainment. 4 acres with 800-foot waterfront, 6 boat moorings, swimming, tennis, sailboats, hammocks, play equipment. Bike rentals, golf nearby.
Location Far E tip of Long Island. 100 m E of NYC. Take Rte. 27 to Exit 8 (1 m past Southampton College) and follow Rte. 52 to Rte. 38 and turn right. Continue to Rte. 114 N to ferry. On Shelter Is., continue on Rte. 114 N to traffic fork and go straight on Cartright Rd. to stop sign. Turn right on Ram Is. Dr., then right turn over causeway to inn.
Restrictions Smoking permitted in lounge only.
Credit cards MC, Visa.
Rates Room only, $165 suite, $85–115 double. Extra person in room, $15. 2-night weekend minimum. Alc dinner, $45.
Extras Ferry pickups. Port-a-crib available.

SKANEATELES

The Sherwood Inn
26 West Genesee Street, 13152

Tel: 315–685–3405

The Sherwood Inn started out as a stagecoach tavern in 1807, owned by Isaac Sherwood. It was purchased by William Eberhardt in 1975, and the current innkeeper is Bernie Simmons. Rates include a continental breakfast.

"Sherwood House is located very handsomely in the heart of this little upstate New York town, right on the shores of a large lake, which gives the community its name (or vice versa). The service is very friendly and reasonably personal, although the inn is large enough so that in two stays I've never had an occasion to meet the innkeeper. However, the staff is cordial, helpful, and very accommodating. The inn's bar and lounge tend to attract many local residents. The lobby has a beautiful fireplace and a setting of antique chairs for fireside cocktails. The restaurant and dining room are part of the inn, and both overnight guests and 'outsiders' come to dine. Rooms are furnished with beautiful antiques; most are quite large, and are very diverse in shape and arrangement. Most have a sitting area and many have fireplaces." *(David A. Kendall)*

"Good breakfast, cordial staff. Our room was fine, but noisy! We were disappointed in our dinner here, but heard that The Krebs, a restaurant close by, is supposed to have the best food in the area." More comments please.

Open All year. Restaurant closed Christmas Eve and Day.
Rooms 5 suites, 4 doubles, 7 singles, all but one with full private bath and/or shower, telephone, air-conditioning, fan. Most with desk.
Facilities Restaurant, tavern/bar, library with TV, screened porch. Pianist in dining room, jazz group in tavern weekends/holidays. Lake swimming across

street; tennis, fishing, golf, waterskiing, boating, downhill and cross-country skiing nearby.
Location Central NY, Finger Lakes. 25 min. W of Syracuse. In village.
Restrictions Light sleepers should request a quiet room. Smoking restricted to tavern.
Credit cards Amex, DC, MC, Visa.
Rates B&B, $90 suite, $60 double or single. Extra person in room, $10. 15% service. Alc lunch, $8; alc dinner, $60.
Extras Pets allowed with prior arrangement. Crib, cot, babysitting available.

STEPHENTOWN

Mill House Inn
Rt. 43, 12168

Tel: 518–733–5606

Long-time owners Frank and Romana Tallet welcome guests to their rustic inn, built on the site of an old sawmill, with rough sawn beams and paneling throughout. Rooms are furnished eclectically, with antiques, period reproductions, and flowered wallpapers. Rates include a continental breakfast of coffee, juice, and cereal or toast, and afternoon tea; a full breakfast of pancakes, or omelets, or shirred eggs is available at an extra charge.

"The Tallets are gracious innkeepers, who did everything possible to make our stay a happy one; our room was clean and comfortable." *(Nancy Thomas)* "Restful, peaceful, clean and comfortable accommodations, with owners who are well suited to the innkeeping business." *(LDP)*

Open May 15–Nov. 1, Dec. 15–March 15.
Rooms 5 suites, 7 doubles—all with private bath and/or shower, desk, air-conditioning. Some with radio, fireplace.
Facilities Dining room, living room. 3 acres, hiking trails, swimming pool. Golf, tennis, lake for boating, swimming nearby. 5 min to cross-country, downhill skiing.
Location E NY, Berkshires. 14 m from Pittsfield, MA. Taconic Parkway to Rte. 295. Go N to Rte. 22. Go N to Rte. 43. Turn right, 1 m to inn.
Restrictions No smoking. No children under 10.
Credit cards Amex, MC, Visa.
Rates B&B, $100–140 suite, $80–90 double, $65–70 single. Extra person in room $15. 3-night weekend minimum July, Aug.
Extras German, Spanish, Slovenian spoken.

TANNERSVILLE

Information please: We'd like to hear more about the **Deer Mountain Inn** (Route 25, P.O. Box 443, Tannersville, 12485; 518–589–6268), a restaurant and inn owned by Danielle Gortel. Built as a ski lodge, the inn offers lunch and dinner to the public; a three-course prix fixe dinner is offered for a very reasonable $18. The building is paneled in wood throughout, with several handsome fieldstone fireplaces. The dining room is simply done with glowing wood floors, walls, and ceiling, and matching tablecloths and curtains, while a lounge invites guests to relax in its overstuffed chairs and couches before the hearth. Guest rooms have a very eclectic decor, with crisp coordinating curtains and bedspreads. Lawn games are available, and plans to rebuild the tennis court and swimming pool on the inn's 15 wooded acres are in the works. Reports?

For an additional area entry, see listing for the **Redcoat's Return** in Elka Park.

Eggery Inn

Tel: 518–589–5363

County Road 16, 12485

Founded in the early 1800s, Tannersville was named after its first major industry, leather tanning; hemlock bark was an essential ingredient in the tanning process, and hemlocks grew in profusion throughout the area. Later in the century, elaborate resort hotels were built. When the railroads allowed the wealthy to vacation farther north, the grand hotels were replaced by boardinghouses offering a mountain vacation for the working classes. The Eggery, once one of these boardinghouses, was converted into a country inn in 1979 by innkeepers Abe and Julie Abramczyk. B&B rates include a full breakfast of eggs, French toast, or pancakes with bacon or sausage, while dinners offer a choice of entrées such as baby salmon stuffed with crabmeat or chicken francaise, and homemade desserts, with cheesecake, apple strudel, and chocolate mousse pie among the favorites.

"Situated opposite Hunter Mountain, the Eggery Inn provided us with a setting fit for a woodsman. The varicolored panorama of the fall foliage, seen from our room, was quite enchanting. In addition to enhancing the inn's 1930s colonial-style architecture with a complete renovation of its heating, plumbing, and electrical systems, the inn's proprietors carefully chose country furnishings and knickknacks to complement the homey atmosphere." *(Joseph L. Giffuhl)*

"Spectacular views of the northern Catskills. The Victorian parlor has lovely wood wainscotting, a wood-burning Franklin stove on a brick hearth, an antique player piano, and Mission Oak furnishings. Rooms have sweet country curtains and print comforters." *(Michael Spring)*

"Breakfasts are hearty, and Saturday night dinner is a delicious dining experience." *(Julie & Dave Holland)* "Immaculate, great food, warm country atmosphere. Abe and Julie go out of their way to ensure their guests' comfort." *(Carol & Dan Alesandro)*

Open All year. Restaurant closed April, parts of May, June, Sept., Nov.
Rooms 1 suite, 13 doubles—all with private shower and/or tub, TV, fan. 6 rooms in annex.
Facilities Dining room; living room with fireplace, TV, games; bar/lounge; wraparound porch. 13 acres. Lake swimming, trout fishing, golf, tennis, downhill cross-country skiing nearby.
Location SE NY, Northern Catskills, Greene County. 125 m N of NYC, 50 m S of Albany, 18 m Woodstock. 1 m from village. From I-87, take Rte. 23 to 23A to Tannersville traffic light. Go left (S) 1½ m to inn.
Restrictions Smoking restricted to bar area of dining room.
Credit cards Amex, MC, Visa.

Rates B&B, $43–45 per person (suite), $75–80 double, $60–65 single. MAP, $65 per person (suite), $120–125 double. Extra person in room, $20–40. Room only rates available. 2-3 night weekend, holiday minimum. Prix fixe dinner, $23–25. **Extras** Annex wheelchair accessible. Spanish, Yiddish spoken. Station pickups sometimes. Vegetarian meals on request.

TICONDEROGA

Information please: Traveling north up the west side of Lake Champlain will bring you to Route 22 and the towns of Westport and then Essex. Westport is home to **The Inn on the Library Lawn** (1 Washington Street, Westport, 12993; 518–962–8666), recommended by *Anne Wichman* as having "unbelievably good food at breakfast and dinner, with rooms that were comfortable (with private baths), but nothing special." The inn sits on the village green overlooking the lake, along with several shops and the library; concerts are held here in summer. A little further north is the pretty village of Essex, its Federal period houses clustered around the natural harbor. Listed on the National Register of Historic Places (along with the rest of the town) is **The Essex Inn** (16 Main Street, P.O. Box 324, Essex, 12936; 518–963–8821). Lunch and dinner are served on the long porch overlooking Main Street; rooms are simple but comfortable. Reports please!

Bonnie View Acres   *Tel:* 518–585–6098
Canfield Road, 12883

Innkeeper Bonnie Dixon runs a small B&B in a new farmhouse, built in 1981 and decorated with lots of family antiques and portraits. All the beds have heirloom wool quilts made by Bonnie's grandmother, who spun and dyed the wool herself. The Dixons' small farm has chickens, a cow, a donkey, a pig, and four horses—available for sleigh rides in the winter. The full country breakfast includes their own eggs and bacon or sausage, plus juice or fruit, and homemade biscuits or bread. Homemade soup and rolls are always available on cold winter afternoons. Winter visitors especially enjoy a moonlit sleigh ride, followed by a hearty country dinner of stuffed chicken breast or ham, mashed potatoes, whipped squash, green beans, corn pudding, several salads and relishes, breads, dessert, and beverage; wagon rides followed by dinner are offered in summer.

"After many stays in Ticonderoga's dull, unattractive motels, I was delighted to find such a comfortable, clean B&B. The atmosphere is warm and caring, the owners very friendly, and the biscuits outstanding." *(Joe Giangola)*

"Breakfast was so delicious, I was only sorry that we couldn't stay for dinner. The Dixons gave generously of themselves, giving us the personalized attention that made this B&B special, and very patiently showed our children around the farm. The kids would happily have spent our whole vacation there." *(Diane Wolf)* More comments please.

Open All year.
Rooms 3 doubles, 1 single, share 1 bath.

Facilities Living room, dining room, living room with TV, screened and open wraparound porch. 52 acres with lawn games, hiking trails, wagon rides, cross-country skiing, horse-drawn sleigh rides, ice-skating pond. 4 m to lake for canoeing, fishing, swimming. 1/2 hr. to downhill skiing.
Location NE NY, at VT border. Approx. 45 m N of Glens Falls. From Ticonderoga, take Rte. 74 W to Putnam Pond Rd. Go left about 1/2 m to Canfield Rd. Turn left 1 m to inn on left.
Restrictions No smoking. No alcohol on premises.
Credit cards None accepted.
Rates B&B, $40 double, $30 single. Children under 5, free; 5–15 1/2 price. Prix fixe dinner, $20, with horsedrawn wagon or sleigh ride.
Extras Port-a-crib available. Station pickups, $5.

TRUMANSBURG

Sage Cottage
112 East Main Street, Box 626, 14886

Tel: 607–387–6449

Owner/innkeeper Dorry Norris opened her B&B in 1984 in a restored Gothic Revival home, built in 1855. Dorry is an expert on herbs, publishing a quarterly newsletter, giving classes, and tending her ever-expanding herb gardens—and 16 varieties of sage line the front walk alone. She describes the inn far better than we can: "My goal is to give people a home to 'go home to.' Nothing fancy. The cooking is satisfying and tasty but not gourmet, although we are happy to meet the dietary needs of our guests. Heart-shaped rosemary biscuits with strawberry-rhubarb jam is about as outré as we get. Homemade granola or old-fashioned oatmeal will never be featured on Julia Child. Sage Cottage is a good place to stay if you're touring the Finger Lakes—wineries and state parks with wonderful gorges, creeks, and waterfalls are nearby. Our village is a friendly one; guests are always startled when the 'natives' speak and smile at strangers."

"All that we needed or wanted, including large fluffy towels, individual soaps, and a history of the house was cheerfully provided. We were welcomed with friendship and iced tea, which we sipped on the shaded veranda. Our room was spacious and contained antique furniture. We especially enjoyed the sun porch where we breakfasted. Delightful food." *(Joan & Norman Graham)* "A well maintained Victorian Gothic cottage, furnished with a plethora of period antiques, books, and dried herbs. Delicious breakfast, especially the French toast with lemon sauce." *(Delmont & Jeannette Smith)* More comments please.

Open All year.
Rooms 4 doubles, all with private bath and/or shower, radio, fan.
Facilities Dining room with fireplace; sun porch; living room with library, games, TV; porches; garden room. 1 acre with herb gardens, off-street parking. Swimming, hiking, golf, cross-country skiing 3–8 m away.
Location N Central NY, Finger Lakes region. 10 m NW of Ithaca. 3 blocks from center of town.
Restrictions Some traffic noise possible in front rooms. No smoking.
Credit cards None accepted.

Rates B&B, $46 double, $43 single. Extra person in room, $12. 2-night minimum some weekends. Tipping not expected.

Taughannock Farms Inn
Tel: 607–387–7711

2030 Gorge Road, Route 89
Taughannock Falls State Park, 14886

High above the shores of Lake Cayuga is the Taughannock Farms Inn, built in 1873 by a wealthy Philadelphian, John Jones, and decorated with furnishings imported from England and Italy. This lavish summer mansion stayed in the Jones family until the 1930s and 1940s, when the land was deeded to New York State for the creation of Taughannock Falls State Park, and the house was sold to Merritt and Maude Agard. Long-standing traditions continue to this day under the management of their grandchildren, current owners Keith and Nancy (Agard) le Grand. Rooms are furnished with Victorian antiques, some original to the house, and the inn is well known for its restaurant. Most tables are on the glassed-in porch, tiered to maximize the lake views for dinners. Specialities include orange date bread, a long-time tradition at the inn, roast duck with black raspberry sauce, pork loin with apples, prime rib, or fresh fish. Dessert favorites include peppermint ice cream pie or chocolate mousse torte.

"When one approaches the inn up the steep drive from lake level, rounds the bend and first views the building it truly is a step back in time. The inn's Victorian presence and beautiful gardens makes one think of a setting from a movie. The views of the forests of Taughannock, the waters of Lake Cayuga and the hills of the Finger Lakes region are breathtaking.

"We stayed in the Garden Room, a large, charming room furnished with antiques and a queen-size canopied bed that requires a small step stool to reach. The Victorian-themed rose-patterned wallpaper is enhanced by drapes of matching fabric. The private bath, stocked with the inn's own fragrant herbal bath grains, adds another special touch. The food is always excellent, artfully served, with homemade touches that you don't find in the typical restaurant. Breakfast is special with fresh fruit, home-baked breads and muffins with the inn's own jam and first-rate coffee, served in the gardens in fine weather. The le Grands are most accommodating; we needed to make special arrangements and all went off without a slip." *(Marion Fay)*

Open
Rooms 2 cottages, 5 doubles—all with private bath, radio, fan. 1 cottage with telephone, air-conditioning, kitchen.
Facilities Restaurant, lounge, sitting room. 7 acres with gardens, on Lake Cayuga. In state park with hiking, wildlife sanctuary, swimming, boat launch.
Location N Central NY, Finger Lakes region. 9 m NW of Ithaca. On Rte. 89 at entrance to state park.
Restrictions No smoking in guest rooms. "Well-behaved children welcome."
Credit cards Amex, MC, Visa.
Rates B&B, $110–175 cottage, $75–100 double. Extra person in room, $20. Prix fixe dinner, $17–26.

Extras Train station pickups. Babysitting available, by special arrangement. Dutch, German, French spoken.

WARRENSBURG

The Merrill Magee House   *Tel:* 518–623–2449
2 Hudson Street, 12885

It's hard to believe that a classic Greek Revival country inn like The Merrill Magee House, set on the village green, is only five miles away from the tee-shirted commotion at Lake George village. Longtime owners Ken and Florence Carrington offer elegant, English-style innkeeping in their antique-filled establishment, which dates back to the early 1800s. Rates include a full breakfast and afternoon tea. Warrensburg is known for its antique shops, and 25 are within walking distance of the inn.

"The Merrill Magee House is a romantic and cozy country inn. The antique floorboards give a friendly creak as you go up the stairs to the old-fashioned bedrooms in the main house. The shared bath is equipped with a huge claw-foot tub, where you can soak up to your neck. The handmade coverlet on the four-poster bed, antique settee, and fireplace gave us a feeling of having stepped back in time. On a return visit, we stayed in one of the new rooms in the addition, and were delighted to find that our room had just as much charm and atmosphere. The owners are most attentive, making us feel very much at home. Whenever they have a free moment, they are happy to spend time chatting with guests by the fire." *(Mr. & Mrs. Dean Holbrook)*

"From the hand-carved antique piano in the foyer, to the beautifully appointed pink and white tables in the dining room, the inn offers relaxed elegance. The menu presents a good mix of traditional fare and nouvelle dishes; portions are generous, well prepared, and nicely presented. Service is well balanced—solicitous but not intrusive. The guest rooms invite one to stay, relaxing by the fireplace with a good book. There's enough space in the rooms to move about freely, and they are clean, pretty, and private. The decor follows a simple country motif and includes handsome, solid wood furniture. Like the main building, it is not overdone. The Carringtons do an excellent job of pleasing their guests, making them feel comfortable and well cared for." *(Nancy Burnett)*

"We enjoyed the spacious elegance of the Lavender Room (in the Peletiah Richards Guest House), and loved the extravagance of the Jacuzzi in the sun room down the hall. It had a camelback loveseat, good reading lamp, canopied bed with hand-crocheted coverlet and eyelet ruffle; the ample closet held a supply of extra pillows. Wine and a platter of fruit, cheese and crackers awaited us when we arrived. The food in the restaurant was superb; the service was friendly and attentive." *(Patricia Moran)*

Open All year.
Rooms 13 doubles—10 with full private bath, 3 sharing 1 bath. All with radio, air-conditioning. 10 rooms in annex, all with fireplace.

Facilities Restaurant; parlor with TV, fireplace; tavern with fireplace, games; porch. Guest house with Jacuzzi. 5 acres with swimming pool. Cross-country ski rentals. Tennis, hiking, golf, fishing, sailing nearby. 1 m to cross-country skiing, 15 min. to downhill.
Location E central NY, Adirondack region. 5 m N of Lake George, 60 m N of Albany. Take I-87 (Northway) to Exit 23 and follow signs to Warrensburg. Go to 3rd traffic light to inn on the left.
Restrictions No smoking in dining room. No children under 12.
Credit cards Amex, MC, Visa.
Rates B&B, $70–105 double. 2-night weekend minimum. Midweek, special tour, ski packages. Alc dinner, $30–35. 15% service added to meals.
Extras 1 room equipped for disabled.

WATERLOO

James Russell Webster Mansion Inn   *Tel:* 315–539–3032
115 East Main Street, 13165

There are a great many cozy and inexpensive B&Bs around these days, but only a few that offer a truly deluxe overnight experience in an antique-filled mansion, at very lofty prices. The James Russell Webster Mansion clearly falls into the latter category. Leonard and Barbara Cohen, both antiques experts, have decorated this 1845 Georgian mansion with an extraordinary collection of eighteenth- and nineteenth-century European and Asian antiques, creating an unusual and quite formal effect. As one might expect, dinner is a multicourse event; menus are discussed in advance with guests. Favorites include lobster stuffed with crabmeat, served with herbed spinach with cheese and potato strudel; dessert specialties include cheesecake with strawberry-raspberry glaze or chocolate fudge cake with whipped cream.

The Cohens are cat lovers, and have an exceptional collection of cat figurines, as well as five of the warm and purring variety. Rates include a breakfast of exotic juices, home-baked bagels, French breads, challah or sticky buns, imported cheeses and fruit, plus coffee and tea.

"The hospitality, ambiance, cuisine, and overall setup created one of the most memorable nights we've ever enjoyed. Who could imagine an English country manor in Waterloo, New York!" *(Richard Greenburg)*

"While the price may be alarming to some vacationers, the quality of service and atmosphere is unequalled. Barbara Cohen is a gourmet cook and her masterpieces fit right into the atmosphere of their home." *(Dan Pigott, also Richard & Paula Soulies)*

Another guest agreed that the mansion was indeed beautiful, but was made uncomfortable by its "museumlike atmosphere and numerous accompanying rules."

Open All year.
Rooms 2 suites—both with private bath and/or shower, desk, air-conditioning, fireplace.
Facilities Dining room, summer dining room, living room, courtyard with flowers. Swimming, fishing, cross-country skiing nearby.
Location Finger Lakes, Seneca County. 45 m from Rochester, Syracuse, Ithaca. 2 blocks E of village center. On Rtes. 5/20, 2 blocks E of Rte. 96, between Geneva

and Seneca Falls. From I-90, take Exit 41 to Rte. 414 S. Bear right at rtes. 5/20; go 7 blocks to inn.
Restrictions No children. No smoking. No shoes in house.
Credit cards CB, DC, MC, Visa.
Rates B&B, $330 suite. No tipping. Alc breakfast, $10–15. Prix fixe dinner, $85 including service. 2-night weekend minimum in season.
Extras Member, Classic Inns by Treadway; Master Chefs Institute of America.

WATERTOWN

Starbuck House   *Tel:* 315–788–7324
253 Clinton Street, 13601

Most people think of B&Bs as places to stay for a weekend or on vacation, but more and more business travelers are realizing what a difference a good B&B can make to their sense of well being while on the road. Although all are welcome at Starbuck House, owner Marsha Eger Brown notes that business travelers make up the majority of her midweek guests.

Built in 1869 for state senator James Starbuck, this 17-room Italianate mansion has been beautifully restored by the Brown family. The decor includes the original gilded pier mirrors, valences, and gas chandeliers in the formal living room, inlaid hardwood floors in the dining room, and a cozy family room with plank floors and a gleaming black marble fireplace. Civil War buffs will especially enjoy the collection of first edition books, including an autographed copy of President Grant's memoirs. The spacious guest rooms are simply furnished with antiques and period reproductions; bathrooms are supplied with thirsty towels, and beds are turned down with a pillow chocolate.

The dining room table is set each morning with china, crystal, silver, and linens on English table mats. Breakfasts are individually presented on silver trays garnished with fresh flowers. The morning meal typically includes spinach cheese squares, fresh fruit, homemade pumpkin bread, banana muffins, blueberry or cranberry nut muffins, coffee, tea and juice; the entrée varies and might include Canadian bacon and Swiss cheese souffle, cinnamon French toast with maple butter, or homemade potato pancakes and apple sauce.

"Marsha Brown is a gracious innkeeper, who did everything possible to make our stay a happy one; our room was clean and comfortable, and the house is furnished with exceptional charm." *(Nancy Thomas)*

Open All year.
Rooms 1 suite, 4 doubles—3 with private full bath, 2 with maximum of 4 sharing bath. All with telephone, air-conditioning. Some with desk.
Facilities Dining room, living room, family room with TV, library, veranda. 6 m from Lake Ontario for boating, fishing. White water rafting on Black River. 1/2 hr. to cross-country skiing.
Location N NY, Thousand Islands. 70 m N of Syracuse, 30 m S of Canada. Take 81 N to Arsenal Street Exit, turn right onto Arsenal Street. Turn right onto Massey, bear left at the triangle. Turn left onto Clinton.
Restrictions No smoking. No children under 12.
Credit cards Amex, MC, Visa.

Rates $70–80 suite or double, $55–65 single. Extra person in room $15.
Extras Wheelchair accessible; some rooms equipped for disabled.

WESTFIELD

Westfield is home to a number of excellent antique shops, and is 10 miles from the Chautauqua Institution, offering a full summer program of concerts, theater, opera, and lectures. The self-proclaimed grape juice capital of the world, it is also home to seven wineries and many antique shops. Lake Erie and Chautauqua Lake are nearby for swimming, boating, and fishing; hiking, golf, tennis and skiing are also easily accessible.

Information please: In nearby Mayville, at the north end of Chautauqua Lake, is the beautifully restored **Plumbush** (Chautauqua-Stedman Road, RD2, Box 332, Mayville, 14757; 716–789–5309) an Italianate villa built in 1865 and laboriously restored as a B&B in 1988. The house is handsomely decorated in period, highlighted by a wonderful collection of curios and collectibles. The reasonable rates include a breakfast of muffins, yogurt, fruit and granola, as well as a never-empty chocolate chip cookie jar. Another possibility is **The Lake Side Inn** (4696 Chautauqua Avenue, Box 83, Maple Springs, 14756; 716–386–2500), a Dutch colonial mansion with 300-feet of waterfront on Chautauqua Lake. Set in a 11-acre wooded private estate just across the lake from the Chautauqua Institution, rates are reasonable and include a full breakfast. Comments?

Westfield House   *Tel:* 716–326–6262
East Main Road, Route 20, P.O. Box 505, 14787

Westfield House is an 1840s-era brick home with a later Gothic Revival addition, framed by old maple trees and overlooking the local vineyards. It's owned and run by Betty and Jud Wilson, earlier contributors to this guide, who turned innkeepers in 1988. Rates include a breakfast of juice, tea or coffee, a hot entrée, and home-baked rolls, bread, and muffins, as well as wine and hors d'oeuvres served from 5 to 6 P.M..

"We were graciously welcomed to this charming B&B, set well back from Route 20, and sheltered behind a double row of stately shade trees. Our room, the only guest room on the first floor, was done in a restful rose and was equipped with a firm four-poster queen-size bed and a lovely fireplace. The Wilsons hosted us to cheese and crackers before dinner. The next morning, breakfast was served on the patio, and included homemade bread and kuchen, blintzes with marmalade sauce, and assorted sliced fruits." *(Beth & Geoff Eggert)*

"Having grown up in the Midwest, I have seen many Gothic Revival homes, but until our visit, I had never seen the inside of one. Fourteen-foot ceilings on the first floor are accented by the pointed arch windows and the grand foyer was furnished with an enormous antique mirror that had—most appropriately for the hometown of Welch's grape juice—carved and gilded grape clusters. We stayed in the Captain's Quarters suite and enjoyed a very comfortable night, kept cool on a hot night by the ceiling fan. The crisp blue and white decor was simply accented by a boat model and several other nautical accents. The bath and dressing room were freshly pine-panelled yet coordinated well with the maritime theme. Breakfast was well-done and very filling; a fresh fruit salad followed by Betty's special French toast and sausage. All in all, the Wilsons have done a good job in their first innkeeping experience of creating a warm, inviting atmosphere."*(NPB)*

One satisfied guest did note, however, that the inn's location (though well set back and shielded by landscaping) on busy Route 20 could be initially discouraging, but that this should not deter guests from experiencing the Wilson's warm hospitality.

Open All year.
Rooms 2 suites, 5 doubles—all with private bath and/or shower, radio, desk, fan. Telephones available upon request. 1 suite with TV.
Facilities Dining room with fireplace, living room, parlor, porch, needlework shop. 1.7 acres with carriage barn.
Location W NY, 2 ½ hrs. NE of Cleveland, OH. 1 hr. SW of Buffalo, 45 min. NE of Erie, PA. 1¼ m E of town center on Rte. 20.
Restrictions No smoking. No children under 12.
Credit cards MC, Visa.
Rates B&B, $85 suite, $60–75 double, $55 single. Extra person in room, $15. 2-night weekend minimum. 10% discount for 4-night stay. Senior discount. Prix fixe dinner, $25.

The William Seward Inn
South Portage Road, RD 2, 14787

Tel: 716–326–4151

The original section of the William Seward Inn was built in 1821, and was bought by William Henry Seward soon afterward. Seward, at that time the agent for the Holland Land Company in Westfield, later became famous as the secretary of state under Abraham Lincoln and Andrew Johnson when he arranged the purchase of Alaska from Russia—known at the time as Seward's Folly. Seward made several additions to the house, including the two-story Greek pillars that give the inn the look of a mansion. In the 1840s the house was sold to George Patterson, who became lieutenant governor of New York, and remained in that family for over 100 years. It was moved from town to its present location about 25 years ago, and was bought by Peter and Joyce Wood in 1986.

"Our room looked out on Lake Erie and was furnished with a four-poster bed and period antiques. Two comfortable chairs at one end provided a small sitting area. The sink was in the bedroom, while the commode and shower were in a closet-size room off the sitting area. There was plenty of space to put things away in the dressers and closet. The bed was very comfortable, with an abundance of blankets and numerous fluffy pillows to lounge on. The atmosphere of the inn is quiet and relaxing. Several delicious breakfast courses were served at a leisurely pace, and both the presentation and the conversation were excellent. Another opportunity for socializing with other guests was provided early each evening, when wine and cheese, hot buttered rum, and appetizers were served in the living room. Best of all is the level of service provided by the owners. There were chocolate hearts on the bedside table, and fresh flowers in our room when we arrived; the selection of magazines in our room was changed daily; every morning while we were at breakfast, the snow was brushed off our car." *(Jim & Cathy Sirianni)*

"We are particularly finicky about cleanliness, and this inn certainly passed with flying colors. Menus are available from nearby restaurants, and Peter is only too happy to call for reservations." *(Carolyn & Bill Myles, also Arlene Lengyel)* "The inn is furnished with a large collection of antiques, giving each room a unique and unduplicated personality. In the morning, we enjoyed an excellent breakfast of 'Plantation Pancakes,' served on beautiful old china in the formal dining room." *(Mr. & Mrs. James Turner)* "Joyce is a very creative cook and has expanded her talents to serving delicious dinners on Saturday nights (off-season)." *(Jim & Nancy Young)*

"We were shown to our room and Peter promptly returned with glasses of ice-cold lemonade. The Woods are available to help or answer questions without intruding on your privacy. We enjoyed selecting a book from their excellent library, then retiring to read in our room. After a fabulous breakfast, we sat with Joyce and Peter, looking through their photo album recording the inn's renovation. They make running a B&B look easy (which it isn't), a sign of professionalism at its finest." *(Robert & Donna Bocks)*

Open All year.
Rooms 10 doubles—all with private bath and/or shower, radio, fan. Some with desk, air-conditioning. Telephone, TV available on request.
Facilities Parlor with fireplace, library, dining room, gift shop. 3 acres.
Location W NY, 2 ½ hrs. NE of Cleveland, OH. 1 hr. SW of Buffalo, 45 min. NE of Erie, PA. 3 m to town. 4 m S of I-90, on Rte. 394.
Restrictions No smoking. No children under 12. Check-in before 8 P.M. requested.
Credit cards MC, Visa.
Rates B&B, $60–94 double, $50–84 single. Extra person in room, $15. 2-night summer/special weekend minimum. 10% senior (over 60) discount, midweek. Theme weekends, special packages. Off-season prix fixe dinner, $16–24.

WHITEHALL

Apple Orchard Inn
RD 2, Box 2458, 12887

Tel: 518–499–0180

The Apple Orchard Inn has been owned since 1986 by Wayne and Judy Jones who report that "they get the best sunsets for miles around." Set between Vermont's Green Mountains and New York's Adirondacks, this quaint country inn is situated in a prime location for hiking, foliage touring, or skiing; it is equidistant between the Killington and West Mountain ski slopes. Lovers of pancakes take note: the Joneses tap their sugar maples every year to make syrup. Guests are invited to participate in the "sugaring off", held in the Jones' sugar house during March and April; for their efforts, helpers receive a pint of the finished product.

Hearty breakfasts with omelets, fruit, homemade sweet rolls, and of course, pancakes, are served daily; on weekends, dinner with salad, homemade bread, an entrée, glass of wine, dessert and coffee is also served.

"The gracious innkeeper did everything possible to make our stay a happy one; our room was clean and comfortable, and the house is furnished with exceptional charm." *(Nancy Thomas)*

Open All year.
Rooms 6 doubles—all with private bath and/or shower. 3 with air-conditioning, 3 with fan.
Facilities Dining room, living room with TV, sun room, porch. 134 acres with swimming pool, maple sugaring house, bicycles, sleds, ice skates, volleyball, lawn games, cross-country skiing. 27 m to Killington, VT ski area.
Location N Eastern NY, Adirondacks region. 25 m NE of Glen Falls, NY; 25 m W of Rutland, VT. 5 m from town. From I-87 (Northway) take Exit 20 and go E on Rte. 149 to Rte. 4 in Fort Ann. Continue on Rte. 4 through Whitehall, heading E toward VT. Turn right on Old Fairhaven Rd. to inn.
Restrictions No smoking on 2nd floor.
Credit cards Amex, MC, Visa.
Rates B&B, $65 double, $45–65 single. Extra person in room, $10. MAP (Fri.–Sun. only), $90 double. Extra adult in room, $45; extra children under age 4, free; extra child age 5–17, $16.50. $10–15% service additional. 10% senior discount. Holiday entertainment.
Extras Pets permitted by prior arrangement. Station pickups. Crib available.

WINDHAM

For an additional area entry, see listing for **Point Lookout Inn** in East Windham.

Albergo Allegria   *Tel:* 518–734–5560
Route 296 P.O. Box 267, 12496

Leonore and Vito Radelich, originally from Veneto Province (once part of Italy, but now in Yugoslavia), ran a restaurant for many years on Long Island. They moved to Windham and, ten years ago, opened La Griglia, a restaurant specializing in northern Italian cooking, with two Italian Renaissance dishes offered nightly. Pork Michelangelo, scallopini of pork with fruit juices, grilled apples, tomatoes, and garlic, is a favorite.

In 1985, the Radelichs completed the total renovation of the Albergo, created from two of the original cottages of the former Osborn House, a summer boardinghouse complex built in 1876. Interior spaces were redesigned to create roomy accommodations, while preserving the original Victorian woodwork, trim, and moldings. Rooms are decorated with period wallpapers and Victorian furnishings. Rates include a breakfast of fresh fruit and juice, croissants, homemade granola, egg dishes, Belgian waffles, or speciality pancakes.

Michael Willis reports that although the Radelichs sold their restaurant, La Griglia, "the food remains as excellent as ever." Meanwhile, the Radelichs, never ones to rest on their pesto, have built an addition onto the Albergo, which "combines period decor and country inn warmth with luxurious new baths with heat lamps and Jacuzzi tubs."

"Most charming. The common rooms were quite nice, and I had a wonderful, clean, comfortable room and bath. The location is convenient to good restaurants, quiet, and very low-key." *(Richard A. Gerweck, Jr. also Steve Koenig)*

Open All year. Restaurant closed Monday.
Rooms 4 suites, 14 doubles, all with full private bath, telephone, TV. 4 in annex. 1 suite with double Jacuzzi.
Facilities Restaurant, 2 large living rooms with fireplaces, games, library, TV. Northern Italian cooking workshops. 4 acres with herb gardens, bocce, badminton, creek with swimming hole, waterfall, trout fishing. ½ m to Ski Windham, 7 m to Hunter Mt. 2 m to cross-country skiing. Golf across street; tennis, lake for swimming, boating, fishing nearby.
Location SE NY, Northern Catskills, Greene County. 1 hr. S of Albany, 2½ hrs. N of NYC. 1 m to town off Rte. 23.
Restrictions Smoking restricted to living room, some guest rooms.
Credit cards MC, Visa.
Rates B&B, $85–175 suite, $55–115 double, $45–95 singles. Extra person in room, $10–15. 2-night weekend minimum. Alc dinner, $30.
Extras Entrance ramp; one bath equipped for disabled. Station pickups. Crib available. Italian, Croatian, Afrikaans spoken.

Key to Abbreviations

For complete information and explanations, please see the Introduction.

Rates: Range from least expensive room in low season to most expensive room in peak season.

Room only: No meals included; sometimes referred to as European Plan (EP).

B&B: Bed and breakfast; includes breakfast, sometimes afternoon/evening refreshment.

MAP: Modified American Plan; includes breakfast and dinner.

Full board: Three meals daily.

Alc lunch: A la carte lunch; average price of entrée plus nonalcoholic drink, tax, tip.

Alc dinner: Average price of three-course dinner, including half bottle of house wine, tax, tip.

Prix fixe dinner: Three- to five-course set dinner, excluding wine, tax, tip unless otherwise noted.

Extras: Noted if available. Always confirm in advance. Pets are not permitted unless specified; if you are allergic, ask if pets are in residence.

We Want to Hear from You!

As you know, this book is only effective with your help. We really need to know about your experiences and discoveries.

If you stayed at an inn or hotel listed here, we want to know how it was. Did it live up to our description? Exceed it? Was it what you expected? Did you like it? Were you disappointed? Delighted?

Have you discovered new establishments that we should add to the next edition?

Tear out one of the report forms at the back of this book (or use your own stationery if you prefer) and write today. Even if you write only "Fully endorse existing entry" you will have been most helpful.

Thank You!

Pennsylvania

Tattersall Inn, Point Pleasant

From the ridges of the Appalachian mountains which cut diagonally across the state to softly rolling farmlands, dense northern woods and quiet river valleys, Pennsylvania offers visitors a wide palette of urban and rural landscapes. Anchoring the southeastern and southwestern corners are the state's cultural and urban centers, stately Philadelphia and a surprisingly revived and lively Pittsburgh.

Eastern Pennsylvania alone has several different geographic areas, all of them with varied cultural and natural attractions and history. These include Bucks County, Chester County, and Lancaster County. (Look under the "Location" heading for each listing if your sense of geography is fuzzy.) Because the listings for each area are scattered throughout this chapter (we list them alphabetically by town), here are a few background notes on the different regions:

Bucks County: Although only 1½ hours from New York, and 45 minutes from Philadelphia, Bucks County is a peaceful rural retreat of rolling green meadows dotted with cows and deep forests, with the beautiful Delaware River running through. New Hope, its best-known town, was founded in 1681. Many of its inns and hotels date back to the 1850s, when the Delaware Canal was in full operation. After the railroad made the canal's mule-drawn barges obsolete, nothing much changed until the end of the century, when some New York artists discovered its charms. Its reputation as an artists' colony really grew during the 1930s, when it was rediscovered by some of New York's most well-known artists and writers.

Although it has its overtouristed side (Main Street in New Hope being the leading example), Bucks County offers fine-quality food and lodging, excellent antique and craft shops, a wide river for canoeing and rafting, lovely walking and hiking trails, and numerous historical sites relating to the Revolutionary War. Rates in Bucks County do not vary with the seasons, but are generally lower midweek and higher on weekends.

Information please: There's no shortage of inns in Bucks County, but we've lacked positive inn reports on several. Overlooking the Delaware is the **Black Bass Hotel**, dating to pre-Revolutionary times, with rooms furnished simply with antiques and a reputation for outstanding food (River Road, Lumberville, 18933; 215–297–5815). On the site of an 18th century grist mill is the **Pear & Partridge Inn**, known primarily for its fine cuisine but offering six comfortable guest rooms (Old Easton Road, Doylestown, 18901; 215–345–7800). Also in Doylestown is the Burpee family estate, still owned by the family and known as the **Inn at Fordhook Farm**. A handsome stone manor house, rooms are filled with family heirlooms and you can even relax in the study where W. Atlee wrote his first seed catalog (105 New Britain Road, Doylestown, 18901; 215–345–1766).

The well-known **Colligan's Stockton Inn** just on the other side of the Delaware River, has undergone a variety of management changes in recent years, and we'd like to hear more from recent guests before reinstating them for a full entry (Route 29, Stockton, NJ 08559; 609–397–1250).

For additional area listings, see the New Jersey chapter, where you'll find descriptions of inns just on the other side of the Delaware.

Chester County/Brandywine Valley: Only 30 miles southwest of Philadelphia, this area of rolling hills and pastures is known for the 350-acre Longwood Gardens, the Wyeth Collection at the Brandywine River Museum, and the collection of American decorative arts and furniture at the Winterthur Museum.

Lancaster County: Also called Pennsylvania Dutch country, this area of rich rolling farmland is known for the Amish people, a religious group that eschews much of the twentieth-century world, including most modern conveniences we take for granted. We are able to learn much about their way of life through the Mennonites, who follow many of the same religious precepts, but feel that it is all right to have contact with the outside world, and are willing to adopt some modern ways.

Although Lancaster County has some tacky tourist traps, the area offers many attractions of genuine historic and cultural interest; if you saw the movie *Witness* you know how beautiful the region is. Accommodations in this area range from historic and elegant inns to working farms with guest rooms—nothing fancy, but they're clean and inexpensive.

Reader tip: "A highlight of my trip was having dinner and spending an evening with Jack and Dee Dee Meyer. These are wonderful plain folk with six children who open up their home to share their life with others. It is an evening not to be missed. Jack can be found at Abe's Buggy Rides near Bird-in-Hand, or write them at 869 West Sunhill, Manheim 17545." *(Dianne Crawford)*

The Poconos: Although some may know the area only by the heart-

shaped beds featured in ads for the "honeymoon capital of the East,"
there is a great deal of natural beauty to be found in the Poconos, from
the Delaware Water Gap, at the entrance to the Poconos, to the areas
further north, around Canadensis.

Wayne County: Trailblazers will head for the pastoral rolling hills of
northeastern Pennsylvania, just south of Binghamton, New York.
Honesdale, the county seat, grew prosperous in the nineteenth century
as the country's largest coal-shipping center; today's visitors are more
likely to be attracted by the county fair, held the first full week of
August. Wayne County's uncrowded roads are ideal for exploring, and
the area is home to dozens of sparkling mountain lakes.

Rates listed do not include the 6% Pennsylvania state sales tax.

ADAMSTOWN

Adamstown Inn   *Tel:* 215–484–0800
62 West Main Street, 19501-0938

Home to more than 2,500 antiques dealers in the spring, summer, and
fall, it's no wonder that Adamstown is sometimes called the "antiques
capital of the world." Aficionados no longer have to break the mood
when it comes to lodging, thanks to the Adamstown Inn. Although the
original house dated back to the early 1800s, the yellow brick home you
see today was largely constructed in 1925. It remained a private home
until 1988, when Tom and Wanda Berman bought it in 1988, and
converted it into a B&B. They spent months adding three new bathrooms, refinishing all the floors and the chestnut woodwork, and wallpapering the rooms in reproduction papers. Highlights include the
elaborate leaded glass windows, added in 1925. Although both Tom and
Wanda gave up careers in finance for innkeeping, they had been collecting antiques for years, and it shows in the handsome period decor.
Guest rooms are furnished with lace and balloon curtains, Oriental
rugs, family heirlooms, handmade quilts, and marble-topped dressers.

"The entire home is warm, cozy, spotless, and beautifully decorated
in genuine antiques. Extra touches include the fresh flowers, fine table
settings, and the genuine friendliness of Tom and Wanda Berman."
(Stan Alekna) "Though a bit off the beaten track, there are places to go
antiquing in Adamstown and outlet shopping in Reading. A great touch
is the coffee waiting at your bedroom door in the morning. Some good
restaurants are within a short distance. The Black Angus was our favorite; they make their own beer and the food was delicious." *(Mary Lou
Paratore)* "Excellent sticky buns, toast, muffins, fruit, cheese, juice and
coffee at breakfast. Good bathroom lighting; convenient, well-lit parking area." *(Nancy Malinowski)*

Open All year.
Rooms 4 doubles—2 with private bath and/or shower, 2 sharing 1 bath, 1 with
double Jacuzzi. All with radio, air-conditioning. 2 with desk. TV on request.
Facilities Breakfast room, living room with fireplace, library, games. ¾ acre
with barbecue pit. Tennis, swimming pool, golf nearby. 20 m to downhill skiing.
Location PA Dutch Country. 20 m NE of Lancaster, 10 m SW of Reading.

Approx. 3 m N of junction of I-76 & Rte. 222. From PA Trnpke. (I-76), take Exit 21 to Rte. 222 N. Exit 222 at Willow Street or Bowmansville Rd; follow to center of town and inn.
Restrictions Smoking in library only. No children under 12.
Credit cards MC, Visa.
Rates B&B, $55–90 double. Extra person in room, $20. Reduced rate for seniors. 2-night holiday/weekend minimum.

AIRVILLE

Spring House   *Tel:* 717–927–6906
Muddy Creek Forks, 17302

Named for the spring that emerges in its basement, this fieldstone house was built in 1798 by a Pennsylvania legislator. It was a falling-down ruin when Ray Constance Hearne bought it in 1971; she restored the entire house, and took care of removing truckloads of debris and decayed wallpaper. She has decorated the rooms simply but elegantly with country antiques, hand-stenciling on walls, quilts, and hand-woven rugs.

Ray says that "Spring House is run with regard for the environment, the seasons, the specialties of the region, the wildlife. Our luxuries are featherbeds that enfold, eggs golden and fresh from free-range hens, a house with simple sculptural spaces that provide a home for books, paintings, weavings, local antiques and pottery, and a collection of musical instruments from around the world. Food is lovingly prepared based on local produce, and guests gather around a large ship's table to converse and share wine and cheese. I am delighted to have guests seeking solitude, a place to contemplate, write, or paint. One can walk or bicycle for miles without encountering traffic."

"The location is very scenic, in a small community, yet within easy driving distance of shopping, museums, antique shops, vineyards, restaurants, and many other fine attractions. Ms. Hearne is a very warm and friendly person, who greets you with a smile and the offer of a refreshing drink. Her hearty full breakfast includes coffee ground fresh each morning, and fresh fruit that she's selected locally." *(Sharon Brooks)*

"Start off with an inspired site—a prerevolutionary stone house in a secluded valley on the fringes of Pennsylvania Dutch country. Add a restoration that blends whimsy (an Etruscan bathroom, stone griffins in the rock garden, and an English setter who gives tours) with country authenticity (creamy whitewashed walls, wood-burning stoves, aromatic sun-dried sheets, and wraparound featherbeds). Top it off with breakfasts that are both imaginative and delicious, and served with a flourish, ranging from Deep South corn pudding to Pyrenees vegetable-egg casserole. It's all infused with Ray Hearne's creativity and personal charm." *(Susan Kalish)* More comments please.

Open All year.
Rooms 5 doubles—3 with private shower, 2 with maximum of 4 sharing bath. All with fan; 3 with desk.
Facilities Dining room, living/family room. 2½ acres with stream for swim-

ming, trout fishing, canoeing, ice-skating. Hiking, bicycling, cross-country skiing from front door. Horseback riding, golf nearby.
Location Pennsylvania Dutch Country. 30 m SW of Lancaster. From Philadelphia, take Rte. 372 across Susquehanna River. Go N onto Rte. 74 to Brogue. Turn left at post office and go 5 m to Muddy Creek Forks. Inn at foot of hill on right.
Restrictions No smoking.
Credit cards None accepted.
Rates B&B, $60–95 double, $50–75 single. Extra person in room, $20; child in parents' room, $15. 2-night weekend minimum. 10% discount for 5-night stays.
Extras Spanish spoken.

BEACH LAKE

The Beach Lake Hotel
Tel: 717–729–8239
Main Street and Church Road, P.O. Box 144, 18405

When Roy and Erika Miller bought The Beach Lake Hotel in 1987, a seven-year search for "the perfect inn" ended, and the real work began. Dating from the 1850s, this simple sturdy building was also home to a tavern, post office, and general store, although it has housed overnight guests since the Civil War. After a top-to-bottom renovation, combining country inn comfort with Victorian decor, The Beach Lake Hotel now offers period guest rooms, supplied with fresh fruit and homemade candies, and decorated with reproduction Victorian wallpapers, lace curtains, restored woodwork, brass or canopy beds, and antique furnishings (all of which are for sale). Common rooms include a comfortable parlor, also furnished in period, a cozy pub, and a pleasant dining room, with tempting dishes at breakfast and dinner. Erika is the chef; breakfast favorites include apple-sausage pancakes with brandied grape sauce, eggs Benedict, and two-cheese omelets, served with breakfast meats, fruit and juice, and a variety of muffins, popovers, and toast. A recent spring dinner included mushroom nut torte with shallots; fettucini with lobster, shrimp, and scallops; and chocolate mousse with raspberry sauce.

"Erika and Roy Miller greeted us with warm smiles and interesting conversation. Our room was immaculate, as was the rest of the inn." *(Clifford Thomas & Sally Jo Glendenning)* "The inn has a romantic little dining room where we found the food to be as good as or better than that at New York's finest restaurants. The menu included a choice of six appetizers, three soups, five entrées, and six desserts—everything we had was delicious and was served beautifully." *(Jim Dowling)*

"We were the first guests to arrive, and had a chance to look through all the rooms. After an hour we decided on the third floor because of the brass bed, larger quarters, and elegant furnishings. The Millers suggested restaurants, sights, shops, and more." *(Anthony Cerzio)* "The baths have clean and modern fixtures, with charming colors and wallpaper to blend in with the historic furnishings." *(Beverly J. Lynch)* "Location is ideal, very quiet, walking distance to lake. Well-lit parking area is right behind building." *(Larry Farley)* Reports, please.

Open All year. Restaurant closed Tues., Wed.
Rooms 6 doubles—1 with full private bath, 5 with private shower. All with air-conditioning; 3 with desk.
Facilities Dining room, parlor, pub, gift shop. 2 acres with gardens; adjacent to lake for swimming, boating, fishing, canoeing. 4 m to Delaware River for canoeing, fishing. 15 m to cross-country, downhill skiing.
Location NE PA. Wayne County, northern Poconos. 40 min NE of Scranton. In center of village. From NYC: Take NYS Thruway to Exit 16, Harriman. Take Rte. 17 W to I-84 to Exit 1, Pt. Jervis. Take Rte. 6 to Rte. 97 N. Go 30 m to Narrowsburg. Bear left at blinking light (Rte. 52 W), down hill to town; cross bridge into PA. Take Rte. 652 4 m to Village View Farm, turn right to 'T' & inn straight ahead.
Restrictions No smoking in guest rooms. No children.
Credit cards Amex, MC, Visa.
Rates B&B, $85 double. Extra person in room, $25. 2-night minimum preferred June–Oct. Alc lunch, $8–10; alc dinner, $30–35. Theme weekends.
Extras Station pickups.

BETHLEHEM

Bethlehem was founded in 1741 by the German Moravian sect, and is known as the home of Bethlehem Steel and Lehigh University, and for its Christmas celebration and Bach Festival in May. The area was industrialized early, and visitors will enjoy a visit to the city's restored eighteenth-century industrial area. We'd like to hear more about the **Bethlehem Hotel**, a premotel-era establishment combining classic elegance with some questionable updating (437 Main Street, 18015; 215–867–3711).

Wydnor Hall   *Tel:* 215–867–6851
RD 3, Old Philadelphia Pike, 18015

Wydnor Hall is an imposing fieldstone manor house, built around 1810, and opened in 1988 after a two-year restoration. Owner Kristina Taylor notes that "we appeal to the sophisticated, discriminating traveler who appreciates the privacy and service we provide." Rooms are furnished with colonial antiques and handsome quilts, and offer good lighting. Rates include a full breakfast, with buffet dishes on the dining room sideboard and a hot entrée prepared to order.

"My large, quiet room was nicely furnished with all the necessities in proper working condition. A good night's rest came in a queen-size bed, attractively made up with peach-colored linens, topped with an elegant peach silk blanket giving a luxurious touch. Breakfast, beautifully served, was a bowl of fresh strawberries, raspberries, and blueberries with cream and delicious bread (a full breakfast is also available). After breakfast, I enjoyed an interesting conversation with the owner. The living room is especially inviting at teatime, with its sofas, chairs, and lovely antiques, done in soft blue, beige, and mauve." *(Edna Huston Johnson)*

"We felt like guests at a very grand and well-staffed home. The quality of the surroundings, service, and food was very high; everything is done with great care and taste, including the linen, silver service, and furnishings. From the coffee tray in the morning with newspaper, through the superb breakfast and afternoon tea (and wine), the comfort of the service and surrounding is on a par with a fine European hotel." *(Mr. & Mrs. Peter Kuyper)* "Best of all was the hospitality of the Taylors." *(Mary Vento)*

Open All year.
Rooms 1 suite, 3 doubles—2 with full private bath, 2 with maximum of 4 people sharing bath. All with desk, air-conditioning.
Facilities Dining room, living room, conservatory. 2 acres with stream, gardens. 10 m from Delaware River for fishing, swimming, boating.
Location 55 m N of Philadelphia. 3 m from Bethlehem. From Bethlehem, follow Rte. 378 to Black River Rd. Turn right onto Black River Rd. and left at Old Philadelphia Pike. Inn is 1/4 m on right.
Restrictions No smoking in guest rooms. No children under 12.
Credit cards Amex, MC, Visa.
Rates B&B, $95 suite, $90 double, $80 single.
Extras Airport/station pickups. French, Hungarian, Spanish spoken.

BLOOMSBURG

The Inn at Turkey Hill
991 Central Road, 17815

Tel: 717–387–1500

Located just off Exit 35 of Interstate 80, the Inn at Turkey Hill provides good food and lodging to travelers on this major east-west route. The main part of the inn is a farmhouse dating back to 1839; most of the guest rooms are in a modern wing, built onto the back of the original structure. The dinner menu is quite adventurous; one of their specialties is rolled duck glazed with orange and ginger and stuffed with wild rice, walnuts, and raisins. The guest rooms face a landscaped courtyard with a gazebo and pond.

"The atmosphere was very warm and relaxing. The staff was more than willing to make us feel at home. Our room was spotless and comfortable. Breakfast, warm and fresh from the oven, is delivered to your door in a basket. The inn is located on the outskirts of town just off the interstate, yet is quiet and peaceful. We enjoy window-shopping along Main Street and visiting the local antique shops. Parking is plentiful and well lit." *(Jennifer L. Amarein)*

"Owner Babs Pruden was so friendly and helpful that we really felt like special guests in her home. She and her father shared the dream of turning their home into an inn, and shortly she will see her son running the inn. Our room was huge, one of only several in the original home. We had a lovely queen-size bed, lots of closets, windows, wing chairs, and a very large private bathroom with a single Jacuzzi.

"Dinner was served in the Stencil Room, one of three dining rooms. The food was beautifully prepared and presented. The inn is very popular with locals, and the Greenhouse room fills up first. Babs, while not hovering, was around the whole time and well aware of how her staff treats her guests. Fresh fruit, pastries, muffins, and toast, along

215

PENNSYLVANIA

with coffee and every kind of tea imaginable, were spread out along with the morning papers. The sun poured in through the Greenhouse windows and the local geese paraded outside by the pond." *(Wendi Van Exan)*

Open All year.
Rooms 2 suites, 16 doubles—all with full private bath, telephone, TV, desk, air-conditioning. Both suites with fireplace and Jacuzzi.
Facilities Restaurant; living room; library with fireplace, TV, games; lounge. 2 acres with patio, gardens, pond, gazebo. Tennis, golf, fishing, swimming nearby.
Location 3 hrs. NW of Philadelphia and W of NYC. 2 m from center of Bloomsburg, at Exit 35 off I-80.
Restrictions No pipe or cigar smoking in dining room.
Credit cards Amex, Discover, MC, Visa.
Rates B&B, $120–140 suite, $68–90 double, $60–80 single. Corporate rates. Extra person in room, $15. Children under 12 free. Alc lunch, $6; alc dinner, $19.
Extras Wheelchair accessible. Cribs, babysitting available. Airport/station pick-ups. Pets permitted.

CANADENSIS

Information please: Built in the 1890s as a summer boarding house, the **Old Village Inn** (Route 390, North Skytop Road, 18325; 717–595–2120) became a country inn in 1925, and was renovated in the 1980s. New owners Otto and Vera Lissfeld, originally from Switzerland, bring years of international hotel experience to the inn, as well as a European accent to the cuisine. Rates for the 11 traditionally furnished guest rooms are very reasonable, and include full breakfast, evening hors d'oeuvres, and dinner. **The Overlook Inn** (Dutch Hill Road, 18325-9755; 717–595–7519 or 800–441–0177) was originally built as a farmhouse in the early 1800s; 100 years later, it was converted into a country hotel. At that time, it "overlooked" the Delaware Water Gap, but now stands of evergreens block the view. Guest rooms are decorated warmly and comfortably with old (but not antique) furnishings. Rates include dinner and a full breakfast. Reports on both these inns would be most welcome.

The Pine Knob   *Tel:* 717–595–2532
Route 447, Box 275, 18325

The Pine Knob dates back to 1847, when Dr. Gilbert Palen built himself a home and started a tannery. In the process he renamed the town (originally called Frogtown—anything would have been an improvement) Canadensis, after the botanical name of the hemlock, whose bark was used in the tanning of leather. The building was turned into a guest house in 1886, and was purchased by Scott and Annie Frankel in 1988. Annie reports that she and Scott share over 30 years in the hotel business, and that they were both born and raised in this area. "My mother

216

helps with lots of the baking—my brother tends bar, and Scott's parents do the bookkeeping and stand in as inn-sitters when we need a day or two away."

Rates include full breakfast, dinner and evening turndown with homemade cookies on the pillow; favorite entrées include rack of lamb with rosemary, duck with green peppercorn sauce, and chicken stuffed with mushrooms and wrapped in puff pastry. From May through October, the Pine Knob sponsors craft and art workshops (additional fee).

"The inn is nicely situated on a fairly quiet road, surrounded by landscaped grounds, with a large swimming pool just across the road. The inn has a light and spacious parlor, hung with lovely watercolors by local artists, an airy dining room—highlighted by the Frankel's extensive collection of antique cookie jars, and a cozy Victorian-style bar. The guest rooms are most inviting, comfortably decorated with brass or carved oak beds, handmade quilts, cheery wallpaper, and period antiques; nearly all the baths have recently been redone, and are clean and fresh. Ample porches run along the side of the inn, facing the flower gardens, and are well supplied with rocking chairs for sitting and chatting." (SWS)

"We had a delicious dinner of duck in green peppercorn sauce with wild rice and chicken Wellington. The duck was perfect, not sweet at all; the chicken was tasty, although slightly underseasoned. For dessert we shared a piece of real pecan pie, with a delicious homemade crust. Service was warm and friendly, with Scott acting as maitre d', and Annie visiting each table to say hello. The Frankels are welcoming hosts, and are working hard to make a nice inn even nicer. Annie is a creator and collector of quilts, and the results of her efforts can be seen on the walls and beds of many of the inn's rooms." (Diane Wolf)

Open All year. Restaurant closed to public Mon.
Rooms 2 suites, 25 doubles, 2 singles—20 with private bath and/or shower, 7 with sink in room and shared bath. All with fan, 1 with desk. 9 rooms in cottage.
Facilities Bar, restaurant, living room with fireplace, TV, piano, books, games. 8½ acres with gardens, woods, swimming pool, tennis court, lawn games, trout fishing, art gallery. Golf, downhill and cross-country skiing nearby.
Location Poconos, Monroe County. ½ m S of center of town. From I-80 W, take Rte. 447 N to inn.
Restrictions No children under 5.
Credit cards MC, Visa.
Rates MAP, $138–148 suite, $110–138 double, $55–74 single. Extra person in room $69. 10% service. Family rates. 2-3 night holiday/weekend minimum. Weekly rates. 3–5 day art, quilting workshops. Prix fixe dinner, $29. Alc dinner, $27.
Extras Bus station pickups.

CHURCHTOWN

Information please: A recently opened B&B, **The Inn at Twin Linden** (2092 Main Street, 17555; 215–445–7619) offers six guest rooms with private baths, and serves meals ranging from Belgian pecan waffles with homemade brandied peach syrup for breakfast to spicy Cajun skewered shrimp over rice for dinner. Reports please.

Churchtown Inn
Tel: 215–445–7794
Route 23
Mailing address: 2100 Main Street, Narvon, 17555

A handsome fieldstone house dating back to 1735 and enlarged in 1810, the Churchtown Inn offers a winning combination—cozy rooms furnished with antiques and handmade quilts plus hospitable innkeepers: Stuart and Hermine Smith, and Jim Kent. Recent changes at the inn include a glass garden room for breakfast; although dinner is not served at the inn, the innkeepers are pleased to arrange dinner with a local Amish family—often a highlight of a visit here.

"Our room was furnished with two beautiful canopy beds. Stuart Smith is a retired choral director who has a great voice and is a master at making everyone feel at home and comfortable. Each breakfast was different—cereal, sausages, and a delightful apple custard pancake. Great coffee and juices. The countryside is delightful, and you can sit on the front patio and watch the Amish ride by in their buggies." *(Stuart Barrett)*

"The friendly ambience is due to Stuart Smith's graciousness; he encourages guests to interact and is an excellent pianist." *(Marilyn R. Watson)* "Our room and bath could not have been cleaner, and hot water and parking were plentiful. The Smiths arranged for us to have dinner with an Amish family, which was a fantastic experience." *(Steve and Betsy Noal)* "Beautiful and spotlessly clean." *(Joel Abrams)* "White baseboards and windowsills that gleamed. A big plus was the very comfortable beds." *(Pat Dusa)*

"We enjoyed a sweeping view of the picturesque countryside from our bedroom. Although it is conveniently located on a major route, the inn is quiet and tranquil. There is ample parking. The hosts are all that is hospitable, and the food surpassed all expectations." *(Valerie Carlos Letelier, also Bill Werner)*

Open All year. Closed Christmas.
Rooms 8 doubles—6 with private shower and/or bath, 2 with maximum of 4 people sharing bath. Most with TV, desk, fireplaces; all with air-conditioning.
Facilities Dining room; 2 parlors, with library, game corner, piano; TV/den room; enclosed porch, patio. Swimming pool, lake, tennis, golf, horseback riding, cross-country skiing nearby.
Location SE PA, Pennsylvania Dutch Country. 16 m NE of Lancaster. Take Exit 22 (Morgantown) off I-76 (PA Tpke.). Go S on Rte. 10, then W on Rte. 23 to inn.
Restrictions Limited traffic noise in 2 guest rooms. Smoking on enclosed porch only. No children under 12.
Credit cards MC, Visa.
Rates B&B, $50–90 double, $45–85 single. Extra person in room, $20. 2-3 night holiday/weekend minimum. Weekly rates.
Extras Limited German, Italian spoken.

CLARK

Tara   *Tel:* 412–962–3535
3665 Valley View Road, 16113   412–962–2992

A Greek Revival mansion built in 1854, Tara was restored by Donna
and Jim Winner in 1986. Their inn re-creates a piece of the old South—
Hollywood style—inspired by the movie *Gone with the Wind.* All rooms
are named and luxuriously decorated with antiques in the style of a
particular character from the story.

"We stayed in the Victorian room, which has a lace-draped satin-
covered bed, an eleven-foot ceiling adorned with a crystal chandelier,
and a gas fireplace; the bath had a galvanized claw foot tub with gold
fixtures. The inn also houses three restaurants—the casual Stonewall's
Tavern, the elegant Ashley's Restaurant, and the family-style Ole
South Room. I ate at the first, and enjoyed freshly made fettucini with
pesto and pine nuts. I heard that the fixed price menu at Ashley's was
good and that the Ole South Room is fun—homemade coleslaw, apple
butter, chicken, real mashed potatoes, and lots more, all served family
style. A tour of Tara is worthwhile, although the place can get crowded
and somewhat commercial in feeling around lunchtime. High tea is a
nice touch—served on the veranda in Miss Ellen's library. I'd also
recommend a drive south of I-80 to New Wilmington to a restaurant
called The Tavern, which serves excellent homemade food." *(Susie
Preston)*

Open All year. Restaurant closed weekdays Jan. through mid-Feb.
Rooms 13 doubles—all with private bath, air-conditioning, fan. Some with
fireplace. Telephone, radio, TV, desk on request.
Facilities Dining room, living room with fireplace, bar/lounge, library, patio. 4
acres with croquet, bocci, carriage rides, sleigh rides, bikes. Lake for watersports.
Golf nearby.
Location W PA. 7 m N of Sharon. From I-80 take Rte. 18 N to Clark. Approx.
10 m.
Restrictions Smoking restricted to certain areas. "Not suitable for accommodat-
ing children overnight."
Credit cards MC, Visa
Rates B&B, $119–150 double. 15% service. 10% senior discount. Weekend rates.
Alc lunch $6, alc dinner $17. Children's menu.
Extras Airport pickups.

COOKSBURG

Clarion River Lodge   *Tel:* 814–744–8171
River Road, P.O. Box 150, 16217   800–648–6743

Owner/manager Skip Williams describes the lodge as having a "spectacular natural setting along the gentle Clarion River, adjacent to Cook
Forest Park, the oldest and largest stand of virgin pine and hemlock in

the East." Built as a private estate, the original house is now the dining area and is highlighted by a massive fieldstone fireplace, log beams, and cherry paneling. A breezeway connects the newly built guest rooms that are decorated with modern Scandinavian decor. Favorite activities include hiking or skiing through the Cook Forest and canoeing on the river. The dinner menu includes a good selection of steaks, seafood, and pasta dishes.

"Highlights were a leisurely stroll on a river road with picture-perfect scenery; carefully selected wines served in front of the fire; deer just outside the windows; a tour of local interest spots—virgin timber, quaint little towns, museums, and craft shops. The food was wonderful; great fish dishes and delicious peanut butter pie. Complimentary breakfast includes juice, cereal, rolls, and endless cups of good coffee. Our room had a balcony overlooking the river, a comfortable king-size bed, and a bathroom with all the latest features—no roughing it here." *(Kathryn Powell)* "Stunning location, away from crowds and traffic. The staff was accommodating but never intrusive, and the personal involvement of the owners in the inn's day-to-day operations was refreshing." *(Greg & Jill Fraser)*

Open All year. Closed Christmas Eve, Day.
Rooms 20 doubles with full private bath, telephone, TV, desk, air-conditioning, fan, refrigerator.
Facilities Dining room, enclosed breezeway with books, magazines, fireplace, bar/lounge, meeting room. 30 acres with river for canoeing, fishing, swimming, hiking, bicycling.
Location Great Forest of NW PA. 2 hr N of Pittsburgh. From I-80 take Exit 13 (Brookville). Go N 15 m on Rte. 36. Turn right on River Rd. Go 5 m.
Restrictions No infants.
Credit cards Amex, MC, Visa.
Rates B&B, $57–99 double. Extra person in room, $15. 10% senior discount. 2-night holiday minimum. Full breakfast $4. Alc lunch $5–7, alc dinner $12–35.

Gateway Lodge & Cabins
Route 36, Box 125, 16217

Tel: 814–744–8017
In PA: 800–843–6862

The Gateway is a rustic log cabin, set among the virgin pine and hemlock forests of Cook Forest State Park. It was built in 1934 and, with the exception of an indoor swimming pool and an added stairway and porch, has not been changed structurally since. Joe and Linda Burney bought the lodge in 1980 and have furnished it comfortably with antiques, hand-hewn chestnut beds, and braided rugs. An additional 13 guest rooms are planned for completion in 1991.

Breakfast, lunch, and dinner are all open to the public. Dinner seatings are at 6 P.M. and 8 P.M. Tuesday through Saturday; 2 P.M. and 5 P.M. on Sunday. Entrées might include chicken and biscuits, baked haddock stuffed with vegetables, and country-style barbecued ribs. Although a wider choice of dishes is offered on weekdays, Linda notes that on weekends, "our custom is that the first caller to make a dinner reservation for the evening sets the menu. Meals are served by the light of kerosene lamps and our staff dresses in colonial costume."

"Dinner was quite good; the lodge's public rooms are rustic and comfortable, and the indoor heated pool looked inviting." *(JP)* More comments please.

Open All year. Closed Thanksgiving week, Dec. 22-25. No dinner served on Mondays.
Rooms 8 doubles—3 with full private bath, 5 rooms with a maximum of 5 sharing a bath. 8 cabins with kitchens, fireplaces (no linens or cooking utensils).
Facilities Dining room, living room, taproom, game room, porch, indoor swimming pool (heated in winter). 16 acres. In 6,000-acre Cook Forest State Park, with hiking, fishing, bird-watching, bicycling, canoeing, tubing, golf, horseback riding, swimming, ice-skating, cross-country skiing, snowmobiling, sleigh and carriage rides.
Location NW PA, Clarion/Jefferson County. Take Exit 13 off I-80, to Rte. 36 N. 14 m to inn.
Restrictions Children welcome in cabins.
Credit cards Amex, MC, Visa.
Rates Room only, $75 double. $65–97 cabin (sleeps 2-8). 2-3 night minimum in cabins. 10% discount Jan.-April cabin rate. Full breakfast $3-6. Prix fixe dinner, $14–18.

EPHRATA

Ephrata's key attraction is the Cloister, a Protestant monastery for men and women founded in 1732 by Conrad Beissel. An early experiment in communal living, the Ephrata Cloister became renowned for its German medieval-style architecture. Known for its prose, poetry, and music, it was a famous colonial printing and publishing center. Tours and craft demonstrations are offered year-round; a musical drama depicting eighteenth-century cloister life is offered summer weekends.

Ephrata is located in the Pennsylvania Dutch Country of southeastern Pennsylvania, 5 miles south of Pennsylvania Turnpike Exit 21, 12 miles northeast of Lancaster, and 15 miles southwest of Reading. It's 1½ hours northeast of Baltimore, MD, and 1 hour west of Philadelphia.

Clearview Farm   *Tel:* 717–733–6333
355 Clearview Road, 17522

We've often driven by big old stone farmhouses, curious to see what they're like inside. Clearview Farm B&B provides one answer to that question. A limestone farmhouse built in 1814, it has been the home and working farm of Glenn and Mildred Wissler for over 30 years. Entering the farmhouse, past the flower gardens and pond with resident swans, may come as a surprise: the inn is elegantly decorated with formal Victorian antiques and detailed window treatments in every room but the cheerful den, which has a country motif, complete with antique farm tools, quilted and stenciled hearts, and braided rug. Despite the formality, the Wisslers have taken care not to place form over function. Comfort took priority over appearance when they searched the area for just the right antiques for each room, and the lace-topped canopy beds, brass and iron beds, and carved walnut bed all have comfortable mattresses and quality linens. Breakfasts are farm-hearty, and vary daily; ham and cheese souffle, French toast with oatmeal apple bread, or waffles with fresh strawberry sauce are among the favorites, accompanied by fresh fruit, muffins or coffee cake.

"Gracious hospitality, warm and inviting home. Tasty breakfast, enchanting rooms." *(JM)* More comments please.

Open All year.
Rooms 5 doubles—3 with private shower and/or bath, 2 rooms with a maximum of 4 people sharing a bath. All with air-conditioning.
Facilities Parlor, dining room, den with fireplace, TV/VCR; porch. 200 acres with pond.
Location From Lancaster take Rte. 222 N to Rte 322 W. Go thru Ephrata, and after passing Family Time Restaurant take 5th rd. on right at Whtaneys Inn onto Clearview Rd. Inn is 1st farm.
Restrictions No smoking. No children under 12.
Credit cards MC, Visa.
Rates B&B, $69 double. Extra person in room, $15.
Extras Airport/station pickups.

The Guesthouse at Doneckers   *Tel:* 717–733–8696
318-324 North State Street, 17522

The Guesthouse and Restaurant at Doneckers opened in recent years as an adjunct to Doneckers's existing complex of retail fashion stores. The Guesthouse was created by connecting and restoring three turn-of-the-century brick houses; an addition, built in 1777 and completed in 1988, has increased the room count by ten. Rooms are individually decorated with hand-stenciled walls, handmade curtains, and English as well as local antiques. The breakfast buffet includes croissants, breads, cheese, fruit, cereals, sausage, juice, tea, and coffee.

The real surprise at Doneckers is the restaurant. In the midst of Pennsylvania Dutch Country, chef Jean Maurice Jugé serves innovative and imaginative French cuisine to considerable acclaim. A possible dinner selection might include an appetizer asparagus custard with tarragon tomato sauce; an entrée of boneless duck with ginger pear sauce or Dover sole with strawberry butter; and a dessert of white and dark chocolate mousse.

"Attractive decor, with nice touches like goose-down pillows, bed turned down at night with chocolate on pillows, Crabtree & Evelyn soaps. Restaurant and shops both excellent." *(Kathy Renck)* "Our room was furnished in antiques with a warm and cozy feel. Breakfast is served in the pantry and consists of small croissants, muffins, fresh fruit and juices, coffee or tea. The ladies who served breakfast and who generally run the inn were nice and made our visit most enjoyable." *(Martin Yaker & Edith Shuan)*

Open All year. Closed Christmas. Restaurant closed Wednesdays, Jan.–Nov.
Rooms 7 suites, 22 doubles—all with private bath and/or shower, telephone, air-conditioning. Some with Jacuzzi, fireplace.
Facilities Parlor with TV, breakfast pantry; small meeting room, balcony/deck. Restaurant with dancing at special events, shops. Swimming pool, tennis courts, cross-country skiing nearby.
Location Center of town. Just off Rte. 322/Main St.

Credit cards Amex, CB, DC, Discover, MC, Visa.
Rates B&B, $125–130 suite; $59–105 double; $51–74 single. Extra person in room, $10; crib, $8. Alc lunch, $6–12; early dinner, $10; alc dinner, $50. Children's menu at lunch.
Extras 5 guest rooms, parlor wheelchair accessible. Cribs, babysitting available. Airport/station pickups. French spoken.

Hackman's Country Inn
140 Hackman Road, 17522

Tel: 717–733–3498

A sturdy brick farmhouse, painted white, with green shutters and trim, encircled by big old shade trees, and sitting on a quiet country road, Hackman's fits just about anyone's vision of the ideal country B&B. Stepping inside, the spell is not broken; the central keeping room has a walk-in fireplace, handsome country antiques, braided rugs, and plain white walls, while upstairs, a similar decor is highlighted by hand stenciling and colorful quilts in traditional patterns.

"The inn is surrounded by fields; we spent many hours on the porch swing listening to the quiet, pierced only by bird songs and an occasional passing car. The farmhouse was built by Mrs. Hackman's husband's ancestors in 1857, and is still a working farm; it has been a B&B since 1986. The plumbing is old but works well. All doors lead to the kitchen, a warm and comforting room where a breakfast of homemade muffins and jam, fresh fruit and juice, and coffee is served. Mrs. Hackman was courteous and wonderfully hospitable; Amish country seems to imbue its inhabitants with a quiet friendliness. The area around Ephrata boasts mostly flea markets and antiquing; the back roads near the inn are ideal for bicycling." *(Maxine Lee Booth)*

"Mrs. Hackman is a caring, lovely person; she's very concerned about her guests' comfort. The food was delicious, ample, and well-served. Rooms are extra clean, bed linens crisp and clean, and there's ample parking and lighting." *(Wilma B. Jessee)*

Open All year.
Rooms 4 doubles—2 with private shower, 2 sharing 1 bath. All with air-conditioning.
Facilities Keeping room/kitchen, porch. Shaded lawn, 90-acre farm.
Location Take Hwy. 222 to Ephrata Exit. Go W on Rte. 322 for 4½ m to Hackman Rd. Turn right on Hackman Rd. at the Agway store and go N to inn on left.
Restrictions No smoking. No children under 10.
Credit cards MC, Visa.
Rates B&B, $50–60 double; $45 single. Extra person in room, $15.

Smithton Inn
900 West Main Street, 17522

Tel: 717–733–6094

The Smithton Inn was built as an inn and tavern in 1763 by Henry and Susana Miller, married members of the Ephrata Cloister. It continued in use as an inn through the Civil War, and stayed in the Miller family for over 200 years. It's been owned by Dorothy Graybill and her partner since 1979; be sure to request a copy of their helpful booklet, *Smithton Suggestions.*

Guest rooms are furnished with antiques and furniture crafted with hand tools in the inn's cabinet shop, hand decorated antique blanket chests, and original paintings and folk art pieces. Amenities include feather beds, guest night shirts, fresh flowers, fruit baskets, oil lamps in the windows, candies, and reading material.

"The peaceful, gracious atmosphere, the comfortable furniture and wonderful rooms, reflects the attitude of innkeeper Dorothy Graybill. Wonderful Amish and Mennonite history was at the tip of Dorothy's tongue whenever asked, and her help in visiting the area around the inn was priceless. To top it off, we were invited to share an evening meal with an Old Order family. We shall always remember the lovely meal, and the experience of talking with and learning about the Plain People." *(Jean Cashen)*

"Our room was spotlessly clean, furnished with antiques and a good, firm, king-size bed, with a fire laid in the fireplace. Upon our return from a delicious dinner at nearby Lincoln House, we found the candles lighted in our room." *(Stuart Rider, Jr.)* "Our beautiful room had a canopied bed, handmade quilts, hurricane lamps, and fresh flowers and fruit. The breakfasts are wonderful and cookies and lemonade were offered each evening along with teas and coffee. Dorothy Graybill is a walking information/visitor's center." *(Dianne Crawford)* More comments please.

Open All year.
Rooms 1 suite, 6 doubles, with private bath, desk, air-conditioning, working fireplaces. Kitchenette, dining area, whirlpool tub in suite. Telephone on request.
Facilities Dining rooms, library, common room. Garden with fountain, koi fish; lop-eared rabbits; patio furniture.
Location 5 m S of PA Tpke., From Exit 21 take Rte. 222 to Ephrata Exit. Go W on Rte. 322 for 2½ m to inn.
Restrictions No smoking. Though on a busy street, the owners have taken exceptional steps to ensure quiet rooms.
Credit cards Amex, MC, Visa.
Rates B&B, $140–170 suite (4 rooms), $65–115 double, $55–105 single. Extra person in room, $35. Family rates. 2-night holiday/weekend minimum.
Extras Limited wheelchair access. Airport/station pickups. Pets permitted with prior arrangement. Cradle available.

ERWINNA

Information please: We'd like more reports on **Evermay on-the-Delaware** (River Road, Route 32, 18920; 215–294–9100) well known for its fine cuisine: "Excellent food; service totally professional; romantic atmosphere. The setting is quite formal—no shorts are allowed in the parlor when sherry is being served!" *(Pat Drake)* Another reader said that his dinner here was one of the best he'd ever eaten, but that the guest rooms were "just OK." More reports welcomed.

Isaac Stover House   *Tel:* 215–294–8044
River Road, P.O. Box 68, 18920

Built in 1837, this eclectically styled mansard-roofed Victorian was restored by television personality Sally Jessy Raphael in 1988; Susan

Tettemer is the resident innkeeper. An inveterate collector, Sally has utilized the "cluttered" style of Victorian decor to showcase her Burmese crafts, Balinese puppets, and other mementos of her worldwide travels. Reproduction wallpapers, lavish curtains, and velvet couches with lace antimacassars complete the decor. Amenities include evening wine and refreshments, plus in-room sherry, robes, lush monogrammed towels, and toiletries.

A typical breakfast might include Italian spinach pie, lemon bread, fruit compote, and cranberry-apricot juice, served in front of the fireplace in the parlor or at one of the marble-topped tables in the breakfast room.

"Our innkeeper was warm, friendly, and caring. The housekeeping was impeccable, as were the grounds." *(James Karangelen)* "Our room had beautiful views of an old mill and the Delaware River about 40 yards from the inn. The bed was very comfortable with lots of pillows and a fluffy down comforter. We breakfasted on cereal and fruit, quiche with potatoes, ham and broccoli, coffee, and pastries." *(John Eckert)*

Some additional comments: "We enjoyed our stay here, but were stunned to learn that the rates were more than doubled from our first visit in 1989 to our unrealized visit in 1990, and stayed elsewhere." Also: "The plumbing was OK but stronger water pressure would have been nice." More comments most welcome.

Open All year.
Rooms 1 suite, 6 doubles—5 with private bath, 2 with a maximum of 4 people sharing 1 bath. Some with desk, fan. 1 with fireplace.
Facilities Parlor with fireplace, breakfast room, TV area with books, games; porch. 13 acres with gardens, lawns. River tubing, canoeing, boating, fishing nearby.
Location Bucks County. 13 m from New Hope. From NJ, take NJ Turnpike S to Exit 14. Take Rte. 78 W to Exit 15, Clinton-Pittstown. Turn left on Rte. 513. Follow Rte 513 S 11 m to Frenchtown, cross over Frenchtown Bridge. Turn left on Rte. 32, and go S 2 m to inn on right, across from Stover Mill.
Restrictions No smoking in guest rooms. No children under 12.
Credit cards Amex, MC, Visa.
Rates B&B, $250 suite, $150–175 double. Extra person in room, $15. 2-3 night weekend/holiday minimum. Corporate rates.

FARMINGTON

Nemacolin Woodlands
P.O. Box 188, 15437

Tel: 412–329–6190
412–329–8555

Less than a decade old, this extensive resort ran into financial problems early on, but now seems well back on track with a full variety of accommodations and restaurants, and a full complement of sports facilities, including a newly opened spa, with services and cuisine to match. Here's what a frequent contributor had to say:

"Our room was beautifully decorated with two queen-size beds, an easy chair, and private balcony. Food in the dining room is good but expensive; service is excellent. The inn is decorated with many lovely antiques and a large fireplace. The well-equipped spa is across from the inn; they supply sweatsuits, slippers, towels, and shampoo. There's a beautiful swimming pool, sauna, whirlpool, steam room, weight and exercise room and more; we were allowed to use the facilities even after we checked out. It was raining when we visited, but we plan to return to enjoy the many outdoor activities." *(Janet Payne)*

Open All year.
Rooms 164 units; 26 suites, doubles in inn; remainder in 1-2 bedroom condo units. All with full private bath, telephone, TV, air-conditioning. Many with refrigerator, balcony, deck, fireplace.
Facilities 2 restaurants, cafeteria, lobby, meeting rooms. 2,000 acres with outdoor & heated indoor swimming pool, sauna, whirlpool, full spa facilities, nature program, jogging trails, golf academy, 18-hole golf course, canoeing, nature program, horseback riding, cross-country skiing, airstrip.
Location SW PA, Laurel Mts. 60 m SE of Pittsburgh. From I-70, take Donegal Exit to Rte. 381 S. Go E on Rte. 40 to resort entrance on left.
Credit cards Amex, MC, Visa.
Rates Room only, $90–260 double. Extra person in room, $10. Alc dinner, $25–40. Extensive list of spa, golf, other package rates.
Extras Airport pickups.

FOGELSVILLE

Glasbern   *Tel:* 215–285–4723
Pack House Road, RD 1, Box 250, 18051-9743   800–654–9296

Glasbern, a reconstructed barn, combines the original foundation, wood beams, and shale rock walls, with cathedral ceilings and a contemporary airy feeling. Beth and Al Granger opened the inn in 1985; since then, they have added a handsome indoor swimming pool, and have expanded to the adjacent Carriage House (née tractor shed).

Dinners are now served at the inn, prepared by Chef Mark Shield, who studied at the Culinary Institute of America in Hyde Park, and the Cordon Bleu in Paris. Recent entrées included sole with shallots, lime, and wine butter sauce; veal scallopini with red onions, leek, and wild mushrooms; and chicken Calvados with apple-walnut stuffing and finished with Stilton cheese.

"Nestled in a quiet valley surrounded by magnificent pine trees, huge windows cover the inn's southern face, hence the name Glasbern— 'glass barn.' The reception area is spacious and open. A large woodburning stove warms guests during the winter, and meals are taken at the oval dining table next to the lounge. A 'country feel' is evident in the dried flower arrangements, candles, baskets, and comfortable furniture.

"Our room was furnished with antiques and modern pieces, and had a queen-size four-poster bed and a beautiful view from the huge windows. Breakfasts were a delight; one morning we had poached pears in custard sauce, the next we had an English breakfast complete with grilled tomato." *(Jon & Kae Tienstra, also Jacquie Gordon)* "We stayed in a suite in the newly renovated carriage house, and loved its gracious and elegant atmosphere, along with the king-size bed, fireplace, and whirlpool tub." *(Mrs. Paula Stubbs)* More comments please.

Open All year. Restaurant closed Sunday, Monday.
Rooms 11 suites, 10 doubles—all with private bath and/or shower, telephone, radio, TV, desk, air-conditioning. 14 with whirlpool, 8 with fireplace. Suites with kitchenette. 7 rooms in annex.
Facilities Common room with fireplace, sun-room, meeting room. 16 acres with heated swimming pool, hot tub, jogging, bicycling, cross-country skiing. Down-hill skiing, lake for fishing, swimming nearby.
Location E central PA. 10 m W of Allentown; 5 min. from intersection of rtes. 22/78 & 100. 2 m from Iron Run Industrial Area. From Rte. 100 N, go W on Tilghman St. Turn right at N. Church St. to Pack House Rd.
Restrictions Children in farmhouse only.
Credit cards Amex, MC, Visa.
Rates B&B, $125–175 suite, $95–145 double, $80–100 single. Extra person in room, $15. 2-night weekend minimum. Alc dinner $35.
Extras Limited wheelchair access. Cribs available.

GARDNERS

Goose Chase
200 Blueberry Road, 17324

Tel: 717–528–8877

Set in the rolling hills of Adams County orchard country, the Goose Chase B&B was opened by Marsha and Rich Lucidi in 1987. Decorated in Williamsburg tradition and colors, this stone house, built circa 1759, is furnished with hand-made quilts, folk art, and 18th-century antiques and reproductions, including four poster and canopied beds. Most walls are hand-stenciled, and wide-planked floors are found in most rooms. Extras include scented soaps and potpourri, toiletries, and fluffy robes. Guests may relax on the patio in summer, or pick their own blueberries. Rates include a full breakfast and afternoon refreshments. The breakfast menu changes daily, although blueberries always appear, a reminder of the inn's address. One morning might bring blueberry pancakes with maple syrup and fresh fruit salad with honey-yogurt dressing, while another might feature melon with blueberry puree; crepes with eggs, mushrooms, tomatoes, and Parmesan cheese sauce; Italian sausage; and banana nut bread.

"Marsha and Rich spent time talking to us and recommending local attractions, restaurants, and historical sites in the Gettysburg area. Careful attention is paid to details. Our medicine cabinet was stocked with every imaginable toiletry, and wonderful chocolates were on my pillow each night. Marsha serves the delicious breakfasts in authentic colonial garb. " *(Dorothy Deluca)*

Open All year.
Rooms 1 suite, 4 doubles—all with private bath, radio, desk, air-conditioning, fan. 2 rooms in carriage house with fireplace.
Facilities Dining room, living room with books, TV. 25 acres with garden, swimming pool, hiking trails, cross-country skiing. 20 min to downhill skiing.
Location S central PA. 12 m N of Gettysburg. From Gettysburg take Rte. 15 N to Rte. 234, turn left at stop sign. Go ½ m, turn right onto Old Harrisburg Rd. Go 9/10 m, turn left onto Oxford Rd. Go 2½ m, turn left onto Blueberry Rd.
Restrictions No smoking. No children under 12.
Credit cards MC, Visa.

Rates B&B, $118 suite, $59–89 double. No tipping. 2-night minimum holiday weekends.

GETTYSBURG

Founded in the 1780s, Gettysburg grew up around the intersection of four major roads and a number of secondary routes; its strategic location led to its involvement in the bloodiest battle of the Civil War in 1863. The battlefield virtually surrounds the town, and is now a National Military Park. There is much to see and do in the area, but don't expect to experience it in solitude, especially on weekends in good weather. Start early in the day, and stop first at the National Park Visitors Center for information; local B&B owners should also be knowledgeable about the battlefield.

Gettysburg is located in south central Pennsylvania, 50 miles northwest of Baltimore.

For an additional area entry, see listing in Gardners, above.

The Brafferton Inn   *Tel:* 717–337–3423
44 York Street (Route 30), 17325

Built of stone in 1786, The Brafferton Inn is one of the oldest homes in Gettysburg and is listed on the National Register of Historic Places. A "new" brick wing was added before the Civil War and now houses most of the guest rooms. Rooms are decorated with eighteenth-century stencils, primitive antiques, samplers, and quilts.

Mimi and Jim Agard bought the inn in 1986 and have done an imaginative job of restoring it. A full breakfast is served in the dining room each morning; peaches and cream, French toast, or strawberry pancakes with whipped cream are specialties. The dining room is highlighted by a hand-painted mural of eighteenth-century Gettysburg.

"A very pleasant inn in the heart of Gettysburg, within easy walking distance of plentiful shopping and dining. A hearty walk takes you to the National Cemetery, site of Lincoln's address, and several historic attractions. Our room was spacious and quiet with an extremely comfortable bed. Our bath was small but charming, with a thrown pottery sink. The dining room was welcoming and warm, and the Agards and their staff are especially hospitable. The tiered decks and herb and flower gardens in back are great places to sit with a book or a glass of wine." *(Judy Lamberti)* More comments please.

Open All year.
Rooms 11 doubles—6 with full private bath, 5 with maximum of 10 sharing bath. All with air-conditioning. Some with desk. 6 rooms in annex.
Facilities Dining room, library, living room with player piano, atrium, back garden/deck. Skiing, golf, swimming, hiking, downhill skiing nearby.
Location Just off square.
Restrictions No smoking. No children under 7.
Credit cards MC, Visa.
Rates B&B, $80–95 double, $65–80 single. Extra person in room, $10.
Extras Wheelchair access. Babysitting available.

The Tannery   *Tel:* 717–334–2454
449 Baltimore Street, 17325

The Swoope family has owned The Tannery since 1920; in 1989 they refurbished the family home, built in the Gothic revival style in 1868. Named for the tannery which once stood at the back of the property, this Gothic revival structure is extremely convenient for touring the Gettysburg battlefield; tour buses leave just a block away. Charlotte Swoope notes that "we are Gettysburg natives and have valuable knowledge about the area which we can pass on to our guests. We help with dinner reservations, secure battlefield guides, and try very hard to make our guests feel at home here." Rates include a welcoming glass of iced tea or lemonade, pre-dinner wine and cheese, and an extended continental breakfast.

"Rooms are sparkling clean, freshly refurbished with modern bathrooms. Although the decor is traditional, the lack of antiques is more than made up by the comfortable setting and well-informed, anxious to please innkeepers." *(MW)* More comments please.

Open April 1 to Nov. 1.
Rooms 4 doubles—all with private shower and/or bath, air-conditioning.
Facilities Breakfast room, parlor, TV room, porch. Off-street parking.
Location 5 blocks from town center. Walking distance to historical interests.
Restrictions No smoking. No children under 12.
Credit cards MC, Visa.
Rates B&B, $70–85 double. Extra person in room, $12.

GLEN MILLS

Sweetwater Farm   *Tel:* 215–459–4711
Sweetwater Road, Box 50, 19342

Sweetwater Farm was established in 1734. Its original section was completed in the mid-1700s; the mansion addition was made in 1815. The house has ten working fireplaces, original oak and pine random-width floors, and a wide sweeping center hall staircase. Rates include a full country breakfast of fresh orange juice, eggs right from the henhouse, bacon, ham and sausage, pancakes or French toast, and homemade coffee cake. Long-time owner Linda Kaat sold the inn in 1989, and the inn's ownership is in flux.

"Although the rates are now on the high side, Sweetwater Farm is a charming old farmhouse, very well maintained. Cats, dogs, sheep, goats, and horses occupy the five-story barn, making for a pleasant, warm country atmosphere." *(Pat Drake)* "Sweetwater Farm is located near Philadelphia and Longwood Gardens, with some of the best antique shops around. *(Earl & Joann Crown)*

Also: "We loved this inn when Linda owned it, and were very disappointed at the high prices and poor value on a recent return visit."

Open All year.
Rooms 4 suites, 5 doubles, 4 cabins—10 with private bath and/or shower, 3 with

maximum of 6 people sharing bath. Some rooms with TV, desk, telephone. All with radio, air-conditioning.

Facilities Tavern room, dining room, library, parlor, country kitchen, porch. 50 acres with meadows, woods, farm animals, swimming pool. Ridley Creek State Park nearby for hiking, fishing.

Location SE PA. Chester County. 10 m N of Brandywine Valley, 20 m W of Philadelphia, 10 m N of Wilmington, DE. Off U.S. 1 at Valley Rd. to Sweetwater Rd.; near Chadds Ford. 20 min. to Longwood Gardens, 5 min. to Franklin Mint.

Restrictions No children under 7.

Credit cards Amex.

Rates B&B, $155 suite, $125–145 double, $145-185 cottage. Extra person in room, $15. 2-night minimum stay on holiday weekends.

Extras Play equipment available. Cabins wheelchair accessible.

GREENSBURG

Mountain View Inn   *Tel:* 412–834–5300
1001 Village Drive (Route 30 East), 15601

While originally built in 1924, with a more recent guest wing, the Mountain View has the appearance and feel of a much older building, partly due to the good taste of the owners, who have furnished it almost entirely with antiques and good reproductions, and partly due to the frame construction, which has resulted in floors that squeak just enough to make it sound much older. Many rooms have lovely views of the Laurel Mountains.

"Our room oozed charm in wallpaper and furnishings, and was large enough to hold our king-size bed with plenty of room around it. Private baths, closets, and excellent maid service made our stay a delightful experience. The inn is a local favorite for dining, justified by the varied menu and excellent food. The staff, from busboys to managers, are exceedingly pleasant and helpful, and can take criticism and complaints in the manner in which they are intended, truly making every effort to make your stay a happy one." *(Jim & Marty Marsden)*

"The welcome is friendly, the service smiling and efficient and the housekeeping displays admirable attention to detail." *(S. Larcombe)* "Our room was extremely quiet; we called room service for dinner, and got the quickest service ever. The food was hot and exactly right." *(Mr. & Mrs. Mark DeLario)* "The staff went out of their way to accommodate our toddler. The tavern is a nice place to go for a casual dinner or drink; it's not rowdy or smoky." *(Cynthia & David Battalia)*

"Our room had a four-poster cannonball pine bed, complete with step-up stool, covered with a white chenille George Washington bedspread. A beautiful pine table spanned the large wall of windows. The colorful floral wallpaper, soft colored wing chairs, and a stunning floral basket completed the room. The bath was spotless and well equipped with toiletries, even a telephone. The inn's dining room is large with one wall of windows, a fireplace, china cupboards and shelves full of antique glassware and china. We enjoyed barbecued shrimp and medallions of veal accompanied with soup, salad, and homemade bread. Service was prompt and efficient. The breakfast menu included several

low-cholesterol choices, as well as light fluffy blueberry pancakes."
(Donna & Peter Christensen)

Open All year. Closed 4 days over Christmas.
Rooms 6 suites, 50 doubles—all with full private bath, telephone, radio, TV, desk, air-conditioning, fan.
Facilities Dining room with pianist, living room, tavern with evening entertainment. 15 acres with grounds for strolling, fish pond. Tennis, golf, cross-country skiing nearby. 15 min. to swimming, trout fishing, white-water rafting. 30 min to downhill skiing.
Location 35 m E of Pittsburgh, via Rte. 30.
Credit cards Amex, CB, DC, MC, Visa.
Rates Room only, $80 suite, $52 double, $47 single. Extra person in room, $5. Family rates. Alc breakfast, $3–7; alc lunch, $6–8; alc dinner, $30.
Extras Wheelchair access. Airport/station pickups. Cribs, babysitting available.

HANOVER

Beechmont Inn   *Tel:* 717–632–3013
315 Broadway, 17331

In 1985, the Hormel family—Terry, Monna, Glenn, and Maggie—active in many local Hanover enterprises, decided to add a bed & breakfast inn to their list of businesses. In April 1986, they opened the Beechmont, having spent the previous six months restoring and redecorating it in a style appropriate to its 1834 Federal-period origins. They used both antiques and reproduction furnishings, primarily of walnut and mahogany, with a rose/green/cream color scheme.

Rates include a full breakfast and afternoon tea. Weekend breakfasts are more elaborate, and might include fresh fruit in summer or baked apples or spiced fruit compote in winter, homemade granola, homemade breads and muffins, and a hot breakfast entrée such as Hungarian sausage strata or herb cheese tart.

"The Hormels are wonderful hosts who provide a comfortable, clean environment. Our room was lovely, decorated in charming colors and fabrics, appointed with antiques and reproduction pieces. Monna even provides an electric blanket for chilly evenings—just one of the many extra touches we discovered. Our suite also had a sitting room in a remodeled porch, and a generous closet with sturdy hangars and lovely sachets to freshen our clothes. Breakfasts were elegant, yet substantial, with a daily offering of homemade granola with yogurt, and a different entrée daily. Our favorite was turkey crepes—creamy and crispy at the same time. The Hormels provide their guests with ample information on antique dealers, area sites and attractions, and menus for restaurants of all types." *(Susan Mavaromatis)*

"I was served tea in the afternoon and a gourmet breakfast with fine china and silver. My room was the Diller Suite, with a working marble fireplace, kitchenette, and a magnificent canopy bed. Monna Hormel is attentive to every detail, including directions to antique shops and historic surroundings." *(Helen Leonard)* "We enjoyed the Hershey Suite, with its lacy curtains, bedspreads, and pillowcases. In one corner is a large antique trunk filled with stuffed animals. Lots of plants and country decor. The room looks onto a nineteenth-century courtyard and herb and flower gardens. We breakfasted in the courtyard, shaded by a century-old magnolia tree." *(Geri Scholtis)* "The innkeepers seem to know just when to be helpful and when to disappear. The location at the edge of the historic area is ideal." *(JH)*

Some minor areas for improvement: "Our bathroom needed some sort of shelf for our toiletries." And: "Although our room had ample closet space, our friends' room had no place to hang clothes."

Open All year.
Rooms 3 suites, 4 doubles—all with private bath and/or shower, radio, air-conditioning. 6 with desk, 1 with fireplace. Telephone, TV on request.
Facilities Parlor, dining room, library with game table. Courtyard, glider swing, garden. Tennis, swimming pool nearby. 3 m to Codorus State Park for swimming, fishing, boating, hiking, cross-country skiing.
Location S central PA, York County. 13 m E of Gettysburg, 40 SW of Lancaster, 60 m NW of Washington, DC. From Rte. 30, go S on Rte. 94 (Carlisle St.) to Center Square. Turn left on Broadway, go 3 blocks to inn on right.
Restrictions No smoking in public rooms. No children under 12.
Credit cards MC, Visa.
Rates B&B, $80–95 suite, $70–75 double, $64–69 single. No tipping. 2-night minimum some weekends.

HOLICONG

Ash Mill Farm   *Tel:* 215–794–5373
Route 202, P.O. Box 202, 18928

Pat and Jim Auslander bought Ash Mill Farm in 1989, leaving the corporate world behind for the more pastoral setting of Bucks County. A B&B for many years, this 18th century manor house, built around 1790 of plaster over fieldstone, overlooks fields of grazing sheep. Random-width wide board floors are complemented by a decor of Shaker-style pencil post and canopy beds; hand-stenciled walls, floors, and trim (some original to the house), Laura Ashley fabrics, and other country touches, including tole ware, baskets, lace, and hand-painted chests. Modern comforts include down comforters, extra pillows, thick terry-cloth robes, and well-stocked medicine chests.

Rates include a breakfast of fresh-baked muffins, fresh fruit and juice, coffee or tea delivered to your room or a full country breakfast served in front of the dining room's walk-in fireplace or on the garden patio. Also included is afternoon lemonade and cookies, or sherry and cheese, depending on the season.

"The farm is located on a major road, but is set far enough back so that traffic noise is not a problem. Sheep grazing in the pasture, cats dozing in the yard, and wicker furniture on the front porch immediately provide a sense of country charm and tranquility. The country theme is carried throughout the whole house. My favorite room is the large one on the second floor with a queen-size bed and daybed. The shared bathroom looks like something from a house decorating magazine. The two-room suite on the third floor is ideal for those desiring privacy. The breakfasts are delicious and filling. I returned for a second visit to find that the ownership had changed, but am pleased to report that the inn is just as nice as before; the new owners are delightful." *(Tom Chang)*

Open All year.
Rooms 1 suite, 5 doubles—4 with private bath and/or shower, 2 with maximum of 4 sharing bath. 5 with air-conditioning, 1 with ceiling fan.
Facilities Dining room with walk-in fireplace, parlor with fireplace, veranda, sun patio. 11 acres with nursery, walking paths, flowers, and sheep. Off-street parking.
Location Bucks County. 4 m W of New Hope; .7 m past Lahaska on right.
Restrictions No smoking. No children.
Credit cards Discover, MC, Visa.
Rates B&B, $100–110 suite, $80–100 double. Extra person in room, $12. Corporate rates. 2-3 night minimum on weekends, holidays respectively.
Extras Airport/station pickups. Some French, Spanish spoken.

Barley Sheaf Farm
Route 202, Box 10, 18928

Tel: 215–794–5104

If you had spent the weekend at Barley Sheaf Farm in the 1930s, Harpo Marx, Dorothy Parker, and Lillian Hellman might have been among your fellow guests; the farm was then owned by playwright George Kaufman, who often invited his many theater and literary friends. The farm dates back to the mid-1700s, although the buildings have been expanded and renovated many times over the years. Don and Ann Mills bought the farm in 1974, and opened it in 1978 as Bucks County's first B&B. The rooms are decorated with exceptional charm, from the somewhat formal colonial parlor to the warm, inviting guest rooms.

"The atmosphere is warm and welcoming, and all the rooms are furnished with lovely antiques. Our room on the third floor was charming and our bathroom was fun—very large, with an old-fashioned tub in the center of the floor with shiny brass shower ring and faucets, and a shower curtain completely surrounding the tub. We enjoyed the main house, but the cottage is also delightful, with three charming bedrooms and a lovely small living room. Breakfast is a standout—fresh fruit, hot breads, perhaps an omelet or French toast with hot apricot syrup and the best ham ever. The innkeeper welcomed us, cooked breakfast, and made our stay extra special. A scrapbook of menus helps one decide where to go for dinner." *(Jack & Billie Schloerb)*

"From the fireplace in our room to the luxurious bath, to its quiet countryside setting, everything was heavenly. Don and Ann are warm and friendly hosts." *(Richard Streeter)*

Open All year.
Rooms 1 suite, 9 doubles—all with private bath and/or shower, telephone, air-conditioning; 3 with desk. 3 rooms in separate cottage.
Facilities Living/family room with fireplace, TV room with fireplace, sun porch. 30 acres with swimming pool, lawn games, farm animals. Near Delaware River for canoeing, fishing, tubing.
Location Bucks County. 90 m S of NYC, 50 m N of Philadelphia, 10 min. SW of New Hope. Follow Rte. 413 to Buckingham. At Buckingham, go left (E) on Rte. 202 to Holicong and inn.
Restrictions No children under 8.
Credit cards Amex, Visa.

Rates B&B, $125–175 suite, $95–155 double. Extra person in room, $17. 2–3 night holiday/weekend minimum. 10% senior discount. 15% midweek off-season discount.
Extras Airport/station pickups. Limited wheelchair access. French spoken.

JERSEY SHORE

Sommerville Farms B&B   *Tel:* 717–398–2368
PA Route 44, RD #4, Box 22, 17740

Bill and Jane Williams invite you to relax at their 200-acre working farm, home to 400 cows, steers, and calves. In the owner's family for over a century, the farmhouse consists of the original 125-year-old plank structure with a more expansive Victorian addition. The elaborate woodwork is original, and much of the decor is antique, some of it the result of Jane's 12 years as an antique dealer. Rates include a breakfast of fruit and juice, granola and yogurt, cereals, homemade muffins, breads, and in cold weather, heartier dishes such as bacon strata. Guests enjoy exploring the pre-Revolutionary Fort Antes Cemetery, with views of the West Branch of the Susquehanna River and the Bald Eagle Range of the Appalachians. *(Betty Norman)*

Open All year.
Rooms 5 doubles, 1 single—all with a maximum of 5 people sharing a bath. All rooms with fan.
Facilities Living room with fireplace, parlor with TV, games; breakfast room. 200 acres with gardens, jogging, walking, bicycling. River nearby for boating, fishing, swimming. Cross-country and downhill skiing nearby.
Location Central PA. 12 m W of Williamsport. From Rte. 220 go S on Rte. 44. Cross river then bear left at fork. Inn on left.
Restrictions No smoking.
Credit cards None accepted.
Rates B&B, $40 double, $25 single. Extra adult $15, extra child (under 17) $10. 2-night minimum, foliage season.
Extras Airport/station pickups. Cribs, play equipment, games available.

JIM THORPE

Wedged into a narrow gorge rising up from the Lehigh River, this town was originally made up of three separate areas, Mauch Chunk, Upper Mauch Chunk, and East Mauch Chunk (*Mauch Chunk* means "Bear Mountain" in the language of the local native Americans), which were renamed Jim Thorpe in 1954 in honor of the famous Olympic athlete. The town's numerous mansions and historic buildings date back to the second half of the nineteenth century, when the Lehigh Valley Railroad brought coal to the big cities, tourists to enjoy the mountain scenery, and considerable prosperity to the inhabitants. Mauch Chunk State Park for swimming, boating, fishing, and picnics is 2 miles from town; it's a 3-mile drive to cross-country skiing and white-water rafting, and 8–20 miles to downhill skiing.

Jim Thorpe is located 30 miles northwest of Allentown, and 60 miles northwest of Philadelphia.

The Harry Packer Mansion
Packer Hill, 18229

Tel: 717–325–8566

The Harry Packer Mansion sits high on a hill in the Mauch Chunk historic district. It was built in 1874 in the Second Empire style as a wedding present from Asa Packer to his youngest son, and is constructed of brick, stone, and sandstone, with cast iron trim. (One wonders what the other sons got!) The inside furnishings include elaborately carved walnut, oak and mahogany woodwork, inlaid oak parquet floors, Minton tile floors, Tiffany stained glass windows, and hand-painted ceilings. Rooms in the recently refinished carriage house have period decor and modern baths. Rates include a full breakfast of scrambled eggs or French toast, with juice, fruit, pastry and bagels, served on the tiled patio in good weather.

Robert and Patricia Handwerk, who have owned the mansion since 1982, describe it as being "in a spectacular setting. Most guests relax on the veranda in the summer, talking to the other guests. In the winter the fire is always going in the reception room. Guests enjoy a glass of wine and a game, or just chatting or reading." The inn has become known for its mystery weekends, with "Murder at the Mansion" scheduled on frequent weekends.

"The mansion is decorated in true Victorian style. Our rooms were both clean and comfortable; meals were delicious and filling. The town of Jim Thorpe provided a great setting. The scenery is beautiful, and there are many shops for browsing, along with an old train station and many outdoor activities." *(Barbara Ann Burden)* More comments please.

Open All year.
Rooms 1 suite, 15 doubles—9 with private bath, 7 with maximum of 4 people sharing bath. All rooms with desk. Some in adjacent carriage house.
Facilities Parlors, dining room, game room, library. Terraces overlooking river. Park, tennis court across street. Swimming, boating, downhill and cross-country skiing 3–6 m away.
Location 2 blocks from center of town. Right at light on Rte. 209 S. 1st left up Packer Hill.
Restrictions No smoking in bedrooms. No children under 6.
Credit cards MC, Visa.
Rates B&B, (midweek) $110 suite, $75–95 double. Special weekend "murder mystery" packages.

KINTNERSVILLE

The Bucksville House
RD 2 Box 146, Rte. 412 & Buck Drive, 18930

Tel: 215–847–8948

This registered landmark dates to 1795, when Captain Nicholas Buck purchased land in what is now Bucks County, and built several stone buildings. The property passed to his son, who built the Bucksville

Hotel in 1840. It became a popular stagecoach shop, and what is now the dining room was probably used then as a wheelwright's shop. The house was a speakeasy during Prohibition, and a tavern in the 1930s. The Bucksville House was bought by Joe and Barb Szollosi in 1984, and is decorated with quilts, baskets, canopy beds, antiques and country reproductions handcrafted by Joe. A full breakfast is served hearthside in the dining room (floored in Mercer tiles) or in the gazebo.

"A charming house in a rural setting. We stayed in a large suite decorated with quilts, a large wooden desk, and an exceptionally comfortable bed. It was part of the original home and was in beautiful condition, especially the wide-board hardwood floors. Joe is responsible for all the restoration work, which has taken about five years to complete—the Szollosi's bought the inn as a 'handyman's special.' They are two of the most sincere and accommodating hosts you will ever meet. They welcomed us as if we were long-lost friends, and took the time to get to known us and share their stories as well.

"Joe makes his own wine and offers it to the guests before dinner. Later, when you've returned from the evening's adventures, there's popcorn or biscuits or some other tasty snack waiting for you on the table. Barb and Joe made great breakfasts, including French toast with strawberries and a rich buttery sauce. Barb has great suggestion for antiques and bargain-hunting as well as good suggestions for reasonably priced dinners." *(Andrew Winand)*

Open All year.
Rooms 1 suite, 3 doubles—all with private bath and/or shower, desk, air-conditioning, fan. 2 with fireplace.
Facilities Dining room, living room, family room with fireplace, games, TV. 4 acres with gazebo, croquet. Nockamixon State Park nearby for water sports, cross-country skiing.
Location Upper Bucks County, 1 hr. N of Philadelphia, about 45 min. N of New Hope. Take Rte. 611 N through Doylestown. Go 14 m N to Rte. 412. Turn left, go 2 m to inn on right.
Restrictions No smoking. No children under 12. Some traffic noise in front rooms.
Credit cards Amex, MC, Visa.
Rates B&B, $120 suite, $84 double, $75 single. Extra person in room $15.

LANDENBERG

Cornerstone B&B
Tel: 215–274–2143
Newark & Buttonwood Roads, R.D. 1, Box 155, 19350

The Cornerstone B&B takes its name from the stone that marked the completion of this historic home in 1820. Records show that the property was granted to William Penn's son in 1704, and that the original house was built in the early 1700s. Quaker masons constructed the house of unusual "plum pudding" fieldstone, while the elaborate fireplace mantels were carved by Hessian soldiers after the Revolutionary War. Now owned by Linda Chamberlin and Martin Mulligan, the Cornerstone is decorated with wing chairs, ruffled curtains, canopy beds, hand-stitched quilts, and highlighted by 18th century antiques. Rates include a full country breakfast and afternoon tea.

"My room was pretty, neat, and clean with a country ambiance. Innkeeper Linda Chamberlain couldn't have been more receptive or cordial, making the Cornerstone a really enjoyable place to stay. The breakfast was good, the coffee great. Service was excellent; plumbing, parking, quietness all fine; the lighting adequate." (Jack H. Marshall)

Also: "The inn was a bit difficult to find; get careful directions."

Open All year.
Rooms 2 suites, 4 doubles—4 with private shower and/or bath. 2 rooms sharing 1 bath. All with radio, TV, air-conditioning, fan. Suites with fireplace. 3 apartments in renovated barn with kitchen, laundry.
Facilities Country kitchen, living room with fireplaces, den, veranda, greenhouse, swimming pool with Jacuzzi. Bicycles, hiking trails.
Location Chester County, just W of Wilmington DE. From I-95, take Exit 4 to Rte. 7 N. Go 7.1 m to Little Baltimore Rd. (traffic light, nursery at corner). Turn left onto Little Baltimore Rd (name changes to Newark Rd. at PA state line). Go 2.7 m to Buttonwood Rd. & inn on far right corner.
Restrictions Smoking in common rooms only.
Credit cards MC, Visa.
Rates B&B, $85–100 suite, $60–85 double, $50–75 single. Extra adult in room, $15. Extra child, $1 for each year old. Weekly, monthly rates for apartments. 10% senior discount. 2 night minimum for suites in fall, winter.
Extras Airport/station pickups. French, German spoken.

LIGONIER

Ligonier and nearby Laughlintown, have a number of historic sites worth visiting: The Compass Museum, a stagecoach stop on the Philadelphia-Pittsburgh Turnpike; the Forbes Gun Museum, with a collection dating to 1450; and Fort Ligonier, a reconstructed English fort built during the French and Indian Wars in 1758. Also of interest within an easy drive is Falling Water, the Johnstown Flood Museum and Memorial, and Linn Run State Park. Kids who've overdosed on history will clamor for a visit to the rides and waterslides of Idylwild Park.

Information please: We'd like to hear more about the **Ligonier Country Inn** (Route 30 East, P.O. Box 46 Laughlintown, 15655; 412–238–3651), where rooms are pleasantly decorated with country-style furnishings, including delicately patterned wallpapers and brass or four-poster bed frames with cozy featherbeds. Rates include a continental breakfast on weekdays and a full breakfast on weekends.

Town House   *Tel:* 412–238–5451
201 South Fairfield Street, 15658

Ligonier dates back to 1758, when it was the site of a now restored British frontier fort built during the French and Indian War. By the time Jacob Frank came along and built a hotel in 1870, the town was relatively civilized and in need of a respectable boarding house. The hotel remained in continuous operation, but by the 1950's the emphasis had shifted to the restaurant business. In 1985, the inn was bought by Dick and Peggy Olson, who concentrated first on the restaurant business. In 1988, they redid the six tiny rooms which shared a single bath on the second floor, remodeling and turning the six into two larger rooms. All furnishings are antique, most original to the hotel. The restaurant continues to be the key activity here, with traditional American cuisine that the Olsons call "grandmother's house recipes." Typical entrées include Amish baked ham, baked scrod, stuffed chicken breast, roast turkey, and prime rib, with homemade bread pudding; apple and pecan pie are dessert favorites.

"Shaded by majestic trees, The Town House is in a quiet residential area right on the edge of the business district, within walking distance of the beautiful town square. Our room had a private bath in the hall adjacent to the room. The room was freshly decorated with period antiques, as was the entire inn; much of the old woodwork and detailing had been retained and restored. The atmosphere was warm, cheery, and welcoming, much like being a guest in a private home. The Olsons are friendly, courteous, and readily available to guests, yet were never bothersome or overbearing. They told us the history of the inn and suggested several local points of interest worth visiting.

"Breakfast included a buffet of fresh fruit, juices, cold cereal, coffee, a selection of teas, real creamery butter and cream, and outstanding baked goods: butterscotch pecan rolls, home baked bread, fruit breads, pecan waffles, muffins and rolls. On request, Dick Olson prepared bacon, ham, sausage, eggs, hot cereal, toasted bagels and cream cheese and more. Special treats included lime marmalade, homemade tomato butter, and Scottish oatmeal with maple sugar. Dinners were equally tasty, highlighted by such unusual condiments as homemade apple butter, cranberry apple sauce, and three-color pepper relish. Several other restaurants are within walking distance; we also enjoyed an Italian eatery called the Ligonier Tavern." (Lisa Craig)

"Guest rooms decorated with a good eye to color and decor; breakfasts are made to order with the best waffles I've ever had." (BC) "Our favorite things: Wicker front porch swing, peach pie, pecan rolls, cross-stitch over the bed which read 'Love is sharing hearts.' Only thing missing: My grandmother; time to stay longer." (Joan May) "Even though the restaurant is the main activity of the inn, guests are made to feel very welcome. There is a comfortable sitting area with books, magazines, TV, and early morning coffee. Our attractive room was tastefully decorated with excellent lighting, and eating in the eating room is always a pleasure." (Betty Norman)

And from the "no-place-is-perfect" department: "Fans don't cool off the bedrooms completely on really hot nights, and in winter, the old steam radiators made our room a little warmer than desired."

Open All year. Restaurant closed Jan., Feb.
Rooms 2 doubles with private bath and/or shower, radio, desk, ceiling fan.
Facilities Dining rooms, common room with TV/VCR, stereo, books, games; library, bar. 3 acres with gardens. State parks for fishing, hunting, horseback riding, downhill, cross-country skiing nearby.
Location SW PA. 50 m SE of Pittsburgh. 2 blocks from center. From PA turnpike take Exit 9. Go 10 m N on Rte. 711.

Restrictions Smoking in designated areas only. No children under 10. Street noise may disturb light sleepers.
Credit cards DC, Discover, MC, Visa.
Rates B&B, $45–65 double. Extra person in room, $10. Family rates. Alc lunch $7, alc dinner $19. Children's menu.
Extras Airport station pickups. Babysitting available.

LITITZ

Reader tip: "While in Lititz, be sure to visit the Wilbur Chocolate Company and the Sturgis Pretzel factory. Sundae Best is an ice cream parlor to die for." *(Dianne Crawford)*

The General Sutter Inn   *Tel:* 717–626–2115
14 East Main Street (Route 501), 17543

Lititz was founded in 1756 as a Moravian community. To ensure the high moral caliber of the town, all inhabitants were required to abide by strict regulations, which prohibited, among other things, all "dancing, taverning, feasting, common sports, and the playing of children in the streets." The inn was built in 1764, and named Zum Anker. The name was changed in 1930 to honor John Sutter, the California gold rush pioneer who lived his last seven years in Lititz. The inn was renovated in 1981 by owners Richard and Joan Vetter; rooms are furnished with Victorian and country antiques. Breakfast and lunch are served in the coffee shop, while American cuisine is served at dinner in the Zum Anker room.

"The General Sutter is a well-maintained old inn with friendly management, on the main street of Lititz. We had a big, comfortable room on the second floor in front. It was freshly painted, spotless, not noisy, and very reasonably priced. The room was furnished with a nice mixture of heavy Victorian pieces and wicker and lots of character. The ceiling was decorated with lovely plaster work and a striking hanging lamp. The only niggle I have relates to an excess of knickknacks and fake flowers. The public rooms are comfortable, and there is a pretty little library on the second floor. We did not eat in the restaurant. The inn is perfectly placed for walking to the beautiful public buildings that remain from the original Moravian settlement, as well as for wandering about the rest of the lovely and remarkably clean old town. Rather than appearing gentrified, Lititz seems never to have gone downhill. There is splendid public park, which was full of fireflies and happy middle-aged square dancers on a summer Friday night." *(Carolyn Mathiason)*

Also: "Lunch was a disappointment, with an uninspired menu and minimal service, and our room was badly in need of refurbishing."

Open All year. Closed Christmas and New Year's.
Rooms 2 suites, 10 doubles—all with private bath and/or shower, telephone, TV, radio, desk, air-conditioning.
Facilities Restaurant, coffee shop, lobby with fireplace, library with table games. Patio with fountain, porch swing, tables, and chairs.
Location SE PA, Pennsylvania Dutch country. 6 m N of Lancaster. Center of town.

239

PENNSYLVANIA

Restrictions Traffic noise could disturb light sleepers.
Credit cards Amex, MC, Visa.
Rates Room only, $120–135 suite, $70–90 double, $55–65 single. Extra person in room $4. Alc lunch, $5; alc dinner, $25.
Extras Cribs available. Airport pickups.

MALVERN

The Historic General Warren Inne   *Tel:* 215–296–3637
Old Lancaster Highway, 19355

Innkeeper Julie De Feo reports that "the General Warren is located in a booming corporate area, yet is enough off the beaten path to offer a very quiet peaceful getaway. We take pride in our reputation for attention to detail and personal service." The inn has been welcoming guests since 1745, and rooms have been recently refurnished with colonial reproductions, original windows framed with period window swags, hand-stenciled walls, and Oriental carpets. Rates include a continental breakfast of fresh juice and fruit, croissants, coffee and tea. The inn is known for its restaurant; favorite entrées include veal with sun-dried tomatoes, mushrooms, cream, and Parmesan cheese; Maryland crab cakes, and grilled chicken breast with lemon pepper sauce.

"My suite here gave me ample space to rest and relax, and was well equipped with modern amenities, yet had real historic charm, unlike the cloned chain hotels I'd stayed in on previous business trips to the area." *(MW)* More comments please.

Open All year. Restaurant closed Sun.
Rooms 8 suites—all with private bath and/or shower, telephone, radio, TV, desk, air-conditioning. Some with fireplace. 1 with whirlpool bath.
Facilities 3 dining rooms, bar/lounge, deck. 2 acres with garden. Boating, hiking, horseback riding nearby.
Location Chester County, 25 m W of Philadelphia. From Rte. 202 take exit for Rte. 29. Go S to Rte. 30, turn left. Go E to next traffic light, turn right onto Old Lincoln. Go ⅛ m, turn right onto Old Lancaster Hwy. Inn is on right.
Restrictions No children under 12.
Credit cards Amex, DC, MC, Visa.
Rates B&B, $85–135 suite. Corporate rates. Alc lunch $15, alc dinner $25.
Extras German spoken.

MANHEIM

Herr Farmhouse Inn   *Tel:* 717–653–9852
2256 Huber Drive, 17545

While we love historic homes of all kinds, from the most extravagant Victorian to the plainest saltbox, we admit to a real soft spot when it comes to fieldstone houses—perhaps because they're so solid, stable, and reassuring. Herr Farmhouse, is just such a place. Built circa 1810, with blue-gray shutters and trim, its original sections date back to 1738.

Owned by Barry and Ruth Herr since 1985, the farmhouse is furnished with colonial charm. Its simple white walls contrast with painted wooden trim in Williamsburg colors, bright quilts, antiques and reproduction furnishings; Oriental carpets complement the soft gleam of the original wide-board pine floors. Breakfasts of cereal, sweet rolls, muffins, cheese, fresh fruit and juice, are served in the dining room, in the kitchen before the huge walk-in fireplace, or in the brick-floored sun porch with wicker furnishings. One favorite guest room has a cherry-wood canopy bed, perfect spot to cuddle up in the red flannel nightshirts provided by the inn, and watch the flickering flames of the fireplace illuminate the room.

"Room, breakfast, service, housekeeping all excellent. Highly recommended." *(Michael & Dina Miller)*

Open All year.
Rooms 1 suite, 3 doubles—2 with private bath, 2 share bath. All with air-conditioning, ceiling fan. 2 with fireplace.
Facilities Dining, living, common rooms with fireplaces, TV; library, game room, sun porch. 11 acres with barns. Tennis, golf nearby.
Location 9 m NW of Lancaster. 1 m from Rte. 283 W take Mt. Joy/Rte. 230 Exit. Turn right onto Esbenshade Rd., immediate right onto Huber to inn on left.
Restrictions No smoking in guest rooms. No children under 10.
Credit cards MC, Visa.
Rates B&B, $85 suite, $65–75 double. Extra person in room $10. 2–night holiday/weekend minimum.

MENDENHALL

Fairville Inn   *Tel:* 215–388–5900
Route 52, P.O. Box 219, 19357

In the heart of the Brandywine Valley, halfway between Winterthur and Longwood Gardens, and convenient to the Brandywine River Museum, is the elegant Fairville Inn, owned since 1986 by Patricia and Ole Retlev. Rooms are decorated in light colors with antiques; rates include a continental breakfast of juices, toast, English muffins and scones, strudel, or muffins—"whatever is freshly baked that morning"—plus afternoon tea and home-baked cookies.

"A lovely inn with friendly staff. Our beautiful room was highlighted by fresh roses. Breakfast was good—fresh fruit, orange juice, toast, banana bread, and coffee. Its country location makes it generally quiet and restful." *(Elizabeth Church, also Betty Norman)*

Open All year.
Rooms 2 suites, 13 doubles—all with full private bath, telephone, TV, air-conditioning. 5 with fireplace; 10 with desk. 10 in annex.
Facilities Living room with fireplace, breakfast room. On 3.5 acres. Canoeing, walking, bicycling, polo nearby.
Location Brandywine Valley. 8 m NW of Wilmington, DE. From I-95 take Exit 7 and go N on Rte. 52. Cross PA state line. Inn on right.
Restrictions No children under 10. Traffic noise in front rooms.
Credit cards Amex, Discover, MC, Visa.

Rates B&B, $160 suite; $95–135 double, single. Extra person in room $10. Corporate rates.
Extras Swedish spoken.

MERCER

Magoffin Guest House   *Tel:* 412–662–4611
129 South Pitt Street, 16137

A Queen Anne Victorian, the Magoffin House was built in the late 1800s, and was occupied by the Magoffin family for over fifty years. Next door is the Magoffin House Museum, and the Mercer County Courthouse is just across the street. The house was renovated as a B&B in November 1985, and has been owned by Gene and Gala Slagle since 1988; Jacque McClelland is the innkeeper. The area is a favorite of antiquers, with shops in all directions. Food in the Magoffin's restaurant is hearty and old-fashioned; a choice of several entrées is offered nightly, and might include chicken and biscuits, beef stew, or stuffed pork chops.

"This large brick home has been beautifully restored and furnished with period antiques. Our room had a mahogany four-poster (with a good, firm mattress), a dresser, a wardrobe with a beveled-glass mirrored door, a comfortable chair, and a fireplace. The McClellands are friendly and made us feel welcome. The menu is interesting—well prepared and nicely presented; herbs are used to season many of the dishes." *(Shirley Noe)*

"Our suite had a sitting room with a bedroom upstairs and a sleigh bed. Amish clothing and handiworks were displayed as art. Breakfast included juice, fresh fruit, coffee cake, croissants, and an egg and sausage quiche. The dining area is quaint, with floor-to-ceiling bay windows. The tables are close together in order to encourage conversation, and the decor includes Victorian print tablecloths and high-backed chairs, some grouped in front of a fireplace. The covered front porch with chintz-covered wicker rockers is a great reading spot. Small town atmosphere—great area for antiquing." *(Karen Hughes)*

"The perfect overnight between New York and Chicago." *(Dave Nelson)*

One area for improvement: Better bedside lighting!

Open All year. Restaurant closed Sun., Christmas, Thanksgiving.
Rooms 1 suite, 8 doubles—7 with private bath and/or shower, 2 with a maximum of 4 sharing a bath. All with radio, TV, desk, air-conditioning, fan. Some with fireplace. 4 rooms in annex.
Facilities Breakfast room; gift shop; veranda. Swimming pool, tennis, waterskiing, boating, fishing, hiking nearby. 20 min. to cross-country skiing.
Location W PA, approx. 50 m N of Pittsburgh. 5 min. N of I-80 & W of I-79, one block from intersection of Rtes. 19, 58, & 62. 1/3 block from county courthouse.
Restrictions No smoking. Street noise in front rooms.
Credit Cards Amex, MC, Visa.

Rates B&B, $90 suite, $50–80 double. Extra person in room, $10. Children under 8 free. Alc lunch, $7; alc dinner, $15. 15% weekly discount.
Extras Crib, babysitting available. Airport/station pickups.

MERCERSBURG

The Mercersburg Inn
405 East Main Street, 17236

Tel: 717–328–5231

Today, when most people would consider a house of 2500 square feet to be spacious and many city dwellers make do with far less, it's hard to imagine a private home of *20,000 square feet.* But that's just what Harry Byron built in 1910. Harry's wife quipped that she knew the house had forty closets, but that she really wasn't sure of the number of rooms. The foyer alone could double as a dance floor, with its gleaming parquet floors, rose marble columns, and curving double staircase. This Georgian colonial mansion, set on a hill overlooking the Cumberland Valley to the Tuscarora Mountains beyond, was converted into an inn in the 1950s. Fran Wolfe bought the inn in 1987, and has done an incredible job of returning the home to its original glory, restoring the original baths, and furnishing the guest rooms with locally crafted king-sized canopied beds.

As Fran describes it, "This is the inn for someone who appreciates history, architectural restoration, and gourmet food. We care about details, from the presentation of each dish in our six-course dinners to the fluffy down comforters on the beds." A stroll through Mercersburg's Historic District, listed on the National Register of Historic Places, is a good way to develop the appetite needed for the inn's acclaimed dinners.

"The most extraordinary features of this inn are the food and the bathrooms. Nothing in your book prepared me for the astounding Brobdignagian scale of our bathroom. It was absolutely wonderful with a great big free-standing bath with mighty taps, plus a huge hip-bath which almost swallowed me whole, an enormous wash basin and a separate shower. Ample towels added to the luxurious feeling. Our bedroom was vast with a huge balcony (complete with table and chairs), a working fireplace, and two enormous walk-in closets. Our king-size four-poster bed resided in lonely splendor, and was very comfortable with night tables and bedside lights on each side.

"Prepared by a young American chef, the food was exceptional in quality. A prix-fixe six-course dinner was inventive, interesting, and absolutely delicious. The service was very good and the meal well paced." *(Ellie Friedus, also Elizabeth & Jerome Thompson)*

One area for improvement: "Although understandably difficult in a house this vast, we found the furnishings a bit sparse, and in some cases uninspired, and the walls bare, as if a lot of things had recently been removed." Comments?

Open All year. Restaurant closed Mon. and Tues.
Rooms 15 doubles all with private bath and/or shower, air-conditioning. Some with desk, fireplace, balcony. Telephone on request.
Facilities Dining room, sun porch, game room with pool table, TV, games, fireplace. 5 acres with gardens. Tennis, golf, swimming, fishing, boating, hiking nearby.
Location S Central PA. Cumberland Valley. 90 min. from Washington D.C. 3 blocks from town center.
Restrictions No smoking. Children by prearrangement.
Credit cards Amex, MC, Visa.
Rates B&B, $70–170 double. Extra person in room $25. 15% service. Fireplace rooms—2-night minimum on weekends, holidays. Prix fixe dinner $35, plus 15% service.
Extras Restaurant handicap accessible. Swiss German, German, French spoken. Babysitting by prearrangement.

MILFORD

Black Walnut Inn
509 Firetower Road, R.D. 2, Box 9285, 18337

Tel: 717–296–6322
800–866–9870

The Black Walnut Inn is a Tudor-style stone house built in 1917, set on a 160-acre estate surrounded by fields, forest, lakes and ponds. Purchased by Stewart Schneider in 1985, this antique-filled manor house offers hearty country breakfasts, afternoon sherry, and nightly desserts with coffee.

"The inn has an enclosed pine porch, and a very large dining room, overlooking the pond and furnished with pretty flowered tablecloths and wicker chairs. In the morning, the pool table was covered, and a fabulous breakfast buffet was set out. In addition to your choice of juices, coffee, and fruit, breakfast included eggs, bacon, and pancakes, toast, English muffins, bagels, cream cheese, lox spread, sliced tomatoes and onions, and more. We saw deer grazing outside as we ate. The resident black labs accompanied us as we walked around the grounds admiring the unusual species of pet chickens and ducks; later, we used their paddleboat to explore the lake. The sitting room has comfortable seating and a beautifully carved brown marble fireplace original to the house. The innkeeper, Hermein Ankersmit, is originally from the Netherlands, and is very charming and friendly; apple pie and coffee was served in the evening.

"Our room was small, with a toilet and sink in the room, and a bath down the hall. It had knotty pine walls, wallpaper, a brass bedstead, and a few antiques. We peeked into a few other rooms; those on the top floor are quite small, while those on the second floor vary in size—the largest seemed to be at the end of the hall, farthest from the stairs. But you don't come here to stay in the rooms, but rather to enjoy the ample grounds and relaxing setting. While not a fancy place, the rates are very reasonable, considering the first-rate breakfast." *(SC)*

One area for improvement: "Better lighting was needed in the room; it was dim, making reading difficult."

Open All year.
Rooms 12 doubles—4 with full private baths, 4 with private half-bath and shared tub, 4 rooms sharing 1 bath. 1 room with TV. All with fan.
Facilities Dining room with pool table, sitting room with fireplace, TV, VCR, piano; enclosed porch with ping pong; hot tub. 160 acres with lakes, ponds, paddle boats, fishing, walking trails. Turkeys, chickens, petting zoo. Canoeing, rafting, golf, horseback riding, skiing nearby.
Location Bucks County. From Rte. 206N cross Milford Bridge and enter PA. Go through light, past Grand Union. Follow Rte. 6, 1 mile to inn's sign.
Restrictions Smoking in living room and porch only.
Credit cards Amex, MC, Visa.
Rates B&B, $53–85 double. 2 night weekend/holiday minimum.
Extras Station pickups. Dutch, French, German, Swiss-German spoken.

MILTON

Hotel Milton   *Tel:* 717–742–7676
101 N. Front Street, 17847   800–326–9382

If you're looking for a comfortable spot for lunch, dinner, or an overnight stay while driving across Pennsylvania, try combining historic charm and a convenient location near I-80 at Hotel Milton. Built in 1902 as a private home, this imposing red brick building—with a turret and many gables—operated as a private club for years, then was converted into a hotel. In 1988, the hotel was bought by LeeAnn and Robert Wallich, who closed the hotel for extensive renovations, reopening it in October 1989.

Room rates include a full breakfast; hearty American food is served at lunch and dinner, with roast beef, broiled scallops, and baked ham among the very reasonably priced entrées. *(MW)* Comments please.

Open All year. Closed Christmas Day, New Year's Day.
Rooms 2 suites, 12 doubles, 1 single—10 with private bath and/or shower. 5 with maximum of 6 people sharing bath. All with telephone, TV, desk, air-conditioning, fan.
Facilities 3 dining rooms, bar/lounge with music weekends. Fishing, boating, swimming nearby.
Location Central PA, Northumberland Country, Susquehanna Valley. Near junction of I-80 & I-180. 15 m SE of Williamsport. Downtown historic district.
Credit cards Amex, MC, Visa.
Rates B&B, $60 suite, $50 double, $40 single. Family rates. Senior discount. Alc breakfast, $2–5; lunch, $5; alc dinner, $17. Children's menu.
Extras Airport/station pickups. Cribs, babysitting available.

MT. JOY

Information please: Within a short distance of Mt. Joy are two other intriguing (and reasonably priced) possibilities. **The River Inn** (258 West Front Street, Marietta 17547; 717–426–2290) offers B&B accommodation in a 200-year-old home in the heart of Marietta's historic district; many rooms have fireplaces, and breakfast is served on the screened-in porch overlooking the gardens or fireside in the tavern room. **The Colombian** (360 Chestnut Street, Columbia, 17512; 717–684–5869 or 800–422–5869) is a turn-of-the-century mansion built in the Colonial Revival style, offering period and country decor, five guest rooms with queen-sized beds, air-conditioning, private baths, and hearty buffet breakfasts. Your reports please!

Cameron Estate Inn
Donegal Springs Road, RD 1, Box 305, 17552

Tel: 717–653–1773

The Cameron dates back to 1805; it was one of the largest homes on the Susquehanna frontier. In 1872 it was purchased by Simon Cameron, Secretary of War under Abraham Lincoln and four-time U.S. senator. Cameron transformed the estate into a magnificent mansion, and planted the grounds with flowers and hundreds of beautiful shade trees.

The mansion was purchased in 1981 by Abe and Betty Groff, owners of the well-known Groff's Farm Restaurant, located a few miles away. The Groffs have restored the inn, and have decorated each guest room individually with antiques and period reproductions. The inn is listed on the National Register of Historic Places.

"A handsome red brick building with a wide porch, situated in a large wooded area. Our second-floor room had a king-size four-poster bed, wide-plank floors, mahogany furniture, wing chairs, and a working fireplace; it was decorated in browns and beiges, coordinating with the Oriental carpet. The bath was tiny but very modern. Breakfast was continental, with breads, pastries, juice, and coffee, while dinner featured locally caught trout." *(MFD)* "Be sure to ask for one of the romantic fireplace rooms. Each is decorated in a different color scheme, and most have antique or reproduction furniture—with canopied or brass beds." *(KFR)* "Dinner at nearby Groff's Farm Restaurant is not to be missed! It's a real Pennsylvania Dutch experience, and the prices are quite reasonable. It's very popular, so make your reservations well ahead, as much as 2–3 weeks for Saturday night." *(SJM)*

"A lovely, secluded spot between Harrisburg and Pennsylvania Dutch country. Gettysburg and the Hershey factory are also within easy driving distance. There is a small first-floor sitting room for guests, and a lovely dining room, decorated in blue and white, supplemented by additional tables on the rose and white sun porch. The guest rooms I saw were quite large, with sitting areas. All were different and elegant; some of the bathrooms had the original patterned tile floors. Our room had a window air-conditioner, and the whole house was cool and pleasant on a 100° day. Dinner was good, and the breads and rolls at breakfast the next morning were particularly good. We lunched at Groff's Farm Restaurant, and enjoyed the table relishes and a wonderful dish of creamed chicken on crispy noodles." *(Susan Schwemm)*

"Easy to follow directions, despite a late-night arrival. We were greeted by the housekeeper with complimentary glasses of wine. The inn is wonderfully located in the midst of farmland with a stream winding through the grounds. Our third floor room was rather small, attractively furnished with antique reproductions, with a spacious modernized bath. The continental breakfast was served in a sunny many-windowed room, and was average in quality. Prices are fair and reasonable, a just reflection of the size and decor of each room." *(Janet Kaufman)*

"A very handsome house in a lovely extremely rural setting. Our large room was very attractive, well thought out in terms of furniture. Dinner is served on one of the enclosed porches which surround the inn on three sides, and was fairly good, although the service was a little off-hand. A self-service breakfast is laid out in the same room, and the food and selection was very nice. In general, the inn was efficient, clean, comfortable and attractive." *(Ellie Friedus)*

While the overall consensus about this inn remains overwhelmingly positive, readers did note a few minor drawbacks: "We received no help with the bags, or turndown service. Those looking for privacy should note that the honeymoon suite is on the first floor, with windows opening onto the tables on a brick terrace outside." And: "We were somewhat disturbed by the noise from neighboring rooms, especially the bathrooms. We also had ample occasion to use the fly swatter thoughtfully provided with our room, perhaps an inevitable by-product of the nearby farms. Interaction between the innkeepers and the guests was minimal, and the staff rather cool; we sought out all information ourselves by inquiring at the reception desk."

Open All year. Restaurant closed Sun. evening, Christmas Day.
Rooms 18 doubles—16 with private bath and/or shower; 2 rooms with maximum of 4 people sharing bath. All with radio, air-conditioning; some with desk, 6 with fireplace.
Facilities Restaurant, sitting room, library/TV/game room, enclosed porch. 15 acres with trout stream, lawn games, hiking trails. Heated swimming pool, tennis court nearby.
Location Lancaster County. 1/2 hr. to Lancaster and Hershey; 3 1/2 hrs. to NYC, 2 hrs. to Philadelphia. From Rte. 283, take Rheems exit to Colebrook Rd. S. Turn right on Donegal Springs to inn driveway on right.
Restrictions No children under 12. No smoking in living room, library.
Credit cards Amex, MC, Visa.
Rates B&B, $55–105 double. Extra person in room, $10. 2-night weekend minimum. Alc lunch, $7; alc dinner, $36.
Extras Airport/station pickups by prior arrangement. Limited wheelchair access.

Cedar Hill Farm   *Tel: 717–653–4655*
305 Longenecker Road, 17552

Although many innkeepers leave city life to put down roots in the country, Russel Swarr's roots are deep. He was born at Cedar Hill Farm, home also to his father and grandfather. Restored as a B&B in 1987, Russel and his wife Gladys have decorated their stone farmhouse simply but elegantly with floral wallpapers and 19th century antiques, many of them family heirlooms. Built in 1817, this working farm overlooks Little Chiques Creek. Cedar Hill has the original white pine floors, an open winding staircase, a walk-in fireplace, and an Indian door.

"This hillside farm has a lovely rural setting, yet is just minutes from town. The atmosphere is cozy and welcoming, and the Swarrs obviously enjoy their guests. The beds are comfortable, the bathrooms amply supplied with hot water. The inn is clean and quiet—we heard nothing of the other guests, even though some left very early to go antiquing. Breakfast, prepared in the farm kitchen from old Pennsylvania Dutch recipes, features freshly baked muffins or fruit bread, cereals, cheese, fresh fruit, and juice." *(Margaret Zieg, also Diana Mimaltse)* "The view from the bridal suite balcony of the snow-covered fields and bridge was worth the trip. The innkeepers are well informed and gave easy-to-follow directions." *(Tom & Sandy Roddy)*

Open All year.
Rooms 1 suite, 3 doubles—all with private bath and/or shower, air-conditioning. 1 with TV, desk.
Facilities Dining room, sitting room, TV room with stereo, VCR, computer, porch. 53 acres with picnic facilities, cross-country skiing, stream for fishing. Tennis, golf, downhill skiing nearby.
Location 25 m SE of Harrisburg, 11 m W of Lancaster. From Rte. 283 take Mt. Joy exit to Rte. 230. Go to bridge at "Welcome to Mt. Joy" sign. Take next left at Longenecker Rd. Cross bridge then take immediate left.
Restrictions No smoking.
Credit cards Amex, MC, Visa.
Rates B&B, $55 double, $45 single. Extra adult in room $10; extra child $7.
Extras Station pickups. Play equipment, games available.

MUNCY

Maple Knoll B&B
Route 220, R.D. #2, 17756

Tel: 717–546–6288

Maple Knoll is a limestone farmhouse, built in 1824, owned by Mick and Shirley Merloe. Its rooms are decorated in colonial colors and decor, with its five fireplaces still very much in use. B&B rates include a welcoming glass of lemonade or cup of tea, and a full breakfast with Maple Knoll's farm fresh eggs and homemade jellies and jams, served in the formal dining room, on the porch, or by the limestone fireplace in the kitchen.

"The Merloes have painstakingly restored their authentic Quaker-style farmhouse surrounded by fields and populated with cattle, chickens, and their Australian shepherd, Bozo, who will steal your heart. Shirley is not only charming and well informed but loves to cook and does wonderful quiches. Don't miss her little antiques shop, stocked with primitive furnishings and accessories." *(Jonathan Douglas)*

Open All year.
Rooms 1 suite, 2 doubles—all with full private bath, clock/radio, desk, air-conditioning, fan.
Facilities Parlor, dining room with fireplace, TV room with fireplace; porch. 11 acres with antique shop, farm animals.
Location Central PA. Approx. 15 m E of Williamsport. From I-80, take Exit 31-N to I-180 W. Go approx. 14 m to Halls/Pennsdale exit. Turn right, go 2 m to inn on left.
Restrictions No smoking. No children under 7.
Credit cards None accepted.

Rates B&B, $80 suite, $55 double, $45 single mid-week. Extra person in room, $15. Corporate rates.
Extras Airport pickups.

NEW CUMBERLAND

Farm Fortune   *Tel:* 717–774–2683
204 Limekiln Road, 17070

In 1785, Peter Hursh purchased 490 acres of land for three of his sons, and called the land Farm Fortune. This was the name Chad and Phyllis Combs chose when they restored the house as a B&B and brought it back to its original appearance. A limestone farmhouse, set high on a hill overlooking Yellow Breeches Creek, legend says the house was part of the Underground Railroad. Rates include a breakfast of fresh fruit, warm breads, juice, coffee and tea; full breakfast is available with advance notice.

"With all the beautiful early American antiques, you feel as if you are staying in a museum—with none of the stuffiness. The Combs are a delightful couple who make their guests feel immediately at home." *(Betty Norman)*

Open All year.
Rooms 3 doubles—1 with private bath, 2 rooms sharing 1 bath. All with air-conditioning. 2 with porches.
Facilities Dining room, family room with walk-in fireplace, terrace, antique shop. 3 acres with tubing, hiking, fishing. 10 m to downhill skiing.
Location Across river from Harrisburg. Just off PA Tpke. and I-83. Call for directions.
Restrictions No smoking. No children under 10.
Credit cards MC, Visa.
Rates B&B, $55–64 double, $47–56 single. Extra person in room $15.

NEW HOPE

See chapter introduction for information on New Hope and Bucks County, as well as additional accommodation suggestions in the general area.

Information please: Listed in earlier editions, the **Centre Bridge Inn** (Star Route, Box 74, 18938; 215–862–9139 or 862–2048) has played to mixed reviews. It offers comfortably furnished rooms, some with canopy beds and river views, and forgettable breakfasts. The restaurant has a good reputation for its pricy French continental cuisine, served on the patio in good weather, offering a lovely view of the Delaware River and Canal.

Right in the center of the gallery and shopping area, the once shabby **Logan Inn** (Ferry & Main Streets, New Hope 18938; 215–862–2300) underwent a $1,000,000 restoration in 1988. Built in 1722 and listed on the National Register of Historic Places, its antique woodwork gleams once again, and an 18th century mural, uncovered during the renovations, has been painstakingly restored. Its 16 guest rooms overlook the river or the town, and combine the colonial charm of four-poster canopied beds with such modern comforts as all new tiled bathrooms, telephones, TV, and air-conditioning. Rates include a full breakfast, and the inn's restaurant offers contemporary American cuisine—pasta, seafood, and hickory-grilled meats. Reports please.

Pineapple Hill
1324 River Road, 18938
Tel: 215–862–9608

In the 1700s the pineapple was a prized delicacy, and an invitation to share one symbolized the warmest welcome. Pineapple Hill, named after this tradition, is a 1780 farmhouse with walls 18 inches thick, fireplaces, and traditional woodwork, furnished with country antiques, American folk art, and Oriental rugs. Converted into a B&B in 1984, the inn is now owned by Linda and Hal Chaize, who purchased it in 1989.

"The house is decorated comfortably with antiques, and the large, well-appointed rooms have excellent reading lamps on both sides of the beds and modern plumbing. The inn has the most beautiful swimming pool we have ever seen, surrounded by the ruins of an old stone barn and planted with impatiens. Beautiful garden and landscaping." *(Carla Cohen)*

"A moderately large old-fashioned farm house, the inn's first floor has a very comfortable dining room and parlor, with period decor. The delicious breakfast might include quiche and sausages, or French toast with apples. We had a chance to see most of the rooms. One had an antique double bed, lots of country antique furnishings, and was done with white walls and blue trim. The large bathroom [has] an old church pew in it; we saw several other bathrooms and all were very modern and clean but with an old farm/country touch to them. Almost all rooms have charming extra touches—one bathroom had a pegboard for hanging clothes, and a shelf with tiny little houses on it; another guest room has lots of hand-stenciling, and well coordinated fabrics. Although the inn is in the midst of various home developments, looking out the back you see some farms, pastures—lots of green and trees. Linda and Hal, the new owners, are very personable and friendly." *(SC)*

"Simply and tastefully decorated authentic farm house. Immaculately clean with an excellent location. Concerned, yet unobtrusive hosts." *(Marlene Capise)*

Open All year.
Rooms 2 suites with private bath, 3 doubles—1 with private bath or shower, 2 with maximum of 4 people sharing bath. All with desk, air-conditioning.
Facilities Breakfast room, living room with books, magazines, games. 5 landscaped acres with flower gardens, swimming pool. Tennis, fishing, canoeing, rafting, tubing, boat rides, hiking, cross-country skiing, golf nearby.
Location Bucks County. 4½ m S of town center off Rte. 32.
Restrictions No smoking. No children under 12 on weekends or under 10 during week.
Credit cards Amex.

Rates B&B, $100–115 suite, $85–95 double. Extra person in suite, $20. No tipping. Reduced rates for 5 or more consecutive nights. 2-3 night minimum, weekends and holidays.

The Wedgwood Inn
111 West Bridge Street, 18938

Tel: 215–862–2570

Carl Glassman and Nadine (Dinie) Silnutzer opened the Wedgwood in 1982; guest rooms are located in two adjacent buildings, one built in 1833, the other in 1870. Carl points out that "our land was the bivouac site of George Washington's army in 1776, before the famous Christmas Eve crossing of the Delaware; four times a year the Wedgwood hosts New Hope's own Revolutionary War reenactment group, of which I'm a member. Memorabilia of the era are on display at the inn."

"The Wedgwood is run with all the comfort and efficiency of a highly professional operation, yet with the warmth and hospitality that personal friends would extend. The innkeepers are inexhaustible sources of advice on all area restaurants and activities." *(David & Joanna Sachar)* "My well-appointed room included a king-size mahogany four-poster pineapple bed with reading lights on both sides and Amish quilts." *(Ronald Jay Leff)*

"We were welcomed with wassail and cookies; they provided dinner recommendations and made the reservations. The continental breakfast consisted of a fresh fruit cup, homemade muffins and croissants with a different filling each day, cinnamon coffee, and freshly squeezed juice. Our beautifully furnished room had hand-blown Italian blue glass lamps, a cozy Victorian-style bed, and evening mints with Carl's secret liqueur. The living room has a wood-burning stove, cozy sofas, and a wide variety of reading material as well as fresh fruit for late-night snacks." *(Chris Torres)*

"The rooms are neat, clean, spacious and charmingly decorated. We love the leisurely breakfast usually shared with other guests around the dining room table, where everyone swaps shopping, antiquing, and restaurant advice. Be sure to ask Carl for the houses's history; he may even throw in a great ghost story for you." *(Bill & Ellen Morrison)*

"We arrived in the early afternoon, and were greeted by Carl and Dinie. There were delicious chocolate chip and lemon cookies on a platter, and iced tea. Our room had a triple-mirror dresser, plant-filled window, soft lighting, and comfortable wing chair. Our bed linens and quilt were charming, and the bathroom very comfortable with good towels, shampoo, and more. After dinner we returned to the living room to read, listen to classical music, munch on apples and cookies, and even made ourselves a cup of tea." *(Jean & Leonard Paul)*

Open All year.
Rooms 2 suites, 10 doubles—10 with private bath and/or shower, 2 with maximum of 4 people sharing bath. All with radio, desk, air-conditioning, fan. 2 with telephone, TV.
Facilities 2 parlors with fireplaces, 2 sun porches, veranda with hammock. 2 acres with gazebo, lawn games, paths, gardens, cross-country skiing. Club privileges for swimming, tennis. Downhill skiing nearby.
Location Bucks County. Historic district, 2 blocks from center. From NY, take

PENNSYLVANIA

NJ Turnpike S to Exit 10; take Route 287 N for 15 miles; Rte. 202 S for 30 m over Delaware River Bridge. Take first New Hope exit; follow Rte. 32 S 1 m to traffic light. Turn right on Bridge St. to inn at top of hill on left.
Restrictions Traffic noise in front rooms. No smoking.
Credit cards None accepted.
Rates B&B, $120–150 suite, $80–125 double, $75–85 single. Extra persons in room, $15. 2-3 night holiday/weekend minimum.
Extras Limited wheelchair access. Babysitting available. French, Dutch, Spanish, Hebrew spoken. Station pickups. Special breakfast menu available during Passover.

The Whitehall Inn
Pineville Road, RD 2, Box 250, 18938

Tel: 215–598–7945

The Whitehall Inn is an elegant country manor house, with high ceilings, wide pine flooring, and wavy-glass windows. Rooms are furnished with antiques, and rates include a multicourse breakfast, beautifully served on fine china, with crystal and sterling; afternoon tea; and evening sherry. Provided in each guest room are bedtime chocolates, velour robes, homemade rose potpourri, Crabtree and Evelyn toiletries, and a bottle of locally produced wine.

Mike and Suella Wass left the corporate/consulting life in 1985 to take over The Whitehall. "The inn was built circa 1794 and has warm and friendly parlors and inviting porches. Mike and Suella Wass make every effort to keep their guests comfortable. Our room was small but cozy. The farm-fresh breakfast included freshly squeezed orange juice, blueberry pancakes, sourdough rolls, and raspberries swimming in heavy cream. Lush rolling hills, stables, a tennis court, and a pool make The Whitehall ideal; it's close enough to New Hope to be convenient, but its location off the main road ensures a peaceful night's sleep." *(Phyllis Farlow)*

Herewith our favorite sort of complaint: "Last year's write-up doesn't do this inn justice. The four-course breakfast is incredible, and the afternoon tea a real treat after a day of shopping in New Hope. Suella and Mike are great hosts, very friendly and helpful. They have thought of everything to make the Whitehall restful and romantic. There are books with guest-written reviews of area restaurants next to sample menus; hand cream, bath salts, perfume and lots of towels in the bathroom, robes in the closets, crystal glasses and chilled wine on arrival, chocolates at bedtime, and we were even sent off with a plate of biscuits and cinnamon bread to snack on in the car. Our room had a canopy bed and fireplace ready to use; the others were equally delightful, individually done in period wallpapers." *(Nancy Wolff)*

Open All year.
Rooms 1 suite, 5 doubles—4 with private bath, 2 sharing 1 bath. Most with desks, some with fireplace.
Facilities Dining room, parlor with fireplace, games, library, pump organ, piano; sun-room. 12 acres with horse farm, swimming pool, tennis court. Horseback riding/instruction.
Location Bucks County. 3 m from New Hope. From Philadelphia, take I-95 N to Newtown Exit, Rte. 332 W. Continue to Newtown and then take Rte. 413 N to Pineville, 6.5 m. Go right at Pineville Tavern on Pineville Rd. The Whitehall Inn is 1.5 m from the tavern.

Restrictions No children under 12. Absolutely no smoking.
Credit cards Amex, CB, MC, DC, Discover, Visa.
Rates B&B, $110–160 suites and doubles. 2-3 night weekend/holiday minimum.
Extras Airport/station pickups.

NEWTOWN

Information please: Ye Olde Temperance Inn (Route 332, 5-11 South State Street 18940; 215–860–0474) was the site of temperance meetings in the 1700s; today it's home to a restaurant and 12 guest rooms decorated in period.

The Brick Hotel
State & Washington Avenue, 18940

Tel: 215–860–8313

Founded in 1684 by William Penn, Newtown offers historic tree-lined streets, but is well off Bucks County's well-trodden tourist path. The Brick Hotel was built in 1764 and was completely renovated in 1985 under the auspices of the National Park Service; it's listed on the National Register of Historic Places. During the Revolutionary War, the hotel was used by George Washington to entertain troops; you can do the same, even if your troops consist only of your spouse and kids. Lunch and dinner are offered in the inn's elegant dining room and glass-enclosed porch, a delightful alternative to the microwaved styroburgers served a few miles away on the interstate. Overnight guests are accommodated in handsome guest rooms, decorated with quality reproduction Victorian furnishings; one room has a lace-canopied bed with dark floral prints coordinating on the wall and beds.

"The hotel sits in the middle of Newtown, a very pretty place. We stopped for a delicious lunch; service was very good, and the waitress helpful with our kids' special requests. Our room combined period decor with good bedside lighting and other modern amenities." *(DW)* More comments please.

Open All year.
Rooms 13 doubles—all with private bath and/or shower, telephone, TV, air-conditioning.
Facilities Restaurant, bar/lounge. Playground 3 blocks away.
Location SE Bucks Cty. 3 m W of I-95 via Rte. 332. About 30 min. (non-rush) from Philadelphia, New Hope, or Langhorne (Sesame Place).
Credit cards Amex, Discover, MC, Visa.
Rates Room only, $95–110 double. Alc dinner, $25. Children's menu.

NORTH EAST

Brown's Village Inn
51 East Main Street, 16428

Tel: 814–725–5522

In the heart of Lake Erie's wine country is North East, a town ideal for enjoying the lake, the four local wineries, and a handful of local festivals. A visit to the Chautauqua Institution, just a half-hour away, is also recommended.

Dating back to 1832, the Federal-style inn once served as a stagecoach tavern and as a stop on the Underground Railway. In 1987 it was converted into a restaurant and inn by the Brown family. Guest rooms have brass and iron beds with down quilts and antique armoires. Rates include such breakfast specials as French toast with blueberry conserve or peaches and cream pancakes. Several dining rooms make up the restaurant (although there is still a private sitting room for overnight guests). Veal, flamed with brandy and oranges or sauced with Dijon mustard, cream, and mushrooms is the house specialty.

"The rooms are homey, clean and bright. All facilities worked well; the parking is more than ample; the overall ambience and atmosphere delightful." *(Richard Barber)* "Our room was appointed with comfortable antiques with a modern private bath. Breakfast was delicious, exquisitely arranged and laid out, with beautiful linens and tableware. The Browns are warm and delightful hosts." *(Richard Streeter)*

"Our room was spacious, the decor bright and cheerful. Rebecca Brown made us feel right at home, and even let us help ourselves to dessert treats late at night when the kitchen was closed!" *(Karen Barton)*

Open All year. Restaurant closed Christmas, New Year's.
Rooms 3 doubles—all with private bath and/or shower, radio, desk, air-conditioning, fan.
Facilities Restaurant, sitting room with TV.
Location 10 m E of Erie on Lake Erie. Downtown location with off-street parking.
Restrictions Smoking in common areas only.
Credit cards MC, Visa.
Rates B&B, $55–65 double, $45–55 single. Extra person in room, $10. Corporate rates, also reduced rates for week long stay. Alc lunch $6, alc dinner $14.
Extras Airport/station pickups. Cribs, babysitting, play equipment, games available. Pets accepted.

NORTH WALES

Joseph Ambler Inn   *Tel:* 215–362–7500
1005 Horsham Road, 19454

The original part of this fieldstone manor house was built by Joseph Ambler, a wheelwright, in 1734, with various additions and outbuildings constructed over the following 250 years. The inn has been owned by Richard Allman since 1983, and is managed by Steve and Terry Kratz. Rooms in the main house, the restored stone barn and adjacent cottage are furnished with period antiques and reproductions. Rates include a full breakfast, with a choice of eggs, pancakes, or French toast.

"Beautiful country setting. Rooms are attractively furnished, and the general atmosphere is most charming. Good food." *(Joan McPherson)*

Open All year.
Rooms 28 doubles with private bath and/or shower, telephone, radio, TV, air-conditioning. Many with desk. Rooms in 3 separate buildings.

Facilities Restaurant, game room with TV, living room/library with walk-in fireplace; lounge. 13 acres with golf nearby.
Location 45 min. N of Philadelphia, 18 m of New Hope. From PA Tnpke. take Exit 26 to Rte. 309 N. Turn right at 2nd light onto Stump Rd. Go left at 1st light onto Horsham. Go left to inn immediately on right. 2 m from town.
Credit cards Amex, DC, MC, Visa.
Rates B&B, $85–140 double. Extra person in room, $15. Corporate rates. Weekend packages. Alc dinner $35.
Extras French spoken.

PARADISE

Also recommended: Intercourse is just a short way from Paradise (sorry, we couldn't resist), where the **Best Western Intercourse Village Motor Inn** (Routes 340 & 772, Intercourse 17534; 717–768–3636 or 800–528–1234) is recommended for those seeking a quality motel.

Maple Lane Farm Guest House
505 Paradise Lane, 17562

Tel: 717–687–7479

Edwin and Marion Rohrer have owned the Maple Lane Farm for 25 years, and built a separate house for guests across the lane from their own 200-year-old stone farmhouse. A stay at a real working farm like this gives visitors a good idea of what the Amish country is really like—a better picture than the area's numerous commercial attractions. The Rohrers farm 250 acres, and the usual sounds guests hear are the lowing of their dairy cattle and the clip-clop of their Amish neighbor's horses going down the road. Mrs. Rohrer can arrange for guests to visit one of her Old Order Amish neighbors who has quilts for sale. The guest rooms are decorated with quilts, hand-pierced lampshades, needlework, and stenciling, all done by Mrs. Rohrer, along with poster and canopied beds. The guest parlor, painted white with Williamsburg blue trim, is furnished primarily with Victorian antiques. Breakfast is a modest offering of rolls, with juice and coffee served in styrofoam cups.

"The Maple Lane couldn't have been more comfortable or more congenial." *(Marjorie Morrel)* "Immaculate, wonderfully peaceful and in beautiful surroundings. We felt as welcome as in the home of friends." *(Doug Campbell)* "Fully endorse existing entry. The Rohrers went out of their way to welcome us, writing beforehand to send maps and tell us about the area." *(Michael Crick)*

Open All year.
Rooms 4 doubles; 2 with full private bath, 2 with maximum of 4 people sharing bath. All with TV, air-conditioning.
Facilities Parlor, guest refrigerator, porch. Spacious lawn with picnic table, wading stream. 100-acre working dairy farm with 120 cows. Tennis, golf nearby; 1 m to Strasberg Steam Railroad.
Location Lancaster County, Pennsylvania Dutch country. 10 m SE of Lancaster, 60 m W of Philadelphia. Turn S on Rte. 896 off Rte. 30. Go 3 m to Strasburg. Turn left on Rte. 896 at traffic light and go 1½ m out of town. Turn right at sign for Timberline Lodge onto Paradise Lane.
Restrictions No smoking or drinking.

Credit cards None accepted.
Rates B&B, $45–55 double. Extra person in room, $5; no charge for children under 3. 2-night weekend minimum.
Extras Cribs, play equipment available.

PHILADELPHIA

Philadelphia has come a long way since W.C. Fields issued his less than complimentary opinions of the city. In addition to fine museums and historical sights, the city now offers many restored neighborhoods, fine shops, and quality restaurants. History buffs will head straight for Independence National Historical Park, a collection of historic buildings including Independence Hall and Congress Hall, then to the Betsy Ross House and Elfreth's Alley, the oldest continuously inhabited street in the country. For more information, call or write the Visitors Center at 1525 Kennedy Blvd. 19102; 215–636–1666.

Also recommended: Although too big at 371 rooms for a full entry, readers report with delight on the luxurious, elegant rooms, and the exceptionally gracious, courteous service of the staff of the **Four Seasons** (1 Logan Square, 19103; 215–963–1500). *(Gerald Bahr)*

Rates do not include 11% state and city taxes.

The Earl Grey B&B   *Tel:* 215–732–8356
2121 Delancey Place, 19103

Although this B&B is located in a registered landmark house dating back to the 1860s, it is not named for a historic figure, nor for the tea, but for Patricia and Richard Boyle's cat: "Earl Grey is a magnificent gray cat and is really the host, although he allows us to think we are." Rooms are decorated with some antiques and great attention to detail—fresh flowers, fruit, sherry, special soaps, bath salts, potpourri, designer linens, and bedtime treats of chocolates, cookies, or fresh strawberries.

Breakfast specialties include French toast with slivered almonds and apricot sauce, soufflés, or a variety of omelets, plus homemade breads and muffins, and fresh fruit and juices served in the garden, dining room, or kitchen.

"Although a private home, this B&B offers every amenity and is owned by lovely people. The Boyles are art collectors, with experiences as writers, lecturers, museum directors, and painters. Their home is beautifully decorated, with lots of books." *(Zacharias Rosner)* "Rooms are eclectically decorated with antiques and modern art; terrific location in a residential area convenient to downtown." *(DW)* More comments please.

Open All year.
Rooms 1 suite, 3 doubles—all with full private bath, telephone, air-conditioning. TV on request.
Facilities Living room, dining room, library, kitchen (limited). City garden. On-street parking; 1/2 block to public garage.
Location Rittenhouse Square area. Between 21st and 22nd sts.; between Pine and Spruce.

Restrictions No smoking. No children under 12.
Credit cards None accepted.
Rates B&B, $110–140 suite, $80–110 double, plus 6% tax. No tipping. 2-night booking preferred on weekends.
Extras French, German, Dutch spoken.

Hotel Atop the Bellevue
1415 Chancellor Court, 19102

Tel: 215–893–1776
800–221–0833

A creative reconstruction of the old Bellevue-Stratford Hotel, built in 1904, the Hotel Atop the Bellevue now occupies the top seven floors of the original building, with the rest used for commercial and retail space.

"Unlike any other hotel we've visited, you experience the Bellevue from the top down. Although the building fronts on Broad Street, you enter via a small side court, where an elevator whisks you to the top floor. After registration, you are then escorted to your room on one of the floors below. Our room was elegantly furnished in period reproductions, in shades of hunter green and cream, with good views over the city. State-of-the-art amenities included three telephones (each with two lines and computer hook-up) terry robes, slippers, and a marble bathroom with its own TV (!). Some bits of the old hotel were evident in the smallish size of our bathroom, and in the silvered full-length mirror that fronted our closet door. We peeked into one of the rooms overlooking the atrium, but much preferred our outside room. The best part of the hotel is its common areas. Breakfast and a reasonably priced pre-theater dinner are served in the atrium conservatory, airy with wicker chairs and palm trees, while the hotel's top floor has the Library Lounge, a clubby looking expanse of dark paneling, leather chairs, and Oriental carpets. Also on the 19th floor is The Founders, the hotel's formal restaurant, but our favorite spot was the Barrymore Room, a light-hearted aqua confection; its ceiling is wonderfully painted in 'contemporary Rococo,' and its windows overlook the city. Come here for afternoon tea regardless of where you're staying." *(SWS)*

Open All year.
Rooms 172 suites & doubles—all with full private bath, telephones, TV/VCR, radio, air-conditioning, minibar.
Facilities Conservatory atrium, library, 3 restaurants, health club with indoor heated swimming pool, squash & racquetball courts, jogging track, Nautilus. Valet parking.
Location Downtown, corner Broad & Walnut Sts.
Credit cards Amex, DC, Discover, MC, Visa.
Rates Room only, $265–400 suite, $200–240 doubles, $180–220 single. Weekend rate, including parking, tax, service, $140. Corporate, package rates. Alc dinner, $20–50.
Extras Member, Preferred Hotels.

The Independence Park Inn
235 Chestnut Street, 19106

Tel: 215–922–4443
800–624–2988

Built in 1856 as a dry goods store, the Independence Park Inn was restored as a small, luxury inn in 1988. Listed on the National Register of Historic Places, this granite structure is now home to a club-like

PENNSYLVANIA

lobby with leather settees and fireplace, where afternoon tea with pound cake and cucumber sandwiches are served daily. In back is a glass-enclosed garden courtyard where guests can enjoy a breakfast of fresh fruit and juice, pastries, croissants, and bagels, coffee, and tea, and the morning paper. Guest rooms are comfortably furnished with quality reproductions. The location and amenities appeal to both business and pleasure travelers alike.

"Our room was clean and comfortable, with a king-size bed with a firm mattress and lamps on both sides of the bed. The writing desk was well stocked, and our large bathroom was supplied with plenty of towels. Guest rooms away from the street are exceptionally quiet for a city hotel, while those facing Chestnut Street have high ceilings and huge windows. The lobby is lovely, but its moderate size and the location of the elevators close to the registration desk makes it feel safe." *(Diane Wolf)*

Open All year.
Rooms 36 doubles—all with full private bath, telephone, radio, TV, desk, air-conditioning. Some with desk.
Facilities Lobby with fireplace, dining room, atrium, meeting rooms. Parking in municipal garage, 2 blocks away. Health club privileges.
Location Historic Independence Square area, 2 blocks from Independence Mall.
Restrictions No smoking in common rooms. Some street noise in Chestnut St. rooms.
Credit cards Amex, DC, MC, Visa.
Rates B&B, $95–120 double, $85–110 single. Extra person in room, $5. 10% senior discount.
Extras Wheelchair accessible. One room equipped for the disabled. Cribs available. French, Spanish spoken.

The Rittenhouse Hotel
210 W. Rittenhouse Square, 19103

Tel: 215–546–9000

Overlooking Rittenhouse Square, the Rittenhouse Hotel has one of the best locations in the city. While not large, this 6.5 acre park is an oasis of green and quiet, yet is just a few blocks from the Academy of Music, and central to the city's business, cultural and shopping areas. A new 33-story building, the hotel occupies its middle floors; the lower floors are filled with retail and commercial space, while the top floors are home to luxury condominiums.

Four restaurants are housed here: 210, an elegant restaurant overlooking the square; TreeTops, a more casual bistro with a similar view; the Cassatt Tea Room, for afternoon tea and evening cocktails, with paintings by Mary Cassatt; and the Boathouse Row Bar, with the ambiance of an old Schuylkill River rowing club. All are very popular with locals and hotel guests alike; *Gila Anderson* reports that the crabcakes with shallot rings and tomato relish served at TreeTops are an all-time favorite.

"We had a chance to see several rooms. Although those overlooking the square have the best view, the others have a pleasant view of the city. All the guest rooms, even the least expensive, are handsome, with carved mahogany desks and rich upholstery. No less extravagant are the marble bathrooms, each equipped with hair dryer, magnifying mirror, terry robes, and its own telephone and television." *(Diane Wolf)*

Open All year.
Rooms 11 suites, 87 doubles—all with full private bath, telephones, radio, TV/VCR, desk, air-conditioning, fan, mini-bar.
Facilities 4 restaurants, lounge with evening entertainment, health club, sun deck. Valet parking.
Location Downtown between Walnut, Locust Sts.
Credit cards All major cards.
Rates Room only, $300–935 suite, $150–260 double, $150–235 single. Extra person in room, $25. Children under 18 free in parents' room. Alc lunch $25, alc dinner, $70.
Extras Wheelchair access. Cribs available. Over 18 foreign languages spoken including French, Spanish, German, Italian, Arabic, Japanese, Russian, and Vietnamese.

Society Hill Hotel
301 Chestnut Street, 19106

Tel: 215–925–1394
215–925–1919

The Society Hill Hotel was built in 1832 to provide temporary accommodation for longshoremen, and later served as a recruiting station during the Civil War. It became Philadelphia's first B&B hotel in 1981, and is under the same ownership as the Society Hill hotels in Baltimore, MD (see listing). Their popular bar/restaurant is ideal for light suppers with a menu ranging from Philadelphia steak sandwiches and burgers to Buffalo wings and nachos.

"If the Liberty Bell and Independence Hall were not so close, you would think you were in Europe. Granted, the rooms are tiny, large enough for only a brass double bed, and desk or small bureau. There is no elevator for this three-story hotel and the stairs are steep. The bathrooms are even smaller, with only stall showers, but come equipped with hair dryers, fancy soaps, and shampoos. Fresh flowers and chocolates are placed in every room, and the housekeeping is impeccable. Hotel guests have their continental breakfast of freshly squeezed citrus juices, and croissant and muffin, and newspaper delivered to the door. Children are warmly welcomed.

"While the hotel is located on a busy and noisy corner, the security is excellent. Guests receive keys, but the public, although they frequent the bar/restaurant, are denied access to the hotel. Live jazz is featured in the bar, and in summer, the crowd spills out onto a sidewalk café. Parking is one block away in a municipal lot, so leave your car and get around the historic area and center city Philadelphia by taxi or public transportation." *(Wendy Robbins)*

"Even though we were on the second floor it was very quiet, despite the bar. The staff was friendly and helpful. Our corner room had a lovely brass antique bed, brass lamps, an antique dresser with local sightseeing information, a round table and two comfortable chairs, and a color TV. What the room lacked in size was more than made up for with little extras. Heavy curtains blocked out noise and light when closed. The best part is the hotel's location—all the historic sites are within a five-minute walk. The hotel is across the street from a park on one corner and the Visitors' Center on the other. Ben Franklin lived next door. The wonderful old homes and the redone streets of Society Hill make for a terrific walk while you work your way down to South Street's shops and restaurants. Downtown is only a short ride away." *(Wendi Van Exan, also Mr. & Mrs. S.L. Herndon)*

Open All year. Restaurant closed Thanksgiving, Christmas.
Rooms 6 suites, 6 doubles—all with private shower, telephone, clock-radio, TV, desk, air-conditioning, hair dryer.
Facilities Bar/restaurant with jazz piano Tues.–Sat. Parking in municipal garage, 1½ blocks away.
Location Historic district at 3rd & Chestnut. Across from Federal Visitors' Center, 2 blocks from Independence Hall. 10 blocks from center.
Restrictions Traffic noise in some rooms.
Credit cards Amex, DC, MC, Visa.
Rates B&B, $100–130 suite, $77–95 double, single plus 11% tax. Light lunches and suppers, $6–10; Sunday brunch. 2-night weekend minimum. Dinner/theater packages.

The Thomas Bond House
129 South Second Street, 19106

Tel: 215–923–8523

A 1769 brick home inside Independence National Historic Park and listed on the National Register of Historic Places, The Thomas Bond House was originally built for Dr. Thomas Bond, who co-founded Pennsylvania Hospital, the first public hospital in the U.S., along with Dr. Benjamin Rush and Benjamin Franklin. After additions in 1824 and 1840, and occupancy by both residential owners and commercial establishments, the Department of the Interior purchased and restored this building as part of the historic park. In addition to a full complement of modern amenities for both business and pleasure travelers alike, extra soundproofing was installed to prevent street and adjacent room noise from disturbing the guests. A full breakfast is served on weekends while the midweek continental breakfast provides a choice of homemade blueberry, apple-walnut, or raspberry muffins.

"Each window even has a 'candle' with a flicker bulb, and our bath was equipped with fluffy towels and a whirlpool tub. Good restaurants are nearby, and the bus and subway are convenient." *(Dianne Crawford)* "Rooms are beautifully furnished with period decor and have lots of storage space. We stayed in both a double and a marvelous suite. The weekday breakfast included homemade muffins, juice, and coffee, with strata and a breakfast meat added on the weekend. The innkeepers were most friendly and welcoming. We were able to talk to the other guests while enjoying afternoon wine, crackers, and cheese." *(Sue & Jack Lane)*

"The Christmas decorations and smells of baking goodies made us feel right at home. Breakfast was tasty and check-in/out procedures small and problem-free." *(David Vroom)* "Excellent service, housekeeping, location, and parking." *(Peter Aaron)*

Some minor niggles: "Rooms vary widely in size and price; some on the third floor are quite small, and not as well equipped with bedside tables and lighting." And: "Although we understood the need for a gas-fueled fireplace (with fake metal logs) because of the building's age, we were a little disappointed." Also: "Pillows are firm, which is apparently how everyone else likes them."

Open All year.
Rooms 2 suites, 10 doubles—all with private bath and/or shower, telephone, radio, TV, air-conditioning. 10 with desk, 3 with whirlpool tub, 2 with fireplace.
Facilities 2 dining rooms, parlor with fireplace, library; antique/gift shop. Municipal parking next door.
Location Historic district between Chestnut and Walnut Sts.
Restrictions No children under 10.
Credit cards Amex, MC, Visa.
Rates B&B, $150 suite, $80–125 double. Extra person in room, $15.
Extras Wheelchair accessible; one room equipped for disabled.

PITTSBURGH

Information please: If you want to stay near the city but not in it, then the **Sewickley B&B** may suit. A century-old Queen Anne mansion owned by Clark and Diane Race, rooms are filled with antiques but are named after pop singers—friends from Race's years in radio and TV (222 Broad Street, Sewickley 15143; 412–741–0107). If you've always wanted to curl up by the fire in an authentic log cabin, then **Cole's Log Cabin B&B** (RD #1, Box 98, Pine Bank 15354; 412–451–8521) may be just the right thing. It's nestled in the country hills and hollows, yet is just 55 miles southwest of Pittsburgh.

The Priory—A City Inn   *Tel:* 412–231–3338
614 Pressley Street, 15212

For 93 years The Priory housed the Bavarian and Benedictine priests and brothers of neighboring St. Mary's Church. In 1986, Ed and Mary Ann Graf restored the building as an inn, decorating the rooms with nineteenth-century antiques.

"A beautifully restored building with a warm, friendly staff. Given the bad weather during our visit, the limo service provided in their vintage Chrysler was very enjoyable. The tasty continental breakfast (fresh fruit, juice, bagels, pastry, muffins, and hot beverages) was served in a lovely large room adjacent to the courtyard. The neighborhood, while still in transition, was not unsafe." *(Anthony & Susan Smith)*

"Lovely spacious rooms, beautifully restored architecture, two parlors with sherry in the evening, quiet back patio suitable for reading. The neighborhood is undergoing active restoration. Good German restaurants in the area; large city park nearby with aviary and playhouse." *(Jack Johnstone)*

"Walking into the Priory is like stepping from the thoroughly modern city of Pittsburgh into another world. From the beautifully restored turn-of-the-century architecture to the sitting rooms furnished with period pieces, it's a monument to the way things used to be. Courtyard rooms overlook a quaint, quiet, red-brick piazza with fountain, while those on the city side have a captivating view of the Pittsburgh skyline, particularly beautiful at night. The rooms are spotless, with high ceilings and elaborate detailing. Modern touches like the televisions are discreetly tucked away in an armoire." *(John & Diane Lally)*

Open All year.
Rooms 3 suites, 21 doubles, 2 singles—all with private bath and/or shower, telephone, radio, TV, air-conditioning. Some with desk.
Facilities Dining and breakfast rooms, sitting room with fireplace, library. Courtyard with fountain, outdoor seating. Off-street parking. Park nearby.
Location East Allegheny/Deutschtown. Across 9th St. Bridge, 1/2 m from center.
Restrictions Children under 7 discouraged.
Credit cards Amex, DC, Discover, MC, Visa.
Rates B&B, $85–130 suite, $75–90 double, $65–75 single. Extra person in room, $5–10. Weekend rates. 10% AARP discounts.
Extras Free limo service to city. Crib, babysitting available. Wheelchair accessible; 1 suite equipped for disabled.

POINT PLEASANT

Tattersall Inn   *Tel:* 215–297–8233
Cafferty and River Road, P.O. Box 569, 18950

Built in 1740, the Tattersall Inn is a plastered stone mansion painted pale lilac with cream trim and deep green shutters. Innkeepers Herb and Gerry Moss have owned the inn since 1985. Rooms are furnished with antiques and decorated with Gerry's paintings and needlework, while the dining room is highlighted by Herb's collection of vintage phonographs, including a 1903 Edison cylinder talking machine.

The Tattersall is only a short walk from a tiny country store where you can buy sandwiches and other picnic supplies, and just a bit farther to Point Pleasant Canoes, where you can rent canoes, rafts, and inner tubes; you travel upstream by bus, then you can float lazily back down to your starting point.

"The Tattersall has four large pillars supporting a balcony that runs the entire length of the second story. We stayed in the Lavender Room, with a four-poster queen-size bed, silk moiré walls, lavender and wood furnishings, and a small foyer and bath." *(PBB, Louise Weiss)* "Herb and Gerry are warm and welcoming hosts and are excellent sources of information on local highlights and tourist attractions. Cider and cheese is served nightly in the common room, where menus from many local restaurants are available for review." *(Kathleen Walther)*

"All rooms have firm mattresses, and extra pillows are provided.

The bathrooms have good facilities and lighting. The location is quiet and parking is ample. We have checked out several other neighboring inns, and we think the Tattersall is one of the most comfortable in the area." *(Kristie Miller & T.L. Hawkins)* "Rooms are quiet and clean, the baths well supplied with towels, soaps and shampoo, with delicious chocolate truffles waiting for you at night. Breakfast included raspberry muffins, croissants, poppy seed bread, jellies, jams, and your choice of hot beverage. Guests sit around the big dining room table and share experiences. It's also interesting to read through their book of guest comments on area restaurants." *(Richard & Celia Schacher)* More comments please.

Open All year.
Rooms 2 suites, 4 doubles—all with private bath and/or shower, air-conditioning. Some with desk.
Facilities Dining room, library, common room with fireplace, guest refrigerator, porches. 1½ acres with flower gardens, lawns. Swimming pool, boating, fishing, playground, hiking, cross-country skiing nearby.
Location Bucks County. 7 m NW of New Hope. 2 blocks from village center. Take Rte. 32 to Cafferty Rd. 150 yds. to inn on right.
Credit cards Amex, MC, Visa.
Rates B&B, $85–95 suite, $75–85 double, $65–75 single. Extra person in room, $15. Senior discounts. 2-night weekend minimum.

POMEROY

Stottsville Inn
Rte. 372 at Strasburg Road, P.O. Box 67, 19367

Tel: 215–857–1133

In the 18th century, the Strasburg Road was a major trade route between Lancaster and Philadelphia. By the 1790s, the Stottsville Inn was a favorite resting place of travelers riding through. The present building was constructed in 1858, and was owned by the Stott family until 1875, when it was bought by Maris Chandler. Chandler kept meticulous journals, and much of the history he recorded can be found at the inn today. The inn was expanded and modernized with the passing years; in 1906 it was the first building in the area to install electric lights.

Now listed on the National Register of Historic Places, the inn has been owned by Raymond Carr since 1987, and is managed by Eugene Principe. Carefully restored in country Victorian decor, the inn clings to the past while providing all modern amenities. Many rooms are furnished in original antiques dating to 1858, including marble-topped bureaus and carved headboards; also on display are old photographs, ledgers, and the inn's original sign. Rates include a breakfast of fresh fruit and juice, croissants, homemade muffins, tea or coffee. The inn's restaurant offers a range of entrées, but with seafood dishes as a speciality. Pomeroy is located off-the-beaten track, yet is convenient to the attractions of both Pennsylvania Dutch country and the Brandywine

Valley. "Consistently fine dining; quality corporate accommodations." *(CWW)* More comments requested.

One area for improvement: Better bedside lighting!

Open All year. Closed Christmas, New Year's Day.
Rooms 11 doubles—all with private bath and/or shower, telephone, TV, air-conditioning.
Facilities Dining room, pub with music Fri., Sat.; verandas. Conference facilities. 21 acres with formal gardens, hiking trails. Lake nearby.
Location Chester Cty. 1 hr. W of Philadelphia, 30 min. E of Lancaster. Take Rte. 30 E to Rte. 10 S. Turn right, go S to Rte. 372 E. Turn left, go ½ m to inn on right.
Credit cards Amex, DC, MC, Visa.
Rates B&B, $50–70 double, single. Alc lunch, $8; alc dinner, $35.
Extras Airport/station pickups. Restaurant wheelchair accessible.

SCENERY HILL

Century Inn　　　　　　　　　　　　　　　　　*Tel:* 412–945–6600
Route 40, 15360　　　　　　　　　　　　　　　　　　　　412–945–5180

Open since 1794, the Century Inn is the oldest continuously operating inn on the old National Road, which connected the eastern seaboard with the western frontier. When Stephen Hill opened the inn, George Washington was president and the Whiskey Rebellion was in full swing; a flag flown by the insurgents is on display in the front parlor. Early visitors to the inn included Andrew Jackson and General (Marquis de) Lafayette.

The inn was purchased and restored in 1945 by Dr. and Mrs. Gordon Harrington; in 1978, their son and daughter-in-law, Gordon Jr. and Megin, took over. Of particular interest are the original kitchen, with its massive fireplace, hand-forged crane, and period cooking utensils, and the innkeeper's room, with its woodwork, plaster, and stenciled walls still intact after almost 200 years. The cuisine is traditional American, with a good selection of fish and seafood.

"The Century Inn has been delightfully restored and filled with antiques. One upstairs bedroom has a permanent display of antique toys and dolls. Breakfast (for overnight guests only), lunch, and dinner are served in several lovely dining rooms, and eating there is a special treat." *(Janet Payne)*

"A delightful country inn, with good food and attractively landscaped grounds. The rooms aren't large and are furnished with antiques and old furniture." *(Barry Gardner)*

Open Mid-Mar. to mid-Dec.
Rooms 3 suites, 6 doubles with private bath and/or shower. 3 rooms in annex.
Facilities Restaurant, parlor with TV, bar; music room. Folk singer or pianist occasional Sat. evenings. 22 acres with gazebo.
Location SW PA. 35 m S of Pittsburgh. From E, take I-70 W to Bentleyville, then Rte. 917 S to Rte. 40. From N take Rte. 19 S to Rte. 519. Go S on Rte. 519 to Rte.

40. From W, take I-70 E to Rte. 79 S. Take 1st exit to Rte. 40. Go E on Rte. 40 to inn.
Credit cards None accepted.
Rates Room only, $73–130 double. Extra person in room, $10. Alc breakfast, $5; alc lunch, $7; alc dinner, $20–25.
Extras Cribs, babysitting available.

SKYTOP

Skytop Lodge
Route 390, 18357

Tel: 717–595–7401
In PA: 800–422–7SKY
Outside PA: 800–345–7SKY

The natural beauty of the Poconos was scourged twice in modern times, once in the nineteenth century by the logging and leather tanning industry, which left the mountainsides bare of trees, and again, more recently, by much of the tourist industry, which reforested the slopes with gaudy billboards advertising tacky honeymoon havens. In this setting, Skytop is an oasis of old-fashioned elegance and good taste unequaled in the Poconos. Continuity is a watchword here: some 80% of its guests are returnees, and Bill Malleson is just the sixth manager at Skytop since it opened in 1928; his dad was general manager before him. From its handsome stone lodge to its 5,500 wooded acres, all conceivable sports and activities are offered, from a full children's program in the summer to private downhill ski slopes and outstanding cross-country ski trails in winter. There's even a steep toboggan run, which rises high above the lake; when the ice is thick, you shoot down the track and across the frozen surface, slowing down in heaps of hay.

A $2 million renovation project, completed in 1989, has produced rooms redone in country-style scrubbed pine furniture, comfortable wing chairs, and nature prints, with excellent lighting and newly retiled baths. Rooms in the main lodge are compact, with large closets, typical of an old-fashioned resort where guests used to come for extended stays and where little time is actually spent in the room. The dining room is spacious but not cavernous and is remarkably quiet, a comment on both the acoustics and the clientele. The lodge and grounds are very well maintained, with an airy indoor pool and a brand-new outdoor one; there's none of the shabbiness found in some resorts of a similar vintage.

"Skytop offers an unusual balance—rural isolation, yet just 100 miles from the city, a welcoming atmosphere for families, yet still a pleasant escape for couples. The staff is very accommodating, and the food, although not gourmet, is exceptionally good considering the number of meals prepared daily. The fresh vegetables, salads, and fruits were especially tasty. My husband enjoyed the old-fashioned 'sporty' golf course, completed in 1928, with its narrow fairways, and my children went charging all over the place with newfound friends, exploring every nook and cranny, trying out every possible activity. The high-

265

lights for me were the easy hike up the Trout Stream Trail to Indian Ladder Falls, and the Lodge's rooftop observatory with 35-mile views in all directions. If you're there on a Saturday night, do not miss the 'Grand March,' a longstanding Skytop tradition unchanged for decades." *(SWS)*

Open All year.

Rooms 185 doubles—all with full private bath, telephone, TV, desk, air-conditioning. Radio on request. Most in main lodge, some in neighboring cottages.

Facilities Lobby, dining room, bar/lounge, library, card room, game rooms, porches, exercise room. 5,500 acres with indoor and outdoor swimming pools, wading pool, hot tub, sauna, 7 tennis courts, paddle tennis, lawn bowling, croquet, badminton, archery, miniature golf, bicycling, children's activity program (summer), 18-hole golf course, lake and stream fishing, canoeing, boating, hiking, ice-skating, cross-country & downhill skiing, toboggan run.

Location NE PA, Pocono Mts. Approx. 100 m from NYC & Philadelphia. 1 m N of Canadensis. From I-84, take Exit 7, & take Rte. 390 S approx. 10 m to lodge on left. From I-80, take Exit 49 to Rte. 191 N to Canadensis, then Rte. 390 N to lodge on right.

Credit cards Amex, DC, MC, Visa.

Rates Full board, $329–$360 suite, $249–259 double, $119–130 single. Extra person in room, $70. 2 children free in parents' room up to age 18 with $10 service charge & 2-night minimum. 10% service charge. Midweek discounts. Senior, sports, weekend packages.

SLIPPERY ROCK

Applebutter Inn   *Tel:* 412–794–1844
152 Applewood Lane, 16057

Too often real estate developers are known for their disregard for the preservation of the past, but in the case of Gary and Sandy McKnight, a desire to maintain a piece of area history led to the opening of the Applebutter Inn. In 1977 the McKnights purchased a 100-acre parcel on which they built a group of homes. But they felt that the boarded-up old farmhouse was an eyesore at the entrance to the development. Rather than tear it down, the McKnights restored it in 1988 as a bed & breakfast inn. The farmhouse, built in 1844, was restored from top to bottom, and a nine-room addition was designed to blend with the original architecture. The handsome result is colonial, not Victorian in appearance, although the inn is furnished in antiques and reproductions dating in style from 1800 to 1870. Kimberly Moses is the resident manager.

"Old-fashioned charm plus modern comforts. Our room, the Steele Room, was beautifully appointed, spotless, and thanks to our gas log fireplace, cozy and warm on cool spring evenings. The breakfast of juice, apple pancakes, homemade apple muffins, and, of course, apple butter was a delight. This quiet area, close to colleges and near quaint Amish farms, was perfect for antique hunting, long country drives, and plain old relaxing." *(John & Diane Lally, also Carolyn Davis)* More comments please.

Open All year. Closed Christmas, Thanksgiving.
Rooms 11 doubles with telephone, TV, air-conditioning, fan. Some with desk.
Facilities Living room with fireplace, keeping room with fireplace, sun-room/parlor, deck. 2 acres with garden sitting areas. Cross-country skiing, tennis, golf, lake for watersports nearby.
Location 50 m N of Pittsburgh. From I-79 take Slippery Rock exit to Rte. 108. Go E 7 m, turn right onto Rte. 173S. Go ¼ m to inn on right.
Restrictions No smoking.
Credit cards MC, Visa.
Rates B&B, $79–105 double. Extra adult in room $15; extra child under 16, $10. 10% senior discount.
Extras Wheelchair accessible. Cribs available. Babysitting with advance notice.

SOUTH STERLING

The French Manor
Huckleberry Road, P.O. Box 39, 18460

Tel: 717–676–3244

During the depths of the Depression—1932 to 1937—most Americans scrimped and scraped to get by, while a very few continued to enjoy great wealth. One of those in the latter category was Albert Hirschorn, who built a lavish summer mansion during those years, using it to house his art collection. They say that "all good things come to those who wait," and this is certainly true here: his art collection is now open to the public as part of the Hirschorn Gallery of the Smithsonian in Washington, and his summer home is now the French Manor inn.

Purchased in 1989 by Lois and Walt Nebel, the manor was built of oak, cedar, pecky cypress, and field stone obtained from the estate's original 600 acres, topped with a slate roof imported from Spain. The rooms are furnished with Henredon and other quality reproduction furnishings, with lavish fabrics and elaborate window treatments. The oak-beamed vaulted Great Room seats 60 people for dinner, while a basement common room provides a more casual setting in which guests can mingle.

A la carte meals are offered on weekdays, with elaborate eight-course dinners featured on weekends. Although off to a somewhat rocky start under its previous owners, the current chef, trained in French cuisine at the Culinary Institute of America in Hyde Park, is winning kudos for his meals. Although there are extensive choices through the menu, a recent dinner included melon with prosciutto, French onion soup, scallops with fresh vegetables, green salad, fruit and cheese platter, sorbet, and roast pheasant, concluded by almond white chocolate apricot cake. Lois notes that the chef has taken care to balance the size of portions so that guests feel pleasantly full, but not overwhelmed at the conclusion of a meal.

"After living in Europe for many years, it was refreshing to visit this wonderful inn. A totally relaxing atmosphere is created by the stone manor house, grounds, and the hilltop views. Looking up at the stars with the city lights far in the distance is incredible. An eight-course dinner is served on the weekends; it takes three hours and is worth it. At night it's elegant, but small and cozy. The innkeepers were formal and calm during dinner; in off hours they were talkative, friendly and sincere. We were the youngest couple there and on Sunday, when all other guests left, we sat outside on the beautiful slate patio, had breakfast, and were able to sit and chat with Walt. He's a great guy. The Nebels have great plans for the inn." *(Cindy McEachern)*

Open All year.
Rooms 7 doubles—5 with private bath, 2 with maximum of 4 sharing bath. 1 in carriage house.
Facilities Great Room, common room with TV, stereo, games; patio. 43 acres.
Location Poconos. From NYC, take I-80 W to Exit 52. Follow Rte. 447 N to Rte. 191 N to S. Sterling. Turn left onto Huckleberry Road.
Restrictions No children.
Credit cards MC, Visa.
Rates MAP, $100–200 double. 18% service.

STARLIGHT

The Inn at Starlight Lake
Route 370, Box 27, 18461

Tel: 717–798–2519

An inn since 1909, and owned by Judy and Jack McMahon since 1974, the Inn at Starlight Lake is a longstanding favorite of many travelers. Judy says that "the turn-of-the-century atmosphere of the inn's interior and the natural appeal of the lake, rolling hills, and fields are key attractions here. With its warm, informal, congenial atmosphere and the excellent food and spirits, the inn appeals to a wide variety of families and couples." Chef Michael O'Neill's continental menu is highlighted by beef en brioche with bordelaise sauce, duck with two sauces, venison, and homemade pastas.

"The best thing about this inn is not the food, although it is delicious; not the ambiance, although is charming; not the rooms, although they are clean, eclectically furnished, and very comfortable; not the setting, although the lake and wooded hills are beautiful in all seasons. The best part is Judy and Jack McMahon—always a smile, always the right word at the right time, always charming and friendly." *(Vernon Lubs)*

"You can sit in a deep, cozy chair and read a book while warming your toes at a fire that has chestnuts roasting in a pan on its grate. You can exercise moderately, strenuously, or not at all. You can be solitary or social. You can change for dinner or come down in ski knickers . . . to sip a marvelous hot 'schnocolate' (peppermint schnapps and hot chocolate) after skiing for hours. Families are welcome, yet couples can dine romantically on the glassed-in porch where there are only tables for two. Special touches include music during meals from Judy and Jack's extensive record collection, fresh flowers, delicious wholesome meals. Our favorites include their wonderful homemade breads and whole-wheat waffles, salads dressed with lemon and pine nut dressing. Starlight soups, full of fresh vegetables, are hearty and delicious, especially after a morning of cross-country skiing.

"The cross-country ski trails are well groomed and marked, winding through meadows and gentle hills, beginning almost at the inn's front door. When there's no snow, we have explored those same Moosic Mountain trails on foot." *(Micki & Jack Ginsberg)*

"We prefer the small but charming rooms in the main house, with its creaking stairs, crackling fireplace, hot buttered rum, great food, comfy chairs, and reasonable wine list. There is great antiquing in the nearby NY towns of Deposit and Hancock. The place always appears freshly painted on the outside and in the dining room. The McMahons recently installed modern shower stalls in the rooms, but had the good sense to leave the rest of the place alone." *(James Smith)* Reports welcome.

Open All year.
Rooms 1 suite with whirlpool bath, 26 doubles in main house and separate cottages—20 with private bath, 7 with maximum of 4 people sharing bath. 3-bedroom house also available.
Facilities Restaurant, bar, reading room with fireplace, game room, TV room. 400 acres with shuffleboard, tennis, biking, hiking, children's play area; 20 m of cross-country ski trails with lessons and rentals. On Starlight Lake for swimming, canoeing, boating, sailing, fishing. Riding, golf, downhill skiing nearby.
Location NE PA, Wayne County. Approx. 35 m SE of Binghamton, NY, 35 m NE of Scranton. From NY, take Rte. 17 W to Exit 87 (Hancock NY). Take PA Rte. 191 S to Rte. 370 W to Starlight.
Credit cards MC, Visa.
Rates MAP, $160–175 suite, double; $64–85 single. Extra person in room, $49; children 7–12, $37; children under 7 free (food extra). Weekly rates. Alc lunch, $5–7; alc dinner, $12–29.
Extras Cribs, babysitting available. Station pickups.

STATE COLLEGE

The Nittany Lion Inn
1274 North Atherton Street, 16803

Tel: 814–231–7500

A colonial-style inn located on the Penn State campus, The Nittany Lion Inn offers modern accommodations and reception facilities to alumni and other campus visitors. Guest rooms come decorated with reproduction colonial furnishings and the usual contemporary amenities. Upstairs rooms overlook the campus, golf course, and distant mountains.

"The warmth of the inn extends throughout the well-appointed rooms, the inviting lounges, the attractive dining rooms, and the friendly staff. It offers great opportunity to relax and enjoy a taste of campus life." *(Betty Norman)*

Open All year. Restaurant closed during school holidays.
Rooms 2 suites, 132 doubles, 6 singles—all with private bath, telephone, radio, desk, air-conditioning.
Facilities Restaurant, bar/lounge with piano; lobby. Off-street parking. Golf, tennis, swimming nearby. Conference facilities.
Location Central PA. 10 m S of I-80. On campus.
Credit cards Amex, DC, Discover, MC, Visa.

Rates Room only, $90–110 suite, $62–90 double, $55–90 single. Extra person in room, $10. 2-night minimum football weekends, graduation.
Extras 3 rooms with wheelchair access.

THORNTON

Pace One Inn   *Tel:* 215–459–3702
Thornton and Glen Mills Road, 19373

Ted Pace, owner of this country inn for the last decade, invites guests to his converted 240-year-old barn for a delicious meal and a quiet evening's rest. The decor is simple but elegant throughout; the original stone walls and hand-hewn beams are highlighted with lots of plants. Guest rooms are cozily tucked under the eaves, and are decorated with antiques and country quilts. The restaurant is extremely popular with locals (advance reservations essential on weekends) and a typical dinner might include an appetizer of Brie, shallots, and tarragon, baked in a puff pastry; an entrée of quail with sausage and black bread stuffing; salad and fresh vegetables; and a dessert of pecan pie with whipped cream.

"Outstanding food, thoughtful service, delightful surroundings. The dining room can be a bit noisy when full." *(Diane Wolf)* More comments please.

Open All year.
Rooms 1 suite, 6 doubles, 1 single—most with private bath and/or shower, desk, air-conditioning.
Facilities Restaurant. 3 acres.
Location SE PA, Brandywine Valley. 20 m SW of Philadelphia. From Wilmington, take Rte. 202 N to Rte. 1 E (right) to Thornton Rd. N (left).
Credit cards Amex, DC, MC, Visa.
Rates B&B, $75 suite, $65 double, $45 single. Alc lunch, $8, alc dinner, $25-30.

TYLER HILL

Tyler Hill Bed & Breakfast   *Tel:* 717–224–6418
Route 371, P.O. Box 62, 18469

Wayne Braffman and Roberta Crane opened the Tyler Hill B&B in 1986, and have worked hard to make it a warm and inviting place to stay.

"Roberta and Wayne are enigmatic, eclectic, even a bit eccentric. They are also the two most fascinating and gracious hosts one could care to meet. The house is as clean and comfortable as could be desired, and its quiet, idyllic setting makes it the perfect place to unwind. You can expect a hearty breakfast par excellence, thanks to Wayne's exceptional culinary talents. Wayne has published a cookbook, or rather a collection of favorite recipes and stories about their early years as innkeepers—fascinating even if you've never cracked an egg." *(Donna & Michael Rosenthal)*

"Despite our midnight arrival, we were greeted warmly with a glass of sherry. Wayne is a gourmet breakfast chef—fresh fruit; light, fluffy pancakes; bread like my mother never made; and good, strong coffee." *(Laura McKenna)* "Wayne and Roberta know the area well, including restaurants and activities. They also encourage guests to enjoy movies from the large videocassette collection." *(Sally Barhydt)*

"The Ephemera Room is an area devoted to vintage newspaper clippings, magazines, and posters. Browsing through the room (items are for sale) and noting the variety of art objects that grace the rooms ensures much discussion with former gallery curator Roberta." *(Sue Bartholomew)*

"The gleaming hardwood floors covered with Oriental rugs and the white walls adorned with paintings by local artists make this a truly charming renovated turn-of-the-century home. The upstairs rooms are furnished with antiques, and beds are piled high with pillows and down comforters. Sunday morning, I met Roberta as I started up the quiet main street for a walk. She had already been to the General Store for papers to be shared by all the guests—another thoughtful touch." *(Suzanne Zivic)*

"Our room was spacious, comfortable, and had lots of reading material. The bathroom was spotlessly clean, with plenty of hot water, and big soft towels in abundance. There's a big front porch where you can sit and relax and watch the coming and going of the Tyler Hill community." *(Laurie Leslie)*

"The rooms have well-chosen antique furniture, prints, paintings, and extra touches such as *Life* magazines from 1940–1960 on the nightstand. There was a beautiful view of the snow-covered Poconos from our rooms. One scrumptious breakfast included homemade sour cream coffee cake, pears with raspberry sauce, and eggs Benedict. After a day of cross-country skiing, I curled up in a rocker, while Roberta fixed us hot fudge sundaes." *(Eric Schmitt)*

Open April through Feb.
Rooms 4 doubles share two full baths; air-conditioning.
Facilities Dining room, living room/library, TV/VCR room, gift shop, deck. 1¼ acres with hammock, gardens, lawn chairs. 2½ m to Delaware River for swimming, rafting, tubing, canoeing, fishing; 8 m to lake with beach; 10 downhill/cross-country ski areas within 25 m.
Location NE PA. N Poconos, Wayne County. 16 m NE of Honesdale, 25 m W of Monticello, NY. 110 m NW of NYC. 2 houses away from general store.
Restrictions Smoking downstairs only. No children under 8.
Credit cards MC, Visa.
Rates B&B, $75–95 double. 2-night minimum holiday weekends.

UPPER BLACK EDDY

Bridgeton House   *Tel:* 215–982–5856
River Road (Route 32), Box 167, 18972

In 1836, Bridgeton House was built on the banks of the Delaware River, facing the old mill town of Milford, NJ. Originally a private residence, it was later converted to a candy store and bakery, and in 1955, to apartments. In 1981, innkeepers Beatrice and Charles Briggs rescued the building and began its restoration. Seventeen layers of linoleum later, the 100-year-old floorboards came to light, as did the original 1836 fireplace. Soundproofing and private baths were added as part of the renovation process; in 1989 they added a third-floor penthouse. Bea describes it as a "plush luxurious room with a fireplace. The marble bathroom has an oversized tub with a separate shower and three large windows overlooking the river for a wonderful view. French doors with private porches offer a similar vista to the other riverfront rooms. Rooms are decorated with fresh flowers, country antiques and primitives, pottery, quilts, and Oriental and rag rugs. Bea prepares a full breakfast, with such goodies as fresh melon, asparagus and cheese omelets, and poppy-seed apple cake.

"We had a very charming and comfortable room overlooking the Delaware and the Upper Black Eddy-Milford Bridge. It had a four-poster bed and was one of the few places we stayed where there were good reading lights in bed." *(MP)* An area for improvement: keys for quest rooms.

Open All year.
Rooms 3 suites, 6 doubles—all with private bath and/or shower, telephone, radio, air-conditioning. Penthouse suite with TV, stereo, deck. Suites with fireplace. 2 bathrooms are quite small.
Facilities Dining room, main room with fireplace, sitting room, library with river views. Swimming, fishing, tubing, rafting, canoeing, boating, sunbathing on riverside terrace. Cross-country skiing, hiking, bicycling nearby.
Location Bucks County; 18 m N of New Hope via Rte. 32 N; 3½ m N of Frenchtown/Uhlerstown bridge. 65 m W of NYC. In village.
Restrictions No smoking. No children under 8 on weekends.
Credit cards Only to hold rooms without deposits; Amex, MC, Visa.
Rates B&B, $110–175 suite, $75–95 double. Midweek rates. 2-3 night weekend/holiday minimum.
Extras NYC bus stop in village.

WASHINGTON CROSSING

Information please: Hollileif (677 Durham Road/Route 413, Wrightstown 18940; 215–598–3100) is just 5 miles west of Washington Crossing and about 15 miles south of New Hope. This 18th century farmhouse has been restored as a B&B with four centrally air-conditioned bedrooms, each with private bath. The country decor is highlighted with antiques, and rates include a full breakfast, afternoon refreshments served before the living room fire or on the shaded porch, and turndown service. Reports please.

Woodhill Farms Inn   *Tel:* 215–493–1974
150 Glenwood Drive, 18977

Bucks County's most contemporary inn was built of stone and cedar in 1978 for use as a B&B, and was purchased by Donald and Mary Lou

Spagnuolo in 1988. A continental breakfast is served weekdays, and a full breakfast on weekends. As you may have guessed, the hamlet of Washington Crossing was named after Washington's famous crossing of the Delaware in 1776. You can get a beautiful view of the area from Bowman's Tower in nearby Washington Crossing State Park.

"Don greeted us warmly, despite our late arrival. He and Mary Lou are always available, but never intrusive. The inn is located in a peaceful residential area, and offers a warm, comfortable atmosphere throughout. On weekends a spectacular breakfast is cheerfully served on fine china with linen napkins and elegant table settings. The homemade breads are not to be missed, and the coffee is both excellent and abundant. Our room had a comfortable queen-size bed and a beautifully tiled bath with a sunken tub. Herbal soups and shampoo were thoughtfully provided. An in-room thermostat (unusual in an inn) added to our comfort. Dining and shopping in the surrounding areas is great, and the Spagnuolo family is always ready with suggestions." (MC) "Wonderful owners, immaculate inn. Wine and cheese awaited our arrival, and the homemade breakfasts were excellent. A terrific experience." (Mark Hughes)

Open All year.
Rooms 5 doubles with private bath and/or shower, radio, TV, air-conditioning, fan, telephone, desk.
Facilities Living room with fireplace, dining room. 10 acres with garden, fish pond, hiking trails, putting green. Delaware River nearby for canoeing, fishing, tubing.
Location Bucks County, E central PA. 15 min. S of New Hope. Exit I-95 at Yardley onto Taylorsville Rd., go N 1 m to Mt. Eyre Rd. and turn left. Go 4/10 m; turn right on Walker Rd. Go right on Bruce Rd; after 4/10 m, go right again to inn.
Restrictions Smoking in bedrooms only. No children under 6.
Credit cards Amex, MC, Visa.
Rates B&B, $85–125 double. Extra person in room, $15. 2-night minimum weekends, holidays. Corporate rates. Senior discounts.
Extras Limited wheelchair access. Station pickups. Cribs, babysitting available.

WILLIAMSPORT

A major manufacturing center, most people visit Williamsport on business, but more than a few detour to see the home of the Little League World Series, and the Little League Baseball Museum next to the field. Williamsport is located in north central Pennsylvania, 90 miles north of Harrisburg, 60 miles northeast of State College, and 30 miles north of Lewisburg.

The Reighard House   *Tel: 717–326–3593*
1323 East Third Street, 17701

Opened in 1986 as Williamsport's first B&B, the Reighard House is a stone and brick Victorian built in 1905, and has been home to Sue and Bill Reighard since 1976. Rooms are decorated with a mixture of Victorian and more recent furnishings.

"The owners are gracious and friendly, but respect guests' privacy. The common rooms are warm and inviting, and during warm weather the front porch is a frequent gathering place. Each bedroom is decorated with a different color scheme and theme: the Lavender and Lace room has a four-poster canopy bed with a white lace spread, lavender and white accents and wallpaper, purple carpeting, and a full bath with purple towels. The Atocha room has a tropical nautical theme accented with artifacts brought back by the Reighard's son, who explored a sunken Spanish treasure ship. The house is spotless." *(NB)*

"A top-notch inn, and Susan is an exceptionally fine hostess." *(Melvin Mailloux)* "In addition to a complete breakfast, the Reighard's offer their guests soda, wine, sherry, snacks." *(William Ennis)* "Bob and Sue are always ready with maps, menus from local restaurants, and whatever else a visitor might need." *(Charles & Marilyn Doebler)* "Nice extra touches, like a coffee maker in one's room." *(Marie O'Neill)* "Every night a small basket of fruit, nuts, and sweets is left in each room. Breakfast is anything the guest wants. There is a den with books, VCR, and a collection of movies. A beer tap is open to all guests gratis. Off-street parking is ample, and the location is a residential/commercial area adjacent to I-180; highway noise is minimal." *(Mort Sternberg, and others)* "Just as good as your write-up promised." *(Jonathan Douglas)*

Open All year. Closed Dec. 25–Jan. 1.
Rooms 6 doubles—all with private shower and/or bath, telephone, radio, TV, desk, air-conditioning. 2 with fan.
Facilities Living room, music room, library, dining room, breakfast room, porch. Complimentary YMCA membership for swimming, health club, hot tub. Bicycle path, hiking, hunting, fishing, canoeing, skiing nearby. Car rentals available.
Location N central PA. 1 m from center of town.
Restrictions Smoking on first floor only (except dining areas). Some traffic noise in front rooms.
Credit cards Amex, CB, DC, MC, Visa.
Rates B&B, $58–98 double, $48–68 single. Extra person in room, $10; crib in room, $5.
Extras Airport/station pickups. Crib available.

The Thomas Lightfoote Inn   *Tel:* 717–326–6396
2887 South Reach Road, 17701

Guests really enjoy the delicious food and warm atmosphere at this inn, listed on the National Register of Historic Places. Built in 1792, the inn fed and housed those traveling on the west branch of the Pennsylvania Canal (1830–1865), and was also a prominent stop for escaping slaves on the Underground Railroad.

"The inn was completely restored by Jim and Rita Chilson, and opened in 1987. The guest rooms are decorated in eighteenth-century style with antiques and reproduction furniture, highlighted by canopy beds, country wallpapers, and hand stenciling. Rooms are very clean with excellent lighting; beds are firm and comfortable. Rita is an exceptionally vivacious and friendly innkeeper who makes her guests feel right at home. Rates include a bowl of fresh fruit in your room and wine and cheese before dinner, or the delicious house specialty, cranberry iced tea. The varied dinner menu is excellent, and you can have dessert sent to your room." *(Michael & Phyllis Johansen)*

"The living room has a large welcoming fireplace, as does the dining room. The owners are friendly yet give you privacy. My spacious room had a high poster bed with a firm and comfortable mattress, a fireplace (lit every night), a wingback chair and a footstool. Everything was very clean, and the bathroom was well supplied with such extras as a razor and hair dryer. The food was excellent; the very full breakfast included a baked apple with cinnamon and cream, apple walnut muffins, and a special blend of tea." *(Keith Gunter)*

One area for improvement: "A second telephone line for guest use would be appreciated by business travelers."

Open All year. Closed Christmas.
Rooms 2 suites, 3 doubles—3 with full private bath, 2 sharing 1 bath. All with telephone, radio, TV, air-conditioning; some with desk. 3 with fireplace. 1 with sun-porch.
Facilities Restaurant, living room with fireplaces; pub/lounge. 4 acres with gardens, gazebo. Susquehanna River park in front of inn for walking, canoeing, boating, cross-country skiing.
Location 3 m from center. From Williamsport, Rte. 220 S to Reach Rd exit. At ramp turn left onto S Reach Road to inn 1 m on right.
Restrictions No smoking on second floor. Traffic noise in back rooms (guest rooms face front and are quiet). Children over 6 preferred.
Credit cards MC, Visa.
Rates B&B, $65 suite; $55–60 doubles; $50 single. Extra person in room, $10. 2 night minimum some weekends. Prix fixe dinner $12–24. Corporate weekly rates.
Extras Restaurant wheelchair accessible. Station pickups. Crib available.

We Want to Hear from You!

As you know, this book is only effective with your help. We really need to know about your experiences and discoveries.

If you stayed at an inn or hotel listed here, we want to know how it was. Did it live up to our description? Exceed it? Was it what you expected? Did you like it? Were you disappointed? Delighted?

Have you discovered new establishments that we should add to the next edition?

Tear out one of the report forms at the back of this book (or use your own stationery if you prefer) and write today. Even if you write only "Fully endorse existing entry" you will have been most helpful.
Thank You!

Virginia

Fassifern Bed & Breakfast, Lexington

Few states equal Virginia's importance in the birth of this country. The first permanent English settlement in America was at Jamestown, in 1619. Eight U.S. presidents were born in Virginia; of the founding fathers of the U.S., Washington, Jefferson, Madison, Marshall, Monroe, and Henry were all Virginians. More Civil War battles were fought in Virginia than in any other state; Civil War buffs will want to visit all the battle sites. There is much of historical interest for all to explore in the state. The Virginia Division of Tourism has helpful brochures specifically dealing with many facets of Virginia history; ask for details when you call or write (see Appendix 3 for address).

Northern Virginia is noted for its historic towns and is known as horse country. The Tidewater area is home to Jamestown, Williamsburg, and Yorktown, plus Virginia Beach. The Eastern Shore is an isolated finger reaching out into the Chesapeake Bay from Maryland—Assateague National Seashore is perhaps its best-known feature. The central and southern portions of the state are rich in history, particularly of the Civil War. In the west, the Shenandoah Valley and Blue Ridge Mountains are where Washingtonians go to cool off, literally and figuratively; the scenery is breathtaking in all four seasons.

Virginia's spa country is located in the Allegheny Mountain Valley towns of Warm Springs, Hot Springs, and White Sulphur Springs, along the West Virginia border. You can soak in medicinal waters, or enjoy the equally recuperative effects of the peaceful mountain air.

Rates do not include the 6% state sales tax on lodging, and the 4% tax on meals. Rates do not change seasonally in most locations, but tend

VIRGINIA

to be highest on weekends and lower midweek. If you plan to stay at an inn for three or four nights during the week, be sure to ask if any midweek discounts apply.

ABINGDON

The Martha Washington Inn   *Tel:* 703–628–3161
150 West Main Street, P.O. Box 1037, 24210   In VA: 800–533–1014

Built in 1832 to house the family of one of Abingdon's first millionaires, the Martha Washington Inn has seen numerous changes: first, in 1858, it housed a women's college of the same name, and then served as a hospital during the Civil War. As student enrollments declined during the 1930s, the building was converted into a hotel. Over the last six decades many changes in structure and ownership occurred, and in 1984 it was sold to its current owners, The United Company. After a $6,000,000 renovation, the hotel combines both antebellum and Victorian decor, with lavish use of gilded trim, velvet and satin furnishings, period reproductions, and antiques.

A major local attraction is the Barter Theatre, America's longest running professional resident theater company (and also the state theater of Virginia). Housed in some of the former college buildings, its name is derived from the original payment to the actors—produce bartered in exchange for theatrical talent. Among the notables who honed their skills here are Thornton Wilder, Gregory Peck, Hume Cronyn, and Patricia Neal.

"The hotel is lovely, both outside and in. Ample parking is provided, and is well lit at night. Elegant, immaculate, well-maintained, and very polished are the only words to describe both the common areas and the guest rooms. The furnishings in our room were lovely—both antiques and reproductions. Our bathroom was supplied with lots of thick, luxurious towels, and we heard nothing from any other rooms or the halls. A newspaper was left outside our door; alarm clocks were provided, along with extra pillows and blankets. Abingdon is a lovely town, well worth visiting." *(Joyce Whittington)*

"The exquisitely decorated restaurant, the First Lady's Table, offers many well-prepared traditional Southern dishes as well as continental cuisine, all served by a courteous staff."*(Betty T. Norman)*

An area for improvement: "Perhaps we hit a bad morning, but our breakfast in the First Lady's Table was disappointing. Eggs, biscuits, and coffee were lukewarm, and our grits were lumpy." Comments?

Open All year.
Rooms 61 suites & doubles—all with full private bath, telephone, radio, TV, clock, air-conditioning. Some suites with whirlpool, steam room.
Facilities Restaurant, 2 lounges with nightly entertainment, lobby, ballroom, meeting room, gift shop. Room service.

278

Location SW VA, Shenandoah Valley. 133 m W of Roanoke, 142 m N of Knoxville, TN. From I-81, take Exit 8 ½ m N to inn.
Credit cards Amex, DC, Discover, MC, Visa.
Rates Room only, $135–360 suite, $82–120 double, $68–110 single. Corporate rates. Children's menu.

ALDIE

Little River Inn
Route 50, P.O. Box 116, 22001

Tel: 703–327–6742

Tucker Withers opened the Little River Inn in 1982, and later learned that it had belonged to his great-grandparents. It was then in poor condition, but he restored it, along with several outbuildings, adding modern baths and decorating the rooms with beautiful antiques— quilts, hooked and braided rugs, spool beds, and 19th-century paintings. The inn consists of the main house and a log cabin, built around 1810, the Patent House, dating to the late 1700s, and the Hill House, a more recent addition with its own herb and boxwood garden.

Tucker's enthusiasm for this region is unlimited: "Aldie's small-town charms include its many antique stores and its working gristmill, built in 1810. It's protected from the urban sprawl and congestion of Washington, only 35 miles away, by the Bull Run Mountains to the east and prime horse farms to the west. Cyclists love our back roads, and there are eight wineries in the area; nearby Middleburg is known as the 'heart of fox-hunting country.' "

"Tucker has taken great care in the restoration of the inn's buildings to generate a beautiful country atmosphere with all the modern conveniences. All the rooms are decorated with country antiques that lend a homey aura, and the staff is friendly and efficient, creating a home-away-from-home feeling. The sleepy little town of Aldie provides country-style peace and quiet. Breakfast is prepared at the convenience of the guest and includes menus such as Dutch apple baby, sausage and eggs, or, my favorite, baked French toast. The breakfast always comes with an assortment of juices, locally made sausages, homemade poppy seed muffins or strawberry bread, and, of course, great conversation. For evening snacks Tucker always leaves an assortment of wine and cheese and other munchies in the kitchen for guests to enjoy." *(Bob Sanchez)*

"I find that the combination of quiet location, nearby attractions, variety of decor in the antique-filled rooms, a warming fire on cool evenings, and the friendliest of innkeepers create an unbeatable combination."*(C.G. McCarty)* "The Little River Inn offers super-clean surroundings in a private atmosphere."*(Gregory Winters)*

"Your entry was totally accurate. The inn has a wonderful atmosphere with a warm, friendly and efficient staff. There are beautiful old quilts and stencilled lamps (each different) in every room, and antiques everywhere." *(Elisabeth McLaughlin)*

Open All year.
Rooms 3 cottages, 5 doubles—5 with full private bath, 3 with maximum of 4 people sharing bath. All with desk; some with air-conditioning. 3 with fireplace.
Facilities 2 sitting rooms (one with fireplace), dining room. 5 acres with gardens, patio, and petting farm. Bull Run Mountain trails nearby.
Location N VA, Loudoun County. 35 m W of Washington, DC, 5 m E of Middleburg. 17 min. from Dulles Airport. From I-495 beltway, take Rte. 66 W to Rte. 50 W 20 miles to Aldie and inn.
Restrictions No children under 10.
Credit cards MC, Visa.
Rates B&B, $110–190 cottage, $75–85 double, $60–70 single. Extra person in room, $20. Tipping "not expected."

ALEXANDRIA

Morrison House
116 South Alfred Street, 22314

Tel: 703–838–8000
In VA: 800–533–1808
In US: 800–367–0800

At first sight, you might assume that the elegant Federal-style Morrison House was built in 1785, not two centuries later when it was actually constructed by Robert Morrison. A European-style small luxury hotel, it is furnished with high quality period reproduction furnishings, brass and crystal lighting, elaborately swagged curtains in tones of soft yellow, green, and peach; modern amenities such as televisions are of course discreetly tucked away in custom-made armoires. The hotel is home to two restaurants, Le Chardon d'Or, for elegant French dining, and the more casual Grill; both are served by the same kitchen, and both have been well received by local critics.

"The perfect combination—period charm combined with every modern amenity. The bathrooms have imported marble vanities, with Lancôme soaps and lotions, with lighting designed for putting on makeup—no fluorescents. Owner Robert Morrison is very pleasant and cordial. He was very much involved in every detail of the design of his inn; to avoid the blank wall usually found at the end of a hotel corridor, he had a window added to provide sun.The inn is on a quiet residential street in the heart of Old Town Alexandria, two to three blocks from the main thoroughfare." *(Frank & Dotty Scarfone)* "The food is outstanding and afternoon tea, delightful." *(Carolyn Myles, also Hope Welliver)*

Open All year.
Rooms 3 suites, 42 doubles—all with full private bath, telephone, radio, TV, air-conditioning. Some with fireplace. Concierge service.
Facilities Parlor with fireplace, library, two restaurants, bar/lounge with fireplace, piano. Health club, pool, sailing nearby. Indoor valet parking.
Location Historic Old Town. Two blocks W of S. Washington St., between King and Prince Sts.
Credit cards Amex, CB, DC, MC, Visa.

Rates Room only, $250–385 suite, $135–195 double. Extra person in room, $20. Children under 12 free in parents' room. Full breakfast, $9. Alc lunch $12–14; alc dinner $35–55.
Extras Wheelchair accessible. Pets permitted by prior arrangement. Cribs, baby-sitting available. French, Spanish, German, Russian, Japanese, Arabic spoken.

AMHERST

Dulwich Manor Inn
Route 5, P.O. Box 173A, 24521

Tel: (804)–946–7207

Built in 1912 with Flemish bond brickwork in the style of an English estate house, Dulwich Manor is Amherst County's first B&B inn. Bob and Judy Reilly, formerly an actor and a public relations expert respectively, opened their house to overnight guests in 1989. Set in the rolling countryside with views of the Blue Ridge mountains, the inn is furnished with antiques and reproductions; beveled glass panels provide a rainbow of light in the entry way and public rooms. Rates include breakfast and afternoon refreshments. Breakfast menus vary daily, but might include cold berry soup, crepes with apple rings, ham, shepherd-ers' potatoes, and homemade breads and muffins.

"Dulwich Manor is located in a quiet, pastoral setting that is easy to find and close to interesting area activities. The innkeepers, Bob and Judy, spent a number of years as guests at B&Bs before opening their own and it shows: everything that they would have wanted for themselves they supply for guests. Judy's country breakfasts seem to go on forever; over a visit of six days we had a different menu each day. The generously-sized rooms have large, working windows that flood the space with light; the period furnishings give a gracious feeling. The plumbing is fine; while it takes a little while for the hot water to arrive, once it does, the supply is ample." *(Rev. & Mrs. Wayne Harnden)*

"All the style and comfort that you could want, topped off by a sumptuous breakfast served with wit and charm by Bob and Judy." *(Susan & Russell Morrell)*

Open All year.
Rooms 5 doubles—3 with private bath and/or shower, 2 with a maximum of 4 people sharing bath. All with radio, air-conditioning. 3 with fireplace, 1 with whirlpool tub.
Facilities Dining room, living room with fireplace, study with fireplace, veranda. 5 acres with lawn, hot tub. Tennis, golf, children's play equipment nearby. James River nearby for rafting, canoeing. 45 m to Wintergreen ski area.
Location Central VA. 50 m SW of Charlottesville, 15 m N of Lynchburg. 1 m from town. From Rte. 29 turn E on Rte. 60 and go ¼ m to inn.
Restrictions Smoking in study only.
Credit cards MC, Visa.
Rates B&B, $65–85 double, $60–80 single. Extra person in room, $10; extra child under age 12, $5. Midweek senior discount. 2-night weekend minimum, special events.
Extras Airport/station pickups, $5–10. Babysitting available.

ARLINGTON

Crystal B&B
2620 South Fern Street, 22202

Tel: 703–548–7652

The Crystal B&B is a Dutch Colonial home built in the 1940s, decorated in a country theme, with handmade quilts in every room. A continental breakfast is served on weekdays, and usually includes owner Sue Swain's homemade croissants and jams, cereal, and fruit; a full breakfast is served on weekends, with omelets, blueberry pancakes or whole wheat yogurt pancakes among the favorite entrées.

"Located in a convenient, pleasant neighborhood just 20 minutes from downtown Washington, the Crystal B&B is cozy, comfortable, and very clean. The owners are warm, friendly people who respect your privacy while making you feel like part of the family." *(Sung Hui Kim)*

"Sue Swain is delightful. We were the only guests and felt very pampered. The inn is located on a quiet residential street, yet just a short distance away is a brand-new mall with Nordstrom's and Macy's." *(Dianne Crawford)*

Open All year.
Rooms 2 doubles, 1 single with shared bath.
Facilities Living room, dining room, TV room. Flower garden. Off-street parking.
Location DC metro area, 20 min. to downtown. 7 blocks to Metro. 5 min. drive to National Airport.
Credit cards Visa.
Rates B&B, $60 double, $45 single. 10% weekly discount.

BEDFORD

With a newly restored downtown and a population of fewer than 6,000 people, Bedford makes a lovely place to overnight when you're traveling the Blue Ridge Parkway along Virginia's western border. It's about 30 miles west of Lynchburg, 100 miles southwest of Charlottesville, and 225 miles southwest of Washington, DC.

The Longwood Inn
517 Longwood Avenue, 24523

Tel: 703–586–2282

This turn-of-the-century Victorian is encircled with porches; the interior features the original oak and pine floors and tiled fireplaces, along with collections of antique lace and glass and an eclectic mixture of nostalgic and contemporary furnishings.

"The front porch is most inviting, with ample current reading material and newspapers, a beautifully manicured lawn, and gentle woodwind music floating from a hidden speaker." *(Eric Bivens)* "A mixture of traditional and modern decor, with a blend of calm colors and soft fabrics. Great food." *(Wink & Becky Glover)* "The inn's fresh, light interior, with plants in the windows, gives it a homey feel, and the collection of framed handkerchiefs are a source of interest as well as a charming touch. All my needs were met—plenty of towels, artistic writing materials, and a delicious, simple breakfast. The inn is surrounded by a well-tended garden—plants are marked with their common names. The inn occupies the highest elevation in town, in a neighborhood of stately Victorian homes." *(Kristen Bedford)* "The inn is within easy walking distance of the restored downtown area. Our room was large and most pleasant, done in beiges and white, with a hardwood floor, reading materials, fresh flowers, full-length mirror, good lighting, and handsome window treatments. Our room was very quiet—we couldn't hear a sound from the other rooms—and our bath was new, with good plumbing. The inn is immaculately clean throughout." *(Mrs. Jack Hammond)* "The beds are big and comfortable; chocolate-chip cookies are there for the eating and sherry is available for a nightcap. Daily newspapers are found in front of the fireplace, where a cheery fire crackles." *(Charles Perry)* "A chocolate lover's dream—there were brownies to greet us when we arrived and chocolates hidden under the pillows. After a wonderful breakfast, we were given more chocolate to sustain us during our hike of the nearby Peaks of Otter." *(Rick Floyd & Andee Rubin)*

"A tremendous amount of work was done remodeling and creating a luxurious hideaway. It's obvious that only the best quality in furniture, bathroom fixtures, and decorations were used. Our bedroom was huge, with a very comfortable sofa, rocker, table and chairs, fireplace, and half-canopy king-size bed. Wonderful bedding and towels." *(Mary Wabeke)*

Important note: Just as we went to press, we learned that the inn has been sold; the comments above reflect guests' experiences under the previous owner, Lou Wright. Reports on how the inn is faring are *most* welcome.

Open Jan. 10 to Dec. 15
Rooms 5 doubles—all with private bath and/or shower, radio, desk, air-conditioning.
Facilities Dining room, parlor, common area with guest refrigerator, porch with swing, glider. 1 acre with herb, vegetable, and flower gardens. Tennis and lake for fishing and swimming nearby. 10 m to cross-country skiing.
Location 9 m to Blue Ridge Parkway, 9 m to Peaks of Otter. 4 blocks to center of town.
Restrictions No smoking.
Credit cards None accepted.
Rates B&B, $50–80 double, $40–70 single. Extra person in room, $10.
Extras Handicap accessible. Cribs, babysitting, swings, games available.

Peaks of Otter Lodge
Blue Ridge Parkway, P.O. Box 489, 24523
Milepost 86, at Route 43

Tel: 703–586–1081
In VA: 800–542–5927

An authorized concession of the National Park Service, the Lodge offers motel-style accommodations that do a surprisingly good job of blending into its beautiful lakeside setting. Restaurant specialties include mountain trout, prime rib, and barbecued ribs.

"What a wonderful surprise this place was. It gets an 'A' on all the usuals—cleanliness, large attractive rooms, good but simple food—and the setting is picture-postcard pretty." *(Mrs. Arnold Miller)*

"The Peaks of Otter loom above the lodge, and offers a reasonably short but surprisingly challenging climb. Make it early enough in the morning and you'll see less tourists and maybe even a deer beside the trail. The lodge sits beside a trout-filled lake beside the Skyline Drive. All-you-can-eat buffets are included in the rates during the off-season. The food is traditional country style—don't expect fancy sauces—but is filling and inexpensive." *(MG)*

Open All year.
Rooms 62 suites and doubles—all with full private bath, air-conditioning, balcony or patio.
Facilities Restaurant, bar, gift shop. On 24-acre lake for fishing, boating; hiking trails, Park Visitors' Center nearby.
Location On Blue Ridge Parkway, at milepost 86; junction of Rte. 43.
Credit cards MC, Visa (not accepted for deposits).
Rates Room only, $75–100 suite, $60 double, $45 single. Children under 16 free in parents' room. Extra adult in room, $4. Rollaway bed, $4.
Extras Wheelchair accessible. Crib available.

CAPE CHARLES

Set near the southwestern tip of Virginia's Eastern Shore, Cape Charles is just a few miles north of the Chesapeake Bay Bridge, 20 miles north of Norfolk/Virginia Beach, and 60 miles south of Chincoteague. Williamsburg is 1 hour away. The town offers golf, tennis, charter boat fishing, antique shops, good seafood restaurants, and charming backroads.

Nottingham Ridge Bed & Breakfast　　　　*Tel:* 804–331–1010
Route 646, P.O. Box 97-B, 23310

Nottingham Ridge is a classically styled colonial brick home, owned by Bonnie Nottingham since 1985. Rooms are decorated with antiques and contemporary furnishings, highlighted by local crafts. Rates typically include a full breakfast with fresh fruit or juice, homemade breads and jams, along with afternoon wine and cheese or cake and coffee.

"Bonnie is a first-rate hostess, with a warm, outgoing personality. The house sits atop sand dunes above their private beach, overlooking Chesapeake Bay. Breakfast is served on the large screened porch facing the bay, and guests seem to prefer this spot for visiting with each other as well. My room held a canopied queen-size bed and had large windows to let in the breezes and the restful sound of waves breaking on the shore. The bath was large and more than adequate, clean and attractive." *(Jane Bowman)* "An attractive, comfortable B&B in just the right location between Norfolk and Williamsburg." *(Mrs. S.I. McKanna)*

Open All year.
Rooms 3 doubles—all with private and shared baths, telephone, radio, desk, air-conditioning, fan. TV available on request.

Facilities Living room, dining room, screened porch. 17 acres with large private beach on Chesapeake Bay. Hiking, biking on grounds. Fishing, golf, tennis nearby.
Location 20 m N of Norfolk, Virginia Beach, 3.5 m N of Bay Bridge-Tunnel. 10 m from town. From Chesapeake Bay Bridge-Tunnel, go 2 m W on Rte. 646 to inn on the bay.
Restrictions Smoking in den, porch only. No children under 6.
Credit cards None accepted.
Rates B&B, $65–75 double, $50–60 single. Extra person in room, $20.
Extras Airport/station pickups by prior arrangement. French spoken.

B&B of Pickett's Harbor   *Tel:* 804–331–2212
P.O. Box 977AA, 23443

"This secluded home is right on Chesapeake Bay, surrounded by pines and dunes. The house is modern (we had a separate entrance and private bath) but with the feel and furnishings of early America. We were greeted with wine and cheese on the screened porch by owners Sara and Cook Goffigon. Sara is a person of many talents, and our delicious breakfast was evidence of one of them. Restaurants are some distance away, so I'd suggest eating before you arrive. Another possibility is to come early and allow time to settle in, take a walk on the beach or go for a swim, then drive several miles to dinner and be back before dusk." *(Mary Hayslip)* Reports most welcome.

Open All year.
Rooms 3 doubles, 1 single—2 with full private bath, 2 with maximum of 4 people sharing bath. All with air-conditioning, fan.
Facilities Living room, dining room, screened porch. Private beach for swimming, fishing, boating.
Location E shore VA. Call for directions.
Restrictions No smoking.
Credit cards None accepted.
Rates B&B, $60 double, $50 single. Extra adult in room, $20; child under 10, $10. Cot, $15.

CHARLOTTESVILLE

Charlottesville is best known as the home of Thomas Jefferson's Monticello and the University of Virginia. Other sights of interest include Castle Hill, Ashlawn, Michie Tavern, Court Square, and the nearby Skyline Drive. The best place for information on all these sights is the Thomas Jefferson Visitors' Bureau, located at the intersection of I-64 and Rte. 20 South. The area also offers lakes for boating and swimming; it's a 40-minute drive to downhill and cross-country skiing. Albemarle County is horse country, with many fox hunts and steeplechase events; there's no shortage of golf courses and tennis courts, either.

Charlottesville is 125 miles southwest of Washington, DC, and 75 miles northwest of Richmond.

Information please: We'd like additional reports on the **200 South Street Inn** (200 South Street, 22901; 804–979–0200), two restored buildings dating from the 1850s, listed in earlier editions. Rooms are comfortably but elegantly decorated with English and Belgian antiques; many have canopy beds and fireplaces. The inn is filled with classic English art, works of contemporary Virginian artists, and historical photographs. A restaurant called Memory and Company serves lunch and dinner in the inn. Although its location is not particularly attractive, it is convenient, just two blocks from the historic district. On the other hand, readers noted that the staff lacked sensitivity to guests' needs, the breakfast was skimpy, and the prices high in relation to what was offered. Opinions?

The Boar's Head Inn & Sports Club
P.O. Box 5307, 22905

Tel: 804–296–2181
800–476–1988

Built 25 years ago as a small country inn, John Rogan's Boar's Head has grown into a large resort hotel and sports complex. Although it's much larger than most of our listings, it is well recommended by quite a few respondents. The public rooms are decorated with some antiques; guest rooms are comfortably furnished with colonial reproductions—some prefer rooms in the original part of the inn. Casual meals are served in the tavern; more elegant ones in the regular dining rooms. The dinner menu includes such regional favorites as spoon bread, country ham, and pecan pie, plenty of beef dishes, plus more adventurous cuisine—rack of lamb and roast duck. Local Virginia wine makes an appropriate accompaniment.

The Boar's Head is a good choice for those who want a vacation that combines history with an active sports program. Keep in mind that reservations are almost impossible to get on fall weekends when the University of Virginia is playing a home football game.

"Restful location in the suburbs of Charlottesville, in an area of gentle hills, with two peaceful lakes. Despite all the sports facilities, it is also a good place to rest and relax. Our large room had a king-size bed and a balcony overlooking the lake." *(Karen Gould)*

"A charming inn with inviting sitting rooms and a homey atmosphere. The meals and dining room service were excellent." *(Mrs. E. Wheatley, also Elizabeth Sommer)*

And some areas for improvement: "My room had not been made up when I arrived at 4 P.M.; the windows were stuck with paint, making it impossible to insert a screen which had been removed." Also: "The food varies—some meals are good, some indifferent. One was really excellent, a luncheon of broiled red snapper." Additional reports welcome.

Open All year.
Rooms 11 suites with fireplaces, 164 doubles—all with full private bath, telephone, TV, desk, air-conditioning. Many with balcony. 75 rooms in annex.
Facilities 4 restaurants, bar, sitting room, tavern with live music, specialty shops. 43 acres with 3 swimming pools, 16 tennis courts (3 indoor), 4 squash courts, 2 platform tennis courts, fishing, golf, jogging trail, exercise room, gardens, duck ponds. Ballooning. Conference facilities.
Location 2½ m to town. 5 min. from U. of VA. From I-64, take Exit 22B to Rte. 250 W. Go W 1½ m to inn on left.
Credit cards Amex, CB, DC, MC, Visa.
Rates Room only, $160–185 suite, $103–155 double, 15% service suggested.

Extra person in room, $20. Pets, $12. No charge for children under 18 in parents' room. Breakfast, $5–8. Alc lunch, $7–14; alc dinner, $20–40. Holiday, sports packages.
Extras Pets permitted. Ramps, special bath facilities for disabled. Airport pick-ups. Cribs, babysitting, kiddie pool available. French, German, Spanish spoken.

Clifton
Route 9, Box 412, 22901

Tel: 804–971–1800

Stay at Clifton if you'd like to treat yourself to an overnight at a Jeffersonian estate. Set on a cliff overlooking the Rivanna River, Clifton was built in 1799 on land originally part of the Jefferson family estate, Shadwell; Monticello can be seen on a neighboring hill when the trees are bare. Thomas Jefferson gave the land to his eldest daughter, Martha, when she married Thomas Mann Randolph, a future governor of Virginia. Owned by Mitch and Emily Willey since 1986, Clifton is managed by Sue Putalik. Guest rooms have the original pine floors, wall paneling, and working fireplaces, with period decor and quality linens. Rates include a multi-course breakfast, and dinners are also available.

"From the friendliness of the staff to the ambience of warmth and welcome, to the unparalleled beauty of the inn and grounds, everything is perfection." *(Joseph Luciano)*

"Our suite was very clean and neat. We used the fireplace throughout our weekend, which added to the historic atmosphere. We were served homemade cookies and tea upon our arrival, and late-night hot chocolate was brought to our room. Breakfast was hearty and delectable, elegantly served on beautiful china. The innkeepers were wonderfully friendly hosts who made us feel as if we were their personal guests." *(Betty Anne Soffin, also Carol & Nick Mumford)*

"The common rooms are magnificent. On our arrival the air was scented with wood smoke from the fires in the drawing room and library, with tempting platters of cheese and other snacks laid out. Our room was lovely, with a fire waiting to be lit in the fireplace, and cotton sheets of a very high quality. Our bathroom was big and bright, with a shower and a plentiful supply of fluffy towels. The innkeepers were well-supplied with up-to-date menus for local restaurants; they re-served a table for us at the Ivy Inn, an excellent choice. *(Ellie Freidus)*

Although readers are delighted with this inn, expectations run as high as their rates. Some suggestions: "Early morning coffee would be a lovely touch. Also, although I had told them that I don't eat meat, breakfast consisted of ham steak with puréed pumpkin, a croissant, and grapes. An egg or some potatoes would have made for a more balanced meal." Also: "Although herbal bath salts were provided, our bathroom just had a shower; although there was room for a tub, a sculpture occupied the place where a bath should go. I love art but . . . " Finally: "The nearest restaurant is about a 15-minute drive; it's a shame there's nothing closer."

Open All year.
Rooms 1 cottage, 3 suites, 5 doubles—all with private bath and/or shower, telephone, desk, air-conditioning, fan, fireplace. 1 room in annex; 3 rooms in cottage.
Facilities Dining room with fireplace, living room with fireplace, grand piano;

library with fireplace, garden room, terrace. 45 acres with river view, private lake, swimming pool, tennis court, lawn croquet, hiking, fishing.

Location 5 m to town. From I-64, take Exit 25 to Rte. 250 E. Turn right on Rte. 729 (Shadwell). Go S ¹⁄₈ m to inn on left.

Restrictions "Non-smokers preferred."

Credit cards MC, Visa.

Rates B&B, $130–165 suite or double. Extra person in room, $15. Summer packages. Group dinners by prior arrangement.

Extras Station pickups. Crib available. French, German spoken.

Silver Thatch Inn   *Tel:* 804–978–4686
3001 Hollymead Drive, 22901

Built by captured Hessian soldiers during the Revolutionary War, the Silver Thatch has been added onto many times during the past 200 years. New owners Mickey and Joe Geller bought the inn late in 1988, and have added top quality sheets, plenty of thick towels, and down comforters to the antique decor. Rates include a breakfast of juice, melon, cereal, granola, muffins, and coffee. The Gellers note that "we are working with Virginia growers and producers and have two wonderful chefs creating modern country cuisine; our wine list features three local Virginia vineyards, and our homemade desserts and breads are fabulous." The menu changes seasonally with daily specials always available.

"Mickey and Joe Geller have created a warm and friendly atmosphere. The three dining rooms are very romantic with candle lit tables, crisp white linens, and soft background music. The staff attended to all my needs, and the food was fabulous. I had Santa Fe chicken, a spicy dish served with corn sticks and a hot black bean salsa. Dessert was a white chocolate mousse filled with raspberry purée." *(Elizabeth Bright)*

"Although under new ownership, we were told by Lisa Workman (a most delightful staff member who was of great help to us) that very few changes have been made. Because dinner was not being served the night we stayed, we were referred to the Galerie, where we enjoyed superb French cuisine. Breakfast was very good and the decor has a pleasant country motif. We stayed in the James Monroe Room with a canopied queen-size bed. Drinks on the patio overlooking the garden was most enjoyable." *(Barbara Hornbach)*

An important note: At press time, we learned that the inn was for sale, due to personal problems. We'd suggest inquiring further when making reservations.

Open All year. Closed 1st 2 weeks Jan.; 1st 2 weeks Aug. Restaurant closed Sun., Mon.

Rooms 7 doubles—all with private shower and/or bath, air-conditioning. 4 with fireplace.

Facilities Restaurant, common room, bar/lounge with TV, fireplace. 1¹⁄₂ acres with swimming pool, tennis court. Fishing, golf nearby.

Location 5 m to town, on Rte. 1520, ¹⁄₂ m E of Rte. 29N.

Restrictions No smoking.

Credit cards MC, Visa.

Rates B&B, $105–135 double, $75–105 single. Extra person in room, $25. Corporate rates. 2-night weekend, holiday minimum. Alc dinner, $45–50.

Extras Airport pickups.

CHINCOTEAGUE

Information please: We'd love to have current reports on the **Channel Bass Inn** (100 Church Street, Chincoteague 23336; 804–336–6148), a luxuriously furnished 10-room inn and restaurant. Guest rooms are well-equipped, attractively furnished with antiques, and the inn is known for outstanding food at both dinner and breakfast. But . . . rooms cost $100–150; breakfast is an additional $30 for two, and dinner will run you another $200. Gulp. Tell us if you think it's worth the splurge; reader reports are mixed on the subject.

Another area possibility is the recently opened **Garden and Sea Inn** (Route 13, P.O. Box 275, New Church 23415; 804–824–0672), about 15 minutes drive northwest of Chincoteague. Dating to 1802, the inn's restaurant specializes in seafood and produce of the Eastern Shore; rates are reasonable and include a continental-plus breakfast and afternoon tea.

The Little Traveler Inn   *Tel:* 804–336–6686
113 North Main Street, 23336

Jim and Priscilla Stam own two inns, located directly across the street from each other—The Little Traveler and Miss Molly's Inn. Miss Molly's was built in 1886, and is named for its long-time owner. Marguerite Henry stayed here while writing *Misty*, and it's said that much of the plot was worked out while rocking on the front porch with Miss Molly and Captain Jack. The history of The Little Traveler is no less interesting: the house was built in the 1850s by two local men, who eventually married two sisters. The sisters didn't care to live under the same roof, so they split the house in half and moved the front half next door; the Stams have joined the houses again with a large garden room. Rooms are furnished in Federal style with the owners' 30-year collection of 17th, 18th, and early 19th century antiques; as you might expect of homes of this era, some of the guest rooms are quite small. Rates include a homemade continental breakfast and afternoon tea.

"The comfortable rooms are beautifully furnished with antiques. Jim and Priscilla Stam were helpful and congenial, offering information and anecdotes about the area. Their inns stood out amongst the area's run-of-the-mill (and rundown) seaside motels." *(Demetra Saldaris & Russell Goodfellow)* More comments please.

Open April 1–Dec. 1
Rooms 13 doubles—2 with private shower and/or bath, 11 with maximum of 4–6 sharing bath. All with radio, air-conditioning, fan. Some with desk.
Facilities Dining rooms, sitting rooms, garden room, fireside room, open & screened porches, gazebo. Courtyard with fountain. 2 acres with rose garden.
Location 2 blocks from center. 4 m from wildlife refuge, National Seashore.
Restrictions No children under 12. No smoking in guest rooms. Street noise will disturb light sleepers in some rooms.
Credit cards None accepted.
Rates B&B, $55–105 double. $45–65 single. Extra person in room, $20. 2-night weekend minimum.

CULPEPER

Fountain Hall B&B   *Tel:* 703–825–8200
609 South East Street, 22701   800–476–2944

An 1859 Victorian house named after Fountain Fisher Henry, a scion of old Virginia, it was reconstructed in 1923 in the Colonial Revival-style by another prominent citizen, Jackson Lee Fray, founder of the local phone company. Owned since 1985 by Steve and Kathi Walker, the inn provides a convenient in-town location just six blocks from the Amtrak station; rail access is available via the Cardinal (Chicago-D.C.) line and the Crescent (New York-Atlanta-New Orleans) line.

"Fountain Hall provides ample common rooms for socializing. The house is decorated to reflect its history; the guest rooms are comfortable, private and quiet. The inn is centrally located for a number of historic and natural attractions." *(Kathleen Rainey)* More comments please.

Open All year.
Rooms 5 doubles—all with private bath and/or shower, telephone, radio, desk, air-conditioning, fan.
Facilities Breakfast room, dining room, living room, game room. 1 acre with volleyball, patio.
Location N VA, Culpeper County. 72 m SW of Washington, DC; 45 m NE of Charlottesville. 1/2 m from town center. Take 2nd Culpeper exit off Rte. 29 S to Main St. Turn left on Main and then left on Davis St. Continue to East St. and turn right to inn on the left.
Restrictions No smoking.
Credit cards Amex, MC, Visa.
Rates B&B, $55–75 double, $45–65 single. Extra person in room, $10. Senior discount 2-night weekend minimum during Oct.
Extras Wheelchair accessible; some rooms equipped for the disabled. Station pickups. Crib available.

FAIRFAX

The Bailiwick Inn   *Tel:* 703–691–2266
4023 Chain Bridge Road, 22030

Built in the early 1800s, the Bailiwick Inn is right across the street from the Fairfax Courthouse; both buildings are listed on the National Register of Historic Places. Restored in 1989 by Anne and Ray Smith at a cost of over $1,600,000, the inn has been lavishly decorated with antiques, reproduction period fabrics, and feather beds. Bedrooms are named for famous and infamous Virginians, and rates include afternoon tea with scones and fruit tarts, turndown service with a pillow chocolate, and a full breakfast of fresh fruit and juice, homemade breads, and an entrée such as a crab omelet or Belgian waffles.

"The restoration of this home is impeccable, the antiques genuine, the food extraordinary. Ann and Ray are delightful hosts; no detail is missing, no comfort overlooked." *(David & Julia Marsden)* "In the middle of a historic city, with fabulous rooms tastefully done." *(Carey Marder)*

Open All year.
Rooms 1 suite, 13 doubles—all with private bath and/or shower, telephone, desk, air-conditioning. 4 with fireplace, 2 with Jacuzzi tub.
Facilities Breakfast room, double parlor with 2 fireplaces. Courtyard with fountain, pond, herb garden, arbor. On-site parking.
Location Historic district. 20 m W of Washington, DC. From Rte. 50 turn S on Rte. 123 (Old Chain Bridge Rd.)
Restrictions No smoking.
Credit cards MC, Visa.
Rates B&B, $185–195 suite, $110–165 double or single. "Tipping not encouraged."
Extras Wheelchair accessible; some rooms equipped for the disabled.

FREDERICKSBURG

Fredericksburg dates back to the early 18th century; it served as an important river port city in the colonial period, and was a central meeting point for George Washington, Thomas Jefferson, Patrick Henry, James Monroe, and John Paul Jones. Sights of interest include Mary Washington's home, James Monroe's law office, the Rising Sun Tavern, and the Kenmore plantation house, as well as the town's many craft and antique shops. Surrounding Fredericksburg are a number of major Civil War battlefields, including Chancellorsville, Wilderness, and Spotsylvania.

Fredericksburg is located in northern Virginia, 50 miles south of Washington, DC, and 55 miles north of Richmond, just a short distance off the Route 3 East exit of I-95.

Information please: When it comes to Fredericksburg's inns, we've had bad news, and we've had bad news. Readers have reported generally unsatisfactory experiences at the inns listed in our earlier editions, and the other B&Bs in town are either very small, or have too many people sharing a bath. Until the situation changes, we'd suggest sightseeing here, then moving on for overnight accommodation. Your reports, suggestions, comments, and new finds most appreciated.

FRONT ROYAL

Chester House Inn   *Tel:* 703–635–3937
43 Chester Street, 22630   800–621–0441

At Chester House, one of the first things that a passerby would notice about this turn-of-the-century home is the boxwood maze in the garden. The care evident in this gardening endeavor is representative of the effort which Ann and Bill Wilson put into their B&B, opened in 1988. Guest rooms are furnished with Sheraton-style pieces, Oriental rugs, and crisply ironed linens. Rates include continental breakfast; on one recent occasion Ann provided homemade popovers, juice, cereal, fruit and coffee.

"Our room had great lamps and overstuffed chairs for sitting and reading. The bath was immaculate and updated, with large, fluffy towels. The expansive public rooms are tastefully furnished with antiques, comfortable chairs, period draperies and an interesting art collection. Breakfast was served in the formal dining room (complete with unusual carved Italian marble fireplace) with silver service, fine china and crisp linens. The inn is a quiet oasis in the center of town, and the garden area is spectacular with a columned arbor with a large fountain and the boxwood maze." *(Susan Guest-McPhail)*

Open All year.
Rooms 1 suite, 4 doubles, 1 single—suite with private bath and/or shower, 5 with a maximum of 5 people sharing bath. 1 with private 1/2 bath & shared full bath. All with radio, air-conditioning, fan. 2 with desk, 2 with fireplace.
Facilities Dining room with fireplace, living room, TV room, veranda. 1 1/2 acres with boxwood maze, fountain. Shenandoah River nearby for fishing, canoeing, tubing. 5 m to downhill, cross-country skiing. Off-street parking.
Location N VA, Warren County. N end of Skyline Dr. 70 m W of Washington, DC. 1/2 block to center of town.
Restrictions Smoking in TV room only. No children under 12.
Credit cards MC, Visa.
Rates B&B, $95 suite, $65–80 double, $55 single. 2-night minimum on some weekends.

HARRISONBURG

The Joshua Wilton House
412 South Main Street, 22801

Tel: 703–434–4464

The Joshua Wilton House, an 1883 Victorian mansion, is within walking distance of the local historic district and James Madison University. Owners Roberta and Craig Moore report that the Wilton House is Harrisonburg's most elegant lodging and restaurant; guest rooms are decorated with period antiques. Rates include an afternoon beverage and a breakfast of homemade pastries, eggs, fresh fruit, and coffee.

"Our room was very clean and nicely decorated. The first floor has a restaurant and small bar, both with fires in the fireplace for a cozy atmosphere. The food in the restaurant was fairly expensive for the area but was excellent, worth the money." *(Sally Sieracki)*

Open All year.
Rooms 5 doubles—all with private bath.
Facilities Restaurant, sitting room.
Location N VA, Blue Ridge Mts. 126 m SW of Washington, DC. From I-81 take Exit 63. Go W on Port Republic Rd. to Main St. Turn right on Main St. and go 1 m to inn on right.
Restrictions No smoking in guest rooms.
Credit cards MC, Visa.
Rates B&B, $85 double.

HOT SPRINGS

The Carriage Court   *Tel:* 703–839–2345
Route 220, Route 2, Box 620, 24445

Carriage Court is a group of old farm buildings that have been remodeled and converted into a country inn and restaurant, set halfway between Warm Springs and Hot Springs. It's been owned by the Aborn family since 1985, and rates include a continental breakfast. Much replanting has been done in 1989 to enhance the inn's flower gardens.

"A charming, comfortable treasure, appealingly decorated with period furniture, pictures, and pottery. It is perfectly situated for taking the waters at Warm Springs and tea at the Homestead, and for walking the roads and trails in the countryside. The management is attentive, with a casual homeyness. Parking is at the door, and everything works as it should. It is quiet, convenient, warm, and friendly." *(Melva Chanslor)*

"We enjoyed our early-morning coffee on our private deck overlooking beautiful rolling hills and woods that contain many hiking trails. We were asked frequently if there was anything we needed. We also appreciated personal touches such as the handmade needlework pictures and ample supply of paperbacks." *(Jane Goldsberry & Judy Abshire)*

"Very good Italian-style food for dinner, and service from people who care about you. A golfer's paradise." *(Elizabeth Matarese)* "Our room was wonderful, clean, quaint, and quiet, with our very own herd of cows out back." *(AMC)* "The private deck was very enjoyable as was the spacious room and sunken bath. Every room is different and the furnishings are very homey." *(Sara Warren)*

"Our room, #8, was spacious, with plenty of lights, books, magazines, a sofa, and rocking chair. French doors led to a private deck overlooking the hills. We had a walk-in closet and a large bathroom with a country print wallpaper, coordinating towels, and a built-in dressing table. Service was prompt—a minor plumbing problem was immediately repaired after we reported it. Breakfast was adequate and the lunch-time salad bar was excellent." *(John & Jocelyn Hayes)*

"I'd suggest asking for rooms 7 or 8, in the Carriage Inn, at the back of the parking lot, away from the main road. They are nicely decorated with antiques and modern decor, and have decks overlooking the cow pasture." *(SHW)*

Open All year.
Rooms 3 suites, 3 doubles—all with full private bath, telephone, TV. Some with desk, deck or porch. Some with kitchenette. Rooms in 2 adjacent buildings.
Facilities Breakfast room, restaurant, deck. 2 acres with flower gardens; swimming pool nearby. 1 m to lakes, rivers, golf, fishing, downhill skiing, ice-skating.
Location Western VA, Allegheny Mts. Bath County, "Spa Country." 200 m SW of Washington, DC, 150 m W of Richmond. On Rte. 220, 1 m from the Homestead and Hot Springs.
Restrictions Traffic noise in front rooms.

Credit cards MC, Visa.
Rates B&B, $59–120 suite; $48–59 double. Extra person in room, $12. Group packages.
Extras Pets permitted. Wheelchair accessible. Cribs available; babysitting by arrangement. Airport pickup by prior arrangement.

IRVINGTON

Reader tip: "Do not confuse The Tides Inn with The Tides Lodge. The resorts are owned by two brothers, and are located across the creek from each other. The Tides Inn is an American plan resort with an MAP option, and is more elegant; The Tides Lodge is more casual. Visiting privileges between the two establishments can be arranged. The Lodge has a full service marina; the Inn has a few boat slips, but rates at the Inn include yacht luncheon cruises aboard the *Miss Ann*, and cove cruises abroad the *High Tide III*. The Inn has a par-3 golf course on the grounds, and owns the Golden Eagle, an 18-hole golf course and restaurant, a few miles away." *(SHW)*

The Tides Inn   *Tel:* 804–438–5000
King Carter Drive, 22480   800–843–3746

"This was our third visit to the Tides, and I relax as soon as I get in the door. A new feature of the inn is a greeter, who meets you at the door, ascertains your needs, and tries to smooth your way. We arrived just in time for the yacht luncheon cruise, and Joyce—the greeter—took care of everything. When we returned from the cruise, the luggage was in our room and the car was parked under a tree and locked.

"The yacht experience is always wonderful. The boat is outfitted in such a way that everyone can have the amount of sun, wind, and temperature they prefer, from totally protected to totally open, with various stages in between. The cove cruise is equally delightful. The employees are genuinely concerned with your happiness and the other guests are usually friendly. Other favorite moments were spent in some of the inn's lovely public rooms, doing needlework, writing postcards, and talking. Glass walls face the view of the Rappahannock River, and the manicured lawns and gardens sloping down to the water really make for a perfect setting. While we were in the living room the first afternoon, Joyce brought us some iced tea, an unexpectedly thoughtful touch in a resort this size.

"Our rooms were pleasant, medium-sized, with hotel variety antique reproductions and standard hotel-style tiled baths. The bathroom amenities were from Lord & Mayfair, and the beds were triple sheeted with down pillows. The twice-daily maid and turndown service was provided without fail while we were at breakfast and dinner.

"The main building is divided into the Main Wing, the East Wing, and the Garden House; nearly all rooms face the water. The East Wing and the Garden House are newer, with better sound-proofing and in-room TVs. The Windsor House and the Lancaster House are at the rear of the property, and are more luxurious, with balconies and larger bathrooms, some with sunken tubs. Best of all is the Lee Suite, with a living room done in Oriental rugs, a mahogany Chippendale breakfront, burgundy velvet wing chairs and cream-colored sofas; the bedroom has two four-poster beds and a huge marble bathroom with whirlpool tub.

"The food is exceptional. Exquisite selections, such as lobster Thermidor, shrimp with crab Imperial, veal medallions, and soft shell crabs—and no surcharges. Overall, their motto of 'quiet quality' holds true." *(Susan W. Schwemm, also Francis Barron)*

"This small resort appeals to families who enjoy tenis, golf, and the beach. Simple, genteel atompshere with Southern charm. Sports-filled days and early nights. Excellent service and first-rate children's programs." *(MDS)*

One tiny niggle: "Although our waitress was lovely, we thought that a few of the others could have been friendlier."

Open All year.
Rooms 111 suites, doubles & singles in 3 buildings—all with full private bath, telephone, air-conditioning. Some with TV, balcony. 1 suite with whirlpool tub. Television available on request in some units.
Facilities Dining rooms, lounge, lobby with entertainment nightly, recreation center, gift shop, clothing shops. Par-3 golf course, 4 tennis courts, shuffleboard, croquet, horseshoes, saltwater swimming pool, sail and paddle boats, canoes, freshwater fishing, yacht cruises, summer children's program. Complimentary van service to 36-hole championship course 2.5 m away. Valet service.
Location E VA, Tidewater region. From Irvington, go W on Rte. 634 (King Carter Dr.) 1/4 m to inn.
Credit cards Amex, MC, Visa.
Rates Full board, $240–270 double, $130–215 single. Extra person in room, $45–60. MAP rates available.
Extras Pets permitted by prior arrangement, $5.

The Tides Lodge   *Tel:* 804–438–6000
1 St. Andrews Lane, P.O. Box 55, 22480   800–24–TIDES

The Tides is an attractive resort, well known for its challenging championship golf course, relaxing atmosphere, good food, and comfortable accommodations. A full program of activities is offered daily. Rates include nearly everything except for golf. A one-to-one ratio of staff to guests ensures attentive service. Rooms are furnished in traditional comfort, most with balconies overlooking the river.

"E.A. Stephens and his staff have created a feeling of welcome, comfort, and relaxation. Somehow he has instilled in his staff a sincere desire to serve and comfort the guests. There is no question that the tone, style, and ambiance of the place comes from the top, but it is expressed by everyone from the doorman to the front desk, to the day and night maids, the wait staff and maintenance crews. Everyone has a warm smile that clearly communicates their desire to make your stay special. The beautifully landscaped grounds border on the banks of Carter's Creek, with fantastic views across the marina docks toward the historic Rappahannock River and Chesapeake Bay. The mixture of sail and motor boats and guest rooms bring interesting folks of all sorts, from families to golfers to retirees.

"The food is wonderful. My waistline tugs at the thought of their honey buns, their 'anything-you-want breakfasts,' and dinners from a menu that changes daily. Even the hamburgers served by the heated freshwater pool are marvelous. Extra temptations include the sandwiches served by the saltwater pool and all sorts of goodies in the Ice Cream Parlor. Extras include the sunsets seen from the decks of the *Binnacle* and the dinner cruises on the *High Tide II*. The wonderful golf course was started in 1959 by Sir Guy Campbell, resident architect of the Royal and Ancient in St. Andrews, Scotland." *(Norman Block)*

Open Mid-March through Jan.
Rooms 4 suites, 60 doubles—all with full private bath, telephone, TV, desk. Some with radio, most with balcony. Rooms in 3 buildings.
Facilities Dining room with evening dancing, lobby, game room, bar, pro shop, yacht cruises. 175 acres with 18-hole golf course, 9-hole par-3 course, heated freshwater swimming pool, saltwater pool, sauna, 3 (lighted) tennis courts, marina, fishing, boating, sailing, bicycling, putting green, horseshoes, croquet, shuffleboard. Children's programs, playground.
Location E VA. Northern Neck; Tidewater area. 60 m E of Richmond. 8 m from Chesapeake Bay. From Irvington, take Rte. 200 N, go left (W) on Rte. 646, left again on Rte. 709, left again to lodge.
Restrictions No smoking in some guest rooms.
Credit cards MC, Visa.
Rates All rates per person. MAP, $171–179 suite, $95–114 double, $145–193 single, plus optional 15% service. Children free Sun.–Thurs.; charged by age x $2 on Fri., Sat. Room only, per person, $146–154 suite, $70–78 double, $105–121 single. Extra person (over age 17) in room, $45. Alc lunch, $7–10; alc dinner, $30. Golf, honeymoon, midweek packages.
Extras Some rooms wheelchair accessible. Small pets permitted in some rooms, $8. Crib, babysitting available. Airport/station pickups, $60.

LEXINGTON

Lexington is a nineteenth-century town with a handsome historic district and the homes of both Robert E. Lee and Stonewall Jackson; Washington and Lee University and Virginia Military Institute are also located here. Nearby attractions include Natural Bridge and the Blue Ridge Parkway.

Lexington is in the Shenandoah Valley, in the western part of Virginia, 54 miles northeast of Roanoke, and 69 miles southwest of Charlottesville.

Information please: Long listed in this guide but one from which we have had little reader feedback is the **McCampbell Inn** (11 North Main Street, 24450; 703–463–2044), one of three Lexington inns owned by Peter Meredith and his family; the others are the Alexander Withrow House, just across the street, and Maple Hall, a short distance from town. Listed on the National Register of Historic Places, the three properties range in age from 140 to 200 years, and all have been fully restored as country inns, with many antiques and historic paintings. Rates include a continental breakfast and afternoon wine; dinners are served at Maple Hall. Comments, please?

Fassifern B&B *Tel:* 703–463–1013
Virginia Route 39, RR 5, Box 87, 24450

Under the ownership of Pat and Jim Tichenor, Fassifern was a real favorite of our readers. The Tichenors have moved on to another B&B called Oak Spring Farm & Vineyard (see listing under Raphine in this chapter). The new owner, Frances Smith, with her daughter and son-in-law Ann Carol and Arthur Perry as innkeepers, seem to be off to a good start. Fassifern dates back to 1867, although it was built on the foundations of a much older building. Guests enjoy wandering about the grounds or sitting on the dock watching the wildlife on and in the pond. Rates include a breakfast of freshly squeezed orange juice, homemade granola, fresh fruit, strawberry preserves, a variety of home-baked breads, muffins, yeast rolls, or croissants, and a baked custard or bread pudding.

"Although the house is over 120 years old and filled with antiques, it was like walking into a brand-new home because everything was fully restored and in mint condition. The stairway, which rises to the third floor, is a showpiece. Thick, thick towels, lace-edged sheets, beautiful four-poster twin beds in our room. Elegant breakfast on china dishes, heavy solid gleaming silver." *(MW)*

"Our Austrian room on the second floor had ornate walnut twin beds with good firm mattresses and matching period furniture. The private bath was fresh and sparkling clean with soft fluffy towels." *(Arlyne & Colette Craighead)* "Stunning dark woodwork, great layout. Our third-floor room had a little sitting room with interesting magazines and wonderful nooks and crannies, perfect for curling up with a book. Be sure to read the history book on Fassifern in the living room." *(BLK)* "The location in the country by a pond is within minutes of downtown Lexington." *(John Roberts)*

"Ann Carol, Arthur and Frances were always able to offer helpful sightseeing suggestions as well as engaging conversation. Breakfast was sumptuous with fresh fruits and freshly baked scones. We found our room to be clean, spacious, and attractively appointed with antique oak furniture." *(Dennis & Alice Davis)* "The ideal inn setting complete with Victorian home, fine furnishings and careful attention to every need of the guests. The proprietors are extremely attentive and concerned that one's stay be as pleasant and carefree as possible." *(Caroline Martin)*

Open All year.
Rooms 5 doubles—all with private bath and/or shower, radio, air-conditioning. 1 with deck. 2 rooms in cottage.
Facilities Parlor, dining room. 3½ acres with gardens, pond, pasture. Swimming, fishing nearby.
Location 2 m from center. From I-64, take Exit 13 to Rte. 11 N. Go 50 yds., and turn W (left) on Rte. 39 toward Goshen. Inn is ¾ m on left.
Restrictions Light sleepers should request rooms away from road. No smoking.

Credit cards Amex, MC, Visa.
Rates B&B, $75 double, $60 single. Extra person in room, $15.

Llewellyn Lodge   *Tel:* 703–463–3235
603 South Main Street (Route 11 South), 24450

Ellen Roberts opened the Llewellyn Lodge as a B&B in her eclectically
furnished 1930s-era home in 1985. She notes that after twenty years in
the travel and hospitality business, she feels she is well aware of travelers' needs. "My aim is to have an inn that I would want to stay at
myself. Judging by the number of repeat guests and referrals, I think
I'm achieving this goal. It's also fun to convert motel travelers into B&B
travelers, which I've done often." Her husband John is a native Lexing-
tonian, familiar with area hiking and bicycling trails, and where the fish
are hiding. Guests are welcomed with a refreshing drink, and breakfast
might include omelets or Belgian waffles with Virginia maple syrup,
sausage, bacon, and blueberry muffins.

"Ellen is a friendly, warm, relaxed, helpful, and interesting hostess.
Her home is spacious and comfortable. After settling into our room we
and other guests enjoyed refreshments and conversation in the living
room. Parking is ample, and all major attractions are within walking
distance." *(Bill & Angela Moreau)*

"My room was a bit on the small side but was well furnished. A
traditional full breakfast was made to order; it was well prepared and
served in a dining room with views of the neighborhood. The morning's
copy of the *Washington Post* was an appreciated accompaniment to breakfast." *(James Utt)* "Completely lived up to your description. The owners
are warm, friendly people. The accommodations are excellent, the
breakfasts outstanding." *(Suzanne & George Zivic)*

Open All year.
Rooms 6 doubles—all with private bath and/or shower, radio, air-conditioning,
fan. 1 with TV, 1 with desk.
Facilities Living room with fireplace, dining room, TV room, patio, picnic table.
Maury River & Goshen Pass nearby for swimming, fishing; hiking on the 7-mile
Chessie Nature Trail.
Location 8-min. walk to historic district. From I-81, take Rte. 11 S to inn.
Restrictions No smoking in dining room or guest rooms. No children under 6.
Credit cards Amex, MC, Visa.
Rates B&B, $55–70 double, $45–60 single. Extra person in room, $10. $5 senior
discount.
Extras Station pickups.

LURAY

Information please: Previously listed in this guide but lacking in cur-
rent reader feedback is **The Ruffner House & The Cottage** (Stonewall
Jackson Highway, Route 4, Box 620, 22835; 703–743–7855), built by
Luray's first settler, Peter Ruffner, for his family in 1739 (his other claim
to fame is that he discovered a cavern opposite the famous Luray
Caverns). Rooms in The Ruffner House are decorated formally with

Victorian antiques, while those in the adjacent cottage have a more relaxed country decor. Rates include a full breakfast of eggs, pancakes, or French toast, breakfast meats, homemade breads, juice, coffee, and tea. More comments, please.

Big Meadows Lodge
Tel: 703–999–2211 (in-season)
703–743–5108 (off-season)
ARA Virginia Skyline Company
Milepost 51.3, P.O. Box 727, 22835

Big Meadows Lodge is one of the two lodging concessions on the Skyline Drive, within the Shenandoah National Park. The other (also in Luray) is Skyland, described in the following pages. Reservations for either must be made months in advance. Big Meadows takes its name from its setting on a high plateau looking down over the Shenandoah Valley. The rustic main lodge is built of wormy chestnut with floors of flagstone and oak; a dining room and bar provide local cuisine and beverages. Miles of hiking trails provide breathtaking views, cool waterfalls, and fields of wildflowers; tours by horse drawn wagon are also available. Evening campfire programs are provided for both entertainment and information. "Huge dining room, friendly staff, fabulous hearty breakfast in a gorgeous mountain setting." *(Carol Moritz)*

Open Mid-May through October.
Rooms Suites, doubles, and cabins—all with private bath. Some with TV. Rooms in main lodge, motel facility.
Facilities Restaurant, bar, lobby with fireplace, TV lounge, mountain craft shop, patio. Ranger talks, wagon rides, hiking.
Location W VA, Shenandoah Valley. At mile 51.3 of Skyline Drive.
Credit cards MC, Visa.
Rates Room only (for 2 persons), $55–63 cabin, $86–92 suite, $39–72 double. Extra person in room, $5. Rollaway bed, $5.

Shenandoah Countryside
Tel: 703–743–6434
Route 2, Box 370, 22835

A custom-designed farmhouse, this small B&B has been owned by Phel and Bob Jacobsen since 1980, who note that "guests are treated as personal friends and members of the family. Our home is located in the shadow of the Blue Ridge Mountains and Shenandoah National Park."

"As you drive up the winding driveway, you have a feeling of relaxation and comfort. Phel and Bob Jacobsen greeted us, and gave us a tour of their lovely new brick home. There are three porches overlooking the Shenandoah Valley; the views are breathtaking. Our upstairs room had walnut twin beds, an overhead fan, and fresh flowers. They even provided us with attractive robes and slippers, since our private bath was across the hall. The bathroom was roomy, had a nice old claw foot tub, with decorative country touches. Phel has a way of coordinating her colors perfectly. Breakfast was served in the lovely dining room, with outstanding valley views. Table settings were so attractive. We were served a waffle topped with sliced banana, fresh peaches, a scoop of cottage cheese, and a sprig of freshly cut mint. We had our second and third waffles plain, topped with Vermont maple syrup. Freshly squeezed orange juice was combined with cranberry and raspberry juices—this ideal combination is Bob's speciality. A perfect B&B." *(Arlene & Colette Craighead)*

Open All year.
Rooms 3 doubles—1 with private bath, 2 rooms sharing 2 baths. 1 room with desk. All with fan.
Facilities Living room, dining room, keeping room, screened porches, deck, recreation room, Finnish sauna. 45 acres with gardens, hammocks, swings, Christmas tree farm, walking trails, bicycles. River and reservoir nearby for water sports. Horseback riding nearby.
Location 4 m SE of Luray.
Restrictions No smoking. No children under 10.
Credit cards None accepted.
Rates B&B, $65 double, $55 single. Extra person in room, $20. No tipping. 2-night minimum holiday weekends, foliage season.
Extras Local airport pickups.

Skyland Lodge   *Tel:* 703–743–5108 (off-season)
ARA Virginia Skyline Company   703–999–2211 (in-season)
Milepost 41.7, P.O. Box 727, 22835

Skyland is one of the two lodging concessions on the Skyline Drive, within the Shenandoah National Park. The other is Big Meadows Lodge (also in Luray), described earlier. Reservations for either must be made months in advance.

"The lodge is rustic, with stone fireplaces (with fires!) and pine paneling; all modern conveniences such as private full bath and heat are present. Most rooms offer a spectacular view of the Shenandoah Valley, and many have a balcony for viewing the sunset and stars. There are no televisions or phones in the rooms. While there, one can easily forget civilization and enjoy nature. There are many trails for hiking. The dining room offers excellent cuisine. I recommend the trout, catfish, and London broil.

"The rooms are clean and comfortable and the hot water is hot! The employees are helpful and courteous. The lodge is designed to be rustic and outdoorsy, so the outdoor lighting and parking in some areas is not too good. The more secluded rooms require a short walk to your car; others have parking right at the door. We like to go in October when the foliage is at its best, but I understand that spring is delightful also." *(Pamela Proffitt)* More comments please.

Open Late March through mid-Dec.
Rooms Suites with fireplaces; cabins, doubles, singles—all with private bath. Some with TV.
Facilities Restaurant, bar with entertainment. Ranger talks, hiking, fishing, canoeing, horseback riding, play areas.
Location W VA, Shenandoah Valley. On Skyline Drive, Mile 41.7
Credit cards MC, Visa.
Rates Room only (for 2 persons), $63–120 suite, $34–70 cabins, $48–76 double. Extra person in room, $5. Rollaway bed, $5. Early Bird, Harvest, Yuletide packages.

MIDDLEBURG

The Red Fox Inn and Tavern   *Tel:* 703–687–6301
2 East Washington Street   Outside VA: 800–223–1728
P.O. 385, 22117

In 1728, Joseph Chinn built this tavern, known then as Chinn's Ordinary. In 1812, the tavern was enlarged and its name changed to the Beveridge House. During the Civil War, the tavern also served as a hospital; the pine bar in the Tap Room was made from an operating table. The name was changed to the Red Fox in 1937, and in 1976, Turner Reuter, Jr. took over the inn and began a major renovation effort. The nearby Stray Fox Inn and McConnell House date back to the 19th century and are decorated with period reproductions; guests preferring a quieter atmosphere should request rooms in either one. The latest addition to the hostelry is the Middleburg Inn, immediately adjacent to the Red Fox, with guest rooms on the second floor above a fine jewelry shop. Rates include continental breakfast.

"We had a lovely room with a working fireplace, pleasantly furnished with reproduction pieces. There was a *Washington Post* outside our door each morning and a dish of chocolate truffles and fresh fruit slices left by the bedside each night. We ate dinner downstairs at a table next to the fireplace, which gave the room a wonderful atmosphere. Our meal was very good and the service friendly. The town of Middleburg is charming, and the surrounding countryside lovely, with rolling hills and thoroughbred horse farms, and very convenient to DC." *(Barbara Hornbach)*

"Delightful, elegant yesteryear inn, which fully measured up to its reputation. Our room was quaint, the bath complete with a bidet, tub, and shower. A delicious dinner was served in an appealing tavern-type dining room." *(Hope Welliver)*

Open All year.
Rooms 8 suites, 15 doubles—all with private bath and/or shower, telephone, radio, TV, desk, air-conditioning. Most with canopy bed; 9 with fireplace. 1 suite with screened porch. 17 of the rooms are in the nearby Stray Fox Inn, McConnell House & Middleburg Inn.
Facilities Restaurant, bar, pub, terraces. Riding lessons, ballooning trips, equestrian events and activities nearby.
Location NE VA, Loudoun County (horse country). 50 min. W of Washington, DC, 30 min. W of Dulles Int'l. Airport, 35 min. E of Winchester. Center of town.
Restrictions Light sleepers should request rooms in Stray Fox Inn or McConnell House.
Credit cards Amex, MC, Visa.
Rates B&B, $150–225 suite, $125–140 double. Extra person in room, $25. 15% gratuity suggested. Alc lunch, $15; alc dinner, $40–50; smaller portions for children under 12.
Extras Limited wheelchair accessibility. Crib, cot available by advance notice, $10–25.

MIDDLETOWN

Wayside Inn Since 1797
7783 Main Street, 22645

Tel: 703–869–1797

The Wayside served as a stagecoach stop through much of the nineteenth century. It was used by soldiers from both the North and South during the Civil War, and thus was saved from destruction, even though Stonewall Jackson's famous Valley Campaign swept past only a few miles away. The two side wings and the third floor date to the early 1900s, when owner Samuel Rhodes changed the inn's name to the Wayside.

Meals still feature colonial-era favorites—peanut soup, spoon bread, prime rib, country ham, pan-fried chicken, served with fresh vegetables and homemade breads and dessert.

"Filled with antiques. We slept in a high rope bed, and our bath had bars of lavender soap and lots of thick new towels. Beautiful antique-filled dining rooms serving original colonial foods. A great place to stay." *(Mrs. Peter Payne, also JL)* Reports needed.

Open All year.
Rooms 2 suites, 20 doubles—all with private bath and/or shower, telephone, desk, air-conditioning.
Facilities 3 dining rooms, sun-room, sitting room, den with TV, library, bar/lounge. 2 acres with patio. Hiking, swimming, fishing, boating, golfing, skiing nearby.
Location N VA, Shenandoah Valley. Approx. 70 m W of Washington, DC. At crossroads of I-81 (Exit 77) & Rte. 11.
Restrictions Light sleepers should request rooms in back.
Credit cards Amex, DC, MC, Visa.
Rates Room only, $125 suite, $70–110 double. Extra person in room, $20. Children under 12 free. 10% AARP discount. Alc lunch, $7; alc dinner, $36.
Extras Ground floor rooms for handicapped. Cribs, babysitting available. Spanish, French spoken.

MILLBORO

Fort Lewis Lodge
HRC 3, Box 21A, 24460

Tel: 703–925–2314

Located on 3,200 acres in the Allegheny Highlands and adjoining George Washington National Forest, the Fort Lewis Lodge encompasses a Black Angus cattle farm, complete with 1850s gristmill and a renovated silo with glassed-in observation tower. The new lodge building, designed and built by owners John and Caryl Cowden, provides views of the spectacular scenery from both the gathering room and the large deck; the compact guest rooms have handcrafted cherry and oak furniture accented with quilts, country plaid blankets, and rag rugs. John reports that "guests enjoy miles of marked hiking trails, bicycling on country roads, river fishing for trout and small-mouth bass, wildlife observation, and great home cooking." They also outfit guests for over-night camping trips and, during the fall months, provide programs for deer and turkey hunting. Rates include breakfast and dinner; blueberry pancakes are a breakfast favorite, while dinners feature their own beef, lamb, or fish. Families are most welcome; the Cowden's three kids—ages 4–10—will happily invite young guests to join them for farm chores like collecting eggs.

"The lodge is beautifully built, finely appointed and immaculately maintained; the food is hearty and delicious; and the owners bend over backwards to make their guests feel welcome. It is quiet, peaceful and wonderfully refreshing." *(Bill O'Connor)*

"The owners, John and Caryl, offer their guests the run of a working farm that includes nearly a mile of scenic riverfront and fishing waters that yield red-eye bass for kids with cane poles, and small-mouth bass and trout for those with fly rods. During the fall season, the lodge draws hunters for wild turkey, deer and bear, with guide service arranged. Bambi lovers can take a careful walk through the woods or an early-evening drive along the country roads for the pleasure of seeing several buck deer, or—if you're lucky—a small flock of wild turkeys. For the less adventuresome, there are the domesticated sheep that roam the hillsides.

"Next door in a restored 1850s gristmill, meals are served buffet-style, with an interesting choice of both domestic and imported wine. You can watch Caryl prepare the meals from your table. We forgot to make arrangements for lunch our first day. When John overheard our predicament, he helped us conduct a raid of the kitchen, making us deer sausage sandwiches. The inn is located only minutes away from the posh Homestead at Hot Springs, but is twice the fun at 1/3 the price. He also introduced us to a fox breeder, who invited us to meet his pet fox and see his other 50, and a taxidermist who showed us his shop." *(MG)*

Open May to Oct.

Rooms 12 doubles—8 with private bath and/or shower, 4 with a maximum of 4 people sharing bath. All with radio, desk, fan.

Facilities Gathering room, deck, observation tower. 3,200 acres with river, swimming pond, woodland, hiking, camping, fishing (catch & release basis). 30 min. to downhill skiing.

Location W VA, Allegheny Highlands. 60 min. W of Lexington, Staunton. From Staunton, go W on Hwy. 254 (at railroad underpass) to Buffalo Gap. Go straight on Rte. 42 S for 29 m to Millboro Springs. Take Rte. 39 W for .7 m and turn right on Rte. 678. Follow Rte. 678 for 10.8 m and turn left on Rte. 625. Go .2 m to sign on left.

Restrictions No smoking in guest rooms.

Credit cards MC, Visa.

Rates MAP, $95–110 double, $75 single. Extra adult in room, $25; extra child under age 12, $15. 10% service. Weekend packages. Prix fixe lunch, $5–7.

Extras Crib available.

MILLWOOD

Brookside B&B   *Tel: 703–837–1780*
Route 723, 22646

Built in 1780 by the great-grandson of "King" Carter (of Carter's Grove in Williamsburg), Brookside offers an intimate retreat in the historic village of Millwood, just adjacent to the millrace and behind the restored Burwell-Morgan Mill. Located in the heart of Hunt Country, the region is noted for its antique shops, auctions, flea markets and proximity to Virginia vineyards. Rooms are decorated with 18th century antiques and reproductions, with queen-size featherbeds (hypoallergenic), down duvets, canopied beds, and working fireplaces. Rates include full breakfast and evening turndown service with antique nightgowns provided.

"The Brookside has what we truly favor: a historic atmosphere in a wonderfully restored 18th century mill owner's house; warm and welcoming hosts Gary and Carol Konkel; fine detailing and furniture, including authentic canopy beds and working fireplaces in all the rooms; and a special breakfast prepared by the hosts. Crossing random-width flooring in order to start a roaring blaze in the fireplace, then crawling back to the soft cloud of the featherbed is our idea of delight." *(Louis Moriconi)*

Open All year.
Rooms 1 cabin, 4 doubles—all with private bath and/or shower, air-conditioning, fireplace.
Facilities Dining room with fireplace, common room with fireplace. 5 acres with herb garden, stream. Tennis, golf, bike route, wineries, antique shops nearby.
Location N VA, Hunt Country, Shenandoah Valley. 60 m W of Washington, DC. In center of town. From Washington go W I-66 to Exit 5. Go N on Rte. 17 to Paris and turn left at blinking light onto Rte. 50. Cross Shenandoah River and take second right marked Boyce/Millwood (Rte. 723). Continue 1¼ m on Rte. 723 to Millwood. Cross bridge and look for Burwell-Morgan Mill immediately on your left. Turn left into mill lot and cross millrace bridge at far end to inn on right.
Restrictions No smoking. No children.
Credit cards Choice, MC, Visa.
Rates B&B, $120 cabin, $95–120 double, $85–110 single. 10% senior discount on request.

MOLLUSK

Greenvale Manor   *Tel: 804–462–5995*
Route 354, Box 70, 22517

The Northern Neck was one of the earliest regions to be settled by English colonists; Captain John Smith sailed up the Rappahannock River in 1607, and described the area as a "fruitful and delightsome land." In 1651 the area known as Fair Weather Neck was deeded to

Anthony Stephens. In 1840 Greenvale Manor was built of cypress with oak joists, resting on the foundations of an earlier house. The Dezendorf family owned the manor from the 1930s to the 1960s, and did much to expand and modernize it, adding a wing to each end of the house, and building the cottages and swimming pool. Little had been done since then to maintain the house, so when Pam and Walt Smith moved from Connecticut and bought Greenvale Manor in 1987, they became full-time painters, sanders, paper-hangers, and landscapers. They've done a lovely job of decorating the rooms with antiques and reproductions, highlighted by Pam's homemade curtains and heirloom quilts. Rates include a full country breakfast of eggs, pancakes, fruit and juice, bacon or sausage. Weekend packages are available; especially popular are those during the summer when a crab dinner is served picnic-style.

The manor is bordered by both the Rappahannock River and Greenvale Creek; guests enjoy the sandy beach on the former, and the dock for fishing and crabbing at the latter. "Captain" Walt charters his Chesapeake Deadrise boat; the design of the boat is unique to the Chesapeake Bay oystering and fishing community—a special flare of the bow minimizes spray in choppy water. Pam reports that many of their guests bring their own "toys," such as small sailboats, canoes, power boats to use on the waterfront.

"The area is completely rural, but there is a lot to do. Several nice restaurants are within a short drive. There are loads of places to hike, including the beach along the river. But the real draw is two-fold—the inn itself and its 19th-century splendor, and its owners, Walter and Pamela Smith. Our favorite room is the Greenvale Suite with its view of the river." *(Gertraud & Frederic Wagner III)*

"A beautiful place in a peaceful location. Food, comfort, cleanliness, and plumbing are all excellent. The Smiths are wonderful people, very warm and truly concerned for their guests' welfare." *(Midge & Hal Mahler)* "The rooms, baths, game room, and sun porch all make you feel comfortable, relaxed, and 'at home.' Our biggest problem was remembering *not* to make the beds." *(Arthur Schatz)* "Breakfast, served on the porch overlooking the river, is a highlight with the innkeepers constantly trying out new recipes." *(Doug & Mary Jo Smith, also Roger & Sandra Will)*

Open All year.
Rooms 5 suites, 5 doubles—7 with private bath and/or shower, 2 with a maximum of 4 people sharing bath. All with air-conditioning. Some with desk, fan. 2 suites with fireplace, 1 suite with kitchen. 2 suites, 3 rooms in 2 cottages; 1 of the cottages with kitchen, living room.
Facilities Dining room with fireplace, living room with fireplace, game room with TV/VCR, games, fireplace; screened veranda. 13 acres with swimming pool, bicycles, badminton, croquet, nature trails, private beach and dock, crabbing; power boat for charters.
Location E VA, Northern Neck. 70 m E of Richmond, 65 m N of Williamsburg, approx 90 m S of Washington DC. 15 min. from town. From Washington, take I-95 S to Fredericksburg, then Bypass Rte. 17 S to Tappahannock, E on Rte. 360 to Warsaw. Then take Rte. 3 E to Lively, right on 201, left on 354. Go 2 m to inn on right.

Restrictions No smoking in guest rooms. No children.
Credit cards None accepted.
Rates B&B, $90 suite, $65–80 double. 2-night minimum holiday weekends. Weekend packages.

MONTEREY

Highland Inn   *Tel:* 703–468–2143
Main Street, P.O. Box 40, 24465

At the turn of the century, travelers came to the mountains of western Virginia to enjoy the cool climate and spring waters. Monterey is a village of 300 people and is surrounded by three million acres of National Forest. The county seat of Highland County, it's known as "little Switzerland." "The total county population of under 3,000 is less than a typical Washington-area high school. Sheep clearly outnumber people in this pastoral setting." *(Joanne Harkleroad)*

Built as a resort in 1904, the Highland is now listed on the National Register of Historic Places, and has been owned by Joanne and John Crow since 1987. In its heyday, guests ranged from Henry Ford and Harvey Firestone to Eric Rommel (the "Desert Fox"), who stayed in the hotel in the late thirties when researching the battle tactics of Confederate General Stonewall Jackson. A three-story frame Victorian with a two-level porch, the Highland features guest rooms furnished with Victorian antiques and some four-poster and canopy beds; rates include a light continental breakfast.

"John and Joanne Crow and their staff are never too busy to visit, never too tired to help, and never too harassed to attend to a guest's request. On one visit we arrived after the dining room and stores in town were closed for the night. Management made sure we had a snack before retiring." *(Philip Ranck)*

"This is the genuine article—a real turn-of-the-century Victorian inn complete with gingerbread porches, pot-bellied stoves, and antique-furnished rooms with modern conveniences.

"The inn's dining room is a favorite gathering spot for local gentry. Local beef, pork, and fowl, as well as mountain trout and catfish, are served along with a generous soup and salad bar. The Crows' trademark is the fresh melon assortment that they miraculously provide 12 months a year. Their desserts are the despair of any calorie counter, with toll house, maple walnut, and blueberry pie among my favorites. The service is as good as the food. The waitresses are polite, friendly, and always at your service—never an empty coffee cup or water glass." *(Capt. & Mrs. Alexander Barton)*

"Every room is furnished with country antiques, stencils on the walls, and a lovely quilt collection. The owners are warm, pleasant people who know how to run an inn, yet are willing to help you in any way they can." *(Nancy Weber)* "A cozy atmosphere, country charm and true Southern hospitality—which in today's society is difficult to find—is alive and well at the Highland Inn." *(Bill & Cynthia LaRue)*

"You can literally fall asleep counting the sheep on the hillside outside the window. A dozen excellent trout steams are within a 15-minute drive, but if you don't know where to go, the owners can easily advise you. The dining room is this county seat's gathering place for local farmers and politicians. Rooms are modest, but so are the prices." *(MG)*

And another opinion: "Please remind your readers of the old adage: 'You get what you pay for.' The Highland has real country charm, but don't expect $100-a-night amenities when you're paying $50."

Open All year.
Rooms 3 suites, 17 doubles, 2 singles—all with private bath and/or shower, fan; some with TV, desk.
Facilities Dining room; bar/lounge with TV, weekend entertainment; banquet room, wraparound porches. Boating, fishing, skiing, hiking, golf, and cave exploring nearby. On-site parking.
Location Western VA, Allegheny Mts., near WV border. Approx. 140 m NW of Richmond, VA; 40 m W of Staunton, VA; 170 m E of Charleston, WV. At intersection of Rte. 250 & Rte. 220.
Restrictions No smoking in dining room.
Credit cards MC, Visa.
Rates B&B, $49–75 suite, $39–55 double, $35–55 single. Extra person in room, $5. 15% service additional. 2-night weekend minimum. Alc breakfast, $3; alc lunch, $4–5; alc dinner, $15.
Extras Crib, babysitting upon request.

MOUNTAIN LAKE

Mountain Lake
State Route 700, 24136

Tel: 703–626–7121
800–346–3334

The present Mountain Lake hotel was constructed in 1936, replacing a 19th-century stagecoach inn. By 1986, its longtime owner and managers had decided it was time to modernize the inn—rooms were redecorated in an elegant, traditional thirties look, new rooms and facilities were built, and, for the first time, the massive stone building stayed open through the winter. The same year, the movie *Dirty Dancing* was filmed here.

"To Mountain Lake 's picture-postcard setting (beside a 23-acre natural lake at an elevation of 4,000 feet, surrounded by mountains), renovation of the interior has brought relaxing comfort and aesthetically pleasing decor. In the dining room, with windows facing the lake, we were served meals delicious in flavor and ample in quantity. And, in spite of its rural seclusion, the hotel is less than 45 minutes from each of two interstate highways." *(Whitfield Cobb)*

Additional reports welcomed.

Open All year.
Rooms 5 suites, 50 doubles, 17 singles, 16 1–3 bedroom cabins—all with full private bath, TV, fan. Some rooms with fireplace, whirlpool tubs.
Facilities Restaurant, parlor/library, card room, TV rooms (1 with VCR), gift shops, recreation barn with pool tables, games, Ping-Pong, video games; pub, health spa with sauna, whirlpool tub, exercise equipment. Evening activities include ballroom dancing, bingo, wine tasting, casino nights, movies. 23-acre lake

with beach for swimming, fishing, boating; 2,500 acres with hiking, golf, tennis, croquet, horseback riding, carriage rides, children's play equipment, cross-country skiing, ice-skating, sleigh rides.
Location SW VA, Allegheny Mts., near W VA border. 50 m W of Roanoke. From I-81, take Exit 37 to Rte. 460 W to Blacksburg, then take Rte. 460 Bypass (left fork) to Rte. 700. Follow Rte. 700 for 7 m to hotel.
Restrictions Casual dress is not permitted after 7 P.M.
Credit cards Amex, CB, Choice, DC, MC, Visa.
Rates MAP (for 2 people), $170–230 suite, $140–150 double, $95–185 single. For 1–3 bedroom cabin, MAP $125–340. Children age 4 & younger, no charge; children age 5–11, $20; children age 12 and over, $35. $5.50 per person daily service charge. 2-night weekend minimum. Children's menu available from 5–7 P.M.
Extras Airport/station pickups. Spanish spoken. Cribs, babysitting available.

MOUNT CRAWFORD

Mount Crawford is located in the Shenandoah Valley of western Virginia, between Harrisonburg and Staunton, about 130 miles west of Washington, D.C. It's a good base for visiting one of the four area colleges—James Madison University, Bridgewater College, Eastern Mennonite College, and Mary Baldwin College, and makes a good center for touring other area attractions in Staunton, Charlottesville, and Luray. Local attractions include horseback riding, canoeing on the Shenandoah River, hiking, and downhill and cross-country skiing.

The Pumpkin House Inn
U.S. Route 11, RR 2, Box 155, 22841

Tel: 703–434–6963

John Craun built this brick home on part of a 120-acre land grant, and it stayed in the hands of his descendants until it was sold at auction in 1941. In 1947, it was bought by the parents of the present innkeepers, brother and sister Tom Kidd and Liz Umstott, and was renovated as an inn in 1986. It's named after the pumpkin patch behind the inn, where pumpkins had been grown for the past 35 years. The inn has wide-board heart-pine floors, carved woodwork, and hand-stenciled walls, and rooms are furnished with antiques (some of which are family heirlooms, while others are for sale). Rates include a continental breakfast, with pumpkin bread a featured favorite.

"An absolutely charming inn in an 1847 restored home located in scenic farm country. Each bedroom has its own beautiful decor—ours was the Quilt Room. Mr. Kidd suggested a nice family restaurant nearby." *(Arlyne & Colette Craighead, also Mrs. Lola Rhea)*

Open All year.
Rooms 7 doubles—3 with private shower, 4 with maximum of 4 sharing bath. 6 with air-conditioning. 4 with fireplace.
Facilities Dining room; lounge with TV, fireplace, library. 43 acres.
Location 4 m S of Harrisonburg, VA. ½ m S of Mt. Crawford on W side of U.S. Rte. 11, between exits 60 and 61 on I-81.
Credit cards Amex, MC, Visa.
Rates B&B, $40–70 double, $35–65 single. Extra person in room, $5.

MOUNT JACKSON

The Widow Kip's Shenandoah Inn   *Tel:* 703–477–2400
Route 698, RR 1, Box 117, 22842

A stately colonial built in 1830, The Widow Kip's has been owned by Rosemary Kip since 1985. Rosemary did a complete renovation—when she bought the house, it had no electricity and minimal plumbing. Now nostalgia and antiques fill the rooms, along with locally-crafted quilts, four-poster, sleigh and Victorian beds, and the original working fireplaces. Two restored cottages, originally a wash house and a hen house, create a charming courtyard with the house. Everything in the inn is for sale, and bears a price tag. Rates include afternoon sherry and a full country breakfast of fruit, eggs, sausage, biscuits or scones, juice and coffee.

"Rosemary Kip is a delightful innkeeper. Each guest room is named for a flower; ours was the Marigold Room, filled with antiques, and with a nice clean bathroom." *(Arlyne & Colette Craighead)* "The ruffled curtains were crisp, the floors glistening, the bathrooms glistening, and the pool sparkling. We could not have been more pleased with both Rosemary and her inn." *(Patricia Pulley)* "We especially enjoyed the apple and peach butters served at breakfast." *(EF)*

Open All year.
Rooms 2 cottages, 5 doubles—all with private bath and/or shower, air-conditioning, fireplace. 3 with desk. 1 suite with kitchenette, TV.
Facilities Living room with fireplace, games; porches, gift shop. 7 acres with swimming pool, gas barbecue grill, horseshoes, bicycles.
Location From I-81, take Mt. Jackson Exit 69 to Rte. 11 S. Go 1.3 miles and turn right onto Rte. 263, then 2nd left onto Rte. 698. Inn is 2nd house on left.
Restrictions No smoking in common rooms. Traffic noise will disturb light sleepers.
Credit cards MC, Visa.
Rates B&B, $70–90 cottage, $60 double. Extra person in room, $7.50. $4 fireplace fee. No tipping. 10% midweek senior discount. Evening snack menu, $3–6.
Extras Pets permitted in cottage. Crib available.

NELLYSFORD

Trillium House   *Tel:* 804–325–9126
Wintergreen Drive,   For reservations (9–5 P.M.) 800–325–9126
P.O. Box 280, 22958

Located near the small town of Nellysford, Wintergreen is a beautiful four-season mountain resort community of 10,000 acres with many condominiums and houses available for both sale and rent. Ed and Betty Dinwiddie designed and built Trillium in 1983, for people who prefer a country inn to a rental condo. Nineteenth-century antiques, reproductions, and contemporary furniture make up the decor.

"The inn has a lovely arched window over the entrance, and lots of wood used inside and out. Just inside the front door is the main living area; a library is located upstairs in a quiet loft setting, and downstairs is a TV room with large-screen television and comfortable chairs and sofas. The dining room seats about forty. The guest rooms are spacious, with all the modern amenities of a nice hotel, including fluffy towels and scented soaps. Dinners are served on weekends, and we found the food to be tasty and a good value. A full breakfast is included in the room rate, and it was hearty and plentiful. Because the Trillium was designed as an inn, many built-in features are excellent: parking facilities, ski racks, great showers, and perfect location for skiing." *(CBG)*

"The rooms are delightful, comfortable, and decorated with tender loving care. Everything is neat and clean. The breakfast room overlooks the trees and golf course; closer to the window are bird feeders attracting numerous and varied birds. The Dinwiddies are helpful and hospitable; they do everything possible to see that every guest is comfortable." *(Corbin White)*

"Just as described. Everyone went out of their way to make us feel welcome. The twice-daily towel service and evening turndown were unexpected and done very unobtrusively. There was always a bowl of fresh fruit and a filled candy dish in the sitting room. Dinner on Friday night was delicious; although the tables were set with linen and candles, the atmosphere was casual and relaxing. The VCR and tapes for the large-screen TV near the woodstove in the sitting area are pleasant on a chilly evening." *(Amy Peritsky)*

Open All year. Dining room open Fri. and Sat. only (single seating at 7:30 P.M.).
Rooms 2 suites, 10 doubles—all with private bath and/or shower, air-conditioning. Some with desk.
Facilities Living room, library, garden room, TV room with VCR. 1½ acres with gazebo, wildflower garden. Wintergreen resort activities available: swimming pools, exercise spa, tennis courts, golf, hiking, fishing, canoeing, horseback riding, downhill skiing.
Location NW VA; Blue Ridge Mts. 3 hrs. SW of Washington, DC. Between mileposts 13 & 14 on Blue Ridge Parkway.
Restrictions Children discouraged.
Credit cards MC, Visa.
Rates B&B, $120–140 suite, $80–90 double, $65–70 single. Extra person in room, $35. 2–3 day peak/holiday weekend minimum. Prix fixe dinner, $22–26.

NORFOLK

Days Hotel Waterside   *Tel:* 804–622–6682
345 Granby Street, 23501   800–522–0976

If you're looking for a place to stay in this Navy city, Days Hotel Waterside, formerly known as Hotel Madison, offers old-fashioned elegance and reasonable rates. Built in 1906, the hotel was the first in Norfolk to have an elevator. The building is decorated in turn-of-the-century style with mahogany and cherry woods, and crystal chandeliers. In 1989 the guest rooms were refurbished with new drapes, bed-spreads, carpets, and lighting.

"On the trolley route, or an easy fifteen-minute walk from the water-front, Days Waterside is an older hotel offering friendly service and neat, clean rooms. Our room was large, with two big windows, a queen-size bed, and ample dresser and desk space. Decor is traditional—not antique but not typical hotel fare either. Large bathroom. We found a great restaurant right nearby, in the renovated historic area, called the Carriage House—terrific food, neighborhood bar." *(Wendi Van Exan)* More comments please.

Open All year.
Rooms 6 suites, 128 doubles—all with private shower and/or bath, telephone, TV, desk, air-conditioning. Some with radio, refrigerator. Parking garage.
Facilities Restaurant, lobby, bar/lounge. Health club, racquet ball.
Location Downtown. On river front. At corner Freemason St., near Granby mall.
Credit cards Amex, CB, Discover, MC, Visa.
Rates Room only, $58–90 suite, $60 double, $55 single. Extra person in room, $5. AARP and September Days Club discounts. Alc dinner $6, alc dinner, $20. Children's menu.
Extras Wheelchair accessible; some rooms equipped for the disabled. Pets per-mitted, $25. Crib, babysitting by arrangement. Airport pickups, $5.

ORANGE

Orange is in north central Virginia, 60 miles southwest of Washington DC, 30 miles northwest of Charlottesville, and 5 miles from Montpelier. From Washington, DC, take I-495 to I-66 west to Route 29 south. Take the Orange exit of Route 29 to Route 15 to Orange.

"This area is rich in history. Montpelier, home of James and Dolley Madison, is ten minutes away and is now open to the public. Ash Lawn, (President James Monroe's home) is about 30 minutes away." *(Carolyn & Bill Myles)*

Information please: The **Mayhurst Inn** (Route 15, P.O. Box 707, 22960; 703–672–5597), an impressive Italianate Victorian mansion, pro-vides B&B guests with an opportunity to explore its fine architecture, most particularly the oval-spiral staircase ascending four floors. Owned since 1982 by Stephen and Shirley Ramsey, the inn has some guest rooms with fireplaces; on Saturday nights a southern-style dinner is served. Although listed in earlier editions, current feedback is needed.

The Hidden Inn   *Tel:* 703–672–3625
249 Caroline Street, 22960

Ray and Barbara Lonick bought the Hidden Inn in 1986, and describe it as being a particular favorite with "young and middle-aged couples

from the Washington, D.C., area who are looking for a romantic getaway. Our inn is quiet, cozy, and a little elegant—there are wicker pieces
on the verandas; Oriental rugs in the public rooms; silver, and lace
tablecloths in the dining room. Our color scheme is rose, white, and
light blue, with lots of fresh flowers."

The decor is largely Victorian, and rooms have brass or canopy beds.
Rates include a full breakfast and afternoon tea. A typical breakfast
might include granola, corn muffins with strawberry jam, grits, eggs,
fried apples, ham, and toast, while the single-entrée dinner offering
might be pâté, cream of broccoli soup, salad, beef chasseur with wild
rice and asparagus, and Oreo cookie cheesecake for dessert.

"Friendly owners Ray and Barbara really try to offer a touch of
old-fashioned elegance. We slept in brass twin beds; they placed a
chocolate on our pillow; breakfast was served in the pretty dining room.
Great service—quiet and peaceful atmosphere." *(Arlyne & Colette Craighead)*

Open All year.
Rooms 4 suites, 5 doubles—all with private bath and/or shower, air-conditioning. 6 with fan, 2 with TV, desk. Suites with Jacuzzi tub. Some rooms in 2
2-bedroom cottages adjacent to inn, with private verandas or living room.
Facilities Dining room, living room with fireplace and TV, wraparound veran-
das. 6 acres with vegetable and rose gardens, gazebo, croquet, horseshoes, and
badminton. 5 m to lake for fishing.
Location N central VA. 30 m N of Charlottesville, 5 m from Montpelier. 3 blocks
from center. From Washington, DC, take I-495 to I-66 W to Rte. 29 S. Take
Orange exit off Rte. 29 S to Rte. 15 to Orange.
Restrictions Morning train might disturb light sleepers. No smoking.
Credit cards MC, Visa.
Rates B&B, $119–139 suite, $79–99 double, $59–79 single. Extra person in room,
$15. 2-night minimum on holiday weekends. Alc dinner $30, plus 15% service.
Picnic lunches.
Extras Spanish spoken.

The Shadows   *Tel:* 703–672–5057
Route 1, Box 535, 22960

A restored 1913 stone house, The Shadows is owned by Barbara and
Pat Loffredo, who have furnished the guestrooms with antiques, lace
curtains and designer bed linens; some bathrooms have the original
claw foot tubs.

"We were greeted with glasses of apple cider. The Shadows is a
beautifully restored farmhouse in immaculate condition. The Loffredos
were perfect hosts who went out of their way to insure that we were
comfortable and enjoying our visit." *(Kinloch McCollum)*

"We stayed in the Victorian Room which was furnished with a white
iron and brass bed with beautiful ruffled sheets and comforter. The
bathroom was scrupulously clean, supplied with toiletries. Breakfast, at
our chosen time, included bananas and strawberries in cream, followed
by stuffed French toast with sausage and fried apples. As we prepared
to leave, Barbara and Pat suggested that we feed a handful of fresh
flowers to their goat who loved them." *(Dana Abdella)*

Open All year.
Rooms 4 doubles—all with private bath and/or shower.
Facilities Breakfast room, living room with fireplace, library; porch with swing. 44 acres with woodland.
Location 3/4 m SW of town on Rte. 20 S.
Credit cards None accepted.
Rates B&B, $70–85 double.

Willow Grove Inn
Route 15 North, 22960

Tel: 703–672–5982

The strong influence of Thomas Jefferson's preference for classic Greek architecture can clearly be seen at the Willow Grove Inn, with its imposing center pediment and four supporting Doric columns. The house dates back to the 1770s, and was originally built in the Federal style, but a brick addition, completed in the early 1800s, doubled its size and gave the house its present look. Now listed on the National Historic Register, and owned by Angela Mulloy since 1987, the house and grounds have been fully restored to their original beauty, with antique furnishings inside, and rolling lawns, formal gardens, magnolias, and willow trees outside. Favorite entrées at the inn's restaurant include Rappahannock trout in lemon butter and game birds with wild rice and mushrooms.

"The house is magnificent, in a beautiful country setting with lovely views all around. Our room, the Washington, was enormous, with six windows, nice old furniture, a splendid bed with lots of pillows, and a working fireplace. The bathroom was equally large with a huge old bath, a sink, and shower. It was all extremely comfortable. The atmosphere was very welcoming and friendly without being obtrusive.

"We had dinner in the candlelit dining room. The staff was helpful and sweet (but not sugary). The food was interesting without being pretentious; they didn't attempt more than they could deliver, and we were happy with everything. There was also a very pleasant music to accompany it—a young man playing the piano and occasionally singing—providing just the right level of sound.

"Breakfast was delivered to the room at the time requested the night before. It was a splendid spread of fresh fruit, yogurt, granola, coffee, and freshly-baked muffins, still warm in their basket. We sat at our table, sipped our coffee, and contemplated the green fields and cows. Angela Mulloy is to be congratulated on her exceptional inn." *(Ellie Freidus, also Hope Welliver)*

Open All year. Restaurant closed Tues., Wed.
Rooms 2 2-bedroom suites, 3 doubles—all with private bath and/or shower, desk, air-conditioning. 3 rooms with fireplace. Telephone on request.
Facilities Restaurant with music on weekends, tavern, music room, TV room. 37 acres with early–19th century formal gardens, barns, outbuildings.
Location On Rte. 15, N of Orange.
Credit cards MC, Visa.
Rates B&B, $105–145 suite, $95–135 double. Extra person in room, $20. Prix fixe brunch, $20. Alc lunch, $8–12; alc dinner, $50; 20% service additional.
Extras Limited wheelchair accessibility. Crib available.

313

VIRGINIA

PARIS

Ashby Inn   *Tel:* 703–592–3900
Route 759, Route 1, Box 2A, 22130

Once called Pun'kinville, this little village took a very small step towards sophistication when the Marquis de Lafayette came to visit in the
late 1700s, and it was renamed Paris in his honor. The inn dates to 1829,
and has been restored by John and Roma Sherman with its Federalist
spirit very much intact. Guest rooms are decorated with early 18th
century antiques and reproductions, including hand-painted ward-
robes, quilts and coverlets, rag and Oriental rugs and blanket chests; all
overlook a hillside where Black Angus and white-tailed deer graze. The
original basement kitchen, with walnut beams and stone fireplace, is
now a taproom, while two upper rooms and an enclosed porch contain
the inn's restaurant. The menu is limited, concentrating on seasonal
foods like asparagus, shad, raspberries, soft shell crab, and game. Breads
and pastas are homemade, much of the produce is homegrown, and
backfin crabcakes are a speciality.

Area activities include horse shows, races, and stable tours, wine
touring in the nearby vineyards, hiking along the Appalachian trail,
fishing and floating on the Shenandoah River.

"A special place, with owners who clearly know what they're doing.
Our large room, the only one with a working fireplace, was furnished
rather sparely but in excellent taste—some simple antiques, two comfortable chairs, a big rag rug, and carefully chosen pictures. The bath
had been nicely done, with sturdy good-quality equipment. The inn has
a most attractive library on the first floor, handsome dining rooms, and
an atmospheric taproom. The food is very good, with lots of game and
well-prepared vegetables. The full breakfast, served between 8 and 10
A.M., was excellent. The Ashby was a fine place to spend a foggy winter
weekend, and is no doubt even nicer in the spring and fall when one
can walk in the lovely surrounding countryside." *(Carolyn Mathiasen)*

"Lovely inn. We ate out of doors under a large awning. Charming
atmosphere, fine food." *(Hope Welliver)*

Open All year. Restaurant closed Mon., Tues., major holidays.
Rooms 6 doubles—4 with private shower and/or bath, 2 sharing 1 bath. All with
air-conditioning. 1 with fireplace.
Facilities Restaurant, library/sitting room with fireplace, taproom, patio, gar-
den. Hiking, fishing, tubing nearby.
Location N VA, Hunt Country, Blue Ridge foothills. 60 m W of Washington,
DC. From I-495 (Beltway), take Rte. 66 W to Exit 5 (Delaplane/Paris). Go 7.5 m
N on Rte. 17, then left on Rte. 701 into village. From Middleburg, take Rte. 50
W. 3 m W of Upperville, turn left on Rte. 759. Paris located at intersection of
Rtes. 17 & 50; inn is at intersection of Rtes. 701 & 759.
Restrictions No children under 10.
Credit cards Amex, MC, Visa.
Rates B&B, $80–135 double or single. Extra person in room, $20.

314

PETERSBURG

Mayfield Inn   *Tel:* 804–861–6775
West Washington Street Extension,   804–733–0866
P.O. Box 2265, 23804

In 1986 Jamie Caudle fully restored this B&B, which is listed on the National Register of Historic Places, decorating it with antiques, reproductions, and Oriental rugs. He describes his inn as being ideal for "guests who can appreciate authentic restoration of an architecturally significant 18th-century house of beauty, luxury, and comfort. Two siege lines surrounded Mayfield during the Civil War, and General Robert E. Lee and his staff stayed here in the closing stages of the war. The house has seven fireplaces, one-inch-thick paneling and wainscotting, and beautiful woodwork."

"Just lovely—a 1750 house that has been completely and very beautifully restored. It is perfect—no water stains on the ceilings, no peeling paint, no flaws anywhere. The guest rooms are charming, and we were served a fine country breakfast in the dining room." *(Sally Sieracki)*

"Convenient for touring the James River plantations, and a delightful stop after a day of hard driving on I-95. The Mayfield Inn has spacious grounds, great for relaxing after a hard day's drive. The beautifully restored and furnished public rooms are a guest's delight—a first-rate B&B." *(Betty Richards)*

Open All year.
Rooms 2 suites, 2 doubles—all with private bath and/or shower, telephone, air-conditioning. 2 with desk.
Facilities Parlor, living room, dining room, all with fireplaces. 4 acres, heated pool, walking areas.
Location SE VA. 22 m S of Richmond. 100 m E of Virginia Beach. 2 m to center. Take Exit 3 off I-95. Go 3 m W to city limit sign.
Restrictions Smoking on ground floor only. No children.
Credit cards Choice, MC, Visa.
Rates B&B, $80–100 suite, $60–80 double. Extra person in room, $15. 10% senior, military discounts.

RAPHINE

Information please: The Osceola Mill Country Inn (Rte. 56, Steele's Tavern, 24476; 703–377–MILL), a converted 1859 flour mill complex in nearby Steele's Tavern, provides a variety of accommodations including a cottage with whirlpool tub and stone fireplace, and a double room equipped for the disabled. Also available is a restaurant, walking trails, and a swimming pool.

Oak Spring Farm & Vineyard
Route 1, Box 356, 24472

Tel: 703–377–2398

Oak Spring Farm is the latest venture of Pat and Jim Tichenor, experienced innkeepers and former owners of Fassifern, a B&B in Lexington (see entry). Pat reports that Jim finally completed all projects and renovations to that much loved inn and decided to take on a new challenge in a more rural setting. Built in 1826, Oak Spring was in need of total restoration; fortunately the farm had only three owners in its lifetime, so much of the original structure was still intact. During the renovation process, which included adding new bathrooms for each guest room, the Tichenors found the original mantel and door for the guest living room, and discovered that one wing of the house was originally a one-room schoolhouse.

The property itself has many interesting aspects: some of the farm is leased to the Natural Bridge Petting Zoo, so a herd of friendly burros are frequently in residence; it is a registered archaeological Indian site; and it has a 5-acre vineyard with both table and wine grapes grown for area wineries.

The Tichenors have decorated the house with an eclectic mix of antiques, 'near antiques,' artwork and accessories collected during their 26 years of world travel during Jim's military career. Rates include a breakfast of freshly ground coffee, fresh fruit or fruit compote, an assortment of homemade breads and muffins, and freshly squeezed orange juice.

"Having heard glowing reports of the Tichenor's former establishment, I couldn't wait to visit Oak Spring. I wasn't disappointed: the hospitality was wonderful, the bath immaculate, breakfast excellent. I truly felt as though I were a house guest." *(Mrs. Paul Stapleton)* "I loved the quiet atmosphere, the view of the surrounding fields, and the non-smoking policy. The Tichenors have the ability to make guests feel at home immediately." *(Susan Nagle)*

Open All year.
Rooms 3 doubles—all with full private bath, desk, air-conditioning.
Facilities Living room with fireplace, dining room, porches. 40 acres with barn, pasture, vineyards, gardens, hiking trails.
Location Central VA, Blue Ridge foothills. 50 m W of Charlottesville, 20 m S of Staunton, 14 m NE of Lexington. From I-81 take Exit 54 and follow Rte. 606 E to Steele's Tavern. Turn right on Rte. 11 and proceed to next crossroad and turn left on CR 706. Inn is 50 yds. on the right.
Restrictions No smoking. No children under 16.
Credit cards MC, Visa.
Rates B&B, $55–65 double, $40–55 single. Extra person in room, $15. No tipping. Discount for 3-night stay.
Extras Station pickups. Some German, French spoken.

RICHMOND

Richmond has had a dramatic history, including such high points as Patrick Henry's famous "Give me liberty or give me death" speech in

1775, the attack by the British not long after, and its tenure as the capital of the Confederacy from 1861 to 1865. The city is still home to several churches of significant historic interest, and a number of historic James River plantations lie within an easy drive, as does the Richmond National Battlefield Park. Also of interest are the Museum and White House of the Confederacy, the Edgar Allan Poe Museum, and other museums devoted to science and fine art. If you're visiting Richmond on a weekend, take the Cultural Link Trolley, connecting most hotels with the city's major attractions; ride all day for only $2.

Information please: A luxurious small hotel is the **Commonwealth Park**, an all-suite hotel with 59 units overlooking the State Capitol. Rooms are elegantly furnished with 18th-century mahogany reproductions, highlighted by brass chandeliers, and weekend rates are available (9th and Bank Streets, P.O. Box 455, 23230; 804–343–7300 or 800–343–7302). Reports?

Reader tip: "Several B&Bs are located in the Church Hill district, a charming enclave surrounded by very poor inner-city neighborhoods. Although the area is only 12 blocks from downtown, night-time strolls are definitely *not* recommended."

Richmond is in the eastern part of the state, 106 miles south of Washington, D.C., and 50 miles west of Williamsburg.

Abbie Hill Bed & Breakfast *Tel:* 804–355–5855
P.O. Box 4503, 23220 804–353–4656

A B&B in a turn-of-the-century Federal townhouse previously known as "Hanover Hosts in the Fan," long-time owners Bill and Barbara Fleming report that "our guests seem to enjoy the high ceilings, period decor, and huge old-fashioned bathrooms supplied with heaps of thirsty white towels. Our grandmothers were the source of most of the furnishings and we even have some of their handmade quilts. Our talented children and friends have made many of the handcrafted but usable items around the house. We have had this house since 1983 and are continually re-doing some room or another, as a place this large always cries out for one project or another." Rates include a full breakfast on weekends, continental breakfast weekdays.

"Charming decor, delicious breakfast, located on a beautiful street." *(Mike & Judi Anderson)* "Clean, airy rooms in a residential area full of shops and restaurants, yet just a short drive from the financial district. Friendly innkeepers are pleasant and on-street parking was easy." *(Norm Topf)*

Open All year.
Rooms 1 suite, 2 doubles—1 with private bath, 2 with a maximum of 4 people sharing 1 bath. All with radio, desk, air-conditioning, fan. TV on request.
Facilities Dining room, parlor with games, guest pantry, TV/reading room, laundry facilities, porch. Off-street parking.
Location Historic Fan district. 2½ m from Exit 14, I-95. Turn right on North Blvd. and continue to Broad St. Turn left and go to 2200 block. Turn right on Monument Ave. to 3rd house on right.
Restrictions Smoking discouraged; restricted to pantry or porch. No children under 12.

Credit cards MC, Visa.
Rates B&B, $115–150 suite, $55–95 double, $45–65 single. Extra person in room, $25. Weekly, group rates. Honeymoon, historic preservationist packages. 2-night weekend minimum, March–Dec.
Extras Airport/station pickups, $10.

Berkeley Hotel

Tel: 804–780–1300

1200 East Carey Street, 23219

The Berkeley is an elegant, small hotel built in 1988 with handsome period decor and a style that gives it the feel of an earlier era. It's located in Shockoe Slip, the city's 19th century warehouse district, and home to the Farmers Market—one of the country's oldest—offering fresh produce and local crafts. Today this area is also home to antique shops and boutiques, comedy clubs and restaurants.

"Elegant accommodations, fabulous breakfast buffet, superb service. Our room had coordinating floral print bedspreads and drapes, and ample comfortable seating. The lobby is dark and clubby, while the dining room is great for people watching in the busy downtown area; it's obviously popular with locals." *(Carol Moritz)*

Open All year.
Rooms 55 suites & doubles—all with full private bath, telephone, TV, radio, air-conditioning, desk.
Facilities Lobby, restaurant, valet parking, business services. Fitness center nearby.
Location Historic Shockoe Slip District, at corner of 12th St. 2 blocks to Capitol.
Credit cards Amex, DC, Discover, MC, Visa.
Rates Room only, $115 double, $105 single. $69 weekend rate. Alc dinner, $25.
Extras Airport/station pickups; downtown shuttle service.

Carrington Row Inn

Tel: 804–343–7005

2309 East Broad Street, 23223

In 1818, most of the U.S. was virgin forest. Yet Richmond was already enough of a city that when the Carrington brothers built homes for their families, they constructed three attached houses in the now historic Church Hill district. Very sophisticated for their day, the houses have separate entrances in front, with a shared veranda overlooking a garden in the back. One of these houses has been owned by Anne and Michael Catalina since 1984, and has been furnished with antiques and period reproductions. Rates include a continental breakfast and evening sherry. Just a block away is St. John's Church, famous as the setting for Patrick Henry's fiery oratory. *(MA)* Reports most welcome.

Open All year.
Rooms 4 doubles—all with private bath and/or shower, telephone, desk, air-conditioning, fan. 2 with fireplace, 2 sharing 1 sitting room.
Facilities Dining room, living room with fireplace, garden, off-street parking.
Location Church Hill historic district. 1 m to center. From I-95 S, take Exit 11 (3rd St. ramp), to 5th traffic light (Broad St.) and turn left. Proceed E to the 2300 block to inn.
Restrictions No children. Traffic noise in front rooms.
Credit cards MC, Visa.
Rates B&B, $73–93 double, $63–73 single. Rates include service.

The Catlin-Abbott House
2304 East Broad Street, 23223

When Jim and Frances Abbott bought The Catlin House in 1980, it had been vacant for eight years and was condemned. Back in 1845, William Catlin had the house built by his slave, William Mitchell, now recognized as Richmond's finest brick mason and the father of Maggie Walker, the first woman to found a bank in America. The Abbotts managed to salvage the beautiful wide-board floors and the fireplaces, but nearly everything else had to be rebuilt in the renovation process. They've decorated the rooms with period antiques, crystal chandeliers, and Chinese rugs; rates include a full breakfast, served on fine china with sterling flatware in the formal dining room or, upon request, in your room.

"A pleasant B&B, with the feel of an inn, not a private home (a plus to us). We were pleased with the suite we had on the first (below the parlor) floor, though it was a bit dark during the day. It had a working fireplace, and diverting magazines. Breakfast was fine—scrambled eggs, bacon, biscuits, decent coffee. Parking was easy on the street in front." *(Rachel Gorlin)*

At press time we learned that a change of ownership is in the works, since the Abbotts decided it was time to take it a little easier. Inquire further when making reservations. More comments please.

Open All year.
Rooms 2 2-bedroom suites (1 with kitchen), 3 doubles—all with private bath and/or shower, telephone, TV, desk, air-conditioning, fireplace. Suites with porch or patio.
Facilities Living room, dining room with fireplaces.
Location Church Hill District. 12 blocks from center. From I-95 S, take Exit 11 (3rd St. ramp) to 5th traffic light (Broad St.). Turn left and go E to 2300 block. From I-95 N, take Exit 10 (E. Broad St. ramp) to 1st traffic light. Turn left on Broad St. and go to 2300 block.
Restrictions No children.
Credit cards Amex, MC, Visa.
Rates B&B, $120–140 suite, $83 double, $73 single including tax and service. Extra person in room, $15.
Extras Station pickups. Airport delivery.

Jefferson Sheraton
Franklin & Adams Streets, 23220

An elaborate Beaux-Arts structure built in 1895, the Jefferson was meticulously restored in 1986 at a cost of $35 million and is listed on the National Register of Historic Places. Even if you can't stay overnight, stop by to see the Tiffany stained glass dome in the Palm Court lobby, and the magnificent marbled two-story Rotunda. "Beautiful building in the heart of Richmond. From the grandeur of the lobby with marble columns and staircase to the period antiques and reproductions in the spacious guest rooms, you are aware of the meticulous restoration which has taken place. The TV and mini-bar are attractively hidden in an armoire so as not to spoil the feel of the room. The atmosphere is gracious and the staff is most attentive to your needs. There is a small ice cream parlor in the lower level, also a coffee shop and a bar. Near the main lobby is a large dining room which serves breakfast, lunch and dinner; they also serve a fabulous Sunday brunch." *(Elizabeth Sommer, also SR)*

Open All year.
Rooms 26 suites, 248 doubles-all with private bath and/or shower, telephone, radio, TV, air-conditioning, mini-bar. 9 suites with fireplace, 2 suites with whirl-pool tub, baby grand piano.
Facilities Lobby, 2 restaurants, lounge with entertainment, meeting rooms. Health club privileges. Golf, tennis privileges nearby. Valet parking.
Location Downtown. From I-95 take Belvedere St. Exit.
Restrictions No smoking in some guest rooms.
Credit cards Amex, DC, Discover, MC, Visa.
Rates Room only, $175–550 suite, $139–149 double, $125–135 single. Extra person in room, $10. Weekend rate, $75–89.
Extras Some rooms equipped for the disabled. Limousine service to airport.

SCOTTSVILLE

Chester B&B
State Route 726, Route 4, Box 57, 24590

Tel: 804–286–3960

Imagine that a friend of a friend invited you to spend a few days in his Greek Revival mansion, built in 1847 and surrounded by equally venerable plantings. Imagine further that two gracious hosts await to make your visit as pleasant as possible. This is much the atmosphere that Gordon Anderson and Dick Shaffer have worked to create in the four years that they have owned Chester. In addition to a full breakfast of fresh fruit and juice, eggs, pancakes, and Virginia sausage, guests may enjoy complimentary wine, beer, soft drinks, tea, or coffee at any time. Dinners are served as well, and guests feel that the delightful food and conversation are the highlight of their stay.

"Dick and Gordon go out of their way to make each guest feel comfortable and relaxed. Their stories of searching for an inn, restoring the house and acclimatization to Scottsville (from New York) make wonderful entertainment." *(Gwynne Daye)*

"We were graciously greeted by Gordon and Dick; they offered us drinks and showed us to our room, as though we were personal friends come to visit. Our room was beautiful, impeccably clean, and charming. The next evening, we had a delightful dinner at the inn. Gordon and Dick took turns serving, and we all talked and laughed through a delicious meal of curry soup, shrimp and rice, and chocolate cake, served on fine china and crystal in the lovely candlelit dining room.

"The house is fully renovated with new plumbing and wiring, decorated with the owners' collections of furniture, and everything is bright and cheerful. Our room was furnished with a high four-poster bed, night stands and a dresser—all of which were antique and in beautiful condition. We also had a fireplace, laid with wood and ready to light." *(Kelly & Michael Warkoczeski, also Denny & Nancy Fish)*

"The owners' Borzois (Russian wolfhounds) are graceful and

320

friendly." *(David & Carole Metzger)* "Our room had many well lighted reading areas and lovely views of the grounds." *(Mary Kleinert)*

An area for improvement: "Air-conditioning would be a welcome addition to the second-floor guest rooms."

Open All year.
Rooms 1 suite, 4 doubles, 1 with full private bath, 4 with a maximum of 4 sharing a bath. All with radio, desk, fan. 4 with fireplace.
Facilities Dining room with fireplace, living room with fireplace, TV; lounge, library, porches. 7 acres with croquet, antique shop. Bicycles available. River for fishing, boating nearby.
Location Central VA, Albemarle County. 18 m S of Charlottesville, in Monticello wine region. From Rte. 20 take Rte. 726 W. Go approx. 1/4 m to inn on left.
Restrictions Children under 9 discouraged.
Credit cards Amex.
Rates B&B, $75 suite, $70 double. Extra person in room, $20. Prix fixe dinner with wine $20.
Extras Pets permitted, must be kept at inn's dog kennel. Airport/station pickups.

High Meadows Inn

Tel: 804–286–2218

RR 4, Box 6; 24590
Route 20 South/Constitution Highway

Peter and Mary Jae Sushka restored High Meadows, doing much of the work themselves, and decorated the rooms with period antiques. The inn is composed of two buildings, one dating from 1832 and the other from 1882, connected by a covered hallway; both are listed on the National Register of Historic Places. The Sushkas describe the inn as being "especially attractive to people interested in history, yet looking for all the modern conveniences. It's the perfect place for people who love to travel but hate to leave home." Dinners are served on weekends, and include a choice of French, Italian, and game dishes along with Virginia wines; weeknights the Sushkas offer guests a supper picnic basket. As their vineyards are now producing five tons of Pinot Noir grapes each August and early September, guests have the opportunity for "hands on" fun and can reap the reward of complimentary meals. Local attractions include the area's numerous historic sights and antique shops, as well as canoeing, tubing, and fishing on the James River, plus winery tours and hiking.

"High Meadows Inn is a unique blend of Federal and Victorian architecture made even more distinctive by Peter and Jae. This Renaissance couple's sense of history is reflected in the meticulous attention to detail they have shown in restoring and furnishing each of the theme bedrooms with authentic antiques. (We slept in an original Jenny Lind bed.) A friendly and gracious atmosphere prevailed in the intimate dining room, where we were served a tantalizing breakfast of fresh fruits, family-recipe muffins, eggs, and a special blend of coffee. Conversing with our hosts, while their son played classical guitar music, made these meals a highlight of our weekend. We walked the grounds, admiring the flowers, azaleas, and dogwood while en route to the gazebo, pond, and vineyard. Closeness to other historical points of interest—including

321

Ashlawn, Monticello, and the University of Virginia—added to the pleasures of our stay." *(Ann & John Glenson)*

"The hosts' attention to cleanliness and manicure extends beyond the inn to its abundant surroundings; beautiful, exotic and rare flowers greet you throughout the grounds. The delicious and unpretentious meals, a rooster from the nearby farm greeting the day, and the gracious attention to guest comfort have great charm and appeal for the city-stressed traveler." *(Roddy & Donna Hiduskey)* "The food was wonderful and Peter's instinct for wine choices is impeccable. He went out of his way to make our stay very special." *(Dana Abdella)*

"We were greeted on arrival with Virginia wine, cheese, and friendly conversation. Our room had a fascinating photo album showing the inn's step-by-step restoration and explaining the origin of its furnishings." *(Becky & Les Crenshaw)* "From the flowers in the rooms to the mints on the pillow to assistance with tours of local wineries and Monticello to a gourmet breakfast, you will truly be spoiled by the Sushkas." *(Mr. & Mrs. James L. Bailey)* "I particularly enjoyed the evening wine-tasting, which gave us the opportunity to relax before the fire, browse through the voluminous 'before and after' photo albums, and read our novels." *(Darian Schulze)*

Open All year. Closed Dec. 24, 25.
Rooms 2 suites, 5 doubles—all with private bath and/or shower, desk, fan. 5 with air-conditioning.
Facilities Dining/breakfast rooms, bar/lounge, library, music room, porches. 23 acres with formal gardens, ponds, vineyards. On the James River for tubing, canoeing, rafting, fishing. Hiking nearby. 40 min. to downhill skiing.
Location Central VA, Albemarle County. 17 m S of Charlottesville, in Monticello wine region. 1 m N of Scottsville, on Rte. 20.
Restrictions Smoking discouraged. No children under 8.
Credit cards None accepted.
Rates B&B, $110 suite, $85–95 double, $70–80 single. Extra person in room, $15. 10% AARP discount. 2-night weekend minimum spring and fall. Weekend prix fixe dinner with wine, $30; 15% service, 4.5% tax additional. Weeknight picnic supper basket with wine, $40 for two; 10% service additional.
Extras Pets occasionally permitted with prior notice. French spoken.

SMITHFIELD

Isle of Wight Inn
1607 South Church Street, 23430

Tel: 804–357–3176

Smithfield is an old river town, best known as the home of famous Smithfield ham—salty and always very thinly sliced. It's not too far from Williamsburg; you cross the James River by ferry between Jamestown and Surry (a lovely ride), and take Route 10 south to Smithfield. Built in 1984, the Isle of Wight is owned by Bob Hart, Marcella Hoffman, and Sam Earl, and furnished with traditional and reproduction furniture. While not exactly a traditional inn, it's clearly a reader favorite.

"Beautifully furnished rooms, continental breakfast in an intimate, elegant dining room." *(Carol King)*

"A real favorite. We were welcomed with great friendliness to this luxurious small motel/inn with an attractive antique shop. Our very large and pleasant room had its own external door, fireplace, small but well-equipped bathroom with large shower and excellent queen-size bed. Breakfast, served in the room, was Smithfield ham rolls (only one each) and good coffee. Be sure to visit Joyner's ham shop, more or less opposite the inn." *(David Felce)* "Exactly as you described it in last year's edition. Extremely helpful and friendly service. Would make an excellent base for visiting Williamsburg. The Smithfield Inn in the center of town provided an excellent Sunday evening buffet supper." *(Michael Crick)*

Open All year.
Rooms 4 suites, 6 doubles—all with full private bath, telephone, cable TV, desk, air-conditioning. Several suites with fireplace, 1 with Jacuzzi.
Facilities Living/family room, with player piano; dining room, kitchen, antique shop. Limousine tour packages. Fishing, tennis, jogging trail, golf nearby.
Location Southeast VA, Tidewater, Isle of Wight County. 12 m W of Newport News, 27 m W of Norfolk. Approx. 22 m S of Williamsburg. 2 m from town, on Rte. 10 near James River Bridge.
Restrictions No smoking in public rooms.
Credit cards Amex, MC, Visa.
Rates B&B, $79–99 suite, $49–79 double, including service. Extra person in room, $10. Senior discounts.
Extras Crib available.

SMITH MOUNTAIN LAKE

The Manor at Taylor's Store   *Tel:* 703–721–3951
Route 122; (mail) Route 1, Box 533, 24184

Although you'd search in vain to find Taylor's Store on a contemporary map, old maps of this region have it well marked, indicating its prominence. Skelton Taylor established a general merchandise trading post here in 1799, and it later functioned as a post office and tavern. The manor, now an inn, dates to the early 1800s, and was originally part of a tobacco plantation. Lee and Mary Lynn Tucker bought the property in 1986, and have fully restored it as a country inn.

"Mary Lynn and Lee clearly have a great affection for their home and share it happily with their guests. They have created a true feeling of the past while maintaining all the modern comforts. We slept in the Colonial Room in a great, canopied four-poster bed. The room was spacious, bright, and well equipped. Like everything here, it was clean, fresh, and inviting. A French door led to a private balcony with a view across the fields that was pure country. Our bath was new, spotless, and well stocked with towels and had a super shower. The first morning we enjoyed an early walk to the ponds in the fields and woods behind the house and stopped to pet the Newfoundlands in their pen. There is a game room with a pool table, and a fine old-fashioned parlor with a grand piano and a comfortable sofa, plus plenty of books for browsing. Our first breakfast was a stack of whole wheat pancakes with ham and

Virginia maple syrup. The second morning Mary Lynn served crepes filled with fresh strawberries and Neufchâtel cheese. For dinner we chose peanut soup, followed by scallops with wild rice and asparagus. The Tuckers are interesting and gracious hosts. Lee's plans include establishing a winery on the premises. We had a long chat about viniculture in general and about its exciting possibilities in Virginia." *(Dick & Erna Loerch)*

"Mary Lynn and Lee have restored, mostly with their own hands, this historic home into an inn of understated elegance. Our spacious, airy bedroom had a huge, extremely comfortable canopy bed, and a large private bath. Most amazing are the Tuckers themselves. Besides being host innkeepers extraordinaire, they are each young career-oriented individuals. Lee is a doctor and Mary Lynn is a college-level nursing instructor who also breeds award-winning show dogs." *(Frank & Prudence Pesce)*

"Extras included cozy bathrobes, chocolates on the turned-down beds, potpourri in the bathroom, evening coffee and dessert, and a game of pool to cap it off." *(Monika Chiaro)* More comments please.

Open All year.
Rooms 6 doubles—4 with private bath and/or shower, 2 with a maximum of 4 people sharing bath. All with radio, desk, air-conditioning. 3 with private porch, 1 with fireplace. 1 cottage with 3 bedrooms sharing 2 baths, kitchen, den, deck.
Facilities Parlor with piano; dining room with fireplace; great room with TV/VCR, fireplace, billiards; exercise room; hot tub; guest kitchen; library. 120 acres with hiking, croquet, volleyball. 6 ponds for fishing, canoeing, swimming. Tennis, golf, boating nearby.
Location SW VA. 15 m E of Roanoke. Take Rte. 220 S to Rte. 122/40. Turn left, following signs for Booker T. Washington Monument. Located 1.6 m past Burnt Chimney intersection, on right.
Restrictions Smoking permitted only in cottage. No children under 12 in main house.
Credit cards MC, Visa.
Rates B&B, $55–80 double. Cottage, room only, $80–140 double; weekly rates available. Extra person in room, $15. 2-night minimum stay in cottage.
Extras Wheelchair accessible; limited facilities for the handicapped. Station pickups. Some German spoken.

SPERRYVILLE

The Conyers House   *Tel:* 703–987–8025
Route 1, Box 157, Slate Mills Road, 22740

The Conyers House dates to 1770, with additions in 1810, and in 1979, when it was bought by Sandra and Norman Cartwright-Brown. Sandra is an avid fox hunter and an active member of the Rappahannock Hunt; she'll happily go out with experienced riders, and can make arrangements for novices at a nearby stable.

"We stayed in Helen's Room, a spacious room with a four-poster queen rope bed with a double-thick mattress, and a small spool servant's bed. The rug in the room was a lovely pastel Oriental. There were several dressers, tables, and chairs, with adequate reading lamps, and a working fireplace. Family heirlooms were everywhere, including a charming palm-sized photo album. Grampie's Room, next door, was medium-sized, with antique furnishings. If you're traveling light, don't mind very steep stairs, and aren't too tall, I'd also recommend the light and airy Attic Room, with private deck and half bath. My other recommendation is the Hill House, delightfully private with a huge bathroom and large Jacuzzi.

"The dining room is large and elegant, with a table that seats at least ten. We were served dinner by firelight. It included a cheese and cracker tray of Camembert and brick cheese, goose paté, and crab spread. Then came potato corn chowder, salad, pork tenderloin with sauerkraut and apples, served with russet potatoes, squash and tomatoes. Dessert was a dark chocolate mousse ice cream pie. While we dined, Sandra lighted the fire in our room, a lovely touch. Breakfast is served family-style during a two-hour period. Eggs scrambled with mushrooms, tiny bran muffins, English muffins, large homemade biscuits, sausage gravy, orange juice, apple cider, and a fruit plate with grapes, kiwi, honeydew, and starfruit made a bountiful selection. Everything was nicely presented and pleasantly served. The living room has a warm clubby feel, with soft overstuffed couches and book-lined walls.

"I thought Sandra was a delightful innkeeper—interesting, friendly, and especially delightful for those who enjoy horses. Her inn is perfect for a country getaway, and the colonial fox-hunting atmosphere gives it a special touch." (SHW)

Some areas for improvement: "Our bathroom needed more attention to detail, and seemed out of character with an inn of this quality. Instead of the little basket of amenities and box of tissues you might expect, we found what was apparently previously started soap, toothpaste, and shampoo. Although clean, the shower curtain around the tub was stained by the mineral content of the water. Prices in this area have been pulled upwards by the Inn at Little Washington. Our dinner was delightful, but at $50 per person, I felt we ate just as well—or better—at some of the other inns you list, and at lower cost."

Open All year.
Rooms 2 cottages, 6 doubles—6 with private bath and/or shower, 2 with a maximum of 4 people sharing bath. 6 with air-conditioning, 3 with porch, 2 with fireplace. Cottages with fireplace or woodstove, 1 with Jacuzzi.
Facilities Dining room with fireplace, living room with fireplace, library; TV room, porches. 2½ acres with pastures. Trail rides; not for novices. Golf, tennis, hiking, climbing, fox hunting nearby.
Location N VA, Rappahannock County. 1½ hrs. W of Washington, DC; 45 m N of Charlottesville. From DC, take I-495 to Rte. 66 W, then exit on Rte. 29 S to Warrenton. Turn W on Rte. 211 and go through Little Washington to Sperryville. Turn left at Sperryville Emporium, then left again at blinking light (Rte. 522). Turn right on Rte. 231 (after cemetery). Go approx. 8 m and turn left on Rte. 707. Go .6 m to driveway to inn.
Restrictions Smoked restricted to living room, porches. No children on weekends; "not suitable for young children." Steep narrow stairs may be difficult for some to negotiate.
Credit cards None accepted.
Rates B&B, $100–170 double. Extra person in room, $25. 2-night minimum, holidays and high season (Sept.–Nov.). Prix fixe dinner, $50 plus gratuity.

Extras Pets permitted in 2 rooms only by prior arrangement. Local airport/station pickups. German, French, Italian spoken.

STANLEY

Information please: Milton House is a 1918 Sears Roebuck mail order Southern colonial home, set among large Norwegian spruce trees. Reasonable rates for the three guest rooms include a full breakfast. Reports?

Jordan Hollow Farm Inn   *Tel:* 703–778–2209
Virginia Route 626, Route 2, Box 375, 22851   703–778–2285

Jordan Hollow is a horse-breeding farm, where plenty of horses are available for riding or "just looking." The dining rooms, where breakfast and dinner are served, are in the 200-year-old farmhouse. Guest rooms are located in two separate lodges built in 1983 and 1990 to complement the other farm buildings. Marley and Jetze Beers have owned and run the farm since it became an inn.

"We arrived at Jordan Hollow in the pitch dark, bedraggled after a long day of traveling. Imagine our thrill the next morning when we awoke to the country quiet, stepped out onto the balcony, and saw stretching before us verdant hills and glens, green meadows sparkling with wildflowers, fine-looking horses grazing with their foals skittering about. We wandered in the barns, roamed the pastures, enjoyed excellent food in the pretty dining rooms, and sipped drinks in the friendly bar/recreation room. We took trail rides through the lovely countryside on their well-trained mounts, hiked in the adjacent Shenandoah National Park, and relaxed on the inn lawns, reading and playing with the resident kittens—and never had to dress up once!" *(SG)*

"The Beers are bright, talented, interesting people who gather you into their home as friends. The service was perfect—delivered by friendly, helpful local residents. The sleeping lodge was new, clean, and comfortable. This is not a fancy, formal facility! It is, in our opinion, a true country inn with all the hoped-for ambience." *(Nancy & Fritz Thompson, also Seymour Solomon)*

"This is a real working farm; three horses, which had foaled recently, were out in paddocks where the guests could watch them for hours. Our room was spotlessly clean and very homey, with special touches like a bottle of wine and nice, colored towels, instead of the standard motel white. The old farmhouse's small dining rooms are decorated nicely in country calico, other odd antiques, and African artifacts. The food was excellent—everything from soup to dessert was cooked to perfection." *(Mike & Doris Donch)* "Two of the cozy dining rooms are the original 200-year-old log rooms. Favorites entrées are the rainbow trout and roasted quail with cream and herbs." *(Mrs. Lola Rhea)*

"After dinner each night we all went to the pub, where there is something for all ages. My five-year-old son loved the pool table, games, and dart board, while we enjoyed conversations with the other guests. The horseback riding is well organized, with riders separated by ability." *(Piper Starr)*

An area for improvement: One otherwise satisfied guest noted that their bathroom fan (which turned on automatically with the light) was noisy, disturbing when the bathroom was used late at night. We'd say a nightlight would solve the problem handily. Comments?

Open All year.
Rooms 1 suite, 20 doubles—all with private bath and/or shower, telephone, desk, air-conditioning. 4 with fireplace, whirlpool tub.
Facilities Restaurant, bar/lounge/pub, game room, library, meeting rooms. Weekend entertainment in pub. 45 acres with trails, horseback riding. Shenandoah River nearby for canoeing, fishing, swimming. Golf, tennis nearby. Cross-country, downhill skiing 15–30 min.
Location N VA, Shenandoah Valley. 2 hrs. W of Washington, DC, NW of Richmond, VA. 6 m S of Luray. From Luray, take Rte. 340 S 6 m. Go left on Rte. 624, left again on Rte. 689, right on Rte. 626 and follow signs.
Restrictions No smoking in barn.
Credit cards CB, DC, MC, Visa.
Rates Room only, $95 suite, $75 double, $65 single. Extra person in room, $10. Children under 16 free in parents' room. Riding packages. Alc lunch $5, alc dinner, $20.
Extras Guest room and bath equipped for disabled. German, Dutch, some French spoken. Cribs, babysitting available. Pets boarded by special arrangement.

STAUNTON

In easy reach of many area sights, Staunton is a popular base for touring the Shenandoah Mountains. Staunton itself has undergone considerable renovation of its historic downtown. In addition to the birthplace of Woodrow Wilson, the Museum of American Frontier Culture has opened recently.

Also recommended: Although we were unable to obtain enough information to complete a full write-up, *Mrs. Lola Rhea* wrote that the **Spiff Inn** (Rte. 1, Box 8, Mt. Sidney 24467; 703–248–7307), located 13 miles north of Staunton, offers four guest rooms with private bath, in a house built in 1835; "the owner is a charming English lady."

We'd also like your opinion of the **Buckhorn Inn** (Route 250, Star Rte. 139, Churchville 24421; 703–337d–6900) located 12 miles to the west. Built as an inn in 1811, it's best known for its buffet dinners, although seven guest rooms offer very modest accommodation at equally modest prices. A country menu is offered at the buffet most nights, although Wednesdays feature German cuisine, and seafood is highlighted on Friday. Feedback so far is mixed, with one frequent contributor reporting that their room was spotless, that both their bed and the food at the buffet were uneven, and that the breakfasts were superb both in quality and the range of choices. Comments?

Belle Grae Inn   *Tel:* 703–886–5151
515 West Frederick Street, 24401

Restored by owner Michael Organ in 1983, the Belle Grae is a rambling brick Victorian mansion with white gingerbread trim, and is Staunton's oldest B&B. In addition to accommodation in two adjacent homes, the Belle Grae offers formal and casual dining in its restaurant and bistro.

"The Belle Grae is a Victorian home on a quiet street very near Mary

Baldwin College and Stuart Hall School. The rooms have all been furnished in period or antique pieces. Parking behind the house is ample, and gives you a nice stroll through a beautifully landscaped garden and terrace area. The inn has recently purchased another old home adjacent to the original. The dining rooms are lovely, the tables set with crystal and silver while the bistro area is more informal and open with occasional evening entertainment. The resident owner, Tom Organ, is a very personable fellow who goes out of his way to make guests feel at home and most cordially welcomed." *(Patricia DeMonte)*

"An attractive Victorian house in an interesting little town, well situated for a walking tour of Staunton's historic center. Our room was in the front of the house, with an attractive bedroom and a very small bathroom. We were glad to sink down with a glass of sherry, provided in a decanter in our room.We enjoyed our dinner in the Victorian dining room. Two menus are available—a simple, bistro menu, and a more elaborate one. We chose the latter and were very satisfied. Service was attentive and efficient. Breakfast is served in the 'bistro' part of the inn, a sixties-style extension to the main house; it's very bright and has nice views of the front lawn with squirrels scampering about." *(Ellie Freidus)*

"Excellent food. Lunch served on garden patio in summer." *(Mrs. Lola Rhea)* "Interesting dinner menu, excellent food and service, informal yet elegant setting." *(Laura Lapins)*

Some areas for improvement: "Although we had reserved a twin-bedded room, we were shown to one with a double bed and a sofa bed, which was unsatisfactory. The owners were on vacation and the young lady in charge was very nice, but inexperienced." Also: "Breakfast was served only between 7:30 and 8:30 A.M.; there was no choice, and our omelet tasted as though it had been on a steam table for some time."

Open All year. Restaurant closed in Jan.
Rooms 12 suites & doubles—all with private bath and/or shower, desk. Some with telephone, TV.
Facilities Restaurant, bistro, parlor with fireplace, sitting room with fireplace, music room, TV room, veranda, courtyard. 1½ acres with veranda. ½ block to tennis court.
Location Take Exit 57 off I-81. Go W 3 m on Rte. 250 to Rte. 254 to W. Frederick St.
Restrictions No children.
Credit cards Amex, MC, Visa.
Rates B&B, $90 suite, $65–85 double. Extra person in room, $25. Alc lunch, $7–9; alc dinner, $17–25.

The Frederick Hotel   *Tel:* 703–885–4220
18 East Frederick Street,   Outside VA: 800–334–5575
P.O. Box 1387, 24401

The Frederick Hotel is composed of three connected town houses, built between 1810 and 1910. It's located right across the street from Mary Baldwin College, and near Woodrow Wilson's birthplace, Stuart Hall, and many shops and restaurants. Joe and Evy Harman restored the inn in 1984, and have decorated it with antiques and reproduction pieces. In 1991, plans are to add a restaurant featuring regional cuisine.

"The rooms were spotless, and innkeeper Evy Harman is a gracious hostess. Our room had a charming antique baby cradle." *(Mrs. Peter Payne, also Patricia DeMonte)* More comments please.

Open All year.
Rooms 5 suites, 6 doubles—all with private bath and/or shower, telephone, radio, TV, desk, air-conditioning, fan.
Facilities Dining room, living room, library. Small vegetable, herb gardens. Free pass (for 2) to Staunton Athletic Club indoor swimming pool, hot tub (next door). Tennis, golf nearby. 45 min. to downhill skiing, hiking, canoeing, Skyline Drive, Blue Ridge Parkway.
Location NW VA. 150 m SW of Washington, DC; 40 m W of Charlottesville, 100 m NW of Richmond. Exit 57, I-81, then Rte. 250 W. Center of town, across from Mary Baldwin College.
Restrictions No smoking.
Credit cards Amex, DC, Discover, MC, Visa.
Rates Room only, $65–70 suite, $55–60 double, $40–45 single. Extra person in room, $15. B&B, $75–85 suite, $65–75 double, $45–50 single; plus 15% service on meals. Extra person in room, $20. MAP, full board available. Children's rates, room only, $17.50; B&B, $20. 10% senior discount on room. Alc lunch, $8.95; alc dinner, $21.95; plus 7.5% tax, 20% service.
Extras Wheelchair accessible; some rooms equipped for the disabled. Crib, babysitting available.

Thornrose House at Gypsy Hill   *Tel:* 703–885–7026
531 Thornrose Avenue, 24401

A gracious Georgian-style brick home, Thornrose has been owned by Carolyn and Ray Hoaster since 1984. Carolyn describes it as a "small, friendly establishment catering to guests who enjoy having a taste of the Old South, and who welcome interaction with other guests and with their host and hostess." Rooms are decorated with period antiques, and rates include afternoon tea and a full breakfast of birchermuesli—a delicious Swiss cereal—followed by eggs, bacon, sausage, and toast. Guests can work off this hearty meal in the 300-acre park across the street, or can relax in a rocker on the shady veranda. *(Patricia DeMonte)* More comments please.

Open All year.
Rooms 3 doubles—all with private bath and/or shower, radio, air-conditioning. 1 with desk.
Facilities Dining room with fireplace, sitting room with fireplace, piano, TV, radio/cassette player; wraparound veranda. Gardens with colonnades, benches. Gypsy Hill Park across street for swimming, golf, tennis (tennis rackets provided).
Location Take Exit 57 off I-64/81. Follow Rte. 250 W for 3.2 m, then turn left on Thornrose Ave. 4th house on left.
Restrictions No smoking. Children not encouraged; infants or children over age 6 only.
Credit cards None accepted.
Rates B&B, $45–60 double, $35–45 single. Extra person in room, $15. 2-night weekend minimum for some weekends.
Extras Crib available. Station pickups by prior arrangement; airport pickup for longer stays.

STRASBURG

Hotel Strasburg
201 Holliday Street, 22657

Tel: 703–465–9191

The century-old Hotel Strasburg offers period atmosphere and a location close to the Skyline Drive. Once a major pottery-making center, it's now better known for the Strasburg Emporium, an enormous warehouse crammed with antiques.

"The furnishings are antique, and the floors creak a little. It feels like a visiting grandmother's house, because of its warmth, age and solid well-being. Our room had a whirlpool tub for two and a magnificent antique bed with half-canopy. You couldn't ask for a more romantic getaway. Dinner was well-seasoned and good; breakfasts were excellent; and the staff is gracious and friendly." *(Judilynn Niedercorn)* "A historic hotel, decorated with beautiful wallpaper in each room." *(Mrs. Lola Rhea)*

An area for improvement: One otherwise satisfied guest notes that the supply of towels was a bit skimpy.

Open May through Oct.
Rooms 4 suites, 23 doubles—all with private bath and/or shower, telephone, air-conditioning. Some with TV. Suites with Jacuzzi, TV. Suites in adjoining Taylor House.
Facilities Restaurant, tavern, lobby.
Location N VA. 75 m W of Washington, DC. Take I-66 W to I-81 S to Strasburg Exit 75. Go S on Rte. 11 approx. 1½ m to 1st traffic light and turn right. Go 1 block then turn left at light on Holliday St. Go 1 block to hotel on left.
Restrictions Light sleepers should request rooms away from the tavern.
Credit cards Amex, DC, MC, Visa.
Rates Room only, $99–149 suite, $69–79 double. Extra person in room, $15. Children under 16 free in parents' room.

SWOOPE

Lambsgate B&B
Route 254, RR 1, Box 63, 24479

Tel: 703–337–6929

Lambsgate is a restored 1818 vernacular farmhouse, owned since 1984 by Daniel and Elizabeth Fannon. Rooms are cheerfully furnished with some antiques, and Elizabeth notes that guests enjoy "our quiet (except for baaing and mooing) pastoral surroundings, the opportunities for hiking and bicycling nearby, the comfortable, informal accommodations, and the convenience of being just eight miles from the interstate."

"Lambsgate is a peaceful and idyllic old Victorian farm, located in the historic and scenic Shenandoah Valley. Our spacious room had a beautiful view of Eliot Knob (second highest mountain in the valley) and the Allegheny Mountains. Elizabeth and Dan Fannon run a lamb farm and both are full of lambing stories that animal lovers are sure to enjoy. Dan takes your breakfast order the night before and cooks up a huge southern country breakfast. Country ham with red-eye gravy and grits are his specialties; the bran muffins were delicious too. Both Dan and Elizabeth are friendly, gracious hosts." *(Lynn Bachenberg)*

"We always look for an inn with well-kept yard. Those who grow flowers, we find, tend to keep an inn with a special touch; the Lambs-gate is such a place, and sits on a hill, alongside a stream. We found good conversation and good books in a country atmosphere." *(Dr. & Mrs. Edward Hayes)*

Open All year.
Rooms 3 doubles, with maximum of 6 sharing bath.
Facilities Dining room, living room. 7½ acres with sheep, lambs; river for fishing (poles provided). Hiking nearby.
Location Western VA, near W VA border. 8 m W of I-81, 6 m W of Staunton. From Staunton, go W on Rte. 254, turn right on Rte. 833 to B&B on right.
Restrictions No smoking.
Credit cards None accepted.
Rates B&B, $36.58 double, $31.35 single, including tax, service. Child in room, $10. No tipping.
Extras Crib available.

TREVILIANS

Prospect Hill   *Tel:* 703–967–0844
State Highway 613, RR 3, Box 430, 23093

Prospect Hill dates back to 1732; by 1840, when William Overton was the owner, the plantation covered over 1,500 acres. The family fortunes were reduced after the Civil War, and the Overtons began taking in paying guests from the city. In 1880 they expanded the Manor House and slave quarters to accommodate guests on a regular basis; today the number of overnight guests has remained small, although up to 100 can be served at dinner.

Rooms at Prospect Hill, in the main house and in various outbuildings, are decorated with antiques and handmade quilts. A full breakfast is served in your room, and dinner is a leisurely four-course (no choice) meal. Mireille and Bill Sheehan have owned Prospect Hill since 1977. Son Michael is the chef, and meals frequently have a French Provençal accent.

"Upon arriving you find a bottle of wine, homemade cookies, and a fruit bowl in your room. A large swimming pool makes late afternoons very enjoyable after trips to Monticello and Charlottesville during the day." *(Mark Goodman)* "The care and concern which the Sheehan's show for their guests was truly evident in the way in which our request for a change in menu (having fish during Lent) was received. Without fanfare, we were served delicious salmon wrapped in spinach in a puff pastry shell. A special place, run by special people." *(Paul Starr)*

"Excellent food well presented by the innkeeper. The grounds are lovely, and you can spend several enjoyable hours just strolling around; there is a graveyard on the property where the slaves were buried. Rooms are very clean and plumbing is excellent. A bit hard to find, but well worth it." *(Pat Drake)*

"We felt welcomed the moment we walked in. Dinner was a treat, with light, elegant cuisine, accompanied by good wine. Breakfast was up to the same standard, with some of the best sausage we've ever had. Our room, the Old Summer Kitchen, was warm, cozy, and had a new bath complete with Jacuzzi, a porch and a wonderful view from the shower. Lighting was good, everything was spotless, and it was quiet." (Kathleen Owen) "Many of the charming accommodations are located in restored dependencies on the grounds, offering a romantic setting and much privacy, but somewhat limiting guest contact. The innkeepers and staff offer a warm welcome and careful attention to creature comforts." (Joan Reid)

Open All year, except Dec. 24, 25.
Rooms 4 suites, 8 doubles—all with private bath and/or shower, air-conditioning. 3 rooms in main house, 9 in 6 outbuildings; 9 with fireplace, 4 with whirlpool tubs.
Facilities 3 dining rooms; 2 sitting rooms; library; veranda. 40 acres with 10-acre arboretum, swimming pool, hammocks, benches. Lake Anna for fishing, boating. James River for tubing, canoeing. 45 min. to Skyline Drive, 1 hr. to Wintergreen.
Location N central VA. Approx. 15 m E of Charlottesville, 90 m W of Washington, DC. From Charlottesville, take I-64 to Exit 27 to Rte. 15 S to Zion Crossroads. Turn left on Rte. 250 E. Go 1 m to Rte. 613, turn left and go 3 m to inn on left.
Restrictions No smoking in 2 dining rooms.
Credit cards MC, Visa.
Rates MAP, $240 suite, $180–240 double. Extra person in room, $35. Midweek discounts. Senior discounts. 2-night weekend minimum. Prix fixe dinner, $25–35.
Extras French spoken.

UPPERVILLE

1763 Inn   *Tel:* 703–592–3848
Route 1, Box 19D, 22176   800–699–1763

Not surprisingly, the 1763 inn was actually built in that year (the portion housing the restaurant); while it can't be verified whether George Washington actually slept here, it is known that he owned this building as part of his Virginia property. Owned since 1970 by Uta Kirchner, the inn has period furnishings and paintings in the appropriately named George Washington Room while the German and French rooms are decorated in a style reminiscent of their countries. Guest rooms are located in several cabins, a renovated stone barn, and the main house. The large, well-known restaurant serves German-American cuisine; veal schnitzel prepared in several ways are popular menu items; rates include a full breakfast.

"Our delightful cabin overlooked grazing horses and cattle, as well as the inn's swimming pool and tennis court. We breakfasted in the dining room, watching a swan gliding on the pond outside. Uta and Don Kirchner are most affable hosts." (Hope Welliver) More comments please.

Open All year. Restaurant open for dinner daily, and for lunch Sat., Sun.
Rooms 3 cabins, 13 doubles—all with private bath and/or shower, radio, TV, desk, air-conditioning. Most with fireplace, whirlpool tub. 14 with telephone. 12 rooms in annex.

Facilities Restaurant with entertainment Fri., bar. 50 acres with swimming pool, tennis court, fishing. 15 m to downhill skiing.
Location N VA. 50 m W of Washington, DC; 22 m SE of Winchester, 23 m N of Warrenton. 2 m W of town on Rte. 50 (Mosby Hwy.).
Credit cards All major credit cards accepted.
Rates B&B, $50–150 cabin, $95–150 double. Extra person in room, $20. 2-night weekend minimum. Alc lunch, $15–20; alc dinner, $35.
Extras Limited wheelchair accessibility; some rooms equipped for the disabled. .

VESUVIUS

Irish Gap Inns   *Tel:* 804–922–7701
Route 1, Box 40, 24483

Built in 1986, the Bee Skep and the Gatehouse are the two buildings that make up the Irish Gap Inns, owned by Dillard Saunders and Susie and Dell Carter. Both buildings have an airy and spacious country look, rustic yet elegant, and both share beautiful views of the ponds, fields, and surrounding mountains.

Dillard Saunders reports that "the people come to our inn to relax and enjoy the quiet privacy we offer. Most who hike our trails are interested in the wildlife, Indian lore, flowers, and our pets. If you don't like animals this isn't the place for you. We have dogs, birds, horses, fancy rabbits, goats, turkeys, chickens, and a llama. The children enjoy gathering the chicken eggs, throwing sticks into the pond for the retriever, and playing with the rabbits. Fishing for bass, bream, and catfish, swimming in the spring-fed pond, tooling around in the paddleboat or canoe, shooting pool, and talking hunting are favorites with the adults. Everyone seems to enjoy going into Lexington for lunch, shopping, and historic tours."

"A marvelous place to stay—comfortable and immaculate, with a delicious hearty breakfast—perfect except for the instant coffee. Young, friendly owners with lots of energy." *(Patsy Anderson)* "We had a delightful room in the Gatehouse cottage and were able to use the well-appointed kitchen. The main house, of post and beam construction, has a large sunny sitting room the size of three ordinary living rooms. Very peaceful location." *(Stephen Thomas)* More comments please.

Open All year. 4-wheel drive vehicle required for winter access.
Rooms 1 2-bedroom suite, 6 doubles in 2 separate buildings. All with private bath and/or shower, TV, desk, air-conditioning, ceiling fan. 1 with whirlpool bath. Rooms in Bee Skep have mini-refrigerator, porch with rocking chairs.
Facilities Gatehouse: great room with fireplace, dining area, TV, kitchen, porches, decks. Bee Skep Inn: great room with fireplace, dining area, game room. 285 acres with farm buildings, wildflowers, woodlands; hiking & cross-country trails; ponds for fishing, swimming, boating, canoeing, and hunting. Bicycling nearby. 30 m to Wintergreen for downhill skiing, golf.
Location W central VA, on Blue Ridge Pkwy. 18 m NE of Lexington, 30 m to Natural Bridge. Turn off Pkwy between mileposts #37 & #38; go N on Rte. 605 to private road sign for inns.
Restrictions No children under 12 at Bee Skep; all welcome in Gate House.
Credit cards MC, Visa.

Rates B&B, $146 2-bedroom suite, $68–98 double, $58–78 single, including service. Extra person in room, $20. Group (8 or more people) and weekly rates for entire Gate House. 2-night minimum May, Oct. weekends, also holiday weekends. Prix fixe dinner (24 hr. advance notice), $18.
Extras Wheelchair accessible; 2 bedrooms/baths equipped for disabled. Crib available. Kennel/stable boarding for pets, $5-20.

VIRGINIA BEACH

Angie's Guest Cottage
302 24th Street, 23451

Tel: 804–428–4690

Long-time owner Barbara Yates describes her B&B as a "large beach house with a casual atmosphere. Guests often describe us as being cute, clean, comfortable, convenient (sorry about all the 'c's'), and friendly. When you're not on the beach or touring, sit on the front porch and watch the people go by, take a bicycle ride, or relax under a tree in the back yard and read a book." In-season rates include a variety of breads, cereal, cheese, fruit, coffee, tea, and juice.

Perhaps best known for its miles of free beaches, and typical tacky beach town honky-tonk, Virginia Beach also offers such interesting rainy-day diversions as the Virginia Marine Science Museum, Life-Saving Museum of Virginia, several restored 17th and 18th century homes, and the nearby Norfolk Naval Base. *(Jason Vogel)*

Open April 1 through Oct. 1
Rooms 2 cottages, 3 doubles, 1 single—1 with private bath and/or shower, 5 rooms sharing 3 baths. All with radio, TV, air-conditioning, refrigerator.
Facilities Living room with library, guest kitchen, porch, deck. Patio with barbecue pit, picnic tales, Ping-Pong. Parking available in driveway or on street.
Location Center of resort area. From Rte. 44, turn left on Arctic Ave. and go 3 blocks to 24th St. and turn right to inn. From Bay-Bridge Tunnel, take Rte. 60 to town and turn right at 24th St.
Restrictions Noise from backyard youth hostel. No smoking.
Credit cards None accepted.
Rates Room only (prior to Memorial Day weekend, after Labor Day), $26 double, $20 single. B&B (Memorial Day weekend–Labor Day weekend), $60 double, $48 single. Extra person in room, $4–10. Weekly rates in cottage. 2-night minimum stay.
Extras Station pickups. Babysitting available. French, German spoken.

WARM SPRINGS

A historic town nestled at the base of Little Mountain in the Alleghenies, Warm Springs offers pleasant streets lined with beautiful old buildings, and makes a good base for exploring the area's natural beauty—and of course, for taking the baths here (the reasonable fee includes use of an old-fashioned bathing suit), or at nearby Hot Springs or Bolar Springs. The town lies along a mill stream, on a quiet loop of Main Street, about four blocks removed from U.S. Highway 220, a heavily traveled commercial route, which runs just outside of town.

Information please: The **Meadow Lane Lodge** (Star Route A, Box 110, 24484; 703–839–5959), with farm animals and even a peacock, provides a relaxing atmosphere in a rural setting. Listed in last year's guide, we'd like to get some additional feedback on the **Three Hills** (Route 220, Box 99, 24484; 703–839–5381), a grand manor house, with cottages, built in 1913 in the Colonial Revival style. Restored in 1984, it sits high above Route 220, with beautiful westward views over the Virginia highlands.

The Inn at Gristmill Square
Route 645, Box 359, 24484

Tel: 703–839–2231

Located right at the center of Warm Springs, Gristmill Square comprises a cluster of five restored 19th-century buildings including the inn's guest rooms, a restaurant, an antique gallery, and a country store. The inn was created in 1972 and has been owned by the McWilliams family since 1981. Rooms are decorated in a variety of styles, from antique to country-comfortable to more modern furnishings. The inn's restaurant, the Waterwheel, is housed in a mill dating back to 1900; both continental and American dishes are offered, but native brook trout is a particular specialty—you can have it smoked, broiled, or pan fried with black walnuts.

"We stayed in the Silo Room, which included a round living area with a couch and fireplace, and plenty of interesting reading materials, adjoined by comfortably sized bedroom and bath. The furnishings were lovely and well kept. The restaurant was very good, and we enjoyed selecting our own bottle of wine from the cellar. The surrounding countryside is picturesque and peaceful. We took some pleasant walks on the country back roads and also enjoyed poking around the nearby town of Hot Springs." *(Linda & Phillip Burcham)*

"The spring which supplied water to the old mill wheel goes around and through the different houses, where the guest accommodations are. The tiny village is delightful and within walking distance of Warm Springs baths. Guest rooms have their own sitting areas, and all are furnished with antiques. We were greeted with a basket of cheeses, crackers, fruit, chocolates, and a bucket of ice. Meals are served in the Waterwheel Restaurant, part of the old gristmill, with the millstones, exposed beams, and grain chutes still intact. The food is delicious, beautifully prepared and served." *(Betty Sadler)*

"We stayed in the Steel House, across the road from the inn. Parking and dealing with luggage was exceptionally easy. The rooms were large, with country-style decor, including quilts, wooden queen-size beds, overstuffed chairs, marble-topped dressers, and fireplace. Our room had rag rugs on hardwood floors; my parents' room had wall-to-wall tweed carpeting. We did not see the innkeeper after arrival, and nor is there a place to mingle with other guests. After check-in, you are left to your own devices unless you request assistance. Our bathrooms were well-equipped with thick, colored towels, and Gilchrist & Soames amenities. Extra touches included an alarm clock, full-length mirror, and wall-mounted hairdryer. Breakfast was delivered to our room within five minutes of our request, and included three kinds of melon, grapes, pineapple, and strawberries, homemade raisin bread, nut bread, and a thermos or coffee." *(SHW)*

"Fully endorse existing entry. They have a surprisingly wide menu with exceptional continental cuisine. For my money, it's better than the Homestead's." *(MG)*

An area for improvement: "The Jenny Payne Room could use a larger bedside table and new lamp shades."

Open All year.
Rooms 2 2-bedroom apartments, 4 suites, 8 doubles—all with private shower and/or bath, telephone, TV, fan, refrigerator. Most with desk, fireplace; some with kitchens. Rooms in 3 buildings.
Facilities Restaurant, bar. 1 acre with sauna, swimming pool, 3 tennis courts, Jackson River for fishing. Golf, horseback riding nearby. 4 m to skiing.
Location From Staunton, follow Rte. 250 to Rte. 254 to Buffalo Gap. Then take Rte. 42 to Millboro Spring, Rte. 39 to Warm Springs. Inn is on Rte. 645.
Restriction Some early morning (7:00 A.M.) traffic noise weekdays.
Credit cards MC, Visa.
Rates B&B, $105–140 apartment (sleeps 4), $80–85 suite or double, $65–70 single. Children under 10 free in parents' room. Extra person in room, $10. MAP, $157–238 apartment, $136–141 double, $88–93 single. Extra person in room, $32.50; extra child under 10, $15. Alc lunch $7, alc dinner $25.
Extras Limited wheelchair accessibility. Small pets permitted; may not be left unattended. Airport/station pickups. Crib, babysitting available.

WASHINGTON

The tiny town of Washington (population 220) was laid out by George Washington over 250 years ago; the street names are unchanged. It is home to several quality gift, craft, and antique stores. Known as Little Washington, it is located in Northern Virginia, in Rappahannock County. Its 60 miles west of Washington, D.C., 13 miles east of the Skyline Drive, and 1/2 hour west of Warrentown.

Information please: For those who'd like to combine a superb meal at the Inn at Little Washington with more reasonably priced accommodation, we'd suggest **Caledonia Farm** (Route 628, Rte. 1, Box 2080; 703–675–3693) just 4 miles away. A Federal-style stone farmhouse built in 1812 and surrounded by acres of farmland, long-time owner Phil Irwin offers a choice of breakfasts cooked to order, evening refreshments, numerous other amenities and fireplaced guest rooms decorated with antiques and period reproductions. Rates are a reasonable $70–100, except for Saturday nights, when they increase by 50%. Reports please.

The Inn at Little Washington
Middle and Main Streets, P.O. Box 300, 22747

Tel: 703–675–3800

Not long after Patrick O'Connell and Reinhardt Lynch opened their Little Washington restaurant in 1978, a Washington, DC, food critic described it as "the best restaurant within a 100-mile radius of Washington." By now the inn has received the highest acclaim from every conceivable source, including five diamond/star ratings from AAA and Mobil. Despite weekend surcharges, advance reservations for weekend dinners are required a month ahead, especially in the fall. If you want to stay overnight, plan two to three months ahead. Given the hoopla, guest expectations run as high as the prices, and reader feedback seems to indicate that many feel its worth it for the ultimate fantasy experience. Use the advance lead time to budget for your excursion, so when you get to the inn, you won't have to think about money at all. Many feel its worthwhile to go the whole nine yards and reserve one of the suites for the most extravagant evening of all.

Rooms are lavishly decorated by the designer of the inn's dining room, with English fabrics, elaborate wallcoverings and *faux* marble painting, antiques, and all possible amenities; rates include a full breakfast. Rooms vary in size, design, decor and style as well as price; the least expensive are compact, while the suites are extremely spacious.

Under the inventive touch of chef Patrick O'Connell, the cuisine continues to win accolades from all. A recent dinner menu selection included timbale of lump crabmeat with spinach mousse, foie gras with smoked goose bread, and ham with black-eyed peas vinaigrette among the appetizers; sweetbreads with chestnuts, cider, and cream, and lobster with orzo among the entrées; and chocolate bourbon pecan torte and apple tart among the dessert choices. These are tough decisions, though, so you might want to arrange for a tasting dinner instead; ask when you make reservations.

Breakfasts are no less tempting. Possibilities might include a wild mushroom omelet with sausage and potatoes, or panfried trout, with thick-sliced bacon and eggs scrambled with smoked salmon.

"At the foot of the Blue Ridge Mountains, the Inn at Little Washington is the place where I try to stop for dinner after any day trip in the area (Skyline Drive, Monticello, Civil War battlefields). It's even close enough for a drive from D.C. on a day off. The dining room is a classic example of gourmet American cuisine at its best." *(Spencer Weber Waller)*

"Long considered competitive with the best French restaurants in Washington, D.C., the Inn at Little Washington is rather more imaginative than most of them. Our room was elaborately decorated and the glitzy bathroom lacked for nothing. The price includes a delicious and very substantial breakfast, with endless choices (no need to eat again until dinner), served at whatever hour you choose in the beautiful William Morris–wallpapered dining room." *(CM)*

"Truly a luxurious, gourmet experience, which is worth the price if you love excellent food. We had dessert in the beautiful landscaped garden, serenaded by the local tree frogs." *(Pamela Young, also Mrs. Lola Rhea)*

Open All year. Closed Mon., Tues.
Rooms 2 duplex suites with balconies, 8 doubles with private shower or bath, desk.
Facilities Restaurant, sitting rooms, covered garden terrace with fountains.
Location Center of town.
Restrictions No children under 10.

VIRGINIA

Credit cards MC, Visa.
Rates B&B, $400 suite, $210–300 double. $80 surcharge weekends, holidays.
Prix fixe dinner, $70 (Sun.–Fri.); $90 Sat.
Extras Member, Relais et Chateaux.

Sycamore Hill House & Gardens
Route 1, Box 978, 22747

Tel: 703–675–3046

Set atop Menefee Mountain (elevation 1,043 feet), Sycamore Hill is a contemporary stone house with a lots of windows and a 63-foot veranda for drinking in the views of meadows and woodland, gardens and mountains. Kerri Wagner—formerly a registered lobbyist—and Stephen Wagner—a free-lance illustrator—left the hustle and bustle of the nation's capital to open this small B&B in 1988. Kerri continues to pursue her interests in gardening and sells the surplus (flowers, fruits and vegetables) to her guests and others. Stephen focuses his personal art on nature and wildlife, and his professional work has appeared in *National Geographic* and the *Washington Post*; originals of his published work hang in the house.

Guest rooms are handsomely decorated with an eclectic touch; the Wagners' interest in Oriental art is evident throughout the house. Rates include a full breakfast which might include sourdough French toast, stuffed pears, or apple soufflé.

"If you're interested in a quiet setting and a magnificent view, surrounded by nature, this is the place. This 18-year-old home is open and airy, full of plants and artwork. Brandy in each room and chocolates each night on the nightstand are nice touches. The owners are friendly and helpful; they provided us with a list of restaurants they enjoy in nearby Warrenton. Their big white dog, "Molly Bean," made us feel right at home." *(Janet Payne)*

Open All year.
Rooms 1 suite, 2 doubles—suite with private bath, doubles sharing 1 bath. All with radio, TV, desk, air-conditioning, fan.
Facilities Living/dining room with TV, stereo, piano, fireplace; veranda. 52 acres with wildlife sanctuary, gardens, woodlands.
Location N VA, Rappahannock County. 66 m W of Washington, DC. On top of mountain, at intersection of SR 683 and Rte. 211.
Restrictions No smoking in guest rooms. No children.
Credit cards MC, Visa accepted only for last-minute reservations; not accepted for payment.
Rates B&B, $145–165 suite, $75–105 double. Extra person in room, $25. 2-night holiday weekend minimum. 10% discount for 4-night stay in suite.
Extras Limited wheelchair accessibility.

WHITE POST

L'Auberge Provencale
P.O. Box 119, 22663

Tel: 703–837–1375

For a touch of southern France in northern Virginia, L'Auberge Provençale is the inn of choice for both food and accommodation. In 1980, fourth-generation chef and owner Alain Borel and his wife Celeste bought this 1750s stone farmhouse, first renovating the downstairs for their restaurant. Over the next seven years, they added a wing with guest rooms and a sunny breakfast room. Guest rooms are eclectically decorated with French art and fabrics, Victorian wicker, and Federal reproductions. The restaurant serves, *bien sûr*, French cuisine; rates include a full breakfast.

"We found staying here like having the best guest room of a friend's well-appointed country house. There was no institutional severity in the bedroom with its random-width floors and four-poster bed, but rather a profusion of pictures, fresh flowers and plants, wooden carvings and magazines.

"If only one's friends served as good food as that of gracious chef-owner Alain Borel. This is really elegant French food in the style beloved by Julia Child. My first course was a mousse of scallops with beurre blanc sauce, threaded with a pretty design of red pepper coulis; my next course was a dish made famous in a Parisian 3-star restaurant—lobster with vanilla butter sauce—shelled and then re-shaped, served with asparagus and the thinnest French beans. My husband had a salad of sweetbreads and wild mushrooms, followed by pigeonneaux with local morels and tarragon. It was well worth the drive from DC, and the big breakfast was wonderful, too.

"The inn is on the way to the Blue Ridge Mountains and Skyline Drive; you could spend the day hiking in the mountains, then retire to the inn for dinner and the night. While not located in a village, it was nice to sit on the porch and gaze at fields of cows, rolling green countryside and the blue hills beyond." *(Carolyn Mathiasen)*

Open Closed Jan. 2 through Feb. 13.
Rooms 6 doubles—all with private bath and/or shower, air-conditioning. Some with fireplace.
Facilities Restaurant, bar, sitting room. 8.5 acres with gardens. Golf, canoeing nearby. 15 min. to downhill skiing.
Location NW VA, Clarke County. 1½ hrs. NW of Washington, DC. Take I-66 W to Exit 5. Go N on Rte. 17 for 9 m to Rte. 50 and turn left. At 1st traffic light turn left on Rte. 340. Go 1 m to inn on right.
Restrictions No children under 10.
Credit cards MC, Visa.
Rates B&B, $175 suite, $135–165 double, $95–135 single. Extra person in room, $20. Tipping encouraged. Alc dinner, $30–50.
Extras Wheelchair accessible; some rooms equipped for the disabled. Airport pickup, $60. French, Spanish spoken.

WILLIAMSBURG

Williamsburg was selected as the new colonial capital of Virginia when it became clear that the original capital at Jamestown was disease-ridden and undefensible. It was planned and built starting in 1700 by Governor Francis Nicholson, and grew rapidly. In 1780, the capital was moved again, this time to Richmond. Williamsburg continued as the county seat and as the home of William and Mary College and the

Public Hospital for the Insane. Fortunately, a large number of 18th-century houses survived, and, in 1926, the Reverend W.A.R. Goodwin persuaded John D. Rockefeller, Jr., to finance the city's restoration. Today, the historic area is operated by the nonprofit Colonial Williamsburg Foundation. All visits to Colonial Williamsburg should begin at the Visitor's Center, for full information on what to see and do.

More than one million visitors come to Williamsburg every year. Remember that Williamsburg is very hot and crowded in the summer; late fall or early spring are probably the best times to visit. If you do visit in the warm weather, try to walk or jog through the restoration early in the morning (around 6 A.M.), before the crowds arrive. Although the weather can be quite chilly and damp, special programs and reduced-rate packages are available from January to early March.

Williamsburg is located 155 miles south of Washington, D.C., and 50 miles southeast of Richmond.

Also recommended: Although not really appropriate for a full entry, we received a rave report on the **Kingsmill Resort** (1010 Kingsmill Road, 23185; 804–253–1703 or 800–832–5665), a conference center and condominium complex on the James River. It's two miles from Colonial Williamsburg, and adjacent to Busch Gardens and the Anheuser-Busch brewery—clearly an ideal family choice. "The resort has 12 tennis courts, an 18-hole golf course, a marina, and a sports club with indoor and outdoor swimming pools, Nautilus equipment, and racquetball. Condos are built of gray cedar, blending well with the surrounding pine forests. Our spacious unit was done in Williamsburg style, with Queen Anne reproductions, and wallpapering in plum and blue-gray. Daily maid service, triple-sheeted beds, and bathroom amenities provided hotel-style comfort. We had an excellent dinner in the Riverview Dining Room, and enjoyed a sumptuous buffet breakfast in the Bray Dining Room. The food was among the best we've had in the area. The staff was extremely accommodating, and the cost of our two-bedroom condo was less than two rooms at the Williamsburg Inn." *(SHW)*

Information please: War Hill Inn (4560 Long Hill Road, 23185; 804–565–0248) is a relatively new B&B, built in 1968 of old bricks and woodwork salvaged from historic buildings. The five guest rooms overlook 32 acres of fruit orchards and grazing Black Angus cattle, and rates include a full breakfast. Children are welcome in this peaceful setting just three miles from Williamsburg's sights.

For an additional area entry, see Smithfield.

Himmel Bett Inn   *Tel:* 804–229–6421
706 Richmond Road, 23185

Located in a brick Cape Cod home, this B&B has been owned by Mary Peters since 1985 and is furnished with Pennsylvania Dutch country antiques and quilts.

"The rooms of Himmel Bett look as though they jumped off the pages of *Country Living* magazine. Mary Peters has a charming collection of country antiques and has furnished each room down to the last detail with wonderful treasures and accessories. The walls of every room are hand stenciled, and the four-poster and spool beds are gorgeous. The house is quiet and extremely comfortable, and is located within easy walking distance of the historic district. Mary went out of her way to be helpful and accommodating." *(Linda Bachrack)*

"Mary Peters made us feel that we were part of the family. Breakfasts are excellent and everything is homey and clean." *(Clyde & Charlene Erler, also Dynele Hay)* "Entering this little brick house on Williamsburg's main road, we were surprised to find a wonderfully cozy home. Breakfast included a muffin or roll with flavored butter, followed by quiche, waffles, or eggs. Mary created a wonderful atmosphere as she cooked, served, and chatted with us during breakfast." *(Geoff & Sue Meisner)*

Open All year.
Rooms 3 doubles—all with private bath and/or shower, TV, air-conditioning, fan.
Facilities Dining room, living room with TV. York and James River nearby for fishing. Off-street parking.
Location 4 blocks from center. Walking distance to restored area.
Restrictions No smoking. No children under 12.
Credit cards MC, Visa.
Rates B&B, $70–85 double, $65 single. Extra person in room, $20.
Extras Airport/station pickups, $10. German spoken.

Williamsburg Inn   *Tel:* 804–229–1000
Frances Street, P.O. Box B, 23187   800–HISTORY

The Colonial Williamsburg Foundation owns and operates 1,000 rooms spread over seven different lodging establishments, including the Williamsburg Inn, the Williamsburg Lodge, the Motor House, the Colonial Houses, Providence Hall, the Cascades, and the Governor's Inn (call the toll-free phone number above for information on all of them). A key asset of all these lodgings is their location, enabling you to stroll the grounds in the early morning or evening, after the crowds have dispersed. The Inn and the Colonial Houses are most highly recommended, with the Colonial Houses way ahead as the first choice of most respondents. Here's a sample of the reader feedback received:

The Inn: The Williamsburg Inn is a very well known full-service luxury hotel, with high standards, and corresponding rates. "Truly the epitome of elegance and good taste. Rooms are furnished in the Regency manner, with muted Schumacher fabrics, original paintings and prints, and brass candlestick lamps." *(Michael Spring)* "Service is impeccable from the front door to the dining room and throughout the inn. Each staff member stands ready to help each guest make their visit more pleasant. The Regency Dining Room serves a very elegant buffet breakfast, and dinner is a highlight not to be missed. The public rooms are very inviting as they overlook a patio facing the golf course; the gift shops are very attractive." *(Elizabeth Sommer)* "Lots of bathroom amenities; enjoyed afternoon tea and cookies at 4 P.M.. The hotel also offers an excellent two-hour walking tour." *(Dianne Crawford)* "Excellent breakfasts, with fine service." *(SHW)*

And less favorably: "Very expensive and noisy. Lots of little extras in the room, but the decor didn't seem special." Also: "Check-in can be cumbersome, especially if the inn is full."

The Colonial Houses: "Furnishings in the Colonial Houses are antique reproductions, as are the artworks. Floors are hardwood, with woven rag rugs. Most have fireplaces and TVs; bathrooms are well equipped with thick towels and amenities, although many are tucked up under the eaves. Beds are triple-sheeted, and there is evening turndown service. All are within a four-square-block walk of the Williamsburg Inn." *(SHW)* "Although expensive, the accommodations are truly outstanding and worth the splurge. The house where we stayed, 3008 Francis St., was a real doll house, beautifully furnished with reproductions. The bathroom was adorable, with its steeply pitched ceiling, fresh flowers, thick towels. Our beds had real feather pillows." *(Mary Wabeke)* "We rented the second floor of a small house on Duke of Gloucester Street in the heart of Colonial Williamsburg. The guest room and bath were large and appropriately decorated, but the best part came in the evening, when we could step out the door of our little home and walk throughout the town, looking into the shops and buildings and pretending to be an actual part of this marvelous 18th-century town." *(Jack & Sue Lane)* "We stayed in the Chiswell-Bucktrout Kitchen (in colonial times, kitchens were often separate buildings), and found it charming, comfortable, and wonderfully convenient. It had a large closet/pantry, brick floor, with a little courtyard." *(Dianne Crawford, also Nick & Carole Mumford)* "Breakfast is included; a delicious one is served at Shields' Tavern. Parking is provided; closet space is plentiful, hidden behind old latch doors; there is even an iron and ironing board for your convenience. I recommend that you outline your desires (large or small bedroom, fireplace, porch or garden, etc.) so that the staff can match a house with your needs. All houses are discreetly marked and one needs a map (provided at check-in) to decipher what is where. One of the staff escorts you to your 'house' and settles you in. The houses are very popular and seem to fill up months in advance; for Christmas there can be a two-year wait." *(Elizabeth Sommer)*

The Motor House: "Delightfully clean. Easy walking distance to local transportation to all events and meals. A wonderful place to be off-season." *(Robert Rieger)*

Open All year.
Rooms 25 suites, 210 doubles—all with full private bath, telephone, radio, TV, desk, air-conditioning.
Facilities Restaurant, 4 lobbies, 2 cocktail lounges, library. Music nightly, dancing weekends. 200 acres. 2 swimming pools, 8 tennis courts, golf, lawn bowling green.
Location Center of town.
Restrictions Smoking restricted in some areas.
Credit cards Amex, MC, Visa.
Rates Room only, $250–500 suite, $165–250 double. Extra person in room, $15. Alc breakfast, $6–16; alc lunch, $11–14; alc dinner, $30–55. Special packages.
Extras Portable ramp for wheelchair access to first-floor rooms; some rooms equipped for the disabled. Airport/station pickups. Crib, babysitting available. German, Spanish, Italian spoken.

Williamsburg Sampler B&B
922 Jamestown Road, 23185

Tel: 804–253–0398
800–722–1169

Helen and Ike Sisane are the young owners of the Williamsburg Sampler, a B&B conveniently located across the street from the College of William & Mary, and within walking distance of Colonial Williamsburg. Their home is a three-story red brick Colonial Revival home, built in the 1930s, decorated with Ethan Allen reproductions, Queen Anne wing chairs, and highlighted by their collections of pewter, framed samplers, and antiques. Guest rooms have either a rice-carved four-poster bed, a cannonball bed, a canopied bed, or mahogany twin beds. Rates include a breakfast of juice, fresh fruit or melon, waffles or raisin French toast, and coffee cake. "Delicious breakfast. Warm and friendly atmosphere." *(GR)* More reports welcome.

Open All year.
Rooms 4 doubles—all with private bath and/or shower, radio, air-conditioning, fan.
Facilities Living/dining room, porches. Off-street parking.
Location Walking distance to Colonial Williamsburg. From I-64, take Exit 57 A/B to Rte. 199 W. At intersection of Rte. 199 and Rtes. 5/31 (at stoplight) turn right. Go .7 m to inn on right.
Restrictions No smoking. No children under 8.
Credit cards None accepted.
Rates B&B, $75 double. $120 for family renting two rooms. 2-night weekend/holiday minimum.
Extras Station pickups.

WOODSTOCK

Woodstock is located in the Shenandoah Valley of northern Virginia, 90 miles west Washington, DC. From Washington, take I-66 west to I-81. Then take I-81 south to Woodstock. Take Exit 72, then follow Route. 42 east into Woodstock.

Reader tip: "The area is full of historic sites, caverns, antique shops, national parks, wineries, and recreational activities. The view from Massanutten Tower is truly magnificent, with the seven bends of the Shenandoah River spread out below." *(Joy & John McCauley)*

Information please: The Azalea House (551 South Main Street 22664; 703–459–3500) is a century-old Victorian home decorated with family antiques. Rates include a full country breakfast, and the backyard swimming pool offers guests a refreshing dip after a day of touring. Reports?

The Candlewick Inn
127 North Church Street, 22664

Tel: 703–459–8008

The Candlewick is a turn-of-the-century Victorian, bought by John, Patricia, and Tom Samford in 1988. Rooms are decorated simply with antiques, period pieces, and country touches, with a light and airy look. Rates include a breakfast of a baked egg dish, bacon or sausage, pumpkin bread, fruit and juice, coffee and tea. Tom notes that their inn is "the old Bargelt house, dating back to the 1880s. Guests enjoy the old-fashioned charm of the random-width pine flooring and parlor window seat with a lovely view of the Massanutten Mountains. The inn sits on a quiet street with shops and stores a short walk in one direction, and pastures, woods and creeks in the other."

"Our hosts quickly made us feel like treasured friends, going out of their way to accommodate their guests' needs. Teresa is very concerned with keeping things spotless. Extra touches include quality linens and complimentary toiletries, fluffy towels and ample lighting for reading and doing make-up." *(George & Zora Payne, also Nancy Gill & Keith Sharon)*

"The friendly owners are well informed about local events and activities. The inn is tastefully and comfortably decorated with beautiful antiques and crafts. The breakfasts were terrific. Fresh fruit was in abundance and each meal was hearty and delicious." *(Martha Blumenthal & Christopher Farrell, also Jeran & Alan Fink)*

Open All year.
Rooms 4 doubles, 1 single—1 with private shower, 4 rooms sharing 2 baths. All with air-conditioning, fan.
Facilities Parlor with books, games; TV room, porch with swing; country kitchen with sun porch. Gardens with patio, badminton. Shenandoah River nearby for swimming, fishing, canoe, and inner tube rentals. 30 min. to downhill skiing. 5 m to Shenandoah Vineyard.
Location Turn left on Rte. 11 (Main St.). and go to 3rd traffic light and turn right on Court St. Go 1 block and turn left on Church St. ½ block to inn on left.
Restrictions No children under 12. Smoking only in public rooms.
Credit cards None accepted.
Rates B&B, $45–55 double, $40–50 single. Additional person in room, $15. 10% senior discount. 2-3 night minimum required during peak season.
Extras Station pickups.

The Country Fare
402 North Main Street, 22664

Tel: 703–459–4828

Built 1772 of log and brick, The Country Fare is a cozy B&B restored in Williamsburg colors and wallpapers, with hand-stenciled designs throughout. Rooms are decorated with a mix of antiques and country collectibles, reflecting owner Bette Halgren's interest in crafts. Rates include a breakfast of fresh fruit and juice, homemade breads and biscuits served served on old family china and silver. "Delightful accommodations, warm hospitality." *(JN)* More comments please.

Open All year.
Rooms 3 doubles—1 with private shower, 2 with maximum of 4 sharing bath. 1 with fireplace, all with air-conditioning.
Facilities Dining room with wood stove, living room, porch with rockers, swing; patio.
Location Walking distance to village.
Restrictions No smoking.
Credit cards None accepted.
Rates B&B, $45–55 double, $40 single. Extra person in room, $10. 2-night minimum fall weekends.

The Inn at Narrow Passage
U.S. 11 South, P.O. Box 608, 22664

Tel: 703–459–8000

Long before Shenandoah Valley travelers rolled down Interstate 81, stagecoaches bumped their way along the Wilderness Road, past what is now known as The Inn at Narrow Passage, site of Indian raids and in 1862 the headquarters of Stonewall Jackson. Portions of the inn date back to 1740, although some of the guest rooms are housed in a recent addition. The inn was restored by Ellen and Ed Markel in 1984, who exposed the original log construction and pine floors. They've furnished the inn with colonial reproductions and queen-size canopy beds. Ellen notes that "the guests we most enjoy having are married couples who appreciate the history and beauty of this area and like the warm, family hospitality we try to provide."

"Located on the banks of the Shenandoah River, the inn is graced with the constant and soothing melody of running water. It is both rustic and delightfully charming, with an almost eerie historical presence. We stayed in the bedroom that Stonewall Jackson used during the Civil War." *(Paul Embroski)* "Our comfortable room had a four-poster bed and working fireplace. The inn is easily accessible from the highway but is far enough away that traffic noise is not bothersome. Best of all is Ed's genuine friendliness and his easy, unobtrusive manner." *(Richard Merritt)*

"The Markels' greeting is as warm as the slow burning fire in the living room and the hot herbal tea they serve on chilly evenings. Breakfasts are delicious, the bacon outstanding." *(Mr. & Mrs. Robert Ward)* "Relax in the sitting room reading or playing checkers, then stretch your legs by paying a visit to the inn's pet rabbit or strolling along the Shenandoah River." *(Fred & Martha Sisk)*

"Ed Markel made us feel welcome from our first phone call to make reservations. Upon arrival, he showed us to our spotless room and invited us to have a look at the other rooms, since we were the first to check in. Most of the accessories were for sale at their shop, as well as locally made crafts. The grounds were well kept, and Mopsy, their rabbit, keeps an eye on guests." *(Lana Alukonis)*

Open All year.

Rooms 12 doubles—8 with private bath and/or shower, 4 with a maximum of 4 people sharing bath. All with radio, air-conditioning. Some with desk, fireplace. Four rooms in annex.

Facilities Living room with fireplace, dining room with fireplace, porch. Country store. 5 acres on Shenandoah River. Fishing, water sports nearby. 30 min. to downhill skiing at Bryce Mt.

Location N VA, Shenandoah Valley. 90 m W of Washington, DC. From Washington, take I-66 W to I-81. Take I-81 S to Woodstock (Exit 72, Rte. 11). 2 m S of Woodstock on Rte. 11.

Restrictions Smoking in living room only. Light sleepers should request rooms away from street. No smoking in guest rooms. "We prefer infants or children over 4 because of stairs and fireplaces."

Credit cards MC, Visa.

Rates B&B, $55–80 double, $45–75 single. Extra person in room, $8. "We appreciate a tip for our housekeepers." 2-night minimum holiday and October weekends.

Extras Cribs, babysitting available.

Key to Abbreviations

For complete information and explanations, please see the Introduction.

Rates: Range from least expensive room in low season to most expensive room in peak season.

Room only: No meals included; sometimes referred to as European Plan (EP).

B&B: Bed and breakfast; includes breakfast, sometimes afternoon/evening refreshment.

MAP: Modified American Plan; includes breakfast and dinner.

Full board: Three meals daily.

Alc lunch: A la carte lunch; average price of entrée plus nonalcoholic drink, tax, tip.

Alc dinner: Average price of three-course dinner, including half bottle of house wine, tax, tip.

Prix fixe dinner: Three- to five-course set dinner, excluding wine, tax, tip unless otherwise noted.

Extras: Noted if available. Always confirm in advance. Pets are not permitted unless specified; if you are allergic, ask if pets are in residence.

We Want to Hear from You!

As you know, this book is only effective with your help. We really need to know about your experiences and discoveries.

If you stayed at an inn or hotel listed here, we want to know how it was. Did it live up to our description? Exceed it? Was it what you expected? Did you like it? Were you disappointed? Delighted?

Have you discovered new establishments that we should add to the next edition?

Tear out one of the report forms at the back of this book (or use your own stationery if you prefer) and write today. Even if you write only "Fully endorse existing entry" you will have been most helpful.

Thank You!

West Virginia

Thomas Shepherd Inn, Shepherdstown

West Virginia is a rural, mountainous state, with areas of great beauty. Most of our listings are in the Eastern Panhandle, a region of historic interest and natural attractions. Because this area is only a 60- to 90-minute drive from Washington, D.C., and Baltimore, MD, it is particularly popular on weekends. Rates are most often highest Friday and Saturday nights, and can be substantially lower midweek. Rates don't usually vary much with the seasons, although October is generally the most popular period.

The rest of the state is also worth exploring, particularly if you have time to drive the backroads and "hollers." Look for rugged scenery, traditional Appalachian crafts, fall foliage that challenges New England's, and towns with names such as "Odd," "Man," "Hometown" and "Paw Paw."

Information please: The **Chestnut Ridge School,** a former elementary school on the outskirts of Morgantown is now home to a four-guest room B&B, each with a private marble and brass bathroom (1000 Stewartstown Road, Morgantown, 26505; 304–598–2262).

We'd also like to add entries in West Virginia's northwest panhandle. Wheeling, long a dreary industrial town, is slowly restoring the hand-some Victorian homes built during the city's prime. B&B accommodation is available at **Yesterday's Ltd. B&B** (823 Main Street, Wheeling 26003; 304–233–2003 or 304–232–0864. Two Victorian homes, the McClosky House and the Hess House are owned by the same people, and both offer period decor in rooms overlooking the Ohio River. The Hess House is particularly striking architecturally, built in the French

347

Renaissance Revival style. Another possibility 45 miles further south is the **Wells Inn** (316 Charles Street, Sistersville 26175; 304–652–1312). Built when this now-sleepy river town boomed with the discovery of natural gas and oil, this historic inn offers hearty meals and basic accommodation at modest prices. Reports?

Another possibility in the well-known resort town of White Sulphur Springs, near the Virginia border in the southern part of the state, is **The James Wylie House** (208 East Main Street, White Sulphur Springs 24986; 304–536–9444). The town is best known for the Greenbrier Resort, which often refers guests to this B&B when it's full. Dating to 1819, this Georgian Colonial-style B&B offers rooms furnished with antiques and country decor; the very reasonable rates include a full breakfast.

Rates do not include 5% state sales tax, plus additional local taxes of 3-4%.

BERKELEY SPRINGS

"We this day called at Ye Famed Warm Springs," says the March 18, 1748, journal entry of sixteen-year-old George Washington, who was traveling with a Virginia surveying group. He was referring to the warm mineral waters of what is now called Berkeley Springs, the nation's oldest spa, which nowadays offers a full range of mineral baths and massage, as well as a regular swimming pool. Other sights of interest include nearby Prospect Peak, with a three-state view; Cacapon State Park, with a lake for swimming and boating, and an eighteen-hole Robert Trent Jones golf course; hiking and riding on Cacapon Mountain; Berkeley Castle; and the historic Chesapeake and Ohio Canal Tunnel in Paw Paw, completed in 1850.

Berkeley Springs is located in the Eastern Panhandle region of West Virginia, 100 miles west of Washington, D.C., and Baltimore, MD, and 165 miles southwest of Philadelphia, PA.

The Country Inn *Tel:* 304–258–2210
Route 522, 25411 800–822–6630

The Country Inn was built in 1932 in a brick colonial style. Rooms are comfortable, with a mixture of period and contemporary decor. The inn restaurant offers American cuisine for breakfast, lunch, and dinner. Most respondents have been delighted with the quality and cost of the food at both breakfast and dinner, and pleased with the inn itself: "Delicious food, charming rooms. Big-city quality and cuisine at country prices." *(CW, also Sally Sieracki)* More comments please.

Open All year.
Rooms 72 suites and doubles with private or shared bath, TV, air-conditioning. Some rooms with sink or half-bath in room.
Facilities Restaurant, sitting room, lounge, garden, art gallery, meeting room, porches. Full spa facilities. Tennis, golf nearby.
Location In town, adjacent to Berkeley Springs State Park.

Credit cards Amex, MC, Visa.
Rates Room only, $70–135 suite, $35–75 double. Extra person in room, $5.
Midweek "3rd night free" package.
Extras Airport/station pickups.

Highlawn Inn   *Tel:* 304–258–5700
304 Market Street, 25411

The Highlawn is a turn-of-the-century Victorian home, owned by
Sandy Kauffman and Timothy Miller. Rooms are decorated with period
antiques and feature designer linens, English soaps, and other bath
amenities. Guests enjoy relaxing on the Highlawn's porch rockers, with
a lovely view overlooking the town.

"Everything is so fresh—the wonderful West Virginia air, the beautiful bedrooms with special linens and appointments, and the magnificent breakfast." *(Virginia Schatken)* "Outstanding breakfast. Very
personal setting—you really feel like one of the family. Rooms very
clean and attractively decorated." *(Pat Drake)* "Bathrooms are loaded
with plump towels and extra niceties. We were served an old-fashioned
country breakfast, cooked to order, beautifully presented. Early morning coffee was available to take to our bedroom, and herbal teas and
coffee are available in the living room throughout the day. Sandy made
our dinner reservations, and helped us reschedule activities canceled
due to a bad storm." *(Judith Kaplow)*

"The inn has a lovely ground-floor room easily accessible to anyone
with difficulty walking. It was comfortable and cozy with period decor
and quality bed linens. Sandy and Tim treated us as guests in their own
home, and made reservations at the baths and with an excellent mas-
seuse. Breakfast included fresh fruit, juice, and home-baked breads—
different each day—with eggs, sausage or bacon and the best biscuits
I've ever eaten. On the last day Sandy surprised us with cherry tarts
made with fruit from her own tree, and wonderful French toast." *(Angela
Mauran)*

Open All year.
Rooms 1 suite, 5 doubles—all with private bath and/or shower, TV, air-condi-
tioning.
Facilities Sitting room with fireplace, games, books, puzzles. 3/4 acre with picnic
table, wraparound veranda with porch swings, rockers. 9 m to Cacapon State Park
for golf, tennis, hiking, swimming.
Location 3 blocks from center, 3 blocks to Berkeley Springs Mineral Baths. From
I-70, I-81, take Rte. 522 to Market St. At the top of the hill on the left is the inn.
Restrictions No children.
Credit cards MC, Visa.
Rates B&B, $90 suite, $70–85 double.

CHARLES TOWN

Charles Town is home to the Charles Town Races and the Old Opera
House. Harper's Ferry National Historic Park and Antietam Battlefield
are both nearby. Charles Town is located on the Eastern Panhandle, 70
miles west of both Washington, D.C., and Baltimore, MD.

Information please: We'd like new reports on the **Carriage Inn** (417 East Washington Street, 25414; 304–728–8003) listed in previous editions of this guide. It was put up for sale last year, and more feedback is needed before we can reinstate it for a full entry. This five-guest room B&B is furnished with country antiques and hand-made canopied beds. Its Civil War history is especially interesting: in 1864, Generals Grant and Sheridan met here to discuss war strategy. At the time of the meeting, a flag carried under the command of Stonewall Jackson was hidden in an upstairs fireplace. Had these been found, the house would probably have been burned down by Union soldiers.

For an additional Charles Town–area entry, see listing for **Gilbert House** under Middleway.

The Cottonwood Inn   *Tel:* 304–725–3371
Route 2, Box 61-S, 25414

Eleanor and Colin Simpson have turned their Federalist-era (circa 1800) farmhouse into an inviting B&B, decorated with antiques and period reproductions. Rates include a full breakfast, with pecan griddle cakes and sausage links, southern-style French toast and bacon, and huevos rancheros among the favorite choices.

"A charming, quiet B&B in the country, a short but beautiful drive through rolling farmland. Our room was comfortable and clean, the owners warm and friendly, the breakfast wonderful." *(Janet Payne)* "Excellent location, with well-kept grounds, comfortable furnishings, and service beyond reproach. The Simpsons are both enjoyable and professional hosts." *(Vickie & Rhea McGee)* "The living room is a quiet, warm place to sit and read." *(Elizabeth Ingles)* "Very sophisticated decor, porch swing a delight." *(Nancy Riker, also JP)*

Open All year.
Rooms 6 doubles—all with private bath and/or shower, TV, air-conditioning. 3 with desk, 1 with fireplace.
Facilities Living room with library, fireplace; dining room with fireplace; porch with swing. 6 acres with stocked trout stream. Fishing, swimming, boating on Shenandoah & Potomac rivers nearby.
Location 6 m S of Charles Town. From Charles Town, take Rte. 9 S. Go 2.6 m to Kabletown Rd. and turn right. Go 3.2 m to silos at fork in road. Take right fork to inn.
Credit cards MC, Visa.
Rates B&B, $75–85 double. Extra person in room, $10. 2-night minimum holiday/craft festival weekends.
Extras Station pickups.

Hillbrook Inn   *Tel:* 304–725–4223
Route 13, RR 2, Box 152, 25414

Hillbrook was built as a private home by Colonel Bamford in the 1920s using timbers and stone from the farm that occupied the site in the 1800s. The Colonel modeled it after an inn in Normandy which he had much admired, and it is an extremely handsome and rambling structure, half-timbered with many chimneys, gables, and leaded glass windows. Owner Gretchen Carroll rescued Hillbrook from the brambles in 1985 with much difficult renovation work. She says that Hillbrook is for romantics of all ages who want to enjoy each others company in quiet, lovely, and relaxed surroundings. Rooms are furnished with Oriental rugs and original paintings; the antique beds have feather pillows and goose down comforters.

"The house is unique in its architecture, built on a hill, all rooms of different levels, only one room wide, with beautiful high vaulted ceilings, massive timbers, huge windows with small panes, plenty of fireplaces. Gretchen Carroll has carefully placed her beautiful objects d'art and antiques collected from all over the world throughout the house. She also has art books and fascinating volumes everywhere. She is clearly a multi-talented person to have done the restoration of the house herself, to cook such excellent meals, and to be such a charming and friendly hostess. The gardens are equally lovely with ducks on the pond, the old spring house, and more. Her New Year's Eve dinner is worth a drive from Washington just for the meal—seven or eight courses, small and beautifully paced." *(Pam Young)* "Classy, classy, classy. The house is spectacular, the quintessential country inn, with thousands of panes of glass in the mullioned windows, and woodland views everywhere. Gretchen met us in the driveway; after helping us stow our luggage she encouraged us to relax by the fire with a glass of sherry. Our rooms, The Lookout and The Point, shared a separate small staircase; the low eaves of The Lookout give a second meaning to its name, in addition to its fine views. With designer sheets, down pillows and duvets, our beds were very luxurious. Each bathrooms is distinctively different, some with clawfoot tubs (the Locke's Nest even has lavender fixtures) and European hand-held shower fixtures, but all are elegant with thick, colorful towels, Potter & Moore bath amenities, and lots of hot water. Gretchen has lived all over the world, and her collections highlights every room; there is original art from Southeast Asia, Africa, and South America.

"Our dinner was a seven-course triumph, with a good wine selection, served at a table next to the window, with a fireplace behind us. Our waiter was very competent, subdued, yet humorous. I was pleased that Gretchen had remembered our request, made months before, to omit certain foods that we cannot eat. Our fish course was a seafood creole with black drum fish, then a pasta course of angel hair and spinach linguine with pesto. The entrée was sautéed chicken with oregano and prunes, followed by a salad of curly endive, pineapple and cucumber with dill vinaigrette. These were accompanied by two fine Hungarian wines. To complete a proper European meal, we were offered a cheese course, and finally, a frozen dark chocolate mousse for dessert.

"Our breakfast, served on the sunporch, was equally inventive: melon, cranberry juice, a paprika and oregano seasoned egg with sliced ham, French toast made with English muffins, and raspberry tea (or coffee). At our request, Gretchen joined us. We found her to be helpful, cheerful, and totally sympathetic. She was happy to spend time with us, but willing to leave us to ourselves. I'd be back there again tomorrow, if I could." *(SHW)*

Open All year.
Rooms 3 suites, 2 doubles—all with private bath.

351

Facilities Restaurant, tavern with music weekends. Living room with 2 fire-places; library. 17 acres with ponds, streams, hammock, gardens.
Location 5 m from town. 1.5 m from the intersection of Rtes. 13 & 611 in Summit Point; 4.8 m from intersection of Rtes. 13 & 51 W of Charles Town.
Restrictions No children.
Credit Cards MC, Visa. Cash or check preferred.
Rates B&B, $150–175 suite, $100 double. 15% service additional. Alc dinner, $50–60.
Extras Some French spoken. Airport/station pickups.

ELKINS

The town of Elkins is surrounded by opportunities to delve deeper into West Virginian highlands and wilderness: the Monongahela National Forest, Bickle Knob, Cheat River, and Otter Creek Wilderness areas are close at hand; not much farther away are Canaan Valley and Blackwater Falls state parks, Spruce Knob, Seneca Rocks, and Dolly Sods Wilderness areas. If that isn't enough to consider for hiking, sightseeing or skiing, Elkins is also home to Davis & Elkins College and the annual Augusta Heritage Arts & Crafts Workshops.

Information please: If you'd like to get even further off the beaten path than Elkins, see if you can find the village of Helvetia (pronounced Hel-vay-sha) in the Allegheny Mountains in middle of the state and close to nothing whatsoever. (Hint: It's about 30 miles southwest of Elkins.) Settled by Swiss farmers in 1869, this tiny village was West Virginia's first district to be listed on the National Register. Innkeeper/restaurateur Eleanor Mailloux notes that "if you want to see something other than beauty, go somewhere else. Come here to relax and do nothing and you'll love it." Meals are available at the Hutte Restaurant, famous for its Swiss specialities and its Sunday brunch. Accommodations are available at Eleanor's **Beekeeper Inn** (Box 42, Helvetia 26224; 304–924–6435), with four rooms furnished in country antiques and quilts. If you want to see the village during an uncharacteristic burst of activity, visit during the Helvetia Fair, the second weekend of September, but reserve well ahead.

An appealing destination for train buffs is the old logging town of Cass, about 50 miles south of Elkins, close to the Virginia border. Restored Shay engines ascend the steep slopes of Cheat Mountain, using reverses and switchbacks to climb an 11% grade. Several museums showcase local history, while shops sell gifts and local crafts. Accommodations are available in two B&Bs: **The Shay Inn** (General Delivery, Cass 24927; 304–456–4652), the restored superintendent's house, with country decor and homestyle food, and in the **Cass Inn** (P.O. Box 68, Cass 24927; 304–456–3464). *Reports most welcome.*

Tunnel Mountain B&B
Route 1, Box 59-1, 26241

Tel: 304–636–1684

Tunnel Mountain B&B, owned since 1988 by Robert and Paula Graglia, is a contemporary, Colonial-style home, built of fieldstone and clap-board, nestled on the side of its own mountain. The house is decorated with antiques, art, collectibles and crafts; each guest room has its own quilt (handmade by Paula's mother) to set a country mood. Paula reports that her breakfast specialty is "homemade waffles with lots of added touches. Ham and eggs and freshly ground coffee are always available."

"The first of many wonderful impressions was the friendliness and warm hospitality offered by Paula & Robert. The living room is the focal point of the house where guests gather to sit, watch the fire, talk, or read. Decorated with antiques from local shops and watercolors from area artists, much of the interior is finished with beautiful pine and wormy chestnut paneling. Our room was spacious, with a homemade quilt, and the bathroom was roomy and warm. Breakfast was simple, but well done; all the guests ended up sitting and talking long into the morning." *(Dr. & Mrs. Richard DeAngelis)*

"While creating a very relaxed atmosphere, Paula & Rob were also great at helping us to make the most of time, directing us to excellent cross-country skiing and good restaurants." *(Kate Freiman & Bill Rezny)* "They made us feel welcome without smothering us—they knew when we wanted to chat and were sensitive to those times when we wanted to be alone." *(Cathy Standard Levy & Rich Levy)* "Very quiet, rustic setting with easy access to town and the more energetic activities of hiking and fishing." *(Robert Mesrobian)*

Open All year.
Rooms 3 doubles—all with private bath and/or shower, TV, desk, air-conditioning. 1 with fireplace.
Facilities Dining room, living room with fireplace, porch. 5 acres, walking/cross-country trails. Swimming, tennis, golf nearby. 1½ m to Cleat River for water sports. 30 min to downhill, cross-country skiing.
Location NE WV, Potomac Highlands. 3½ hrs. W of Washington D.C. 4 m E of Elkins on Rte. 33.
Restrictions No smoking. No children under 8.
Credit cards MC, Visa.
Rates $50–65 double. Extra person in room, $15. Holiday/weekend minimum.

LEWISBURG

The General Lewis Inn
301 East Washington Street, 24901   *Tel:* 304–645–2600

Listed on the National Register of Historic Places, Lewisburg is associated with both the Revolutionary and Civil wars. The inn is composed of a home built in 1834 housing the inn's restaurant and lobby and the main section of the inn, which dates to 1929.

"Wonderful hospitality. We enjoyed afternoon tea with strawberries, short biscuits, and cream on a beautiful veranda. Dinner was excellent—a pleasure to find a chef who knows how to cook salt-cured country ham properly!" *(Mr. & Mrs. A.D. Moscrip)*

"The exterior of the inn is a long, lovely white-pillared affair. The public rooms are extremely pleasant and comfortable." *(MFD)* "Antique-filled guest rooms with comfortable beds. Attentive owner and innkeeper, delicious home-cooked meals, and very reasonable rates." *(Joyce Whittington)*

Open All year.
Rooms 2 2-bedroom suites, 26 doubles—all with full private bath, telephone, TV, air-conditioning. Some with desk.
Facilities Living room, restaurant, porch with rocking chairs. Pioneer items & stagecoach on display. 1 acre with gardens. Fishing, swimming, white-water rafting, hiking, golf, tennis nearby.
Location SE WV. 103 m E of Charleston, WV, 72 m W of Lexington, VA. Historic district. 2 blocks to center. From I-64 Lewisburg Exit, go S on Rte. 219 to 1st traffic light (Washington St.), then left 2 blocks.
Credit cards Amex, MC, Visa.
Rates Room only, $80 suite, $55–75 double, $45–55 single. Extra person in room, $5. Family rates. Alc breakfast, $3–6; alc lunch, $6; alc dinner, $22. Picnic baskets.
Extras Pets with prior approval, $5. Cribs, babysitting available.

MARTINSBURG

Martinsburg prospered with the coming of the railroad in the 1850s; fruit orchards and woolen mills became its principal businesses. Although the apples are still growing strong, the textile business has faded. More recently, several old woolen mills have been refitted as outlet centers, especially popular with shoppers at Christmas; of particular interest is the store selling fine glass made in West Virginia in the Blue Ridge Outlet Center. Outdoor activities include hiking, golf, tennis, canoeing and white water rafting, and exploring the area's historic sites.

Martinsburg is located in the eastern West Virginia panhandle, 75 miles northwest of Washington D.C., and 75 miles west of Baltimore.

Information please: The Dunn Country Inn (Route 3, Box 33J, 25401; 304–263–8646) is a stone farmhouse dating back to 1805, with a more recent addition built in 1873. Rooms have individual motifs, some with 18th century antiques, another done in "Roaring Twenties" decor. The inn has a quiet country setting, and rates include a full breakfast and afternoon refreshments. An in-town possibility is **Aspen Hall** (405 Boyd Avenue, 25401; 304–263–4385), a 200-year-old Georgian-style home built of limestone and listed on the National Register of Historic Places. Eleven miles south of Martinsburg is a historic B&B called **Prospect Hill** (Route 51, Box 135, Gerrardstown 25420; 304–229–3346). Surrounded by 225 acres of fields and orchards, this Georgian mansion was built in 1795, and sits at the base of North Mountain. The main house offers two guest rooms with private bath and fireplaces, while the restored slave quarters offer the facilities of a small house. Fueled by a hearty breakfast, guests can pick their own fresh fruit, or fish in the pond. Reports would be most welcome.

Boydville: The Inn at Martinsburg   *Tel:* 304–263–1448
601 South Queen Street, 25401

Built in 1812 by Elisha Boyd, a general in the War of 1812, the estate was almost burned down by the Union Army during the Civil War. Only a last minute personal telegram from President Lincoln diverted the disaster. After the war, the house served as a family home for U.S. senators and ambassadors, changing hands only twice in its 175-year history.

Innkeepers Owen Sullivan and Ripley Hotch purchased the property in 1987, and after months of work, they re-opened Boydville as an inn. The original woodwork and 19th-century wallpaper have been restored, complemented by the owners' lifelong collection of art and antiques. Breakfasts include such specialties as puffed apple pancakes, frittatas, and homemade breads and muffins, and guests note with pleasure that repeats are rare.

"We received the grand tour, and were shown the original wallpaper shipped from France, the moldings of crafted pineapples, and the beautiful mural in a paneled bedroom (a similar one by the same artist is in the White House). We wandered all over the house, but the family room with a huge fireplace was our favorite. You can sip a glass of sherry, socialize, or just sit and read." *(Paula Abramson)*

"The spacious rooms are brimming over with antiques. On each visit a guest can discover some curio not noticed before. The inn holds a wonderful art collection of paintings, glass, and porcelain. The library contains volumes to keep one busy for hours." *(Philip Wilson)* "Rip and Owen are always there when you need them, yet are unobtrusive hosts. The house is clean and well-maintained, the atmosphere relaxed, and the location convenient. We shopped in the factory outlet stores two blocks away, and visited Harper's Ferry National Park nearby." *(Steven Golob)* "The inn is immaculate, beautifully furnished, set at the end of a tree-lined drive. From the moment you step in the door you have sense of being welcomed into someone's home, with every special whim being catered to." *(Winston Sharples)*

Open All year.
Rooms 6 doubles—all with private bath and/or shower, desk, air-conditioning, fan.
Facilities Dining room, living room with fireplace, stereo; music room, game room with TV, library, porch. 15 acres with plantation outbuildings. Lake and river nearby for fishing, rafting, canoeing, swimming. Cross-country skiing nearby.
Location From I-81 take Exit 13. Go E on West King St. Turn right on South Queen St. Go 3½ blocks. Inn on right.
Restrictions Check-in before 10 P.M. No smoking. No children under 12.
Credit cards Amex, MC, Visa. 5% discount for cash, check.
Rates B&B, $100–115 double. Extra person in room, $20. 2-night minimum holiday weekends.
Extras Station pickups. French spoken.

MIDDLEWAY

The Gilbert House
Tel: 304–725–0637

Mailing address: P.O. Box 1104, Charles Town, WV 25414

Middleway, a village dating back to the 1700s, is one of West Virginia's oldest settlements. The Gilbert House was built of stone around 1760, and is listed on the National Register of Historic Places; the oldest flagstone sidewalk in the state is in front of the inn. Jean and Bernie Heiler have owned this B&B since 1984, and have decorated it with antiques, tapestries, original paintings, and Oriental rugs. Jean says, "We specialize in romance and celebrations. Refreshments such as tea, wine, crackers and cheese, cake, cookies, etc., are available at any time. Breakfast includes fresh-squeezed juice, fruit, homemade breads and muffins, omelets, plus a meat or fish dish. Historical documents and records of the area are available in our guest rooms."

"The Gilbert House is a quiet, refined bed & breakfast somewhat off the major tourist trails. Our room was furnished with a comfortable bed with down pillows, quaint rugs, and country accents. The bath was large, with fresh towels provided twice daily." *(Donald Staley)*

"One of the nicest examples of Georgian-colonial hospitality I have ever had the pleasure to encounter. The inn, parts of which were built in the 1760s, is wonderfully restored, with the added convenience of modern plumbing." *(Kathleen Barry)*

"Bernie and Jean are very warm, enthusiastic people. Jean just loves sitting down and getting to know her guests. She likes to regale them with the legends of the era, and loves to feed everyone. After a day of sightseeing, we were greeted with a fire, hot mulled cider, and stollen. Our room had a fireplace, a sitting area, and a huge bathroom with modern plumbing, along with fresh flowers, candies, and champagne. Many of the antiques throughout the house are for sale. Walking in the back of the property we discovered old cemeteries and a waterwheel. Breakfasts were delicious and unusual—bratwurst and mushroom scrambled eggs, fresh spinach, chocolate croissants, all delicious." *(Rebecca & Jeff Ward, also Brian & Cynthia Unwin)*

"Jean is very active in the historic preservation efforts in Middleway and takes guests on an informative walking tour of the historic district. Special touches include calligraphic place cards made by Jean, fruit, candy, and beverages in your room, and the special feeling that you are truly a guest in their home. We used Gilbert House as a base to explore the area, and particularly enjoyed visits to the Skyline Drive, the castle in Berkeley Springs, Antietam Battlefield, Harpers Ferry, antique shops and malls, and factory-outlet centers." *(Andy & Karen Menzyk)* More comments please.

Open All year.
Rooms 2 suites, 1 double—all with full private bath, radio, air-conditioning. Telephone, TV on request. Some rooms with desk, fireplace.
Facilities Living/family room with piano, games; library/parlor; dining room; kitchen. Canoeing, rafting, hiking, golf nearby.
Location E WV, Eastern Panhandle. Near Harper's Ferry, 5 miles from Charles Town. In historic district, at juncture of Rtes. 1 and 51, halfway between I-81 and Charles Town.
Restrictions No smoking in public rooms. No children.
Credit cards MC, Visa; plus 5% service charge.
Rates B&B, $130 suite, $85–100 double. Extra person in room, $20. Weekly discount. $20 surcharge if staying Sat. night only.
Extras German, Spanish spoken.

MOOREFIELD

McMechen House Inn
Tel: 304–538–2417
109 North Main Street, 26836

McMechen House is a part Federal, part Greek Revival–style building completed in 1855. As the fortunes of war shifted back and forth in the region, it served as staff headquarters for both the Union and Confederate troops. It was being used as an apartment house when Art and Evelyn Valotto bought it in 1984. The Valottos have furnished it simply, with many Victorian pieces. Rates include a continental breakfast of cereal, fruit, juice, coffee, and homemade rolls and muffins.

"Moorefield is located in the Potomac Highlands, an ideal base for swimming, canoeing, fishing, and rafting in the South Branch of the Potomac River, for hiking and hunting in the surrounding hills, and for treasure hunting at Saturday morning country auctions. When Art and Evelyn Valotto decided to give up the frantic pace of a large metropolitan school district and open a B&B, they did us all a great service. The Valottos have spent untold hours and dollars restoring this lovely brick Federal-style house, built over 100 years ago. It's squeaky clean. Be sure to allow some time to sit on either of the two back porches and enjoy Mrs. Valotto's flower garden and visit with other guests." *(Phil & Nora Eramo)*

"Breakfast is always started with a fruit compote or fresh fruits in season followed by Evelyn Valotto's pastries, which are legendary. The house is quiet and peaceful, with a wealth of reading material; it's fun to look at the old-time tools and artifacts." *(Byron Brogle)* "The high ceilings and antique furnishings create a real sense of the past, combined with the comfort provided by air-conditioning and modern baths. Everything was sparkling clean and well-maintained, with no chipping or peeling of paint or wallpaper. The buffet breakfast of blueberry pancakes with sausages and homemade pastries was tasty; the owners are present but never obtrusive." *(Jill Reeves)* "We stayed in the suite, a real bargain. The decor combines antiques and traditional pieces. The most unusual feature: when the Valottos stripped the old wallpaper, they discovered Civil War–era graffiti underneath and left one wall exposed for people to see." *(Mary Wabeke)*

And a word to the wise: "The inn is for sale, and we only hope that the new owners do as good a job." Inquire further when making reservations.

Open All year. Closed Dec. 15–Jan. 15.
Rooms 4 2-bedroom suites, 3 doubles—all with private bath and/or shower, telephone, TV, desk, air-conditioning.
Facilities Parlor with games; dining room. Lawn furniture, hammock, games. Tennis, golf, hiking, caving, fishing, swimming, white-water canoeing, rafting nearby. 45 min. to cross-country skiing.
Location E WV, Potomac Highlands. 110 m W of Washington, DC, 160 m NW of Richmond, VA. In town at junction of Rtes. 220 & 55.
Restrictions "Only noise after 9 P.M. is on Friday nights if the Yellow Jackets team wins." No smoking.

357

Credit cards Amex, MC, Visa.
Rates B&B, $50 suite (accommodates 4), $45–50 double, $35 single. Extra person in room, $15. No tipping. 2-night minimum holiday weekends and Heritage Weekend (last weekend in Sept.).

PARKERSBURG

An industrial center since the 19th century, Parkersburg's most interesting attraction is the Blennerhasset Island Historical Park in the middle of the Ohio River, reached by a sternwheel paddleboat. "Blennerhassett Island, where Aaron Burr planned the government's overthrow with Harmon Blennerhassett, now features the rebuilt mansion (originally constructed in 1810), an oil and gas museum, and the Middleton Doll Factory. A short distance up the river, in Williamstown, is an antique mall, and the Fenton Art Glass Museum and factory gift shop." *(SHW)*

Information please: Parkersburg's first B&B is the **Harmony House,** located in a restored turn-of-the-century home listed on the National Register of Historic Places. Rooms are decorated with antiques and Oriental rugs, and the very reasonable rates include such breakfast treats as Belgian waffles with whipped cream and fruit (710 Anne Street, 26101; 304–485–1458). Reports please.

Blennerhassett Hotel *Tel:* 304–422–3131
Fourth and Market Streets, P.O. Box 51, 26101   800–262–2536

The Blennerhassett took six years to build and opened in 1889. Nearly a century later, it underwent a one-year restoration and expansion, reopening in 1986; the hotel changed hands in 1988, and was bought by Ken Vincent. The goal of the renovation was to recreate the hotel's turn-of-the-century atmosphere, adding all the modern facilities and amenities expected by 20th-century travelers. The public rooms are decorated with period antiques, collected from buildings in New York and England, and the guest rooms are furnished with reproduction Chippendale furniture and period English and American original prints.

"The lobby is fairly small, but with lots of nooks and crannies that contain antique furniture and lots of books on the shelves. There is a lovely gift shop that features a collection of Middleton dolls. All the woodwork is original and has been polished till it gleams. The staff is very helpful, courteous, and friendly.

"The restaurant is named after Harman Blennerhassett. Harman's, the most elegant restaurant in the area, specializes in continental cuisine. It is long and narrow, with a banquette the full length of one side; the decor is dark green with white tablecloths; the wall treatment is a cream-colored faux embossed tin with large mirrors and Audubon prints. Our meal was first quality and of excellent value. Our entrées included shrimp sautéed with mushrooms and artichoke hearts in garlic sauce, boned baby quail, and veal with fettuccine. For dessert we had bananas Foster prepared table side with a hazelnut liqueur.

"We also visited on Easter Sunday for the buffet; this is truly one of the most spectacular that I have seen anywhere. The dessert table had enormous strawberries dipped in white and dark chocolate, assorted pies, cakes, truffles; the fruit trays had passion fruit and kiwi in addition to the other standards. The food is wonderfully prepared, reasonably priced, and service is cheerful, even enthusiastic. The staff seem to really want you to have a good time and love their restaurant as much as they do.

"Rooms in the older section are spacious with high ceilings, and reproduction Chippendale furniture; bathrooms are remodeled, motel-style. The most interesting rooms are the corner rooms with curved walls and extra-tall windows, and the two-story suite on the 4th floor, which can connect with three other rooms—it would be perfect for a family reunion. Guest rooms in the modern section at the rear of the hotel are quieter and smaller; they overlook a 3-story atrium and court-yard, and are inviting to women travelers." *(Susan W. Schwemm, also Janet Payne)*

Open All year.
Rooms 3 suites, 81 doubles, 23 singles—all with full private bath, telephone, cable TV, desk, air-conditioning, fan.
Facilities Restaurant, lounge, library, ballroom, meeting rooms. Sternwheeler boat, fishing, bicycling, and carriage rides nearby.
Location W central WV. Mid–Ohio River Valley, Allegheny Plateau. 75 m N of Charleston, 110 m SE of Columbus. Downtown. Take Rte. 50 E to Market St., turn left; hotel ½ m on left.
Restrictions Light sleepers should request rooms at back.
Credit cards Amex, DC, MC, Visa.
Rates Room only, $125 suite, $55 double. Extra person in room, $6. 16% service additional. No charge for children under 12 in parents' room. Senior discount. Corporate rates. Weekend packages. Alc breakfast, $4–7; alc lunch, $10; alc dinner, $35.
Extras Wheelchair accessible. Airport/station pickups. Crib available.

ROMNEY

Hampshire House 1884
165 North Grafton, 26757

Tel: 304–822–7171

The Hampshire House 1884, a restored 19th century brick Federal-style home, is owned by Jane and Scott Simmons. An extensive renovation took place before the inn opened: central heat and air-conditioning was installed, and the walls sound-proofed. The interior was professionally decorated to reflect the ambiance of 1884, and most of the furnishings are either Rococo, Renaissance, or Eastlake, all popular styles of the day. Dinners are available by advance reservation; a sample menu might include cream of leek soup, chicken with couscous, salad, steamed vegetables, and apple pie.

"The inn provides ready access to some of West Virginia's finest scenery, including Romney, West Virginia's oldest town. The Sim-monses have an excellent supply of information on recreational and touring opportunities in the area; the State School for the Deaf and Blind is a short walk away, and the town has a fascinating Civil War history. Each bedroom is furnished in a historically distinct decor, with the exception being modern bathrooms and carpeting; everything is immaculately clean. The guest sitting room has an extensive library, with books of historical interest, video tapes, and other literature about the area. The snack area is certainly appreciated by early risers—you can make your own tea or have a snack without disturbing others.

"Scott's breakfast is a highlight of a visit—choices range from home-made granola, fruit, omelets, French toast, oatmeal or blueberry pancakes, and muffins to the more standard eggs and bacon. Scott willingly and capably caters to special dietary needs and personal preferences; we particularly enjoyed an omelet with a goat cheese and herb filling. Jane and Scott are fascinating and interesting hosts who make their guests feel truly welcome." *(Waldemar & Beth Scherer)*

"The rooms are clean, bright, comfortable; the service is impeccable; there is off-street parking in a quiet, pleasant neighborhood not far from the center of town. Best of all are the Simmonses—warm, bright, competent, and considerate hosts." *(Dr. & Mrs. J. Allan Hovey, Jr.)*

Open All year.
Rooms 4 doubles—all with private bath and/or shower, TV, air-conditioning, fan. 3 with desk.
Facilities Dining room, tea room, living room with library, TV/VCR, games. Guitar, banjo music occasionally. Covered veranda, patio. Swimming, tennis, golf, canoeing, horseback riding nearby.
Location NE WV, Eastern Panhandle. 2½ hrs. W of Washington, DC, 1 hr. W of Winchester, VA. 1½ blocks N on Grafton St. off Rte. 50.
Restrictions No smoking.
Credit cards Amex, DC, MC, Visa.
Rates B&B, $60–65 double, $50–55 single. Extra person in room, $10. MAP, $85–95 double, $63–95 single. Extra person in room, $23. 15% service on meals. Prix fixe lunch, $9; dinner, $9–18.
Extras Airport/station pickups, fee charged by distance.

SHEPHERDSTOWN

Shepherdstown, West Virginia's oldest community, was founded in 1730. Area attractions include the Old Opera House in Charles Town, Harper's Ferry, Antietam Battlefield, and the races at Charles Town and Summit Point, plus golf, tennis, horseback riding, white-water rafting and canoeing, and jogging and walking on the old C&O Towpath across the Potomac River.

Shepherdstown is in the upper Shenandoah Valley of the Eastern Panhandle, at the Maryland border. It's 8 miles from Harper's Ferry and 4 from Antietam Battlefield. Washington, D.C. and Baltimore, MD are an hour and a half away by car. From Washington, take I-270 to Frederick bypass, then onto I-70 to Exit 49. Turn left at Route 34 in Boonsboro to Sheperdstown.

Bavarian Inn and Lodge *Tel:* 304–876–2551
Route 1, Box 30, 25443

The Bavarian Inn includes a handsome stone colonial, built as a private residence in 1930 and converted into an inn in 1962, and four chalet-style structures, built since 1981. The guest rooms are luxuriously decorated with oak furniture and canopied beds; all have tiled fireplaces and balconies overlooking the Potomac. The Bavarian theme in food and accommodation was introduced by innkeeper/owner Erwin Asam, originally from Munich. Keeping up with the times, the Asams have added non-smoking dining rooms, entrées for vegetarians and dieters, and wild game dishes in season.

"This neatly constructed stone inn rests back off the main road. The four additional 'chalet-style' guest houses perch over the Potomac River. Noted especially for the original German dishes served in the elegant restaurant, the menu also provides wild game entrées and an extensive wine list. Service can be a bit slow but innkeeper Erwin Asam will seat you. Much of the flavor of West Virginia's historic landmarks and antique and craft shops are nearby." *(Natalie & Jonathan Birbeck)*

"We stayed in one of the spotless new chalet-type buildings. Our room had a fireplace with a gas fire—clean, neat, though not the same as wood. The handsome furnishings are a mix between German oak and early American oak reproductions. The highlight of our stay was the excellent dinner." *(Sally Sieracki)*

"This is the place for a relaxing getaway but plan ahead—usually two months—for a weekend reservation; the rooms (and even the swimming pool) have wonderful views of the Potomac. The food is excellent, and reasonably priced; from September through March the restaurant has a 'game festival' with a special menu featuring roast venison, pheasant, wild boar, and rabbit." *(Lana Alukonis)*

Open All year.
Rooms 18 suites, 24 doubles—all with private bath, telephone, TV, radio, desk, air-conditioning, balcony. Most with queen-size canopy bed, fireplace. All suites with whirlpool tub. Guest rooms in 4 separate chalets.
Facilities Restaurant, bar, conference room, gift shop. Live music in bar/lounge Fri. and Sat. nights. 11 acres with gazebo, heated swimming pool, tennis court. Golf nearby. Jogging on C&O towpath across river.
Location In town.
Restrictions Smoking restricted in some areas.
Credit cards Amex, CB, DC, MC, Visa.
Rates Room only, $95–120 suite, $70–95 double. Additional person in room, $10. Family rates. 2-night holiday/weekend minimum. Alc breakfast, $4–8; alc lunch, $6–10; alc dinner, $15–25.
Extras Wheelchair accessible. Crib, babysitting available. German, French, Spanish spoken.

The Thomas Shepherd Inn *Tel:* 304–876–3715
300 West German Street, P.O. Box 1162, 25443

The Thomas Shepherd Inn was built as a parsonage in 1868, and was restored in 1984 as a B&B. A long-time reader favorite, it was sold in

WEST VIRGINIA

1989 by Ed and Carol Ringoot to Margaret Perry and Robert Ellrott. This white brick Victorian home, with wide plank floors and a real double parlor, is elegantly furnished with period antiques, old prints, and Oriental rugs. Margaret prepares an imaginative array of breakfast dishes; one morning's menu included fruit compote, a mushroom omelet with sour cream and dill sauce, and croissants; on another occasion she served sparkle punch, poached pears with cranberry-pecan sauce, and Belgian waffles with whipped cream and fresh fruit.

"The inn is wonderfully decorated with post-Civil War antiques; I especially enjoyed the atmosphere of the living room and the sherry, tea, and snacks served there by Margaret. The entire inn is immaculate and well-stocked with linens, towels, soap. Most of all, I really liked the friendly atmosphere—Margaret and Bob are very welcoming and witty." *(Pat Cunningham)* More comments, please.

Open All year.
Rooms 6 doubles—4 with private bath, 2 with maximum of 4 people sharing bath. All with air-conditioning, some with desk.
Facilities 2 dining rooms; living room with fireplace; library with TV, porch. Bicycles, with 24-hr. notice. Golf, fishing, white-water rafting, canoeing, hiking, bicycling nearby. 4 m to cross-country skiing.
Location Historic district. In center of town.
Restrictions No smoking. No children under 12.
Credit cards MC, Visa; plus 5% service charge.
Rates B&B, $74–79 double, $63–69 single. Extra person in room, $25. 5% senior, AARP discount. $10 surcharge for 1-night weekend stay. Picnic lunch with 24-hr. notice, $9. Prix fixe dinner, $20–35.
Extras Station pickups.

SUMMIT POINT

Countryside
Hawthorne Avenue, Box 57, 25446

Tel: 304–725–2614

In 1981, Lisa and Daniel Hileman decided they'd had enough of big-city life and opened Countryside, West Virginia's first B&B. They've decorated it handsomely with an eclectic mixture of antiques, collectibles, and original art. Rates include a continental breakfast of coffee, juice, rolls, cereal, and fruit, plus afternoon tea. Lisa and Daniel pride themselves on providing a romantic atmosphere at very affordable rates.

"Our room was charming and filled with teddy bears, quilts, and cross-stitching, plus books, magazines, and games. We were welcomed with a pot of hot tea and cookies. The inn is located on a dead end street in a quaint little village, set between a sweet-smelling apple orchard and the railroad tracks." *(Charlotte & Gary Craig)*

"The breakfast consists of country muffins, spiced ham, cereal, and tea, served on wicker trays with nice china. Soft drinks, candies, and other snacks are always available." *(Maureen & Scott Zeiss)*

"The house is spacious and quaint, with lots of interesting knick-knacks all around. The porch is an excellent place to read and relax and looks out on a large backyard with flower gardens and trees. The living

362

room, also a nice place in which to read, is heated in the winter by a wood-burning store. The kitchen is a large, open room and is the focal point for friends to relax and chat with the owners. Breakfast is served wherever and whenever you request it. The bed is extremely comfortable due to a feather mattress (on top of a regular firm mattress), and a feather comforter for warmth. A choice of pillows is provided. The ceiling fan is useful in all seasons. The bathroom is small but adequate." *(Teri Rawlins)*

"Fully endorse existing entry. Lisa has made the rooms cozy and warm, and her personal touch is everywhere. The inn is very clean, and the breakfast good." *(Laura Lapins)*

Open All year.
Rooms 2 doubles with private bath. Both with radio, desk/table, air-conditioning.
Facilities 2 parlors with woodstove, books, magazines, TV, stereo, games. Terrace with patio furniture. 3 acres adjacent to 400-acre apple orchard. Near Shenandoah and Potomac rivers for fishing, canoeing. Hiking, bicycling.
Location E WV, Eastern Panhandle. 14 m from Harper's Ferry. 6 m from Rtes. 7 & 340. In town.
Restrictions No smoking. No children.
Credit cards MC, Visa.
Rates B&B, $40–60 double. 2-night holiday weekend minimum.

We Want to Hear from You!

As you know, this book is only effective with your help. We really need to know about your experiences and discoveries.

If you stayed at an inn or hotel listed here, we want to know how it was. Did it live up to our description? Exceed it? Was it what you expected? Did you like it? Were you disappointed? Delighted?

Have you discovered new establishments that we should add to the next edition?

Tear out one of the report forms at the back of this book (or use your own stationery if you prefer) and write today. Even if you write only "Fully endorse existing entry" you will have been most helpful.
Thank You!

Appendix 1

PLACES THAT WELCOME FAMILIES

The inns and hotels listed below usually offer cribs, baby-sitting, games, and/or activities kids will enjoy. Most but not all can accommodate infants and toddlers. Nearly all offer free or reduced rates to children. Unless specifically noted under "Restrictions," our other entries will also accommodate children, but don't welcome families with either special prices or facilities, and typically don't feel "equipped to take young children, especially on busy weekends."

DELAWARE
Rehoboth Beach—The Corner
   Cupboard Inn

DISTRICT OF COLUMBIA
Bristol Hotel
The Canterbury Hotel
The Hampshire Hotel
Hay-Adams Hotel
Henley Park Hotel
Jefferson Hotel
Normandy Inn
The River Inn
The Windsor Inn

MARYLAND
Baltimore—Admiral Fell Inn
   Peabody Court
   The Shirley Madison Inn
Chestertown—The Inn at Mitchell
   House
   The White Swan Tavern
Denton—The Sophie Kerr House
Stevensville—Kent Manor Inn

NEW JERSEY
Cape May—Chalfonte
   The Wooden Rabbit
Montclair—Marlboro Inn
Pittston—Seven Springs Farm B&B
Spring Lake—The Chateau
   The Normandy Inn
Summit—Grand Summit Hotel

NEW YORK
Albany—Mansion Hill Inn
Blue Mountain Lake—Hemlock Hall
Cazenovia—Brae Loch Inn
   Lincklaen House

Chestertown—The Balsam House
Cooperstown—Creekside B&B
   The Inn at Brook Willow
   The Inn at Cooperstown
   The Phoenix on River Road
East Hampton—Bassett House Inn
Fredonia—The White Inn
Geneva—Geneva-on-the-Lake
   The Inn at Belhurst Castle
Hague—Trout House Village Resort
Hillsdale—Swiss Hutte
Keene—The Bark Eater
Millerton—Simons' Way Village
   Inn
New Paltz—Mohonk Mountain
   House
New York City—Doral Tuscany
   Dumont Plaza
   Hotel Algonquin
   Hotel Empire
   Hotel Iroquois
   Hotel Plaza Athénée
   The Lowell
   Parc Fifty-One
   Park Avenue Sheraton
   The Stanhope
North Hudson—Elk Lake Lodge
North River—Garnet Hill Lodge
Poughkeepsie—Inn at the Falls
Saratoga Springs—Adelphi Hotel
Skaneateles—The Sherwood Inn
Ticonderoga—Bonnie View Acres

PENNSYLVANIA
Bloomsburg—The Inn at Turkey Hill
Ephrata—Guesthouse at Doneckers
   Smithton Inn
Fogelsville—Glasbern
Greensburg—Mountain View Inn

Jersey Shore—Sommerville Farms
B&B
Lititz—The General Sutter Inn
Mercer—Magoffin Guest House
Milton—Hotel Milton
Mt. Joy—Cedar Hill Farm
North East—Brown's Village Inn
Paradise—Maple Lane Farm Guest
House
Philadelphia—The Rittenhouse
Scenery Hill—Century Inn
Skytop—Skytop Lodge
Slippery Rock—Applebutter Inn
Starlight—The Inn at Starlight Lake

VIRGINIA
Abingdon—Martha Washington Inn
Alexandria—Morrison House
Amherst—Dulwich Manor Inn
Bedford—The Longwood Inn
Peaks of Otter Lodge
Charlottesville—The Boar's Head Inn
& Sports Club
Clifton
Hot Springs—The Carriage Court
Irvington—The Tides Inn
The Tides Lodge
Luray—Big Meadows Lodge
Skyland Lodge
Middleburg—The Red Fox Inn and
Tavern

Middletown—Wayside Inn Since
1797
Millboro—Fort Lewis Lodge
Monterey—Highland Inn
Mountain Lake—Mountain Lake
Hotel
Mount Jackson—The Widow Kip's
Shenandoah Inn
Norfolk—Days Hotel Waterside
Orange—Willow Grove Inn
Smithfield—Isle of Wight Inn
Stanley—Jordan Hollow Farm Inn
Staunton—The Frederick Hotel
Strasburg—Hotel Strasburg
Swoope—Lambsgate B&B
Vesuvius—Irish Gap Inns
Virginia Beach—Angie's Guest
Cottage
Warm Springs—The Inn at Gristmill
Square
Williamsburg—Williamsburg Inn
Woodstock—The Inn at Narrow
Passage

WEST VIRGINIA
Lewisburg—The General Lewis
Inn
Parkersburg—Blennerhassett Hotel
Shepherdstown—Bavarian Inn and
Lodge

Appendix 2

RESORTS

We defined the word *resort* quite loosely here to mean an inn or hotel that serves both breakfast and dinner (usually lunch as well), and has, at a minimum, both a swimming pool and a tennis court, which are often near a golf course. Typically, water sports, fishing, hiking, horseback riding, or skiing are also readily available.

NEW YORK
Hague—Trout House Village Resort
Hillsdale—Swiss Hutte
New Paltz—Mohonk Mountain
  House
North River—Garnet Hill Lodge

PENNSYLVANIA
Canadensis—The Pine Knob
Farmington—Nemacolin Woodlands
Skytop—Skytop Lodge
Starlight—The Inn at Starlight Lake

VIRGINIA
Charlottesville—The Boar's Head Inn
  & Sports Club
  Clifton
  Silver Thatch Inn
Irvington—The Tides Inn
  The Tides Lodge
Mountain Lake—Mountain Lake
  Hotel
Nellysford—Trillium House
Williamsburg—Williamsburg Inn

WEST VIRGINIA
Shepherdstown—Bavarian Inn and
  Lodge

Appendix 3

PLACES THAT HAVE RESTAURANTS

The inns and hotels listed below have restaurants open to the public. While advance reservations are always recommended, they are essential for some of the smaller ones. In some cases, 24-hour advance notice is required, and you may even be asked to specify your choice of entrée.

DELAWARE
Rehoboth Beach—The Corner
  Cupboard Inn
Wilmington—Christina House

DISTRICT OF COLUMBIA
Bristol Hotel
The Canterbury Hotel
The Hampshire Hotel
Hay-Adams Hotel
The Henley Park Hotel
The Jefferson Hotel
The Morrison-Clark Inn
The River Inn
The Tabard Inn

MARYLAND
Baltimore—Admiral Fell Inn
  Peabody Court
  Society Hill Hotels
Buckeystown—The Inn at
  Buckeystown
Frederick—Turning Point Inn
Georgetown—Kitty Knight House
Grantsville—The Casselman
Havre de Grace—Vandiver Inn
Oxford—Robert Morris Inn
St. Michaels—The Inn at Perry Cabin
Snow Hill—Snow Hill Inn
Stevensville—Kent Manor Inn

NEW JERSEY
Cape May—Chalfonte
Hope—Inn at Millrace Pond
Montclair—Marlboro Inn
Princeton—Peacock Inn
Summit—The Grand Summit Hotel

NEW YORK
Albany—Mansion Hill Inn
Amenia—Troutbeck
Averill Park—The Gregory House

Berlin—The Sedgwick Inn
Blue Mountain Inn—Hemlock Hall
Cazenovia—Brae Loch Inn
  Lincklaen House
Chestertown—The Balsam House
Clarence—Asa Ransom House
Dover Plains—Old Drovers Inn
East Hampton—Hedges Inn
  Maidstone Arms
  1770 House
East Windham—Point Lookout
  Mountain Inn
Elka Park—Redcoat's Return
Fredonia—The White Inn
Geneva—Geneva-on-the-Lake
  The Inn at Belhurst Castle
Groton—Benn Conger Inn
Hadley—Saratoga Rose B&B
Hillsdale—L'Hostellerie Bressane
  Swiss Hutte
Ithaca—Rose Inn
Leonardsville—The Horned Dorset
  Inn
Millerton—Simmons' Way Village
  Inn
New York City—The Box Tree
  Doral Tuscany
  Dumont Plaza
  Hotel Algonquin
  Hotel Beverly
  Hotel Empire
  Hotel Iroquois
  Hôtel Plaza Athénée
  The Lowell
  Parc Fifty-One
  Park Avenue Sheraton
  The Pierre
  The Stanhope
  Wyndham
North River—Garnet Hill Lodge
Pittsford—Oliver Loud's Inn
Rhinebeck—Beekman Arms

Saratoga Springs—Adelphi Hotel
Schroon Lake—The Schroon Lake Inn
Shelter Island—Ram's Head Inn
Skaneateles—The Sherwood Inn
Tannersville—Eggery Inn
Trumansburg—Taughannock Farms Inn
Warrensburg—The Merrill Magee House
Windham—Albergo Allegria

PENNSYLVANIA
Beach Lake—The Beach Lake Hotel
Bloomsburg—The Inn at Turkey Hill
Canadensis—The Pine Knob
Clark—Tara
Cooksburg—Clarion River Lodge
Ephrata—Guesthouse at Doneckers
Farmington—Nemacolin Woodlands
Greensburg—Mountain View Inn
Ligonier—Town House
Lititz—The General Sutter Inn
Malvern—The Historic General Warren Inne
Mercer—Magoffin Guest House
Mercersburg—The Mercersburg Inn
Milton—The Hotel Milton
Mount Joy—Cameron Estate Inn
Newtown—The Brick Hotel
North East—Brown's Village Inn
North Wales—Joseph Ambler Inn
Philadelphia—Hotel Atop the Bellevue
The Rittenhouse Hotel
Society Hill Hotel
Scenery Hill—Century Inn
Starlight—Inn at Starlight Lake
State College—The Nittany Lion Inn
Thornton—Pace One Inn
Williamsport—Thomas Lightfoote Inn

VIRGINIA
Abington—The Martha Washington Inn

Alexandria—Morrison House
Bedford—Peaks of Otter Lodge
Charlottesville—The Boar's Head Inn & Sports Club
Silver Thatch Inn
Harrisonburg—The Joshua Wilton House
Hot Springs—The Carriage Court
Irvington—The Tides Inn
The Tides Lodge
Luray—Big Meadows Lodge
Skyland Lodge
Middleburg—The Red Fox Inn and Tavern
Monterey—Highland Inn
Mountain Lake—Mountain Lake Hotel
Nellysford—Trillium House
Norfolk—Days Hotel Waterside
Orange—The Hidden Inn
Willow Grove Inn
Paris—Ashby Inn
Richmond—Berkeley Hotel
Jefferson Sheraton
Stanley—Jordan Hollow Farm Inn
Staunton—Belle Grae Inn
Strasburg—Hotel Strasburg
Trevilians—Prospect Hill
Upperville—1763 Inn
Warm Springs—The Inn at Gristmill Square
Washington—The Inn at Little Washington
White Post—L'Auberge Provencale
Williamsburg—Williamsburg Inn

WEST VIRGINIA
Berkeley Springs—The Country Inn
Charles Town—Hillbrook Inn
Lewisburg—The General Lewis Inn
Parkersburg—Blennerhasset Hotel
Sheperdstown—Bavarian Inn & Lodge

Appendix 4

STATE AND PROVINCIAL TOURIST OFFICES

Listed here are the addresses and telephone numbers for the tourist offices of the Middle Atlantic states covered in this book. When you write or call one of these offices, be sure to request a map of the state and a calendar of events. If you will be visiting a particular city or region, or if you have any special interests, be sure to specify this as well.

Delaware Tourism Office
99 Kings Highway
P.O. Box 1401
Dover, Delaware 19903
(302) 736–4271 or (800) 441–8846
(out of state) or (800) 282–8667 (in Delaware)

Washington, D.C. Convention and Visitors' Assoc.
Suite 600, 1212 New York Avenue, N.W.
Washington, D.C. 20005
(202) 789–7000

Maryland Office of Tourist Development
217 E. Redwood Avenue
Baltimore, Maryland 21202
(301) 333–6611 or (800) 543–1036

New Jersey Division of Travel and Tourism
C.N. 826
Trenton, New Jersey 08635
(609) 292–2470 or (800) 537–7397

New York State Division of Tourism
1 Commerce Plaza
Albany, New York 12245
(518) 474–4116 or (800) 225–5697 (in the Northeast except Maine)

Pennsylvania Bureau of Travel Development
Department of Commerce
453 Forum Building
Harrisburg, Pennsylvania 17120
(717) 787–5453 or (800) 847–4872

Virginia Division of Tourism
202 North 9th Street
Suite 500
Richmond, Virginia 23219
(804) 786–4484 or (800) 847–4882

Travel West Virginia
West Virginia Department of Commerce
2101 East Washington Street
Charleston, West Virginia 25305
(304) 348–2286 or (800) CALL WVA

MAPS

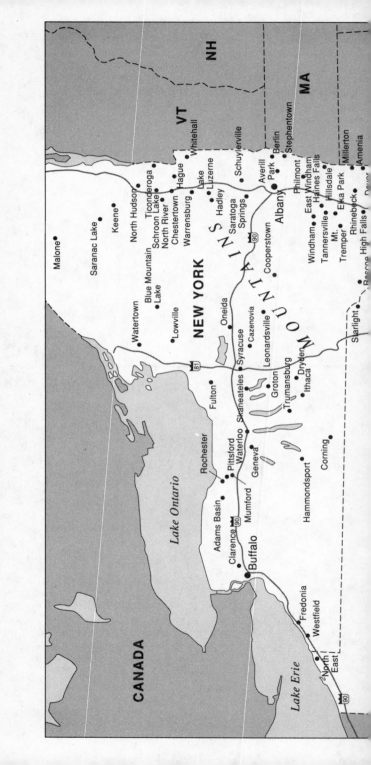

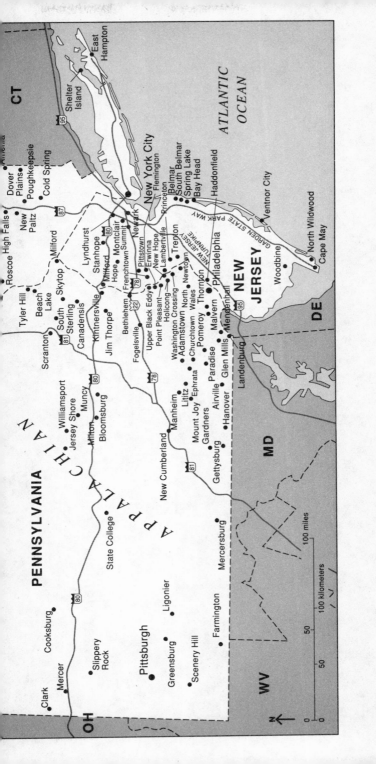

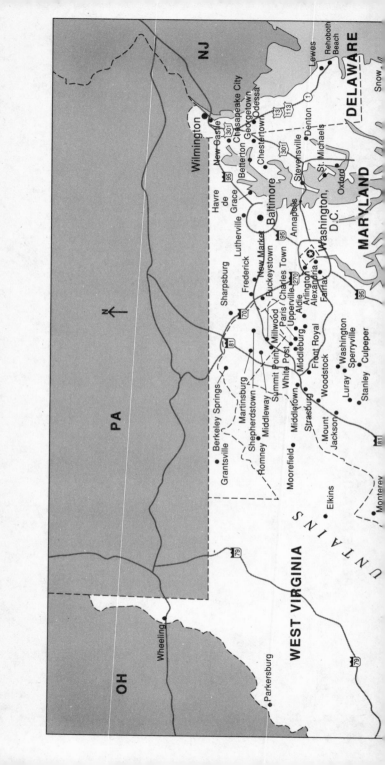

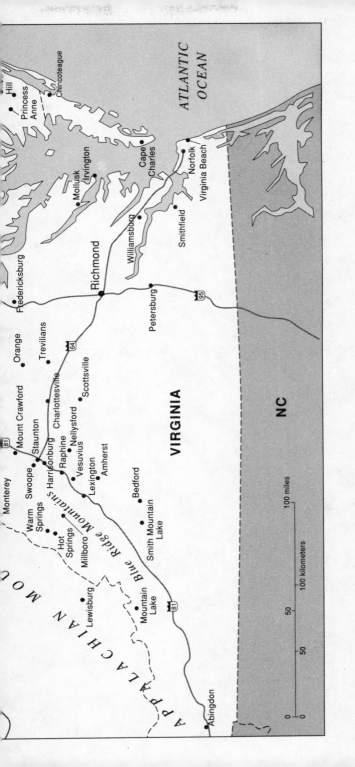

Index of Accommodations

Congratulations!

We are delighted to announce that we have mailed over 500 copies of the *America's Wonderful Little Hotels & Inns* guides to our most helpful respondents. These were people who sent us particularly insightful or useful reports, either positive or negative, on two or more establishments.

Hotel/Inn Report Forms

The report forms on the following pages may be used to endorse or critique an existing entry or to nominate a hotel or inn that you feel deserves inclusion in next year's edition. Whichever you wish to do, don't feel you have to use our forms, or, if you do use them, don't feel you must restrict yourself to the space available. All nominations (each on a separate piece of paper, if possible) should include your name and address, the name and location of the hotel or inn, when you have stayed there, and for how long. A copy of the establishment's brochure is also helpful. Please report only on establishments you have visited in the last eighteen months, unless you are sure that standards have not dropped since your stay. Please be as specific as possible, and critical where appropriate, about the character of the building, the public rooms, the accommodations, the meals, the service, the nightlife, the grounds, and the general atmosphere of the inn and the attitude of its owners. Any comments you have about area restaurants and sights would also be most appreciated.

Don't feel you need to write at length. A report that merely verifies the accuracy of existing listings is extremely helpful, i.e., "Visited XYZ Inn and found it just as described."

On the other hand, don't apologize for writing a long report. Although space does not permit us to quote them in toto, the small details provided about furnishings, atmosphere, and cuisine can really make a description come alive, illuminating the special flavor of a particular inn or hotel. Remember that we will again be awarding free copies to our most helpful respondents.

There is no need to bother with prices or with routine information about the number of rooms and facilities, although a sample brochure is very helpful for new recommendations. We obtain such details directly from the hotels selected. What we are eager to get from readers is information that is not accessible elsewhere.

Please note that we print only the names of respondents, never addresses. Those making negative observations are not identified. Although we must always have your full name and address, we will be happy to print your initials, or a pseudonym, if you prefer.

These report forms may also be used, if you wish, to recommend good hotels in Europe to our equivalent publication, *Europe's Wonderful Little Hotels & Inns* (published in Europe as *The Good Hotel Guide*). Reports should be sent to *Europe's Wonderful Little Hotels & Inns*, St. Martin's Press, 175 Fifth Avenue, New York, NY 10010; to P.O. Box 150, Riverside, CT 06878; or directly to *The Good Hotel Guide*, 61 Clarendon Road, London W11. Readers in the UK can send their letters postage-free to *The Good Hotel Guide*, Freepost, London W11 4 BR.

To: *America's Wonderful Little Hotels & Inns,*
    P.O. Box 150, Riverside, CT 06878.

Name of hotel_____

Address_____

Telephone_____

Date of most recent visit_____ Duration of visit_____

☐ New recommendation   ☐ Comment on existing entry

Please be as specific as possible about furnishings, atmosphere, service, and cuisine. If reporting on an existing entry, please tell us whether you thought it accurate, and whether you would return. Unless you tell us not to, we shall assume that we may publish your name in the next edition. Thank you very much for writing. Report (use your own stationery if you wish):

I am not connected directly or indirectly with the management or owners.
I would stay here again if returning to the area. ☐ yes   ☐ no

Signed_____

Name_____
                         (Please print)

Address_____
                         (Please print)

_____

MA91

To: *America's Wonderful Little Hotels & Inns,*
   P.O. Box 150, Riverside, CT 06878.

Name of hotel_____

Address_____

Telephone_____

Date of most recent visit_____ Duration of visit_____

☐ New recommendation   ☐ Comment on existing entry

Please be as specific as possible about furnishings, atmosphere, service, and cuisine. If reporting on an existing entry, please tell us whether you thought it accurate, and whether you would return. Unless you tell us not to, we shall assume that we may publish your name in the next edition. Thank you very much for writing. Report (use your own stationery if you wish):

I am not connected directly or indirectly with the management or owners.
I would stay here again if returning to the area. ☐ yes   ☐ no

Signed_____

Name_____
                    (Please print)

Address_____
                    (Please print)

_____

MA91

THE INNGOER'S

Europe's Wonderful Little Hotels and Inns, 1991, *Great Britain and Ireland*
◄

Europe's Wonderful Little Hotels and Inns, 1991, *The Continent*
►

America's Wonderful Little Hotels and Inns, 1991, *U.S.A. and Canada*
◄

America's Wonderful Little Hotels and Inns, 1991, *New England*
►

America's Wonderful Little Hotels and Inns, 1991, *The Middle Atlantic*
◄

America's Wonderful Little Hotels and Inns, 1991, *The South*
►

America's Wonderful Little Hotels and Inns, 1991, *The West Coast*
◄

America's Wonderful Little Hotels and Inns, 1991, *The Midwest, The Rocky Mountains, and The Southwest*
►